BLACK COUNTRY CINEMAS

CLIFTON

GRAND OPENING TO-NIGHT 7-30

Ned Williams

STAGE & SCREEN IN SOUTH STAFFORDSHIRE
& THE BLACK COUNTRY
VOLUME 1

URALIA PRESS

2011

Black Country Cinemas

is dedicated to

Kiran and Kate

This book is produced
in a limited edition.

The first 500 copies
are numbered and signed

168

Ned Williams

Text typing: Tracey Ward.
Setting and page layouts by the author.
Cover design by Roger Crombleholme

Black Country Cinemas
(Volume 1 of "Stage & Screen in South
Staffordshire & The Black Country")

ISBN: 1 898528 09 8

First published by Uralia Press, 2011
23 Westland Road
Wolverhampton
WV3 9NZ

Printed by Imagery, Kings Norton

This book is also dedicated to all those who worked in Black Country Cinemas, and particularly to those who shared memories and information with me.

Here we see Derek Simmonds lacing up the projectors at The Danilo, Stourbridge, where he was taught the art of projection by George Salt. I first met Derek when he opened a little shop in Stourbridge Road, Holly Hall, to hire out and sell 16mm and 8mm cine films. He immediately shared his enthusiasm for projecting films, collecting films, discussing films! His enterprise went on to become Derrann Films of Dudley.

Ned Williams

Foreword

One of my earliest memories is of tramping through the snow with my aunt to a local 'picture house' which I think was The Majestic on Bearwood Road. I was about five, and I remember with great clarity the heavenly sensation of thawing out in the rich, red warmth of the cinema and then the utter thrill, as the lights went down, my aunt shoving a wine gum into my mouth as the film began; it was "Lady and the Tramp". I was mesmerised by the characters, the vivid Technicolour, and, of course, the story, and there began my love of the cinema.

Fast forward just a few years, into the early sixties, and "Carry on Cleo" was the film. "All the one and nines out" was the cry as the manager marched down the aisle and attempted to put out a smouldering seat in the front row whilst simultaneously ejecting several rowdy, scoffing teenagers. This was the Prince's Hall cinema in Smethwick on a Saturday night, where the chatter and shouts from the audience often drowned out the film dialogue, and a baffling variety of missiles hurled through the air. I remember half a cucumber and a man's sock landing on my lap at one performance. There was more going on off the screen than on!

I was born about five years after cinema attendance in Britain passed its peak, but have been lucky enough to appear in a number of films and the whole business of "going to the pictures". By the time "Educating Rita" was reaching Black Country screens in the early 1980s there were only a few cinemas left in the Black Country – and yet such films could fill a cinema, as well as have the power to change a few lives.

Fortunately, since that time a handful of multi-plex cinemas have opened in the Black Country and cinema attendance has started to improve once more. I was glad to hear that some of the films in which I have appeared, like "Calendar Girls", and "Momma Mia", and the "Harry Potter" films have led to long queues forming outside Black Country cinemas – just like "the old days". And I am pleased to welcome you to Ned's book which tells the stories of our local cinemas.

Julie Walters CBE

Photo: Sven Arnstein

3

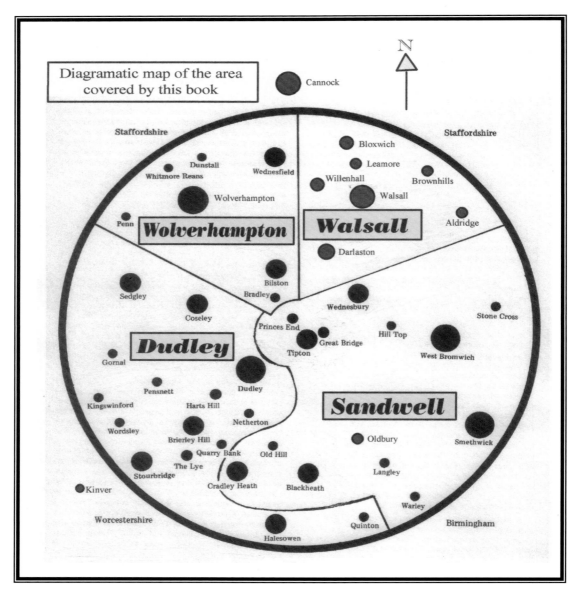

Diagramatic map of the area covered by this book

N

Cannock

Staffordshire

Staffordshire

Bloxwich

Leamore

Dunstall

Whitmore Reans

Wednesfield

Willenhall

Brownhills

Wolverhampton

Walsall

Penn

Wolverhampton

Walsall

Aldridge

Darlaston

Bilston

Sedgley

Bradley

Wednesbury

Stone Cross

Coseley

Princes End

Hill Top

Dudley

Great Bridge

West Bromwich

Tipton

Gornal

Dudley

Pensnett

Sandwell

Kingswinford

Harts Hill

Netherton

Wordsley

Oldbury

Smethwick

Brierley Hill

Quarry Bank

Old Hill

The Lye

Langley

Stourbridge

Kinver

Cradley Heath

Blackheath

Warley

Worcestershire

Quinton

Birmingham

Halesowen

This book is divided into sections based on the boundaries of the Metropolitan Boroughs created in 1974, shown diagrammatically above.

The tour starts in Sandwell and takes a clockwise journey through Dudley, Wolverhampton, Walsall, and then finally takes in the cinemas within South Staffordshire. The dots represent towns that had one or more cinemas.

Cinemas often go through a number of name changes. To find the text about a particular cinema, search the names listed in the Contents by town.

CONTENTS

Introduction

Welcome to this book about Black Country cinemas. The two things that you might notice straight away are that the book covers a slightly wider area than the Black Country itself, and that the book is designed to complement a companion volume about local theatres. The total project is designed to look at the history of "stage and screen" entertainment in The Black Country and South Staffordshire. Although one can try and separate them, the history of theatres and cinemas intertwine, and similarly their history does not quite fit into neat geographical boundaries – hence the epic scope of the project!

In 1982 I produced a book called *"Cinemas of the Black Country"*, which went out of print fairly quickly. Ever since then I have been trying to produce a new version that would bring the story up to date, and add detail to the story as told in 1982. At the same time I tried to "mop up" the histories of some cinemas that had been left out in 1982 on the grounds that I did not feel they were really in the Black Country. This led to the publication of *"Cinemas of Aldridge & Brownhills"* in 1984, and *"The Kinema at Kinver"* (written jointly with Bill Parker) in 1986. These stories can now be brought together.

Another result of the publication of *"Cinemas of the Black Country"* arose from the fact that I had included cinemas owned by Pat Collins, the famous fairground showman. Fairground enthusiasts were outraged that I had drawn people's attention to his cinema activities when really his life on the fairground was what needed recording! Via a devious route, this led to the production of a biography of Pat Collins, written in association with Freda Allen and published in 1991. After that three more books followed on the fairground.

The result of becoming interested in the fairground was that I started to take account of the world of the circus, and any entertainment that was presented on a "Here today, Gone tomorrow" basis. This led to a fascination with bioscopes and then the mysterious world of portable theatres. I discovered a small dedicated bunch of enthusiasts who were trying to put the history of portable theatres "on the map." It then seemed natural to study the history of the "permanent" theatres that came in their wake. I had now come full circle as I was back in a world where theatres sometimes became cinemas and visa versa. It was time to try and put the whole picture together.

"Cinemas of the Black Country" was produced at a time when the cinema business seemed in terminal decline. There were only about seven cinemas left in the Black Country when the book came out, and some of those closed soon afterwards. Then the mutli-plexes came along and the story seemed to go into reverse. Instead of just writing a new edition to list a few more closures, this book has to record some new exciting cinema openings!

The other thing that has happened since 1982 is that our historical perspective has changed. The life of some cinemas now seems incredibly short – could then have really come and gone so quickly? And not only that, their passing is now much longer ago – there are less and less people around who remember them. Add all this to the fact that the Black Country has changed enormously since those times and you will see that this book is in danger of becoming incomprehensible to any reader under sixty five at the time of publication. The cinemas described were part of a world that might seem "pre-historic" to future generations. How will they understand that we had to rush out of a cinema before the National Anthem began because we dare not miss the last trolleybus home? How will they understand that to my generation the phrase "home cinema" is a contradiction in terms"?

This book celebrates the cinema-going days of the past, but does not wish to ignore the fact that a twenty-first century version of cinema-going is alive and well. The study of cinema history has also made great strides, thanks to the work of bodies like the Cinema Theatre Association. Some cinemas are now recognised as being of historic interest and are "listed". Others have been restored like the wonderful Plaza at Stockport. In other places cinemas have been preserved, and in some the old fashioned aspects of film presentation are deliberately re-created – from festoon curtains to sales staff who carry trays of ice cream into the auditorium.

When Edward Hewitson opened the Windsor, Smethwick, in 1930, he wrote:

"Here then is the answer to those who ask, 'Why all these places of amusement?' They are centres of mental and physical relaxation, the reflex of hard industrial organisation. The more a people must work, the more it should play."

and of his new cinema he wrote:

"No one can cross its threshold without feeling a sense of exhilaration. It is a triumph of architecture graced by the art of the scenic decorator, a veritable place of luxury, comfort, and beauty. Here music, colour, soft lighting, all combine to provide an atmosphere of joyousness in which the mind can more easily cast aside those worries and problems of the office, the casting shop or the lathe."

All that — before the film has even begun its own seductive effect! A great deal of attention is paid to the films themselves. This is a book about the places in which they were shown. In this book you are asked to stand with your back to the screen and admire the auditorium itself, the exterior of the building, the men who designed and built it, the staff who ran it, the companies that invested in it, the patrons who supported it, the forces of destiny that opened it and closed it.

It might be asked how does a "furriner", who has only lived in the Black Country for half a century, come to be writing such a history, and then re-writing it? The short answer is that in April 1980 I drove past the Coliseum, Dudley Road, Wolverhampton to find the place being demolished. In the stalls a huge bonfire was consuming the paperwork accumulated in the cinema. It was a potent image that reminded me of many such occasions I had experienced since coming to this area in 1962; one arrives somewhere to find it "gone". I felt that it was now or never, so many buildings had already disappeared, probably so many people had passed on, so much had never been recorded. I resolved to put the matter right without further delay.

The long answer concerns my own long relationship with the cinema, as an eager patron. In London I lived half way between two cinemas: the Odeon, Gants Hill, and the Coliseum, Manor Park. Ironically I later discovered they were designed by the same architect, George Cole, at opposite ends of his career. They were so different, one a magnificent super-cinema, the other a grubby flea-pit, that I learnt from an early age that no two cinemas were the same and that their variety provided as much enjoyment as the films themselves. At the Odeon I joined the Minors' Club on Saturday mornings. Who can call themselves educated who have not been brought up on children's matinees ? But at the Coliseum I encountered a more intriguing mystery concerning cinemas. The seediness of a run-down flea-pit attracted disapproval that suggested film going to such establishments might initiate one into the forbidden mysteries of the adult world. I longed to be old enough to understand what *"I Was A Teenage Werewolf"* was all about! Perhaps it provided the mysterous key to being an adult. Attempts at pretending to be an adult in order to see X films seldom fooled the lady in the box office.

During my teens I was fortunate to belong to the State Film Society: a cinema co-operatively owned by its staff and patrons, in Leytonstone. Eventually bingo was played on five nights of the week and our films were screened only on Wednesday evenings, but what wonderful evenings they were. I learnt that it was possible for people to love a cinema and that some individuals would make almost any sacrifice to enjoy the act of putting an image on that sacred screen. It was as if films left in their cans died of neglect!

When I came to the Black Country I found myself exploiting the variety of cinemas that still staggered into the sixties to do battle with declining audiences and advancing Bingo. It was still possible to catch a trolleybus from my new home in Dudley to the Clifton, Wolverhampton, catch the blue and cream No. 74 bus in search of the Queens, West Bromwich, or mount a motorcycle to try and find the Royal, Cradley Heath, or Lyttleton, Halesowen. Later in life I was able to explore cinemas on a wider basis – from Australia to Albania! The wider the variety of cinemas I have encountered, the stronger I have felt the urge to write about them, or photograph them, and share what can be known about

Right: The author presents the original "Cinemas of the Black Country" at a launch at The Odeon, Wolverhampton in October 1982. A "Supplement" was published in the Spring of 1984, and a booklet was produced to mark the closure of The Odeon in July 1983.

9

them. Once something seems to be disappearing it seems logical to try and put things "on the record".

The result has been that I have spent many years enaged in extremely exciting work. It has been a process of assembling a fairly large and complex jig-saw from very tiny pieces. Cinema histories cannot be compiled from single sources and the quest for any sources at all has been as enthralling as those matinee serials. While I have spent much time buried in newspapers and records in libraries and archives, I have also engaged in so much social activity that I thought I would never have time to write everything down. I have met as many cinema proprietors, managers, usherettes, patrons, builders, projectionists, and "chuckers-out" as I could find. Everyone has been generous with their time, energy, and information, not forgetting cups of tea. I am still amazed about how much devotion people have felt towards their cinemas, whether they were patron or staff.

I have sometimes felt worried that people have imagined that I have arrived on the scene to denigrate or scorn their flea-pit, blood tub, or bug-hut, but readers will realise that the more obscure the cinema the more I have been fascinated by it. If I am guilty of displaying any negative feelings towards any local cinemas it is more likely to be a frustration with the anonymity of a super-cinema on a national circuit!

Some large cinemas that closed before I knew them still seem unknown quantities to me. On the other hand a glorious local flea-pit like the Rex, Whitmore Reans, or The Forum, Pensnett, really exercises the imagination.

The cinema is the marriage of technology and magic. After all that restless material progress of the nineteenth century man deserved to sit back in some comfort and turn his inventions to the serious business of enjoying dreams and being "entertained". It is a cliche to describe the cinema as an art of illusion, but the statement becomes more interesting if it is applied to the entire business of "film-showing" and "film-going"rather than simply the process of "film-making".

This book celebrates two illusions that were quite distinct from the movement of light and shadow on the screen. The first illusion concerns the environment in which the event takes place, it is revealed in their early name: the "picture palaces." The showman's art was to provide an illusion of taste, comfort, luxury, and personal attention, that could all be yours for the price of an admission ticket. The second illusion was a trick played upon the showman himself: the illusion of profit! Individuals and companies set out to build palaces and super-cinemas at tremendous cost because they themselves were carried away by this illusion. A few were lucky, or astute enough, and turned the illusion to a reality, but others struggled for years to pay off mortgages long after the illusion had crumbled.

I suppose I was once naïve enough to believe that

cinema proprietors were in the buisness because they simply loved showing films. Investigation has suggested that they were simply interested in making money, and perhaps showing films was a way of doing it. On the other hand all the usherettes, and lonely projectionists, or "operators" as they seem to prefer to be called, have often presented themselves to me as vicitms of the illusions of the cinema buisness. They never made a fortune but they seem to have enjoyed being "in entertainment". Think also of those folks who appeared on stage. Fame and Fortune were both elusive – sometimes as elusive as the week's paypacket if we are to believe James Mason's account of his week in Bilston! You might be overwhelmed by the many names that are inlcuded in this book – some are provided to show how so many aspects of the business were interlinked through peoples' lives and careers, but other are here so that future family histrorians can find confirmation that Great Grandad was "Second Operator" at an almost forgotten cinema.

In the early days the "palaces" were often called "the Electric Palaces", due to their ability to flood their exterior in light, or generate their own power to put a picture on the screen. On reflection I wonder if the phenomenon that was really "electric" was the relationship between the events of the screen and the audience. The shared gasp, the huge hall-full of laughter, the mutual sitting on edges of seats, in a cinema, are things that television or a DVD can never satisfactorily re-create. I hope this book helps you relive that excitement as I tell you the stories of these Black Country palaces and the people who ran them.

Ned Williams
Summer 2011

Section 1
A Cast of Thousands

1. THE EXHIBITORS

Pat Collins 1859 – 1943

It is fitting that we should begin by considering the life and work of a fairground showman because the fairground was probably the place where the first cinematograph pictures in the Black Country were seen. Films were first "exhibited" in Britain at the Lumiere Brothers demonstration in London, early in 1896. The commercial and entertainment potential of cinematography was recognised by people like Randall Williams – a fairground showman already able to present optical illusions to a paying audience in the form of "The Ghost Show". Early in 1897 Williams started travelling his cinematographic show in what became known as the "bioscope". In the remaining three years of the century the invention spread like wildfire and several fairground showmen immediately recognized its potential.

One such man was Pat Collins. He had been born into fairground life and grew up travelling the towns of Staffordshire, Cheshire and Lancashire, working on his father's roundabout. His Bloxwich-based biographer E.J. Homeshaw, wrote, "He was a cheerful lad and a born optimist. At 21 he had a hand-turned roundabout, a horse, a wife, and a few shillings in his pocket. His home was a horse drawn flat under which he slept at night."

In 1882 he had decided to settle in Walsall and began to prosper. He understood that the working population of urban areas like the Black Country sought escapism and excitement when they came to the fair. Pat Collins introduced new attractions and was quick to adopt any new technology that he could use on the fairground, for example the steam traction engine and generator. He bought a car, as soon as such things were available, to keep an eye on all his interests. In the late 1890s he observed the bioscopes appearing on the fairground. These things are not well recorded but we know that such a show appeared at the Bloxwich Wake in 1899, and by the end of that year Pat had bought the show. In the mid 1900s he commissioned his own new bioscope shows – Wonderland No.s 1 and 2 – as described in the chapter on "bioscope days".

It has also become apparent that Pat Collins dabbled with presenting films in cinema-like style in 1910, after the passing of the Cinematograph Act. He opened an "Electric Picture Palace" in converted premises in Lichfield on 31st. October 1910, managed by Joe Bate, who recalled the event in Worlds Fair of 13th February 1937! Unfortunately fire destroyed the enterprise on 5th April 1911, so we do not know how committed Pat was to showing films on a permanent site at that time.

During the First World War Pat moved the headquarters of his empire from Walsall to Bloxwich, and searched for a wartime activity that would compensate for the fact that his fairs had ceased travelling. Almost next door to his base in Bloxwich he discovered the Electric Palace, built by Thomas Jackson of Wolverhampton. As the war came to an end Pat acquired the Bloxwich cinema, plus two others in the Black Country – one at Dudley Port, and the other at Darlaston. He also ran the cinema in Oakengates and acquired interests in other far-flung theatres, skating rinks, and dance halls.

Left: Pat Collins

In Bloxwich he set about building a brand new cinema to replace the one he had bought- and this became The Grosvenor – as fully described in the chapter on Bloxwich. By that time his life was also taking off in other directions and that story has been told elsewhere. What we need to recognise here is that Pat, having been part of bioscope history, went on to be cinema proprietor in the Black Country for a time in the 1920s.

Waller Jeffs 1861-1941

The invention of the cinematograph was also seized by another breed of showmen, the presenters of travelling lectures, travel talks and magic lantern shows. These toured the drill halls and temperance institutes of the land while the fairs toured the wakes grounds. Their "educational value" gave them a respectability that no doubt the fairground lacked.

One man who was widely acclaimed as a travelling speaker and presenter of the lantern slide lecture was Waller Jeffs. At the turn of the century his shows at Birmingham's Curzon Hall were extremely popular. The Curzon Hall, at the top of Suffolk Street, was later the site of the West End Cinema, but it had been built to house dog-shows. Political meetings, boxing, variety, religious services, circuses, all came to the Curzon Hall. In May 1901 Waller Jeffs presented a complete programme of moving pictures, although it is possible that he had included short pieces of films in earlier shows. The programme of Edison films ran for two hundred performances and Black Country folk, as well as Brummies, flocked to see it.

Jeffs made his own films of local events and of local visits by celebrities like General Buller or Buffalo Bill and screened these. The fact that he was probably doing this before the turn of the century is suggested by the fact that he became a member, and later President, of the Cinema Veterans Association. He also arranged complete film shows in other towns, probably including the Agricultural Hall, Wolverhampton and the Public Hall in Dudley. His seasons of film shows continued at the Curzon Hall throughout the 1900's. In 1908, for example, he filmed a Wolverhampton-Birmingham cycle race and photographed the event from a car that dashed along in front of the cyclists.

His manager at the Curzon Hall was Irving Bosco and later, when Mr. Bosco became a cinema proprietor, Waller Jeffs returned the compliment and managed one for him. This was at the Picture House, Harborne. About 1921 Waller Jeffs moved to the Picture House, Stratford-on-Avon, again in association with Irving Bosco, to whose family he was "Uncle Wally". Eventually Sidney Clift bought the Stratford-on-Avon Picture House and Waller Jeffs' new association with the emerging Clifton Circuit brought him back for at least one significant visit to the Black Country.

Above: Waller Jeffs (Author's collection)

In his seventies, he came to the opening of the Regal, Wednesfield, on the 14th October 1935, and two of his films taken in 1908/9 were presented as the first part of the programme. He was always a man that was loved and respected, and his kind gentlemanly manner endeared him to everyone he met. He died, at the age of eighty, on 1st July 1941 and is buried at Brandwood End Cemetery, Kings Heath. It is not clear if any of his films have survived.

Irving Bosco 1870 — 1946

I have mentioned Irving Bosco in the previous section of this book. His name is occasionally to be found in the few printed references that are made to the life and work of Waller Jeffs, but I feel his part in bringing the cinema to the Black Country needs to be more widely recognised. He was a striking man with an equally striking assumed name. He was born as William Morris Bainton, on 13th October, 1870, at Keighley in Yorkshire. How he adopted the name Irving Bosco is an intriguing mystery, although it may have been a name found somewhere in his family's history, or a circus name.

Towards the end of the last century he was to be found touring Ireland with Bosco's Circus. In his role as the Ring Master he introduced many of the leading acts of the day. He had also toured Britain with some kind of entertainment and had visited Dudley in the early 1890's. When the cinematograph was displayed in

Above: Irving Bosco (Author's collection)

London in the middle of that decade he had turned his inventive skill to perfecting a machine of his own. He eventually patented part of the mechanism but later sold the idea to a London firm. It seems likely that he made his own films and showed them with the travelling circus.

The turn of the century saw him working with Waller Jeffs at the Curzon Hall, after which he seems to have toured with a cinematograph show for the Navy League. He was definitely in this area again by 1908 for the cycle race that has already been mentioned, and in 1909 he married Miss Ducie Saunderson. She also came from Yorkshire and was a mezzo-soprano, actress and dancer. She was appearing twice-nightly for sixteen weeks "non-stop" at the Curzon Hall. Waller Jeffs was the best man and that evening he brought the couple on stage at the Curzon Hall.

Mr. and Mrs. Bosco Bainton settled in Tipton and it seems likely that Irving Bosco showed films in Dudley sometime in 1909. Christmas film shows at Dudley's Public Hall were presented by Professor Wood but as soon as the Cinematograph Act became law it seems that Irving Bosco acquired the necessary licence and began his regular shows at the Public Hall as from 31st January, 1910.

He was also showing films at the Picture Palace, West Bromwich before the coming of the Cinematograph Act helped by his brother, James Bainton. This new venture

needs to be recognised as the Black Country's first cinema.

In the years leading up to the War he broadened his operations considerably. In June 1911 he opened the Cape Hill Electric, a purpose-built cinema, and in April 1912 he began showing films at The Rink, Smethwick and The Empire, Dudley. The latter became the headquarters of "Bosco's Pictures Ltd.", which was formed in 1913. He moved to Smethwick as his interests began to include cinemas in the Birmingham area; the Picture House, Harborne and the Picture House, Villa Cross. Shows at the Public Hall, Redditch were also presented by Bosco's Pictures.

During the First World War, or just after it, Irving Bosco relinquished his interest in the West Bromwich cinema, to Thomas Leach, and abandoned Dudley's Public Hall. Some pioneers, such as Professor Wood and his son decided to expand, but it seems that Mr. Bosco felt unsure of the industry's future. In October 1920 Kine Weekly reported that he was putting his cinemas up for sale. In a subsequent edition it reported that he certainly did not intend giving his cinemas away but a buyer materialised and Bosco's Pictures Ltd. was wound up at a special general meeting on 17th December 1920.

The man who bought the Empire, Dudley, the Rink and the Cape Hill Electric, the two Birmingham cinemas and the Public Hall, Redditch was E. C. Shapeero of the Record Cinema Circuit based in Nottingham. Although this deal marked the end of Irving Bosco's association with Black Country cinemas it is interesting to recall what happened next. From the same Mr. Shapeero, and a partner named Mr. Cook, Irving Bosco acquired the Picture House in Stratford-upon-Avon, and installed Waller Jeffs there as the manager. This cinema had opened in 1913 and had developed a few problems that its new owner was quite equal to solving.

To his staff at Stratford Mr. Bosco was always the "Great White Chief" and he regularly visited the cinema on Saturdays to see Waller Jeffs and see how business was going. Very quickly it became apparent that the unreliable electricity supply was the cinema's main problem. A power cut on Whit Monday 1921 while queues waited outside the hall convinced Irving Bosco that there was only one answer: they would generate their own power. A gas generator was installed and the staff trained in its use. A lamp was erected at the top of a flag pole to proclaim their triumph and even during power failures in the mains supply they could announce, "Bosco's Beacon shines nightly!". In 1924 he sold out, but he made sure that Waller Jeffs' position at the cinema was to be permanently safeguarded, as recorded in the previous section.

Like many of his fellow-members of the Cinema Veterans Association, Irving Bosco was definitely a great showman. He was a big impressive man with an engaging outgoing personality. He could combine a shrewd business sense with generosity, fairness and a sense of humour. These attributes, plus his continual inventiveness, made him an ideal pioneer of the new medium. He retired before the advent of the talkies, and when he died in 1946, many of the buildings in which he had shown films had disappeared or changed their use. His most lasting monument in the Black Country was the Cape Hill Electric, which survived into the mid fifties.

The Woods of Bilston:

Professor Joseph Wood (1842 - 1927) & Thomas Wood   (1868 - 1938)

If life took you into the Bingo club in Bilston's Lichfield Street, you would have noticed a monogram consisting of a single "W" at the centre of a very theatrical proscenium arch. One or two assistants talked of the building being haunted by the ghost of a professor and some of the elderly Bingo-players claimed to remember the professor "reading their bumps". Unravelling these "mysteries" unfolds the story of the men who brought films to this part of the Black Country, one of which became one of Bilston's leading citizens.

Joseph Wood was one of four brothers born on a smallholding in Northumberland. He was born in 1842, had a "working childhood", and received no education. About the age of 10 he set off in search of a brighter future in Liverpool and found work in a flour mill. He then set about acquiring some education with all the drive and energy that some Victorians brought to the task of improving themselves. He studied anatomy and physiology and from an interest in medical matters he

ventured into a number of subjects such as mesmerism, phrenology, palmistry and the interpretation of handwriting. He was largely self-taught but progressed far enough to be able eventually to make a living from demonstrating his skills and lecturing on them. These lectures, from the mid 1880's onwards, were accompanied by lantern slides.

The Professor's son, Thomas Reay Wood, born in 1868, became the projectionist, and in 1887 acquired an elaborated machine that could dissolve one image into the next and add movement, such as falling rain etc., to static views. A travelling show consisting of the Professor's demonstrations and his son's magic lantern slides was a success in the industrial towns of the North West and then in Staffordshire.

In 1896 Tom Wood immediately recognized the potential of R.W. Paul's cinematograph, the Professor purchased a projector in the October of that year and they put on their first programme of animated pictures at Bury. By this time they had settled into a routine of living and working in Douglas, Isle of Man, each summer and touring the mainland industrial towns in the winter. Although strict Wesleyans there was no rest for them on Sundays, for on that day they presented sacred concerts!

While Tom purchased and projected films, the Professor produced his own book, "Scientific Palmistry" published in Douglas in 1897. The future patrons however, seemed likely to find more enjoyment in animated pictures than in having bumps read. Tom was anxious to make his own films and eventually acquired his first camera, a Prestwich, in 1900. Like many of his fellow members of the Cinema Veterans Association, he was both exhibitor and film-maker. In 1902 he went down to London and made his own film of Edward

The Wood Family, at their Bilston home: Standing left to right: Thomas Wood, and his father Joseph Wood. Seated: Reay Wood, Mrs. Nellie Wood, (Tom's wife) and Angela Wood. Details of the life of Nellie Wood, once a variety theatre artiste, are included in Volume 2 on local theatres.

(From the collection of Angela Bird.)

VII's coronation, sending the results back to Douglas for screening at the Grand Theatre, the next night! He also made a successful film of the King's post-coronation tour, including a visit to the Isle of Man.

While managing the Grand Theatre in Douglas in the early years of this century Thomas Wood met many of the show business personalities of his day. It was also probably where he met Miss Zella Vondi, an accomplished pianist. Her real name was Miss Nellie Hewitt, and she came from Handsworth. They married in 1906.

The winter tours with the travelling cinema continued and the Woods updated their technology as the years went by, adding a heavy electric generating set to their equipment that had to be transported from hall to hall. Bilston Town Hall was on their circuit, as were the Public Hall in Dudley and other halls in the Black Country. They settled in Bilston in 1910 and rented a room in the Town Hall to be the first "Wood's Palace".

In the next four years they looked round for a suitable site for a permanent purpose-built cinema. About 1912 they found a site on the Wakes Ground at Willenhall but nothing came of this, although, after the Great War they leased the Coliseum, Willenhall, for a time. During the War itself Thomas Wood joined the St. John's Ambulance Association and performed duties with the Special Constabulary. He was also acting-manager at Leon Salberg's Alexandra Theatre in Birmingham for a while. As soon as peace returned he turned his attention, once again, to the expansion of his entertainment business.

In 1919 the Woods leased the tiny Electric Palace, opposite the Town Hall, in Church Street, and as materials became available again they set about building the magnificent Wood's Palace in Lichfield Street. In 1921 their shows in the Town Hall ceased and their purpose-built cinema opened. The full details are described in the section on Bilston's cinemas. They did not rest there; they acquired the lease of the Alhambra, in the High Street, and showed films there until 1927 when they opened their new purpose-built "Savoy" on the opposite side of the road.

In the meantime they acquired the Theatre Royal in 1924, briefly showed films in Bloxwich, and, towards the end of the twenties, took over the Queens at Bradley. Thomas Wood was also a director of the Palace Cinema in Wednesbury and the Palace, Melton Mowbray. Added to all this activity he had become an important figure in the civic life of Bilston. He had been chairman of the Urban District Council in 1925/7 while also serving on Staffordshire County Council, and acting as a local magistrate. He was a Rotarian, and was on numerous committees, including the Childrens Holiday Camp Fund, the District Nursing Association, the Horticultural Society, and Swan Bank Methodist Church!

In January 1928 he held the first of Bilston's "Cinema Balls". The British film actress Marie Ault came to the Town Hall to judge the fancy dress competition and to join the four hundred and fifty revellers. They continued annually into the thirties and raised funds for the charities with which Thomas Wood was associated.

Professor Wood died in 1927 and Thomas Wood consolidated the business of "Woods Picture Halls" from then onwards rather than continue the expansion. His brother-in-law Leon Hewitt, acted as general manager in order to give "T. R." time for his many activities but even so he was often to be found at his office in the Palace.

As the thirties unfolded he installed sound in his cinemas and converted the Theatre Royal to a cinema as the talkies gained popularity. It later became a theatre again. He also took part in the organisation and planning that led to the rebuilding of the Palace in Wednesbury.

In 1933 Bilston had become a Borough and Thomas Wood became its Mayor in November 1935 and spent a busy year in this office. Perhaps it is not surprising that at this time he decided to retire. The super-cinemas and the growth of the circuits were overtaking family businesses. On 29th August 1936 the three Bilston cinemas: the Woods Palace, the Savoy and the Queens, were leased to C.S. Joseph's Astel Pictures for twenty-one years. Before leaving his office at the Palace, Alderman Wood gave an interview to Quaestor of the Express and Star. In this he reviewed his career from the days of travelling lantern-slide shows to the eve of the practical use of television. "Films", he said, "have made home conditions better, improved behaviour, and made people dress better." What would he say today?

His civic life continued; for example he opened Bilston's Library in March 1937, in his sixty-ninth year. He died on 16th December 1938 and at his funeral were to be found mourners representing all aspects of the cinema, past, present and future, ranging from Charles Pindar, the Wednesbury member of the Cinema Veterans Association of Pre-1903 exhibitors, to John Davies who represented Oscar Deutsch, but who was later to rise to great heights in the Rank Organisation.

T.R. Wood's heirs continued to be the landlords of the picture houses while C.S. Joseph ran them on his twenty-one year lease. Thus in the mid fifties when C.S. Joseph chose not to renew the leases, they returned to the family. The Theatre Royal, Bilston, closed and the Forum, Bradley, was sold to Mr. and Mrs. Woodroffe, but Thomas Wood's son, Reay Wood, took over the Savoy, hoping that a buyer would be found. No buyer materialised and thus Reay Wood kept the family's association with cinemas going right into the sixties. For a time he added the Rialto, Wednesbury, to his task of running the Savoy, but the late fifties were difficult times to be running cinemas and their closure became inevitable. The Rialto enjoyed a further short lease of life in other hands, but the Savoy closed in 1963.

The Odeon, late Wood's Palace, which had been trans-ferred directly from C.S. Joseph to Oscar Deutsch back in 1936 had seen its lease renewed by the Rank Organisation. It closed a year after the Savoy and became a Bingo Hall. Its connection with Woods Picture Halls was finally severed in 1971 when the Rank Organisation offered the Hutchinson Group a package deal of five halls that included the Dunstall Odeon and the Bilston Odeon. This brought the Wood family's association with Bilston to an end.

The Poole Family

The pioneers of cinematography were showmen from a variety of backgrounds: the fairground, the lecture hall and the music hall. What they had in common was that they invariably travelled the length and breadth of the land while providing their entertainment. The building of permanent "cinemas" provided a break with this tradition and heralded the demise of that way of life. People like Irving Bosco, Benjamin Kennedy and the Woods then put down some roots in the Black Country. The same cannot be said of the Pooles, but as they contributed to the history of early film-showing in the Black Country they deserve to be included here.

This story begins in 1837 when a man named M. Gompertz formed a partnership with two brothers, George and Charles Poole. Legend has it that the former, a travelling presenter of "panoramas", met the two brothers while they were busking on the promenade at Margate. They teamed up so that they could provide a musical accompaniment to the show, which consisted of painted pictures being rolled across the stage. Some of the pictures were very elaborate and expensive, others used trick effects such as moving components, and they usually depicted great battle scenes, epic disasters and contemporary events.

Eventually the Poole Brothers took over the business entirely and were joined by a third brother, John Poole. John Poole's son, Charles W. Poole became the manager and they adopted the term "Myriorama" to describe their moving tableaux. The show was accompanied by an orchestra and included variety acts between each tableau. The show travelled from town to town and hired a public hall for a week. Special trains and fleets of horse-drawn pantechnicons had to be organized to move the elaborate equipment and growing numbers of personnel. By 1900 seven such shows were on tour. About the same time films were introduced and included among the vaudeville turns while the next panorama was being mounted. Some of these films had mechanically coupled sound-on-phonograph, yet they still were only considered in third place, in terms of entertainment value, after the panorama and the variety acts.

Poole's Myriorama visited the Black Country on tour each year but their headquarters were established in Gloucester, so a stronger association with the area did not come about until they gradually started acquiring some of the halls they visited on a more permanent basis. Charles Poole and his son, John R. Poole, started running cinemas very soon after the passing of the 1909 Cinematograph Act.

They opened the Kings Hall in Stourbridge in November 1911, and the Queens Hall, Brierley Hill in May 1912, and eventually had cinemas in Edinburgh, Aberdeen, Oxford and Ipswich. "Pooles Perfect Pictures" never quite penetrated the Black Country as thoroughly as other early concerns, but their presence at Stourbridge survived the coming of sound and the advent of the super-cinema. The only male member of the fourth generation of the family, John K. S. Poole, born in 1911, was trained in all aspects of the cinema business and preserved his family's traditions. After celebrating the centenary of the business he set about rebuilding the Kings Hall as a modern super-cinema.

They were an old-fashioned family business and their employees often enjoyed a long association with them, for example Harry Wharton and Harry Morris in Stour-bridge. Other people associated with cinemas in the Black Country, for example Cecil Couper in Brierley Hill and Jim Davis in far away Wednesfield, began their cinema-careers with Pooles. (Cecil Couper was related to the Poole family). Their connection with local cinemas was severed in the mid-fifties when their Stourbridge cinema was sold to the Rank Organisation.

Benjamin Kennedy 1867 – 1939

Ben Kennedy came to the cinema via the music hall, but he was not born into a theatrical tradition, nor was he born in the Midlands. He was born in London, the son of a furrier. It was intended that he would go into his father's business but legend has it that he ran away at the age of thirteen and joined a travelling waxworks show. Once established in the Black Country in the 1900s we find that his name pops up all over the place, leasing places and eventually building his own premises. His life creates several problems for us. First of all: was he a "cinema man" or was his heart in "theatre"? Secondly, how does one tell his story? Despite being involved in the story of so many venues he left us with very little trail to follow. He probably didn't regard the first question as valid – he was simply a showman and therefore interested in "entertainment". In practice he generally favoured "cine-variety" – shows that combined films with live acts. As for the second problem, Ben probably created it! He seems to have deliberately chosen to be a shadowy figure. Nevertheless, you will find a more complete account of his life in Volume Two.

You will find Ben Kennedy mentioned many times in this book when exploring places like: The Olympia, Wordsley; The Hippodrome, Cannock; The Kings Hall, Willenhall; The Borough Hall, Wednesbury; The Coliseum, Bearwood, and The Empire, Smethwick. At one time he claimed to have connections with thirteen halls.

Kennedy's name is particularly associated with Dudley. In October 1920 he acquired the Opera House, and the adjacent Scala ten years later. The Scala was demolished and rebuilt as a super-cinema called The Plaza, opening in May 1936. About six months later the Opera House was burnt down. Ben Kennedy then set out building his ultimate achievement. From the ashes of the Opera House a huge brand new theatre – The Hippodrome - was built to stand alongside the Plaza. He was then in his seventies, but in December 1938 he struggled to attend the opening of the Hippodrome in an invalid chair. It was a brave and proud gesture to build such an immense theatre when super-cinemas seemed to rule the entertainment world.

Not long afterwards, on 10th April 1939, Ben Kennedy died at his home in Wollaston, near Stourbridge. His sons continued to run the halls in Dudley, and one in West Bromwich, but the Plaza was eventually sold to Miles Jervis and the Hippodrome closed on 15th March 1958, as far as the Kennedys were concerned. The Hippodrome was sold and re-opened for a short time as a theatre but was not a real success. All is revealed in volume Two.

Above: Ben Kennedy – from a photograph that appeared in the opening brochure for the Dudley Hippodrome. His lucky horse-shoe tie pin, said to be a gift from his father, was something he wore all his life!

Edward Hewitson 1874 – 1936

It presents a very neat straightforward picture for the historian if one person can be given the credit for bringing the cinema to a particular town; for example Professor Wood, and his son, in Bilston. Smethwick seems to have been equally fortunate. In this case Edward Hewitson introduced films to the town.

Edward Hewitson came to Smethwick in 1897 to be manager of the Theatre Royal, Rolfe Street, on its opening. He was, therefore, a man of the theatre, as much as the cinema, and it was in the Theatre Royal that he first showed films, introducing them after the stage show about 1905. Like other early exhibitors he also made his own films and occasionally hired the Town Hall in which he put on shows. Following the passing of the Cinematograph Act he does not seem to have rushed into the business of showing films on a full-time basis. Films still mingled with the theatrical offerings at The Theatre Royal and at Ben Kennedy's rival theatre, The Empire.

Irving Bosco opened the first purpose-built cinema in Smethwick, at Cape Hill, in 1911, just at a time, presumably, when Edward Hewitson was making up his mind that exhibiting films had a future. Edward Hewitson left the Theatre Royal on 2nd December 1911 after a Benefit evening held in his honour. A few months later he opened "Pictureland" at the Town Hall while his own cinema was being built. The new cinema, The Prince's Hall, was built nearby, on the site of an old post-office. This opened on 19th December 1912 and the shows at the Town Hall ceased.

During the same period Thomas Jackson, in Wolverhampton, was expanding like wildfire, but Edward Hewitson proceeded more slowly. He added the Majestic, Bearwood, early in 1916. Perhaps its completion had been held up by the outbreak of war. By the end of the First World War he had also acquired The Coliseum, Bearwood, and the Ring Palace, West Smethwick. I do not know whether he had any wish to purchase Irving Bosco's two Smethwick cinemas, the Rink and the Cape Electric, after the war. In the event the only further addition to his "chain" was the Empire, Smethwick, acquired in 1922 and turned into a cinema.

Running five local cinemas, he was now an exhibitor of some importance and he became a prominent member of the local Cinema Exhibitors Association and joined such battles as the campaign for Sunday opening. He became the C.E.A.'s National President in 1927 and also entered the world of politics. His interest in his cinemas was still strong and towards the end of the twenties a great deal of activity took place, anticipating the coming of sound and the super-cinema.

First of all the Coliseum was replaced by an entirely new cinema, built just across the road. This new hall was The Windsor, opened in September 1930 with the wonders of sound, and a Compton theatre organ. Three months later a new Prince's opened in Smethwick itself as a fine replacement for the old Prince's Hall. The Windsor, however, was the company's 'flagship' and the head office was established there. The Rink, Windmill Lane, was also re-opened in 1930 by Gaumont British, and thus Smethwick enjoyed three new large cinemas, each containing a Compton organ !

The Empire was updated with sound equipment but the Ring Palace was abandoned after a short period of survival as a "silent" cinema surrounded by sound ones!

Edward Hewitson's civic life was still to reach its summit. He became Smethwick's Mayor in 1935. Unfortunately, a few days after the end of his year of office, he died on 19th October 1936. Thus he did not live to see the last part of his cinema empire join the Windsor and the Prince's as a modern super-cinema. The final touch was the rebuilding of the Majestic, which was completed just before the beginning of the Second World War.

Surrounded by the growing circuits, the four halls now run by Edward Hewitson's son, Alan, provided an oasis of independence and remained as such until their closures, thus linking the family's name indelibly with cinema entertainment in that borough.

Below: Edward Hewitson (Author's collection)

Thomas Jackson 1869 - ?

The men who built the first cinemas and recognized that films could bring profit to permanent establishments were not always men from the traditions of the theatre, or travelling showmanship. Sometimes local entrepreneurs were simply businessmen who seem to have alighted on the new toy just at the right moment and who adopted it as their main concern. One such man was Wolverhampton's early film magnate: Thomas Jackson, who had been born in Coseley on 20th March 1869.

On leaving school he served an apprenticeship in the wholesale grocery trade that led to setting up his own business in Whitmore Reans, an industrial suburb of Wolverhampton. He obviously had talents in building and running businesses because he soon had several grocery shops in Wolverhampton. In 1894 he decided to go into the bakery and confectionery trade and built his "Hygienic Cake Factory" in Whitmore Reans. He invested in "state of the art" baking machinery, powered by his own gas engines and was soon employing over one hundred people. Twenty horse-drawn vans were required to deliver his products. In 1902 when interviewed by the Wolverhampton Journal he listed music and singing as his "recreations".

While the Cinematograph Bill was going through Parliament it appears that Mr. Jackson was still baking

Below: Thomas Jackson (Author's collection)

cakes at his bakery in Whitmore Reans, but maybe by then he was looking for something new in which to invest his energy and talents. He lived nearby the bakery, at 78 Gatis Street and his world still seemed to centre on Whitmore Reans. Perhaps inspired by the success of the Quigley's at the Olympia, he decided to convert his bakehouse, or part of it, into a cinema. This became The Strand, opened in 1912. Following its success he opened the Alhambra in Bilston and the Electric in Bloxwich. He formed a company called Wolverhampton, Walsall and District Cinemas, with a capital of £15,000. His meteoric rise was accompanied by the building of larger premises, considered quite a novelty because of their size; The Coliseum, Wolverhampton and the Cinema de Luxe, Walsall. We cannot be quite certain how large an empire Thomas Jackson was planning. Recently it came to light that was planning to build a purpose-built cinema in Netherton in 1913 or 1914. The plans are preserved in Dudley Archives.

In a bewildering maze of activity the Midlands County Cinema Circuit Ltd., was also formed early in 1914. This company had its headquarters in Market Harborough, Leicestershire, and owned both of Mr. Jackson's Walsall cinemas, the De Luxe and The Palace, the Coliseum, Wolverhampton, and the Picture House, Kidderminster – where he employed Percy Lloyd as manager, who had previously managed The Pavilion, Wolverhampton. The Palace, West Bromwich and the Little Picture House, Victoria Street, Wolverhampton, were also brought under his control. The latter became his headquarters, and, at some stage he moved from his home in Whitmore Reans to a grand house in Merridale Road: "The Firs". Apparently Thomas Jackson managed to supervise all his cinema interests personally, with the help of his daughters, and a speedy chauffeur-driven car!

In May 1922 Kine Weekly announced that he intended selling his chain of six cinemas and "The Firs". The six cinemas at that time were the Picture House and Coliseum, Wolverhampton, the Palace and the Cinema de Luxe, Walsall, and the cinemas in West Bromwich and Kidderminster. The Strand was to be re-built as The West End, the Alhambra, Bilston, was by then being run by Thomas Wood and the Bloxwich cinema had passed to Pat Collins. It seems that Mr. Jackson wished to move to Leicestershire and concentrate on his interests there.

No sale was forthcoming and it seems that he was forced to form a new company to run the circuit. He went into partnership with a Mr. C.D. Allen and formed Jackson Allen (Cinemas Consolidated) Ltd. Unfortunately the partnership did not thrive and on 16th March 1923 Pathe Freres presented a petition for the liquidation of the new company. It was heard at Wolverhampton County Court on 6th April and the company was compulsorily wound-up. Further court proceedings occupied the remainder of 1923 and Thomas Jackson's bankruptcy was finally recorded in

the 1926 Kine Year Book. The Midland Counties Circuit - run by L.A. Thompson, then operated the six cinemas mentioned above as the official receiver.

The rise and fall of this Black Country cinema proprietor is interesting in several respects. Firstly it illustrates the attraction that the new medium had for anyone of an entrepreneurial disposition, and the fact that the prospect of great wealth was possibly an illusion. Maybe the day-to-day administration of such a scattered and quickly established empire created problems, although men like Irving Bosco and Benjamin Kennedy had managed it. Later men built circuits of cinemas each separately financed by individual companies, but the cinema business was always a world where distant profits were often preceded by daunting initial capital investment. Another aspect of Thomas Jackson's career is the speed with which such a man can "disappear" into history. Just over thee quarters of a century after his difficulties, his life and work seem as remote as King Arthur and the Round Table! I have spoken to a few of his ex-employees and to a few of the patrons of his cinemas from those far off days before the First World War. Yet as a person I know very little more about him than I first imagined on initially encountering his name in those cryptic entries in the Kine Year Books. A few people alive in the 1980s remembered eating his cakes, popularly known as "kill-me-quicks"! He transformed himself from a baker to a showman. He adopted the tricks of men like Irving Bosco and Thomas Wood. For example, in July 1914 he filmed Wolverhampton's annual flower show and screened the results at the Strand, the Picture House and Coliseum. Yet today few people know his name or can provide memories of the man himself.

If he left Wolverhampton about 1924,1 wonder what became of him? Perhaps he did manage to pursue his interests in Leicester. I have heard other more romantic stories including one in which he emigrated to Canada and ran cinemas in Saskatchewan!

The Bray Family and Wally Davies

When I first came to the Black Country in the early sixties I remarked to someone on the number of little cinemas that had closed in the area around Dudley. The stranger said that all the cinemas belonged to either "the Brays or the Coupers" in the south west of the Black Country. It was not quite true, but the names had obviously become part of the folklore regarding local cinemas and nearly two decades later, I began to sort out who these people were and which cinemas were which!

At the turn of the century the Brays were an established business family in Dudley. They had no previous show business connections but cinematography obviously attracted a young Sidney Bray. Mr. Bray's sister married another local man, Walter Davies. Mr. Davies' grandfather had been a noted Netherton brewer and early this century his father kept the Criterion Public House in the Market Place, Dudley. Music hall entertainment was to be found at the Criterion and eventually films. At some stage it ceased to be a public house altogether and the entire site was converted into a cinema, only about thirty feet wide, but nevertheless a cinema. By this time Sidney Bray had already established himself as a cinema proprietor, by putting on shows at the Drill Halls in Halesowen and Langley and at the Palace cinema in Brownhills.

Wally Davies, born in Springmere, Dudley in 1891 and educated at Holly Hall School, had started work at "The Earl's" (Round Oak Steel Works) in 1907 as a clerk and draughtsman. He first joined his brother-in-law Sidney Bray, in the cinema business on 30th January 1911. After work he made his way to the Drill Hall, Halesowen, and described what happened next in his diary:

"At 6.30 p.m. I opened and started to take the money for the pictures. It was a terrible scramble; they knocked my pay office over and the money on the floor. At the two houses I took £7.10.0 in about fifty-five minutes. (I was very ill, I, foolish-like, had a glass of bad ale)".

From August 1913 onwards he was running Sidney Bray's Langley Cinema in the Drill Hall in that town.

As from the beginning of January 1915 Sidney Bray became the licensee of the Criterion on his homeground in Dudley, but it seems that the cinema was still only a very part-time interest of brother-in-law Wally. Wally Davies was extremely inventive and persuaded Sidney Bray to be his partner in a number of schemes. First of all he became the first Dudley aviator when he took off from a field near the Priory on 27th May 1911! He built his machines in the large workshop space available at Sidney Bray's home at 90 Aston Road, Dudley. In September 1913 he had emerged from this workshop with a glider which was tested at Lapal, near Halesowen.

While Sidney Bray was establishing his place in the cinema world, Wally Davies was involved in more technical matters and the First World War took him away from the area while employed by the Bournemouth Aviation Company in their design team. After the War Sidney Bray turned his attention to rebuilding the Criterion while Wally Davies turned his attention to hydroplanes. Once again these were built at 90 Aston Road and the two men tested them on the River Severn. Sidney Bray's son, Bernard, born 1910, used to come along for the ride, and inherited his uncle's love of speed.

The Criterion opened in November 1923 but, as far as I know Wally Davies, had nothing to do with this particular venture. His involvement in cinemas was re-kindled the following year when he became Sidney

Bray's partner at the Palace, Brownhills, and this somehow became his cinema while the Brays were more pre-occupied with their interest in the Black Country itself. Sidney's younger brother, Clifford Bray, had taken over the management of the Criterion, which left Sidney more time, to concentrate on their interests in Halesowen.

Following his success at the Drill Hall, Sidney Bray had acquired the Picture House, Halesowen, from the Rose Brothers. In February 1924 it was gutted by fire, doing £3,000 worth of damage. It took over three years to rebuild the cinema, by which time the local cinema proprietor was facing the advance of the combines and the impending arrival of sound. These threats were felt particularly strongly in Dudley and the Criterion was sold to A.P.P.H. that was about to be merged into P.C.T. at the end of 1927. Clifford Bray left Dudley to develop his interest in the Central at Stourbridge and Sidney Bray continued to concentrate his activities in Halesowen.

After re-opening the Picture House, Sydney Bray also acquired the Cosy Corner in Peckingham Street, thus establishing his monopoly in Halesowen. In the early thirties he also showed films at the Victoria Palace in Lye for about four years. Clifford Bray's work in Stourbridge was more spectacular. The building of the Central was undertaken by a public company, as the Criterion had been. F. J. Ballard, an important local businessman, was on the board of both, and both cinemas were built by the Dudley firm, A. J. Crump of Aston Road. It was built on a scale and grandeur that could rival the work of the combines. (For example, it was certainly as good as P.C.T.'s new hall in Dudley; The Regent!). It opened in May 1929, shortly before the talkies arrived.

As the manager of the Central, Clifford Bray earned the popularity of the well-liked genial local cinema manager never quite acquired by his brother. He organized money-raising charity shows for local hospitals and was often in the foyer to greet his patrons, although by the mid thirties he no longer enjoyed good health. He died on 23rd April 1937 at the early age of 52, having been confined to bed for the last few weeks of his life. In the same year Oscar Deutsch acquired the Central and in 1938 it became the Odeon.

During the mid thirties Sidney Bray still fought for the cause of the independent private cinema proprietor! In Brownhills, he and Wally Davies bought their rival, the Regent. The demolition of the Palace helped pay for extending and improving the Regent. In Halesowen the Cosy Corner seemed to be running into difficulties and its licence was only renewed temporarily in 1935 because it was understood that Sidney Bray was intending to build a brand new cinema in Halesowen. In the 1930's this was easier said than done by a lone individual but somehow the Lyttleton, as the new cinema was called, managed to reach completion and defiantly opened in April 1938. It was a very attractive cinema, a small super-cinema in fact, built in the prevailing "modern" style, and a fitting conclusion to Sidney Bray's career. His son, Bernard Bray, was old enough to manage the cinema, and at the end of 1940 he inherited both Halesowen cinemas on his father's death. He also became Wally Davies' partner in the Regent, Brownhills.

Wally Davies had never ceased experimenting with hydroplanes and hydro-gliders. For example, in 1938 he had built a fairly large craft at Aston Road, which was sold to the Maharajah of Bhopal. During the Second World War both Bernard Bray and Wally Davies worked hard with an A.T.C. squadron in Halesowen building a ground-model training aircraft which was copied all over the world. Bernard Bray's interest in speed and mechanical matters usually took the form of motoring and rally-driving. A fast car parked outside one of the Halesowen cinemas was a sign that he was "in residence".

The Halesowen cinemas prospered throughout the War years. Bernard Bray making a particular success of the new Lyttleton. Like most other cinemas they suddenly encountered new circumstances in the mid fifties. Bernard Bray died at the early age of forty-nine, thus escaping the final decline of his cinemas. The Picture House closed soon afterwards, but the Lyttleton struggled on, owned and run by his daughters, and his widow. It made a spectacular survival through those difficult times and into the seventies. After the new owners turned it into a Bingo Hall, films still made a "come back" for a short period.

Wally Davies also survived into the seventies. He died at 90 Aston Road, Dudley, in the house that had once belonged to Sidney Bray, in 1972. In his lifetime he had witnessed, and participated in, almost the entire span of the Brays' involvement in local cinemas.

A picture of the Brays, and Wally Davies appears on page 195 in the chapter of the Lyttleton, Halesowen, where they are seen at the opening of that cinema.

Cecil Couper and Mr. Bishop

Cecil F. Couper's name appears in the old Kinematograph Year Books in a number of entries concerning the small cinemas in the south western corner of the Black Country. One cinema, the Savoy at Netherton, was a joint venture with another local exhibitor: Mr. Bishop. It seems sensible to bring their careers together in this section although their business association was fairly brief.

Cecil Couper was actually a native of Southampton and was born in 1885. He was a nephew of one of the Poole's and presumably via this connection eventually found work with the travelling "Myrioramas". He became one of the lecturers who addressed the audience while the panoramas were presented. As they were interspersed with variety acts he became well acquainted with the artistes from the world of "variety". He married "Inez" of "Inez and Pim", a famous acrobatic team.

In 1912 the Coupers came to Brierley Hill to manage the Queens Hall — the Poole's new cinema in the Town Hall, which replaced Mr. Colin's variety shows, known as "The Tivoli". Mr. Couper's cheerful showman's geniality won him many friends and a year later he took over the lease of the Queens Hall in his own right, and continued to enjoy their support. It also seems that about 1914 Mr. Couper took over the Palace Theatre on the other side of Brierley Hill's High Street.

Further immediate expansion was interrupted by the First World War. During the War Cecil Couper served in the Army and as a result of his service suffered ill health for the rest of his life. However, once peace was restored he vigorously set about expanding "Coupers Enterprises".

Left: Charles Bishop, Cecil Couper, "Ma" Couper and Kathy Clarke (cashier at The Coronet, Quarry Bank) photographed at the Couper's home in Brierley Hill.
(Gladys Bishop collection)

First of all they leased the Cinema Hall, High Street, Tipton, and then in 1923 they acquired the Olympia at Wordsley near their base in Brierley Hill. The Coupers' home was at "The Firs" in Albion Street, Brierley Hill, and therefore, this outpost in Tipton must have seemed quite remote from the rest of their operations. The Queens Hall, the Palace, and the Olympia were within easy reach and were very much under his personal supervision. Cecil Couper ran matinees for the children and special Christmas shows in the grand showman's tradition.

He rebuilt the Palace sometime in the mid twenties and, thereafter, it devoted more time to presenting film than live theatre. His daughter, Irene, accompanied the films and Mrs. Couper played a large part in the management of the halls. In September 1928 Irene Couper married Harold Roberts and Mr. Couper's new son-in-law became involved in the cinema world! The wedding at St. Michael's Church was hailed as the first such occasion in Brierley Hill to be recorded on film. The film was subsequently screened on their three local screens so that patrons could share the family's happy event. Charles Poole himself was present and a representative of the Cinema Veterans Association, of which Cecil Couper was a member. Irene's younger sister, Celia, was a bridesmaid. Later her wedding was filmed by Pathe and screened at the Coronet and Savoy.

With the coming of sound Cecil Couper abandoned his outpost in Tipton and later at Wordsley. He began a programme of building small cinemas ideally suited to the village communities of that part of the Black Country.

Early in 1933 he opened the Coronet in Quarry Bank. The four shareholders in this enterprise were Mr. and Mrs. Couper and Mr. and Mrs. Roberts — their daughter and son-in-law. Mr. Roberts maintained his connection with the Coronet for its entire life. Then Cecil Couper began his business association with Howard Bishop of Netherton. Mr. Bishop had been presenting films at the Netherton Institute since before the War. He had also presented films at Dudley's Temperance Hall and at Cradley Heath's Institute, usually presenting films under the banner of "Pictureland". In the early thirties business was bad and Howard Bishop sought Cecil Couper's help in installing sound to bring the talkies to Netherton and regain a reasonable audience. With sound installed the hall became the Imperial. (Everyone in Netherton simply knew it as "Bungies"!)

Business picked up at the Imperial but the future of the lease was uncertain. Howard Bishop died, but his son, Charles Bishop, carried on his father's cinema activities, while working for the Great Western Railway by day. To overcome the uncertainty of the Imperial's future Mr. and Mrs. C. Bishop joined forces with Mr. and Mrs. Couper to build a new cinema almost "next-door". This cinema was the Savoy, and was opened in 1936.

Mr. Couper's final achievement was the building of the delightful little cinema in Pensnett; the Forum. Ill health prevented him from attending the opening of the Forum in January 1937 and he died not long afterwards at a nursing home in London.

The funeral was at Holy Trinity Church, Amblecote. The family were joined by mourners representing many branches of the cinema world, including the Cinema Veterans Association, Charles Bishop, his Netherton associate, D. H. Pass representing the Odeon circuit, and Mortimer Dent of the Danilo circuit (both circuits were now present in Brierley Hill), and the general manager of Poole's Theatres Ltd., along with Harry Morris from the Kings Hall, Stourbridge.

His early death, at the age of 52, robbed the Brierley Hill area of its enterprising showman who had built "village cinemas" where no super-cinema would have dared to venture. These three new purpose-built cinemas carried on but the Queens Hall and the Palace closed. (The former may have closed earlier). The Olympia had been sold to Mr. F.C. Leatham.

The Savoy continued to be run by Mr. and Mrs. Bishop, although Mrs. Couper booked the films for a time, then Irene Roberts did it. Harold Roberts ran the Coronet, and Kitty Stewart and her husband Alfred managed the Forum. The Stewarts were variety artistes who had worked for Poole's way back in the past. Mrs. Couper died in 1947, before the little cinemas began to suffer any decline in their popularity. The Forum was then sold to Mr. F.C. Leatham. It was the first of Cecil Couper's little cinemas to close, in 1959, but by then it was in other hands. Mr. Roberts struggled on at the Coronet until early in 1960 and Mrs. Bishop kept the Savoy open until the end of 1960. The Coronet and Savoy have been demolished, but The Forum survived as a building until the summer of 2011.

Miles Jervis: Father, Son, and Son

As individuals, and endless names, are introduced through the pages of this book you will develop some idea of how everything inter-connects. Some names – like that of "Kennedy" pop up all over the place both geographically and over a number of decades. Others, like "Jackson" appear in a number of locations but only over a short time span. (Thomas Jackson's career in Black Country cinemas lasted for only twelve years.) When we encounter the name "Jervis" we find that it connects the diverse worlds of fairground, cinema, theatre and even Bingo! Often the surname "Jervis" is preceded by the name "Miles" – but it might not always be the same Miles! To clarify which Miles Jervis I am describing, I have adopted the trick of numbering them. This is purely my own invention, and obviously was not used by the Jervises themselves.

Above: Miles Jervis II (1905 – 1985)
(From his own collection)

Miles Jervis I began his association with the cinematograph in the days of the fairground and travelling show. Although he loved the fairground, he realised the potential of permanent cinemas. His brother Edward (Ted) Jervis had been showing films in the Market Hall at Chase Town, firstly just on Saturday night, and then for five days a week and then, when the market ceased to be held, on a full six day week. It was known as the Palace de Luxe. During 1920 Miles Jervis I purchased the Palace from his brother and began to build up a small circuit of cinemas. In 1925 he opened the Chase Cinema at Sankey's Corner. He acquired cinemas in Hednesford from a Mr. Bayliss, and one in Walsall Wood. Edward Jervis built the Regent in Brownhills, which was later sold to Wally Davies and Bernard Bray, before coming to Miles Jervis III at the end of its life!

Miles Jervis I did not concentrate all his attention in the area of the Cannock Chase Coal Field. He made one interesting excursion into the Black Country, by acquiring the Alhambra at Dudley Port. He took it over from Pat Collins in about 1926, and, at the end of the silent era sold it again. But this was not to be the last connection between the Jervis family and Dudley Port's cinema. Miles Jervis I was probably more committed to the world of the fairground than the cinema, but subsequent generations seemed to put the fairground world behind them.

Miles Jervis II was born in 1905 and started work in his father's cinema business in 1926. He acquired his first

cinema in 1937; the Valentine, at Kidsgrove in North Staffordshire. He "joined up" during the Second World War but returned to Kidsgrove when demobbed in 1945. His wife had looked after it during the War.

His debut as a Black Country cinema proprietor came very quickly after the War was over. At the Grand Hotel, Birmingham, on 26th July, 1946 he purchased the Queens and St. George's, West Bromwich, and the Savoy, Oldbury, by putting in the top bid of £25,575 at an auction of the estate of the late Tom Leach. These three cinemas had been leased to the F. J. Emery circuit, a Lancashire-based firm, and the leases still had twelve years to run.

As owner of the freehold Miles Jervis II first took a closer look at the cinemas and found them to be fairly run-down. He therefore went to see the lessee, Sir Frederick Emery, and while discussing the state of the cinemas he discovered that Sir Frederick was willing to relinquish the leases. Sir Frederick's son, who had acted as general manager of his circuit, had been killed during the War while serving with the R.A.F. The father had no enthusiasm for continuing the operation of these particular cinemas.

Thus Miles Jervis II's career as a local independent exhibitor began in these three ancient cinemas, all of which had been rather eclipsed by the emergence of the super-cinemas of the 1930's. However, the next decade gave Miles Jervis II the opportunity of acquiring more modern halls. At the beginning of 1952 he acquired the Alhambra, Dudley Port, from S.T. Cinemas. Mr. Suffolk, of S.T. Cinemas, had acquired the original Alhambra from Miles Jervis I but the cinema that now changed hands was a new replacement that had opened on the site in 1935.

Two years later, in 1954, Miles Jervis obtained the Plaza, Dudley, from the trustees of the estate of Benjamin Kennedy. Collecting cinemas, and therefore acquiring a larger number of seats, was one way of improving one's place in the pecking order of cinemas for an independent exhibitor. However, the major circuits still had first use of the films, and a film could be well exposed to the public by the time an independent exhibitor was able to show it. Strangely enough, at the time of acquiring the Plaza, the independents were seizing an opportunity to fight back. The major companies were reluctant to make any major re-investment in the cinemas, and one circuit had fallen out with a film company. The result was that the introduction of Cinemascope gave people like Miles Jervis II a chance to screen new pictures unseen at Rank Cinemas. Miles Jervis II made a deal with Twentieth Century Fox for the exhibition of their films and felt that the problems and expense involved in showing cinemascope films would be worthwhile. When "The Robe" opened at the Plaza in summer 1954 he was proved right. The Odeon, directly opposite, looked on as huge queues formed outside the Plaza and the film was retained for a second week.

In 1954 Miles Jervis II became deputy chairman of the local branch of the Cinema Exhibitors Association. He seemed youthful compared with many of the other members, but no-one could deny his commitment to the cinema business. He regarded this commitment as the secret of his success. He looked at other exhibitors, such as Arthur Griffin, from whom he later acquired the Imperial, and decided that, for them, running cinemas was only a sideline. After all, even Pat Collins had only run his cinemas as a sideline because his heart was in the fairground. The families that had 100% devoted themselves to their cinemas, the Brays, the Coupers, the Woods, the Hewitsons were now disappearing, or had already left the cinema business. Miles Jervis II was unique in that he preserved this commitment through the most difficult years ahead and passed on the enthusiasm to Miles Jervis III.

Miles Jervis I had died in 1948 and the cinemas at Chase Terrace and Chase Town were then administered by his widow. Although these suffered the misfortunes and decline of the 1950's, Miles Jervis II's Black Country empire continued to expand. In 1957 he acquired the Kings, West Bromwich, from the trustees of the estate of Benjamin Kennedy, and, a few years later, the Imperial from Arthur Griffin. West Bromwich therefore, became the centre of his local operations.

He obtained Dual Pictures and Haven Pictures from C.S. Joseph and took on leases of The Palace, Wednesbury, and The Haven, Stourport. (At the former he ventured into Bingo when the 1960's developed a taste for such things). At one time or another he also controlled cinemas in Cheshire, and one in Bedworth. In the Black Country, the Savoy, Oldbury and St. George's, West Bromwich had closed by the end of the fifties – the closure being presented as symbolic of Miles' objection to the issue of "Entertainment Tax". The Queens and Kings in West Bromwich prospered, possibly because films could be shown a week after they were seen in Birmingham and thus seemed reasonably new.

Following some ill health in the mid sixties, the control of the cinemas gradually passed from Miles Jervis II to his son. Miles Jervis III realised what was happening during the sixties; the "family audience" was disappearing quickly and the tastes of the 18-25 year old age group would determine the future success of cinema programming. He developed the necessary skills in film-booking to keep the business going. Miles Jervis III inherited his father's dedication to the cinema, and in the early seventies when Compulsory Purchase Orders and the wholesale redevelopment of West Bromwich threatened to close the Kings he took the brave, and unusual, step of fighting for a new cinema to be included in that redevelopment.

When the Kings closed the Imperial abandoned Bingo to enjoy showing films again while the new Kings was being built. The Kings opened in June 1975; a brand new purpose-built triple screen cinema, opening at a

time when many other important local cinemas had become history.

By the 1980s Miles Jervis III was running the business, but Miles Jervis II was still very much present in a consultative capacity, and could justly feel proud of his family's record of loyal devotion to showing films, and particularly of their continued success in doing so in the Black Country. Subsequently Miles III's son Paul entered the business and kept The Kings going until the redevelopment of central West Bromwich isolated the cinema and hastened its demise. (Miles Jervis III died on 11th September as this book went to print.)

Above: Paul Jervis outside The Kings, West Bromwich, displaying despair at the effect of building works on the cinema's business. (Gary Stevens collection)

Sidney Clift - (1885 - 1951) & The Clifton Circuit

Three names of Black Country cinemas stand out among the super-cinemas built in the nineteen thirties: the Cliftons, the Danilos, and the Odeons. Each was developed by Birmingham men, and, of course, the Odeons became a national circuit. The story of Oscar Deutsch and his Odeons has become well known, but the story of the other two circuits is less known and belongs very much to Birmingham and the Black Country.

Sidney Clift was a Birmingham solicitor whose association with the cinema business went back as far as 1914. His father-in-law, William Astley, had opened The Empire at Stirchley and Sidney always claimed that this was where his interest began. During the War he became a prominent member of the Cinema Exhibitors

Sir Sydney Clift. (Doug Withers' collection)

Association in Birmingham and at the beginning of the sound era worked hard in their battle with the authorities for "Sunday-Opening in the city". The battle was won at the end of 1932, and a few years later he became chairman of the C.E.A. in Birmingham. When he became its national president in 1944 he was the first Brummie to occupy that post.

In the 1920s he became involved with cinemas in far-off places like Stratford on Avon, but as the 1930s began to unfold his activities began to centre on Birmingham and the Black Country. The Clifton circuit was not "born": it "evolved" in quite a complex way.

The circuit that bore his name, began to emerge in the early thirties, as construction of super-cinemas gained momentum. He became associated with the construction of The Grove at Smethwick, opened in 1932, and the The Rock, in Birmingham. While possible projects were multiplying Sidney Clift joined forces with Leon Salberg, a theatre proprietor often associated with Birmingham's Alexandra Theatre and the production of pantomimes. They were the two directors of The Regal Cinema (Wednesfield) Ltd., which, despite its name, was really one of the first Cliftons! It opened in 1935. (Leon Salberg was drawn into cinemas by the arrival of sound. He had acquired the New Theatre Royal in Bilston Street, Wolverhampton, only to find that the practicality of operating it as a theatre was going to be undermined by the public's thirst for "talking pictures".)

As the subsequent cinemas were opened, each was owned by a separate company and this has led some people to feel that the word "circuit" is incorrect.

However, the management of the cinemas was handled by a single company, they shared a common house-style, and usually the same name: Clifton. The management company was formed in 1934 as Cinema Accessories Ltd., and was responsible for staffing and equipping each cinema as well as for booking the films and purchasing all the ancillary sales.

As time went on Sidney Clift and Leon Salberg were joined by other directors, and some cinemas, such as the Rosum, Walsall, were built as a result of Sidney Clift's partnership with a local entrepreneur. In this case the directors were Sidney Clift, Edgar Summers and the architect, Ernest Roberts, and the cinema opened in 1936. The architects, Ernest Roberts and Roland Satchwell, had particularly strong ties with the Clifton Circuit and helped establish its house-style. Both men also became directors of some of the companies. The circuit rapidly developed in many parts of the West Midlands, and even further afield, but the Black Country cinemas that are this book's concern developed as follows.

In 1937 the Cliftons at The Lye and Sedgley opened. The former was the only Clifton to materialize in the south western corner of the Black Country but others were planned, for example at Amblecote. These sites were in the villages rather than the large towns of the area and in the following year, 1938, Cliftons opened in areas of the Black Country that were, in a sense, "surburban", firstly at Stone Cross, and then at Fallings Park. Other sites were chosen and plans drawn but the cinemas did not materialize. The last brand new Clifton to open in the Black Country was at Coseley, in July 1939, not long before the declaration of War, and the end of the age of building super-cinemas. Again it was a village site but the cinema boldly faced the Birmingham-Wolverhampton "New" Road as if future patrons would drive to the cinema from miles around in the new age of private motoring. It was clear that Odeons and Gaumonts might dominate the centres of larger towns, but the Cliftons were going to make a point of occupying "out of town" locations or village positions.

Other local cinemas were brought under the control of Cinema Accessories Ltd. The New Theatre Royal in Wolverhampton ultimately became a town-centre "Clifton", the Empire and the Classic in Walsall joined the clan but retained their existing names. In 1939 the little Alexandra in Lower Gornal became part of the group.

During the Second World War the Clifton cinemas made a striking contribution towards the War Effort, led by Sidney Clift, who had two daughters in the services. Concerts and special shows raised large sums of money for war-time charities. A collection to raise the money to build a Spitfire collected £5,000 in no time and the new plane was duly named "Clifton Cinemas"! Sidney Clift's other great interest in life was poultry and this led him into war-time work that earned him a knighthood, awarded in 1947 "for services to charity and agriculture". He was not a pretentious man and I doubt whether he insisted on being called Sir Sidney Clift anymore than he had insisted on being "Captain Clift" before that. (He had acquired the rank of Captain while serving in the First World War, in the Royal Artillery and the R.F.C.). Ken Jones, the General Manager of the circuit always regarded him as a good friend, ready wit, and sympathetic listener and said that Sir Sidney was always known as "The Guvnor".

During the forties "The Guvnor" operated over thirty cinemas and continued his work for the C.E.A. and the Trade Benevolent Fund. He never saw the industry decline, as he died on 18th October 1951. He collapsed at Birmingham's Snow Hill station, on his return from a business trip, and died before the arrival of the ambulance. After his death the circuit continued to be managed by Ken Jones for at least another decade, after which the closures began.

(A more detailed account of the work of Sidney Clift, and the circuit that bears his name will be presented in an edition of "Picture House", the occasional magazine of the Cinema Theatre Association, published at the same time as the publication of this book.)

Below: David Ludlow, Ken Jones, Mr. Smith, Captain Sidney Clift, Jim Davis line up at The Regal, Wednesfield, on the occasion of the visit of Marjorie Westbury (far left).
(Mrs. Charlesworth collection)

Mortimer Dent (1875 – 1958) and the Danilo Circuit

Captain Clift often appeared at the opening of his Cliftons, and at special events. In the same way Oscar Deutsch was an identifiable figure associated with the Odeons. When it comes to the Danilo circuit, the man behind it seems a much more shadowy figure at this distance of time.

It seems from recent research that he was born in 1875 in Lymington, Hampshire and grew up in that county. He may have been given the name Hamilton Henry Mortimer Dent, and there is little evidence that he used the "Mortimer" part of his name in early life. In his early twenties he may have gone to London to study law. What is still a total mystery is what happened between the early 1900s, when he was in his twenties and living in London, and his arrival as "Mortimer Dent" on the Birmingham cinema scene just after the First World War.

Mortimer Dent, also sometimes known as "Micky" Dent, seems to have created the name Danilo in an attempt to recall the name of Dan Leno, the legend being that he was a fan of this variety artiste who had died in 1904. Other theories are that it is an Italian place name! Whatever the explanation, Mortimer Dent built Danilos. The cinemas themselves were as grand as the Cliftons and Odeons but the circuit was a much smaller affair and its history seems more obscure.

Above: A Clifton Cinemas long service medal – one of only six made! David Ludlow, seen on left, received one, and Doug Wither,s the circuit's engineer, still has this one!

26

It seems that Mortimer Dent had been in the cinema business since just after the First World War. In the early twenties he joined Joseph Cohen to form C.D. Cinemas Ltd., the initials taken from each surname. They built up a circuit by purchasing old theatres and converted skating rinks, mainly in Birmingham but including a few in the Black Country such as the Olympia, Darlaston. The smartest hall they ran in the Black Country was the Plaza, West Bromwich. By the time they opened the Plaza, in September 1927, the circuit was running fourteen halls.

At the end of the silent era Joseph Cohen and Mortimer Dent decided to go their separate ways. As a result of a good offer from ABC they "sold up", all their cinemas apart from two city-centre halls which later became "News Theatres". Joseph Cohen went on to build his own super-cinemas in Birmingham while Mortimer Dent appeared to look further afield. In the next decade he built eight "Danilo" cinemas, three of which were in the Black Country.

The first was the Danilo, Brierley Hill, which opened at the end of 1936. The Danilo, Quinton, opened in August 1939, became Mortimer Dent's headquarters as it was relatively close to his Edgbaston home, and the Danilo, Stourbridge had the distinction of being the last of the circuit to open, in May 1940. By that time, the other Danilo cinemas were operating at Redditch, Cannock, Stoke, Longbridge, and Hinckley.

They were large elegant buildings observing the traditions of the super-cinema: staff in distinctive uniforms, a house-style established in the furniture and fittings, a place in the community on the scale of an Odeon or Clifton. Is it possible that the man responsible for building eight such palaces remains so obscure? He visited his cinemas, sometimes bringing two huge dogs with him, and often personally appointed his staff, but has left no imprint on history to compare with Oscar Deutsch or Sidney Clift.

At the end of the War the Danilo circuit was acquired by S.M. Super Cinemas Ltd., the expanding empire of Mr. Southan Morris. In 1961 they passed to the Essoldo group and the Black Country survivor, at Quinton, is now part of the Reel circuit. Having sold his circuit to Mr. Southan Morris, Mortimer Dent retired. As far as we know his last appearance in the Midlands was at a Cinema Exhibitors Association gathering in Birmingham on 19th November 1957. He died in Eastbourne far away from Birmingham and the Black Country in the early months of 1958, aged 83.

Oscar Deutsch (1893 - 1941) and the Odeon Circuit

Much has been written about Oscar Deutsch, and the story of the Odeons is the one aspect of cinema history that seems to have reached a relatively wide audience. He was born in Birmingham, in 1893, the son of a prosperous scrap metal merchant who had enjoyed some association with the places of entertainment of the Black Country.

During the twenties Oscar Deutsch realised that an exhibitor's major problem was obtaining the right "product" and knew that power as an exhibitor could only be acquired if one controlled or owned enough cinemas. Some of the principal exhibitors, for example Gaumont, were also involved in film production and thus exhibited their own products. Oscar Deutsch hoped that he would be able to deal directly with the producers and obtain favourable terms by having a big enough "circuit", and by not being seen as a rival producer. This he eventually achieved in a deal with United Artists.

The Black Country can be proud that his first purpose-built cinema was opened in the area. This was the Picture House, Brierley Hill, opened in October 1928. It was not his first cinema, nor his first Odeon, but as it was the first brand new cinema built for Oscar Deutsch it surely deserves a place in history.

With the arrival of the talkies Oscar Deutsch set out on his ambitious plan to build a cinema in the High Street of every reasonably sized town in the British Isles. At first no strong house-style emerged and the first Odeon, opened at Perry Barr in 1931, was in an exotic style more associated with the twenties. Oscar Deutsch commissioned a variety of architects, many of them famous names in cinema-design.

Once again the Black Country played a significant part in his progress. At Warley, on the very border of the Black Country and Birmingham, Oscar Deutsch's new cinema was designed by Cecil Howitt and the Birmingham firm of Satchwell and Roberts who were

Left: Oscar Deutsch. (Author's collection)

responsible for so many local cinemas. Harry Weedon was asked to act as a consultant on the interior decor. Within a short time Harry Weedon had become the Consultant Architect to Odeon Theatres Ltd., and his office produced the house-style that has become so well known.

In passing it is interesting to note that the other directors of the Warley Cinema, as it was called when it opened in 1934, included Captain Clift and W. H. Onions, both of whom played a part in developing cinemas in the Black Country! Further Odeons were built in the Black Country at Dudley and Wolverhampton, both in 1937, and both superb examples of Harry Weedon's style. It is also interesting to note that the Blackheath Odeon, opened a couple of months before the Warley, was the product of a Black Country architect and, therefore, not in the established style. Odeons to other people's designs also came into being by acquisition, for example The Dunstall, Wolverhampton, The Central, Stourbridge, Woods Palace, Bilston and The Grosvenor, Bloxwich.

The classic Odeons of the rapidly growing circuit that poured off the drawing-board in Harry Weedon's office were built in a particular way. After all, the economy had barely recovered from the 1929 — 1931 slump, and the introduction of the talkies made the capital invest-ment needed to build a cinema even more daunting than it had been in the twenties. Each super-cinema was the property of a separate company. A local builder, grateful for such a major contract, would offer to work in return for payment partly in debentures, or even a seat on the board. Once a tenth of the work had been completed Eagle Star provided a mortgage and construction carried on. Oscar Deutsch only had a nominal liability and interest in each company but at the same time developed a strong interest in the companies that supplied fittings and equipment to each cinema, and the management company.

The house-style replaced the eclectic styles of the early cinemas and was much more related to the function of the building. As the style developed the proscenium arch, for example, disappeared and the walls swept directly to the large screen in a way that dramatically focused attention on the film. Sight lines and acoustics were improved, fussy decorative light fittings disappeared and were replaced with hidden lights, and exterior facades began to reflect the influence of art deco and the Modern Movement. Neon lighting added the final touch to these buildings and the name Odeon has become strongly associated with the lettering used ever since the thirties.

The Warley Odeon looked particularly impressive at night, standing at the new gateway to the Black Country — the commencement of the "New Road" which had opened in 1927 to herald a motoring age. By 1937, when the two major Odeons of the Black Country were opened, Odeons were opening at the rate of two or three per week and the event was often treated with the great excitement nowadays associated with the hysteria that greets pop stars. Two years later the pace had slowed down and the approaching prospect of war was to bring further expansion to a halt.

In December 1941, a decade after the opening of the first Odeon at Perry Barr, Oscar Deutsch died at the age of forty-eight. By this time he had opened one hundred and forty cinemas and had acquired about as many existing ones. He had successfully challenged the existing national circuits such as Gaumont British and A.B.C. His initials were now preserved in the name of these superb super-cinemas and, for many, "Odeon" had become a common noun to be used for any such cinema. The name was also exploited as an acronym and was explained as: "Oscar Deutsch Entertains Our Nation".

His financial interests passed to his widow and in 1942 they passed to J. Arthur Rank, who became the new chairman of the board. J. Arthur Rank had been on the board since 1939 and also had a controlling interest in Gaumont British. John Maxwell of ABC had also died in 1941 and Mr. Rank had tried to buy the family's holding in that company, but failed to do so.

J. Arthur Rank became as famous a name as Oscar Deutsch in post-war Britain. By 1947 the Rank Organisation embraced over eighty allied companies. The three hundred and five Odeon cinemas plus the two hundred and forty G.B. cinemas, when combined, out-numbered the four hundred and fifty-eight operated by ABC.

The organisation of the two circuits was amalgamated in 1948 into the Circuits Management Association. In that year the C.M A. controlled five hundred and sixty- four cinemas. Oscar Deutsch's dream of a cinema in every major High Street was outstripped by the reality of the Rank Organisation often owning two cinemas in each town centre! In Wolverhampton the number was four, plus two more nearby. Not only that, but the Rank Organisation was directly engaged in film-production, something not taken up by Oscar Deutsch.

My own views on monopolies in a capitalist economy colour my attitudes towards the suitability of such organisations to provide entertainment in the changing social scene that followed the War. Meanwhile many others have questioned whether monopolies have been good for the cinema business from the patron's perspective.

By the mid- fifties the closures had begun. Cinemas like the Criterion, Dudley, and the Cape Hill Electric closed after a quarrel between the Rank Organisation and the Government on the question of entertainment tax. It began the process that has continued ever since, in a series of waves, and often it has seemed to happen without any relevance to the ability of a local cinema to supply a local need or respond to a local situation. In the meantime the circuits' stranglehold on distribution had done much to affect the survival of everyone else. Many small Black Country cinemas knew they would never get the chance to screen some of the films presented by the major circuits and thus ended up with "foreign films", and strange low budget films.

The Rank Organisation had also "rationalised" in the sense that where they had two cinemas close together, one would have to close. For example, in Stourbridge The Kings seems to have closed simply to consolidate the position of The Odeon, in Wolverhampton The Odeon remained open at the expense of The Gaumont.

ABC

Although Associated British Cinemas became Britain's largest single cinema "chain" of "circuit", its development had no special origins in the Black Country. However, ABC was well represented locally by the process of taking over existing cinemas and by building new ones. The company's key architect designed the Savoys in both Wolverhampton and Walsall. In the latter town ABC was particularly well represented as a result of taking over the Walsall Theatre Company's cinemas. The familiar white, blue and red triangle trademark of the ABC circuit was seen at one time or another in most parts of the Black Country. The symbol disappeared in 1969 when ABC was taken-over by EMI.

2. OTHER EXHIBITORS

Cyril Joseph   1898 - 1987

Cyril Stanley Joseph was born on 22nd March 1898, lived in Edgbaston all his life, and was educated at the King Edward Grammar School in Birmingham (also attended by Oscar Deutsch and Sidney Clift). By the mid-twenties he was a sales representative for Ideal Films and by the end of that decade he had entered the world of exhibitors in Shrewsbury, having acquired a lease on the Central. During the thirties he built up a small circuit of nine cinemas, eight of which were in the Black Country. While others were building super-cinemas he built up his circuit by acquiring older existing cinemas and re-vitalised them in time to enjoy the boom of the late thirties and early forties.

Separate companies existed to operate two or three cinemas, but each was administered by the same three directors. The three men who pooled their talents were Mr. Joseph himself, as leader and "showman", Mr. Harry Gompertz, who was an accountant, and Mr. Alfred Parton Smith, a solicitor. They made their Black Country debut by acquiring the Picture Palace at Great Bridge in 1933 in the name of Storer Pictures.

The major development came at the end of August in 1936 when, in the name of Astel Pictures, they acquired a lease from Thomas Wood on Woods Palace, The Theatre Royal, The Savoy, and The Queens, Bradley. The lease on Woods Palace was sold, in turn, to Oscar Deutsch. This helped finance improvements to the cinemas and further expansion. For example, the Queens was refurbished and became the Forum.

A year later it was possible to lease The Palace at Wednesbury in the name of Dual Pictures. The company re-building the cinema at the time had run out of funds and C. S. Joseph stepped in to complete the cinema and re-open on 27th September 1937. Very soon afterwards similar events led to the acquisition of The Rialto, also in Wednesbury, in the name of Clifford Pictures. Early alterations in 1927 and 1931 had still not brought The Rialto up to date. Cyril Joseph acquired the lease from Mr. I. Kraines, reconstructed the place in six weeks, and re-opened on 17th August 1938.

Cyril Joseph's interests in the Black Country were completed in 1939 with the formation of Pine Pictures to acquire the Olympia and Coliseum in Wolverhampton. Compared to the new super-cinemas many of the halls on the circuit were "flea pits" doing poor business in poor districts of the Black Country, but Cyril Joseph put them back on their feet with a degree of showmanship coupled to refurbishment and better programming. He used stunts and promotions to advertise his shows. For example, the first fifty ladies coming to see a "weepie" like "The White Rose" were given paper roses, an old £5 car was set alight to advertise "The Great Fire". In this way he competed with the elaborate promotions mounted by the managers of the supers, and it brought success to his cinemas. He also followed the example of other successful early cinema proprietors and kept a watchful eye on his enterprises by visiting them regularly.

The eight Black Country halls, plus The Haven, at Stourport, prospered as an independent circuit through the War and the period immediately following it. In the mid-fifties the twenty-one year lease on the halls in Bilston expired and was not renewed. In Wolverhampton Pine Pictures was sold to V.J.H. Wareing, along with the Palace, Great Bridge. The lease on the Palace at Wednesbury was acquired by Miles Jervis. The Rialto was acquired by Reay Wood. As an exhibitor he had the remarkable good fortune of acquiring the cinemas at what turned out to be an opportune time and parted with them before their final decline. His showmanship had earned him a long retirement on Dudley Golf Course perched on a windswept ridge high above the Black Country! He and Henry Parton-Smith spoke to me about their cinemas while I was writing "Cinemas of the Black Country" – a reserved solictor and an extrovert showman! Both regretted that they had no photographs of their cinemas.

Cyril Joseph died in October 1987, at the age of 89.

F. C. Leatham 1902 – 1962

While commenting on the career of Thomas Jackson of Wolverhampton, I drew attention to the fact that some people connected with local cinemas simply seem to "disappear". Their names stare at us from the contemporary entries in the old Kine Year Books but research can fail to bring them back to life in the imagination of the historian. F.C. Leatham is another such intriguing character. Read through those dusty trade directories and his name appears all over the place, undoubtedly earning him a place in this account of Black Country cinemas, but when some kind of bio-graphical jig-saw is assembled I still feel the man is remarkably elusive. I still feel this after many years research and several conversations with his relatives and a few people who knew him!

Frederick Charles Leatham was born in Cardiff on 19th May 1902; he was one of four children, two sons and two daughters. His father, Frederick William Leatham, who had been born in Dudley, was a leather belt maker in the days when most industrial machinery was driven by such belts. The family came to the Black Country during the First World War. As a child he had constructed make-believe theatres from old cardboard boxes to entertain his family but otherwise had no family tradition of "showbusiness" that might have directed him towards the world of running cinemas.

His principle interest was music and after qualifying as a music teacher he gave piano lessons in Dudley. His encounter with the cinema world appears to have come via Mrs. Jones of The Picture House at Princes End, Tipton, later known as The Bruce. At this little cinema he found employment playing the piano accompaniment to silent films. Later he relieved Mrs. Spicer at Dudley's Criterion and played in the orchestra at that grand establishment.

In October 1927 he became the manager at the Rialto, in Wednesbury, newly "re-opened" by Mr. and Mrs. Jones. He stayed there for about three years, until purchasing his first cinema; "The Cinema", High Street, Tipton. Presumably he acquired it as a silent cinema from Cecil Couper, and one of his first tasks was the installation of sound. He then sold it to his father and never again showed much interest in the place, even when the twists and turns of fate brought him back to another Tipton cinema.

At this stage he may have briefly acquired a cinema in Longton, but his next appearance in the Black Country came in the mid-thirties when he again acquired The Olympia, Wordsley, from Cecil Couper. He ran this hall until the beginning of the War when he became associated briefly with the Scala in Stourbridge. It seems that he was interested in taking on a lease at The Queens in Brierley Hill after Cecil Couper's death but there were too many arguments with the Council about who would be responsible for what in terms of refurbishing the place.

Sometime during the War he acquired the Victoria at Horseley Heath, Tipton. To me this seems something of a "come-down" after the Scala in Stourbridge, but it must be remembered that in the early forties the Scala was very much the "poor relation" of Stourbridge's cinemas, surrounded by three "supers". It was also a very low point in Mr. Leatham's fortunes. Apparently he had hoped to move into the world of live theatre, and had intended re-opening the Theatre Royal in Rolfe Street, Smethwick. For a time he lived in a flat "converted" from the dressing rooms in the theatre that had once been managed by Edward Hewitson but the project collapsed, and Mr. Leatham returned to Tipton.

At the Victoria Mr. Leatham was not only proprietor, but also chief operator. Although this had the possible advantage of being a "reserved occupation" and Mr. Leatham was back in business, it hardly seems a good position from which to continue the pursuit of the glory of live-theatre or the illusive fortunes to be made in the cinema business.

At the same time his father, and brother Leonard, were running the Cinema, in High Street, Tipton, not very far away, but Fred Leatham seems to have little to do with that enterprise. When his father died the latter passed to Mrs. Leatham and ultimately the four children, the Cinema was managed by brother Leonard, but still Fred Leatham had little to do with it.

Immediately after the War some improvements were made to the Victoria and a manager installed to run the place while Mr. Leatham went on to further projects. He acquired the Forum in Pensnett, again following in the footsteps of Cecil Couper, and the West End in Whitmore Reans, then operating as The Park. At the latter, refurbishment and new sound equipment gave the place a fresh start when Fred Leatham re-opened it as the Rex in August 1947.

It seems possible that the cost of the work on the Rex was Fred Leatham's downfall. The post-war decline in cinema fortunes was perhaps just too far away to be predictable. It seems a good example of a cinema proprietor investing in a cinema on the basis of the prosperity it had enjoyed during the war. Apparently Fred Leatham himself felt that television would only be a "passing phase". Ironically, at last he was truly a cinema magnate — with three little cinemas under his control, in Tipton, Pensnett and Wolverhampton. He lived in Wolverhampton in a house called "Edenfield", now demolished, but not far from the author's home.

Possibly he felt his career was still ascending. In August 1952 he disposed of the Forum to two old associates, F. Ward and R. Eggington, and took over the Plaza in Dover. The latter held over a thousand patrons and perhaps he felt at last he had acquired a "super-cinema".

As usual he set about making improvements and installed cinemascope about the same time as closing the Rex and putting it up for auction.

Things went wrong. The Rex could not be sold having failed to reach a reserve price at the auction on 20th January 1953. Presumably Fred Leatham had to leave Dover and try and restore some value to his two remaining Black Country cinemas. In 1956 he bravely installed cinemascope at both the Rex and the Victoria but the decline could not be halted. A last minute attempt to remain in the cinema business involved a "swop" with the Victoria and a cinema in Market Drayton but this did not work out successfully. The Victoria then became difficult to dispose of as the Council refused to grant the necessary "change-of-use" that would have made it a potential industrial property. When his appeal was heard by the Ministry of Housing and Local Government he claimed that he had lost a "terrific amount of money" in the cinema business, including £4,000 on the sale of the unfortunate Rex. His appeal, in 1958, was lost, but ironically today the site has been put to industrial use.

The quiet pianist whose career as a cinema proprietor had crossed the histories of so many diverse Black Country cinemas for a time became a rent-collector for Wolverhampton Council, but later returned to business in a Bilston hardware store. As with the cinemas, he had already sold that one and acquired another by the time he died in November 1962. Apparently he had never enjoyed good health.

Unlike some of the men described in this part of the book, he died without obituaries recording his part in the operation of local cinemas. Even within the trade I doubt he was a well known figure, but his restless career in so many Black Country cinemas deserves to be remembered as a tribute to the small independent exhibitor, tenaciously pursuing financial survival in an industry where even the major exhibitors found it difficult to adapt to the social changes that overtook their trade.

Charles Dent and John Marshall Dent

To clear up any confusion between Charles Dent and his heirs and Mortimer Dent of the Danilo circuit, it is worth detailing the careers of the former who became associated with two Black Country cinemas. Charles Dent had first become an exhibitor at the Grand, Tamworth. By 1919 he also owned the Palace, Erdington and entered the Black Country by acquiring the Palace in Freeth Street, Oldbury.

A decade later, on the arrival of sound, Mr. Dent opened a brand new, much larger, Palace at the same address, and his son, John Marshall Dent, became its manager. John Marshall Dent not only inherited the cinemas, but

also expanded his interests in the Black Country by taking over the Regent at Langley Green. His son, Malcolm Dent, worked in both cinemas. J.M. Dent also had plans drawn up by Hurley Robinson for a cinema in Warley but this was never built.

During the War J.M. Dent had the rare distinction of being able to build a cinema. This was the Lido at Lichfield, which had to be rebuilt after a fire, started, according to local legend, by an American serviceman's cigar! No such excitement interrupted the lives of the Palace or the Regent and they both survived until the end of the troublesome fifties without incident. About that time J.M. Dent opened La Reserve Restaurant and provided cabaret entertainment there. Perhaps its success led him to convert the Regent to a variety club. Meanwhile, The Palace, Oldbury, defected to Bingo.

J.M. Dent died in 1970 and the cinemas had to be sold to pay death duties. The Regent went on to have a remarkable old age and even became a cinema again for a while.

Thomas Leach

Not far from Mr. Dent's "Palace" at Oldbury stood the Picture House, Birmingham Street. This had begun its life as a converted market hall in the spring of 1911, when it was known as The Picturedrome. By the end of the year Thomas Leach had acquired it and turned it into something much more like a cinema and reopened it as "The Picture House".

Thomas Leach therefore became an exhibitor about the same time as Thomas Jackson in Wolverhampton. Although he survived much longer he is now an equally shadowy figure, despite building up a small empire in Oldbury and West Bromwich.

Just after the First World War he acquired the St. George's Hall in the centre of West Bromwich and at some stage ran both The Queen's and the Hill Top Cinema. It also seems that he had at least two cinemas in the Birmingham area. In the mid twenties The Picture House in Oldbury was substantially rebuilt becoming a very lofty building into which a far bigger audience could be crammed. When the talkies were introduced in this building in early 1930 the acoustics were found to be awful, and I have the feeling that the thirties saw a decline in the fortunes of the cinemas of Tom Leach. About 1937 the Picture House, the St. Georges and the Queens were leased to F.J. Emery, owner of a Lancashire-based circuit.

By 1946, when Miles Jervis acquired these cinemas Thomas Leach had passed away and his estate was being auctioned. Despite energetic management by Miles Jervis these cinemas were relatively early casualties, only the Queens surviving into the sixties.

Thomas Cooper, Walter Williams & Benjamin Priest

In the south western corner of the Black Country three towns became associated with individual independent exhibitors.

Blackheath became the province of Thomas Cooper, a strict Methodist, who like J. Arthur Rank, was said to have never watched a film! Cradley Heath's cinemas are usually associated with the name of Walter Williams, and in Old Hill we encounter Benjamin Priest. The latter also ran cinemas in Kidderminster and Kinver.

Each of these gentlemen, at some time, ran more than one cinema, but never became exhibitors on the scale of the people described in the previous chapters. Their work is described in more detail in the chapters relevant to each cinema.

Mr. & Mrs. Woodroffe

Although it seems inconceivable, in the light of cinema's decline over the years, that anyone should have entered the business during the 1950's and built up a small "circuit" of local cinemas in that era, but that is just what happened in the Black Country.

Mr. Ken Woodroffe and Mrs. Doris Woodroffe acquired the Alhambra Bilston in the early fifties just before national audience figures were about to plunge. With some drastic modernising and refurbishing the cinema was a success.

In 1955 they acquired the Bruce, in Princes End, Tipton, and refurbished it. When C.S. Joseph declined to renew the lease on the Forum at Bradley in 1957, they purchased the building from Woods Picture Halls and again kept that cinema alive while commercial television came to the Midlands and a set became an essential part of every home. All three cinemas were small, and enjoyed a very local patronage. The Bruce and the Alhambra were pre-First World War buildings and the Forum belonged to the first wave of cinema building after that War.

Somehow they continued to thrive as if the super-cinema, never particularly close by, had never come into existence. Like Cecil Couper's three little cinemas of the thirties, I think they correctly fitted the particular "cinema-needs" of the communities they served: they were village cinemas.

The Bruce, closed first, followed by the cessation of regular shows in the Alhambra, and the Forum became a Bingo Hall, all in the early years of the sixties. The Woodroffc's little "circuit" of three cinemas seems like the last brave stand of the small independent exhibitor, although less dramatic than the survival of Miles Jervis or the indestructability of the Royal at Cradley Heath.

The Final Generation

While Mr. and Mrs. Woodroffe valiantly ran one of the last independent Black Country cinema enterprises towards the end of the fifties, a new generation of film goers was emerging to challenge the prevailing orthodoxy of the major circuits. Their enthusiasm for the cinema was going to keep several cinemas alive for the next two decades. By the mid fifties the Asian minority in the Black Country was large enough to demand its own films and film-shows. The Indian cinema industry was in the process of becoming one of the world's largest film industries, and was developing a relationship with its patrons that reflected the relationship between Hollywood and the English-speaking world a decade earlier.

The first products from the Bombay studios to come to the Black Country were screened by J.S. Sidhu's Eastern Film Society on Sunday mornings in Darlaston. A sympathetic manager, Leslie Taff, and an independent cinema provided the ideal location. Later the Eastern Film Society moved to The Alhambra, Bilston. At first they hired the cinema from Mr. and Mrs. Woodroffe but later bought the cinema and began showing Indian films more regularly, again with some help from Leslie Taff.

Meanwhile Ajit Singh Bains had presented a few Indian films at The Olympia, Wolverhampton, while Vincent Wareing tried to run the place in the twilight of its existence. It was impossible to buy The Olympia after Mr. Wareing's departure in mid 1960 and Ajit Singh eventually persuaded the owner to lease him her other cinema, the moribund Coliseum, Wolverhampton. The poor old Coliseum had suffered badly since Mr. Wareing's last bold attempt to revive it, and Ajit Singh had to put in a great deal of work to make it a cinema for the last time. He reopened it in 1963 and ran it for over a decade.

On the far side of the Black Country The Beacon, Smethwick, had been showing Indian films since the late fifties and continued to do so until December 1980. A number of proprietors had run the place, and towards the end, shows were reduced to Sundays only, but it had shown Indian films for as long as some local cinemas had shown English-language ones! Also in Smethwick, Nirmal Singh Sanghera made a success of running The Princes from 1970 until February 1980. It must not be assumed that the Indian patron supports the Indian cinema indiscriminately simply because the films are in his own language. The Indian exhibitor had to gauge the popularity of certain films and obtain them early enough in their release to earn success.

One exhibitor's name appears in the history of a number of Black Country cinemas; Tarsom Singh Dhami. As a child he had watched travelling cinemas erect their shows, couple their heavy equipment to their generators, and put on film shows. He developed a passion for films and the art and business of showing them. When he came to the Black Country in 1953 he systematically visited the great variety of cinemas still operating at that time, from the Odeons to the struggling independents like The Rex and Carlton in Wolverhampton. His career as an exhibitor began in 1962 at The Clifton, Stone Cross. At first occasional Sunday shows were presented, but from 1964 to 1968 he presented regular programmes until Ladbrokes acquired the premises.

By organising shows at the Dale, and with the cooperation of J. S. Sidhu at the Alhambra, llilston, Tarsem Singh Dhami was able to book Indian films on their first release in this country and bring them to these three Black Country screens.

Later, in partnership with others, he leased The Queens, West Bromwich from Miles Jcrvis. For just over the last three months of its life The Queens showed only Indian films, while the owners and lessee waited for the C.P.O. to take effect. On Sunday 27th. July 1969 the demolition men started work while the audience was watching an Indian film inside the cinema!

In 1972 Mr. Dhami formed the Silver Cinema Company and purchased the Odeon, Wednesbury. It ran for two years, showing films in English and Hindi, until purchased by Ladbrokes in 1974. His enthusiasm for the cinema was unabated and in April 1978 he acquired the Grove, Smethwick. However, as the decade came to a close, the Indian audience disappeared as Video swept the land. The last film was shown at the Grove in November 1981 and the Black Country's last generation of exhibitors gave up the battle. Even the erstwhile Eastern Film Society which was still showing Indian films at the Wolverhampton Civic Hall on Sunday afternoons at the beginning of the eighties gave up in August 1981.

A few other Black Country cinemas had shown Indian films at one time or another. In Walsall the Imperial and The ABC had put on occasional shows, and Surinder Kumar opened the short-lived Rex. In Langley Mr. Gupta acquired The Regent and leased it to several others making a fine "last stand" in the mid seventies, showing English-language films as The Astra, and finally Indian films as The Milan.

The most interesting result of Indian cinema coming to the Black Country might have been the building of a brand new purpose-built cinema, the "Raj", at Pleck, but the project never materialised, partly due to planning objections.

Below: The leaders of The Eastern Film Soicety join Lesley Taff outside The Regal Darlaston in the late 1950s.
(From the collection of Gurdial Sahota who is in centre of picture as the group's chairman.)

3. THE MUSICIANS – including, THE ORGANISTS

No "silent" film was ever shown in silence. Literate patrons read the subtitles aloud, in Black Country dialect of course, for the benefit of those who could not read or could not afford spectacles, and often the action encouraged a certain amount of cheering and hissing. Meanwhile, the management provided some form of musical accompaniment. The piano was the minimum that would suffice. A trio, piano, drums and violin, for example, were preferred. The bigger cinemas might provide a seven piece orchestra which had rehearsed the official score.

An army of part-time musicians devoted their time to providing this music, and for many, the bitterest blow in their lives was the coming of the talkies. Many were so good that the patrons came to the cinemas to hear them play rather than to see the films and today, about three quartes of a century later, their names or becoming forgotten.

Alfred Van Dam at the Queens, Wolverhampton, had a huge following. As leader of the orchestra, and as a violinist, he become a local legend. In Stourbridge two orchestras and their leaders vigorously competed: Norris Stanley at the Kings Hall and Charles Bye at the Scala. Both went on to establish reputation in the musical world when times changed. The third jewel in Stourbridge's crown was Mr. Barrs Partridge, a brilliant pianist, violinist and organist. He came from Cradley Heath and had played at The Royal. He graduated to Birmingham's West End but in 1929 came to The Central, Stourbridge. When sound arrived at The Central he stayed on as organist, but in 1938 he joined the B.B.C. He was finally leader of the second violins for the City of Birmingham Symphony Orchestra. His work included composition, including a comic opera, and maybe his career is still waiting to be re-discovered and re-evaluated.

In Halesowen, Bert Holden's career was typical of the rise and fall in the fortunes of a local musician. He first played the piano for Mr. Bray at the Drill Hall. Matters improved and he was joined by Mrs. Wood on the violin. In 1927, when Sidney Bray opened the newly rebuilt Picture House, Bert Holden went there to be part of an orchestra until the talkies arrived. Afterwards he survived by playing the solo piano at the Cosy Corner while it struggled on as a silent cinema into the mid thirties. Finally he became a projectionist. That pattern was duplicated by many others. In Dudley, Syd Griffiths brought some of the plaster down from the Criterion's ceiling with his drumming while **"Ben Hur"** was on the screen. He believed that Mr. Anton at the Castle Cinema was a brilliant conductor, illustrating his theory that minor cinemas often enjoyed major talents. Perhaps that is why patrons went to the Olympia, Wordsley, just to hear violinist Lena Wood, the same lady that had joined Bert Holden in Halesowen!

Above: The "orchestra" from the Olympia in Wolverhampton, on 17th September 1916: Charles Lowe.pianist; E. Cadman on clarinet; William Bowyer on violin and Walter Fisher on double bass.

(Jane Parker's collection)

Above: Young Sidney Wallbank at the console of the Wurlitzer at the Regent, Dudley, opened by John Howlett .(He was followed briefly by Reginald Dixon.) (From the collection of Mrs. G.C. Wallbank)

The Organists

The first cinema organ in the Black Country was also the first Wurlitzer to be installed in Great Britain. It was opened by Jack Courtnay at the Picture House, Walsall, in 1925. Fifty years later it was removed and made its way to Devon via Sedgley. The two-manual, six unit instrument still exists today in a church at Beer.

From the mid twenties onwards many new cinemas did not feel complete unless they had an organ and a full orchestra. The fashion, for their installation, lasted about a decade, but their popularity lasted much longer, and today I would regard it as something of a cult. An illuminated console rising mysteriously from the stage into the spotlight was undoubtedly something very magical, and if the chambers were correctly arranged in the building, and if the acoustics were right, the full-bodied sound of a large cinema organ was an overwhelming experience. But this was true in all parts of Britain and to conern ourselves with Black Country matters we must look only at the organs and the organists of this area.

The men associated with the organs at the Regal, Darlaston, and the Majestic, Cradley Heath, will be described in a moment. First let us survey the other instruments once to be found locally.

When the Gaumont in Wolverhampton opened in September 1932, the Compton organ was opened by Frederick Bayco. Again, it was the first instrument of this kind to be opened in the Black Country and was much more than a three-manual and pedal organ.

After bringing himself and the organ up on the electric lift, the organist could produce virtually any sound effect he wanted from the machine buried below. He could also control the volume by controlling the louvres to the chamber, hidden from the auditorium by a gauze "wall". In building this organ Compton had used over a thousand pipes ranging in length from three quarters of an inch to sixteen feet. If all the copper wire was unwound from the organ it would have stretched from Wolverhampton Low Level to Paddington, and over five thousand silver contacts in the instrument had been soldered by hand. Frederick Bayco was succeeded on this magnificent instrument by Leslie Taff, moving from the Rink, Smethwick. To some extent the tradition of an organ on this site went back to the days of the Agricultural Hall where a straight organ had existed since 1916. The Compton stayed at the Gaumont until 1966. When the Gaumont closed in November 1973, Graeme Hawkins played a special organ farewell to the cinema on a Rodgers theatre organ specially installed for the final week.

Meanwhile, in Dudley, a great Wurlitzer had been filling the Regent with sound for several years. Although work on it was not quite finished, this instrument was opened by young John Howlett when the cinema opened in September 1928. When new, this Wurlitzer cost £4,000 but probably played its part in establishing the popularity of this cinema. By the early seventies it was dilapidated and forgotten and many of its six ranks of pipes had been stolen. The Rank Organisation considered that the cost of restoration was too high and were glad to sell it to Roy Mosley. He removed it in 1975, and began its painstaking restoration and installation at Peterborough Technical College. With a great sense of history, John Howlett was to have reopened the organ in its new home on 8th March 1981. In the event, it was reopened by John Mann, but John Howlett, prevented by ill-health from attending, sent a recorded message to everyone there.

John Howlett had only stayed at the Regent for a few weeks. He was followed by none other than Reginald Dixon who went on to fame in Blackpool. When Reginald Dixon left Dudley in May 1929, he was replaced by Sidney Wallbank, who had already been "orchestral organist" at the cinema since its opening. Sidney Wallbank had been Musical Director on a P. & O. liner on the run from Tilbury to Sydney. At the latter city he had gained some experience on a Wurlitzer at the Prince Edward Theatre. P.C.T. sent him to Dudley. He stayed until 1932, when he went to London, finishing his career at the Gaumont, Holloway, when it was bombed in 1940. He died in May 1980 just after the research for this book began, but before I could make his acquaintance. The last resident organist at this cinema was Stanley Harrison, seen in the picture of organists at The Rink.

In Stourbridge, John Howlett returned to open another Black Country organ at the Central. (In the meantime he had been to Belfast and Preston). This time he found himself opening a Compton organ, on 16th May 1929. It was a three-manual, ten-unit instrument, and again cost about £4,000. It was later played by Mr. Barrs Partridge but when the Odeon circuit took over the theatre its importance declined. It was broken down and removed in 1958 and I believe parts of it are to be found in Netherton Parish Church.

Wilf Gregory became quite well known at the console of the organ at The Tower. He was been born in Bradmore, Wolverhampton in 1907, and by the age of fifteen was organist at St. Marks Church, Chapel Ash. By the end of the 1920s he was playing the straight theatre organ at Wolverhampton's Agricultural Hall — and was probably the last man to play it when the hall closed in 1931 to make way for The Gaumont.

Staying with APPH/PCT in the 1930s, Wilf worked at The Picture House, Walsall on the Wurlitzer, after which he joined ABC and worked at many of their Midlands cinemas. It was ABC that moved him to The Tower, West Bromwich, during the Second World War — managed at the time by Frank Attoe, with whom he collaborated to produce the cinema choir's "Savings Song"! Although still playing the organ at The Tower in the early fifties he realised that organ-playing days were over and went into relief management.

The organ of the Tower, West Bromwich, will be mentioned again in relation to Leslie Taff. He opened it when the cinema opened in December 1935. It was a three-manual, ten-unit Compton, with a Mellowtone electronic attachment. With the illuminated surround to the console it was the archetype of the cinema organs that patrons love to remember. The organ in Darlaston and Cradley Heath will also be dealt with subsequently. It remains for us here to consider the organs of Smethwick.

Edward Hewitson's replacement Princes Cinema was being built just at the time that organs seemed so important and although the talkies had arrived a Compton organ was installed. It was a two-manual, five- unit instrument, and was opened by Wilfred Southworth. In 1936 it was moved from the Princes to the Empire and rebuilt with six units. It was re-opened by George Hunt. Arter The Empire closed as a cinema it was removed piece by piece by the boys of Holly Lodge Grammar School with the intention of rebuilding it at the school.

When Edward llewitson replaced The Coliseum with The Windsor, in Bearwood, he again installed a Compton organ. It was a three-manual, eight-unit instrument and was opened by Reginald Maynard on 29th September 1930. In his comments on the organ in the opening brochure, Mr. Maynard revealed that the organ consumed fifty thousand cubic feet of air per hour. It was removed in 1960 to Oxley Parish Church, newly built in Wolverhampton. Only seven units were installed but once again a local organ found a permanent home in the Black Country.

Just over two months earlier Gaumont British's new Rink opened in the Cape Hill area of Smethwick. G.B. particularly favoured Compton organs and equipped their palatial new cinema with a three-manual, nine-unit instrument. Leslie James rose into the spotlight to open the organ when the cinema opened on 7th July 1930, and apparently stayed all week to play in this two thousand seater cinema. It probably survived in regular use longer than the Smethwick's other two Comptons, but was removed in 1961, and survives at Quinton Parish Church.

A few small cinemas were not to be outdone by the new super-cinemas, their organs, and the wonders of sound. For example, the West End, tucked away in Whitmore Reans, Wolverhampton, revived their "orchestra" on Friday nights for old time's sake after sound had made them redundant. Later the proprietors, O. G. Pictures Ltd., introduced their own "home-made" organ complete with illuminated console. It was basically a Hammond model A, and it had to stand permanently beneath the centre of the screen but the organist, Arthur Collett, played nightly to an enthusiastic audience. He received some coaching from William Davis who was then playing the organ at Wolverhampton's Gaumont. Like many other cinema musicians, he eventually realised there was a better future in other aspects of the business and went to the ABC to become a projectionist.

William Sykes 1890 - 1975

As the reader will have gathered, the theatre organs in the super-cinemas were often played by a whole succession of organists. It is interesting to consider, therefore, two men that devoted their careers to the Black Country. In the case of the Majestic, Cradley Heath, which remained independent of the circuits throughout its life, one man devoted twenty-five years of service to the cinema and its community. That man was William Sykes.

William Sykes was born in Mirfield, Yorkshire, and trained under Edward Bairstow, the organist at York Minster. He joined the Army in 1916, and in France he formed the 5th Brigade Remount Depot Concert Party and gave concerts around Calais.

He first provided music in a cinema at The Crescent, Dewsbury Road, Leeds, when that opened in August 1921. He stayed there until he came to the Black Country in 1933. He was attracted to the new Christie organ being installed at the Majestic because it was the first Christie organ in Britain with an all-electric action and was the largest of its kind to be built up until then. It was a three-manual instrument with ten extended and distinctive units and a fifteen hundred seater super-cinema seemed a good opportunity.

The organ and the cinema were opened on 27th March 1933 when Mr. Sykes began the proceedings by playing the National Anthem to a capacity audience. His family settled in Stourbridge but he devoted his life and work to Cradley Heath. By the end of 1933 he was appointed Manager of the cinema as well as organist. As well as his administrative duties, he still performed every night for half an hour on the organ before the shows, and took special pride in organ interludes during the programmes. He made his own slides to be projected on the screen while he played below, and wrote his own compositions. The Majestic's reputation for good music spread and trade papers described Cradley Heath as "a centre of musical activity".

During the Second World War all this musical activity greatly increased. For two War-time Christmases he organised recitals at the Majestic that raised money to buy over seven hundred five shilling postal orders that were sent to ex-patrons that were then serving overseas in the Forces. They were accompanied by a letter which said:

"Be of good courage, you are not forgotten, and the time may not be far distant when victory will be ours and you can return home to a better world and to the ones you love. William Sykes".

He was appointed Musical Director for Rowley Regis during the "Holidays at Home" scheme and organised Sunday concerts at the Majestic for the Mayor's Forces Fund. Someone suggested that the Hallelujah Chorus should be heard from the stage of the Majestic and the Cradley Heath Choral Society was formed. "Judas Maccabaeus" was performed on 14th November 1943 and then they began work on "The Messiah". Isobel Baillie and Kathleen Ferrier came along to augment the local principals. The C.H.C.S. provided two hundred voices in the chorus and Mr. Pecks conducted the forty piece Reddal Hill Orchestra. Joined by Mr. Sykes on the Christie it must have filled the Majestic with a mighty sound on 6th February 1944. Kathleen Ferrier was so popular, she returned to the Majestic on 29th October in "Elijah". Mr. Sykes later confessed that he had sometimes been tempted to leave the Black Country but he had created too many strong bonds.

He stayed at the Majestic through the post-war era when the circuits made it difficult for an independent cinema to acquire reasonable films, and organs became unfashionable. In 1955 he invited members of the Cinema Organ Society to come to the Majestic to hear the Christie. He dazzled the audience with his skill in extemporisation and treated them to one of his own compositions: "Moorland Mists". He was still very proud of his cinema, and only the year before it had celebrated its coming-of-age, by introducing reduced prices for pensioners at matinees.

He retired in 1958 and was thus spared the agony of running the Majestic for the last few years of its existence as a cinema. Immediately after its closure it became a Bingo Hall and the Christie languished. Fortunately, during the seventies, it was restored by Mel Edwards, and the organ returned to life just before William Sykes' death on 20th August 1975 at the age of eighty-five. He had lived near Bristol while writing and composing in his retirement, but was brought back to the Black Country for burial at Stourbridge Cemetery.

The Christie was played regularly at the Bingo Club, and is the only Black Country organ to have survived in its original home. However it is currently in very poor condition, has been vandalised, and it is very unlikely that it can be saved.

Leslie Taff   1910 - 1973

Born in Tividale on the outskirts of Tipton, Leslie Taff began his long career in the cinema at a picture house of that town. He obtained an associate degree of the London College of Music when he was twelve years old, and started to play piano accompaniment to silent films at The Victoria Cinema, Railway Street, when he was fourteen. He worked every evening at the Victoria for over four hours and worked in a mineral water factory by day!

A year or two later he graduated to the post of orchestral pianist at The Palace, Oldbury, and from there he moved to The Empire, Dudley. Provincial Cinematograph Theatres owned three cinemas in Dudley and Leslie Taff played in all three, passing from The Empire, to The Criterion, and finally to The Regent.

While he played in The Regent's orchestra he watched the Wurlitzer organ being installed. John Howlett opened the new organ but Leslie Taff was allowed to practice on it, with the encouragement of P.C.T.'s Musical Director. This led to his appointment as an organist and he left the Black Country to play at The Regent, Swindon.

Right: Leslie Taff at the console of the Compton organ at the Regal, Darlaston. (Author's collection)

At the end of the twenties, an up-and-coming organist had to be prepared to move around and from Swindon he returned to this area to play at The Rink, Smethwick, and The Gaumont Palace, Coventry. In 1932 he appeared at The Gaumont, Wolverhampton, not long after it had opened.

P.C.T. had become Gaumont British by this time and Leslie Taff left the company at the end of 1935 to open The Tower, West Bromwich. This cinema's Compton organ was opened on 9th December 1935 and Leslie Taff not only opened it — but also returned to close it thirty years later. His first number at The Tower, where he was billed as "Our Singing Organist", was "Tea for Two", and this became his signature tune.

He left The Tower after it was taken over by ABC and on 19th September 1938 he opened The Regal, Darlaston, The Regal's organ was a Compton Theatrone electronic instrument and became famous when Leslie Taff began B.B.C. broadcasts from The Regal. The first was on Boxing Day 1938.

At The Regal he had entered the world of cinema management and over the years this gave him less time to appear at the organ console. The organ itself grew unreliable and by the time The Regal had turned to Bingo it had been replaced with a modern electric organ.

His last recital was on The Tower's organ. In December 1970, this organ, which he had opened and closed at the cinema, was installed and reopened at Marston Green Hospital. Despite ill health it was a memorable recital, within four days of the anniversary of his debut at The Tower. When he died, three years later, the world lost not only a notable organist, but also a man who had given almost fifty years service to the entertainment industry. He played the organ, played the piano to accompany Alfred Van Dam, organised concerts, managed a cinema and helped organise the earliest specialist Asian film shows in the Black Country — a career truly spanning the history of the cinema.

4. THE PATRONS

While conducting the research for this book a great many people have contacted me not because they worked in cinemas, but because they were part of the audience. It might be thought that a dark building, in which one often did one's courting, would not have attracted much attention from the patron, but this does not seem to have been the case. Many patrons have recalled their cinemas and the staff who worked in them, in great detail, and sometimes the staff have returned the compliment.

Not much can be said that would not be true of the audience in any part of Britain. The cinema set out to acquire enough respectability to attract customers who could afford to pay to come in. Bringing tea and biscuits to the patrons in their seats, and later providing elegant cafes was as important as reassuring everybody of the good taste of the films themselves. The survey that follows will show how each cinema strived to do this.

Many Black Country cinemas, however, exploited a very local patronage and had no need to feel ashamed of providing entertainment for a working class audience that preferred action, melodrama and excitement, to romance and theatrical adaptations. Many small cinemas were called "The Blood Tub" as a mark of their success in providing a suitably violent and melodramatic diet.

If you arrived late at the Electric, in Church Street, Bilston, you risked walking through the beam of light from the projector, and if your silhouette appeared on the screen there would be cries of, "Shif your yed out the rode!"

In such cinemas the films always seemed to be breaking and the audience could hardly be expected to endure such matters in polite silence. Of course noisy rowdy audiences enjoying themselves seemed very immoral to some, and the chucker-out was appointed to deal with the situation. When the Regent replaced the Tivoli in

Right: Wilf Gregory on the console of the Compton organ at The Tower, West Bromwich.

Wilf was born in Wolverhampton in 1907. The first cinema organ that he played was at the Agricultural Hall in Wolverhampton. He later played in a number of APPH/PCT cinemas and came to The Tower about 1940. He later moved into relief management for ABC.

(Evelyn Franks' collection)

Owen Street, Tipton, the proprietors went to great trouble to publicly state that the rowdiness of the audience in the former theatre would not be tolerated in the new one!

When the cinema matured and sound arrived, a quiet and respectful audience was more deserved and for twenty years, from 1930 to 1950, a hushed audience was carried away be some of the greatest films of all time, enjoyed by all social classes, and by all age groups. The period that followed was a difficult one, not only because audiences declined, but the social fabric of postwar Britain was changing and has continued to change. The second release of "Rock Around the Clock" slashed its way through the cinema seats of the Black Country as it did elsewhere, and many a cinema proprietor seems to have seen it as the beginning of the end. Perhaps it did mark the emergence of the teenage audience as an important component of cinema history. By the end of the sixties the remaining cinema-goers were predominantly in the sixteen to twenty-five age group, plus a few pensioners at the matinees. Even the multi-plexes have not radically changed that although individual fims do attract distinctly different age groups back to the cinema.

Two great legends concerning the patrons have become part of the folk-lore of the cinema: bugs and "regulars". Many a local cinema was nick-named the "Bug Hut" or "Flea-Pen". (The word "flea" is pronounced "flay".) Managers and proprietors always adopted the same policy regarding this matter. If a patron complained about the bugs it was politely pointed out that the patron had brought them in. The usual practice was to spray the auditorium with a perfumed disinfectant between the shows, and from the White City in Willenhall to the Scala in Dudley, to the Cosy Corner in Halesowen, patrons have recalled the perfumed scent of that spray more vividly than a D. W. Griffith's classic. The other eduring legend is that of the "regular patron". This involves someone who always expected and demanded the same seat, and in some cases a named patron might have been there when the cinema opened – and was there when it closed.

One sub-group among patrons deserves special mention: children. Children have traditonally provided with their own matinees: the "Penny Rush", later the "Tuppenny Rush", since the beginning of the cinema business. The earliest adverts for The Queens Picture Palace in West Bromwich – up and running in the year before the arrival of the Cinematograph Act – include mention of shows provided for children.

The price of admission often paid for oranges, sweets, comics and special prizes given out to children, and the audience was seldom docile. Usually they were admitted by the side entrance to the cinema, used by patrons reaching the cheapest seats. The noise and the litter problem were both enormous but it was a recruiting ground for future patrons and few local cinemas failed to provide such shows. The first super-cinemas, particularly the Cliftons, carried on this tradition throughout their lives, but the Odeons and ABC Savoys were a little more cautious and introduced them from wartime onwards. (Cliftons took their cinema clubs seriously with all the devices of badges and membership cards etc – and members received a birthday card though the post at the appropriate time!)

The Odeon, Blackheath, claimed to be the first Odeon to start a children's club but I do not know whether this is true. The transition from "matinee" to "club" needs further inverstigation. The town-centre super-cinema moved the show forward to Saturday morning, and to a post-war generation it was always known as "The Saturday Morning Flicks". They spread through the larger cinemas during the forties. For example, ABC's "Minors' Club" did not start at the Tower, West Bromwich, until 1947. The first member still keeps his membership card and can sing the club's song on demand!

As late as 1960 three thousand children went to the Saturday matinees in Wolverhampton alone. At the ABC Tim Whittaker claimed he had a thousand members. Rank's cinemas were doing so well they were about to divide the patrons. John Alexander was going to look after the under 13's at the Gaumont while the teenagers were directed to Reg Felton's care at the Odeon. Two years later the pattern was reversed and the Gaumont played such shockers as "Rock Around the Clock" to teenagers that were about to become Beatle Maniacs. Only six years earlier the same film shown to an "adult" audience had resulted in calling the police!

The last children's matinee in the Black Country was presented while "Cinemas of the Black Country" was being researched. At the Odeon, Wolverhampton, Colin Hunter issued the last ticket (for 15p) to an eager patron on 12th July 1980, after thirty-six years of such shows. They had ceased at the ABC, Stourbridge, one week earlier. How will future Black Country folk ever acquire the habit of cinema-going?

The multi-plexes have revived the chidrens' matinee in as much as suitable films are often shown on Saturday mornings while parents go shopping, and some multi-plexes have arranged specific screenings for mothers with very young children. An interesting twist in the world of "special matinees" has been the "silver screen" phenomena. Senior Citizens are invited to special shows at reasonable prices and often receive free refreshments. These have been popular at the former Danilo, Quinton, and at the Merry Hill cinema.

(The subject of children's cinema has been told in "All Pals Together" by Terry Staples, Edinburgh University Press, 1997.)

5. MANAGERS & STAFF

By the time the architect and builder had done their work, but not always before the last piece of paintwork was dry, a cinema had to have a manager and staff to greet the patrons. Of course, in some of the smaller cinemas the proprietor and manager were one and the same person. In the early days, whoever did the job, was in fairly uncharted waters, but as decades passed management became more professinal, and a stereotype picture of the manager emerged. He was well-groomed, distinguished and worthy of respect if only because of the variety of skills he had to bring to his job. He would have to in the foyer to greet patrons and show concern for their well-being and an interest in their entertainment. To the staff he had to be like a benign ship's captain: a sociable disciplinarian. To his employer he had to be enterprising, resourceful, efficient and honest. To his family, he was probably unknown – he was always at work. He might be agood idea if he knew how to operate the projector or stoke the bolier, and sometimes he was required to display "showmanship". The circuits often expected managers to find ways of promoting particular films and sometimes awarded prizes for success in doing so. The old local newspapers often contain amusing stories of these "promotions".

The stereotype was also "male" but women did take on cinema management – such as Eleanor Webster at The Coliseum, Wolverhampton, Minne Wallace at The De Luxe, Walsall, and Mrs. Woodroffe at the Alhambra, Bilston plus two other cinemas. Women also made it into the projection room, particularly during the Second World War. Many are mentioned in the text.

In the early days cinema managers were often very young. Ivor Griffiths was appoited as Chief Operator and Acting Manager at the Imperial, Walsall, at the age of seventeen in 1918, at a slary of £4 per week. (a "fortune" for a seventeen year old at the time.) He progress was typical – he had worked in the re-wind room, before leaving school. On leaving school he became an operator (or projectionist) and learnt a lot about the electrical side of the business.

Occasionally a manager ran a cinema through-out its life. For example Harry Crane at the Clifton, Coseley, or Frank Bills at the second Alhambra, Dudley Port. More often they graduated to a cinema and then stayed there for life – such as Jim Davies at The Regal, Wednesfield. In some cinemas this meant joining a cinema when it was thriving and having to live through a long period of decline. In this respect some careers seemed to run in reverse. Imagine how Charlie Kettle felt in December 1935 when was the new manager at the opening of The Tower, West Bromwich. By September 1937 he was at the opening of The Palace, Wednesbury. At The Palace he worked for Cyril Joseph, but after the boom years of the Second World War he was struggling to make the best of running The Olympia in Wolverhampton which faced chronic problems of film supply. Through the difficult fifties he was respected and liked as a manager who cared about films and preserved the traditional qualities of a cinema manager. Then Pine Pictures' lease on the Olympia expired and Mr. Kettle found retirement forced upon him.

Below: Staff lined up at The Olympia, Darlaston, in 1951. Manager Billy Gamble sits in front of "Chief", Joe Butler, who is flanked by Alf and Arthur! (Joe Butler collection)

Sometimes a manager had proprietorial aspirations. For example, Cecil Couper, who came to the Black Country as a manager for Pooles then became an entrepreneur. Similarly, Fred Leatham had worked as part-time pianist at the Princes End Picture House then gone to the Rialto, Wednesbury, as manager, but seemed to be driven by a compulsion to own cinemas. The arrival of sound led many cinema musicians to loose their jobs, but a few moved into management as a way forward. Organists sometimes became managers; the two most outstanding examples, William Sykes and Leslie Taff, having been described earlier, but operators tended to stay in their boxes, except in small cinemas, where the job of management often included some work in the projection room, sometimes stoking the boiler and a hundred and one "odd jobs".

In the cinemas of the larger circuits, managers often had to move from cinema to cinema, not only within the Black Country, but sometimes nationally. Even so, three Wolverhampton managers, Cliff Lloyd-Davies, Tom Lloyd and Mr. Felton, managed to establish a local permanence by only making very local moves. Earlier Harry Shawcross had worked at a number of Wolverhampton cinemas until ending his career at the Penn. In the Dudley, Brierley Hill and Stourbridge area several Odeon managers established long Black Country careers. Some managers moved "upwards" within the circuits. For example, Ken Jones managed the Cape Hill Electric and the Grove before ascending to the position of General Manager of the Clifton Circuit, in which position he visited their Black Country halls. More recently Euan Lloyd, from Wombourne, one time assistant manager of the ABC, Walsall, has risen to become a film-producer, and once appeared on the stage of a Black Country cinema to introduce his work!

Many a manager must have had a tale to tell if his career went back to the pre-cinema days. Jack Riskit briefly managed the Palace, Wednesbury, but his vaude-ville background made it sensible for Cyril Joseph to transfer him to the Theatre Royal at Bilston which abandoned films and returned to live theatre. Charles Pindar, who also managed the cinemas of Wednesbury, a member of the Cinema Veterans Association, and therefore must have had tales to tell of films before 1903.

Sometimes a local man without theatrical or early cinema background could seem right for the job. One such man was Harry Wharton from Stourbridge. While working fourteen years as a seedsman for Messrs. Webbs at Wordsley, he had vigorously pursued his interests in amateur music and dramatics. When Pooles opened their skating rink in Stourbridge in 1911, he was put in charge of it and almost immediately it became a cinema presenting both films and variety. Harry Wharton was such an energetic man and so full of ideas that he was forever organising concerts and carnivals and raising money for local charities. During the twenties he transferred to The Scala for a time, changing places with Harry Morris, an equally popular figure who once been a scenery painter. Just as Thomas Wood

introduced "cinema-balls" to Bilston, Harry Wharton once did the same for Stourbridge. Perhaps we shall never see their like again.

Without much chance of earning fame or a named place in history, the rest of the staff of a cinema were really as important as the manager and many notched up a long record of service. Sometimes a cinema could come and go within an individual's working life. Two Wolverhampton cinemas witnessed first and last films projected by the same operator: Cyril Moore at The Penn, and Harry Bayliss at The Dunstall, the latter specially invited back to perform the task. Many an operator showed bravery and quick thought in dealing with burning film and one operator died in a local cinema fire; Frank Danks of the Alexandra. Many worked in cramped conditions and all worked unbelievably antisocial hours.

Presenting a film show was a craft, and like all crafts it had to be learned via a long apprenticeship which began with re-winding films, carrying films to the station, speeding newsreels between cinemas on a bike in all weathers, or keeping the operating room clean, yet it was a job many a fourteen year old school leaver felt would be worthwhile. If you joined the business during one of its rapid periods of growth, 1910 — 1914, or 1932 — 1939, and had your wits about you, there were opportunities for advancement. Harry Bayliss began work at Woods Palace the same day as he left school. He learnt the trade from the "chief", Reg Lloyd, an ex-Pat Collins employee, and entertained John Tyler of Willenhall who often visited Woods Palace before setting up his own cinema, the Dale. When John Tyler built the Dunstall, Harry went to become its chief just before his twenty-first birthday!

The age of the super-cinema demanded a great deal of the operator and often shows were rehearsed to work out cues, volumes, timings, etc. in great detail. If anything went wrong a watchful manager immediately rang the box. Large cinemas sometimes had large operating staff and the "chief" was a very exalted figure. Often he exercised a tyrannical insistence on the absolute spotlessness of his projection suite. As managers and chief operators both seemed such powerful figures, it can be imagined that occasionally some personalities did not get on well with each other. During the Second World War Herbert Morrison recognised the work of a "Chief" as a Reserved Occupation but other operators could be conscripted. In their place came a generation of lady-operators and many a "chief" had to make an adjustment to the fact.

Like other trades, it was sometimes passed on from father to son, or from brother to brother, and one family could collect considerable experience of the Black Country's cinemas. For example, James Powell worked at The Public Hall, Dudley, for Irving Bosco and went with him to The Empire. When Gaumont British eventually took over The Empire he worked for them and transferred to The Regent when they showed the

Right: Vic Court and Jan Bruton at the ABC Stourbridge in March 1982. Vic's 50 year career included work at The Temp in The Lye, The Kings in Stourbridge, and 28 years at the ABC. Jan started her career at The Danilo, Brierley Hill and was deter-mined to become a "Chief". She showed the last film at the ABC on 6th November 1982. (County Express)

first talkie in Dudley. Ultimately he transferred to Poole's at The Kings Hall in Stourbridge. Meanwhile his son, Bernard Powell, had trained as an electrical engineer with Gaumont British, at The West End in Birmingham.

When Gaumont British found themselves short of operators, Bernard Powell was asked to become a relief operator and he travelled far and wide in the Black Country, on his motorbike, working at The Cape Hill Electric and The Rink in Smethwick, or The Empire and Criterion in Dudley. At The Empire, where his father had worked for many years, he met the girl who was to become Mrs. Powell. The cinema staff worked unsociable hours but were often happy together as a group. The G.B. staff thought nothing of holding their own dances at midnight on Saturday night, collecting their G.B. colleagues from other cinemas, and dancing into the small hours. Sunday-closing was important and the staff often used to assemble for Sunday-morning bicycle rides or day trips to the sea.

Bernard Powell followed his father at the Kings Hall in Stourbridge and in 1939 saw the new cinema being constructed around the old one. He liked working for Pooles but by the end of the War had accepted a job at The Clifton in The Lye. At this cinema he was occasionally summoned by Mr. Entwistle to come and solve a problem at The Temp. He then left the cinema business for a while but returned to be a relief operator for the Odeon circuit, working at such places as The Warley Odeon. Between them, James Powell and Bernard Powell had witnessed almost the entire history of the cinema and worked for a variety of employers in every type of cinema, and their experience was by no means unique!.

Few patrons ever met their operators to thank them for the show. The patrons' relationship with their cinema tended to focus on the other staff; cashiers, attendants, ice-cream girls and doormen.

Muriel Morgan was an usherette at Quarry Bank's Coronet but had set her heart on working in Brierley Hill's Danilo. Mr. Roberts of the Coronet encouraged her and she obtained the job at The Danilo. She was in a team of eight usherettes and acquired a made-to-measure uniform. At the Danilo cinemas the girls dressed in smart emerald green frocks, trimmed with orange and gold lace, and their coats had brightly polished brass buttons. As well as showing patrons to their seats she sold the chocolates, and loved every moment of her eight years work. There was a pride in being at the point of contact between the glamorous world of show business and the public. For many girls it followed a daytime job elsewhere, and the rush from the days work to the cinema could not be so hurried that one's appearance suffered, as a good usherette also took pride in her hair and makeup.

The doorman and male attendants were the descendants of that great Black Country tradition: — the "Chucker-out". Some of the earliest Chucker-outs seemed to be chosen for their eccentricity, deformity or physical handicaps if the legends are to be believed. The business of maintaining good order, as well as being a suitable front-of-house "presence", was sometimes combined in the skill and personality of some latter-day doormen, such as Albert Brookes of The Regal, Wednesfield.

Even the cleaners played a vital part in the history of every cinema and ultimately it would be impossible to name every person who had worked in every Black Country cinema. However, as each cinema is described in more detail I have tried to recognise and name the staff where appropriate. Those mentioned are merely examples of the many many others that there is neither time nor space to name.

Bioscope Days

The first few faltering steps in the history of cinematography are well charted. The story begins with a show presented by the Lumiere Brothers in Paris in December 1895. Early in the following year cinematography makes its debut in Britain.

On 20th February 1896 the Lumiere Brothers' 'Cinematographe' was demonstrated in London – in the Marlborough Hall of the Regent Street Polytechnic.

By the end of 1896 film is being screened before provincial audiences either in special presentations of the new medium, or slipped rather quietly into variety shows. We know that on Christmas Eve, December 1896, a film was shown between variety acts at the Corn Exchange in Wolverhampton. This may have been the great historic moment when a film was first seen in the Black Country, but the Express and Star, when reviewing the show just after Christmas granted little importance to it. Therefore, other demonstrations of cinematography may also have been given little or no attention.

Meanwhile, at least one showman from the fairground world had seen some potential in this new technology. Randall Williams had a background in travelling and presenting shows that exploited optical equipment. He had presented a "Ghost Show" making use of the concept of "Pepper's Ghost" – an illusion that exploited the refractive index of glass. Randall Williams was presenting ghost show at Royal Agricultural Hall, Islington, over Christmas 1896, and decided to include "animated pictures" using the Lumieres' Cinamatographe. According to The Era's report on the event at the Agricultural Hall, the ghost show was soon dispensed with altogether and Randall Williams then began his commitment to "animated pictures".

On 14th February 1897 the annual fairground travelling season "kicked off" at Kings Lynn Mart and Randall Williams was there with his animated pictures. Audiences flocked to see the shows and the race was on: other showman immediately set out to present such shows. Very quickly the term "bioscope" was coined to describe these shows – ranging from simple ground level booths to grand wagon-fronted shows. From then onwards it was most likely that Britain's citizens were first entertained by cinematography at the fairground, rather than the public hall or variety theatre,

The obvious question is therefore: Who presented the first bioscope shows in the Black Country? A search through the local newspapers of 1897 is not likely to produce the answer because the first shows were slow to advertise and the newspapers did not report on what was to be found on the fairground at the time – it was not considered to be "news"!

The Rev. Thomas Horne wrote a report on the Birmingham Onion Fair of September 1897 for The Era and from this report we know that Wadbrook's bioscope and Lawrence's show were both present. This suggests they had also made an appearance in the Black Country. We have documentation to prove that Lawrence's marionette show was widely seen in the Black Country so we can assume the same is true of the family's bioscope show.

Pat Collins' name is strongly associated with the fairground scene in the Black Country and his business was well established by the 1890s. One of his flagship events was the annual Bloxwich Gala held in August. Shows were regarded as an important part of this event but the bioscope is not listed among the advertised attractions until the August of 1899. The show belonged to Messrs Wall & Hammersley and later that year it was purchased by Pat Collins – a proof of its popularity. Unlike many local fairs, the Bloxwich Gala did receive the attention of the press, but unfortunately the reporter for the Walsall Free Press was so captivated by Purchase's Menagerie in August 1899 that he gave scant attention to anything else.

Although the press seems to have underestimated the importance of the arrival of cinematography, newspapers did like reporting on local disasters such as fires. The bioscopes continually operated under the threat of an outbreak of fire as the film, made of celluloid nitrate, was extremely inflammable and was passing through machine in close proximity the light source and its accompanying heat. Projectionists were well trained in coping with fire if one broke out as the film passed through the machine, but the situation was compounded by the fact that an audience might panic, and the show was built of wood and canvas!

In July 1898 Captain Payne was travelling his pioneering bioscope show through the Black Country and we would probably have no record of this but for a fire. His show was built up in the Market Place at Bilston – a venue much used by travelling shows. During one of his shows there was some kind of minor "explosion" in the projection equipment and someone in the audience shouted "Fire!" Captain Payne was standing at the back of his show, by the projection booth, and immediately set out to restore order and evacuate his large audience from the show in an orderly manner. Even so, his projection equipment and films were completely destroyed by the fire, as was the canvas roof of his show. He was recognised as the hero of the situation, and received help in getting his show "back on the road".

Walter Payne came from Aston under Lyne and, in the tradition described above, had converted his wagon-fronted ghost show into a bioscope show sometime in 1898. He experienced several fires and replaced the show several times. It travelled until just before the First World War and Walter Payne retired to Knutsford and operated a chain of permanent cinemas in Cheshire.

The first generation of bioscopes looked very much like the menageries, marionette shows, art galleries, waxworks and travelling theatres that had preceded them. Three horse-drawn wagons were drawn up in a line. The middle wagon was usually at right angles to the two flanking wagons and would form the entranced to the "auditorium". In front of the left hand wagon was a primitive organ, and in front of the right hand wagon was the steam engine that would driving a generator to provide the show with electricity. The steps would occupy the central area of the show's frontage up into the show and the platform or stage from which the qualities of the show could be proclaimed. There was an art in enticing the audience to come and see the show on the basis of the free entertainment provided on the front of the show.

The auditorium usually had wooden walls and the roof was a large canvas tilt. The projection equipment usually stood on a wooden platform at the rear of the auditorium and gradually was more "boxed in" to keep it out of sight from the audience.

One question that arises concerns the nature of the films shown in the early bioscopes. What did our Black Country predecessors see for their hard earned penny? The 1900 newspaper advertisement for the annual Bloxwich Gala tells readers that the films will include scenes from the Boer War and "Local Views of Works in the District". Although Pat Collins will have promoted these as his own films, specialist sub-contractors usually made them. A century later the discovery of the films made by Messrs Mitchell and Kenyon has thrown considerable light on this subject and we have been able to see the films themselves although once thought to be "lost". The "factory gate" film was one of the most successful genres exploited by Mitchell & Kenyon, but local football matches and crowds emerging from church services were also popular. The cinematographer had to film as many local people as possible, knowing that they would then come to the fair and spend a penny at the bioscope to see themselves on the screen.

As we proceed into the 1900s a second generation of bioscope shows evolved. On these larger shows the organ was moved to the centre of the frontage and steps moved to the two sides – in line with two entrances. After 1900 the stage area was usually larger in and there were many general improvements all round. More tiered seating was introduced, even some kind of heating could be provided. Larger steam road locomotives, or showmen's engines, travelled with the show to provide electricity generation and to haul the show from ground to ground. The first decade of the twentieth century was the "golden age" of the bioscope.

The 1900s were also slightly better documented than the 1890s. The World's Fair began weekly publication in 1903, and another trade paper, "The Showmen", provides us with more information. Generally local newspapers still took little notice of the bioscopes.

Luckily Pat Collins, a major figure in the fairground world, had made the Black Country his home – firstly in Walsall, and then, after the First World War, in Bloxwich. Pat loved to have the latest and the best of fairground equipment. Having dabbled with the bioscope world from 1899 onwards, the middle 1900s saw him take the plunge. In 1907 and 1908 he launched two large bioscopes. (In the meantime he had used two other shows about which we know less. One, of 1901 vintage, was sold to Messrs Sagar & Scott in 1907 and during that year toured a few Black Country towns before being taken to Yorkshire.)

The No.1 "Wonderland Show" was built by Messrs Orton & Spooner of Burton on Trent and featured a Marenghi 104 key organ. It made its debut at Wrexham Fair in April 1907, and was generally regarded as Mrs. Flora Collins' show. The latest Gaumont "Chronophone" projection equipment was used and no expense was spared. After appearing at prestigious fairs far afield, "Wonderland No.1" made its debut in the Black Country at the Bloxwich Gala of August 1907. Even the local newspaper covered such an important event!

At Christmas 1907, and running into January 1908, "Wonderland No.2" made its appearance. Once again, a Merenghi organ and surrounding coloured lights formed the centrepiece of the frontage. Pat Collins's son, "Young Pat", seems to have been given the task of managing and presenting this show, but once both shows were on the road, it is not always clear from adverts which show was actually being presented at any one particular fair. Generally, Young Pat's "Wonderland No.2" probably made more appearances in the Black Country. It is the organ from the No.2 Show that has survived into preservation – one of the few tangible links we have with the bioscope shows once seen in the Black Country.

At the Whitsun Fair of 1908 on the market patch in the centre of Wolverhampton, the reporter from, "World's Fair" was ecstatic about the qualities of the Wonderland show and reported that:

"Again the organ of Pat Collins is the outside attraction at his large cinematographic show, and the fit up of the concern, together with his attendants, attired in black frock coats and silk hats, offer a completeness so neat and artistic, that, from a monetary point of view also, success is at once assured."

At the end of his report he adds that Annie Holland presented her "Palace of Light" on the North Street side of the fair; "Pitched for its first time in Wolverhampton". In other words two of the best bioscopes in the country could both find enough business to justify attending the Wolverhampton Fair of

1908. Not only was Annie Holland's "Palace of Light" a well known bioscope, Annie herself was none other than the daughter of Walter Payne, whose bioscope had caught fire in Bilston in 1898! Annie was born in 1844 and was therefore in her sixties when she brought her bioscope to Wolverhampton from her base in the East Midlands (Swadlincote).

The mention of Annie Holland's show raises the question of how many other showmen presented bioscope shows in the Black Country? Fleeting glimpses of such things are suggested by brief comments in World's Fair. For example in November 1907 a report on the Wakes at Deepfield, near Coseley, tells us that "Living Pictures" were being presented by John Cordwell. John Cordwell was based in North Wales but his travels occasionally brought him to the Black Country. He may have been showing films, in a fairly modest show, since 1899. Later, his son, also named John, travelled for many years as a tenant with Pat Collins, but not with a show.

Writing in World's Fair, "Southdown" once recalled seeing Chipperfield's Electrograph at Sedgley in 1907. *"... Mr. J.H. Chipperfield was presenting pictures and variety. At this period the Electrograph had a very nice double wagon front, a fine trumpet organ, and a smart Fowler engine. Mr. Chipperfield used to accompany the organ on his trombone for the various parading numbers which were carried out by Clown George and Miss Revell."*

Worlds Fair had two correspondents with a particular interest in the Black Country. One used the pen name, 'Southdown', and the other used the initials, 'JBT'.

Both these man would report on contemporary events and then reminisce about the past. For example, just after the outbreak of the Second World War, in 1939,

Above: Pat Collins' no.1 "Wonderland" bioscope show built up without its huge proscenium arch. (From the collection of the late Jim Boulton)

"Southdown" reports on a visit to Sedgley where he was disappointed to find that the annual Wakes had been cancelled.

"Southdown" seemed anxious to convey the impression that he could provide information about bioscope and portable theatre days from memory. For example in February 1945 he tells Worlds Fair readers: *"It is many years since we last saw theatrical plays being performed on our fairgrounds, though at one time the mumming booth was the principal feature of many fairs."* He goes on to recall Holloway's "Empire Theatre" being open at the Lichfield Bower Fair. He also claimed he had been a projectionist in bioscope shows.

"Southdown" was really Arthur Sellman, and he was born in Mill Street, Cannock, on 1st April 1891 – the son of Mary Sellman from Penkridge and Arthur Sellman Snr who was associated with the Sellman family of well-known Cannock funeral directors. By 1901 his father had died, but he still lived with his family in Cannock. He was still a teenager when the bioscopes were at their zenith in the mid to late 1900s. (For example his description of Chipperfield's show quoted above is based on something he observed at the age of sixteen.) Later he moved to the south coast – hence his "pen name", and he also used the pen names "APS" and "Arthur Fay" when writing about fairground matters. He died in Brighton towards the end of 1970 without anyone asking him to clarify just how well he really knew the bioscope world.

"JBT" was Joe Bate of Tipton who regularly contributed to "Worlds Fair" through out the 1930s, and frequently informed readers about his memories of earlier fairs, and shows in particular. Joe Bate was born in Tipton on 16th December 1874 and thus has a much better chance of being able to recall bioscope days. At the age of thirteen he was selling brandy snap at the Tipton Wakes of 1887 and seems to have gone on to work for many different shows and showmen. Sometimes this work was in the "publicity department" as a bill poster, but he also seems to have assisted in the presentation of shows – both "theatrical" and "cinematic". When Pat Collins decided to cautiously venture into the permanent cinema business at Lichfield in 1910 Joe Bate seems to have been involved as manager. He later made it clear he had worked at Dudley's Empire Theatre, and Douglas Phelps' attempt to use the Alhambra, Dudley Port, and at Smethwick's Theatre Royal.

Joe Bate's wife, Eva, whom he met in Bath, claimed to have once dressed Vesta Tilley so perhaps she came into the story with theatrical connections. Joe also worked closely with Kitty de Smilo (real name: Kate Flanaghan) whom he had first met in 1896 when she was the "target" in a knife-throwing routine presented on Texas Bill's Wild West Show, while at Willenhall. Kitty also paraded on the front of the Wall & Hammersley bioscope show that appeared at Bloxwich Gala in 1899, subsequently acquired by Pat and Flora Collins. This may have been Joe's introduction to bioscopes and to the prospect of occasionally working for Pat Collins.

On the basis of this amazingly complicated life, JBT could file a report for Worlds Fair in the 1930s and provide readers with a unique glimpse of the past. For example, while reporting the Tipton Wakes of July 1933, he adds:

"I can remember the old style Tipton Wakes very well, I attended them with showfolk as far back as 1887. Johnson's Peep Show, Russell's and Hayes' Horses, W. Davies, Stockton's, Antill, J. Caddick, Lallo, Parker's Ghost Show, Wakeman's Theatre, Chittock's Dogs – in fact most of the old travellers have attended it. For many years it was controlled by Mr. Whitehouse of the Golden Cross Inn adjoining, but for many years Mr. Collins has controlled it."

As made clear in Volume 2, references to Wakeman's Theatre are extremely rare and even here Joe Bate provides us with no further information. Unfortunately "glimpses" are all that Joe provides, but he is one of the few local people who searched his memories to provide us with a few links with bioscope days. Joe Bate died in Burntwood Hospital on 20th January 1945, having left a note of his "CV" with his son Arthur in 1943. "Southdown" wrote *It was with regret that I read in last week's Worlds Fair of the passing of the old time showman, Joe Bate, whom I had known for quite a long time, and whom I had last met when he was carrying out publicity work for the late Alderman Pat Collins".*

JBT's mention of "Hayes' Horses" in 1933 brings us to another interesting question: Was there a bioscope show that had specifically Black Country origins? The answer seems to be "yes", if only we could find out more about the Hayes Family.

Once again we have to turn to "Southdown". In the Worlds Fair of 7th July 1945 he writes: ….."*A regular reader of this journal wanted to know something about Hayes' Cinema Show and Ghost Illusion. I take it our friend is referring to Mr. Jack Hayes' show which toured the Black Country, working both privately and the gaffs. This exhibition was built in Hayes' yard at Kates Hill, near Dudley, nearly fifty years ago. It had a double wagon front, with a light engine on one side, and a large trumpet organ on the other. (The organ had at one time been on Hayes' Gallopers i.e. the "horses" mentioned by JBT.)*

The show booth was made and painted by Mr. Hayes, but the front of the show was made and painted by that splendid artist, Mr. Taylor, who was at that time in much demand. About the first gaff attended was Dudley, the fair being held in the market place. This visit to Dudley was marked by an unfortunate incident for now sooner had the organ and the drums struck up than a horse bolted and scattered the crowds…

…..When I saw Hayes' Show for the last time it was erected ready to open at the Wakes Ground in Hednesford, and on the front was painted the words, 'Hayes Coronation Bioscope & Ghost Illusion'. I am not sure that the pictures were always combined with the ghost illusions, but when Hayes did feature the ghost dramas they had with them such well known mummers as Jack Radford and the late Billy Parker, and for publicity purposes (and tober hunting) Mr. Hayes had a brightly painted two wheel trap on which was painted, 'Hayes Grand Ghost Show'."

This gives a more detailed picture of a bioscope show than we are likely to find anywhere else, but ironically no photograph has yet been found of Hayes' show and we have virtually no record of the travels undertaken by this show.

———

When the Cinematograph Act came into force at the beginning of 1910 the bioscope proprietors found they were required to obtain a fresh cinematograph licence every time they built up the show in a new town. The licence could not be granted until the show had been inspected and thus the whole business of travelling a bioscope show became very difficult. In desperation Mrs. Collins converted her bioscope to a Lion Show in the menagerie tradition. The other "Wonderland" show persevered for a while. For example it was still showing films at Pat Collins "Onion Fair" in September 1910 in Birmingham. It was also advertised as being present at Pat Collins' November Fair in Dudley, where it was called "The New Picture Palace", featuring the latest films and of course the "Electric Orchestron", i.e.: the organ.

Another tale of what eventually happened to a bioscope show will be told as we look at the strange cinema history of Cheslyn Hay – as late as 1913.

The "Bioscope Era" ran from 1897 until 1910, but films were also seen elsewhere during that period. Films were presented by companies that had already created a following for shows put on in public halls such as magic lantern lectures, and films were occasionally presented as part of a variety show in local theatres. Examples of this will be found later in this book.

We know from our study of Tom Wood's career that he and his father had travelled in the Black Country with "magic lantern" shows and that from the 1900s onwards these had included some use of film. The Woods booked short seasons in local town halls and thus in 1910, as the Cinematograph Act comes into force, they start using Bilston Town Hall as their first proper cinema.

The other people who made early use of cinematograph were the presenters of "dioramas" and "panoramas". These shows had begun by exploiting moveable scenery. The most famous example, mentioned on several occasions in this book, was Pooles' The Poole family, of which there were many members and several generations, presented their panoramas and dioramas in public halls like the Agricultural Hall in Wolverhampton. Always keen to try the latest forms of visual entertainment, they ventured in to Ghost Show world when that was popular in the 1870s and 1880s.

We should not be surprised that they ventured in variety shows and the use of variety acts to augment the dioramas. As soon as cinematography became a possibility they experimented with that medium. It was Harry Poole's "Myriarama Show" that included a demonstration of the cinematograph in the Christmas Eve show at Wolverhampton's Corn Exchange in December 1896. After the passing of the Cinematograph Act the Poole family open cinemas in Stourbridge and Brierley Hill.

In the December of 1897 George Arundale included the cinematograph in a variety show presented in the "temporary" wooden circus building that had been erected in Wolverhampton's Lichfield Street in 1896. "Hamilton's Excursions" may have presented "living pictures" more or less at the same time in the Public Hall in Dudley. There is good reason, therefore, to suppose that just as the travelling bioscopes introduced Black Country folk to cinematography, there were chances of seeing the same phenomenon in several other settings.

As the first decade of the twentieth century unfolds local theatres also occasionally include cinematography in their variety presentations. This can be found at the Empire, Wolverhampton, The Theatre Royal and New Hippodrome, West Bromwich, and even the Opera House in Dudley. When trying to identify where films were seen in each Black Country town, one has to consider the world, of bioscopes, the fairground, public halls and trade halls, and the theatres.

Above: Mrs. Holland, on top of steps, far right, is seen here on the ex Edwin Lawrence bioscope show fitted with an organ from her own show which had been partly destroyed

by fire in in 1912 at Hednesford. Although late in the day in terms of presenting a bioscope, Annie Holland had bought this show, and was still "on the road". (S. Smith)

After the Bioscopes:

From Electric Theatres to Multi-plexes

Conveniently for the historian the transition from the world of bioscopes and early theatrical presentation of cinematography to the business of providing cinema entertainment on a permanent site was accompanied by the passing of the 1909 Cinematograph Act. From 1st January 1910 onwards cinemas had to be licenced and observe various regulations, to receive such a licence. From then on the cinema has a charted history, however hard it may be to find the documentation today.

From 1910 to the First World War a variety of premises found themselves becoming cinemas. Shops, chapels, factories, and public halls were converted. Theatres installed projection equipment. The first purpose-built cinemas were constructed, and regional and national "circuits" emerged. All aspects of industry grew and developed at a great pace. Very basic cinemas that were crude conversions of exsiting buildings were acceptable in 1910 but were later despised as flea-pits and were usually known by derogatory nick names. In the Black Country think of "The Smack" in Wednesfield, or "The Bruce" (Brew House) in Princes End – both old chapel buildings. Yet by 1914 circuits were building fine purpose-built cinemas like APPH's "Picture Houses".

The First World War checked the progress of the rapidly expanding cinema business. A few small cinemas operating in converted premises found it difficult to keep up with ever more stringent safety regulations and sometimes found themselves holding too few patrons to operate economically. They were often regarded as second class cinemas by their bigger rivals, who dismissed them as "Penny and a Pass" establishments. They "faded away" by 1920 when the building industry returned to life. As materials gradually became available again, work was resumed on building new Picture Palaces and on extending old ones. There was sometimes opposition from those who felt that homes should be built before cinemas. There was also a considerable lack of confidence in the trade itself. Many felt the cinema had a poor future. When Tom Wood built Woods Palace in Bilston he encountered both views, and to take account of the latter it was built as a theatre as well as a cinema.

The cinemas of the early twenties began to establish an appropriate "cinema style". Woods Palace, Bilston, The Criterion, Dudley, and the Scala, Stourbridge are good examples. When P. Morton Shand came to write "Modern Theatres and Cinemas" at the end of the decade he denounced the vulgarity and eclecticism of such buildings and welcomed modernism with open arms. Yet many of them enjoyed a harmony with their

High-Street-neighbours that "supers" failed to achieve. The transitional period at the end of the twenties possibly produced the most exciting variety of cinema-design, in my opinion. It was also the period of transition from "silence" to "sound". Musicians found themselves out-of -work while the public rushed to see and hear the first talkies in town. In some cinemas the orchestra pit was already overshadowed by the magnificent new theatre organs. Popular cinemas like the Regent, Dudley, and the Central, Stourbridge, opened as "silent" cinemas, but with fine organs, but soon installed sound equipment. An indication of the flurry of activity at this time is represented by events in Smethwick. Between September 1929 and December 1930 four substantial sound super-cinemas opened within the borough. All four, The Windsor, The Princes, The Rink, and The Beacon, although considered "modern" in their day, really illustrated the quality and variety of cinemas just before the dawn of modernism.

The following decade, the thirties, produced the "Super-Cinema", a term at first used to denote a degree of luxury and a seating capacity in excess of one thousand, but later strongly associated with the emerging architectural styles. Design became more functional, and often influenced by "Art Deco" styles. This survey includes some fine Gaumonts and Odeons of the 1930s, and buildings like The Tower, West Bromwich, or The Regal, Daraslton. There were also the "imitators" of this style – the Cliftons and the Danilos.

In search of what has been special about Black Country cinemas, perhaps the reader has to think about the late 1930s when amazing cinemas of the Granada and Astoria chains were being opened in the London area. Here we were still building little cinemas like The Forum, Pensnett – just "sheds" in which enertainment was provided on a modest and very local scale. Hence the importance of The Limelight in the Black Country Museum: a representative of the "sheds"!

The years of the Second World War provided a peak in cinema-going. Cinemas were full and queues were the order of the day. In town centres, if you didn't get in at one cinema you had to make a dash to see if you could join a queue to gain admission to another! This has been recalled in several places in this book. The war also saw almost all cinema building come to an end. The Danilo in Stourbridge opened at Whitsun in 1940 – in black-out conditions. A decade later it was possible to look back and imagine that this event was the end of a chapter, and that no more new cinemas would come to the Black Country. (As it turned out, this was not to be the case.)

Above: A palace is under construction near you! And when it is finished you will be invited to attend as often as possible – to enjoy a film luxury surroundings! Local builders and sub-contractors used locally made bricks and locally made steelwork – and it would last forever. Many did not last forever but this one became a listed building and still survives – but not as a cinema! Mr. Bennett Clarke took this picture on 8th April 1937 in Skinner Street, Wolverhampton, to record the construction of the Odeon cinema. (WTC collection)

With hindsight it is possible to imagine that some cinemas built in the 1930s might not have survived had it not been for the war. The wartime boom in cinema-going affected super cinemas and flea pits alike. It looks as if everyone was able to pay off their mortgage! In some cases this led flea-pit proprietors to imagine that in the days when the war was over they would be able to rebuild themselves as super-cinemas. A number of instances of this are described in the book. Unfortunately the post-war years told a different story.

Audience figures began to decline not long after the Second World War was over, and the long sad story of the industry's decline has been considered many times. The reasons were complex and this book does not provide a space to debate them. The Black Country, like many other areas of Britain provides many examples of what happened in subsequent decades. The small local cinemas, that had once been so closely entwined in the lives of the communities they served, suffered when increased mobility and prosperity robbed them of the role and status they had once enjoyed. Conversely some of the large suburban fortress-like super-cinemas became victims of their own scale and grandeur.

Closures dominate the story of the post-war decades but here and there you will encounter optimistic entrepreneurs who grabbed cinemas when they were going "for a song", and staged dramatic re-openings in the belief they could reverse a cinema's fortunes. Look at the cinemas bought by Vincent Wareing (The Coliseum, and Olympia, Wolverhampton, The Palace, Great Bridge, etc...) or look at the amazing revival of the Kinema at Kinver. Look at the position of the "independents" who invested in Cinemascope in the mid 1950s.

By the 1960s some cinemas had closed after a life of only twenty or so years, while others had closed simply because large circuits had absorbed rivals and wished to rationalise. Then came the curious business of Bingo. For a time Bingo was a grim reminder to the cinema enthusiast that film-presentation had ceased, but later Bingo had to be regarded as an acivity that had actually preserved some of the buildings we had loved. Even in the 1980s a cinema like the Odeon, Wolverhampton, which had been savagely "tripled" in the seventies, was closed and then beautifully restored as a home for Bingo.

Elsewhere it has been noted that West Bromwich played a siginificant part in local cinema history by witnessing the opening of the Black Country's first permanent cinem almost a year before the arrival of the first Cinematograph Act. In the 1970s West Bromwich found itself once again making an interesting impact on local cinema history. At a time when it was becoming clear that cinemas might never reverse the decline in the audience numbers, and that Bingo was possibly "here to stay", Miles Jervis opened a brand new purpose-built three screen cinema: The Kings.

Most multi screen cinemas at the time were attempts by the major cinema cicuits to convert existing cinemas into something more viable. The Black Country had its share of tripling and doubling, and an example of that survives at the time of writing at The Reel, in Quinton. Elsewhere such cinemas did not survive the 1980s.

To everyone's amazement the cinema business did eventually reverse its fortunes by the opening of the multi-plexes, of which the Black Country now has four. In some parts of Britain the art-house cinema also provided an unexpected route to cinema survival. The Black Country's example of that is The Light House in Wolverhampton.

It can be difficult to know what to make of the multi-plexes. In all four of our local examples I have had cause for complaint on many occasions. Who knows how we will assess their contribtuion to cinema history in years to come?

Many of the staff who joined the trade in the 1930's stayed for the rest of their careers in the cinema business – sometimes in the same cinema. Try to imagine a career that began with the glamour and prestige of the business at that time, and which ended a quarter of a century later in such sad circumstances! Harry Crane, manager of Clifton Coseley, throughout its life, always wore evening dress every night even to the bitter end, and could always oblige the patrons with a tap-dance routine on the steps. Such a man was given a week's notice and had to find work elsewhere. There was no great financial reward for working in the cinema, but even when some of the glamour had faded there was always great comradeship and friendliness. On days off managers and usherettes alike would often go to the pictures, and share "intelligence" with friendly rivals down the road! And what of the patrons – in this book you will find examples of patrons who attended the opening of their local cinema before the First World War, attended every show on a twice-weekly routine, always sat in the same seat and were there when their cinema closed in the 1970s or 80s!

In the 1980s it was still possible to interview people who had worked in local cinemas in virtually every decade since 1910. Now it is difficult to find someone who can recall the introduction of the talkies. Fewer and fewer buildings survive to remind us of cinema history. While the human story, and the bricks and mortar of cinema history "fade out" in the the twentyfirst century, we have to face the fact that cinema-going is still possible in the Black Country – one 1930s building is still in cinema use, four multi-plexes are in business, one art-house cinema is celebrating its twentyfifth birthday, and beyond the Black Country, out at Cannock a cinema is open today that can trace its history back to 1914! And the Harts Hill Limelight is still showing films at the Black Country Living Museum.

As this book goes to press in the summer of 2011: You can still see the latest movie in a late 1930s super cinema, like The Reel at Quinton, or watch a "silent" comedy classic in the Harts Hill Limelight "shed-like" cinema of the 1920s – re-created at the Black Country Living Museum.

Section 3
Cinemas of Sandwell

We begin our tour of the Black Country and surrounding area by crossing the Birmingham border into Sandwell, one of the four Metropolitan Boroughs of the Black Country created in the local government reorganisation of 1974. This brought together the six towns of Smethwick, West Bromwich, Wednesbury, Tipton, Oldbury and Rowley Regis. The last named borough crossed the high ridge that separates the two halves of the Black Country and brings Blackheath, Old Hill, and Cradley Heath into Sandwell.

Above: The Warley Odeon at night on the 31st April 1935, four months after it had opened. This cinema was a "gateway to the Black Country" for travellers leaving Birmingham by the Hagley Road and joining the Wolverhampton New Road at this point. The word "Odeon" was placed below the word "Warley" on the tower soon after the picture was taken. The picture proves how cinemas could look particularly attractive at night. (John Maltby, CTA Archives))

51

The Birmingham Border

Although the Cape Hill end of Smethwick feels more like Birmingham suburbia than part of the Black Country the city's boundary is just to the south and east of Grove Lane and therefore our tour of the Black Country begins by taking the old Dudley Road out of Birmingham and across the border of what was once Staffordshire.

This route into the Black Country provides us with an immediate encounter with a cinema: The Grove. To the west of The Grove, the main road becomes Cape Hill and passes the site long associated with Mitchell & Butler's Brewery but now occupied by housing. On the right of Cape Hill was the Electric Cinema with a history stretching back to the early days of Black Country cinema. At the end of Cape Hill we come to a major road junction. To the right Windmill Lane takes us to more cinema history represented by The Rink, in two versions, and straight ahead would take us onto central Smethwick, which we will deal with later. Remaining closer to the border with Birmingham we take the Waterloo Road to Bearwood where there is more cinema and theatre history to unfold. Finally, we will take the Hagley Road out of Bearwood, to the site of the Warley Cinema. The Birmingham/Black Country boundary actually runs along the centre of the Hagley Road as it approaches the junction with the Wolverhampton New Road and therefore both the Warley Odeon and the The Grove can equally claim to be cinemas at the "Gateway to the Black Country.

The Grove

Dudley Road, Smethwick, at the junction with Grove Lane.

The site on the corner of Grove Lane and Dudley Road was first seen as a potential location for a super- cinema by Sol Levy. It was surrounded by a densely residential area and the little Cape Hill Electric was regarded as unequal to the task of serving this community. Sol Levy had been associated with Birmingham cinemas as early as 1914 when he opened the Scala in Smallbrook Street, but he died in 1929 at the age of fifty four leaving others to take over the Grove Lane site. The project was taken over by the Grove Cinema Company under the chairmanship of George Parker. More significantly, two of the principle directors were Sidney Clift and Leon Salberg and their interest in the Grove can be seen as one of the the starting points for the creation of the Clifton circuit.

The huge 1700 seater cinema, designed by Roland Satchwell, was far bigger than the Cliftons later built in the Black Country "proper", perhaps reflecting the trend already established at the new Rink in Windmill Lane

Below: The Grove, photographed in 1981 before final closure. (Ned Williams)

(opened July 1930) – at the other end of Cape Hill: the nearer to Birmingham, the bigger the super-cinema. It had been built at a cost of about £40,000. Unlike later Clifton cinemas that favoured BTH equipment, the Grove opened with sound by Western Electric.

The first manager of The Grove was Mr. A.W. Smith who had come directly from The Robin Hood at Hall Green, but had also been at Birmingham's Futurist. Shortly after the opening Ken Jones left his job with Gaumont British at the Cape Hill Electric and moved into the mighty Grove. From the position of manager he rose to be General Manager of the entire Clifton circuit.

The Grove opened on 22nd August 1932 with *"Arsene Lupin"*, starring Lionel and John Barrymore. The opening ceremony was performed by Chairman George Parker, also mentioned in this book in relation to the company that promoted the Scala, Stourbridge. Messrs Clift and Salberg seem to have remained in the background.

As far as it is known The Grove was not provided with an "opening brochure", so some details of the cinema's construction do not seem to be "on the record". For rexample, it is not clear who was repsonsible for building The Grove. Before the cinema opened the Smethwick Telephone had given its readers some idea of the qualities of the building. The paper described the frontage as being "in the French Style", and beautifully lit with floodlights. Green was the colour that dominated the auditorium and attractive pictures had been painted on the side walls by a local artist. The carpet was in crimosn and black and the paper was particularly enthusiastic about the proscenium curtains which were described as "most artistic".

Due to its position out on the frontier, little of the history of the Grove seems to have been recorded by the local press in Smethwick. Its "presence" gradually emerged once other local cinemas closed! By the nineteen seventies the newly formed Borough of Warley included not only the Princes, in what had been the heart of the town, but also such diverse and far flung cinemas as the Grove and the Royal, Cradley Heath. When the modern Metropolitan Borough of Sandwell was created in 1974 the Grove found itself to be within the Black Country once and for all.

In keeping with the Grove's gradual "movement" towards the Black Country, on 9th April 1978 it was sold by the original company to Tarsem Singh Dhami, the Bus Inspector from Wolverhampton. He inherited a cinema that had remained remarkably unchanged since the thirties. Lloyd-Loom chairs still stood in the balcony lounge and display cabinets etc. still had an unmistakeable Art Deco appearance. Cinemeccanica equipment had been installed the previous year so at least the Grove was technically up-to-date. He showed English language films during the week and Indian films on Sundays.

In the following years the remaining audience seemed to gradually melt away. The last regular film presentation, featuring *"Happy Birthday to Me"*, took place on 24th October 1981. Sunday shows had been presented by various lessees and specialist martial-arts programmes had tried to make a last stand, but without success. The very last Indian film was screened on 14th November 1981. I last visited the Grove on 7th November 1981 and a magnificent historical epic from the Bombay studios was playing to half a dozen people.

The Grove became a large D.I.Y kitchen & bathroom. store and in that form the building has survived until the present day.

The Cape Hill Electric

Cape Hill, Smethiwck, at the junction with Rosebery Road.

The Grove was very much a 1930s cinema of the "sound era", but its nearest neighbouring cinema was a small first generation cinerma, linked to Irving Bosco – one of the Black Country's cinerma pioneers. The Electric was the first purpose-built cinema in Smethwick and very much a product of the Black Country rather than Birmingham! Irving Bosco's activities centred on Dudley at the time and his new cinema was designed by the Dudley architects, Messrs. Gammage and Dickinson, and built by the Dudley builders, Messrs. Oakley and Coulson. (Mr. Coulson later became involved with the Grand, Kingswinford.) Its opening was reported in as much detail in the Dudley Herald as in the Smethwick Telephone!

Smethwick was in the middle of Coronation celebrations by the time Irving Bosco's cinema was ready to commence business and his first programme included films of that event. Local citizens were told to, "Bring the little ones to see the Coronation". In the week before the cinema opened the Smethiwck Telephone told its readers:

"Cape Hill is an excellent centre for a picture house, and the one which has been erected on the site at the corner of Rosebery Road will open its doors on Monday next with every prospect of success." And the cinema's own advert told readers it would be: *"The most cosy and comfortable picture house in the Midlands"*

The opening took place on Monday afternoon, 19th June 1911. The Mayor of Smethwick had a seat in the balcony and came to the stage during the interval to make his speech. The local paper described the occasion as a *"brilliant success"* with which *"everyone was delighted"*.

The Cape Hill Electric held 680 patrons at the time, and slightly fewer as years went by. A "Ladies Tea Room" originally adjoined the balcony. Irving Bosco was anxious to make it clear that he was solely interested in presenting pictures. There were no variety acts. At first there were three shows daily at 3, 7 and 9 o'clock, and manager Chas Herrick was left in charge of the place. In order to live up to its name the cinema frequently acknowledged the source of their "electricity" — the Birmingham and Midland Tramways Committee!

Along with Irving Bosco's other cinemas, the Cape Hill Electric passed to Mr. Shapeero in 1920 and then, in March 1928, to the Gaumont British subsidiary Denman Picture Houses Ltd. Denman (Midlands) Cinemas paid £125,000 cash plus a number of shares for about a dozen cinemas. This ended Mr. Shapeero's interests in Black Country cinemas but his Nottingham based company continued to have other property interests in the area.

Gaumont British therefore had the task on converting the cinema to sound. The cinema was equipped with British Acoustic sound equipment. One of GB's managers, Ken Jones, left The Electric to go to the rival Grove cinema and rose to the position of General Manager of the Clifton Circuit. In 1932 the manager, Mr. J. Bowgem, was identified in the local press when hosting a party for eight hundred children and the Mayor, Alderman Mrs. Sands. (She also attended a similar function at The Rink.) Subsequent managers came and went but on 10th December 1954 the Smethwick Telephone reported that Amy Beardall had just retired as manageress of the Cape Electric after fourteen years in the job - during which period she was the only woman in such a post in the Smethwick area. She was replaced by Les Holder from The Rink.

As part of the Gaumont Circuit the Electric found its way, via the Circuits Management Association, formed in 1948 to deal with the management of the former Gaumont and Odeon circuits, into the Rank Organisation.

Neither Mr. Shapeero, nor G.B., nor the Rank Organisation ever seemed to feel any desire to change the Electric's name to anything more modern and one is given the feeling that it was rather a backwater as far as these large organisations were concerned. To its staff it was "small and friendly", to Rank it was probably considered small and old fashioned and it was therefore abandoned in autumn 1956 when the company closed a number of such halls, including the Criterion, Dudley.

The last show, on 29th September 1956, featured ***"Angels One Five "***, starring Jack Hawkins. The building was demolished completely and now offices stand on the site.

The Rink, later known as The Gaumont

Windmill Lane, Smethwick

On 4th September 1909 a large skating rink opened in Windmill Lane. It was promoted by a company formed of local businessmen and was designed by local architect, G. Bowden. It was a timber-framed building clad in corrugated iron but was built on too large a scale to be dismissed as a "tin shed". From the outside it seemed to be finished in a half-timbered effect.

In 1912 it was acquired by Irving Bosco, the cinema entrepreneur who had opened his first cinema in Dudley in 1910, but had then shown an interest in the Smethwick area. Irving Bosco's first cinema in the Smethwick area was the Cape Hill Electric, which he ahd opened in the summer of 1911. He overhauled and reconstructed the building in Windmill Lane, and installed 1500 seats. It opened as the Rink Picture House on 8th April 1912 with a programme that

Right: The Cape Hill Electric on 16th June 1957, almost a year after closure. This cinema had changed very little over the years. (J.H. Harvey)

Right: The original version of The Rink in Windmill Lane, Smethwick in 1929. Irving Bosco had converted the building from an skating rink. (W.H. Elvis, Sandwell Archives)

included a Western, a Comedy and a documentary about wild birds that was in colour.

Along with the Cape Hill Electric, it passed from Irving Bosco to Mr. Shapeero, of Nottingham, in 1920, and then to the Denman Picture Houses section of Gaumont British in 1928.

Manager J.F.Tooley addressed the audience on Saturday 13th May 1929 to tell them that the cinema was about to close and be demolished in order that a brand new super cinema be built to replace it. He introduced Mr. F. W. Davies who had been a patron for many years. In turn Mr. Davies paid tribute to Mr.Tooley who had been manager for 17 years - since the Rink had been converted from a skating rink into a cinema in 1912.

After the manager's announcement the cinema was duly closed and demolition eventually began in November 1929. The contractor moved onto the site on 15th December and work furiously began on building the brand new cinema. Within six weeks two hundred tons of steel, provided by Braithwaites of West Bromwich, were erected and the outline of the cinema could be seen. One or two aspects of this outline were reminiscent of the original Rink!

Below: The new version of The Rink., opened in 1930. Note the peacocks above the windows. (Kevin Wheelan Collection)

Left: The interior of The Rink, Smethwick in "Bingo Days", about 1981. Now known as The Victoria Suite, this area is now occupied by dining tables, but the décor has been preserved including the peacocks in the Moorish arch and the proscenium arch.

(Ned Williams)

The new Rink was designed by W. T. Benslyn. A plasterer who worked on the building, for Bryans Adamanta, told me that Mr. Benslyn had won the commission in competitive circumstances, and his winning interior design had been inspired by ideas produced by his young daughter! Both the interior and exterior of the new Rink were, and are, splendid. The curved brickwork of the frontage, one hundred and twenty feet in length, is relieved by impressive window surrounds in Portland stone. One of the most interesting features of the facade is the use of rnonumental stone peacocks, all of which are excellently preserved. The Architects Journal described it as, "Modern in appearance, with a suggestion of the Italian Renaissance".

A large foyer and generous crush halls anticipated large audiences and the staircases to the balcony greeted patrons with huge murals painted by the scenic artist, Frank Barnes. The huge auditorium held 1,300 patrons in the stalls, and 650 in the balcony. The side walls featured elaborate collonaded Moorish arches cleverly lit with concealed lighting. British Acoustic sound equipment was installed, and a Compton three manual, nine unit, organ with the console mounted on a lift. Somehow the entire building was constructed in seven months, which was considered as a Midlands record for a building of such size. When it opened it brought the talkies to Smethwick, two months before the Windsor, and eight months before the new Princes. Although Smethwick's three new super-cinemas opened within such a short time of each other they really served quite different areas.

The Rink, "The Wonder Talkie House", was opened on 7th July 1930 by Smethwick's Mayor, Councillor Sam Smith, and the programme featured *"Flight"; "the screen's all talking pageant of the air"*. Leslie James, who was resident for the entire first week, opened the new organ and patrons filled those acres of seats for 6d in the stalls, and 9d upstairs.

At the risk of offending supporters of other Gaumonts, I feel that the Rink was the finest Gaumont cinema in the West Midlands, although I also feel that I knew its colleagues in Wolverhampton and Wednesbury much better. I do not even know if building the Rink on such a lavish scale was ever justified. It has the grandeur, and "confidence" of the later Odeons, and also something of their anonymity! Another contender in the competition between Gaumonts must be the Gaumont Palace built in Birmingham at Colmore Circus. This was the first to use the "Gaumont Palace" name, and was also designed by William Benslyn. It was opened just seven months after The Rink.

As with other large circuit-run cinemas, it can be difficult to find details of its day-to-day existence. The Rink did receive some attention from the local press in January 1932 when the manager, T.J. Smylie, held a party for eleven hundred local children at the cinema. They were shown two Mickey Mouse films and a feature called "The Utah Kid" starring Rex Lease. The Mayor, Alderman Mrs. Sands, came along, and John Madin, the resident organist, provided some music. The event seemed to inspire a similar party at The Electric! The Mayor went to both.

The Rink became known as The Gaumont, Smethwick, on 31st July 1948, following the installation of Duosonc Sound, and seven years later celebrated its twenty-fifth anniversary with an appearance of a local children's choir from the Saturday chldren's Matinee Club, accompanied by Reg Johnson on the organ, and with film star Bill Owen cutting the Gaumont Cake. Bill Owen was introduced by the manager. Mr. J. Linz, and was invited because he was the star of the film, *"The Ship That Died of Shame"* which was being shown that week. I am sure no-one could then have believed that such a cinema would cease showing films within a decade.

The Gaumont closed on 1st February 1964 with *"Bitter Harvest"* and *"Tiger Bay"*. Apparently the closure came as quite a shock to the manager; Jim Gower. He had recently been chosen as the circuit's top manager in the West Midlands for his work in publicising the cinema and promoting films! In fact the Gaumont had recently retained *"From Russia With Love"* for two weeks, such was local demand. Poor Mr. Gower had come to Smethwick from the Odeon Dunstall which had eventually become a Bingo Club. He had operated Bingo sessions three afternoons a week at the Gaumont, but had never expected complete apostacy.

At least the Gaumont's conversion to Bingo preserved the building and its magnificent interior, but Bingo ceased in the summer of 2008. The building had been re-roofed and still had plenty of life left in it – it has subsequently become a pub. The Compton organ went to Quinton Parish Church about 1961, and later was rebuilt in several far-flung private homes until broken up for spare parts in about 2000.

Bearwood

At the major five-way road junction at the end of Cape Hill, from which it is possible to look down Windmill Lane and spot The Rink, the trams on their way from Birmingham to the Black Country went straight ahead into Smethwick High Street. Before we take that route, we will turn into Waterloo Road and make our way to Bearwood Road. The latter runs very close to the Birmingham boundary, but Bearwood was definitely in Staffordshire until 1974. At the southern end of Bearwood Road we encounter the Hagley Road at a crossroads known to everyone locally as The Kings Head. The Birmingham boundary runs down the centre the centre of Hagley Road and The Kings Head was always recognised as a significant "border point".

We will look at the two buildings in Bearwood Road, that once stood on either side of the Dunsford Road junction: the Windsor and the Coliseum – historically, the latter comes before the former! We will then progress to the "high street" section of Bearwood Road to look at The Majestic. From there we will take the Hagley Road out into Warley where we encounter yet another cinema right on the border of the Black Country: the famous Warley Odeon.

The Windsor

Bearwood Road, Bearwood

As stated above we describe The Windsor before dealing with The Coliseum to maintain a geographical logic rather than a historical one. Really the Windsor was built to replace the Coliseum and to establish Edward Hewitson's presence in the Bearwood area of Smethwick. We will encounter Edward Hewitson again as we describe the cinemas in the centre of Smethwick, and an outline of his career is provided in the introductory section.

The Windsor was an entirely new cinema/ theatre and was the summit of Edward Hewitson's achievements. As at other locations, Mr. Hewitson called upon the services of the Birmingham architect Horace Bradley, and the builder, William Jackson. Mr. Bradley designed a super-cinema that was attractive from all elevations, as opposed to the dull rectangular box that looked splendid as long as one looked at its frontage! The exterior was finished in stone and rusticated brick and the entrance faced the corner of Dunsford Road and Bearwood Road rather than the latter only. The curved corner entrance, enhanced by an elaborate canopy bearing the hall's name, was particularly attractive, and crowned with a stunning turret and dome. Leaded glass windows abounded and even the dome featured leaded lights that illuminated the balcony lounge just above the cafe.

The 1750 seater auditorium featured decorative plaster-work in white, gold and cream plus two huge murals on either side of the organ grilles. A simple rectangular proscenium enclosed a large screen, up to forty feet wide if required, and there was a 60' x 25' stage and full dressing room facilities. Seats were upholstered in old rose velvet, carpets were rose and mauve, and the curtains were old rose and green. As with the new Prince's in central Smethwick, owner and designer both felt their hall was "modern", but really its charm was its exploitation of the features of the "traditional" 1920's picture palace.

Naturally the Windsor was built as a sound cinema from the out-set, and BTH equipment was installed in its relatively spacious operating room. It opened with Kalee No. 8 projectors. The Windsor also featured an organ; a Compton three manual, eight unit instrument, and the actual organ loft was placed above the stage, the grilles forming an arc between the proscenium and the ceiling.

The work should have been completed by August but the opening was delayed one month. The Windsor was opened on Monday 29th September 1930 by the Mayor, Councillor Sam Smith, the proprietor of the foundry behind the Prince's in Smethwick. The first programme featured, *"Chasing Rainbows"* starring Charles King and Bessie Love. The organ was opened by Reginald Maynard.

At the opening of The Windsor Edward Hewitson could not conceal his pride in the enterprise and said:

"Here then is the answer to those who ask, 'Why all these places of amusement?' They are centres of mental and physical relaxation, the reflex of hard industrial organisation. The more a people must work, the more it should play."

And of his new cinema he said:

"No one can cross its threshold without feeling a sense of exhilaration. It is a triumph of architecture graced by the art of the scenic decorator, a veritable place of luxury, comfort, and beauty. Here music, colour, soft lighting, all combine to provide an atmosphere of joyousness in which the mind can more easily cast aside those worries and problems of the office, the casting shop or the lathe."

The Windsor became the headquarters of the Hewitson group, and of course its flagship. Even so its history ran curiously in reverse. Many buildings that had opened as theatres, closed as cinemas. The Windsor was contrary. Variety acts were gradually added to some film shows and after the War films were abandoned altogether in favour of revues and variety shows. Many stars that are now well known made early appearances on the stage of the Windsor.

Towards the end of its life, Geoffrey Hewitson, the son of Edward Hewitson, presented repertory by a resident company from 1957 onwards. With its grand opening as a cinema long forgotten the Windsor closed as a theatre on 6th February 1960 at the end of the run of the Christmas Pantomime: *"Mother Goose".* The organ was removed and is now in Oxley Parish Church, Wolverhampton.

The later history of The Windsor is therefore described in more detail in Volume Two.

Above: The Windsor, Bearwood, as seen in a commercial postcard of the 1930s. The building made good use of a corner site, and survives as the Sandwell Snooker Centre. While some theatres were subsequently cinemas, The Windsor worked in the reverse order, providing plenty of contempories with memories of it as a theatre. (Ken Rock) Left: Posters for the final pantomime: Mother Goose..

The Coliseum

Bearwood Road, Bearwood

The Coliseum occupied the corner of Dunsford Road and Bearwood Road opposite the corner eventually occupied by The Windsor. For some reason relatively little documentation on the Coliseum seems to exist.

It was promoted by Ben Kennedy's company that had opened the Smethwick Empire in 1910, but was a much more modest building. (Ben Kennedy's life and work is covered in the Introductory section.) It was designed, like The Empire, by Mr. Bowden, to hold a mere 875 patrons on a single floor. From the photograph reproduced here it would seem that the projection room was added later.

Ben Kennedy applied for a kine licence in April 1911 and when his application came before the magistrates it met incredible opposition. Witness after witness, including Edward Hewitson, claimed that there were already sufficient places of amusement in the area, and then local churchmen stood up to cast doubts upon the propriety of such entertainment. Despite all this it seems that the licence was granted and that the Coliseum quietly opened soon afterwards. No account seems to survive of the actual opening

Despite Mr. Hewitson's views on the abundance of local cinemas and theatres in 1911, he seems to have been

Above: The Coliseum, Bearwood Road, in 1929. The Majestic under construction on the left. (S. Smith, Sandwell Archives)

happy to acquire the Coliseum in 1917, and show films there for the rest of the silent era. The Coliseum was managed by Mr. B. Wesley for Edward Hewitson.

Towards the end of the twenties Edward Hewitson decided to build a brand new super-cinema in Bearwood Road. At first the "replacement" was to be called the "New Coliseum", but it materialised as the Windsor.

The Coliseum closed on Saturday 27th September 1930, to make way for the Windsor's opening on the Monday. The last film shown was a Ken Maynard Western called ***"The Phantom City"***.

Eventually the building was sold to the Staffordshire Territorial Association, but it seems they did not use it. During the Second World War it seems that it became a dance hall, and this continued after the war. In the Autumn of 1947 dances were still taking place, featuring Frank Hobson and His Orchestra. He may have stayed until September 1955 when the Coliseum closed for a couple of weeks to have a new maple dance floor installed. There were complaints by local people about "Teddy Boys" visiting the Coliseum at the end of the 1950s but these were dismissed by the manager who welcomed locals to visit his well-run dance hall at any time! In more recent times the site became a garage.

Left: The Majestic, Bearwood in 1959 – as the ground floor was about to become a market hall. This frontage dated from 1939 and it is not clear what the original frontage of the building looked like. This has now been demolished and retail developments have now obscured the site of the cinema.
(Joe Russell)

The Majestic

Bearwood Road

Having provided central Smethwick with the Prince's Hall in 1912, it seems that Edward Hewitson turned his attention to Bearwood. (This pattern was repeated the new Prince's was followed by the building of The Windsor.) Next-door to the headquarters of the Midland Red Omnibus Company, in Bearwood Road, he found a site on which to build the Majestic. By this time the First World War was underway and little seems to be recorded about its construction or design. It was probably built by William Jackson. It accommodated 1000 patrons in the stalls, and 336 in the balcony.

The Majestic was opened on 7th February 1916 by the Mayor, Councillor G. E. Ryder. The first feature film shown was *"The High Road"*. The cinema was particularly proud of its orchestra, led by Herbert Povey, which was described as, "Second only to the one at the Scala, Birmingham".

The Majestic was to experience two more "openings" during its otherwise uneventful lifetime. It closed for a month in 1939 while a new frontage was built on the theatre in an attempt to modernise it. The new front elevation was designed by Roland Satchwell. It was carried out in black, primrose and green Vitrolite, which was not quite as strong as it sounds. Primrose predominated with narrow bands of green, while black only appeared at the base of the facade. The work was

completed by William Jackson. New BTH equipment and a new screen were installed. It reopened in this form on August Bank Holiday Monday, 7th August 1939 with *"Little Tough Guys in Society "*.

Twenty years later the cinema business was going through hard times. The Majestic quietly closed on 21st February 1959 with *"What Lola Wants"*. The ground floor of the cinema became a Market Hall and later a ballroom, but that was not quite the end of the Majestic. By the mid seventies the Majestic and the Midland Red Depot were owned by a property company hoping to undertake wholesale redevelopment of the entire site. Apparently to help prevent vandalism they wished to find someone to lease the cinema for eighteen months, the first six months "rent free"! Michael Flook acquired planning permission to create a small 250 seater cinema using the former circle.

As "The Studio" it opened on 31st March 1977 with *"Gumball Rally"* and *"Lets Do It Again"*. Recent events are not necessarily easier to research than ones long past and Michael Flook and "the Studio" seem to have faded away within a year without leaving us the date of the final show. (Probably at the end of September 1978.)

The auditorium was demolished at the end of 1978 and the frontage followed early in 1979. Nothing remained by March 1979.

Right: The foyer at the Majestic, Bearwood. It looked as if you were entering the baronial home of the Hewitsons rather than a 1930s cinema! (Geoff Hewitson)

The Warley Odeon

Hagley Road/Wolverhampton New Road, Warley.

The Warley Odeon, as it was generally known, stood symbolically at the "Gateway to the Black Country". A Blackcountryman returning from Birmingham felt "at home" once he had passed the massive cinema that stood at the junction of the Hagley Road and the Birmingham-Wolverhampton "New" Road, even if the real Black Country air could not be breathed until passing under the railway bridge at Langley. The "New" Wolverhampton Road was opened in the autumn of 1927 by the Prince of Wales, replacing the old routes from Birmingham into the Black Country represented by the roads through Smethwick and West Bromwich, the latter being part of Telford's trunk road from London to Shrewsbury and Holyhead.

In the 1930's this site was located within the boundaries of the Borough of Oldbury, and few people today could be precise about the original location of "Warley". It remained a relatively undeveloped part of the Black Country until the twentieth century. From then on the use of the name "Warley" gained more currency, and in 1966 when Oldbury, Smethwick and West Bromwich were brought togther as one new County Borough the name "Warley" was used, only to disappear again in 1974.

The original company that set out to build a cinema on this site included Sidney Clift and W.H. Onions. Their involvement presumably accounts for the fact that Roland Satchwell was the original architect. Mr. Onions also played a part in promoting the Tower at West Bromwich, and the Clifton at Stone Cross. At Stone

Cross and Warley it seemed his original intention was to simply called his building "The Cinema". Maybe this was contentious because at one stage it was going to be called The Warley, and then The Warley Cinema!

At some stage the company seems to have run into financial difficulties and Oscar Deutsch was invited to join the scheme. He became the chairman of the company and the Warley played an important part in defining the emerging Odeon style. Originally the new cinema was going to be built to designs provided by Ernest Roberts and Roland Satchwell, but Oscar Deutsch had his own ideas about this. Ironically the Roberts/Satchwell partnership was dissolving at the time. The main elevation was designed by Cecil Howitt, but of greater significance was the fact that Harry Weedon was asked to plan the interior. Harry Weedon engaged 23-year-old Cecil Clavering to actually come up with the designs, and out of this melting pot the straightforward modernism of the Odeons was born.

The Warley was built by J.B. Whitehouse and Son, whose only other cinema-building work in the Black Country was later at the Clifton, Lye. Mr. Whitehouse also became a director of the company. By the time the cinema opened W.G. Elcock had joined the Board, and he later joined the companies building the Odeons in Wolverhampton and Dudley.

The Warley opened on 22nd December 1934, with *"Evensong"* starring Evelyn Laye. On stage were Oscar Deutsch, R.H. Morgan M.P., Councillor Wallis, the Chairman of Oldbury U.D.C. and Mr. and Mrs. Whitehouse. However the actual opening ceremony was performed by the Earl of Dudley. The Earl had quite a lot to say. He felt that more films should portray industrial life and social problems such as housing for the working classes. He added, *"Before the War, when work was over, there was hardly anything else left to do except to get drunk. Now, instead of spending five shillings in getting drunk, we spend sixpence on the pictures, — and a very good substitute it is too!"*.

Everyone admired the huge 1530 seater auditorium, decorated in terracotta and green, and, years later, some patrons can recall the strong scent of carnations in the foyer. It was equipped with BTH equipment, favoured by both Oscar Deutsch and Sidney Clift. Oscar Deutsch seems to have regarded it as an ideal showplace, conveniently close to his home in Edgbaston. He organised special shows on Sundays for his private house parties, and always came personally to thank the chief, Mr. Matheson, and the second operator, Frank Harvey, for their services. The Earl of Dudley also "borrowed" films, and the services of the operators, from The Warley when entertaining guests in his private cinema at Himley Hall.

Very quickly the original name was dropped and it became an Odeon. The name "Odeon" was simply added to the tower beneath the word "Warley". With this comparative "anonymity" I feel it slipped into the

Below: The Warley, April 1935. (John Maltby)

role of serving the Birmingham suburbs whatever its position in relation to local government boundaries. However, as a result of its location it was landmark cinema familiar to Brummies and Black Country folk alike.

The Warley Odeon lasted until 25th November 1961, closing with **"Victim"**, starring Dirk Bogarde, supported with **"Attempt to Kill".** Work started immediately on turning it into a bowling alley at a cost of £200,000. As the Warley Bowl it lasted less than a decade. The last skittles fell on 29th April 1970 and this once elegant building stood boarded-up for a couple of years, while the huge areas of faience on the main elevation began to show their age. It was finally demolished in 1973.

Naunton Developments obtained planning permission to build a 120 bedroom hotel on the site but the building that eventually materialised was a massive office block which became the headquarters of Messrs Albright & Wilson, the Oldbury-based chemical manufacturer. It opened as Albright House in 1974, and won an "Office of the Year" award in 1975.

Strangely enough, after the Warley cinema's closure, the Quinton cinema seemed to have made a virtue, and financial success, of showing films on the fringe of Birmingham's suburbs, but that cinema will have to be dealt with in the section on Dudley as a result of the strange meanderings of local government boundaries.

Central Smethwick

Having dealt, in the previous section, with cinemas close to the Birmingham border, we now move on to the centre of Smethwick. Like many other towns in the Black Country, Smethwick started life as a fairly scattered assortment of hamlets, and by 1800 could only boast a population of about one thousand people. But events during the second half of the previous century had already sewn the seeds of change. The main road from Birmingham, through Smethwick, to Dudley had been turnpiked in 1760. Brindley's canal stretching from Birmingham out into the Black Country towards Wednesbury also opened in the 1760s. Industrialisation had begun and the population began to grow.

Administratively Smethwick had been part of the Parish of Harborne, but in 1856 it gained its own "Local Board of Health", and subsequent development of local government reflects the growth of the town. Like many Black Country townships it was given "Urban District" status in 1894, but recognised as a "Borough" only five years later. By 1907 it had become a "County Borough". Steam trams began running the length of the old turnpike road in 1885, and the route was electrified in 1904. The development of so much urban infrastructure meant that Smethwick could make rapid progress as a self-contained Black Country industrial town, and develop residentially as a result of its proximity to Birmingham. Little wonder that the town acquired places of entertainment.

Left: William Jackson has erected his board to explain that a new "Prince's Hall is under construction. Note the narrow entrance to the former building and the outline of the auditorium.

From the Theatre Royal to Pictureland.

The Theatre Royal was opened in Rolfe Street, Smethwick, on 20th September 1897 – about the same time that other Black Country towns acquired purpose-built variety theatres. It was almost entirely used as a theatre and therefore its history will be covered in Volume Two, but its significance in the story told in this volume is that its first manager was a man named Edward Hewitson.

Edward Hewitson may have experimented with the use of the cinematograph as a variety act during the first decade of the twentieth century, and may have presented the occasional late night film presentation after acquiring a cinematograph licence in 1910. While Edward Hewitson was nurturing his interest in cinematography, Benjamin Kennedy was opening a rival theatre close to the other end of Smethwick's High Street. The Empire opened on 5th September 1910 and Ben Kennedy was well-disposed to the concept of "cine-variety". Perhaps they discussed the merits of live theatre versus the delights of film – they certainly had the opportunity because they later became neighbours for a time!

By the end of 1911 it seems that Hewitson had decided that specialising in showing films was a viable proposition. After a special benefit performance held at the Theatre Royal in his honour, he left to show films in the Town Hall. These shows began on 25th March 1912 and were advertised under the name of "Pictureland". The Cape Hill Electric was already in business, and the Skating Rink in Windmill Lane started showing films the following month, but the Town Hall was located in the centre of Smethwick.

The Town Hall had been built in 1867, and like many such halls built just before the establishment of proper local government, it was designed to include space that could be used as a "Public Hall". (It may well have been used for film presentation before Edward Hewitson moved in.) Its use as "Pictureland" compares with similar use of Town Halls in Bilston, Brierley Hill, and the Public Hall in Netherton. In all such cases the tenant inevitably moved on to "better things".

Having established Pictureland in the Town Hall, Edward Hewitson began planning something more ambitious: The Prince's Hall. Pictureland closed when the new cinema opened.

The former Town Hall is now used as a Public Library and therefore it is still possible to visit the location of Mr. Hewitson's "Pictureland". The lending library occupies the former "public hall" space.

The Prince's Hall

Smethwick High Street

While his film shows were running successfully at the Town Hall, Edward Hewitson organised the construction of a purpose-built cinema. He commissioned F. J. Gill to design the building, and Messrs. Dallow and Son to build it. It was erected on the site of the old Post Office. Only a narrow entrance actually presented itself to the High Street, but a reasonably large auditorium was constructed to hold 950 patrons in tip up seats on a raked floor.

The Prince's Hall opened on Thursday evening 19th December 1912, in the presence of the Mayor and leading townsfolk. Patrons paid 3d, 6d, 9d or 1/- to see a programme that included *"Jasmine"* and *"Fire at Sea"*.

One or two local people can still recall the popular Saturday afternoon children's matinees. The hall was usually packed and halfpenny nougats were sold in great numbers. When Miss Washington, the pianist, arrived she was always greeted with deafening cheers.

From these beginnings Edward Hewitson's empire gradually expanded. By the end of the silent era it no doubt seemed old fashioned and therefore it was replaced with something more modern. Just as the Coliseum in Bearwood had to be replaced with The Windsor, the Prince's Hall had to be replaced with The Prince's. The Prince's Hall is sometimes forgotten but for eigthteen years of the silent era it was Smethwick's town centre cinema. The Prince's Hall closed on 27th April 1930 with *"The Wright Idea"*. William Jackson, the builder, moved in immediately to erect its successor.

The Prince's Cinema

The Prince's was designed by H. G. Bradley and is one of those fascinating cinemas caught in a transition period, reflecting something of the twenties, heralding something of the thirties. Mr. Hewitson told the press, *"The whole building, in fact, expresses the modern spirit of architecture, that there shall be no beauty without use, and nothing useful that is not beautiful"*. A faience-treated facade crowned in a pediment and featuring ornate leaded windows may not have struck some people as pure modernism. Once again, as in its predecessor, a narrow entrance led to a huge auditorium hidden by neighbouring shops. The new Prince's could accommodate 1500 patrons in some luxury. The latest BTH equipment was installed, but the talkies had already arrived at other local cinemas by the time it opened.

It opened on 26th December 1930, Boxing Day, with a film called *"Dynamite"*. A feature of the Prince's was the two manual, five unit, Compton organ. The instrument was opened by Wilfred Southworth. Six years later, however, it was moved to The Empire.

Although more modern cinemas later opened in Cape Hill and Bearwood, the Prince's was central Smethwick's premier cinema throughout its life. It was very nearly destroyed in the Second World War when a land mine almost landed on it. Sam Smith's foundry, just behind the cinema was hit, throwing a length of steel girder into the air which came crashing down through the roof and ceiling of the cinema. The Prince's closed for a short time for repairs and the girder has been "preserved" to this day as a souvenir.

Below: The Princes late 1980. (Ned Williams)

After the War Edward Hewitson's son, Geoffrey Hewitson, was not very keen on installing cinemascope so he put in an extra large 42' x 21' screen instead. Even so "scope" had to be installed eventually. The Prince's was still busy enough in 1966 to warrant spending money on redecoration and re-seating. The 360 seats in the circle were replaced and 300 removed from the stalls to make it more spacious. A short time afterwards a massive programme of house-clearance in the area near the Prince's suddenly removed the local patrons to distant parts of the borough. Attendances dropped drastically overnight.

The Prince's closed on 27th June 1970 with *"Carry On Cruising"* and *"Carry On Teaching"*. Geoffrey Hewitson sold it, at what he considered to be a bargain price, to Nirmal Singh Sanghera. It reopened in April 1971 and was a very successful and profitable cinema for its new owner. Although basically committed to presenting Indian films, the Prince's did show some English language films again during the week, for a time. By the end of the decade it was only in use at weekends, and closed once again about February 1980.

The Princes went through another reopening on 14th January 1994 with **"Demolition Man"**. Once again screening English language films did not seem to work and the cinema returned to Asian films with a further reopening on 8th December 1995. By 2001 The Princes was once again "temporarily closed" having been defeated by Asian film presentation elsewhere.

Despite these reopenings and closures time was running out for the Princes partly because the Sikh temple next door was anxious to expand. In the end it was demolished and the temple did indeed expand across the site.

The Empire

St. Pauls Road, Smethwick

The Empire Theatre Company, under the chairmanship of Ben Kennedy, opened the Empire on 5th September 1910. The building was designed by the local architect, Mr. G. Bowden and was conceived as a theatre. The facade, described as "free-renaissance style" survives to this day and feels "theatrical". It was built by John Dallow and Sons.

Ben Kennedy held a kine licence for the Empire and certainly films were presented there early in the theatre's life. About 1915 it seems to have passed to Messrs. Black and Hicks, who continued to present cine-variety. The same gentlemen took over the Kings Hall, Darlaston from Ben Kennedy. Contrary to other published accounts of this theatre's history, I do not believe it was acquired by Edward Hewitson until 1922. It seems that he purchased it for £14,350 at an auction on 22nd September of that year.

At that time it was said to have 1334 seats and eighty-seven years of its lease to run. It seems that Edward Hewitson may have reopened the Empire three months later for more cine-variety, but in 1924 he set about considerably altering the theatre to make it a full- time cinema. The extensive refurbishing and the new cinema equipment warranted a ceremonious reopening on 6th October 1924, by Smethwick's Mayor, Alderman Betts. The opening feature film was *"Scaramouche"*, accompanied by an orchestra led by Caradoc Davis. The variety tradition could not be broken and the opening also featured *"Henriette and Selina"* on stage. Alan Hewitson, Mr. Hewitson's son, became the manager. So, despite being so "theatre-like" the Empire now settled down to being a silent cinema.

Right: The Empire in St. Paul's Road, Smethwick, about 1920. There seems to be no long canopy on the front of the theatre in this picture. Compare it with the picture in Volume 2.
(Ken Rock)

Like the other halls in the Hewitson group, when sound arrived the Empire installed BTH equipment, and then went one stage better by adding an organ. The two manual, five unit Compton organ from the Prince's was installed at the Empire, with an additional unit. It was opened by George Hunt,, and remained in its new home until 1959 or 1960. It was then removed to Holly Lodge Grammar School.

The Empire's position among Hewitson Theatres was somewhat reduced by the opening of the new Prince's and the Windsor, and finally by the modernising of the Majestic. Perhaps if the Second World War had not come along the Empire might have been next on the list.

As it turned out it was an early casualty of post-War problems. It closed on 13th April 1957 with "*Too Bad She's Bad*", starring Sophia Loren, plus "*Card of Fate*" starring Gina Lollobrigida. The building became a hardware and D.I.Y. store. For years the stage stored scenery for an amateur theatrical group and the elegant leaded glass canopy reminded people of the building's past. It still stands, proudly bearing its name, the canopy modified, its red brickwork much painted, but still unmistakeably a one-time place of entertainment, although now a Sikh temple.

Outer Smethwick

Once Edward Hewitson had acquired the Empire in 1922, he had cinema entertainment in Central Smethwick, and Bearwood, under his control. The might of Gaumont British invaded Cape Hill by taking over The Electric, and replaced Irving Bosco's Rink with something more splendid in Windmill Lane, but Edward Hewitson seems to have kept the larger companies out of Central Smethwick in the same way that Thomas Wood retained control of a Bilston empire in his own lifetime. Out on the fringes of Smethwick were two other cinemas – The Ring Palace in West Smethwick and the Beacon in Brasshouse Lane. The former was taken over by Hewitson, but the latter became an outpost of the ABC empire.

The Ring Palace

Oldbury Road, West Smethwick.

This little-known cinema was in West Smethwick not far from the railway station of the same name. It was originally owned by George Devey, but whether it was purpose-built, or was converted from an older building is not clear.

The Ring Palace opened on Saturday 27th March 1915 and offered, "Warmth, Comfort and Civility", as well as screen entertainment. It was taken over by Edward Hewitson two years later, March 1917, apparently simply to buy-out any opposition, although the Hewitsons seemed to look down on their acquisition and dismissed it as a "flea-pit". Mr. Peake was sent along from the Prince's Hall to run the place and for a time it was re-named the "Picture Playhouse".

By the end of 1917 it advertised itself as "The Palace", which was very confusing as Oldbury's "Palace" was going through numerous minor changes of name at the same time. By the end of the War both settled on calling themselves The Palace! To the locals there was no problem — it was always called "The Ring".

The Ring's finest moments ironically came just as it was about to close. When the Prince's Hall closed to be rebuilt the orchestra was transferred to West Smethwick! By the beginning of 1931 when all neighbouring cinemas were presenting talkies, The Ring stressed in its adverts: *"The only house for silents with an orchestra"*.

The light on the screen faded and the orchestra took their final bow on 5th March 1932 with a showing of *"Motherland"*. After standing empty for a time the building became a warehouse, but has long since disappeared without trace.

Right: The Ring Palace in August 1934 – after its closure as a cinema, having tried to make a virtue of showing silent films after the arrival of sound!
(F. Parkes, Sandwell Archives)

The Beacon

Brasshouse Lane, Smethwick

The Beacon seems remote from central Smethwick, let alone the rest of the Black Country, but I like to think that perhaps its name has some local significance. The promoter of the cinema was Percy Dyche, a Birmingham man connected with other cinemas in the city, but whose only other excursion into the Black Country appears to have been briefly at the Cosy Corner, Halesowen.

The Beacon was designed by Harold Scott and built by T. Elvins. The following description appeared in the Smethwick Telephone:

"The new house has a dignified simplicity both without and within. Nondescript ornamentation is entirely absent; the whole building gives a delightful impression of beauty and spaciousness. The colour-scheme represents a beacon, though sunset colours are also suggested. The green carpet and deep blue curtains edge the bronze of the lower walls, that merge into russet-red and amber, while the ceiling is mottled sky blue".

Mr. W. E. Lawrence J.P. opened the Beacon, on Monday 30th September 1929. He was joined on stage by Percy Dyche, James Hill J.P. and the local vicar, Rev. F. K. Roberts. The programme included *"Give and Take"* and *"The Politic Flapper"*. The auditorium held just under a thousand patrons at 4d and 6d in the stalls, 9d and 1/- in the balcony. The projection room contained Ernimann Imperator 200 machines, and the orchestra pit contained a small ensemble directed by H. J. Miller. Mr. A. S. Anderton was General Manager.

The year after the Beacon opened Smethwick's three super-cinemas opened their doors, but the Beacon's isolation probably enabled it to serve a quite distinct community. (The "other side of the tracks"?). It kept abreast of the times by installing Western Electric sound equipment in the summer of 1932, and claimed to be the first cinema in Smethwick to put on matinees for the unemployed. They were admitted for 3d. It also offered three programmes per week at a time when other cinemas offered two. In early sound days The Beacon made much of the fact that it was going to screen James Whale's "Frankenstein" which it declared was "The Film of the Year"!

Sometime early in the 1930's the cinema became part of the County Circuit, which, in turn, was absorbed by the Mayfair Circuit. At the end of August 1943 the Beacon found it self in the ABC Circuit. The latter collected quite a few ancient or obscure Black Country cinemas! Even as part of the ABC circuit, the Beacon seems to have led quite a quiet life and was seldom mentioned in the local press. In August 1955 the manager, Harold Morris, left to go to the Gaiety in Brum, and was replaced by Ken Howe from Derby.

The reason this was reported was that Harold was a very popular figure locally. He had formed a club for pensioners known as "The Silver Ling Club". Perhaps the Beacon has to be remembered for putting on shows for the unemployed and its pensioners' club! As an outpost of ABC, it managed to outlive their Palace, Walsall, and Olympia, Darlaston, but closed on 15th February 1958, with *"The Lady And The Tramp"*.

The Beacon was sold, for £10,000, to Mohammed Firdar, and he spent another £15,000 modernising, redecorating, and re-seating the place. Even a new screen was installed. It reopened, showing Indian films, on 3rd November 1962. In the following years it was leased to various people, but at least it survived, and played quite an important part in the brief story of Asian cinemas in the Black Country. It closed for a short time in 1978, by which time it was only open four nights a week. The manager, Ragbir Singh carried out various improvements demanded by Sandwell Council, and business resumed.

It was very much on its last legs when I first visited it in the summer of 1980, and I was not surprised to learn that it had closed by the end of that year. Another casualty of the video revolution; the building became a clothing factory.

Right: The Beacon, Brasshouse Lane, Smethwick, in 1980. At the time the cinema was still being used to screen Asian films, but was looking rather sorry for itself. (Ned Williams)

The Beacon

Scott Arms, Great Bar.

As a strange result of how local government boundaries were drawn in 1974, Sandwell, could be said to have had another "Beacon" cinema! The Scott Arms, on the Birminmgham – Walsall A34 main road feels very much like a north western suburb of Birmingham, but as the area is in modern Sandwell, we better include a mention of The Beacon.

The Beacon was opened 9th March 1938, with *"Oh Mr. Porter"*. It was designed by Roland Satchwell to accommodate 1228 patrons, and was built by one of the companies associated with the Clifton Circuit. It was one of the Roland Satchwell designs that had quite an Odeon feel about it, particularly because it featured a tower.

The Beacon closed 16th December 1972, with *"Nympho"*, two years before it could be counted as a Sandwell cinema, but the building survived another ten years before being demolished to provide land for housing.

West Bromwich

Like Smethwick, West Bromwich was once a scattered gathering of small settlements unified fairly rapidly by the processes of industrialisation and urbanisation in the nineteenth century. The Borough of West Bromwich was created in 1882, later becoming a County Borough in 1889. Similarly to Smethwick, we can think of West Bromwich as a town encountered on the way from Birmingham into the Black Country. In this case the road that makes this journey was more than just a local turnpike – it was the route chosen by Telford in his plan to provide a direct route from London to Holyhead, crossing the Black Country via West Bromwich, Wednesbury, Bilston and Wolverhampton (the A41).

The tramway from Birmingham traversed the High Street through the centre of West Bromwich and divided at Carters Green – one route making its way to Dudley via Great Bridge, the other heading for Wednesbury via Hill Top. All these place names are relevant to understanding the location of cinemas.

In this section of the book we will look at the cinemas that developed in the centre of West Bromwich, and then deal with a couple quite remote from that centre, at Hill Top and Stone Cross. Lastly, we travel to the northern border of West Bromwich in the village of Great Bridge. The centre itself was very "linear" – a mile of High Street stretching from Dartmouth Square to Carters Green. In dealing with the cinemas virtually in order of their arrival, we will begin the survey in Carters Green.

West Browmich has a special place in the history of Black Country cinemas. First of all the town can claim to have provided a home for the Black Country's first permanent cinema – opening almost a year before the Kinematograph Act became law and proper cinema history began! Secondly, something happened in West Bromwich in the 1970s that was completely against the general trends in cinema history. While others were trying to abandon the cinema business the citizens of West Bromwich were treated to a brand new purpose built three screen cinema: The Kings. Just to make matters more interesting we begin the survey in a corrugated iron building that never seemed clear about whether it was a cinema or a theatre.

The New Hippodrome/Olympia

High Street, Carters Green, West Bromwich.

The Hippodrome was a large corrugated iron building, indicating that its promoters were not sure how permanent it might be. Possibly financial caution had also led them to adopt an "out of town" site. Unfortunately, the story of how it came to be built, and who was behind it remains obscure. The Midland Chronicle recorded that it was built by Messrs. Richardson and Carlmark but It is not clear whether they mean the "building contractors" or the proprietors! The paper is quite clear in stating that Mr. T.M.Sylvester is Managing Director of the company owning The New Hippodrome. The surnames Calrmark and Sylvester appear among the names of local businessmen. The theatre seems to have had links with the Coventry Hippodrome, so may not have been an entirely local enterprise. (See Vol. 2, pages 65/66.)

The Hippodrome opened on August Bank Holiday Monday, 6th. August 1906 with an afternoon matinee show which was a complete sell-out. The Midland Chronicle told readers: *"The entertainment was of a very high class – there was not a touch of vulgarity or suggestiveness in the whole show."* We also learnt that the orchestra was directed by a Mr. Wright, and the day to day management of the theatre was in the hands of a Mr. H.W. Player. As well as the live variety acts presented the show included pictures presented by Mr. Rowe on the "Hippograph". This information is important as it makes it quite clear that cine-variety was presented from the start. It also had implications for the Theatre Royal, closer to the Town Centre. James Moore, who was in charge at the Theatre Royal immediately introduced twice-nightly shows – at the sames times as those presented by the New Hippodrome, and added "Ruffell's unrivalled pictures" to the shows! Most interesting of all was that James Moore started calling his theatre the "Theatre Royal and Hippodrome" perhaps explaining why the folks at Carters Green had to call their enterprise the *"New Hippodrome"*. James Moore defended his policy by saying that he often presented shows that included equestrian acts.

Above: Black Country folk assemble on horse-drawn breaks for a day out – turning their back on The Olympia – seen in the background. Note the Olympia's poster on the right of the picture. (Chris Clegg)

The Mildand Chronicle was not able to ignore the fact that the New Hippodrome was a corrugated iron building despite Mr. Sylvester stating, "It is the only new building for amusement in West Bromwich." He also explained that the management was keen to replace it with a permanent £20,000 building if public support seemed to justify the investment. After the opening the Chronicle wrote:

"This very striking building which has just been erected at Carters Green opened its doors on Monday afternoon, and a large audience assembled to enjoy a brilliant programme.

A word, however, should be said about the building. Many people who have watched it during the course of its erection will be astonished on going inside at the beauty, comfort and commodiousness of the place. I certainly had not anyhting so elabrate from an iron structure. Inside, no one would imagine it to be an iron building erected for only temporary use."

Following the opening, the New Hippodrome announced that the enterprise had been an "unparalleled success". As people had been turned away from some shows, an additonal Saturday afternoon matinee performance was going to be introduced. The second week's show included the well-known Harry Tate as well as the ubiquitous performing dogs so loved by variety theatres. After that the theatre ceased regular newspaper advertising leaving us to wonder how long success was enjoyed. Although plans were drawn for a permanent building, the "temporary structure" remained in place.

The original company seems to have handed over the task of presenting shows at the New Hippodrome after

a copuple of years. The new presenter was R. Colin, who also provided film and variety at the Empire, Dudley, and Tivoli, Brierley Hill. "Colin's Famous Electric Pictures" were a feature of entertainment in Carters Green by the time the Cinematograph Act became law at the beginning of 1910.

By 1911 the lease seems to have been transferred to Benjamin Kennedy who was busy building an empire of entertainment venues in and around the Black Country. (See introductory section on Ben Kennedy.) Both R. Colin and Ben Kennedy were keen exponents of "cine-variety" making it difficult retrospectively to decide whether they are part of cinema history or theatre history!

The name appears to have changed to the Olympia in 1914. A new company, West Bromwich Olympia Ltd., had been registered in September 1913, and appears to have partly rebuilt the theatre in time to re-open as the Olympia on 1st June 1914. This coincides with Ben Kennedy's opening of The Empire much closer to the town centre. Ben Kennedy actually had an announcement printed in the Midland Chronicle to make it clear that his energies were now focussed on his new town centre theatre:

"Mr. Kennedy wishes it to be understood that he is not connected in any way with The Olympia after 30th

May. Kennedy's only place of amusement after that date will be the New Empire."

The Managing Director of the new company resident at The Olympia was Will Devey, and the day-to-day management of the place was in the hands of F.G. Fenn. They opened with a programme of variety acts and film – promising to change the film contents of the show every Monday and Thursday. The opening programme included two George Formby films: *"No Fool Like an Old Fool"* and *"Adrift in Life's Tide".*

Just after the First World War The Olympia appears to have been used by Ben Kennedy again until it suffered a fire and possibly remained closed until its demolition during the late summer of 1922, After demolition Guest Motors, the local Ford agent, built a showroom on the site. It has two claims to local fame. First, people remember a huge balloon that was tethered to the place, when new, but which sailed away one day when the cable snapped. Secondly, the tin roof, that produced so much noise when it rained, once collapsed under a weight of snow!

The Palace, known as The Queens

Queen Street

The Hippodrome / Olympia was really a theatre that flirted with the new medium of cinematography. The town's first cinema was undoubtedly the Palace, and, although not purpose-built, I would regard it as the first cinema to open in the Black Country. The building had been Josh Bailey's printing works but was converted to a cinema by none other than Irving Bosco, the Black Country cinema pioneer. It opened on Saturday 23rd January 1909, almost a full year ahead of the great burst of cinema-opening activity. As the "Picture Palace", its first programme included *"Rifle Bill"* and many and varied short films. It was managed by Irving Bosco's brother, James Bainton, and probably Irving's wife appeared there to provide song accompaniment to some of the films.

Irving Bosco introduced "benefit shows" at the Picture Palace, just as he did later at Dudley's Public Hall. In February he held a show to raise funds for the local hospital, at which the Mayoress, eleven year old Miss Edith Field, was presented with a bouquet. Later, she, and her brother Charles Field, worked at the cinema. Edith sold penny toffee bars from a tray and Charles worked in the pay box, or, if necessary, in the operating box, where a hand-cranked Pathe projector struggled to present the films without too many fires!

The name "Queens" seems to have been adopted about May 1910, perhaps to avoid confusion with the new purpose-built rival in the High Street, the Electric Picture Palace. Certainly the Queens was quick to compete on any front imaginable. When the new cinema advertised its bright coal fire installed in its lounge the

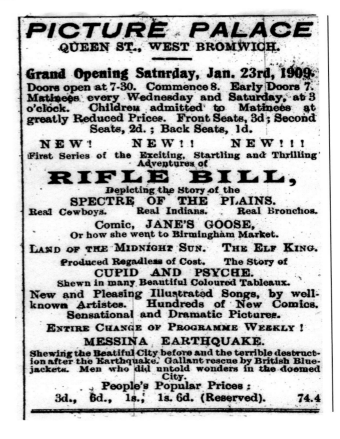

Queens claimed, "N.B. The Hall Is Comfortably Warmed". During the summer of 1911 it closed for a week to be re-seated and to have better use made of its space, after which it claimed, "N.B. The Coolest Hall In The Midlands!".

It thrived on the "penny and a pass" system of filling its seats and advertising its shows, and by enterprising programming. For example in December 1910, the first Christmas after its rival had opened, the Queens presented *"Puss In Boots, plus Pictures"*, and in the January: *"Sleeping Beauty plus ten Pictures"*

Irving Bosco seems to have parted with the Queens earlier than his other Black Country cinemas. About the time of the end of the First World War it was sold to Thomas Leach, who rebuilt the place into the basic form which survived until 1969, increasing its capacity from about 800 to 1200. With the aid of his brothers, and brothers-in-law, Tom Leach built up quite a circuit of local cinemas, and in West Bromwich both the Queens, and the St. Georges, were eventually leased to the F. J. Emery circuit, sometime in the 1930's. By then, of course, it was a sound cinema, using British Talking Pictures equipment.

During the Second World War the Queens appears to have declined. Its seating capacity dropped to a thousand which suggests that F. J. Emery was more generous in the space allowed per patron than Tom Leach, or maybe seats wore out and were not replaced. Local folk tales abound concerning rows in which some seats were missing altogether, and unsuspecting patrons fighting their way along the row to a non-existent place!

Above: The Queens, West Bromwich, about 1948, before Miles Jervis had improved and modernised the canopy. However much improvement took place, The Queens never managed to look very cinema-like as a result of being a conversion of an existing building. (Miles Jervis' Collection)

Possibly the usherettes knew no better, and again local legends suggest a high turn-over of such staff in the early forties. The Queens became known as "The Banger" and "The Bug and Blanket".

In July 1946, along with the other cinemas that formed the estate of the late Tom Leach, the freehold of The Queens was sold, by auction, to Miles Jervis II. This marked a change in its fortunes. Miles Jervis II persuaded Mr. Emery to relinquish the lease, and began to improve The Queens. First of all he installed a more effective sound system (British Acoustic), and added new G.B. Kalee GK 18 projectors.

About 1949 Miles Jervis II improved the frontage of the Queens with a new, longer canopy and, in 1952, Modernisation Ltd. were invited to refurbish the interior. Miles Jervis found that The Queens was the most successful of his Black Country cinemas and it became his headquarters for a time, as well as the scene of his innovations. A "Synchro" screen was successfully tried at The Queens and, in 1956, automated projection was introduced. At first, the chief operator, Peter J. Evans, was proud of the new equipment but in the course of time it turned out not to be very successful. It was, however, the forerunner of more successful systems.

In 1957 Miles Jervis acquired The Kings and became

even more firmly established in West Bromwich. The Kings was much more impressive than the Queens but the latter showed no sign of immediate retirement. By the mid sixties, however, its future looked less secure. I visited it once in 1965 and a bleak programme, *("The War Game"* plus *"Four in the Morning")* perhaps made the cinema seem more dismal than it really was. Possibly even then it was realised that redevelopment would force its closure, hence the signs of neglect.

The Queens showed its last regular programme on Saturday 5th April 1969, closing with the interesting Vincent Price film, *"Witchfinder General"*. The Queens was used on Sundays for the presentation of Indian films, organised by Tarsem Singh Dhami and his colleagues, and these shows continued. Mr. Dhami recalls these shows as being extremely successful and remembers having to rush to the Kings to obtain further supplies of ice-creams to feed his packed house.

The council compulsorily purchased the Queens from Miles Jervis and it was demolished in the August of 1969. Mr. Dhami claims that the demolition contractor came along to start work while the last Indian film show was still taking place!

"The Banger", the Black Country's first cinema on a permanent site, had lasted sixty years. Following its demise, the Imperial returned to the business of showing films and plans were being formulated for a brand new cinema to perpetuate the tradition of film-exhibition established in West Bromwich by Irving Bosco way back in 1909.

The Electric Palace
(later known as The Palace)

High Street, West Bromwich

In the chapter on the Electric Palace, Walsall, we will encounter a company called Electric Picture Palace (Midlands) Ltd., a company that set out to build half a dozen purpose-built cinemas in the area, and who opened their second hall in West Bromwich. It was built, near the junction of Paradise Street and the High Street, to accommodate 1200 patrons, and was designed by Messrs. Hickton and Farmer. It was built by Messrs Hopkins & Sons. The main entrance was originally in Paradise Street.

It opened at three o'clock on Whit Monday, 16th May 1910. Mr. Simpson, the manager, entertained his first patrons with eleven films concerning the life and recent death of Edward VII —

"No better selection of pictures could be made for the opening week, for tragedy in various forms, the romantic, and the comic phases of life are all represented".

Continuous performances were presented from 3.00 p.m. to 10.30 p.m. and it was described as, "A pretty as well as a cosy theatre". A rivalry grew between the Queens and the Palace, but it seems the latter genuinely offered more comfort and luxury.

Towards the end of 1912 the cinema became the property of United Electric Theatres but the current manager, Roland Lea, retained his post, and during the following year saw the Palace improved with the addition of a new entrance. On 27th October 1913 this new entrance, in the High Street, was opened and Roland Lea booked the best films he could find to celebrate the occasion, including *"A Message from Mars"*.

The High Street facade was lavish indeed. The Midland Chronicle recorded that, replic*"The Cornices and Griffins adorning the palisters are an exact a of those used in decorating the great London Opera House"*. The work was done by John Dallow and Sons and made great use of Messrs. Doulton's tiling. Unfortunately no photograph of the Palace frontage seems to exist.

Thomas Jackson of Wolverhampton acquired both the Palaces, Walsall and West Bromwich, and, after the First World War, stressed the quality of music to be found at both. In 1920 a new musical director, Owen Moore, was appointed and advertisements claimed the Palace had, "One of the best orchestras in South Staffs". In addition Fred Diggle performed on a two-manual Mustel Organ.

Following Thomas Jackson's financial troubles in 1923 the Palace was probably administered by Mr. Thompson, the official receiver of the Midlands Counties Circuit. It was managed by Percy Norton, from

Wolverhampton. In the autumn of 1930 it was sold to the Hockley Picture House Company, also encountered in the Black Country at the Picturedrome, Darlaston. For a time in the early thirties The Palace became one of the few local cinemas at the time to have been managed by a woman: Mrs. D. Burgess.

Mr. V. Olliver, of the Hockley Picture House Company, had over-all control of both the Palace and the nearby Imperial for this company until both cinemas were brought under the control of Messrs. Griffin, Wilson and Bassett. In turn Arthur Griffin's company, Griffin Cinemas Ltd., ran the Palace.

These changes of ownership only concerned the building itself as the freehold belonged to Horton Estates of Birmingham. The site was right in the centre of town and yet somehow the Palace never seems to have quite dominated the town's cinemas as one might have expected. Percy Norton used to advertise it as, "The super cinema with super productions", but it always seems to have been eclipsed by its rivals. As it only held about nine hundred patrons perhaps it did not quite deserve to be recognised as a "super cinema". It introduced sound by Western Electric on 16th December 1929, with *"A Dangerous Woman"* but the talkies had already arrived in West Bromwich at the Plaza.

Under the control of Griffin Cinemas it prospered with its colleague, The Imperial, during the Second World War but as business declined it seemed redundant. It is not surprising, therefore, that the Palace should abandon the cause when its lease expired in 1957. It closed on Saturday 28th September 1957 with *"The Lonely Man"*, a western starring Jack Palance. Horton Estates then redeveloped the site and, compared with its old rival, the Queens, the Palace seems forgotten. Arthur Griffin still maintained the Imperial, nearby, until ending his association with local cinemas in 1963.

The Imperial

Spon Lane, West Bromwich

A group of local West Bromwich men assembled to form the Imperial Picture Palace Company after watching the success of the Queens and the Electric Palace. They engaged local architect, Albert Bye, to design their cinema, and employed local builder, Messrs. Dallow and Son, to construct it, on a site next to the Dartmouth Hotel in Spon Lane. Other local firms were used wherever possible, including Messrs. Mallin and Co., who produced the fibrous plasterwork, and Messrs. Chance Brothers who provided glass tiles that were used to decorate the foyer.

The thirteen hundred seater cinema was built in approximately two months and was well and truly worthy of its name. The facade consisted of four shops facing Spon Lane, with the cinema's entrance in the centre. The whole facade was extremely decorative, and was dominated by the figure of Electra bearing an electric torch above the porch. (Echoes of the

Wednesbury cinema of the same name!). The auditorium, set back behind the shops and the facade, also presented a highly decorative appearance as seen from Spon Lane, and claimed to be one of the first buildings in the town to have an asbestos slate roof! Inside luxury and ornate decor prevailed. A raked floor, and upholstered tip up seats throughout housed the audience before the large screen surrounded by amazing ornate plasterwork.

The Imperial Picture Palace opened on 8th April 1912. Patrons were greeted by the manager, Harry Mears, and entertained by an orchestra led by Ralph Powell. (Mr. Powell was later replaced with Percy Hesp.) However, the "official" opening did not take place until 17th April, when the Mayor, Councillor Kenrick came along to perform the ceremony and see a programme that included *"A Question of Seconds"*. As the official party left the cinema they were filmed and the results were later screened.

Despite being such an impressive place, the Imperial was almost completely rebuilt after the First World War. Only portions of the original side walls of the auditorium were retained. The front of the building was brought forward to a facade in Spon Lane that extended to the full height of the cinema. Once again the architect was Albert Bye and he described the style of his new Imperial as "Georgian". Pillars, balustrades, palisters,

Right: The Imperial, Spon Lane, West Bromwich on 4ᵗʰ March 1973 while showing films once again during the period in which Miles Jervis was building a new Kings Cinema.
(Terry Cresswell)

Above: A rather grey picture of the interior of the Palace, West Bromwich reproduced from a pre-First World War local guide. Pictures of this cinema are very rare and no picture has been found of its entrance.

etc., were all treated in a striking white glazed terracotta, with intervening panels of purple brick. It was vulgar, highly eclectic and to a perverse cinema-lover, wildly beautiful!

A proper balcony could now stretch across the lengthened and heightened auditorium, replacing the small corner "boxes" that had existed before, and was reached by an oak-panelled staircase. New seats were upholstered in royal blue velvet. The ceiling was panelled and decorated with owls and bats flying overhead. The doors were draped in black velvet curtains trimmed in amber, and the usherettes wore dresses to match the curtains! The orchestra pit was moved to the side of the screen, rather than in front of it, and Mr. F. Rigby became the new musical director.

The £25,000 reconstruction was completed in time for a grand re-opening on 2nd March 1921, when a one-day screening was presented, followed by *"Aylwin"* on the first three days of normal shows. The company may have paid a lot more than originally intended, but nevertheless felt satisfied. The directors of the Imperial Company were George Arthur Griffin, William J. Wilson, Bill Bassett (the footballer) and Edgar Hounsell (also to be encountered at the Scala, Wolverhampton, and Regent, Tipton). Mr. Griffin, the father of Arthur Griffin of the Dart Spring Company, had been interested in making films and made one short production which

resulted in Sax Rohmer suing him for "pinching" the story!

In the early thirties the Imperial appears to have been leased to Mr. V. Olliver of the Hockley Picture House Company. He ran both the Imperial and the Palace until joining those who wished to build The Tower, at Carters Green. While at the Imperial he installed Western Electric sound equipment. After his departure it presumably returned to the original owners, and then, after Mr. Griffin's death in 1938 it passed to Arthur Griffin. Thus it was to Arthur Griffin that Miles Jervis went in 1963 to acquire the Imperial. Griffin Cinemas showed their last film, *"Blood, on His Lips"* on 28th September 1963, and the Midland Cinemas Bingo Club opened its doors on 24th October. But the Imperial was now owned by a man dedicated to showing films so the story does not stop there.

On Easter Monday, 7th April 1969, the Imperial made a triumphant return to life as a full-blooded cinema. The Queens had closed on Easter Saturday and the manager, Bruno Tomana, crossed Paradise Street to open a transformed Imperial. Bingo had ceased six weeks earlier and Modernisation Ltd., had arrived to completely refurbish the place. Eight hundred bright red super armchair seats, 1380 yards of new luxury carpet and a new Perlux screen went into the auditorium. New sound and projection equipment was supplied by Rank Audio Visual and John Wood, long ago a manager of the Imperial, became the new "chief". The £20,000 conversion from Bingo back to films was celebrated with Rex Harrison's *"Doctor Doolittle"*.

I visited the Imperial several times in the early seventies and was really impressed by the place, particularly by the gleaming white exterior, little changed since 1921,

74

apart from modern signs. (See illustration). While the Kings was being replaced the Imperial preserved Miles Jervis' cinema-presence in the town, and, unfortunately it closed on Friday 27th June 1975, the day before Kings I and II came to life.

It was purchased by the Council for demolition in 1978 order to complete the road improvements associated with the redevelopment of the area, but I cannot help feeling that the destruction of that facade was a sad loss. *"Breakout"*, starring Charles Bronson, was the last film to flicker across that six year old screen in the fifty-four year old building.

The St. George's

Paradise Street, West Bromwich.

The first cinema in West Bromwich to open after the First World War was not a grand purpose-built place like Woods Palace, Bilston, or the Kings, Blackheath. It was a very old building, and the act of converting it to a cinema actually unearthed a box of one hundred year old coins! It may have been a Wesleyan chapel and a school somewhere in its long history, but, in 1859 it was established as the Public Hall. It served as a public meeting place until 1875 when the new Town Hall was opened, but continued to be used for occasional concerts and meetings until 1891. Then it became a wire works!

After the War a company was formed to convert it into the St. George's cinema by Mr. A. A. James. He already

owned the place as a factory, and is alleged to have already had interests in at least three Birmingham cinemas. Work began at the beginning of 1920 and somehow a reasonable auditorium to seat seven hundred patrons was created in the old building. The decor was described as being in a, "rich dark Italian style", featuring hand-painted panels in "Arabesque style". A St. George and dragon motif was supplied to reflect the cinema's identity.

The St. George's opened on 26th July 1920, under the management of Harry Jordon, and with an orchestra led by Mr. Westworth. Programmes were presented in separate performances rather than continuously. Mr. James had organised a private gathering on the day before, a Sunday, in order to show the place to friends and guests. I have no information on films shown on either the Sunday or the following day.

Only one month later adverts appear in the local paper announcing a "re-opening" on 21st August, "Under New Management" and that phrase was frequently repeated in its advertising. It closed altogether for four weeks in summer 1922, re-opening again on 4th September with another new manager: William Singer. One of these early changes probably marks the acquisition of the St. George's by Thomas Leach, although in a Midland Chronicle report of 28th January 1944 it is claimed that Mr. Leach had owned the cinema from the start!

Below: The St. George's, in Paradise Street, next to the arcade. 1960. (R.Hood)

While owned by Tom Leach a BTP sound system was installed (His other cinemas used the same equipment.), and along with the Queens, and the Savoy, Oldbury, it was eventually leased to J. F. Emery. Together with those cinemas it was acquired by Miles Jervis in 1946.

Miles Jervis II never lavished attention on the St. George's as he did with the Queens. Apart from using it as a place to put on a second week run of a particularly successful film, he seems to have regarded it as fairly redundant, and possibly too overshadowed by the Kings on the opposite side of the road. He did remove the BTP equipment, which he disliked, and replaced it with a G.B. Duosonic system. Perhaps it is not surprising to discover that the St. George's was an early casualty. It appears to have closed on 18th June 1955 with a Swedish film called "*Unmarried Mothers*", advertised as "a vital message to every young woman".

This was not quite the end of the story. Mr. B.K. Puri persuaded Miles Jervis to allow him to use the cinema to show Indian films. It reopened on Sunday 24th September 1955 as the Krishna Cinema. A packed house watched "*The Savage Princess*" and similar shows followed for about thirteen weeks.

The last film was therefore shown at the end of 1955 but the building was not demolished until August 1962, leaving a few local legends to survive into the eighties. Several people have recalled a "chucker-out" at the St. George's who did his job in reverse. People were frightened to pass him outside the cinema as he was known to press-gang passers by into the cinema!

The Sandwell Cinema

Sandwell Road, West Bromwich.

At the other end of the High Street, near Carters Green, another "conversion" produced West Bromwich's second cinema to open after the First World War. An old chapel, dating from 1812, complete with graveyard, had lain derelict and unused in Sandwell Road for some time.

It appears that it was bought by a Mr. J. Hughes and converted to a cinema. An entirely new frontage was built in front of the ex-chapel and the latter was converted to an auditorium capable of accommodating nine hundred cramped patrons. The Sandwell Cinema was opened by the Mayor, on 24th August 1922 although the event does not seem to have been reported. Will Smith, from Liverpool, was the new manager.

All does not seem to have gone well, and in February 1924 Albert Smith, of West Bromwich, took control of the cinema and, with his wife's help, tried to revitalise the cinema with promotional advertising gimmicks and local premiers. His advertisements continued to appear in the Free Press until early 1925 and then all was as quiet as the graveyard adjoining the cinema. Children who had made their way through the graveyard to reach the entrance to the cheap seats grew up to tell legends of a manager absconding with cash, and cashier, but I have been unable to find out any factual information about the Sandwell's demise.

For another quarter of a century the building remained derelict again, served a short life as a Council store and was then demolished in the mid fifties.

Right: The Sandwell Cinema, redrawn by Tony Wright from a very poor photograph of the building – taken long after its demise as a cinema.

The Empire
(later known as The Plaza, the Kings and the new Kings)

Paradise Street, West Bromwich

Just before the First World War Benjamin Kennedy set out to provide West Bromwich with a first class purpose-built theatre, in the town centre. The Olympia, at Carters Green, was too far from that centre and presumably not really grand enough. Plans were drawn by Messrs. Wood and Kenrick and the £10,000 theatre was built by Messrs. Dallow and Sons. The Empire opened, as a theatre holding 1800 patrons, on Whit Monday in June 1914. Its history as a theatre is covered in more detail in Volume Two.

The reason that it appears here, between the details of the Sandwell and the Tower, is that its life as a cinema began in 1927. In that year it was leased to C.D. Cinemas, a partnership established between Mortimer Dent and Joseph Cohen. (The career of Mortmer Dent is desrcibed in the introductory section.) They reopened it as the Plaza Super Cinema on 26th September 1927. Then, and for the whole week, the Plaza presented "*Love Me and the World Is Mine*" with Jesse Hackett singing the title song and Mr. Grainger leading the new orchestra.

The claim to be a "super cinema" was justified as the place had been redecorated and re-seated with eleven

hundred plush tip up seats. As with many theatre-conversions the operating room was very high and the screen had to be tilted, but the theatrical atmosphere became a very positive quality at the Plaza, and later as the Kings.

By 1929 C.D. Cinemas had sold out to the ABC circuit and the new lessees were glad to acquire a position in West Bromwich. They installed BTH sound equipment and ran the Plaza until they were able to acquire The Tower at Carters Green. With ABC's departure in 1936, the lease reverted to Ben Kennedy just at the time he was preparing to open his own brand new Plaza in Dudley.

Ben Kennedy continued to use the Plaza as a cinema but was surrounded by competition from the surrounding four cinemas, let alone the Tower.

After the War the Plaza returned to its former way of life as a theatre. In the post-War era that was not an easy option and the place declined. Like the Hippodrome, Dudley, and Royal, Bilston, the Plaza found that "*Strip, Strip Ahoy!*" (a navel revue!) and the "*Phyllis Dixie Show*" attracted some patrons but led many others to "write off" the place completely.

It was rumoured that the Clifton Circuit may have been interested in acquiring the Plaza, but Miles Jervis II beat them to it. The grand final show, as a theatre, was presented on 2nd February 1957. It was called, "*Thanks For The Memory*" starring Hetty King, Randolph Sutton and Billy Danvers, a fitting farewell tribute to "Variety".

Below: The Kings, 4th March 1973.
(Terry Cresswell)

Miles Jervis then started work on the theatre's second conversion to a cinema. He rebuilt the projection room and equipped the theatre for cinemascope. He reseated the stalls, redecorated, and gave the exterior of the building a facelift. A modern canopy was erected and, after much correspondence with the Council Planning Department, the facade was transformed at night with a flood of neon lighting, by Claudgen Neon Signs.

It opened again, this time as The Kings, to complement the Queens, on Monday 11th March 1957. *"Between Heaven and Hell"* was presented in Cinemascope, and its future as a cinema seemed bright. As stated above, the theatrical atmosphere served to heighten the experience of visiting the Kings and my memories of the place seem bathed in bright red and gold even in the mid sixties when other converted theatres, like the Clifton, Wolverhampton, seemed much the worse for wear. Local amateur operatic society shows were performed at the Kings so the stage facilities did still see very occasional use.

When substantial redevelopment threatened the Kings, only Miles Jervis III's determination to continue in the cinema business saved the day. Unfortunately the original Kings had to go, but the hard fought battle to make sure there would be a replacement was won. The Kings was expected to close on 10th March 1973, but

its life was extended to 28th April when it finally closed with *"The Aristocrats"* and *"The Legend of Young Dick Turpin"*. Patrons we were re-directed to the amazingly revived Imperial, while the Kings was demolished and construction of its successor began.

The new Kings was to be a purpose-built triple screened cinema: up until then the only entirely new cinema to be built in the Black Country since the War. It was designed by Keith Davidson and Partners and was as plain as the Imperial and old Kings were ornate. It was built by Costain Construction Ltd., of Coventry and the interior decor was by Modernisation Ltd.

On 28th June 1975 the first two screens were opened. Kings I, with 320 seats, presented *"Shampoo"*, and Kings II with 280 seats presented *"The Yaguza"*. Kings III, the largest auditorium, with 442 seats, opened on 20th July 1975 with *"The Godfather, Part 2"*. Rank Audio Visual supplied new Cinemeccanica equipment, and as before, renewal and innovation saw technical modifications made in the following years. Eventually large horizontal platters were installed in the operating rooms to bring the Kings right up-to-date.

The new screens opened during a heatwave and business was slack, but matters improved and the Kings became a well patronised cinema. It could also be recommended for the advantage of seeing films in purpose-built auditoria. (Not a "botched conversion" beneath the balcony of a fifty year old "super"). It boasted a bar with colour television and programming that often provided the Black Country with its only genuine variety and choice from the 1970s into the early 1980s.

The Kings became a remarkable survivor – outliving most local cinemas and eventually co-existing with the first multiplexes. Management passed from Mile Jervis III to his son Paul Jervis. For a time day to day management was provided by Gary Stevens. Gary was the son of a projectionist who had worked at the ABC Wolverhampton, where his mother was also a cashier! Once introduced to the cinema business he became enthusiastic about joining it, even if it seemed in a state of decline. His dream was to own a cinema, meanwhile The Kings provided experience in "surviving".

The wholesale redevelopment of the centre of West Bromwich which had created The Sandwell Centre and the new Kings in the seventies, eventually qualified for refurbishment. This was to be accompanied by the rebuilding of the bus station – right on The Kings' doorstep. Ironically, work that was designed to regenerate West Bromwich had an adverse effect on the accessibility of the cinema.

Below: The new Kings – opened in 1975 as a purpose-built three-screen cinema, on the edge of the Sandwell Centre. (Ned Williams)

The Kings appeared to have closed quite suddenly on Sunday 8th September 2002 after months of being dogged by building work going around the cinema - and losing its adjacent car park to the new bus station. The front of the cinema was plastered with "Open - Business as Usual" notices but attendances had just drained away. The last films shown were *"Spy Kids"* and *"The Guru"* - projected by Tommy Watkins who had worked in the operating rooms of several Black Country cinemas, and had worked at The Kings since 1989.

A postscript on film presentation in the centre of West Browmich.

Cinema and theatre history in central West Bromwich did not completely come to an end with the closure of the old Kings, or its brave successor, the new Kings. During the 1970s a community arts organisation called Jubilee Arts had been very active. Out of the organisation's work grew a "big idea" that would put West Bromwich and Sandwell on the map and would provide space for theatrical and film presentation into the future – as well as being a general "arts space" and massive agent of regeneration. The proposed building eventually became known as "The Public" and construction of the new centre – in New Street – began in 2004. Everything about the project became a matter of controversy – from the design, by Will Allsop and Julian Flannery, to the mounting costs of construction. The project had to endure public hostility, changes in management, and eventually a financial crisis. Despite all this it opened in 2008, and was completed in 2010.

Already many fine events have taken place in The Public, and for film fanatics a monument to Madeleine Carroll has been provided alongside the giant pink building. This memorial was the result of many years campaigning by Terry Price, and Terry, along with Bill Thomas (Leader of Sandwell Council) and Carl Chinn, unveiled the stone on 21st February 2007. Any future account of cinematic and theatrical entertainment in West Bromwich will have to include the contribution of The Public.

As this book goes to press in 2011, the possibility of new purpose built cinema being built in West Bromwich has again been the subject of local stories. Reel Cinemas may build a six-screen cinema close to The Public. The Express & Star of 10th Feb 2011 suggested it might open by October 2012.

Above: The Tower photographed during opening week. (Ken Rock postcard collection)

The Tower,
later known as the ABC

Carters Green, West Bromwich.

The Tower, or "The Bloody Tower", as it was known to its rivals, was a super cinema in a class of its own. It dominated the street scene at Carters Green, where the clock tower, which inspired the cinema's name, had once dominated a major Black Country tramway junction. The clock tower still survives, built in 1897 by the citizens of West Bromwich to show their respect and gratitude to the town's first mayor and major public benefactor: Reuben Farley. All trace of the cinema has gone.

The Tower was promoted by, and built for, West Bromwich Cinemas Ltd. The directors were V. Olliver, who already had strong connections with the town as a result of managing the Palace and the Imperial, W. H. Onions, a Birmingham cinema entrepreneur also connected with the Warley Cinema and the Clifton, Stone Cross, and Mr. and Mrs. C. O. Brettell. The Brettells, and Mr. Olliver had established the Birmingham based "Piccadilly Circuit" and ran the Piccadilly itself in Sparkbrook, the New Palladium, Hockley, the New Imperial, Moseley Road and, in the Black Country; the Picturedrome at Darlaston. Later they built the Regal, Darlaston.

They engaged Harry Weedon to design their new super-cinema and Cecil Clavering imposed the style on it that

he had helped Harry Weedon develop for the Odeon cinemas. It seems that Oscar Deutsch may have considered joining the venture but appears to have disliked the location. Therefore, despite its appearance, it never had anything to do with the Odeons.

The site was not cleared until May 1935 and the huge cinema was built very quickly, completed by J. R. Deacon Ltd., in seven months. It had originally been conceived as a 1560 seater, but extra land became available just before construction began and it was enlarged to hold 2000, 750 of which were accommodated in the circle. Due to the simplicity of its design, it is its size that made it so imposing. The huge facade was treated in biscuit coloured faience, above a base of black faience tiles. Four small pillars dividing the flight of steps that extended across the entire frontage were similarly treated, as can be seen in the photograph. They originally supported little shrubs! Above the balcony lounge windows the name sign provided essential relief to the huge area of faience. Without it the building has looked rather bare and ugly. A huge foyer, elegant staircases, a cafe in the balcony lounge, all impressed the patron long before he or she entered the auditorium which was bathed in blue and gold. All the fibrous plasterwork was in the Modern style and concealed lighting was cleverly employed.

80

In the centre of the "orchestra pit" was the illuminated console of the three-manual, ten unit, Compton organ, mounted on a lift. The organ itself was in a basement beneath the stage. Up in the operating suite Kalee projectors were installed, and sound was by Western Electric. The owners felt it was better equipped and more genuinely sumptuous than the Odeons. Charlie Kettle was appointed as manager, and Leslie Taff was appointed organist, coming to the Tower from the Gaumont, Birmingham.

It might be expected that such a magnificent super-cinema would be given a civic opening but Mr. Olliver and the Brettells did not seem to go in for such things, although a lavish souvenir brochure of the Tower's opening was produced. Business commenced at 6 p.m. on Monday 9th December 1935. A Laurel and Hardy short, a Walt Disney Cartoon, and Gaumont British News started the programme. Then Leslie Taff rose into the spotlight on the illuminated console of the organ. The organ had an "Electrone" attachment, and the audience was told, *"With it sounds of unprecedented and surpassing beauty, which have never previously been heard by the human ear may be created."* The main feature was that magnificent Hitchcock film, *"The 39 Steps",* starring Robert Donat and Madeleine Carroll. Madeleine Carroll was born in West Bromwich on 26th February 1906. After studying at Birmingham University and a short spell of teaching her acting career took off. Her first film role was in "The Guns at Loos". (This was a silent British films made for Stoll Pictures in 1928 and shown at the Imperial in February 1929.) She died in 1987 but is now commemorated in West Bromwich with a monument erected in New Street, alongside The Public.

The Tower's independence did not last long. ABC, who had cultivated a presence in the town at the Plaza, bought out the directors in the following year, and gradually installed their own staff. As part of a major circuit it had the advantage of visits by film-stars, expensive and elaborate promotions and publicity campaigns, and its size and grandeur no doubt gave it some importance on the circuit but I have often wondered if ABC found being in Carters Green was not quite the same thing as being in the centre of West Bromwich. People from Oldbury and Wednesbury have told me that they visited the Tower when they wanted to go somewhere "posh", but less people in West Bromwich have mentioned it!

Leslie Taff left The Tower in 1938 to go to The Regal, Darlaston. Several organists came and went until about half way through the Second World War when Wilf Gregory arrived from the cinema in Wylde Green. Wilf was born in Wolverhampton in 1907 and first became a cinema organist at Wolverhampton's Agriculturall Hall. He later played the Wurlitzer at Walsall's Picture House, and gained experience at several other cinemas. At The Tower he introduced a wartime "Request Interlude" and forces newspapers carried the story: *"If you come from Birmingham (!) write to The Tower, West Bromwich and have Wilf Gregory unite you with your relatives by playing your favourite tune on the organ."*

Wilf worked well with The Tower's manager – Frank Attoe – and they formed an ABC Minors Club choir after the war to sing their own National Savings song! Wilf wrote the music and Frank wrote the words. Wilf remained organist until 1951 when he decided there was more future in relief management.

From War-time onwards its history consisted of anniversaries, at least one of which was celebrated with a huge cake that was an accurate model of the cinema, and details like the inauguration of the ABC Minors' Club in June 1946. Among the stars that come to the Tower were Old Mother Riley, who came on 17th May 1952, and Richard Attenborough who came along on 3rd April 1948 to promote *"Brighton Rock".*

In March 1951 RCA High Fidelity Sound was installed. Ten years later, in July 1961, it dropped its name, the Tower, and simply became the ABC. I visited it once, in the mid-sixties, to see *"Morgan, A Suitable Case for Treatment"* but I am ashamed to admit that the building made no impression upon me. By then the organ had gone. A farewell concert had been held on 14th November 1965. Leslie Taff returned to play on it, plus Mel Edwards, but it is believed that Trevor Bolshaw played before it sank back into the pit it for the last time. It was bought by Arthur Large, who unfortunately died soon afterwards, but the organ was restored and rebuilt at Marston Green Hospital. Since then it has had several homes and currently (2011) it is a Fentham Hall, near Henley in Arden.

The Tower/ABC closed on 28th December 1968, with **"Hot Millions"**, starring Peter Ustinov. It reopened as an EMI Bingo and Social Club on 18th January 1969. As the seventies progressed its exterior grew increasingly shabby and the Bingo Club eventually closed., and the building was demolished.

Below: Frank Attoe, (in centre of picture) with his staff at The Tower, West Bromwich in the nid 1950s. Staff include Joe Butler (projectionist), Mrs. Plummer and Miss John-son (cashiers). (Joe Butler Collection))

Outer West Bromwich

The Hill Top Picture House (also known as the Rex)

Hill Top, West Bromwich

The Tower, at Carters Green, represents the northern boundary of central West Bromwich. From there Telford's road made its way through small villages that have since become industrialised but their names still stir the imagination: Swan Village, Guns Village, Black Lake and Hill Top. The latter's name is self explanatory, and from the crest of the hill good views are obtained of Wednesbury. Despite the view, Hill Top belongs to West Bromwich.

Two West Bromwich men, Messrs. Bellingham and Jackson, formed a company, with the intention of bringing the cinematograph to the village community of Hill Top. It was no hurried conversion, but a proper purpose- built 750-seater cinema. It was designed by Howard Tipler and was certainly unique in style and appearance! The frontage was finished in a strong red terracotta brick, with a tunnel-like arch round the main entrance, flanked by shops. For many years the words, "The Regal Academy of Reel Art" were inscribed on the

surface of this arch. The interior decor was originally carried out in chocolate and gold. It was equipped with a "Reflecta" screen and Motiograph projectors. It cost about £20,000.

It was opened on Wednesday 27th July 1921, six months later than intended. The first manager was Vincent Hopcroft, who had managed cinemas in Leicester and Merthyr. At the opening there was a full orchestra but subsequently the accompaniment was provided by a piano alone for several years. How long Vincent Hopcroft stayed is not clear, as the owners soon leased the cinema to Tom Leach. For most of the first half of its life it was managed by Joe Robbins, believed to be Tom Leach's brother- in-law. (He had previously managed the Queens for Tom Leach).

A picture of the Hill Top cinema in those days was given to me by Bill Priest who told me:

"On entering was the pay box, on each side were steps leading to the 9d and 6d seats. The 4d seats were reached by a passage-way that came out half way down the hall. The cheap seats were wooden benches in three rows with two central gangways, but the "posh" seats were ordinary tip-ups. It was a single storey building with no balcony.

At one time my three aunts; Kate, Dolly and May Cooper had taken the tickets, which I also did for a spell. We were paid 9d a night and 6d for a matinee, and most weeks we had to ask for our wages. The orchestra was just a piano until one Saturday night it was announced that the Bijou Orchestra would be an added attraction. This consisted of piano, violin and drums. On Monday nights the back row of the wooden benches was where the young mothers brought their babies, and out would come their breasts to feed them. Some thought they were shameless hussies but I didn't think so.

As I write I can still smell the tang of orange peel and the scent of those atomizer sprays, and can still recall the flickering gas jets. When the flame went down the fans were turned on to clear the air. Things got bad towards the end of the silent era. I remember seeing "The Lash of the Law" when there were only two of us paying customers in the 4d seats.

However, finally the cinema was converted to BTH sound and from then on we saw mainly Paramount films".

Poverty-row "B" westerns and strong melodramas were successful at little cinemas like the one at Hill Top. The stars of these films are still loved and remembered by patrons like Bill Priest, half a century later.

The estate of the late Tom Leach ended the lease on the Hill Top Cinema at the end of 1938. It then closed for renovations and re-opened on 2nd January 1939. The original owners appear to have formed a new company, the Reel Academy Ltd., to run the cinema.

HILL TOP PICTURE HOUSE,
WEST BROMWICH.
GRAND OPENING, WEDNESDAY, JULY 27th,
5.30 p.m. to 10.30 p.m.
The Only Hall of its kind in the Midlands.
PERFECT PROJECTION combined with COOLNESS, CLEANLINESS and PERFECT CONTENTMENT.

H. Bellingham was now the Mayor of West Bromwich, and a fellow councillor, A. Guest, became the new manager. The reopening was therefore performed by the Mayor, or the proprietor, depending on which role Councillor Bellingham saw himself taking. Just to confuse everybody he also assumed the role of an attendant and, grabbing a torch, escorted several patrons to their seats.

The cinema now aspired to greater respectability and advertised itself as "The Family House at the top of the hill". Male attendants were replaced by female usherettes dressed in attractive light blue uniforms with beige facings. Some time after this it began calling itself the Rex, although exactly when is not clear. It was certainly known by that name in 1944 when it was purchased by Arthur Griffin. He formed a separate company, Arthur Griffin Ltd., to run the Rex rather than incorporate it with Griffin Cinemas Ltd. As soon after the War as possible he put up a neon sign saying "Rex".

It was successful for a time but audiences declined quickly in the mid fifties and it operated for two or three years at a loss. It appears to have survived until December 1960 when it probably closed with "*The Vikings*". It seems impossible to be more precise about this. The building was sold to the Dart Spring Company for use as a stores. The rather bizarre building stood for at least another fifteen years. About 1976 it was sold to David Siviter of Dudley Street Motors Ltd., and was demolished to make way for an extension to his premises.

Below: The former Hill Top Cinema being used as an Agricultural Division warehouse by the Dart Spring Co. of West Browmich not long before demolition. (May Siviter)

The Clifton

Stone Cross, West Bromwich

Stone Cross, between West Bromwich and Walsall, rapidly developed between the Wars as a surburban residential area. It seems that W. H. Onions, having been "bought-out" by ABC at the Tower, Carters Green, came to the area in search of a site for a new modern super-cinema. He was joined by Captain Clift, who became the company's chairman for a time, by Ernest Roberts, who was to design the cinema, and Edgar Summers, also to be encountered at the Rosum at Walsall.

An old smithy that previously occupied the site was demolished and Messrs. J. and F. Wootton constructed the new super-cinema using the established methods exploiting a steel super-structure and concrete. The auditorium was capable of holding 896 patrons in the stalls and 306 in the balcony, in green upholstered tip-up seats. The modern plasterwork was finished in pastel shades of silver, pink and orange. Like other Cliftons, it used BTH equipment. The exterior of the auditorium was finished in red brick and, due to its position on a small hill, its massive presence can be seen from afar. The entrance and crush hall were greatly extended from the auditorium and had their own striking curved facade, adjacent to some shops.

The Clifton was opened on Saturday 16th July 1938, with a special one night showing of "*'Whoopee'*" starring Eddie Cantor. The opening ceremony was performed by the British film actress, Miss Valerie Hobson. She was given a film-star's reception by crowds outside the new cinema and by the capacity audience within. Her latest film, "*The Drum*" was to be shown at the Clifton shortly. Regular three-day programmes began the following Monday with "*Return of the Scarlet Pimpernel*".

The manager, when the cinema opened, was Philip Cleife, and the chief operator was Jimmy Edwards. The latter stayed at the Clifton for almost its entire life. Like other suburban Cliftons it had a fairly short and uneventful life but there were several slight changes in its ownership. At some stage W. H. Onions ran the Clifton independently of the Clifton Circuit, that is, without the services of Cinema Accessories Ltd., and it was managed for him by Ernest Highland.

The Clifton had one dressing room and an 18 feet by 40 feet stage. The stage facilities came into their own during the Second World War when Sunday variety shows were regularly presented. The bookings for these shows were organised by Jack Riskit – best known as the manager of the Theatre Royal Bilston. (His career is described in Volume Two.) After the War the stage was used less often. One record I have found of it being used was during March 1958 when amateur variety acts were supplementing the films. Perhaps this was a sign of the times! The following year when Mr. Onions was

objecting to his rate assessment he publicly complained that his cinema often had to wait six months to screen popular films, by which time they had been seen in West Bromwich, Wednesbury and Walsall. An independent exhibitor starved of films, losing patrons, and isolated in the suburbs faced many problems.

Eventually the Clifton was brought back under the wing of the "circuit", by then administered by Theatre Administration, but its days were numbered. Bingo was introduced on Thursday nights, surrounded by three programme changes per week. Occasional Sunday morning shows of Indian films were presented by Tarsem Singh Dhami and his colleagues.

The closure came on Saturday 7th March 1964, with "*Doctor No*" starring Sean Connery in the part of James Bond. Regular sessions of Bingo commenced the following Tuesday, run by Harry Whitehouse, of the Lyttleton, Halesowen, and Avion, Aldridge. During this period, 1964 — 1968, Tarsem Singh Dhami's Indian film shows were presented more regularly on Sundays.

In 1968 the Clifton was acquired by Ladbrokes, and they operated the Bingo and Social Club there, followed by Mecca, until the end of 2003. It was a very smart club indeed and much of the decor of the cinema was extremely well preserved. The shaded plaster band round the balcony and extending to the very rectangular ante-proscenium was still a feature of the decor, as was the concealed lighting system above the site of the rear stalls, housed along the main balcony girder. The 1930's murals had vanished from the crush hall but the place was still worth a visit. Sandwell MBC gave permission for the building to be demolished in May 2004, and a visitor to the location today finds a modern block of apartments.

Above: A picture of the entrance of the Clifton, Stone Cross taken from the opening brochure. At the time only the name "Cinema" appeared on the tower. Soon afterwards the word "Clifton" was added and the word "Cinema" moved down the tower!

Above: The Clifton, Stone Cross as a Bingo and Social Club in 1981. (Ned Williams)

Below: A wartime band concert advertised at The Clifton Stone Cross.

Below: A complimentary "bill pass" issued by The Clifton, Stone Cross. These passes were issued to local shop-keepers who displayed a copy of the Clifton's weekly advert on their premises. Note – if you wanted to take a friend it had to be fortnightly!

CLIFTON CINEMA
STONE CROSS.

SUNDAY, NOVEMBER 2nd, 1941

At 6-0 p.m.   Doors open 5-0 p.m.

WELCOME RETURN VISIT of THE   (CODDON)

R.A.O.C. Dance Orchestra

Leader : L/Cpl. ERIC JACUBS, late B.B.C.
(By kind permission of the Commanding Officer)

AND 14 BRILLIANT MUSICIANS now serving in R.A.O.C. from such Bands as Jack Harris, Wally Dewar, Billy Merrin, Hawaiian Serenaders, etc.

Compere : Cpl. WILLKIE HUNT
(Late Magical Society and Principal Halls)

EVERYTHING NEW with

Pte. GORDON HOMER	Pte. STELLA MORRIS
Late Billy Merrin	The A.T. with " I.T."
Cpl. SONNY ROSE	L/Cpl. KEN TUNSTALL
Late Jack Harris and B.B.C.	B.B.C. Accordionist, etc.

" TAFFY "
The Sportsmen's Dilemma.

THE R.A.O.C.ky MOUNTAINEERS

VERNON AND RALSTON	THE TWO VICS
In Side-Splitting Comedy.	Comedy Duo.
JOAN BUTLER	LEONARD ROWE
West Brom's own Silver-Voiced Star.	The Marvellous Juvenile Accordion Wonder. In all New Numbers.

ENTIRE PROCEEDS IN AID OF THE R.A.F. BENEVOLENT FUND and a substantial donation to the CHARLEMONT SOCIAL CLUB to provide Xmas Cheer for our own Local Boys now serving with the Forces.
A GRAND SHOW — FOR A GRAND CAUSE.   DON'T MISS IT

TICKETS NOW ON SALE.   PLEASE BOOK EARLY
PRICES OF ADMISSION : STALLS and CIRCLE, 2/6. BACK STALLS, 1/6 and 1/3. (All including Tax).
EARLY ARRIVAL FOR SEATS IS ADVISABLE. The 2/6 Seats can be booked in advance.   Box Office open every day and on Sunday, November 2nd,

STONE CROSS
CINEMA
WEST BROMWICH

COMPLIMENTARY
BILL PASS

ADMIT
ONE PERSON PER WEEK
OR TWO PERSONS FORTNIGHTLY

SUBJECT TO CONDITIONS
AS SET FORTH ON BACK

Parkes & Mainwarings Ltd., Doe St. Works, Birmingham 4

Great Bridge

It may surprise readers to find that the little cinema in Great Bridge has to be included in the chapter on the cinemas of West Browmich. Its all to do with boundaries! Although Great Bridge is often associated with Tipton, the boundary between Tipton and West Bromwich actually divided the village in half, the boundary being based on the course of the River Tame. Slater Street, and its junction with Great Bridge Street, is firmly in the West Bromwich half of the village. The most exciting way to approach Great Bridge, until 1964, was to arrive by train at either of its unbelievably antiquated stations. However, its cinema, the Palace, has a history stretching back to the days when the electric trams rolled past on their way to Dudley from Handsworth.

The Palace

Great Bridge at the corner of Slater Street.

Most of the history of the Palace seems very obscure. Only some of the small very short-lived cinema-halls of the Black Country give the historian a bigger headache than the Palace! Even when I quizzed its patrons they said very little about the place itself. The fact that a cinema was built at this location is another example of a site becoming historically associated with entertainment, because it seems that the same plot of land may have been the site of Wakeman's Portabale Theatre in the nineteenth century. (See Volume Two.)

In the days when steam trams struggled through Great Bridge it seems that the site of the Palace was occupied by a Toll House which became a barbers shop. This was demolished and a hall erected but whether it was specifically built as a cinema seems very doubtful. There is some evidence that it was an Odd Fellows' Hall. Whatever happened, by the spring of 1910 films were being shown there, a licence being issued by Tipton U.D.C. at the end of March. The licence was transferred several times during the next year or two, but The Palace is thought to have been actually owned by E. J. Crinnian.

It was a small hall with a total capacity of about 750, reduced to 629 by the end of its life. It had a small balcony, and an octagonal foyer with an entrance facing Slater Street. (The main auditorium ran parallel to Great Bridge rather than at right angles to it.) In 1912 an operator named Arthur Barnes was appoointed by Mr. Crinnian, and he stayed at The Palace until 1943. Arthur's son, George Barnes, has been able to provide a picture of the life and times of his father's work at The Palace:

"When my father joined The Palace Mr. Crinnian seemed to be in charge, but he probably shared the ownership of the enterprise with a Mr. Evans and a Mr. Spittle. The latter may have also had an interest for a

time in the cinema in Owen Street, Tipton. When Mr.Crinnian died the cinema was run by his son – Eddie Crinnian until the early 1930s.

My father was something of a 'Jack of all trades'. Apart from his job as operator, he also did the bill-posting on the cinema site. This involved hanging a huge poster on the side of the cinema building, as well as two smaller hoardings. When the regular bill-poster, Billie Short, was on holiday, my father would do his round which extended from Swan Village to Horseley Heath. My father also re-wired the cinema in the late 1920s – possibly for the arrival of the talkies.

In the 'silent days' the films had been accompanied on the piano by Arthur Cook – an unassuming and kindly man who once had the chance of a brilliant career as a pianist but ended up at The Palace!"

I assume that Eddy Crinnian remained the proprietor until the sound era. It seems that sound was installed by 1931, only a couple of years before the cinema was acquired by Cyril Joseph and his partners, this time using the name Storer Pictures. This was the first step taken by Cyril Joseph in forming his small Black Country chain of cinemas – as described in the introductory chapter.

Below: The only picture to come to light providing us with a glimpse of The Palace, Great Bridge, showing the cinema under construction.

The little foyer, designed by Messrs. Gaskell and Chambers, may have been added by Cyril Joseph. He made similar improvements to the foyer and entrance at the Forum, Bradley. The changes to the foyer also led to changes in access to the projection box – home to a BTH system. Even as late as the mid fifties various improvements were made to the Palace. For example, early 1955, none other than the Harry Weedon Partnership drew up plans for an improved projection box.

Storer Pictures (Cyril Joseph) ran the Palace until 1958 when it was acquired by Vincent Wareing, at the same time as he acquired the Coliseum and Olympia, Wolverhampton, also from Cyril Joseph, and the Forum, Caldmore Green. It seems a strange moment for someone to have embarked on a career of running four rundown Black Country Cinemas. However, no doubt they seemed irresistibly cheap.

Cyril Joseph had a large hoarding built at the side of the auditorium, facing the main road. Details of the programme were pasted up every week, but Vincent Wareing decided to save £15 a week by putting up a permanent poster. For the last two years of its life, this hoarding proclaimed, "Bring Your Alice To Our Palace".

Like other cinemas that had survived into the second half of the fifties there seemed, at the Palace, to be a dramatic decline in attendances at the end of the decade. Mr. Wareing blamed a budget after which a television could be obtained on payment of a single instalment rather than a third deposit. It seems that the Palace closed on 16th April 1960 with "Valley Of Fury" starring Victor Mature.

At one time it seemed that the Catholic Church might have bought the place although Mr. Wareing thought it unadvisable to try and bring Christianity to Great Bridge at this late stage. They joked about changing the hoarding to read "Bring Your Alice To Our Chalice"! In the end, the site was purchased by developers, the Palace was demolished, and a parade of shops was built there. Vincent Wareing went on to show films at the Mayfair Cinema in Bungay in Suffolk, where he died in the early 1980s.

Below: Usherettes from the Majestic, Bearwood. Their uniforms feature an "H" monogram – for "Hewitson's Cinemas" (Author's collection)

Wednesbury

Just as we travelled north-westwards from Smethwick to look at the cinemas of Oldbury and Langley, it makes sense to travel on a parallel journey from West Bromwich (out through Hill Top) and on to Wednesbury.

Wednesbury today is part of the Metropolitan Borough of Sandwell. At one time a town of over thirty thousand inhabitants, it obviously never regarded itself as part of *anywhere* else. However, the local government changes of 1966 and 1974 have brought Wednesbury into Sandwell. Topographically it dominates the eastern half of the Black Country with its two churches standing proudly above the plateau and visible from almost *everywhere* else. As the M6 meets the M5, the motorist travelling northwards feels the eastern half of the Black Country closing in around him and these two churches are a signal to the Blackcountryman that he is nearing home. It is worth climbing the hill to the grimy stonework of St. Bartholomew's, or the red and blue brick of St. Mary's to take in the views. Looking westwards, once upon a time across the roof of the Rialto, you can see Dudley Castle and the central ridge of the Black Country stretching from the Rowley Hills to Sedgley Beacon.

Wednesbury is at a crossroads, where Holyhead Road from Birmingham to Wolverhampton (Telford's "A41") crosses the Dudley to Walsall Road which was once the beginning of a principle link between the Black Country and the East Midlands. The South Staffordshire Railway crossed the Great Western Railway at Wednesbury, and nearby the Patent Shaft and Axletree Company built their steelworks. All these things have gone; similarly Wednesbury no longer has a cinema, or a town hall in which a local council meet.

As in other towns, Professor Wood used to bring his travelling show to Wednesbury Town Hall during the first decade of this century, and films also appeared between variety acts at the local theatre; in this case the New Theatre Royal, which in 1910 changed its name to the Hippodrome. We will also encounter Ben Kennedy yet again, but he did not maintain a presence in Wednesbury as he did in West Bromwich and Smethwick.

No place of entertainment in Wednesbury really has a straightforward history and before we dismiss the Hippodrome as being part of theatre history it is worth noting that when H. J. Barlow's repertory company began to face declining audiences in the fifties, the Hippodrome did try showing films at the beginning of the week with live drama at the end of the week! They even tried to install Cinemascope! The Hippodrome disappeared in the 1960s and will be described in Volume Two, but its history is another reminder that the stories of theatrical and cinematic activity are often intertwined.

The Kings Hall, The Borough Hall and The Rialto

Earps Lane, Wednesbury

The story of this institution is typical of the bizarre history of Wednesbury's cinemas. In 1860 a very primitive theatre was built in Earps Lane called The Royal. For a while it served as a kind of public hall and was hired to any touring show prepared to use it. One lessee was "Fiddler Joss", a revivalist preacher who used the hall as his headquarters in 1866. In 1883 it was purchased by the Salvation Army but in 1909 they were able to move to a new citadel, and the building was sold to Benjamin Kennedy.

It was reopened about September 1909 as The Kings Hall. Ben Kennedy also used this name for the hall at which he showed films in Birmingham. Together with Bosco's "Palace" in West Bromwich, it provides an example of films being shown regularly in permanent premises just before the Cinematograph Act. Variety acts were still used between films but the Kings Hall presented itself as a cinema. It was managed by Cinema Veteran, Charles Pindar. One young lad who helped Len Kelly, the operator, during the First World War, can still recall the night that a bomb dropped on Wednesbury from a Zeppelin. He claims someone dived over the balcony when hearing the explosion.

Ben Kennedy seems to have relinquished some of his Black Country halls at the end of the War, including the Tivoli, in Tipton, and the Kings Hall, Wednesbury. It was sold to Messrs. Black and Hicks and substantially rebuilt to open as the Borough Theatre. It changed hands at least once more before being acquired by a Birmingham man, Mr. I. Kraines, who probably owned a building firm. He seems to have acquired it from the Adams Family who ran it during the 1924-26 period. Mr. Kraines substantially renovated the place and then leased it to Mr. and Mrs. Jones of the Picture House, Princes End.

Newly adopting the name "Rialto", it opened under Mr. Jones' care on 24th October 1927. The first film was ***Nostromo*** and, in the freshly decorated hall, the audience enjoyed the film and the music of an orchestra led by Harry Stradd. The assistant manager of the Rialto from October 1927 to April 1930 was none other than Fred Leatham whom we will encounter at numerous venues in the Black Country. He had left the keyboard at Princes End, was gaining experience of running a cinema, and then left to embark on an amazing career as a cinema proprietor, as described in Section One.

1930 was a hectic year at the Rialto. The cinema closed altogether for a month in the spring, reopening on Whit Monday, 9th June, with ***The Drake Case*** supported by a stage act, ***The Musical Monarchs***. Sound was introduced with a special charity show on Sunday 2nd November of the same year. Mr. Kraines reappeared in 1931 and set about rebuilding the place yet again.

Possibly one reason for doing this was to improve the sound as it is believed that Mr. Kraines installed BTH equipment at this stage.

When it was closed on this occasion, on 27th June 1931, advertisements promised that it would be *"much enlarged and vastly improved"*. This time Mr. Kraines managed to lease the Rialto to ABC and they commenced business on 14th September 1931. They may have taken on the lease with a view to assessing the potential of business in Wednesbury. At first they retained the services of Mr. Jones. Quite what happened next is delightfully obscure. It is quite possible that ABC decided not to continue running the Rialto and by 1936 or 1937 it had closed yet again. Mr. Kraines, although not apparently interested in running a cinema himself, never gave up. Another spate of major rebuilding began. In six weeks an imposing new frontage was built, believed to be designed by Ernest Roberts. A new stage and the latest type of glass-beaded screen were installed, as well as new seats for nine hundred and fifty patrons. The work was carried out for the new lessee, Cyril Joseph. On this occasion, Cyril Joseph called his enterprise Clifford Pictures. (See Section One for more information on Cyril Joseph.)

The reopening, on Monday 15th August 1938, was a suitably grand affair. The ceremony was performed by Wednesbury's mayor, Councillor Charles Collins, but Charlie Kettle, from the Palace, opened the proceedings by introducing the new manager, Frank Ellis. (The Palace had also been brought under the control of Cyril

The Rialto awaiting demolition in 1973.
(Andy Rutter)

Joseph.) Cyril Joseph told his guests, including Tom Wood of Bilston, that the Rialto was now a "super-cinema" and everybody sat back to watch *"They Gave Him A Gun"* starring Spencer Tracy.

This restless cinema settled down to an undisturbed life under the control of Clifford Pictures until Cyril Joseph began dismantling his empire in the mid-fifties. The Rialto returned to the trustees of the estate of the late Mr. Kraines. With a nice twist of history it was then leased to Reay Wood. Tom Wood's son had found himself running the Savoy in Bilston and by leasing the Rialto he commanded enough seats to secure reasonable films.

He installed Cinemascope and tried to cope with dwindling audiences but admitted defeat on 30th March 1957 with *"Somebody Up There Likes Me"* starring Paul Newman. The following Monday Syncopating Sandy Strickland used the cinema to try to break the 134 hour non-stop piano playing record! When he broke the record the following Saturday, people paid a shilling to go in and see him do it. Ironically, every seat was taken.

The Rialto lay dormant for a time but a cinema with so many openings and closures was not beaten yet. On 10th November 1958 it was reopened by Neville Wright, with *"Smiley"*. It was redecorated again and Neville Wright boldly embarked on a six year lease. In the first year he prospered and installed the first non-carbon projector lamp in the Black Country into his machines. Somehow he managed to improve attendance, but as the new decade began, matters soon

89

worsened. He kept the Rialto alive until 8th July 1961 and then organised a special farewell presentation with "something for all the family". The last programme began at 5.55 p.m. and included *"Journey To The Centre Of The Earth"* plus *"Young and Dangerous"* and other films, plus a live musical group on stage; *The Renegades*. Neville Wright made special presentations to two teenagers who had helped him run the cinema, Michael Griffiths and Vincent Docherty. This really was the last film show in Earps Lane.

As from Friday 21st July 1961 Miles Jervis II operated his Midland Cinemas Bingo Club in the Rialto and this activity continued into the early seventies, by which time much of the housing in the area had been demolished. In 1971 the new ring road had to be "bent" to avoid the Rialto. Wednesbury Council were now the landlord but Miles Jervis' lease was still operative. Demolition finally caught up with the Rialto in June 1973. Earps Lane disappeared under a newly landscaped grassy bank.

The Palace

Upper High Street, Wednesbury.

As films were proving successful in 1910 in the rather unsatisfactory Kings Hall in Wednesbury's Earp's Lane, it was not surprising that several local businessmen came together to build a proper cinema. They formed the Wednesbury Imperial Picture Company and the local architect, Mr. C. W. D. Joynson, drew up plans for a hall in Upper High Street to hold six hundred patrons.

Messrs. Summerhill and Jellyman built the new cinema, starting work in May 1912. The exterior was treated in white cement and was carried out in "free renaissance" style. The facade was crowned with a life-size female figure bearing an electrically lighted flare. It had a fully carpeted raked floor and scarlet plush tip up seats throughout. Every patron was guaranteed a perfect view of the screen. The Kings Hall still offered crowded benches and poor sight lines.

The grand opening took place on Monday 7th October 1912. Mr. Joynson presented the Mayor, Alderman Pritchard, with a silver key, and asked him to declare the cinema open. An "augmented orchestra" provided accompaniment to *"The Man of the Wilds"* and Edison's *"Relief of Lucknow"*.

As its full name was "The Imperial Picture Palace" it was sometimes known as The Imperial" and sometimes "The Palace". In 1927 when Mr. Jones became manager and lessee of "The Boro", as the Kings Hall was then known, Charles Pindar preserved his association with Wednesbury by moving to the Palace, and stayed there until the first closure in 1937. Considering it was the town's first purpose-built cinema it had lost some of its prestige when the Picture House was opened. It was the last of Wednesbury's three cinemas to introduce sound, towards the end of 1931.

Below: The Palace, Wednesbury in 1937.
(Peter Eardley Collection)

The Palace. Wednesbury. 1937 – interiors.   *(From the Collection of Peter Eardley)*

The original building closed on 29th May 1937 with *"Not So Dirty"*. By then Thomas Wood had acquired a controlling interest in the Palace. However, his plans to reconstruct it unfortunately coincided with his sudden retirement and the leasing of all his cinemas to Cyril Joseph.

Ernest Roberts had drawn up the plans for the new Palace. The former cinema was to form the crush hall to the new auditorium constructed at the rear of the original one. This would then provide accommodation for just over twelve hundred patrons. (895 in the stalls, and 354 in the balcony.) The construction work was carried out by J. & F. Wootton. The original entrance to the Palace was retained, but altered to give it a more modern appearance, and transformed by the effect of neon lighting. BTH equipment was installed.

The new Palace was opened on 27th September 1937 with Cyril Joseph, calling himself "Dual Pictures", as the host. Thomas Wood, now an Alderman of Bilston, came along to pay tribute to the original Palace and to recall the even earlier times when he and his father had presented their travelling shows at the Town Hall. The cinema was declared open by Wednesbury's Mayor, Councillor Jack Smith and everyone enjoyed *"Gold Diggers of 1937"* starring Dick Powell and Joan Blondell.

The Midland Advertiser described the Palace as *"The last word in modern cinema construction"* and Charlie Kettle must have felt that he had not done too badly in coming from the mighty Tower in West Bromwich to manage the splendid "Palace". The Ideal Kinema magazine commented on the pastel shades of green and gold terra cotta, used to decorate the fan-shaped auditorium, and the rose du barry velvet upholstery used throughout. Kalee Model 11 projectors were observed up in the projection room – used in comjunction with BTH sound.

Both Cyril Joseph's cinemas in Wednesbury must have felt slightly overshadowed by the new Gaumont but the popularity of film-going during the War kept all three cinemas busy. During the War, Miss Fellows moved from the Rialto to manage the Palace while Charlie Kettle moved to the Olympia, Wolverhampton. Miss Fellows stayed at The Palace until Cyril Joseph's lease expired in 1958.

Miles Jervis II replaced Cyril Joseph as the lessee of the Palace and tried to tackle the problem of declining audiences. Wrestling was presented on Wednesday evenings, but when this failed to gain popularity, bingo was introduced in the spring of 1961. The freehold of the building now belonged to G.H. Luce, a Wolverhampton businessman, but, while Miles Jervis was introducing bingo, the cinema was being sold to a Manchester firm of property developers.

Miles Jervis seemed reluctant to abandon his presence in Wednesbury, even if only to present bingo. By July 1961 he added a Sunday session of bingo at the Palace and had leased the Rialto to present Friday to Monday sessions of the game. By the end of the year he was persuaded to give up his lease on the Palace and the last film show was screened on 9th December, featuring *"Goliath and the Dragon"* and *"The Fourth Square"*.

On Monday 11th December 1961 the building was auctioned and the fittings were sold a few days later. Some demolition began and then ceased. The boarded-up remains of the Palace survived as an eyesore until wholesale demolition of the Upper High Street prepared the way for development in 1964. Although not completed by him, it was Tom Wood's last cinema project in the Black Country. His son, Reay, felt that it was a tragedy that such a fine and costly building lasted only twenty-four years.

The Picture House,
The Gaumont, later known as The Odeon and the Silver

Walsall Street, Wednesbury.

Perhaps a measure of the importance of Wednesbury was that A.P.P.H. chose the town as a site for one of their cinemas, or perhaps it was the loyalty to their homeland of a number of A.P.P.H. executives that prompted them to bring "wholesome amusement" to this part of the Black Country.

The plans for the Wednesbury Picture House were drawn by the London architects Messrs. Atkinson and Alexander. The front elevation in Walsall Street, was carried out in Carra Ware and inside the presence of much polished wood panelling and tapestries gave the place a very luxurious atmosphere. Construction started in 1914 and was then suspended when the War began. Work was then resumed, but meanwhile rumours had apparently been spread that A.P.P.H. was a German company, all of which had to be strenuously denied when the cinema opened.

The Picture House was opened by the Mayor, Councillor Bishop, on 25th March 1915. The nine hundred guests, occupying every seat in the cinema, were welcomed by Mr. Newbould of A.P.P.H. who stressed that the company was British, that the Managing Director, Dr. Jupp, was from Walsall, and that the company was safely in the hands of South Staffordshire men. It was their nineteenth cinema to open. The first programme of films included *"The Man In The Street"*, *"Andy And The Redskins"* by Edison, *"The Middleman"* and a Keystone comedy *"The Face On The Bar Room Floor"*. Afterwards the Wednesbury Herald commented: *"That such a building should have* been provided in Wednesbury is a compliment to the town".

Like all A.P.P.H. cinemas, the one in Wednesbury later flew the flag of P.C.T. and then Gaumont British, but generally The Picture House had a less chequered history than the Palace or the Rialto. The Picture House introduced the talkies to the town on 11th November 1929 with Al Jolson in *"The Singing Fool"* on the R.C.A. system. (P.C.T. introduced sound at Dudley's Criterion on the same day).

Whatever its prestige or position in the pecking order of cinemas, the Picture House was still in Wednesbury. It therefore seems inevitable that it should close, be transformed, and reopened, at least once! On Saturday 8th January 1938 The Picture House closed with *"History Is Made At Night"* starring Jean Arthur and Charles Boyer. The local paper explained:

"The word went forth, the Picture House was to come down, only for a finer building to arise in far more glorious array on the site of the old one".

The replacement, the Gaumont, was designed by Messrs. W. E. Trent and W. S. Trent and W. S. Trent, assisted by H. L. Cheey of G.B.'s Architect's Department. The new "super-cinema" to accommodate 1594 patrons, was built in just over six months at a cost of about £45,000. The Ideal Kinema claimed, *"(it) has achieved a standard of design, suitability, beauty and accommodation which will be difficult to improve upon".* The facade was faced with cream faience slabs with a thin blue tile insert to form regular squares. The building was dominated by a sixty foot high tower. The large canopy and the tower were much enhanced at night by the use of neon light.

The large entrance hall, with its peach coloured walls swept the patron past the central paybox and down steps to the main foyer, from which central doors led to the stalls and side staircases led to the circle. The auditorium, decorated in peach and blue, which tapered towards the screen, was relatively plain, reflecting the contemporary realisation that concentration should be directed towards the screen. A simple diamond shaped pattern was carried out in the plaster work. Gaumont British Magnus projectors and the latest Duosonic equipment were installed. Very minimal facilities were provided for live performances.

The Gaumont was opened by the mayor, Councillor Collins, on Monday 10th October 1938, supported by Graham Moffatt and Moore Mariott, who also appeared in the feature film, *"Convict 99"* starring Will Hay. Councillor Collins had already opened the new Rialto during his year of office and on this occasion made special mention of the work the construction of the Gaumont had brought to local people. About one hundred local men had been employed by McLoughlin and Harvey, the contractors, and the structural steel work had been made by Rubery Owen at Darlaston.

Sidney Clulow, who had managed the Picture House, was retained at the Gaumont, joined by several other staff who had worked there many years. In two years, the town's three cinemas had been completely renewed and all could now settle down to compete with one another and fight the local council on the question of Sunday opening.

Below: The Gaumont, Wednesbury. 1954. (Sandwell Archives)

Perhaps it was inevitable that a cinema as fine as the Gaumont should outlive its rivals. On the 9th March 1964, after the other two had closed, Wednesbury's surviving cinema changed its name to the Odeon. By then it was being managed by Tom Lloyd who had watched his employer close Wolverhampton's cinemas, and must have wondered how long life could continue in Wednesbury. Like the Rialto and the Palace, the Odeon enjoyed an unexpected extension to its life.

The Rank Organisation "closed" the Odeon on Saturday 29th January 1972, but the cinema reopened the very next day as the Silver. Odeons have not very often been sold to anyone wishing to continue their operation as a cinema, but in this case the Silver Cinema Co. Ltd. bought the place and carried on. One of the principal members of the new company was Tarsem Singh Dhami, whose career is described elsewhere.

The Silver presented English language films six days a week and Indian films on Sundays. The reprieve was short. Ladbrokes purchased the cinema and continued the shows until they obtained a gaming licence. The last English language film show was on 18th May 1974, featuring **"Easy Rider"** and **"Barry Mackenzie"**, although the last Indian film may have been shown a week later.

As a Ladbroke's Bingo and Social Club the building survived and eventually it passed to the Dale Leisure & Bingo Club organisation who installed a Hammond organ but confused everybody by briefly ressurecting the name "The Silver"! In turn it became part of the Walker Group. The ex Gaumont finally closed as Walker's Bingo Club on 28th February 2010 - after thirty

Below: Outside the Gaumont, Wednesbury in February 1964. (Sandwell Archives)

Years! The manager, Barbara Toy, had worked at the hall for twenty-eight years and her assistant, June Perry, had completed twenty-three years. The oldest regular customer was 96.

The Cinema Theatre Association urged the Sandwell MBC to include the cinema in a conservation area, or make it "locally listed" because the quality of its modernist façade – seemed to be "threatened" following the demise of Bingo.

Sunday opening and "Wednesbury Reasonableness"

When APPH applied to Wednesbury Council for Sunday opening in the 1940s, the Council gave permission but stated that nobody under the age of fifteen was to be admitted to such shows. APPH appealed against this limitation and the appeal eventually went to the House of Lords. Law Lord Greene issued a landmark ruling in favour of the Local Authority. He laid down the principle of law stating that a corporation can only be classed as acting unreasonably if no other reasonable authority would ever carry out such an act. This became known as the "Wednesbury Reasonableness" Test.

Tipton

Tipton is very much in the centre of the Black Country, and displays many of the essential characteristics of a Black Country town. One of these characteristics is that the town is really made up of a number of smaller townships, villages and communities. Other characteristics are the importance of coal, of subsequent industry, and the growth of transport based on the emergence of the canals. (Tipton is the "Venice of the Midlands".)

The Urban District of Tipton was another product of 1894 local government legislation, and it went on to acquire Borough status in 1938. In 1966 it joined up with West Bromwich, and thus in 1974 made its way into Sandwell MBC. These changes did little to dampen local civic pride and sense of identity.

Five cinemas existed in the area, untroubled by invading Odeons or Cliftons and not really competing in any way with each other, such was the intensity of their relationship with very localised communities. (Some folks would claim there were six cinemas in Tipton by claiming that The Palace, Great Bridge, was in Tipton. In this book we have had to recognise that The Palace was really in the West Bromwich half of Great Bridge.)

The histories of Tipton's cinemas are often obscure but all of them are fascinating. The cinemas' lives were not only often poorly documented, but some were seldom photogaphed. The rebuilt Alhambra at Dudley Port was the nearest the area reached to producing a 1930's super-cinema, but probably the grandest cinema in Tipton was the Regent in Owen Street, an area with the strongest claim to being the centre of Tipton. Few photographs exist of either establishment.

Below: The Regent as rebuilt in 1920.

Not too far from the Regent was the Cinema in the High Street in a converted school building with a talent for survival. In quite separate communities, the Picture House, known later as The Bruce, served Princes End, and The Victoria served Horseley Heath. Not one of these places exists today as a cinema, or even as a building in other use.

The Tivoli — The Regent later The Regal

Owen Street, Tipton.

As Owen Street was the principal shopping street of the Borough of Tipton it is not surprising that the town's "premier" cinema was to be found there. The original building began life as a market hall, but on 30th May 1910 Benjamin Kennedy acquired approval from the Urban District Council for his plans to convert it into a cinema. The plans were drawn by Messrs. Scott and Clark. As with all "conversions" at this time, the work was accomplished very quickly and Mr. Kennedy was issued with his kine licence on 27th July 1910 and then presumably opened for business as The Tivoli, although I have not been able to discover a precise opening date. Just before Christmas he was granted a stage licence, at first for a temporary period of three months, and the Tivoli was able to present films and variety. As we have seen in previous chapters, "cine-variety" was particularly favoured by Ben Kennedy.

The Tivoli is next heard of in mid July 1913 when plans, by G. Bowden, were approved for adding a raked floor to the auditorium. The U.D.C. minutes recorded that it would, *"Certainly be an improvement".*

Above: The Regent, Tipton, just before its post-war alterations, in which the projection box was re-housed in a more stream-lined extension, and a modern canopy was provided.
(W.G. Langdon)

Apparently The Tivoli was a great success and I have been told the building was packed to capacity when the first Zeppelin raid struck Tipton and bombs dropped in Union Street in the First World War. At the time it seems that it held about 1400 patrons, some of whom had a reputation for rowdiness.

Towards the end of the First World War, and immediately afterwards, the story of The Tivoli, and its successor, the Regent, becomes extremely complicated. It has been difficult to assemble the facts from the fragments of information available. Eventually The Regent was owned by Edgar Duckworth, son of the Lancashire cinema pioneer Joshua Duckworth. Some years later, Edgar's son, David Duckworth, told a local paper that they acquired the cinema directly from Benjamin Kennedy.

Other records seem to suggest that Benjamin Kennedy was neither proprietor nor operator of The Tivoli by the end of the War. It may have been operated by a Mr. Spittle, who may have also had an interest in the Palace, Great Bridge, and then acquired by Edgar Hounsell of the Midland Amusements Company. This Company also briefly acquired the Scala, Wolverhampton, in 1919 and then at the end of that year, sold both cinemas to Midland Entertainments Limited. Oscar Deutsch later held a controlling interest in Midland Amusements, when most of its activities were in Coventry, but his name is sometimes mentioned in connection with The Regent and The Scala. As I understand the fragments of information I have come across, Midland Amusements had shed both cinemas by the time Oscar acquired his

interest. This view is supported by an article in "Picture House" of Spring 1983 in which Dickie Dewes oultines the early history of Midlands Entertainments.

Midland Entertainments were certainly responsible for closing the Tivoli as from 1st January 1920 and for building its replacement, to be known as The Regent. The Regent was not entirely new, but it was a very drastic "rebuilding" job. The contractor, a Mr. Edwards of Dudley, regarded it as extremely awkward. In fact the work was not completed for the opening. Bryans had to come and complete the plasterwork at a later date. The raked floor of the stalls had to be extended, a new balcony was installed, and an imposing new frontage was erected. Fifteen hundred new tip up seats were provided.

The Regent opened on Monday 16th August 1920 at 2.30 p.m. The opening was performed by the Chairman of Tipton Urban District Council, Councillor W.W. Doughty, who had his own cinema interests at the Victoria. He had been entertained beforehand with a luncheon at the Black Cock, and joined the patrons who had been admitted free of charge, for a screening of ***"The Gentlemen Riders"*** supported by *"**The Spiral of Death**"*. At the evening performance the proceeds were donated to the local War Memorial Fund.

Midland Entertainments Limited also poses some mysteries. Some records state that it was a Manchester-based firm and therefore may have had something to do with Edgar Duckworth. However at the opening the company was represented by two directors; Messrs. Emmott and Hinchcliffe. Edgar Duckworth seems to have taken the cinema back from Midland Entertainments about 1924 and for the remainder of the twenties his name actually appeared as "the proprietor" on the Regent's advertisements. Edgar Duckworth entered the business in 1903, when he was sixteen, and this just qualified him to be a Cinema Veteran. His expansion from Lancashire into the Midlands does not seem to have been very significant. Perhaps he is better remembered in Derby, where Duckworth Square is near the site of one of his cinemas.

In Tipton he ought to be remembered for organising Sunday charity shows for the local "Boot Fund". For example, when the Regent closed for a short time in 1930 to have Western Electric sound equipment installed, Edgar Duckworth "reopened" on Sunday 21st September with one of these concerts. He brought the Colne Town Board down from his Lancashire home to entertain the Tiptonians.

Meanwhile the local patrons eagerly awaited the events of the following day: the arrival of the talkies. Sound came to Tipton with *"Paris"* starring Jack Buchanan and *"Smiling Irish Eyes"* starring Colleen Moore. Soon afterwards the theatre was leased to the ABC circuit. It was their only interest in Tipton and, until the opening of the new Alhambra, Dudley Port, its position as the town's premier cinema was unchallenged.

Early during the Second World War it seems that ABC did not renew their lease and for a time the cinema was operated by the Marks Circuit of Manchester, a firm which was briefly interested in two cinemas in Wolverhampton in the early forties. After the War it seems that Edgar and David Duckworth resumed responsibility for running The Regent. It must be assumed therefore that they were the real owners of the building throughout these changes.

In December 1948 they replaced the existing sound system with new RCA equipment and put in new Ross projectors and arcs. From photographs it would appear that alterations to the operating room also took place and rather spoiled the frontage of the building. Further improvements were on the way. On 28th June 1954 the Regent became the "New Regal Cinema" and reopened with a cinemascope presentation of *"The Flight of the White Heron"*, a film of the recent Royal Tour.

In becoming The Regal, the front of the cinema was given a facelift that successfully obscured the alterations mentioned above. A new canopy now supported a fin with "Regal" spelt vertically in neon lights on each side, placed in the middle of an arc-shaped facade that hid the protruding projection room. A slightly 1930's look was thus imposed on the centre of the building, the 1920

facade flanked either side of it and somewhere in the building some remnant of the original Market Hall probably existed! In its new form the Regal survived the fifties.

The end came on Saturday 3rd December 1960 with *"Jazz Boat"*, starring Anthony Newley supported by *"Kill Her Gently"*. David Duckworth had sold the cinema to Capital and Commercial Limited, a company that proposed redeveloping the site. The equipment was removed and then the empty building was left to the mercy of local vandals. By September 1961 scrap-dealers openly parked their horses and carts in Wood Street and raided the building for whatever they could find. Meanwhile the new owners complained that their planning applications were being kept waiting.

Eventually the sad remains of the Regent /Regal were demolished and new shops have been built on the site, but the sorry tale of decay and dilapidation lasting too long, and redevelopment being a long time coming, became a familiar story in Owen Street. At the time of writing some considerable redevelopment of the area has, at last, taken place, but Owen Street has never become a bustling commercial centre of activity as it once was.

After the publication of "Cinemas of the Black Country" in 1982 I was contacted by Ron Fellows who came to the Regent in 1946 during the period that the Duckworths had leased the cinema to the Marks Circuit. At the time the cinema was managed by a Mr. Davies who had been there since the first period of direct control by Edgar Duckworth in the 1920s! As well as being Chief Projectionist, Ron Fellows was given responsibility for publicity work and was given a second-hand Austin 8 van in which he had to drive around and promote The Regent. Ron Fellows was of the view that The Regent always disappointed anyone who attempted to run it. When he witnessed the installation of cinemascope and stereophonic sound he felt the changes had little impact. *"The Robe"* was booked for a fortnight, knowing that the Regent's screen was larger than the one at The Plaza, Dudley where Miles Jervis had successfully run *"The Robe"* for two weeks. In Tipton the film played to empty houses during the second week! Ron himself was appointed as manager for the last years of The Regent's life and Billy Parker took over as Chief Operator. They sadly observed the Bruce and The Cinema doing better business than The Regent.

97

The Cinema

Tipton High Street

Tipton is sometimes called the Venice of the Midlands. At Factory Junction the Brindley and Telford levels of the Birmingham Canal Navigation are reunited and at Tipton Junction the line from the Dudley Tunnel meets the B.C.N. Leaving the Regent in Owen Street and heading for Dudley the traveller had to traverse a bridge over the canal and pass through an area that might conceivably be regarded as "Venetian" to reach High Street. The area has been transformed in the past few decades but a few landmarks, like The Wagon and Horses, have stood long enough to give us some bearings.

About a hundred yards from the Wagon and Horses, on a site that is now a car park for Sedgley Steels, once stood "The Cinema". It never aspired to a more imaginative name. In the summer of 1913 an existing school on the site was converted into a cinema. The architect, A.T. Butler, of Dudley, drew up th plans for the conversion, and, as seen from the sketch, produced something that had the appearance of a cinema. At first it held four hundred and fifty patrons but as seating was improved this fell to just over three hundred.

I have been unable to trace the original proprietor, nor an opening date, but it seems certain that it was in business by October 1913, and at some time in its very

Above: Elsie Willetts, seen on the right, and Rita, on the left join the manager's daughter, (in the centre, in the kiosk at The Regent, on its last night. Elsie and Rita were usherettes.
                    (Elsie Willetts via Keith Hodgkins)

early life it was owned by Messrs. Bradley, Nichols and Beese. Its story successfully eludes the historian until the early twenties when Cecil Couper, of Brierley Hill, took it over as a distant outpost of his empire. He continued to operate it during the remainder of the silent era, his daughter sometimes providing the piano accompaniment. About 1930 Cecil Couper sold it to Fred Leatham who set about installing a sound system, using Gyrotone equipment. Fred Leatham then sold the place to his father, F.W. Leatham who ran it for a time in partnership with a Mr. Hinkinson. The latter was eventually bought out and it became very much a family affair. F. W. Leatham's other son, Leonard, was the operator, and later the manager. Although a modest cinema serving a very local clientele, it seems that it prospered through the Second World War.

Programmes changed twice weekly except under unusual circumstances. For example, *"Showboat"* was so popular it ran for a full week and returned later for a second run! I doubt the patrons appreciated that its director was born nearby in Dudley.

When F.W. Leatham died the cinema was shared by his four children but Leonard Leatham effectively ran the place. His stubborn refusal to abandon it probably accounts for its survival through the difficult times of the mid fifties. Leonard Leatham confessed to the local paper that audiences were often fifty or less. Ironically, I have sat in much smaller audiences in currently surviving cinemas!

Another irony, considering the decline in the 1950's, concerns Leonard Leatham's original intentions, after the War, of replacing the old converted-school with a brand new super-cinema. In 1949 he commissioned Roland Satchwell to produce plans for a magnificent cinema that would have been called the Regal. Roland Satchwell's plans made ingenious use of the awkward site and the Regal would have held 837 patrons. The project compares with Mr. McDonald's similar proposals for the little cinema in Princes End.

Making obscure calculations from assorted hints and suggestions it seems that The Cinema showed its last film on Saturday 21st June 1958, saved from further agony by a Compulsory Purchase Order from the council. As at the Victoria, Horseley Heath, there had been a sudden switch to RCA equipment just before The Cinema's demise, but cinemascope was not installed. Leonard Leatham's modest little cinema faded away into obscurity a decade after he had dreamed of building something more grand.

Below: The Cinema, Tipton High Street: A drawing by Tony Wright based on the original architect's sketch by A.T. Butler. The elaborate frontage concealed a very basic auditorium.

The Alhambra

Dudley Port

The main road from Dudley to West Bromwich leaves the former town at the romantically named Burnt Tree Island and passes through three small communities on the eastern fringe of Tipton, each one supporting a local cinema. After a spectacular hump-back bridge over the Brindley level of the Birmingham Canal the traveller comes to the site of The Alhambra. The road at this point is called Dudley Port, and the Alhambra stood on the corner of Groveland Road.

A quarter of a mile further on, the Telford level of the Birmingham Canal crosses this road on an aqueduct near the windswept station of Dudley Port and beyond this the traveller comes to Horseley Heath, home of the Victoria.

Returning to the Alhambra, its site was occupied at the end of the last century, by a Salvation Army Citadel constructed in corrugated iron. What happened next is really part of local theatre history and will have to be examined again in Volume Two. John Morton who ran a theatre in Cradley Heath apparently wanted to extend his empire to Tipton. On August Bank Holiday 1902 the old Salvation Army building became the Colosseum. It seems that John Morton wished to deliberately confuse people who may have already come across John Clement's Colosseum in Trindle Road, Dudley, but which was not in theatrical use in 1902.

To add to the mystery, Douglas Phelps, of the Alhambra, Stourbridge, agreed a contract with Poole's Myriarama show to bring it to the Dudley Port building in 1904. On this occasion there is no evidence that the Myriama show also included films, but Douglas Phelps returned to the Alhambra later, after an intervening period when it was used as a skating rink. During Douglas Phelps second apperance in Dudley Port he may have included some presention of film material, and its "temporary management" was in the hands of Joe Bate, whose life is described in the chapter on "Bioscope Days".

At a meeting of the planning committee of Tipton U.D.C. on 24th October 1910 a sketch was submitted to the committee to approve the conversion of what was then described as a skating rink into a cinema. The committee insisted on seeing proper plans!

A meeting of the full council took place the next day and granted a kine licence to the "Dudley Port Skating Rink", and as usual in dealing with the cinemas of Tipton, the thread of the story then becomes difficult to follow. At a further planning committee meeting on 31st October, only one week later, the surveyor reported that proper plans had been submitted by Messrs. Stonehewer. The timber and galvanised corrugated iron structure was regarded as satisfactory but the plan was rejected as the provision of emergency exits was not thought to be satisfactory.

I do not know how quickly modifications were made, nor how quickly the Alhambra managed to become a "proper" cinema. Presumably it was towards the end of 1910 or the beginning of 1911. It is also not clear who was the proprietor at the time of becoming a cinema. The early history of the Alhambra is frequently associated with the name of Pat Collins, but, as will be seen, he entered the scene a little later. Having started its life as a cinema called the Alhambra, that name was dropped for a time and it became the Palace of Varieties. Jas Tyrer of Oldbury may have leased the place for a time. In the chapter on The Palace, oldbury, I have noted that the he told the Oldbury Weekly News in September 1912 that he had theatrical interests at Dudley Port. Later in the First World War it appears to have been operated or owned by Messrs. Round and Hipkins.

All we know about Round & Hipkins is that George Edward Hipkins appeared before Dudley Bankruptcy in January 1916. He told the court he had entered a partnership in Septemeber 1915 to run the Alhambra, Dudley Port, but after nine months he was bankrupt. He said he should have known better because he had run a 'pictures and variety' house in Wolverhampton in October 1912 for three weeks and had lost money!

Certainly, by the time matters returned to normal, Pat Collins was definitely proprietor of the Alhambra and advertised the fact in the cinema's advertisements, reviving the original name. For some time it was managed for Pat Collins by James Styles, a gentleman

unknown to most people today, but well known in the fairground world between the Wars. He cultivated the skills of writing and painting and wrote material for the Worlds Fair, including, in December 1943, an epitaph to Pat Collins.

Pat Collins owned the Alhambra it until December 1927 when he sold it to Miles Jervis I of Chasetown. The latter installed Frank Bills as manager and Frank stayed at the Alhambra through its first closure, rebuilding, changes of ownership and until its final closure while in the possession of Miles Jervis II!

While writing "Midland Fairground Families" in the mid 1990s I was able to interview Bessie Hazell who was born into a South Wales fairground family in 1902. Bessie was able to recall matters from about 1905 onwards when her teenage sister had run away to marry a Midlands showman named Miles Jervis. I usually refer to him as Miles Jervis I as his son and grandson all took the same name and each played a part in local cinema history – particularly in West Bromwich and out on Cannock Chase. Bessie had a very strong visual memory of an event in late 1927 when Miles Jervis I appeared in Swansea after a trip to the Black Country:

"You'll never guess what I've just done!" said Miles to his family and friends in Swansea. The fortune-teller on the ground at the time was a Mrs. Davies. According to Bessie, Mrs. Davies looked up and said, "You've bought a cinema from Pat Collins." Bessie also implied that Miles' friends felt it was not a good investment!

Miles Jervis I must have continued to operate the cinema as a silent hall into the sound era and then, about 1933, sold it to Sheridan Film Services of Burton-on-Trent. The directors of this company were S.A. Suffolk, F.S. Suffolk, Fred Bailey and H. Armson. Mr. Suffolk's association with the Black Country included an interest in the cinema at Caldmore Green, Walsall.

The new owners demolished the old corrugated iron building, caring little for the patrons who liked to hear the rain pattering on the roof while watching "silent" films. The intention was to build a modern sound cinema, a precursor and mini-version of the super-cinema. During demolition they came across the original foundation stones of the Salvation Army Citadel and carefully returned them to that organisation, or to the people who had originally laid them!

Ernest Roberts was engaged to design the new building and William Jackson of Oldbury was contracted to build it. The result was very pleasing. Ernest Robert's apparent love of terracotta brickwork relieved with some work in patent stone worked well on a building of this size. Leaded lights, by E. Showell Trickett, were also a pleasing feature and the cinema's name in leaded glass survived until the building was demolished. It was built on the system that was then becoming established as the mode for building cinemas. Structural steelwork, by Rubery Owen, and reinforced concrete floors were now the order of the day. Externally, local bricks from

Pratts of Oldbury, and internally, plasterwork by Bryan's Adamanta, disguised the straightforward functionalism of the building. One slightly old-fashioned touch was the atmospheric treatment of the interior, painted by George Legg. These murals depicted mountain scenes on the side walls. Rose pink curtains of oriental silk provided a touch of luxury, and naturally all the seats were upholstered tip-ups. Seven hundred seats downstairs were in brown plush, two hundred and twenty seats in the balcony were in green plush. Accommodation was later listed as 830.

The new cinema was opened on Easter Monday, 8th April 1935, with an official reception at 5.30 and the ceremony at 6.30 p.m. Frank Bills, the proud manager of the new building, introduced Fred Bailey, Chairman of Sheridan Film Services, who was on stage with Mr. Suffolk and William Jackson. The opening was performed by Councillor A. F. Welch, the Chairman of Tipton U.D.C. who said that he regarded the new cinema as part of the process of beautifying that part of Tipton. Unfortunately, Ernest Roberts was absent, due to illness, but everybody else sat back to enjoy Gracie Field's performance as "Grace Platt" in the film *"Sing As We Go"* specially written for her by J. B. Priestley. Music and songs reached the audience via an RCA Photophone system.

The Alhambra was now Tipton's finest cinema but its location was relatively poor. The Regent, then in the hands of ABC, was more centrally placed. The Alhambra hoped for trade from West Bromwich and Dudley as it was easy to reach from both places, but both towns had bigger modern cinemas of their own.

Sheridan Film Services later became S. T. Cinemas, a partnership between Mr. Suffolk and a Mr. Thornton, still based in Burton.

However, at the beginning of 1952 the Alhambra became the property of Miles Jervis II, the son of the man who had bought the original Alhambra from Pat Collins! It must be rare for a cinema to be once owned by the father of a man who later becomes its owner – by which time it is no longer the same building.

As stated earlier, Frank Bills continued to manage the place through all these changes. In the opening brochure he had stated, *"I will do all in my power to make this theatre so inviting, so cosy, that you will feel insidiously drawn towards it whenever you feel the need for amusement. I want your patronage regularly, consistently throughout the year."* How he felt as the audience declined in the fifties is not recorded. The new owner felt frustrated by the cinema's location, and, by the end of that decade, by its six day licence.

Frank Bills had at some time served on the local council and sometimes gave people the impression that he resented the local authority's inspections and restraints. Nevertheless, he and Miles had to go "cap-in-hand" to Tipton Council and beg to be allowed to show films on the Sabbath. The Council delayed making the decision. While other local cinemas won the right (in Sedgley for example), and the Regent closed down, Miles Jervis waited two years for the issue to be resolved.

Below: The Alhambra, Dudley Port, in 1981 as an electrical wholesaler's store. (Ned Williams)

Above and below: The interior of the Alhambra, Dudley Por from the screent.

Pictures from the archives of the CTA. (Strangely there is no picture of the exterior)

A public meeting was called for September 1961 and all the evils of film-going on the Sabbath were recited public as if time had stood still in Tipton for fifty years. Only the Bruce and the Alhambra were still in business! The former had no intention of opening on Sundays and so the issue only affected the Alhambra. Very dramatically Miles Jervis was refused admission to the meeting on the grounds that he did not live in Tipton and Frank Bills braved the meeting alone to state the cinema's point of view. After all that, Sunday screenings were rejected. With a nice sense of irony Sunday Bingo sessions commenced at the Alhambra on 23rd October 1961 under the flag of the Midland Cinema Bingo Club. (Miles Jervis flew the same flag in Wednesbury).

The Bruce closed the following year leaving the Alhambra as Tipton's sole surviving cinema. A few yards from the cinema extensive road works began as the canal bridge was widened, and a final decline in the Alhambra's audience set in. The end came on 3rd. August 1963 and the last film shown was *"Sparrows Can't Sing"*.

The building still survived as a warehouse for G.A. Nicholas Ltd. The pay box could still be seen in the tiny foyer and the staircase that used to go to the balcony and some plasterwork was still obviously cinema-like in that unmistakeable 1930's style, but decorative details of the auditorium were completely obliterated. It lasted in this form for another quarter of a century, but the building was eventually vacated and was demolished in May 1989. I negotiated with the demolition contractor and it was agreed I could preserve some of the decorative leaded glasswork, including the name "Alhambra". Unfortunateley, before I could take delivery, local lads used the abundant piles of bricks on the site to smash every piece of glass.

The Victoria

Railway Street, Horseley Heath, Tipton

As our survey takes us to the remoter corners of Tipton the quest for information about the local cinemas becomes like looking for cigarette ash in a projection room. Perhaps this publication will encourage others to dig more deeply, if that is possible. Meanwhile the story of the Victoria seems somewhat sketchy.

Railway Street left the main road through Horseley Heath just beyond the Post Office. In 1859 the Primitive Methodists erected the Railway Street Chapel to hold a congregation of three hundred and eighty people. Early this century they moved to new premises, known as the Centenary Chapel on the main road. (Known to everyone as "The Rhubarb", the chapel closed in March 2004.)

Meanwhile, back to the building in Railway Street. On 21st February 1912 the planning committee of Tipton U.D.C. studied plans, drawn by Messrs. Scott and Clark,

for converting the chapel into a picture palace. Approval was granted subject to exits being provided leading directly onto the street opposite the balcony stairs on each side of the building. It seems therefore that the small balcony was inherited from its days as a chapel, as was a mural of an angel! The balcony, which only contained about five rows of seats ended in two boxes, apparently popular with courting couples. (The cost of a box in 1945 was nine pence.)

Once again no opening date seems to be recorded but presumably it was sometime in mid 1912. Its first licence was issued to a Daniel Darby in June 1912. The cinema seems to have been the property of William Wooley Doughty, a local councillor and J.P. He lived nearby in Horseley Heath Villa, and owned the Horseley Heath Hinge Works. He was a strict disciplinarian and took a personal interest in preserving order at his little cinema. He was also patriotic and liked to give away Union Jack badges between the films, and was philanthropic to the extent that during depressed times he sometimes sustained his audience with tea and biscuits or threw handfuls of pennies into the street!

When W. W. Doughty died his sole beneficiary was his housekeeper, Mrs. Smith, who thus became the owner of the Victoria. At the time the piano was played by Jimmy Jones and the second projectionist, Bill Wassell, had the nightly duty of re-whitewashing the plaster-of-paris screen. He believed it was the first of its type in Britain. Once a month he also had to clean an elaborate chandelier that was a feature of the hall. Leslie Taff began his distinguished career playing the piano at the Victoria.

How long Mrs. Smith remained the proprietor is not clear. A record exists showing that in 1932 it was sold by Messrs. Dixon and Hopkinson to a Mr. W. A. Webb, and that up until then it had remained a "silent" cinema. Mr. Webb refurbished the place and supplied new seats. More importantly, he installed the Classitone Sound System and on Boxing Day 1932, it was reopened as the Victoria Talking Theatre.

As it only seated three hundred patrons and served a very local community, The Victoria never elaborately advertised its existence or announced changes of ownership. The final owner of the building as a cinema was Fred Leatham. It appears that he bought the cinema in the early forties. He was responsible for installing Gyrotone equipment, as used by his brother at The Cinema. As soon as the War was over, Fred Leatham tried to radically improve the Victoria. The original chapel had been just under fifty feet in length, but an entrance hall had been added, presumably by Mr. Webb, by extending another ten feet towards Railway Street. Now a thirty foot extension was tacked on to the rear of the building, and the floor level raised. At balcony level the building was extended towards the street to match the ground floor. Much improved, it re-opened on 14th April 1947 with *"Dodge City"*.

The improvements were a heavy investment to make at

a time when the future was relatively uncertain. Fred Leatham was taking on a large mortgage at the Victoria about the same time as he took on the Rex, Wolverhampton. His brother-in-law helped out for a time by running the Victoria and later his sister and her son helped at the Rex but they were difficult times. For one period Fred Leatham managed to organize a "swop" with Sidney T. Collett of Market Drayton's "Town Hall", called the Ritz by Fred Leatham. Mr. Collett met disaster at the Victoria, and Fred Leatham returned to face its final struggles. There was a last minute switch to RCA equipment and the installation of cinemascope but really the battle was lost and the Victoria "faded away" sometime in 1955 or 1956.

Mr. Leatham wished to convert the building to industrial use in order to pay off his mortgage but planning permission for the change of use was refused. Although it seems ironical today, Tipton's Town Clerk at the time insisted that Railway Street was a residential area. Mr. Leatham appealed against the Council's decision and the Minister's Inspector heard the sad tale of his £4,000 loss on the sale of the Rex, Wolverhampton. In 1958 the fact remained that it was a residential area, and no extenuating financial circumstances seemed relevant to the inquiry.

Two years later, in 1960, the Victoria was finally sold to Horseley Bridge and Thomas Piggott Limited and was used as a store for wooden patterns. During the following decade the residential nature of Railway Street suffered considerable demolition and by 1974 the Victoria was left standing in glorious, but dilapidated, isolation. The name "Victoria Palace" and some of the ornamental frontage remained. Suddenly in about 1975, the building was demolished, Railway Street was truncated, and the area redeveloped for industrial use.

The Picture House — The Bruce

New Hall Street, Princes End, Tipton

In another far-flung part of Tipton, the Dudley to Wednesbury Road made its way through Princes End. The Tipton / Coseley boundary ran along the centre of the main road just at the time when the two Urban District Councils sat down to discuss the letters they had received from the County Council informing them of the Cinematograph Act and the delegation of power to issue licences to a very local level. New Hall Street is at right angles to that main road, opposite Bradley's Lane, which brought the Bruce closer to Coseley's cinemas than to the others in Tipton.

Leaving the main road, the Bruce was a small cinema to be found on the left-hand side of New Hall Street, although nothing is to be found of it today. Locally it is always said that it was originally owned by Joseph Pearson. He certainly owned it from the time of the First World War until 1922, but the original proprietor, according to the records was a Mr. B.T. Parsons. In July 1912 he submitted plans to the local council for the conversion of a chapel into a cinema. Little is known about Mr. Parsons other than that he appears to have lived in Pensnett, and he had a "sleeping partner", a Mr. Rhodes, when it came to financing the cinema. As far as the chapel is concerned it is thought to have been a Baptist Chapel of 1871.

The former chapel opened as the Princes End Picture House on 18th November 1912, and Joseph Pearson, mentioned above, was probably the first projectionist, although working as a chain-maker by day.

The Victoria, Railway Street, Horseley Heath, Tipton, 5th August 1968. (Alan Price)

Sometime early in its career as a cinema the frontage was heightened and the name "Picture House" appeared across the top of the facade. The apex of the original gable end can be seen rising above the centre of this facade in the illustration. The small entrance was flanked by boarded-up windows that were covered in boards advertising the programmes; Monday to Wednesday on the left, Thursday to Saturday on the right. This tradition was preserved even when purpose-built display cases, by Girosign, were added in 1948. In the early days five hundred patrons were squeezed into the building but when seating improved this was reduced to three hundred and fifty.

It was an unpretentious cinema in an unpretentious working class area but it had a magic all of its own. To the locals, its plain appearance earned it the nickname, "The Brewus" or "Brew-House", as small out-buildings used for making home-made beer were called in the Black Country. It was therefore unique in the sense that its nickname eventually became its real name.

"The Brewus" or "The Pictures" served Princes End in the same way that the Victoria, or "Darby's" or "Page's," or "The Bump" all served their local communities. In 1920, while Joseph Pearson was running The Picture House, his position in Princes End was threatened by the proposed arrival of a new much larger purpose-built cinema. This would have been called The Victory and would have had the advantage of occupying a prominent site in the High Street. It was promoted by Mr. Thornton and designed by Harold Tomkys, but it never materialised. Mr. Thornton eventually appeared in Tipton as a partner to Mr. Suffolk in the acquisition of the Alhambra, Dudley Port. Joseph Pearson, unfortunately, went bankrupt running the Picture House and gave up the task towards the end of 1922, blaming the cost of films and the effect of unemployment on his takings

He was followed by Mr. and Mrs. Jones who seemed undaunted by Joseph Pearson's problems and, in fact, they went on to make a great success of the Picture House, and even expanded their cinema activities to include leasing a cinema in Wednesbury for a while. They introduced Fred Leatham to the cinema business by asking him to play the piano accompaniment in silent days, and became local legends themselves.

The Picture House opened its doors seven days a week for a time because on Sundays it was used by the Rev. John Young, Minister of the New Hall Street Baptist Church, for talks and lantern-slide shows after evening service, and possibly some enthusiasts were there seven nights of the week as one ex-resident of the street remembers seeing the same people going night after night! This period, in the mid-twenties, has often been recalled in letters to the local press and many people have written to me about it. I will quote one letter, from Eddie Jones, recalling the fascination of Princes End's cinema:

"It was a very low small place, but heaven to us kids and the folks around. It had long hard benches at the front, more benches in the middle, padded and plush covered, and rows of "select" chairs at the back with elbow rests: 3d, 7d and 9d in old money. My mates and I would go to the Saturday afternoon show and Mrs. Jones would walk around with a very long cane to rap anyone misbehaving. Half way through the show a smoked glass slide was flashed on the screen. The writing on the smoked glass slide was scratched with a pin and on the screen was :—

Grand Talking Film Monday — Come Early.

Round about that time the talkies were just being installed around Birmingham. Comes Monday night we managed to get in, "standing up". The big picture came on accompanied by some scratchy music, and a man's voice trying to keep up with the man on the screen. I could hear one of my mates trying to stifle a laugh with his fist in his mouth. It was obvious we were being swindled. There must have been a man and woman and an old wind-up gramaphone hidden up there. Well, there were cat-calls of, "Change the Needle!" and, "Put a cowboy on!". After five minutes a woman in the film began to sing, in silence, and on went the scratchy record. Ironically, the song was called "Am I Blue?", which did not fit at all.

Well, it finished up silent. We were disappointed but we had a good laugh. Funny, but Mr. and Mrs. Jones left early in the car.

Eventually the talkies did come and that episode was forgotten, or was it? There was always some comic in the audience that used to belt out, "Am I Blue?" on suitable occasions".

Sound came to the Picture House on BTH equipment, but those benches lasted until after the Second World War! By such time Mrs. Jones had disappeared from the scene and the cinema was owned by a Mr. MacDonald who ran the place with the aid of his family. Legend has it that his son was named Bruce and that he thought his name was being given to the cinema when he heard it called "The Brewus". The legend of Robert the Bruce was evoked by a spider-motif that appeared on Mr. MacDonald's notepaper.

After the War, Mr. MacDonald had ambitious plans for the rebuilding of his little cinema. In the summer of 1947, the architect, Edmund Wilford, (of Lyttleton, Halesowen, fame!) produced plans for a magnificent new super-cinema. It would have held just under a thousand patrons and would have changed the face of Princes End. The project was dropped and Mr. MacDonald settled for a change of name.

The Picture House officially became The Bruce at the beginning of 1948, with its new name mounted on the front of the cinema to prove it. Internally it had been considerably renovated. The low tunnel-like single floored auditorium was transformed by removing old Tentest panelling and treating the exposed bare brick

Above: The Bruce, Princes End in the 1950s.
(Doris Woodroffe)

walls with rough cast and stippled, the base colour being pale green and the relief gold and red. The dado, to a height of six feet, was painted a purple red and varnished to give some feeling of warmth. Old gas-fired radiators were removed and some basic central-heating installed. The entrance hall was also improved. Thus renewed, the Bruce marched confidently into the post-War era.

When Mr. MacDonald Junior sold the Bruce to Mr. and Mrs. Woodroffe in 1953 it was still a very busy place. They found it was sometimes impossible to pack everybody in! They refurbished the Bruce again, using the services of Modernisation Ltd., of Sheffield, thus bringing the son of one of the pioneers of cinematography, Mr. Friese-Green, to this little cinema.

With a certain amount of pride the Bruce outlived the Regent, and even before 1960 had once proudly recruited two girls who had worked at the Regent. With trade falling at the Alhambra it seemed likely that the Bruce would be Tipton's last surviving cinema, even though it never advertised in the press nor expected to serve anyone outside Princes End

If redevelopment threatened the cinema's existence, it first seemed likely that such a threat would come from

Allen's the nearest factory and employer of many of the patrons. However, it seems the Council had other ideas.

One local legend tells that the place was deliberately set on fire to speed up its demise as Princes Enders would never have forgiven anyone personally responsible for depriving them of their little cinema.

It has been difficult to establish the facts. It seems that it closed after the Council refused to renew the licence. Some items from the cinema were stored in the house next door and on 31st May 1962 a fire was started by vandals amongst some cushions stored there. The fire caused some damage to the cinema itself, and soon afterwards it was compulsorily purchased by the Council.

No one, after exhaustive enquiries, seems to be quite certain when the last film was shown. The Tipton Herald, reporting the fire, said that the cushions had been in store since Saturday 26th May 1962. Possibly that was the date of the last film show at the Bruce; if not, it was probably during that month. Considering this is one of the few such cinemas where the opening date has been established, and considering that it lasted into the sixties, it seems amazing that the date of its last show can only be guessed — but that is part of the intriguing character of the cinemas from the smaller Black Country communities.

Oldbury and Langley Green

Having entered the Black Country at Smethwick, at the beginning of this section, it is logical to continue further into the region via the old Birmingham – Dudley road – known to local readers of a certain age as the B87 bus route. This brings us through West Smethwick, where we encountered the Ring Palace, and on into Oldbury.

Oldbury was rather overshadowed by the progress of Smethwick and West Bromwich. It became an Urban District, in Worcestershire, in 1894, and acquired "Borough" status in 1935. As a town it was heavily industrialised, and suffered badly when these industries declined. It had a well-defined centre, but the population which supported it moved away as result of all the urban upheavals of the twentieth century. In local government terms it ceased to exist as an autonomous authority when subsumed into "Warley" in 1966.

Several developments revitalised the old central area of Oldbury – e.g. the arrival of the "Savacentre" in 1980 (A joint Sainsbury's and BHS project) started a retail revival, and in the late 1970s Oldbury was chosen as the place to accommodate a new Civic Centre for the new Metropolitan Borough of Sandwell. Law courts, a new ring-road, and further retail developments have continued the process of "destroying Oldbury in order to save it"! On land developed by the Black Country Development Corporation, who had their headquarters in the old Accles & Pollack's offices in Oldbury, hoardings were erected in the 1980s to announce the arrival of a huge multi-screen cinema, but so far nothing has materialised. Meanwhile the Oldbury that included the cinemas described in this chapter has almost disappeared under the new landscape.

Once we have looked at the cinemas once to be found in the centre of Oldbury, we will venture out to the village of Langley Green, close to the Albright & Wilson chemical factories, and the home of BIP – British Industrial Plastics.

The Palace

Freeth Street, Oldbury

Oldbury has returned to life in recent times with the building of the Savacentre but the new development obscures the site of Oldbury's first cinema: The Palace.

The story begins at The White Swan, popularly known as "The Museum", in Church Street. In 1910 the licensee was Jas Tyrer and Music Hall entertainment had long been provided at the White Swan. He applied to make alterations to the building in order to show films, but before doing so he acquired a seven year lease on premises in Freeth Street. (For subsequent events in Church Street; see "The Grand").

Once established in Freeth Street, Jas Tyrer spent £350 converting the new premises into a cinema. The conversion was designed by G. Bowden, of Smethwick, and was carried out by H. Banner. The Palace opened, a week later than intended, on Monday 7th November 1910, with a programme that included "Lady *Helen's Escapade* " and "*Fun on the Tom-Tom* ". It was managed by the proprietor's son, Billy Tyrer, later to manage the Cosy Corner, Halesowen, and various Odeons, including the one in Bilston.

An item appeared in The Stage of 2nd November 1911 indicating that the Palace Oldbury was celebrating its first anniversary on that day. This was an Anniversary Benefit for Mr. Tyrer and proved very successful.

A cryptic report appears in the Weekly News for 14th September 1912: Jas Tyrer denies that his cinema is to close and assures everybody that he now has a fourteen year lease. He then adds, "I have recently taken over similar places of amusement at Dudley Port and Pensnett". The former refers to the Alhambra during a chequered period of its early history, but the latter is more of a mystery. (See the section on Pensnett.). It also marks the beginning of a confusing period of this cinema's history.

In 1913 it appears to have been operating as the Cosy Picture Palace. By 1915 it was "Tyrer's Palace" and the proprietor was identified as Mrs. Tyrer. On 17th April 1916 it reopened as the Premier Kinema, having been reconstructed for a Mr. G. H. Gosling. It seems that a balcony was put in at this time, with accommodation for 85, and 345 tip-up seats were installed downstairs. The work was carried out by a Mr. Bailey, and the Premier Kinema opened with "*Whom the Gods Would Destroy*".

It closed yet again in 1917 and reopened on 13th August 1917 as the Palace Theatre, with *"East is East"*. Some continuity is implied by the fact that the proprietors were Premier Cinemas Ltd. By the end of the year another change had taken place and it became the Palace of Varieties, controlled by Joe Day.

After all these changes some stability was restored towards the end of 1919 when it was acquired by Charles H. Dent. Eventually he replaced the original building by erecting a brand new cinema behind it. This was a much larger hall, capable of holding just over a thousand patrons, and had basic stage facilities incorporated in its design. I have not discovered who was the architect but it seems that the builder was William Jackson.

The "New Palace", opened on Easter Monday, 9th April 1928, with *"The Phantom of the Circus"*. It was managed by Charles Dent's son, John Marshall Dent. The follothwing year the New Palace brought the talkies to Oldbury on 9th. December 1929 with *"The Trial of Mary Dugan"*. The better known *"Broadway Melody"* ran for the second half of the week. BTP equipment was used.

*Right: The Palace, Oldbury, awaiting demolition in the latter half of the 1970s. This is the 1928 frontage of the much rebuilt and enlarged cinema. Unfortunately no picture of The Palace in its earlier incarnations has been found.
(Ken Day)*

*Bingo players queue up outside the former Palace, Oldbury, for a last night of Bingo. Second from the left is Lucy Day who had been a regular player at the club.
(Ken Day)*

Having extended his cinema interests to the Black Country it seems that Mr. Dent looked around for further possibilities of expansion. In 1933 Mr. Hurley Robinson produced some plans for him for a cinema in Warley but the scheme was dropped when the Warley Cinema materialised. However, in the spring of 1935 it became possible to acquire the Regent at Langley, and from then on John Marshall Dent ran both cinemas. Mr. Dent retained an interest in live "Variety" and sometimes the cinema insisted on being called "The Palace of Varieties".

When film business declined Variety still seemed an alternative. The Palace closed on Sunday 30th April 1961 with a one day showing of "*The Private War of Major Benson*", starring Charlton Heston. The adverts claimed that it was closed for, "Repairs and Renovations".

It re-opened later as the Palace Variety Club but gradually forsook Variety for Bingo. The "variety" element was compered by Ron French, and "stars" sometimes made an appearance if they could be brought over to The Palace from the Langley Variety Club. The stars included Vince Hill, Ray Alan, and even Matt Munro.

In the early seventies it was acquired by the Noble Organisation, who continued to run it as a Bingo Club for a few years until it was demolished. For a while it had dominated the devastated approach to Oldbury from Brades Village and then it seemed to vanish overnight. The location is now obscured by the building of the "Savacentre", which has its back to Freeth Street. Freeth Street itself looks out on Sandwell's new Civic Centre.

The Picture House
(later known as the Savoy)

Birmingham Street, Oldbury

Following Mr. Tyrer's success in bringing cinema to Oldbury, others tried to emulate his example. In the Spring of 1911 Alfred Griffiths applied for a licence to show films at the Portway Hall, the matter was adjourned and presumably failed. Albert Bradley acquired the Market Hall next to the canal bridge in Birmingham Street and was granted a licence to show films there at the end of April.

Using the name, Picturedrome, the ex-Market Hall appears to have opened as a cinema on 1st May 1911. Jas Tyrer, at The Palace, had opposed both licence applications, but from now on he had to accept competition. Such a state of affairs may not have lasted very long as the Picturedrome ceased advertising in July. It appears to have closed in order to be rebuilt to make it more like a cinema. Messrs. Harper and Sons carried out the work and by the time they had finished it could hold 400 patrons.

It reopened as the Picture House on 25th November 1911. A Mr. Sam Leonard came from Lancashire to run the place, but it is not clear for whom! The anonymity of the new undertaking suggests that possibly Thomas Leach had acquired it, the Picture House was certainly his by the First World War. Sam Leonard continued to present the twice nightly shows of "*Animated Pictures & Comedy Acts*" for a time, but Mr. A. Robbins, another of Mr. Leach's brothers-in-law eventually replaced him.

During the mid-twenties the Picture House was entirely rebuilt to the plans of Mr. Way Lovegrove. He produced a building of considerable height in order to accommodate more than one thousand patrons on a fairly small site. Miles Jervis II later complained that the seats were extremely close together and even a person of average height was forced to squeeze into his seat sideways. Even the operators worked in cramped conditions. Wilf Hollyhead recalls working there in a tiny room barely six and a half feet high and lacking adequate ventilation. Despite all its faults, the facade was quite impressive as can be seen from the illustration.

The "new" Picture House opened in 1926, three years before the "new" Palace. When the latter installed BTP sound equipment the Picture House did the same thing, introducing talkies on 27th January 1930. Towards the end of the thirties it was leased to F.J. Emery, and generally seemed run-down compared with the Palace. On becoming part of F.J. Emery's circuit it seems to have become the Savoy.

In 1946 Miles Jervis II acquired the freehold, and then the lease. He had few illusions about the Savoy and was not particularly impressed with Oldbury as a town in

Above: Behind this "Peace Procession" of the period immediately after the First World War, it is possible to catch a glimpse of the Picture House, Oldbury, before its replacement with the building seen below. (Ken Rock)

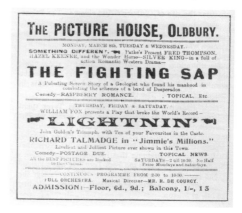

Below: Thomas Leach's new Picture House, Oldbury, as rebuilt in 1926 to the plans of Mr. Lovegrove. It was a lofty building with a steeply raked balcony. (Chris Clegg)

The 1926 interior of The Picture House, Oldbury, complete with orchestra pit where

Mr. De Courcy led the "full orchestra". (Kevin Weelan Collection)

which to show films. Miles Jervis found that the auditorium was so lofty that it was impossible to keep warm and the acoustics were terrible. He installed BA equipment and added extra speakers including special dimensional speakers to face the balcony but to no avail.

Perhaps it is not surprising that the Savoy closed on 22nd March 1958, by which time Miles Jervis was much more committed to West Bromwich. Jack Palance starred in *"I Died A Thousand Times"* on the final night, but the first half of the last week had paid tribute to cinema history with a revival of *"Gone With The Wind"*. After the cinema had closed a notice appeared on the entrance doors exclaiming:

"Closed — At least until the result of the budget is known".

The budget produced a small cut in entertainment tax but apparently it was not enough to persuade Miles Jervis to reopen a cinema for which he had no particular liking!

The Savoy was sold to the Midland Electricity Board but a decade later people were complaining that it had ceased to be used and was becoming an eyesore. It seems that Warley Council purchased it towards the end of the sixties and it was demolished in May 1970.

The Grand

Church Street, Oldbury

Oldbury's least known cinema was to be found next-door to the White Swan in Church Street. (The pub still exists at the time of writing). As explained in the chapter on the Palace, Jas Tyrer had managed the White Swan during the first decade of this century and the place had incorporated a "music hall" for some time. In 1912 the Wolverhampton and Dudley Breweries Ltd., proposed separating the entertainment facilities from the public house by building a purpose-built hall alongside it. Plans were produced by Frank Jones.

On 17th December 1912 Ben Kennedy applied for a music and singing licence for the hall and it was granted. Presumably as soon as possible after that date he opened the hall, calling it "The Tivoli". (See the chapter on Ben Kennedy to appreciate the growth of his Black country empire.) It seems to have become the Grand when it was reopened on 15th February 1915 by a Mr. W. H. Vaughan. He included films between the variety acts and claimed, "Our aim is respectability". I am not sure whether this deterred patrons or attracted them, but Mr. Vaughan had intended the latter and had gone to some trouble to refurbish the hall and decorate it in the flags of the allies. Mr. Vaughan ran the Grand until the early twenties.

In 1923 the proprietors had become Messrs. Redfern and Stoddard. They owned a Birmingham typewriter firm but ran cinemas as a sideline. They had one in Coventry, and, for a time, one in Willenhall. By a twist of fate the Grand was managed for them by Jas Tyrer until February 1924. The Grand carried on until at least 1926. No-one seems sure when it closed, or ceased showing films, but it seems to have well and truly faded from the Oldbury scene by the time the talkies arrived in 1929.

Langley & Langley Green

Langley sits above the Eastern Boundary Fault, where the Ten Yard Seam suddenly drops to greater depth beneath the surface originally putting it "out of reach". Consequently, to the southeast of this fault towns like Smethwick are not part of the Black Country according to the geological definition! Langley grew rapidly after the building of the Titford Canal and the opening of the Langley Forge. The Forge premises, the Canal and other interesting buildings, like the Maltings, still exist but the area has been transformed many times. When I first encountered Langley's Regent cinema it stood almost alone in Crosswells Road as if Langley had been mysteriously removed from around it. Langley became a ward within the Urban District of Oldbury as created in 1894, and subsequently became part of the Borough of Oldbury. Langley, home of The Institute, and Langley Green, home of The Regent, were separated by the railway which arrived in the 1860s.

Below: The 1920 version of Langley's cinema

The Langley Institute, later The Palace

High Street, Langley

The first cinema in Langley was the result of an early venture by Sidney Bray. Films were shown in the hall of the Langley Institute, which had been built as a Temperance Hall in 1878. The shows may have started as early as 1910, and legends tell of films being made featuring local people and being shown at the Institute Hall. All the facts seem obscure but it seems certain that from 1913 onwards Wally Davis was running the place for his brother-in-law. It seems likely that he returned after the First World War and may have presented films in Langley until taking control of the Palace, Brownhills, in 1924.

The Institute Hall then seems to have been taken over by Mrs. B.L. Clamp, and the kine licence was renewed in her name up until 1931. I am not even certain when it was first called "The Palace". The earliest advertisements I have seen using that name date from summer 1927.

The Palace was still showing films three nights a week in December 1930 and had apparently experimented with "sound-on-disc", but seems to have admitted defeat with the coming of the sound era. For some reason it was known locally as, "The Snob" and one legend that still survives in Langley concerns the female "one-man-band" that accompanied the films for a time. Apparently she played six instruments at once — better than a "Bijou Orchestra"!

The Regent
(later known as the Astra
and the Milan)

Crosswells Road, Langley Green

After the First World War the Langley Cinema Company was formed to provide the community with a proper purpose-built picture house. Among the directors were Dr. Broughton, a leading local public figure and member of Worcestershire County Council, William Jackson, who was about to build the cinema, and Abel Round, a Birmingham architect who designed it, and Edward Bayliss. They acquired a site in Crosswells Road on land which had once been part of Showell's Crosswell Brewery of 1870. The maltings associated with this brewery, but on the other sie of the railway have become well known local landmarks and are listed.

Dr. Broughton performed the official opening at a ceremony held on 26th January 1920, and the first film was, *"Out of the Shadows"*. It seems that William Jackson, the builder, had made the major contribution towards creating the cinema by actually building it and was probably paid in shares, thereby taking control of the cinema and the company. It was known at first simply as "The Langley Cinema".

It did its best to keep up with the Oldbury cinemas even when they were renewed as the twenties went on. The talkies arrived in Langley four months after coming to the Picture House, Oldbury. Langley's first talkie, *"The Rainbow Man"* opened on 7th April 1933.

Below: The Regent, Langley, as opened in 1933.

Perhaps the success of the talkies convinced William Jackson that the cinema business had sufficient future to make it worth rebuilding the Langley Cinema on a grander scale. It closed on 27th May 1933 with *"After the Ball"* and rebuilding started straight away. The original balcony was enlarged, a new ceiling supplied, a new lounge and cafe put in, and a new impressive frontage was erected. This has looked austere in recent years but in 1933 was relieved by an elegant canopy and by the cinema's new name across the top of the facade. Obviously the work was done by William Jackson, and proceeded very quickly.

Thus renewed, the auditorium could hold 1200 patrons and was internally decorated in rich cream and pale green. New sound equipment by British Acoustic was installed, and Langley now had a cinema that could easily compare with the two rivals in Oldbury. From now on it was to be called "The Regent". The Ideal Kinema for 9th November 1933 reported on the rebuilding of Langley's cinema:

"How effectively a kinema can change its appearance from just an ordinary entertainment centre into a superstructure possessing all the comfort and amenities one associates with the 1933 home of entertainment is aptly demonstrated at Langley....

The front elevation is carried out in rustic brick, with stone surrounds to the entrance, and white cement facings at the sides and around the windows, whilst the whole is topped with a massive stone top in which the theatre title has been cast. There is an ample canopy running the whole length of the front of the house, above which are four long narrow windows glazed in warm-toned glass.

In the auditorium the decoration scheme is bold, carried out in acoustic plaster following the panel style of design, using pastel shades against the general design of deep orange shading through to pale lemon. The screen curtains are an old gold tone, having a deep border and a hand-painted jazz design, in which gaily-coloured balloons etc., take a prominent position.

The projection department is housed on the third floor level, and is equipped with BTH sound apparatus, which functions with the latest Ross projectors."

The Regent opened at 3 p.m. on 4th September 1933. William Jackson welcomed everybody from the stage, accompanied by Edward Bayliss and F.S. Sandover, the General Manager, and both directors of the original company. Mr. Sandover later left the Regent to take over the West End, Whitmore Reans. Mr. Jackson regretted that Dr. Broughton could not be present, and declared the cinema open. The first programme featured **"Just My Luck",** starring Ralph Lynn.

Barely two years later, in April 1935, the Regent was acquired by Mr. Charles Dent and therefore joined forces with one of its Oldbury rivals; the Palace. From then on it seems to have survived successfully and uneventfully until circumstances changed almost thirty years later.

Its first closure came on 14th August 1965, when **"I've Got A Horse",** starring Billy Fury, was shown, supported by **"Carry On Teacher".** From that date onwards its history is as obscure and as complicated as that of any tiny pre-First World War cinema. Charles Dent's son, John Marshall Dent, first converted the Regent into a Variety Club and began for a week's trial run in that capacity at the beginning of November 1965. Over the next four years it opened and closed as a Variety Club several times.

The projectionist at The Regent, Langley Green, from 1955 until the late 1960s was Les "Taff" Evans, who was also well known as a drummer in local pubs. He combined work in the operating box with stoking the boilers and generally acting as caretaker and "key holder" for the cinema. When Marshall Dent decided to give up showing films and converted the premises to the Langley Variety Club, Les decided to stay and became involved with the day to day running of the club. His son Malcolm recalls that many of the stars who came to the club such as Bob Monkhouse, the Beverley Sisters, Mike Yarwood, Jess Conrad and the ventriloquist, Savine, parked their cars in his father's double garage nearby. Malcolm Evan's brother later married Rita Bradbury who had worked in the kiosk while the Regent was a cinema, and who also stayed to work at the club. The compere of the club was Ron French.

In the end Mr. Dent seems to have decided that business was better as a cinema. New luxury seating was intalled, a new wide screen and stereo sound. On 19th July 1969 it reopened as The Astra, with **"The Magnificent Seven".** It must .have closed yet again because on 30th

July 1970 it had a further reopening. This time it was decided to abandon the family audience and provide "adult films" on a club basis. Mr. Dent told the local paper that he thought the Astra would replace the late Prince's, Smethwick!

Mr. J.M. Dent died later in 1970 and the Palace and the Regent/Astra had to be sold. Tarsem Singh Dhami considered purchasing it but decided not to. It was eventually bought by Mr. Gupta, best known in the Black Country as a garage proprietor, but the story is still far from simple as he then leased it to a number of people.

On 3rd November 1973 it reopened as The Milan at 10 a.m. to present a children's matinee featuring **"Submarine X—L"** and **"Thunderbirds 6",** then all was quiet until the next day, Sunday, when **"A Clockwork Orange"** hit the screen. Once again it had been re-seated and redecorated, only holding 650 patrons, and Kalee 21 projectors were installed, having previously been in the Dale. I visited it early in 1974 and was very impressed with its bright cleanliness, the personal courtesy of the staff and its determination to survive. One surprise was that it was now calling itself the Regent once again! Surrounded by a demolished Langley, the staff told us that they hoped Brummies would drive out to the Regent to catch up with popular films they might have missed in the city.

Below: The Regent Langley in 1971 as "The Astra".

The last English-language film was probably shown in February 1976. It then adopted the name, "The Milan", once more and enjoyed some success in presenting Indian films. In fact Binesh Patel, one of the lessees, was "overwhelmed" by the Milan's success. In February 1978 the Milan was ordered to close by the Sandwell Health Department until various improvements were made. It seems that the problems were overcome and that films continued to be shown until the end of 1979 or beginning of 1980. The Express & Star of 14th January 1980 reported on the closure without being specific about date!

In March 1980 the Council approved an application to turn the cinema into a clothing factory from Mr. M. Lall. Stripped of any ornament the building survived a little longer. In March 1994 a fire destroyed part of the building and it was eventually demolished. Langley, as a village has seen some regeneration and has become home to The Barlow Theatre which began holding occasional film shows in 2010 – but that's another story.

Rowley Regis

The last part of Sandwell that we have to consider takes us to a completely different part of the Black Country. To an outsider there must seem to be no logic in the fact that Sandwell's boundary sweeps from Tipton, through part of Tividale and then up and over the ridge that physically divides the Black Country into two separate halves. Having crossed this ridge, the boundary of Sandwell encloses some small townships: Blackheath, Old Hill and Cradley Heath – townships that made up the old Urban District of Rowley Regis. This creates the odd situation in which the traveller from Dudley to Halesowen leaves the modern Dudley MBC at the boundary of Old Hill, once having crossed a stream called The Mousesweet Brook. While in Old Hill one is in Sandwell, although continuing southwards into Halesowen one is back in Dudley!

The reason for all this is that when Sandwell MBC was created in 1974 it was decided to include the former borough of Rowley Regis within its frontiers. The logic behind this was that the 1966 boundary changes had already brought Rowley Regis into the newly created County Borough of Warley, and Warley was logically going to be a constituent of Sandwell. If all this makes your head hurt it can be made worse by realising that Rowley Regis, traditionally part of Staffordshire found itself to be in Worcestershire from 1966 to 1974!

Cinemas were to be found in Blackheath, Old Hill and Cradley Heath, and each township will be dealt with in that order, rather than throw them all together into a "Cinemas of Rowley Regis" stew.

Blackheath

Blackheath has two faces. When approached from Quinton via Long Lane, passing the site of the Odeon, it seems a suburb of Birmingham. When approached from Dudley via Rowley Regis it seems part of the Black Country. The Kine Year Books usually listed Blackheath's cinemas in with those of Birmingham. This book restores them to the Black Country and puts on record the work of Thomas Cooper.

The Picture Palace

Cardale Street, Blackheath

The first cinema in Blackheath was the Picture Palace. It opened on Saturday 9th July 1910, when scenes from the life and funeral of Edward VII were included in the programme. Seats were sixpence and threepence, children were charged twopence. In its advertising it claimed to be, *The first cinema in the Midlands, and the finest*. It was certainly not "first" in the historical sense! It was managed by Mr. T. Kimberley, and probably operated in converted factory premises. However it has not proved possible to establish who had been responsible for creating it, and subsequently owning it.

It was still open at the end of 1912, but after the Pavilion opened in 1913, Thomas Cooper bought out the Picture Palace and closed it, presumably as just a matter of destroying any competition. It became a bakery and later a factory again.

Below: The Cardale Picture Palace photographed from a tethered baloon about 1912.

The Pavilion

High Street, Blackheath

The first purpose-built cinema in Blackheath was provided by Thomas Cooper. It seems that he owned the land at the time, and the cinema business seemed to be booming, therefore, he built one in the last four months of 1912. The Electric Picture Pavilion opened on 4th January 1913, with a programme that included *"Fire At Sea"*.

Following his success with the Pavilion, Thomas Cooper erected a cinema typical of each of the cinema-building eras. The Kings arrived in 1923 and the Rex in1938. When the latter opened, the Pavilion closed, but the story did not quite come to an end.

The building remained unused through the War years but after the hostilities Thomas Cooper planned further use for it. In 1948 plans were drawn by N. Hadley and Son to convert the Pavilion into a News Theatre. When this seemed too limited a use for the premises it was re-conceived as a multi-purpose ballroom.

It was re-opened in this capacity in May 1951 with a Staffordshire County Police Ball. The County Express 12th May 1951 wrote, *"The Rex Ballroom opened in Blackheath last Tuesday. The hall was the earliest cinema in the district and had remained un-used for many years. There is a new ceiling and floor, and patrons dance to Reg Heathcote and his band."*

However, as well as accommodating three hundred dancers, it was also hoped that plays and films would be presented there. The projection room and balcony seating were retained. A start was made in 1952 on installing new equipment and removable seats were made so that it could still be a News Theatre three or four nights a week. Then the idea was dropped.

A Cee Jay supermarket later occupied the site, almost opposite the Post Office, but for many years the exterior outline of the auditorium's roof could still be clearly seen from The Causeway, running behind the High Street.

The Kings

Long Lane, Blackheath.

After the First World War Thomas Cooper decided to build a larger, more impressive cinema. Like others at the time, he felt slightly uncertain about the future of the business and, therefore, built the hall as a fully equipped theatre.

Unfortunately details of the architect have not been found, but it was built by Thomas Willetts, a local builder who built several striking facades in terra-cotta and brick – i.e. not just the Kings, but also the Birmingham Road Methodist church.

It was certainly an imposing building, although the entrance was fairly modest. The Kings opened on Monday 2nd April 1923 with **"Dick Turpin's Ride To York"**. As a reflection of its size and importance it had an orchestra of six or seven musicians.

Despite the theatrical facilities, it was dedicated to showing films. It seems that it was only used as a theatre for about five weeks of its entire life! It was used a few times by a local amateur operatic society and once T.C. Pictures ran their own pantomime for a week.

Right: Mothers and children were invited to a show at the Kings Cinema, Blackheath, by the proprietor, Thomas Cooper in July 1929. They were not going to enjoy "Easy Payments" as advertised on the left of the entrance, but were going to watch Govern-ment made educational fims about childcare. Note the seats do not have upholstered backrests, and the entrance had not acquired a canopy at this time.
(Anthony Page Collection)

115

The Kings, Blackheath, in 1981. The canopy dates from cinema days. (Ned Williams)

Edibell Sound equipment was installed, and on 31st March 1930 the talkies arrived in Blackheath with *"The Broadway Melody"*. Its position in the town remained unchallenged until the Odeon opened in 1934. Thomas Cooper decided to fight back by building his own super-cinema; the Rex. Consequently the Kings slipped into third place in the town's pecking order of cinemas.

Ironically the Odeon was the first to close, perhaps reflecting the relative obscurity of its location. But if the Odeon could not survive long into the sixties, what chance did the Kings stand? The last show advertised in the County Express was for 3rd November 1962 when the beautifully elegiac *"Guns in the Afternoon"* was shown, but it seems that the Kings may have continued in business for anything up to another two or three years. (Local enthusiasts state that it closed during the winter of 1964/5 with *"The Absent Minded Professor".)*

It would be nice to think *"Guns in the Afternoon"* was the final picture because Randolph Scott and Joel MaCrea symbolised the kind of films that could endear the Kings to its patrons. Obviously Mr. Cooper put his best films in the Rex, but the "B" Westerns that ran at the Kings were more "popular" in a perveerse kind of way. After film presentation ceased the premises were used as a Bingo and Social Club in the auditorium, and as an amusement arcade in the entrance foyer.

Bingo ceased in 2010 and the building was closed.

The Rex

Halesowen Road, Blackheath.

As stated earlier, the arrival of the Odeon, in Long Lane, in 1934 upset Thomas Cooper's local monopoly of cinema entertainment in Blackheath. In building the Rex in Halesowen Road he re-asserted his position as Blackheath's "cinema king". The Rex was much closer to the centre of Blackheath than the Odeon.

The Rex was designed by Sidney H. Wigham, a Birmingham architect, and was built, by J. M. Tate and Sons, to accommodate fourteen hundred patrons. Its fortress-like solid brick presence is only relieved by six vertical windows at the balcony level. The four windows of the balcony lounge do not continue any verticals established at entrance level and it does not, therefore, enjoy the pleasing symmetry of some Satchwell and Roberts cinemas. Perhaps its regality was established by the stone window surrounds and cornices. Its name was certainly chosen to recall the royal associations of the local authority's name; Rowley Regis.

An organ chamber, and console pit in front of the stage, were provided but no organ was installed as Thomas Cooper was of the opinion that patrons came to see films, not hear music! The auditorium was finished in warm tones of russet and rose du barry in shaded plaster bands, above a green and black dado. New Kalee 11 projectors were installed but in about 1946 they were moved to the Kings, and were replaced with Kalee 12 machines. The British Acoustic sound system apparently did not suit the Rex and was eventually replaced with hybrid equipment that worked better.

The Rex opened on Sunday 25th September 1938 at 8p.m. with a special charity concert. Celebreties appearing at this concert inlcuded Harry Pell, Joseph Farrington, Austin Penzer and Gladys Slater. Gladys – lead soprano with the BBC singers – was a local girl from Springfield Road, Halesowen. Films commenced the following day with **"Owd Bob "** starring Will Fyffe.

Sunday concerts must have been a feature of life at The Rex, particularly when fund-raising was so important during the Second World War. One concert scheduled for 26th November 1944 starred Anne Ziegler and Webster Booth, supported by Jan Berenska's "salon orchestra", the Rowley Regis Girls Choir and local entertainer Harry Benet. The stars were delayed on their journey from Birmingham by extremely dense fog and Harry had to improvise an extra act.

As with other cinemas that opened just before the Second World War, its history was fairly uneventful and involved no major changes of structure or ownership. Small details changed, for example a larger screen was installed mid-week during the showing of **"Genevieve"** in the early fifties, but generally the Rex enjoyed a quiet life.

Below: The Rex, Blackheath, as a Bingo and Social Club in 1981. (Ned Williams)

The general decline in cinema business caught up with the Rex in 1968. On 6th July of that year it closed with a screening of the controversial film, **"Ulysses"**. The Rex advertised it as "The Film Sensation of All Time"! The chief operator, Bill Birch, who had also managed the cinema for the past eleven years, was sorry to leave. He had been in the cinema trade for twenty-two years and still hoped that he would find another job in that line. Also in the projection box on the last night was Fred Moore who had worked in The Rex in the mid 1950s. He later became well known as organiser of the annual Black Country B Western Festival, which brought Hollywood cowboys to meet their fans in Rowley Regis.

The Rex was leased to a company who turned it into a Bingo Club but it retained much of the appearance of a cinema, particularly in the fully-seated balcony. It was said that the projection equipment has remained up in the operating room as if waiting to return to life.

Bingo was presented at The Rex from 1968 until 1996, and this was followed by demolition. During the demolition the projectors were indeed found in the projection room, and were removed with the intention of being sold for further use. It seems that they were then smashed while being lowered from the projection room!

117

Odeon

Long Lane, Blackheath

During the period between the opening of the first Odeon at Perry Barr, and the opening of the Warley at the end of 1934, Oscar Deutsch had cinemas designed by a variety of architects without clearly establishing a recognisable house-style. After 1934 it was a different story, but Blackheath's Odeon belongs to that early stage of the development of the Odeon circuit.

The Perry Barr Odeon, in its strange Moorish style, had been designed by Stanley Griffiths, whose name will be familiar to Black Country folk, and Horace Bradley, an architect favoured by the Hewitsons in Smethwick. Stanley Griffiths was commissioned to design the Blackheath Odeon and produced something quite different to the cinema being built at the same time a mile or two away at Warley.

The long auditorium running parallel to Long Lane featured a cinema entrance in the centre of the side of the building, flanked by shops. The entire side wall, entrance and shops were finished in striking cream faience with black borders. When new, the effect was stunning, as can be seen in the photograph. The Art-Deco influence was strongly felt in the design of the leaded glass windows, and particularly in the abstract, but very geometrical, decoration of the interior. The auditorium contained 1,232 seats and was a striking exploitation of the stadium style, used again by Stanley Griffiths for the Kings at Stourbridge. It was built by Housing Ltd., and, like other Odeons, was fitted with BTH equipment.

The Odeon opened on 20th October 1934. Two local councillors shared the opening ceremony. Alderman J. B. Downing, Chairman of Halesowen U.D.C. made the first speech in which he praised the beauty of the cinema and pointed out that 1,200 houses had recently been built in the area surrounding the cinema. He was supported by Alderman B. Hobbs, the Mayor of Rowley Regis. Mr. R. H. Morgan, the M.P. for Stourbridge, and a veteran of cinema openings added a few remarks. Up in the operating room Harry Willis laced up the first films, including *"The Rise of Catherine the Great"*

starring Douglas Fairbanks Junior, and Frank Harvey began to familiarise himself with BTH equipment to prepare himself to open the Warley in six weeks time. Both men became veterans of Odeon openings, and Mr. Harvey later distinguished himself as manager of the Forum, Caldmore Green. It is also interesting to reflect on the fact that Oscar Deutsch opened seventeen cinemas in 1934!

The manager of Blackheath's new Odeon was Charles Crathorn who had come into cinemas via the world of dance hall management. He had cultivated an "Uncle Charlie" personality to attract junior patrons at one of his previous appointments, which proved useful in establishing the children's club at this cinema. He later managed the Odeon, Dudley.

Compared with town-centre Odeons, the one at Blackheath seems to have led a quiet backwater existence. It had a large car park and presumably hoped to serve more than the immediate local surrounding area, but it was possibly over-shadowed by the Warley Odeon and the Danilo at Quinton. It claims to have been the first Odeon to introduce a Children's Club but apart from that I have learnt little about its twenty-six years of life.

It closed on 19th November 1960 with *"Wild River"*, and then stood empty for a long time. In 1962 the idea of turning it into a bowling alley was considered, and Bingo was tried from 10th February 1967 onwards. Its most exciting further lease of life came when it was turned into a ballroom, but ballrooms are not popular with local residents and presumably they have found life quieter since the building became retail premises.

By the 1980s it had become a D.I.Y. supermarket run by the B. & Q. organisation. The exterior was preserved in general outline, and even the leaded windows survived. The Art Deco tiles were obscured by paint and the original harmony of the "frontage" was lost. Virtually nothing of the cinema interior remained. In 1984 the building was gradually cleared and it was decided to demolish the former Odeon. During demolition faded paintwork on the gable end of the adjoining building was exposed – revealing large Odeon lettering on the brickwork.

Left: The Odeon, in Long Lane, Black-heath, photographed in 1934. This was an Odeon that had the distinction of being designed by a Black country architect. (John Maltby)

Above: The impressive stadium-style interior of the Odeon, Long Lane, Blackheath, in 1934. *(John Maltby)*

Old Hill

Visitors to the Black Country who believe what they read on official signs will have noticed that in recent times Old Hill ceased to exist. It became part of Cradley Heath, in Warley, in Sandwell! Not so long ago the population of Old Hill was slightly larger than that of Cradley Heath, but perhaps an indication that the place was doomed to obscurity, was the fact that it only ever enjoyed the services of one cinema!

The Grand

Halesowen Road, Old Hill

The "Grandowd'ill" should be pronounced as one word as far as the local people who knew the place are concerned. For them the place has become a local legend, but for the historian the Grand is poorly documented.

Everyone associates the Grand with Benjamin Priest, and the nut and bolt manufacturing business that existed just behind the cinema. The Benjamin Priest, who founded the original firm in 1854, was the grandfather of the Benjamin Priest associated with the cinema. The latter was born in 1881, in Old Hill, and entered the family firm after completing his education. He seems to have developed an interest in the theatre, and later in the cinema, that led him to build the Grand. Whether it was purpose-built or converted from an existing building is not clear but, at the time of opening, it definitely saw itself as both theatre and cinema.

The Grand opened on Bank Holiday Monday, 4th August 1913, with members of the local council in the audience. They sat down to watch a programme of variety acts, which included the screening of Part One of a film called *"Our Navy"*. Part Two was screened the following week!

Left: The local Salvation Army band leads a Sunday School procession past the doors of The Grand, Old Hill. This entrance and the surrounding shops were built in front of the auditorium – as shown in the picture on the next page. (Ken Rock)

During the War Benjamin Priest met a factory inspectorwho had been an actor, James Broadhurst. It is said that it was he who introduced Ben Priest to the possibility of filming the Reverend Baring-Gould's novel, *"Bladys of the Stewponey "*. This heavy Victorian melodrama, written in 1897, had plenty of cinematic possibilities and Ben Priest, as soon as the War was over, formed his own production company to make such a film. James Broadhurst earned himself a part in the film.

"Bladys" went into production in 1919, directed by Lionel McBean, and photographed by Arthur Kingston, both of whom received praise for their work. The finished film ran for an hour and a half, and was given a press-preview at the Grand on 18th September 1919. Although the filming had created quite an interest locally, when the crew and cast descended on Kinver, the finished product does not seem to have caused so much excitement. After showing it at the Grand, Ben Priest did find a national distributor for the film but whether it was a great financial success seems extremely uncertain. It appeared at Black Country cinemas but was not strongly exploited for its local connections. It came to the Empire, Dudley, for example, for three days in 1922 without special attention.

The operator at the Grand when *"Bladys"* was first shown was Leonard Morgan. He worked at the Grand until 1946 and remembered the film being kept at the cinema. It is thought to have disappeared during structural alterations in 1958. Another view is that Ben Priest felt it was dangerous to store nitrate film in premises close to his factory during the second world.

He ordered the print of *"Bladys"* to be removed and destroyed. The problem with this theory is that the cinema would have been holding nitrate film on the premises anyway – just in the normal course of its business. (Film was not generally available on celluloid stock until after the war.)

In the years following the production of *"Bladys"*, the Grand still presented variety as the major part of its programmes. Films seemed to have a stronger future with the prospect of adding sound, and towards the end of the silent era Ben Priest expanded his cinema interests to include the Grand and Futurist at Kidderminster. For a time he also ran the Kinema at Kinver.

Western Electric equipment was installed at the Grand, and the talkies came to Old Hill on 5th December 1932 with *"Tarzan, the Ape Man"*. From then on it was mainly used as a cinema, although the stage was used by Cradley Heath Operatic and Dramatic Society on occasion.

For many many years the manager of the Grand was George Smith. He was there so long that he saw three generations of his patrons come to his cinema. He was a manager in the great tradition; smart and well dressed, always present to attend to the patrons. He had been an operator at the Royal, Cradley Heath, before going to the Grand, and at the latter he stayed until closure.

Early in 1950 advertisements started proclaiming, "Big Live Shows Coming Shortly". The last film was shown on Saturday 18th March 1950, *"The Small Black Room"*, starring Jack Hawkins. The following Monday

Right: The Grand, Old Hill, after closure as cinema and theatre, about 1960, as the front of the building was about to be rebuilt to re-open as the Plaza Ballroom.
(Fred Guy)

live shows started. They only appear to have lasted for about a year, but during that time there were several incidents on stage which attracted the attention of the National Press.

The Grand then languished, unused for a time, during which Ben Priest died on 23rd May 1954. He was buried at Kinver. His company was anxious to use the Grand as a warehouse and sought planning permission to do so in 1956. The council rejected the application on the grounds that Old Hill needed recreational facilities. In 1958 the company, therefore, submitted new proposals which involved using the ground floor as a warehouse, and using a first floor as a "public hall".

About 1960 it was sold by the Priest family and Mr. J. Regan converted the building to a dance hall; The Plaza Ballroom. The original facade, which included two shops as well as the cinema's entrance, was now obscured by a completely new frontage, designed by no less than Hurley Robinson and Son.

It enjoyed some success as the Plaza Ballroom, but in 1970 Halesbury Enterprises Ltd., applied for a Gaming Licence and the Plaza became a Bingo Club. It still survived in that role into the 1980s. The auditorium, which held just under nine hundred patrons, was cahanged completely but the exterior, behind the Hurley Robinson frontage, was a reminder of the Grand as a cinema. On a side wall a painted sign on the brickwork had almost weathered away, but a message concerning the price of the tip up seats was still just about discernable.

Bingo survived at the Plaza until Mrs. Regan's death in 2008. Once the building became unused it looked as if it

would finally disappear, but a surprise was in store. On 28th May 2010 the Plaza re-opened in a much-modified form as "The Platinum Plaza" with a Temptations tribute band taking centre stage. The club has been created by Ashok Kumar and the interior has been completely transformed for him by Nigel Cooke of IC Projects. Even the exterior of the building has enjoyed a complete "make-over" with aluminium cladding that gives the building a "platinum" appearance. One has to marvel at the ability of this building to re-invent itself again and again!

The Grand Old Man of the Cinema

This was the headline above the obituary of George Smith printed in the County Express as week after his death. George Smith was born in Cheltenham on 18th September 1880. He seems to have come to live in the Cradley Heath area by 1900, but left the area altogether in 1902 to work as an accountant in Nigeria. He was back, "on leave", about 1910 but contracted meningitis and never returned to Africa. Eventually he recovered and had to look for work.

He joined Walter Williams as a projectionist at either The Royal or The Empire, and may have been at The Royal when it opened on 3rd February 1913. The Grand, Old Hill, opened later in the same year and soon afterwards it seems that George left Walter Williams in order to take over management of The Grand. He stayed there for the rest of his life!

He had married Emma Louise Priest in 1912 and the family home was established in Halesowen Road, Old Hill where they had four daughters. The daughters had more to do with the cinema than their mother – who

121

regarded herself as a "cinema manager's widow". George had to be at the cinema six nights a week, and even if the family took a holiday in Kinver he still had to travel back to The Grand each night! George also spent a lot of time in Birmingham at trade shows etc., and became well known in the film trade where his booking skills were acknowledged in the days before film distribution was so "fixed up" in favour of the larger circuits. When Ben Priest took over the two cinemas in Kidderminster (The Grand and the Futurist) George booked for all three cinemas – but had little to do with Ben Priest's venture in Kinver.

As described above, films ceased at The Grand in 1950, but George Smith still had to book films for the Kidderminster cinemas. The Grand at Kidderminster closed on 7th February 1959, but the Futurist was still going strong when George died on 26th May 1960. George had died in his eightieth year, and films had not been presented in Old Hill for over a decade, but he was still working away at what he loved best – booking films!

Below: George Smith

Cradley Heath

In each of the towns surrounding the Stour Vale the local cinemas were dominated by the efforts of one man; in Cradley Heath it was Walter Williams; in Halesowen, Sidney Bray; in Old Hill, Benjamin Priest; in Blackheath, Thomas Cooper.

Cradley Heath has a long association with the iron trades in this part of the Black Country, namely the manufacture of hand-made nails and hand-made chain. Life in Cradley, on the opposite bank of the Stour, at the turn of the century has been vividly described by the late Cliff Willetts in his books, *"When I Was A Boy "* (published by Dudley Teachers Centre), and life in an industrial village was far from idyllic, and almost totally lacking the amenities associated with twentieth century urban life. However, Cradley Heath, on the northern bank of The Stour, seemed more "civilised", the growth of its late Victorian housing that followed the coming of the railway, and its High Street reflected a greater material prosperity. In Cradley Heath, theatres and cinemas became part of life on the northern slopes of the Stour Vale. We go from Old Hill which managed only one cinema to Cradley Heath which had several cinemas and a claim to several theatres even if only temporary ones!

The Palace

Spinners End, Cradley Heath

It is difficult to say with certainty who showed the first films in Cradley Heath but it seems likely that the honour fell to an obscure little cinema in Spinners End, between the St. Lukes vicarage and the G.W.R. Goods Yard. The space occupied by the cinema still exists today just to tantalise the historian who can find out so little about its past, but the fabric of the present building is less than thirty years old, and may be slightly larger than the original.

It may have been presenting cine-variety at the time of the passing of the Cinematograph Act. Walter Williams' son felt it was in business before his father started showing films at the Central, and that was in 1910. A brief report in the Dudley Herald of 20th May 1911 mentions that Sam Williams was continuing to put on good films and variety acts at the Palace, but the name normally associated with the Palace is Mr. W. Barnes. Locally it is sometimes still referred to as "Barnes' Palace".

Just one isolated advert in a Dudley Herald of 3rd February 1912 proudly claims that programmes of films and variety at the "New Palace" were presented twice nightly and patrons were advised that, "Trams pass the door"! Mr. W. Barnes claimed to be the proprietor and the manager was D. E. Barnes. From Mr. Barnes' licence application in August 1913 we learn that he could accommodate two hundred and fifty patrons in his Palace. One news item appearing in the County Advertiser of 21st February 1914 relates to a case in the local Police Court in which a wife accused her husband of desertion, but really this was an argument about finding theatrical digs. They are both described as actors appearing at the Spinners End Hippodrome. All these names and obscure snippets of information are all there is to be found regarding the story of this strange enterprise in Spinners End.

How long it continued to exist I do not know. I imagine that it closed sometime during the First World War. It seems that Walter Williams purchased its projector and possibly some of the benches.

The Central

Foxoak Street, Cradley Heath

At the turn of the century Walter Williams was a gentlemen's outfitter, who had premises in Cradley Heath High Street. He was fascinated by the world of theatre and variety, and eventually by cinematography and still photography.

Early in 1910 he rented a hall that had been used as a roller-skating rink behind the Empire known as The Empress Skating Rink. He opened this as "The Central". It could accommodate about eight hundred patrons and had an entrance in Foxoak Street, where it adjoined the Salvation Army Barracks, and a narrow entrance reached from Newtown Lane. The original opening date is obscure but 25th September 1910 was advertised in the press as a "Grand Re-opening".

In 1912 Walter Williams planned a new "Central Picture Hall", but this became the Royal when it opened early in 1913. He does not however, seem to have closed the Central immediately because he renewed its kine licence in August 1913.

The Royal

Bank Street, Cradley Heath

As mentioned above, in 1912 Walter Williams decided to build a brand new purpose-built cinema behind his premises in the High Street. The site was originally occupied by the chain shops associated with these premises in earlier times. The original front entrance of the building faced Bank Street, a small side-street from Cradley Heath High Street.

Behind the usual concertina metal gates, steps led up to two entrances on either side of a central box office. At that time the auditorium was a single floor and the entire building, including the stage, occupied an area that later formed the auditorium alone. Even so it was claimed that it could hold nine hundred and fifty patrons. (Cradley Heathens must have expected a squash whenever they sought entertainment). The Royal Electric Theatre opened on Monday 3rd February 1913 with *"Dante's Paradise"* and *"The Black Mask".* The following week The Royal presented the famous silent film of the life of Christ: *"From the Manger to the Cross".* Four prices of admission ranged from fourpence to a shilling, but later these were reduced. After the first shows variety acts were included between the films, presented on a very temporary stage with a proscenium arch made of canvas. The relatively large stage and fly-tower were added after the 14/18 War.

When a large section of Cradley Heath High Street collapsed and subsided early in 1914, The Royal was quick to take advantage of the situation. On 21st February 1914 it advertised that the following week's shows would include locally made films of the disaster. These were films shot by Walter Willaims and his projectionist – and they would be regarded as real treasure if rediscovered somewhere today.

Walter Williams always took a very personal interest in running the Royal, and did not install a manager. He made films himself of local scenes, such as workers leaving local factories, and showed these at the Royal. Apart from the proprietor, a few other people made a name for themselves at the Royal, including Mr. Barrs Partridge who went on to the Central, Stourbridge and, eventually the City of Birmingham Symphony Orchestra. As he was a Cradley Heath man, the Royal was proud of the fact that he had played the violin for a time at the local cinema. On 23rd. December 1923 the

Right: The Royal, Cradley Heath, as seen from Bank Street in 1981. Note the fly-tower and very strange emergency exit from the balcony seats. By this time the entrance to the cinema was on the extreme right of the picture, as the High Street entrance led only to the amusement Arcade.
(Ned Williams)

The Royal. Cradley Heath: Top left: The Royal as seen from Bank Street in the 1920s. (Ken Rock) Top Right, unknown operator with the Simplex projector. Walter Howard Williams in the Projection room. (Mrs. Williams) Left: The High Street entrance in 1981.

Opposite page: Contrasting styles of cinema entrances at the Royal, Cradley Heath:
Top left: A 1920s post card view of the Royal's original entrance in Bank Street. (Ken Rock)
Bottom left: The 1930s entrance in Cradley Heath High Street, photographed in 1981 when it only provided access to the amusement arcade established in the foyer.

Right: Simpex projectors in the Royal's ground floor operating room. The gentleman in the lower picture is Walter Howard Williams, son of the original proprietor. (Mrs. Williams)

----

chief operator, Harry Johnson, distinguished himself with his prompt action in dealing with a film fire. In an incident that many operators encountered every now and again, he tore the burning film from the machine and extinguished the fire with only a brief interruption to the performance. He was also well known locally as a champion ox-roaster! Joe Cockin was well known as the chucker-out but his other duties included stoking the boiler. One day he was found dead in the firebox door.

It seems that the circle was added sometime after the First World War, possibly at the same time as the stage and fly-tower were built. This was another case of a local cinema hedging its bets and installing stage facilities just in case the audience grew weary of films. The Royal added sound when the talkies arrived but had to put up a notice stating, "Silence while the talking pictures are on", as the patrons were used to explaining the story to each other and commenting on what they saw! The first talkie shown at The Royal was presented on 24th January 1932. The major updating of The Royal came in the late thirties when it was decided to build a new entrance in the High Street. The plans were drawn by Clarence Bloomer, and were approved in November 1936. The work was completed in time for a grand reopening on 29th August 1938 with ***"Heidi"***, starring Shirley Temple.

The new entrance, and various alterations made at the same time, brought The Royal up to a new standard. British Acoustic Duosonic Sound was installed, plus new festoon curtains, modern chandeliers etc. The owners claimed that this had nothing to do with competition from the Majestic! Apparently The Royal did not suffer any great fall in attendance after the opening of its new rival. Even so, The Royal had installed its own small organ for a time, played by Nelson Dingley, as if they acknowledged that William Sykes was establishing a powerful reputation at their nearest rival cinema.

Walter Williams was helped in running the Royal and Empire by his son, Walter Harold Williams, and by his

daughter who worked in the pay-box at the Empire. However, towards the end of the War he decided, with the family's agreement, to sell the Royal.

On 30th June 1945 the Royal was sold to Howard Lee, but within a year or two of acquiring it, Mr. Lee died, and his daughter, Isobelle Dorsett, had to run it, on behalf of the trustees. The Royal thus proved itself to be one of the great survivors of the cinema business. It outlived the Majestic and all the other surrounding cinemas. Once the last in line to receive new films due to "barring", the Royal survived into an age when such considerations were almost irrelevant.

In the long battle to survive, Mrs. Dorsett, and her son Michael Dorsett, tried many experiments to encourage business at the Royal. A Saturday Morning Film Club for children was operated for a time, and, as recently as March 1976, Sunday night variety shows were tried. Sunday-opening never came to Cradley Heath and so the cinema operated on a six-day licence. However the variety shows were presented as club-nights and for sixty pence members could enjoy monthly shows. It was the first use of the stage for variety for fifty years! The stage had not been used for any purpose at all since one week in 1945 when the local Operatic Society had last mounted their show on its boards. The experimental Sunday shows were short-lived.

Michael Dorsett felt he had really had to start taking care of The Royal as early as 1962, and later recalled how they had struggled to revamp the cinema, as well as try to encourage new business. He remembers buying the festoon curtains and some seats from the Regent, Brownhills, when that cinema closed.

Later the entrance and foyer facing the High Street were converted to an amusement arcade and fruit machines and space-invaders provided "somewhere to go" for young Cradley Heathens. The balcony was closed but three hundred people could be accommodated in the stalls and reached their seats from an entrance in Bank Street – an entrance sligthly to the side of the origianl entrance. History turns full circle! Two ageing Simplex projectors ground away in the original operating room at the back of the stalls and while waiting for the film to start it was interesting to look around and wonder what might date from 1913, from the twenties, or the late thirties.

I enjoyed several memorable visits to the Royal. One Sunday afternoon, 25th January 1970, myself and my fellow members of Uralia Films of Dudley, went to see the premiere of a 16 mm. film called ***"Amber"*** made and presented by "Film Group 32", another bunch of local amateur film-makers! The Royal was packed, even the Mayor of Warley, Councillor Harold Jackson, was present. The thirty minute horror film was well received, and it seemed fitting, even then, that the Royal should be the scene of such an unusual event. On another occasion I sat in the balcony one Saturday night and saw a cat walk across the stage in front of the screen. Such bizarre moments are seldom witnessed in

125

mighty Odeons and all who love little independent cinemas should have made at least one pilgrimage to the Royal before it was too late.

In November 1979 a planning application was made to Sandwell Council to turn the building, or the site, into a supermarket or "market hall". There was opposition from other local traders and the planning committee did not approve. With the strange momentum the Royal possessed, it was still showing films when the region's first multiplex opened at the nearby Merry Hill Shopping Complex in 1988. By then Michael Dorsett had modernised the projection facilities by installing two Phillips FP7 projectors. At first it looked as if the arrival of the multiplex at Merry Hill was not going to damage The Royal.

This feeling did not last long. In October 1988 The Royal "faded away". This term is used to describe the process because – amazingly – no one seems quite certain when the last film was shown! At the time films were being shown from Fridays until the following Wednesday. (The cinema did not open on Thursdays.) Two part-time projectionists were working at The Royal. Jim Spittal worked on Monday nights, and John Boast worked the other nights. The projectionists' log book shows that *"Jungle Book"* was being shown during the penultimate week but audience figures were so low that occasional shows were being cancelled. The one or two people who turned up were sent home. It looks as if a film called *"Frantic"* opened on Friday night, 29th October 1988. That evening was the last to be recorded in the projectionists' log book. What happened on the Saturday is not clear. Michael Dorsett himself cannot remember. On the Monday Michael Dorsett rang Jack Spittall to say, "Don't come in – we're closed." And that seems to be the end of that. What a sad demise for one of the Black Country's great cinema survivors.

Even while awaiting demolition The Royal seemed to "hang on", and was not finally demolished until 2006. The whole area once dominated by The Royal is now a vast Tesco store and associated carpark.

The story continued in a sad vein as The Royal awaited its fate. I visited the closed cinema on several occasions – always expecting each visit to be the last. Michael Dorsett would often show me a feature of the cinema I had not previously appreciated. I remember one occasion when I was invited to take a close look at the plasterwork of the cinema's arch-like ceiling. My finger went right through it as what looked like plaster was really tightly stretched canvas coated in several layers of white paint! Even during the last visit Michael was still delighting in demonstrating the re-wind equipment in an otherwise empty and abandoned projection room. Sometimes Jim Spittal would also reveal a little more cinema history. His brother Jack was then still projecting films at the Quinton cinema, but Jim would talk about his father and grandfather who had also projected films at The Grand, Old Hill.

The Empire

High Street, Cradley Heath

The Empire was opened, as a theatre, on 11th September 1893, thus illustrating that Cradley Heath had sufficient urban aspirations by the end of the nineteenth century to support such a venture. It may have only been a small brick facade that concealed a large corrugated iron auditorium but it had a certain grandeur inside that impressed the local population. Huge stone angels, holding lights aloft, stood one each side of the proscenium, and even the brick frontage was treated with plaster to create a stone-like surface.

It is said that some melodramas were taken so seriously by the local chainmakers that they would wait outside the theatre for the villain, and actors needed police protection. It was pioneered by a Mr. Morton, but by the time Walter Williams was showing an interest in bringing film and yet more variety entertainment to Cradley Heath, it was owned by Mrs. Susie Cranston and managed by Sidney Cranston. Whether they were any relation to the M. J. Cranston that ran the John Bull in Dudley in 1916, I do not know.

The Empire held a kine licence and, during the spring of 1913, for example, Douglas Phelps of the Alhambra, Stourbridge, had his films shown there amongst the variety acts. During the second half of the First World War The Empire was acquired by Walter Williams. It "re-opened" under his management on 14th February 1916 and continued presenting melodramas and variety for a short time. Walter Williams then closed it until he could modernise and reconstruct it to be re-opened as a cinema. The projection equipment was already installed, and even as a cinema, it then presented cine-variety, so really very little changed. Mr. Edward Lucas came up from the Victoria at The Lye to manage The Empire for a time, and it seems to have flourished up until about 1937. The best date I can suggest as the clsoure of the Empire is 30th January 1937, after a screening of *"Strike Me Pink"*. (This film, starring Eddy Cantor as someone struggling against the odds to run an amusement park, was made in 1936.) Possibly The Empire's closure was also the result of Walter Williams decision to concentrate on modernising the Royal.

Certainly it had closed by the time The Royal's new entrance opened in August 1938. Although variety had flourished at the Empire, it closed as a cinema. (Ironically, sound at The Empire was acoustically better than at the Royal.) An interesting point concerning sound at The Empire was that shortly before the talkies arrived films were presented with sound effects provided by a man with a gramophone just beneath the screen. His synchronisation was always better in the second performance than during the first.). The building appears to have remained standing until after the Second World War, but no-one I have spoken to seems to be sure of when it was demolished.

A car park next to the Holly Bush Inn occupied the site

of The Empire, making it possible to work out where it had stood, and how it related to glimpses obtained of the building in pictures taken during the great women chain-maker's strike of 1910. However, car parks, the Holly Bush, and The Royal itself have all had to be swept away to allow a giant Tesco supermarket to provide salvation for Cradley Heath.

The Institute
(Also known as Pictureland)

The Workers Institute was opened by the Countess of Dudley on 10th June 1912. The trustees of the Institute included Mary MacArthur of the Anti-Sweating League, who had led the striking women chain-makers in 1910. The fact that they had found a voice and a new confidence was reflected in the building of the hall. It seems that, when planned in 1911, it was to be the Women Workers Institute, funded by women in the Trade Union Movement, and using funds left over from fund raising during and immediately after the 1910 dispute.

However, it seems that building the Institute had proved expensive and the large hall was leased to Howard Bishop to help repay some of the costs involved. Quite when Mr. Bishop began using the hall for his "Pictureland" is not clear. Like the other Pictureland in Netherton, it was usually known locally as The Stute, but a sign saying "Pictureland" was put up over the side-door. Films, particularly serials, were often shared between the two concerns and travelled backwards and forwards between Netherton and Cradley Heath on the trams.

The twice nightly programmes began with a two-reel silent comedy that was really shown in silence. The pianist, one was a Harry Raybould, would arrive to accompany the feature. The serial always came last and then the hall was cleared for the second house. In some respects the Cradley Heath "Stute" seems to have been more cinema-like than Netherton. For example, it appears that the floor was raked. However, it never went sound, unlike Netherton, and it seems to have closed in 1933, a few weeks after the opening of the Majestic.

Towards the end it had become a paradise for skylarking by the local children and the chucker-out, Mr. Haitland, appears to had to work hard to maintain order. Mr. Bishop tended to look after the shows at Netherton, and therefore, Harry Wild looked after Cradley Heath's Pictureland for him.

Later the hall was used for boxing, and later still, after the floor was levelled, billiard tables were installed. The building survived until threatened by the possibility of a new ring-road coming to encircle the centre of Cradley Heath, and to provide access to the new Tesco supermarket. The ring road would not have run right through the site of The Institute but Sandwell Council seemed to think was close enough to warrant demolition. This caused quite an outrage and many people pleaded for preservation of the building. An answer was eventually found – The Institute was moved brick by brick to the Black Country Living Museum!

Above: The Institute, Cradley Heath, now at the Black Country Museum. Below: The Majestic, Cradley Heath, from a drawing in the opening brochure.

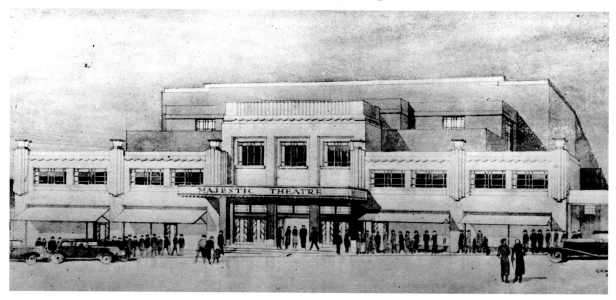

The Majestic

Cradley Road, Cradley Heath

The real proof that Cradley Heath was no forgotten backwater of the Black Country came in 1933 with the opening of a very elegant super-cinema: The Majestic. The Majestic Cinema (Cradley Heath) Ltd., was a company of local men led by Dudley's Alderman F. J. Ballard, whom we will encounter later in connection with the Criterion, Dudley, and the Central, Stourbridge. Since being in the chair at the opening of the Central in 1929, he had also been involved in building the Central, Kidderminster, opened on 5th October 1931. The invasion of Dudley by P.C.T. does not seem to have deterred him from investing in independent super-cinemas, or made it difficult to find other local businessmen to join him in such ventures. On this occasion the architect joined the Board, plus "outsiders" like Mr. J. H. Male of the well-known local haulage firm and two other local councillors, Messrs. Millward and Frost.

The Majestic was designed by Messrs. Webb and Gray of Dudley, who had designed the two "Centrals". It was built by J. M. Tate and Son, a local contractor, and made good use of its site in Cradley Road, not far from the Five Ways, which had become the centre of the town.

As a result of the narrowness of Cradley Road it has been impossible to stand back and appreciate the symmetry of its facade. The central entrance was flanked by shops and they have encroached upon the impact of its canopy and the beautiful stained glass leaded lights of the windows of the balcony crush hall. The most beautiful window, by T. W. Camm of Smethwick, is in a relatively obscure side wall, but when driving up Cradley Road from the Stour's valley at night, it can still be seen in all its glory.

The Majestic was built to hold fifteen hundred patrons, just over a third of which were in the balcony. The auditorium was fan-shaped, and treated in a modern style when compared with Messrs. Webb and Gray's earlier work. The plaster-work was carried out by the West Bromwich firm of John Malin and Company. From the start it was purpose-built for sound, using the Western Electric system, and the building enjoyed good acoustics. The Majestic was proud of its up-to-date projection suite, fitted with Ernemann III machines fitted with Zeiss lamps and lenses.

One of the most important features of the Majestic was its organ. It was the only Christie organ to be found in the Black Country, apart from Eldon Firmstone's instrument at Wordsley Manor, and was a three-manual, ten unit instrument. Of course, all this should be written in the 'present tense', as it is the only Black Country cinema-organ to still reside in its original location at the time of going to press. However, it is currently in very poor condition. At the opening the sight of the organ

Above: William Sykes at the console of the Christie organ at The Majestic, Cradley Heath.   (Mrs. Drinkwater's Collection)

console rising on its pneumatic lift in the centre of the orchestra pit absolutely astounded the audience.

The "inauguration" of the cinema, as the event was called, took place on Monday afternoon, 27th March 1933, in a packed auditorium. Alderman Ballard made a few opening remarks and then handed over to Councillor D.M. Chapman, Chairman of Rowley Regis U.D.C., to perform the opening ceremony. After two short films an organ recital was given by the new resident organist, William Sykes. The afternoon ended with the British feature film, ***"The Flag Lieutenant"*** starring Henry Edwards and Anna Neagle. The proceeds were donated to the Cradley Heath Friendly Society and the local Carnival Committee.

The cinema's manager, at the time of opening, was Mr. Godwin Longthorn, who had also opened the Criterion and P.C.T.'s Regent, but after a short time William Sykes was appointed Manager as well as organist. William Sykes' career is described elsewhere. He worked at the Majestic from 1933 until 1958 and was largely responsible for its success. As a manager he maintained reasonable prices without any increase until the War, and fostered many links between the cinema and the local community. As a musician he educated the musical tastes of the Cradley Heathens. The first cashier at the Majestic is recorded as Elsie Jukes, but she was replaced with Joan Giles. Joan's husband, Frank Giles, was the cinema's chief operator.

As Mr. Sykes' organ interludes began, the page-boy would come on stage with the title of the music printed on a large card. The console would rise into the spotlight, and slides, made by Mr. Sykes, were projected onto the screen above him. The organ interlude between films was always treated as an integral part of the programme; it was not just a matter of playing before the programme. His work during the War is recorded in the chapter on organists.

As independent cinemas, both the Majestic and the Royal suffered from barring practices after the War. For a super-cinema the Majestic faced an early decline in its fortunes and when Stanley Harrison took over as organist and manager after William Sykes' retirement the cinema seemed to be fighting a losing battle. The organ itself became less and less used and signs of the desperate search for an audience came when wrestling was introduced for a time on Wednesday evenings. The cinema was too "majestic" for Cradley Heath in the sixties and the inevitable closure came on 2nd November 1963. The last programme consisted of *"Jumbo"* starring Doris Day, and *"Kill or Cure"*.

The "cure" for the Majestic was Bingo, and it reopened as the Majestic Casino on 7th November. The bingo provider was the Star group. The council had privately discussed acquiring the building but quietly dropped the idea. With the idiosyncrasy the reader may have come to expect of Black Country cinemas, the Majestic did briefly present films again after its "closure". These films took the form of Saturday morning matinees, introduced in January 1964, and operated until the kine licence expired. Six hundred children attended the first show, which hardly filled such a large cinema, but was a good house for a cinema that had just decided its future lay in Bingo.

The story does not end there. Mel Edwards took over the organ and fully restored it over a period of three or four years with the co-operation of the lessees, Star Bingo. By 1973 it could be played once again and became a feature of Friday evenings at the Bingo Club. The Majestic then passed to Jarglen Ltd., another local bingo provider, in July 1975. Some alterations were made to the stage area and proscenium but, as mentioned earlier, the basic architectural features of the building, including the windows, were preserved.

In 1984 there were two well-attended organ concerts at The Majestic, one featured Phil Kelsall, and the other featured Doreen Chadwick and also included the AGM of the Cinema Organ Society.

Although Bingo helped cinema buildings like The Majestic survive, even Bingo has become a victim of the historical process of change. Gala Bingo had taken over the building in 1999 and were just about to set about refurbishing the building when they discovered such a project would be much more costly than they had anticipated. They announced the building would be "permanently closed" as from 31st March 2000.

In the post-bingo era the Majestic has been used as a warehouse by Hawk Cycles – whose headquarters is the old Cradley Heath bus garage. However that does not mean that the cycle company focuses on preserving historic buildings! At the time of going to press The Majestic still stands – over forty years after last showing films.

Right: William Sykes brought many notable singers and musicians to the Royal – as seen in the wartime concert handbill.

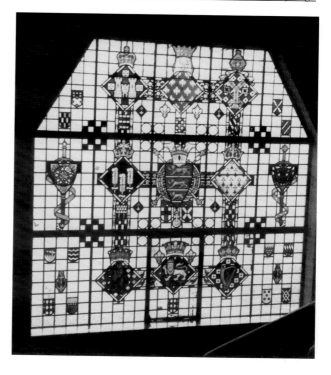

Above: The leaded glass window overlooking the stairs to the balcony in Cradley Heath's Majestic. (Ned Williams)

Above: Music comes to the Rex, Blackheath, in November 1944.

William Sykes "at the Christie organ" was mentioned in Majestic advertising, and Eldon Firmstone of Wordsley Manor, who claimed to have been organist at the Majestic seems only to have been there for three days!

Left: Stanley Harrison followed William Sykes at the Majestic and is seen here at the console. (Eric Maley)

Section 3
Cinemas of Dudley

Harry Arnold Hickman on the Compton organ at the Odeon, Stourbridge, in 1955.

From Sandwell we move on to the present Metropolitan Borough of Dudley. Having just looked at cinemas in the Old Hill and Cradley Heath area it does mean there is some logic on moving on through the Black Country in this way – gradually covering the region in a grand clockwise circular tour. There would be some logic in entering Dudley MBC at Halesowen and working our way round to Coseley to maintain this circular pattern. However, within Dudley itself it seems logical to work in a slightly different direction – reflecting its growth and expansion and changing definition in terms of local government boundaries.

The "original" Dudley was a town established right in the centre of the Black Country – the famous castle being built on a hill which forms part of the ridge bisecting the Black Country from north-west to south east, i.e. from Sedgley Beacon to the Rowley Hills. As the ridge crosses Dudley it is "broken" into separate hills: The Wrens Nest, Castle Hill, and then Kates Hill/Bennetts Hill. These breaks in the ridge allow the town to occupy a key crossroads position in which an east to west line of communication crosses a line that would follow the ridge. Thus, in everyway Dudley was able to claim it held a central position among surrounding towns, although not everyone might agree that it was capital of the Black Country.

Dudley's altitude could also be a problem – both the railway and the canal system had to burrow beneath the

town to traverse the ridge! Water supply was also a problem and in the early to mid nineteenth century, when the town was expanding quickly, it was regarded as an unsanitary and unhealthy place to live. Matters were not helped by the fact that fairly inefficient town commissioners administered it. Everything was turned round in 1865 by creating a new Borough of Dudley and the authority began the long task of putting things right. In 1888 it became a County Borough – in recognition of its growing size and importance, and in recognition that it was making good progress. Although totally surrounded by Staffordshire, Dudley remained part of Worcestershire until 1974.

Meanwhile Dudley had expanded its frontiers in 1928 and 1953. In 1966 it had amalgamated with Brierley Hill, Sedgley and parts of Coseley, all formerly Urban Districts. Thus, in this section of the book we will deal first with the cinemas in the old County Borough of Dudley (including Netherton), and then go on to Sedgley and Coseley and then to Brierley Hill. The 1974 reorganisation brought Stourbridge and Halesowen into the new Metropolitan Borough so we will then proceed to deal with the cinemas in these two areas.

As it happens, within Dudley MBC's boundary we find two of the Black Country's four multi-plex cinemas, so this section of the book finishes by taking account of the new cinemas at Merry Hill and Castle Gate.

Dudley

As explained on the previous page, this survey of cinemas in the current Metropolitan Borough of Dudley begins within the boundaries of the original Dudley Borough as established in 1865. Netherton was included within this boundary, and was also therefore part of Worcestershire until 1974.

When I first arrived in Dudley in the Autumn of 1962 the town seemed like a prosperous bustling market town, famous for its castle and zoo. At first I did not perceive quite how "industrial" Dudley really was, nor did I understand its proximity to the surrounding coalfield. Now I have a better understanding of Dudley as a proper Black Country town, but the initial deception is interesting: Dudley has had something about it that makes it different to surrounding towns!

Perhaps, therefore, we should not be surprised to find that Dudley has an abundance of theatre and cinema history – ranging from the days of the nineteenth century portable theatres, through the building of a variety theatre and an Opera House, to the progress of cinematography from bioscopes to multi-plexes. Into this rich history we have to throw the life and times of Dudley Hippodrome, dealt with in detail in Volume Two. Dudley has been the birthplace of Eliza Bennett, Clarkson Rose, Billy Dainty, James Whale and Lenny Henry!

Where did Dudley folk first see films? During the first decade of the twentieth century there were three places where films might have been seen. The first possibility was that films were presented in bioscope shows that came to the Pat Collins fairground on the corner of Trindle Road and Claughton Road – an area known as The White Knobs. Secondly, films were occasionally presented at the Opera House, and maybe at The Empire in Hall Street. The third "film venue" was created by

Below: A drawing of the Public Hall and Institute from Blocksidge's Dudley Guide.

and Thomas Wood, or by Hamilton's Excursions. These people came to the Public Hall in Wolverhampton Street, or the Temperance Institute in the High Street.

Once the Kinematograph Act came into force on 1st January 1910 it was going to be interesting to see who opened Dudley's first cinema. The race was won by Irving Bosco at The Public Hall. Our survey begins there and stays within the old Borough to introduce each cinema in a chronological order. The only exception to all this is that we leave the story of Netherton's cinemas to the end.

The Public Hall

Wolverhampton Street, Dudley

The Public Hall started life as a Mechanics' Institute. Films were certainly shown there before the passing of the Cinematograph Act but it is not always clear by whom, or even exactly what was being presented. Showmen were careless with phrases like "Animated Pictures" and "Living Pictures" – sometimes this referred to real cinematography, sometimes it just meant that ingenious technolgy was being applied to what was basically a "magic lantern" type show. For example, from Christmas Eve 1895 onwards, for a short season, the show in the Public Hall was presented by "The Lyric Living Pictures and Grand Variety Company". Before leapingto the conclusion that this might, in part, have been a film show, we should remember that the Lumiere Brothers did not present Britain's first cinematogaph show until early in 1866.

From the early 1900s onward it is more likely that such shows did include some material on film. In October 1907 and again at the same time in 1908 20th Century Pictures ran a season in the Public Hall. This was a company associated with Waller Jeffs. His career is described in the Introductory Section, but what needs repeating here is that Waller Jeff's "right-hand-man" was Irving Bosco who was about to play an important role in Dudley's cinema history as well as that of the Black Country in general. From Christmas 1909 into the 1910 New Year Professor Wood was presenting a "Musical and Pictorial Combination", but he had decided, by that time, to settle in Bilston. It fell to another pioneer, Irving Bosco, to be the first to present *regular* film-shows in Dudley, at the Public Hall.

During 1909 Irving Bosco had established a cinema in West Bromwich, but he had visited the Black Country long before that and may have presented travelling shows at the Public Hall. He was granted his kine licence for shows at the Public Hall on the day the Act came into operation: 1st January 1910.

He opened the Public Hall as a cinema on 31st January 1910, and his wife, Ducie Saunderson, sang between the films. Irving's policy was to "keep one step ahead of

Birmingham", and the Public Hall appears to have been a great success. Shows were presented twice nightly and the hall accommodated up to eight hundred patrons, a year later quoted as 630! Irving Bosco became a well known local personality and showed the usual showman's interest in raising money for local charities.

It is known that Irving Bosco made his own films, and during the early days at the Public Hall he screened material he had shot on the Priory Fields when Baden Powell had come to inspect local scouts. Unfortunately we have to assume such material, shot on nitrate film, has been lost.

On 19th October 1911 he persuaded the Mayor, Dudley's M.P., and the Earl of Dudley, to attend a benefit show. The films shown are not recorded, but again Ducie Saunderson sang for the enthusiastic audience. Irving Bosco later expanded his empire but continued to present shows at the Public Hall until sometime in 1919, or possibly the summer of 1920. Films continued to be shown at the Public Hall by Edwin Griffiths but in 1922 his application for his kine licence was refused and he was told that the premises were not considered suitable for that purpose anymore.

On 22nd April 1922 Mr. Griffiths advertised, "This Hall is now to let as a cinema", despite his difficulty in obtaining a licence! In the event the Public Hall reopened as a dance-hall on 27th November 1922. During the 1930s the dance hall was run by the Kennedy family thus establishing a connection between The Public Hall and two Black Country pioneers of cinema and theatrical entertainment. It later had a very prolonged existence as a derelict shell of a building, boarded up and waiting for death. Demolition has removed all trace of it and the area is now a public car park. Many old people in Dudley still recall the shows at the Public Hall, and its name is more frequently evoked than Dudley's other early cinemas.

The Colosseum
(later known as The Gem, The John Bull, The Scala and The Plaza)

Castle Hill, Dudley

Six kine licences were issued on 1st January 1910 in Dudley but the first purpose-built cinema did not open until almost the end of that year.

The Colosseum was created by John Maurice Clement (28th December 1840 - 25th February 1912). He is most well known as the founder, proprietor and manager of the Dudley Opera House, opened in September 1899. At some stage he had purchased "Lloyd's Circus" just round the corner in Trindle Road. He converted it into a theatre, using the name Colosseum, until its closure at the turn of the century. It later became a skating rink. (See Volume Two.)

In 1910 he revived the name Colosseum for a small five hundred seater cinema built next-door to his Opera House. It was a "tin-shed" construction suitably disguised by an elaborate frontage. The "Grand Opening" took place on Christmas Eve, and from then on shows were presented twice nightly at seven and nine. Life did not run completely smoothly and it seems that it may have closed briefly in 1911, although Mr. Clement renewed the licence in 1912. He died in February 1912 and the cinema closed again.

It was reopened as the Gem on 15th December 1913 by George Lovatt of Wolverhampton, who had been unsuccessful in attempting to build a cinema in his home town. The opening programme featured "*The Battle of Gettysburgh*" and ladies were invited to attend free of charge at the first afternoon show. The advertising claimed that the Gem was *"Dudley's Cosiest and Prettiest Picture House"*.

Even so, the cinema changed hands again nine months later, acquired by a John Nisbet, and yet again in October 1916 when it was acquired by a Mr. Cranston of Birmingham. (See Empire, Cradley Heath).

Mr. Cranston reopened on 2nd December 1916 with *"Infidelity"* starring Theda Bara, and re-named the cinema "The John Bull". Another two years passed and the cinema changed name for the third time. On 17th December 1918 it became the Scala and was now in the hands of Ernest Davies, a local auctioneer and estate agent, who was also running the Opera House by that time.

Below: The Colosseum, Castle Hill, about 1911. (Dudley Archives)

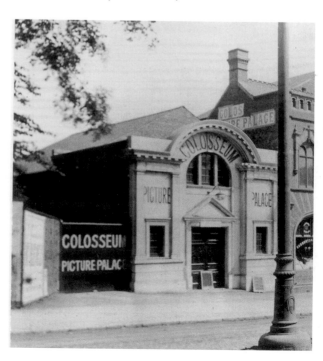

In 1920 Ernest Davies sold the Opera House to Benjamin Kennedy, but the Scala continued to change hands a number of times. By the mid twenties it was being run by Walter McMillan, who had opened the Castle Cinema in the old Temperance Institute, and, while both cinemas were in the same hands, Harry Crane gained some local experience of cinema management at both places that later stood him in good stead when he moved to the Cliftons at Sedgley and Coseley.

During 1931 the Scala seems to have been acquired, at last, by Benjamin Kennedy and underwent its final change of name to the Plaza. A few years later it was demolished to make way for Mr. Kennedy's new purpose-built super-cinema, but many people have happy memories of the place as the Scala, and have nostalgically recalled the perfumed deodorant of the scent sprays and its films in the "Blood Tub" tradition.

The new Plaza was quite different from its predecessor and illustrates how far its architect, Mr. Hurley Robinson, had adopted a functional approach to cinema design by the mid thirties. Its unadorned brickwork must have looked odd next-door to the Opera House, but about five months after the cinema opened the Opera House was burnt down, to be replaced by a new theatre designed by Mr. Hurley Robinson.

The architect's sketch on the front of the silver opening brochure suggests that the original frontage was more effective than the present one. The cinema's name was more centrally placed and the large brickwork flanks were relieved by monogram motifs. It would be interesting to know if they did ever appear on the cinema as built. The construction was carried out by Parsons and Morrin Ltd., of Edgbaston. However plain its exterior, it was described as "palatial" inside, and

fifteen hundred patrons were said to be accommodated in the maximum comfort. The auditorium tapered towards the screen and this was thought to be good for acoustics. Sound was produced by Western Electric equipment.

The opening was held on Thursday 28th May 1936 and Benjamin Kennedy entertained the Council, the Town Clerk, and invited guests, to a presentation of *"Top Hat"* starring Fred Astaire and Ginger Rogers. Inspired by *"Top Hat"* which was retained until the programme change in the middle of the following week, Mr. Kennedy advertised the Plaza as, *"Joyously different to ordinary cinemas"*.

Ben's son Maurice was given the job of "manager", and his brother Bob was described as licensee and film-booker. Both had worked closely with their father in The Opera House. Benjamin Kennedy went on to open the new Hippodrome as the summit of his achievement, but died shortly afterwards in April 1939. His sons continued to run the theatre and cinema through the War years and into the fifties. On one side of Castle Hill stood the theatre, cinema and zoo. Opposite stood the Odeon. Both the Plaza and the Odeon entertained patrons from a very wide area and the whole Castle Hill area, including the zoo, became an "entertainment zone" of regional importance.

Early in 1954 Miles Jervis obtained the Plaza from the trustees of the late Benjamin Kennedy's estate. He took Castle Hill by storm by installing Cinemascope and

Below: The Plaza, Castle Hill, in 1981, between the Zoo's entrance and The Hippodrome, as a two screen cinema. (Ned Williams)

Right: The Plaza, disguised as "The Odeon" in October 1990 – just before closure. Simon Davis, manager, and Jean Hughes, cashier, stand outside their cinema. The cinema was a victim of competiton from the multi-plex at Merry Hill, but would not have survived the opening of The Showcase at Castle Gate – a few yards away. (Ned Williams)

Right: Mel Grafton, Chief Operator at the Odeon/Plaza in the projection box for Screen 1 in October 1990 – just before closure. (Ned Williams)

advertising **"The Robe"** with a huge display that engulfed the Plaza's facade. Large queues developed of eager patrons, and no doubt the new screen format seemed to have come as the industry's salvation. *"The Robe "* opened on 14th June 1954 and was so successful it was retained immediately for a second week. Miles Jervis felt his success was a triumph for the small independent exhibitor, and justified their willingness to adopt wide screen technology at a time when the large circuits seemed a little reluctant to invest. Even so his stay at The Plaza was short.

So successful was the Plaza that Gaumont British purchased it in autumn 1955 and thus, eventually, the Plaza and Odeon were united within the Rank Organisation. As time went on many people felt that Rank would be more likely to abandon the Plaza than the Odeon. They were wrong. On 3rd February 1973 work started on twinning the Plaza; the first such conversion in the Black Country. The conversion cost £35,000, and it was remarkable in that it was carried out

without the Plaza ever closing. Both screens opened on Sunday 29th April 1973. Screen 1 which used the old balcony and existing screen opened with **"The Triple Echo"**. Screen 2 opened with **"Young Winston"**. The two auditoria held 551 patrons and 199 patrons respectively, although I have seen slightly different figures quoted recently. Modern Cinemeccanica equipment had been installed.

The Plaza outlived the Odeon and become Dudley's sole-surviving cinema until the arrival of the multi-plexes. I visited the Plaza frequently in the sixties and I will always remember one particular night. In the middle of **"Boccaccio 70"** the picture faded from the screen. There was much shouting and banging of feet. Then a tiny figure clambered onto the thin strip of a stage in front of the screen. He quelled the noise by waving his torch and shouting that there had been a power-cut but we should stay in our seats. This shadowy little figure then began telling jokes. Soon tears were running down our faces. When the film resumed we

135

gave him a spontaneous standing ovation as he came up the aisle and disappeared.

Just to totally confuse everyone the Plaza was suddenly renamed Odeon at the very end of its life!

The Odeon, (i.e. the former Plaza) closed on Sunday 28th October 1990 with Walt Disney's *"The Little Mermaid"* in one screen, and *"Bird On A Wire"* in the other. Organs and organists were hired for the occasion and the audience as invited to join in singing "Auld Lang Syne" as the credits rolled for the last time! Simon Davis, and his twenty staff were made redundant. He explained to the press, *"We've suffered from competition from the Merry Hill multi-plex – even though it's a pound cheaper to see our films."*

The Opera House and The Trindle Road Rink

As stated in the previous section, John Maurice Clement ran a theatre in Trindle Road, called the Colosseum, during the 1890's. He abandoned this interest sometime after his magnificent Opera House opened in September 1899. The timber framed building in Trindle Road became a skating rink and seems to have enjoyed many and various uses in the field of popular entertainment. On 1st January 1910 William Harper obtained a kine licence for the rink. The licence claimed that a thousand people could be accommodated. It was renewed in 1911 and then lapsed. I imagine that films were occasionally shown in cine-variety programmes.

At the same time J. M. Clement obtained a kine licence, for the Opera House. Films had occasionally been shown there in 1907, and possibly earlier. They were used as a summer attraction. During the summer of 1910 twice nightly shows were presented at the "Opera House Picture Palace and Electric Theatre", invoking three names simultaneously to confuse later historians! The kine licence for the Opera House was renewed right up to the time of Ben Kennedy's arrival, but it is not known how much this was exploited. The story of the Opera House, its destruction, and its replacement by the Hippodrome is described in Volume Two and briefly in this volume in the section on Ben Kennedy.

The Temperance Institute, The Crown and Pictureland (later known as The Temple and The Castle)

High Street, Dudley

The Temperance Insitute was a hall built in Dudley's High Street, and opened on 21st November 1900.Whatever went on at the foot of Castle Hill, Irving Bosco's real cinema competitor was to be found at the

The Temperance Institute in the town centre. Like the Public Hall, it was visited by travelling shows and, therefore, already had established some identity as a "cinema" before the Act. From November 1909 until Christmas the Picture World Company were presenting their "animated films" in competition with Professor Wood at the Public Hall.

On 24th October 1910 the Crown Electric Picture Company commenced a season with their "Entirely new flickerless projectors". Their first programme included *"The Revolution in Lisbon", "Egypt in the Time of the Pharoahs"* and *"Range Riders"*. The season of showing films continued into November by which time the hall was advertising itself as The Crown Cinema, but then it seems to "fade away", or at least cease advertising.

Exactly one year after Irving Bosco had established himself at the Public Hall, the first permanent film-exhibitor arrived at "The Temp". This was Howard Bishop, already successfully showing films in Netherton. He opened his "Pictureland" at the Temp Hall on 30th January 1911. A thousand people came to see a two hour show which included *"Sexton Blake"* and a colour film of Niagara Falls.

Howard Bishop loved the theatre, variety, concerts etc., and usually presented variety acts as part of his film-shows. He made great use of the tramway system by dispatching the performers to Netherton and bringing them back by tram. He usually presented shows twice nightly in Dudley and once nightly in Netherton. Later he juggled with the films themselves when he started shows in Cradley Heath. At least once he organised an outing to Kinver for all his patrons, who boarded the trams outside the Temp and enjoyed the rural virtues of the Kinver Light Railway. Not to be outdone by Irving Bosco, he also organised benefit shows for charity. Howard Bishop was also proud that he had allowed a young violinist named Barrs Partridge to make his debut at Pictureland.

After the First World War the entire Temperance Institute was bought for £15,000 by a Mr. W. L. Moore, who intended turning it into a real cinema. Temple Cinemas Ltd., was registered in January 1920 and began the £7,000 improvement scheme. A lounge and cafe were provided in the basement and the auditorium, now reached by a flight of stairs, was raked and fitted with silk velvet tip up seats throughout. Axminster carpet added to the new feeling of luxury, and two new powerful Kalee projectors were installed.

It opened in May 1920 and Kine Weekly recorded that two thousand people attended the event. The licence permitted audiences of 690. Wilford Cheetam came from the Empire in Hall Street to manage the place, but by July was replaced for a time by Stourbridge's Harry Morris. For some reason The Temple was not a success. Its losses were blamed on "the depression". Shows ceased sometime in 1923 and then the Temple Cinema Company was wound-up in the October of that year.

All was not lost, and, at the beginning of December 1924, a licence was issued to Mr. Walter McMillan to reopen the hall as The Castle. It reopened on 15th December 1924 with *"The Arizona Express"* and advertised its orchestra directed by Leonard Singer. The identity of the new proprietors is somewhat obscure, but, at some stage Ernest Grenville Jones, of the Alexandra, Lower Gornal, seems to have become associated with the Castle. From late 1929 it was managed for five years by Harry Crane, who later appeared at the Clifton, Sedgley.

At least it now enjoyed a more stable existence and kept itself up-to-date by installing British Acoustic sound equipment when the talkies arrived. It must have been rather over-shadowed by the splendid Regent when that opened a few yards away, in September 1929.

However, its tasteful advertisements, featuring Dudley Castle, continued to appear regularly in the Dudley Herald until the end of April 1936. Whether it closed then, or continued a little longer, is very obscure. Only a few months earlier proposals had been made concerning a plan to double its size and improve the sound equipment. It seems possible to me that its demise may be connected with the sale of Mr. Jones' Alexandra, and his possible retirement, but I have no evidence which could confirm that. The Castle eventually became a dance hall, with the cellar in use for a time as a roller-skating rink. By the 1980s it was a Thorns' Superstore, and the frontage, particularly above shop level seemed to indicate it had been rebuilt in the 1960s. Now (2011) that frontage is all boarded up and the premises seem to be vacant. When the building is viewed from the rear it is possible to imagine the outline of the Castle cinema from the current shape of the roof!

The Empire

Hall Street, Dudley

There was a tradition of presenting entertainment in or near Hall Street going back to circus entertainment in the second half of the nineteenth century. Even the building described here as The Empire was actually a replacement for an earlier corrugated iron building. All this is explained in Volume Two as the story has nothing to do with the presentation of film.

At the beginning of this century the original Victorian "Music Hall" seemed a thing of the past. If a town was modern and up to the minute it built a "Palace of Varieties" for the popular entertainment of the working classes! Such a building was erected in Hall Street for a Mr. Tom Prichard. On 3rd April 1903 he invited Dan Leno and the Mayor, John Hughes, to come along and lay foundation stones. It was Dan Leno's first visit to Dudley but he promised to return for the opening of the Empire.

Somewhat amazingly it was planned to have the theatre open at Easter, just a month away. The schedule was kept and on 6th May 1903 Dan Leno returned. He travelled down to Dudley in the morning, took part in the opening ceremony and the first matinee and then hurried back up to London to appear there. The theatre was far from finished at the opening. Ornamental plaster-work had not been applied and permanent upholstered seats had not been installed, but nobody complained.

Below: The Empire, Hall Street, Dudley, awaits demolition in 1970 having last shown films thirty years earlier. (Ned Williams)

The building was designed by a Dudley architect, Arthur Gammage, and held 1,100 patrons in the stalls and 900 in a huge steeply raked gallery. Part of the roof could be rolled back, and in the summer a little sunshine and fresh air were allowed to circulate before the matinee. Despite its popularity it seems to have changed hands a number of times, or possibly a variety of people leased the place. This is particularly true of the period following the passing of the Cinematograph Act. On 1st January 1910 none other than Irving Bosco obtained a kine licence for the Empire but does not seem to have shown films there himself for over two years. While he enjoyed success at the Public Hall, a number of people tried showing films at the Empire. For example, towards the end of 1910 R. Colin was presenting "Colin's Famous Electric Pictures". Mr. Colin provided similar fare in Brierley Hill and West Bromwich. Cine-variety and pure variety tended to alternate until 6th January 1912 when the last live variety show was staged.

It began life as a full-time cinema on 8th January 1912 with a film called *"Fools of Society"*. The presenters were the Pantheon Syndicate. They renovated the Empire and experimented with various short-lived changes of name. By March it was advertised as "Under Entirely New Control" but was quickly in trouble again.

Irving Bosco took over on 8th April 1912. Bert Dawes, who had worked for Waller Jeffs, and for Irving Bosco at the Public Hall, became the manager, and some permanent order prevailed at last. A new electric projector was installed to replace the hand-cranked machine. For a few years it was known as "Bosco's Picture Pavilion" but by the end of the First World War it was the Empire again.

At the end of 1920 Irving Bosco sold his cinemas to a Nottingham-based syndicate led by E.C. Shapeero. A separate company was floated to run the Empire which then installed back projection equipment in the Autumn of 1922, having built a little corrugated iron extension on the rear of the building to form an operating room. They gained a few seats in the auditorium by removing the existing operating room but by the twenties people hoped for a little more leg-room and comfort, and the capacity came down to about thirteen hundred.

Like other ex-Bosco-owned cinemas run by Mr. Shapeero, it was sold to Denman Picture Houses in March 1928. It looks as if Mr. Shapeero had decided to withdraw from the cinema business in advance of the arrival of sound. Denman Picture Houses, the new owners, were was a subsidiary of Gaumont British, and were willing to wire such cinemas for the talkies.

The Empire provided plenty of nostalgic memories for Dudley citizens. Some remember the Saturday afternoon matinees and the crowd of children who could not afford one penny for admission. They gathered in Dudley Row and took turns at looking through a chink in the large exit doors. Patrons also remember the potted palms placed each side of the screen and the three-piece orchestra. In the April of 1922 the locally produced film *"Bladys of the Stewponey"* was given its Dudley premiere at the Empire, and later the same year they screened a film made in the Bean car factory, which was fairly close by.

As The Empire and The Regent were owned by the same company by the time the talkies were arriving it is interesting to see how The Empire was used during the week in August 1929 when The Regent was showing its first sound film (*"The Singing Fool"*). At The Empire they played DW Griffiths' "Orphans of the Storm" almost as if to assert the superiority of silent film!

Having acquired the cinema at the beginning of the sound era, Gaumont British set about preparing the Empire for the new medium. They abandoned Mr. Shapeero's back projection equipment and built a new projection room at the back of the balcony. At first the Cinephone Sound system was installed but later this was replaced by British Acoustic. Some variety acts were still under contract to appear at the Empire after G.B.'s acquisition and the screen had to be "flown" when these acts appeared on stage. This created problems when sound films were being presented and the large horn speakers had to slide into the wings when the screen was flown! The first talkie was projected at the Empire by Abner Parker, who had previously been second operator at the Arcade in Worcester. It was the beginning of his long career in Dudley's cinemas.

For a time in the 1930s Gaumont British advertised the programmes of the Empire, the Regent and the Criterion together in one block: Dudley's "Big Three". However, G.B.'s three Dudley cinemas were hardly three of a kind, and I feel the Empire was always the "poor relation". An antiquated ex-Variety theatre, hurriedly built in 1903 was obviously going to be the first to be abandoned. The Empire closed on 2nd November 1940 with *"Let George Do It"* starring George Formby, which seems an appropriate finale as his father had been a popular star at the Empire in its early days as a variety theatre.

During the War it was used as a factory and warehouse, and for years was occupied by the Dudley engineers, Herman Smith. The peeling remains of the building survived until the beginning of the nineteen seventies. Following demolition, redevelopment was fairly slow, but a brand new Tesco supermarket was built on the site, now replaced by Cousin's furniture store.

The Criterion

High Street, Dudley

The Criterion is presented out of chronological sequence simply because most people will think of the 1923 cinema rather than its almost forgotten predecessor that started showing films regularly even before the Empire. The Criterion, at the turn of the century, was a public-house which offered "Music Hall" entertainment in rather cramped conditions. It was run by Wally Davies' father, a fact which may have had some part in the hall finding its way to Sidney Bray.

A kine licence was issued to the Criterion Electric Theatre at the beginning of 1911. It could hold 253 patrons and is thought to have been the assembly room at the rear of the public house premises. As such it opened on 27th February 1911 with a programme that included *"Jerusalem and the Mount of Olives"* and *"The Little Mother"*. Admission to Dudley's "Most Up to Date Theatre" cost 3d and 6d.

At the beginning of 1913 it was much enlarged by extending the auditorium back towards the Market Place and building a proper entrance and pay box, with operating room above. Having become just a cinema, and nothing else, it managed to increase its capacity to 570. The kine licence changed hands several times and it closed briefly towards the end of 1913 to be reseated and redecorated. It reopened on Boxing Day and from then on seems to have been in the hands of Benjamin Kennedy, until taken over by Sidney Bray. This was accomplished by the beginning of 1915 and marks the moment when Dudley's own cinema magnate established himself in his home town. His other interests were at Halesowen, Langley and Brownhills.

After the War Sidney Bray launched his ambitious plan to replace the Criterion with a fine new cinema. By building a large auditorium behind the existing cinema it was possible to continue business at the latter until about six weeks before opening its replacement. The old auditorium could then be replaced with the crush hall entrance, and balcony level cafe for the new Criterion.

The Criterion Picture House (Dudley) Ltd., began raising their £40,000 capital in the Autumn of 1922. Sidney Bray's original fellow directors were F. J. Ballard (prominent in the industrial and civic life of Dudley and later associated with three other cinemas), A. J. Crump (the building contractor about to start building the cinema), W. Lloyd (an accountant), J. Mason (an industrialist) and Tom Hanson, the Dudley brewer.

The building was designed by Joseph Lawden, of Birmingham, and Howard Cetti of Dudley. The Dudley Herald told its readers, *"The general trend of the design follows the lines of the Greek work of the Renaissance period"*. The huge hoardings across the front of the cinema were pulled down just before the opening and

Above: The Criterion, Dudley. The entrrance was only of shop-width but this led into a large auditorium. (Author's Collection)

the public was suitably over-awed by the dignity of the facade. By everyone working up to the last minute, it was possible to open on Saturday 17th November 1923, with a special presentation of *"Hearts Aflame"* and a locally made film of Mayoral Sunday celebrations. Viscount Ednam came along to perform the opening even though he was suffering from a broken collar bone acquired while hunting. The Mayor, Alderman Tanfield, and Corporation occupied the 1/3d seats in the balcony. Sidney Bray presented Viscount Ednam with a silver paperweight made by Ivo Shaw of Dudley Art School. Horace Watson directed the newly formed orchestra and everybody felt confident that they were sitting in Dudley's finest picture palace.

Normal public shows started on the Monday and great claims were made about the Criterion's intention of showing film of a Japanese earthquake — *"for the first time in Dudley"*. The Empire quickly organised a charity show on the Sunday and showed the same film while the Criterion was closed!

The Criterion was not so easily beaten. It could accommodate twelve hundred people in the greatest luxury Dudley had yet seen. Its cafe, open from 10 a.m. to 10 p.m., incorporating an "American Soda Fountain", made the place a social centre and the kind of respectable establishment usually associated with A.P.P.H. Picture Houses. Sidney Bray eventually handed the day to day management of the Criterion over to his brother, Clifford Bray, and the orchestra found a new popular leader in Stanley Pendrous. The orchestra also featured a Mustel organ.

Nothing challenged the supremacy of the "Cry", as it was called, until P.C.T. announced their intention of building The Regent at the top of Dudley's High Sreet. The approach of a large combine often upset an independent exhibitor like Sidney Bray. Clifford Bray decided to devote his energy to the Central in Stourbridge; Sidney Bray decided to make sure of his position in Halesowen by concentrating his energy on building a super-cinema there. He had just spent a large sum on rebuilding The Picture House in that town. Maybe it made sense to sell The Criterion to P.C.T – or its subsidiary A.P.P.H.

By the time P.C.T. opened The Regent in September 1928, they had already acquired the Criterion through their subsidiary A.P.P.H. in 1927. P.C.T. were shortly to become a subsidiary of Gaumont British and by the end of the decade the Criterion, The Empire and the Regent were bedfellows. Sound came to the Criterion on 11th November 1929 with *"The Glad Rag Doll"*, starring Dolores Costello, not far behind the Regent. The British Acoustic System was used. Despite the presence of The Regent, and later The Odeon and Plaza, The Criterion enjoyed a very central position almost overlooking Dudley's busy market place, it therefore deserved to survive. Its happy family atmosphere often attracted long terms of service. The Chief, Ab Parker, put in over twenty years at the Criterion and particularly remembers

Below: The remains of the auditorium of the Criterion as seen from Hall Street, 1980.

(Ned Williams)

how "spick and span" his box was kept by his second and third operators, Beryl Byfield and Iris Robinson. In total Ab Parker worked over thirty-five years for the Company, having come to Dudley to work at The Empire.

The end came suddenly in 1956 after the Rank Organisation had threatened to close theatres if the Government did not abolish entertainment tax. They rationalised the circuit by closing the oldest halls in towns where they had several screens. The Cape Hill Electric, Smethwick, and the Criterion, Dudley, both closed on 29th September 1956. The last film at the Criterion was *"Reach for the Sky"* starring Kenneth More. As Ab Parker laced up *"Reach for the Sky"* for the final performance he, and the manager, Mr. Toole, must have found it ironical that the film was playing to a packed house and had done terrific business throughout the last week.

The property was later sold to Broadmead, supplying radio and electrical goods. Only the entrance to the cinema was converted into the shop. The auditorium, stripped of its seats, continued to exist as a giant warehouse. Broadmead's shop opened on 26th April 1957. The frontage is still to be seen today, later part of the Wigfall's chain of shops, but the auditorium was demolished in the autumn of 1980 and has now been replaced with a furniture store facing King Street.

When I visited the auditorium in June 1980 I was amazed to find the ornamental plaster work still intact. Elaborate, cornucopia were abundant although rather dusty. Four grinning faces peered down at me from the plaster work of the proscenium arch. A quarter of a century had passed since the last patrons had sat there enjoying the exploits of Douglas Bader. That part of the building was then demolished but the frontage facing the High Street still exists and in 2011 is used by Shipley's Amusements as a gaming arcade.

The Regent
(later known as The Gaumont)

High Street, Dudley

The Regent was one of those cinemas built just as the silent era was coming to a close, and just as the new decade was about to produce a new taste in simplicity in cinema design. It was designed by W. E. Trent, and built by Messrs. McLaughlin and Harvey in eight months. A large sweeping "stadium" style auditorium was provided to accommodate sixteen hundred patrons. The front of the theatre was treated in white stone and an iron and glass canopy, cleverly lit, made it most impressive. This effect was lost over the years as the canopy was replaced, and the shops which shared the frontage became a greater distraction.

The auditorium, crush hall and entrance featured relatively "modern" plaster work, painted in delicate blends of mauve, blue and ivory. Stage facilities and dressing-rooms were provided, plus space for a large orchestra and, of course, a Wurlitzer organ. Considering the whole affair was a P.C.T. enterprise, a surprising number of local people found work there, particularly from the Criterion! Stanley Pendrous came to conduct the orchestra, Beatrice Holmes came as cashier, and Mr. H. Godwin Longthorn arrived as manager. He must have been a gentleman who specialised in opening new halls. He opened the Criterion, and the Majestic, Cradley Heath, but never stayed at a newly opened cinema for long. The paybox at the Regent was a small glass booth, about the size of a telephone box that stood in glorious isolation in the centre of the foyer. To the left of the foyer was the sweets and drinks counter.

The Regent was opened on Monday evening 3rd September 1928 by that cinema-minded Mayor, Councillor F.J. Ballard. There was not enough space to accommodate everyone who wished to be there. Twenty-two year old John Howlett opened the Wurlitzer while the packed house waited for the Mayor to make his speech. Quite a variety of entertainment then followed; short films, vocal solos, organ interludes, and an orchestral "turn". The feature film was *"The Magic Flame"* starring Ronald Colman and Vilma Banky.

An opening brochure was produced for The Regent, in which it stated:

"The Regent is a place of high class entertainment, in which cheerfulness, good taste and comfort are happily blended. It is dedicated to lovers of wholesome amusement, to people who lead busy lives and who need relaxation. Occasionally there may be pictures of a deep human interest which will put you in a serious mood, but always there will be pictures which grip your interest, pictures which will make you glad, and fill your soul with laughter, and will eliminate from your system the day's accumulation of household or business anxieties."

From the opening brochure patrons would have learned that *"The Magic Flame"* had a truly international cast but this did not matter, as it was, of course, a silent film.

Below: The Regent, Dudley. This was another cinema where the auditorium was rather hidden well behind the entrance.

(CTA Archives)

It told a "Romeo and Juliet" style story in a circus setting and provided two parts from Ronald Colman: as a clown, and as a villainous count! The following week's programme also reflected the international nature of silent cinema – culminating on 17th September with a week's showing of F.W. Murnau's *"Sunrise"*, a film that has recently been re-released and re-evaluated by modern critics. Perhaps the Regent really did live up to the promises made in its opening brochure.

People certainly travelled from far and wide to hear the new organ, and a year later they flocked to hear sound as *"The Singing Fool"* introduced the talkies to Dudley on 12th August 1929. Western Electric equipment was installed. Organists moved about frequently at that time, gaining experience and reputations, and a number of famous men appeared at the Regent briefly: Reginald Dixon, Leslie Taff, really an orchestral pianist at the time, Sidney Wallbank, Harry Farmer, Norris Bosworth and Clifford Baggott. Even after the opening of the Odeon many patrons remained loyal to the Regent because of its organ. One also has the feeling that The Regent had a kind of personality and intimacy that some of the supers that followed lacked, despite its size.

On 25th November 1935 James Whale's *"Bride of Frankenstein "* began a six day run after a long publicity run-up. It was billed as *"Dudley's own thriller, directed by Dudley's own director".* It had been banned by most surrounding authorities, but Dudley Watch Committee decided that local patrons over the age of sixteen should be allowed to see a local man's work!

Above: The interior of Dudley's Regent/Gaumont on 23rd. February 1969 when the Wurlitzer was played for the last time before members of the Cinema Organ Society. Perfomances were given by Steve Tovey, John Bee and others. Although Bingo was in operation the original cinema seats were still place!
(John Sharp)

Perhaps the wonderful scene in which the monster is introduced to his bride and her resulting scream was a more exciting cinematic event than Al Jolson singing to his mother seen in the film screened a few years earlier.

By the end of the thirties the Gaumont British presence was clearly established in the advertising, uniforms and monthly programme leaflets but the name "Regent" remained in use until 6th March 1950. While it was officially known as The Gaumont for the next decade, as with most such name changes, the force of tradition was too strong, and most people still label it "The Regent" in their memories.

At the end of the War, Bill Greaves took over as manager and during the settled period that followed many employees put in long periods of unbroken service. Three sisters, Beatrice, Freda and Margaret Morton worked there for many years. A good example of the kind of devotion to be expected from the staff was to be found in the Chief of Staff, Fred Hewitt, who looked very smart in his Gaumont uniform. He had been a carpenter and joiner. He had taken a temporary job at the Criterion and then stayed there over six years. While he was there he built a new sales kiosk which he installed at The Odeon, Blackheath. It was constructed entirely from re-cycled scrapped display materials. When he came to The Gaumont he made another one! The last resident organist at The Gaumont was Stanley Harrison, who worked there from 1947 to 1951, and later went to The Majestic, Cradley Heath.

The Regent opened a GB Junior Club for children aged between seven and fourteen on 7th October 1944 despite the fact that there was already a well-established children's club at the Odeon. As the cinemas were at the opposite ends of the town centre perhaps this did not matter.

When the little Savoy in Netherton died just before Christmas in 1960, Bill Greaves hoped that Netherton cinema-goers would come to the Gaumont. Perhaps he had no idea that his own cinema would close seven months later. I am sure he could never have anticipated how little attention the closure of Gaumont was going to receive. The Dudley Herald gave the Savoy a frontpage obituary, the Gaumont's passing was ignored!

The last film show was on Sunday 16th July 1961 and consisted of a one-day showing of *"Man of the West"* starring Gary Cooper in his last film, plus *"Submarine Seahawk"*. Not a moment was wasted in turning the premises into a Bingo and Social Club. It opened eight days later, on Monday 23rd July, as the Top Rank Bingo Club. It continued to operate in that capacity for over three decades.

At some stage there was talk of reviving the organ, but by the early seventies this was regarded as an impossible task. Replacement parts seemed too costly or even impossible to acquire. Many of its six ranks of pipes had been stolen. Even the cost of trying to remove the remains for scrap seemed daunting. An organ enthusiast from Peterborough, Mr. Roy Mosley, purchased it in 1975 and no doubt the proprietors heaved a sigh of relief.

Preservationists are never daunted, as railway enthusiasts who have heard of Barry Scrapyard will testify, and the Regent's 2 manual, 6 unit Wurlitzer has been lovingly restored at Peterborough Technical College. It was reopened on 8th March 1981 by John Mann. It was hoped that John Howlett himself would venture out of his semi-retirement to perform the ceremony. Unfortunately he was prevented from doing so by ill health. He sent a recorded message to the gathering, admitting his great affection for the organ. "I've seen it since its restoration and felt as if I was meeting an old friend", he said.

The old Gaumont, still known to most Dudley folk as "The Regent", reopened as the Venue, an Asian wedding and conference centre in the Autumn of 2002 and is currently (2011) still serving that purpose.

The Odeon

Castle Hill, Dudley

The last cinema to be built in Dudley represents what many people believe to be the zenith of cinema design: a late thirties Odeon designed by the Harry Weedon office. This particular Odeon seems to have been the work of Budge Reid who had proved himself with work on other Odeons at Wrexham and Crewe. Its strong stylistic simplicity is just as impressive as those Odeons with their fins and towers.

A site for Dudley's Odeon was found on Castle Hill directly opposite the Plaza. The cream faience treatment of the Odeon's frontage stood face to face with the huge unrelieved brickwork facade of the Plaza and, in my opinion, proved the more attractive. The only disadvantage that the Odeon appears to have suffered is that the rising ground of Castle Hill somewhat buried the impact of this frontage. It looked as if the building had sunk into the hillside, coyly hidden behind some ornamental gardens. (It was best seen from half-way up the chair lift in Dudley Zoo).

It was built by Housing Ltd., of Blackheath, who also built the Wolverhampton, Blackheath, and Kingstanding Odeons. It is reputed to have cost about £31,500. It held 1,876 patrons, 1,234 in the stalls and 642 in the circle – making it Dudley's largest cinema. Like other Odeons it was fitted with BTH equipment.

Thirty seven Odeons were opened in 1937, including the flagship cinema in Londo's Leicester Square. This represented a huge volume of human activity, of which the the work in Dudley was only a small part. The Odeon was opened on 28th July 1937 by Dudley's Mayor, Alderman J. Hillman. After his speech there was a musical interlude provided by the Band of the First Battalion, Royal Scots Regiment, followed by a charity collection on behalf of the Dudley Guest Hospital. The the films began with *"British Movietone News"* and a cartoon. The feature was *"Beloved Enemy"* starring Merle Oberon. Mr. and Mrs. Deutsch attended the opening despite such events now becoming rather numerous.

The first manager was Charles Crathorn, who apparently later became a radio and television personality. The first chief, Harry Willis stayed at the Odeon for years. The two men had worked together before at the Odeon, Blackheath. Even one of the patrons was so loyal he became an unpaid member of staff! This was Fred Hemmings, who had visited the Odeon every week since the opening, and, at his own expense, offered to look after the ornamental garden in front of the cinema!

The size and architectural grandeur of the Odeon immediately established it as the town's major cinema. It exuded a confidence that led you to believe that it would last forever, even when surrounded by competition. From then on its history was simply one of

143

stability and success, punctuated with anniversaries and a few special events. In 1941 the Minor's Club began and attracted over a thousand members.

At the end of 1952 two new BTH projectors were installed. Work began after the last show on Saturday night, and the Mayor, Alderman A.M. Silcox came in on Monday to switch them on! The Manager, Mr. Alexander, described them to the local press as "the very latest thing". Perhaps this was ironical in view of the success of cinemascope across the road at the Plaza two years later. Of course, cinemascope came to the Odeon eventually.

Abvove: Two John Maltby pictures of The Odeon, Dudley, taken in July 1937. (CTA Archives)

By the time the Odeon was preparing to celebrate its twenty-first birthday, in 1958, Donald Pass was the manager. He ordered a 150 lb. cake to be made by the Dudley Co-Operative Society with a replica of the cinema on top. In order to find a film with a suitable title, he acquired Carol Reed's ***"The Key"*** direct from the Berlin Film Festival.

Right: Inside the Odeon Dudley: Looking towards the screen in one of John Maltby's 1937 photographs, and below, looking back in the opposite direction after a complete refurbishment by the Jehovah's Witnesses. The organisation has refurbished a number of cinemas in Britain and the USA, photographs of which are proudly displayed at the former Odeon.

In the sixties, after many cinemas had closed, it was still possible to find queues at the Odeon and one had the feeling that its patrons still came from a very wide area. It was best to arrive early to be sure of even finding accommodation in the cinema's spacious car park. When the Plaza was twinned at the beginning of the seventies people began to wonder about the future of the Odeon but business, to an outsider, seemed good. The Saturday Morning Club still had eight hundred members. The last children's matinee was presented on 8th February 1975.

The Odeon closed completely on 22nd February 1975 with the popular musical *"Oliver"*. It was rumoured that the building was going to be pulled down and replaced with an office block. While a few people began to insist on the architectural interest of the building it remained boarded-up and unused. Dudley Council rejected Rank's application to demolish it.

In 1976 an unlikely purchaser materialised who was willing to conserve the building and put it back into regular use, not as a cinema, but as a Kingdom Hall. The local Jehovah's Witnesses have certainly extended

considerable love and attention to their Odeon, both internally and externally. They had to buy 1,600 cinema seats from Rank just to get started although they have since been replaced.

The work has made the auditorium very bright and colourful without being gaudy. The Jehovah's Witnesses themselves seem so pleased that they sell a souvenir set of post-cards of their work! Interesting touches abound. The mock orchestra pit has become a baptismal pool. The projection suite has become residential accommodation and the one-time flag-pole has been replaced by a bird table that, for a time was delightfully at odds with the well-preserved facade, but it was later discreetly re-sited.

The most interesting living proof of the power of cinema traditions to survive is to be seen at a meeting at mid-day on Saturday. Packed lunches are brought into the auditorium on trays swinging from the shoulders of well-groomed volunteers. If only the lights were dimmed you could still imagine that ice-creams and trailers and the "main feature" were on the way!

145

Netherton

Although a part of Dudley it seems quite wrong to think of Netherton as a suburb of Dudley in the way that Stone Cross might be a suburb of West Bromwich, or Penn a suburb of Wolverhampton. Netherton is an industrial village with its own identity, and complex character. When I arrived in the Black Country in 1962 I had never heard of Netherton but I soon found myself visiting the place again and again, to explore tow- paths, the Netherton Tunnel, Cobb's Engine House and all the wonders of Windmill End and Withymoor Basin. Netherton is enclosed in a huge horseshoe of the Dudley Canal, and the highest point within that horseshoe is crowned with the parish church, dedicated to St. Andrew, in which can be found some remains of the organ from the Odeon, Stourbridge. The entire hill and church looked, during the sixties, as if open-cast mining would obliterate them, but the landscape has been restored.

All around Dudley the Parish Churches stood on hills, safely within sight of one another, but remote from the industrial activity and social life of the villages below them. Non-conformists and publicans, and later cinema providers, brought their services much closer to people's work and homes, and a bustling community was to be found on either side of the main Dudley to Halesowen road which became Netherton's "High Street".

Netherton has been part of Dudley since the Borough was incorporated in 1865, but often acted as if it was a separate community. If the Council provided something in central Dudley, the cry from Netherton was usually, "We should have one of those too!" This applied to things like parks, modern street lighting, and libraries, reading rooms and public meeting places. This was the spirit that led to the building of The Public Hall and Institute in the centre of Netherton which was opened on 24th july 1894. It provided a library, reading room, and most important of all, a large hall. This where cinema first came to Netherton.

The Institute
(also known as Pictureland and
The Imperial)

High Street, Netherton, Dudley

The Netherton Institute was a large public hall built at the end of the last century, after the Countess of Dudley had carefully laid the foundation stone on 5th July 1893. When opened in 1894 cinematography had yet to be invented but public halls provided a space which organised entertainment was willing to fill. Robert Colin tried briefly presenting cine-variety in the autumn of 1908 while doing the same at Brierley Hill Town Hall, and at the New Hippodrome, Carters Green.

On 1st January 1910 Howard Bishop obtained a kine licence for film shows in the public hall of the Institute.

At first these were irregular, presumably dependent on when the hall could be booked for that purpose. These shows were advertised as taking place at the "Picture Palace, Netherton". By the end of the year it seems that Mr. Bishop had managed to acquire a more permanent lease and regular shows began on Monday 14th November 1910. The advertisement announced that Jesse Hackett, a celebrated local vocalist, would be present at the opening of the Electric Pictureland.

"Pictureland" was the name used by Howard Bishop not only at Netherton, but also at the Temperance Institute in Dudley and the Working Man's Institute in Cradley Heath. Locally people preferred to call it "The Stute", and later the nickname "Bungies" became so popular that it became a legend.

Howard Bishop provided all the services one would expect from a cinema operating in its own premises. The children's matinee was particularly popular and the usual rules prevailed: a penny downstairs, twopence in the small balcony. The man taking the money used to

Left: The Public Hall and Institute in Netherton, known today as The Netherton Arts Centre, but when the main hall was used as a cinema it was known to most of the locals as "Bungies". A picture of the interior appears in Volume 2. (Ned Williams, 1981)

shout, "Tak 'im back, 'e ay five", and try and keep order. If the film broke or a reel had to be changed the noise of stamping feet and whistling usually brought Mr. Bridgewater out of the library next-door to appeal for silence. At some point Mr. Bishop himself usually came on stage and banged the floor with a broom handle until the audience was silent. He would sometimes announce that the following week everyone would get two free comics! After the show several tons of monkey-nut shells had to be swept up before the evening's performance.

Throughout the twenties Pictureland continued to present films in Netherton although the shows at the Temperance Institute in Dudley had finished at the end of the War. Mr. Bishop was able to obtain seven year leases on the hall in Netherton and therefore he persisted in Netherton, where he lived, although unbale to continue at his other venues. It held about seven hundred patrons, including a few in the balcony but the ground floor of the hall was un-raked and is presumably little changed from how we see it today. In this respect it is difficult to imagine it worked so well as a cinema.

By the end of the twenties business had declined and Howard Bishop joined forces with Cecil Couper, from Brierley Hill, to bring the hall up-to-date by installing sound equipment. It is believed the Morrison system was used. Now a sound cinema, the name was changed to the Imperial, and it is thought to have opened as such about 1932.

In the event Howard Bishop died shortly afterwards and his son, Charles Bishop, took his place. By this time the hall could only be obtained on one year leases and there was always some uncertainty regarding the future of the Imperial. The result was the building of the Savoy, which opened in August 1936 but even that did not lead to the immediate closure of the Imperial.

When Charles Bishop took over his father's interest in the Imperial, his wife began working in the cash desk during the afternoons to learn about the business. She undertook the task of learning everything, including operating the machines, and stoking the boiler. All this knowledge was later put to good use at the Savoy! For the two or three years that the Savoy and the Imperial were both open Mrs. Bishop used to organise the matinees at the Imperial then leave it in the hands of the staff while she went to open-up the Savoy. By the beginning of the Second World War the Imperial had closed but I have been unable to trace any date for a final show or details of the last programme.

After the war the "Stute" became the Netherton Arts Centre, and professional theatre was featured for a time. Its stage was then adopted by Dudley Little Theatre for amateur productions. Although in many ways an antiquated building, it has survived and enjoyed considerable refurbishment, most recently becoming the head quarters of Dudley Performing Arts.

The projection room beneath the balcony has occasionally been used to present 16 mm. films, and there have been attempts to show film digitally in the hall, but flat floors and lofty ceilings do not make congenial surroundings in which to see films. This was something that was quite obvious way back in the late sixties when there was an attempt to run a film society in the hall. Therefore "Bungies" has really been relegated to the world of local legend, and a generation used to multi-plexes will find it hard to believe that the hall could once have been used as a cinema.

Below: The Savoy, Northfield Road, Netherton, 1953. (Gladys Bishop)

The Savoy

Northfield Road, Netherton, Dudley

As stated above, the Savoy partly grew out of Mr. Bishop's dissatisfaction with the terms on which he could obtain the hall in the Institute. But seen in terms of Mr. Cecil Couper's career it was a logical part of his 1930's policy of building purpose-built sound cinemas in Black Country villages, a process he had started in 1933 at the Coronet in Quarry Bank.

Mr. and Mrs. Charles Bishop and Mr. and Mrs. Cecil Couper formed the directors of the new company: Savoy Cinema (Netherton) Ltd. Stanley Griffiths of Stourbridge designed the building and it was built by J.M. Tate of Cradley Heath. It was built in Northfield Road, only a few yards from "the Stute". Five shops faced the road and the entrance to the cinema was reached by a grand flight of steps, and a covered shelter was provided for waiting patrons across the Recreation Street end of the building. There was no balcony and the five hundred and ninety patrons were accommodated on a single raked floor that sloped against the natural slope of the hill on which the cinema was built! A fairly modest nameplate over the entrance and a small sign advertising the current programme were the only adornments to the overall "snowcreted" surfaces of the building.

The Savoy was opened on Wednesday 26th August 1936 at 7.30 p.m. by Councillor Hillman, Mayor of Dudley. (Later during his term of office he opened the Odeon, just by way of contrast!). The Savoy was floodlit for the occasion. For the opening evening only *"Naughty Marietta"*, starring Jeanette MacDonald and Nelson Eddy, was booked but for the rest of the week *"First A Girl"* starring Jessie Matthews, was screened. Ironically, the patrons in Netherton seemed to prefer American pictures which gave the proprietors many headaches when trying to fulfil quota regulations. They were an audience who wanted plenty of film for their money, and generally wanted plenty of "action" in the films. Mrs. Bishop cites the Gaumont British News as an example of something too intellectual for the Savoy!

The art in running the Savoy successfully lay in persuading the patrons to wait for the films to arrive and not sneak off and see them earlier in Dudley. The Savoy also boldly advertised its shows alongside those of its big rivals in Dudley itself without any of the modesty of some Black Country village cinemas. The Savoy assured its patrons that it was the home of good family entertainment.

After the War the equipment was modernised and the Chief, Tommy Willetts, found himself in charge of an RCA LG220 sound system coupled to Ross GC1 projectors, replacing the Morrison sound system favoured by Cecil Couper. The Savoy survived the first winds of change that began to blow through the industry in the fifties. Even in 1958 business was good during the school holidays, and when suitable programmes could be booked. Cinemascope had been installed to keep the cinema up-to-date.

The Savoy never opened on a Sunday and ran two programmes per week throughout its life. Many of the regulars expected to occupy the same seat everytime they attended, including one fat lady at the matinees who regularly occupied two seats. Everything was efficiently supervised by Mrs. Bishop, and everybody could have "lived happily ever after", but the end of the fifties changed everything and by the end of 1960 the Bishops felt they could no longer fight a losing battle.

The Savoy closed on Christmas Eve, 24th December 1960 after wishing everyone a Happy and Prosperous New Year! The last programme consisted of *"The Iron Sheriff"* and *"Hidden Fear"*. Mr. Bishop was interviewed by the Express and Star, and the Dudley Herald gave the Savoy's closure front page headlines. Few other similar cinemas closing at roughly the same time received any attention at all; the Savoy must have been "special" after all.

The building remained standing and for many years was used as a carpet store and warehouse. During that time the exterior of the building remained unchanged. Internally, details like the portholes of the projection room remained a feature of the building. When the old cinema was eventually demolished in 2004, the site was cleared and a new community facility was built – providing a home for health and educational initatives as well as playing a part in Netherton's regeneration. The new building is called "The Savoy Centre!

I Interviewed Gladys Bishop in 1988 and this is what she had to say:

The Savoy opened with Nelson Eddy and Jeanette MacDonald in "Naughty Marietta". It was lovely! It was a packed house and all the councillors were there, and they were entertained to light refreshments afterwards. It was a very happy evening and we met all the guests personally and chatted with them when they came into the office for a drink and a bite.

We ran the performances every night from 6 o' clock and we ran the programme through twice, and we did matinees on Mondays and Thursdays, and for a long we did matinees for children on Saturdays. As time went by we were asked to open on a Sunday but we absolutely refused. We said that six days a week was good enough for anybody!

We were classed as a "C" cinema. The Odeon took priority over everyone and we had to wait until the big cinemas had run the films but they eventually came to us. We educated our audience by saying, "Now if you wait we shall have the film in your cinema and it will save you going into Dudley. They did wait and we used to pack them in nightly. We had the Gaumont British News and our audience appreciated that, and we had to sometimes make up the programme with cartoons. At times we had to take shorts whether we showed them or not just to get the feature film we wanted.

I did all the matinees myself, and I looked after things. On the odd occasion I operated the projectors that I had taken the trouble to learn about. We had a very good operator, a Mr. Fletcher, and I used to go into the operating box to watch him. He was a grand fellow and very tolerant of me and one day he said, "Have a go!", but the only times I really had to put films through was in times of sickness. Whatever happened, I could always fill in; I could even go on the door, because in this business you have got to be adaptable. When it came to directors' meetings, I could always put my say in, as I knew what I was talking about.

We also ran the Imperial at the Public Hall. My husband's father rented the hall for years, and carried on until his death. I came to Netherton in 1934 and it was well established then. It was rented for seven years at a time.

It was a very busy time when we had both cinemas. On the matinee days I started the Imperial at 2pm and then had to go down to start the Savoy at 2.30. and I was backwards and forwards all afternoon. Mr. Bishop Senior had spent a lot of money installing sound at the Imperial and was not very happy when the council said they wanted him to vacate the hall, in what turned out to be the last year of his life. Even we eventually found we were running the Savoy at loss, despite having the latest equipment, and eventually we had to sell the building. They were happy years for my husband and myself, and on six evenings a week we would contentedly climb Church Hill on the way home together.

Netherton: What might have been.

Just before the First World War a purpose-built cinema was proposed for Netherton by Thomas Jackson – a local cinema pioneer who had entered the business in Wolverhampton but who had subsequently built up quite a widely dispersed Black Country empire. His chosen site was somewhere in Netherton's High Street – i.e. between The Stute and Cinder Bank, at the Dudley end of Netherton. Plans were drawn by Messrs. Hickton & Farmer of Walsall, and permission sought but it all came to nothing – probably because of the outbreak of the First World War, and the collapse of Jackson's empire soon after the war. Had the plans come to fruition, Netherton would have had a rather more complex cinema history!

Right: Maud Gardiner, nee Revill, and the author stand outside the door to the re-wind room at the back of the Harts Hill Limelight Cinema in January 1982. Note the door to the projection room on the left.
(Photo: Tom Hetherington)

The Harts Hill Limelight Cinema

51A Vine Street, Harts Hill, Dudley

Half way between Dudley and Brierley Hill is the village of Harts Hill. Ribbon development on the main-road and the growth of housing estates before and after the last War have obscured the identity of such small communities. But in the early twenties Harts Hill was quite distinct from neighbouring Holly Hall, or Woodside, and fields separated them. In the other direction the railway and The Earl of Dudley's Ironworks separated Harts Hill from Brierley Hill. Harts Hill managed to straddle the boundary of Worcestershire and Staffordshire! Therefore one small part of Harts Hill was in Brierley Hill, but the section of the village that included Vine Street was quite definitely in Dudley.

Industry followed the mining of coal and a glassworks was built in Harts Hill. In turn this was replaced by the Dudley Drop Forging Company, Harts Hill was also home to Hingley's ironworks, and at the end of Canal Street was Hill and Smiths who also worked in iron. Opposite the "Dudley Drop" were Cartwright & Paddock, who employed a versatile engineering fitter named John Henry Revill.

John Henry Revill (1881 — 1965) was a local man who built his own house behind numbers 49 and 51 Vine Street. To amuse his children he would show them films in the living-room of this house, projecting from outside the house through the window. From these humble beginnings grew Harts Hill's little cinema

Mr. Revill built himself a cinema on the land adjacent to his house. It was a brick shed-like edifice with two entrances / exits in the side wall and a small operating room at one end. It appears to have cost just under £100 to build, and about as much again to equip. (At 1920's prices!). John Henry Revill recorded every single item

of expenditure from two shillings and sixpence paid for five dozen brass wood-screws to thirty pounds for an Ernemann Bioscope and twenty pounds for a Dreadnought Bioscope. Mr. Revill did not carry out all this work all alone – he enlisted the help of his nephew, Leslie Ball. Leslie Ball was a commercial vehicle mechanic who rose to become foreman at Pensnett Transport - hence his skills in dealing with the Limelight's gas engine. He lived close to the old Conservative Club in Pensnett and eventually opened his own business behind his cottage.

The Dudley Council issued a kinematograph licence for the premises on 30th August 1921 and it is to be assumed that Mr. Revill opened his cinema as quickly as possible after that date. The licence allowed 103 patrons to occupy the building but audiences may have sometimes been twice that size! All the front seats were benches but later, when the building was extended, there were about twenty-four tip ups at the back. Seats were 2d and 4d, later rising gradually to 3d and 6d. The screen was high up on the end wall of the building and lost the two top corners as a result of the slope of the roof. The plastered brickwork inside was gaily painted.

It was operated very much as a family affair. Leslie Ball helped to project and was a genius with the gas engine used to generate power. Mr. Revill's wife, Mary Elizabeth, ran the pay box and pasted up the local advertising hand-bills. Their daughters, Violet and Maud, worked on the gramophone used to provide musical accompaniment.

Outside work, life in Harts Hill had consisted of visiting pubs or chapels, of which there were plenty of both, playing football or racing pigeons. When the Limelight opened in 1921 life gained a new dimension. The cinema was a great success in the local community, and a tribute to the versatility and enterprise of John Henry Revill. In Harts Hill and Holly Hall today old people can recall the shows vividly. Serials like **"The Monkey's Paw"** and **"The Count of Monte Cristo"** were popular even though they seemed old then! Mr. and Mrs. Revill recorded details of many of the films shown in their own note-book and listed their own stock of "stand-by films".

Like other cinema proprietors they ran a popular Saturday matinee performance, and the shop at the front of 49 Vine Street did a roaring trade in sweets. Sometimes their takings at the matinee appear to have been greater than at the evening performance! Versatile Mr. Revill even printed his own hand-bills and letter-headings, and advertised his cinema on a large hoarding on the far-side of the main Dudley-Brierley Hill Road.

The approach to the Limelight Cinema was along a "drive" next to 49 Vine Street. An entry enabled patrons to pass through a wall and into the yard occupied by the cinema. In the yard a small wooden pay box was erected, and two sheds containing gas engines. Mrs. Revill sat in the wooden paybox, in splendid isolation from the auditorium. Originally they used one projector and screened a slide while changing reels, but later bought two projectors, with "modern" carbon-arcs. They also extended the cinema by sixteen feet in 1926, and enlarged the projection room slightly.

Contrasts: Left: Maud surveys the auditorium of The Limelight in January 1982. (Note poster on the billiard table.) Below: The auditorium re-created at the Black Country Living Museum, complete with bench seats and screen painted on wall, and "orchestra pit". Below left: John Henry Revill, proprietor of the Harts Hill Limelight Cinema.

In its early days The Limelight made a profit of about £2 per week, and generally all it went well up to 1928. In 1929 eveything changed, the cinema began operating at a loss, and patrons were tempted to go further afield in search of the talkies! Mr. Revill's family helpers were growing up and meanwhile the audience was dwindling. There seemed to be no point in converting the Limelight to sound.

It seems that the Limelight closed in the July 1929. Mr. Revill later used part of the auditorium to keep his collection of tropical fish. One night during the Second World War he coaxed the gas engine back into life and managed to revive a projector to show a few films to his daughter and her husband, to mark the occasion of their wedding, and then all was quiet once again.

The absolutely amazing thing about the Harts Hill Limelight Cinema is that it remained in existence right up to the time of writing Cinemas of the Black Country! I visited the premises in January 1982, over fifty years after its closure. It was one of the most astonishing events connected with my research into this subject. The screen was still on the wall, the projectors were still in the operating box. The gramophone was still in the auditorium — once filled with the sound of the Destiny Waltz and the Skaters Waltz. Reels were in their place in the rewind room, and the engine room and pay box still stood where they had always been. One tip up seat, the Limelight only had about two dozen, was still in the auditorium. My guide was Maud, John Revill's daughter and on the day after my visit she completed the sale of the property to William Round – a Harts Hill based haulage, removals and storage company. Their premises surrounded the Limelight – obviously they wished to acquire it, demolish and make logical extensions to their premises.

Immediately after visiting The Limelight I wrote to the Director of the Black Country Museum to see if he thought it worth trying to save the building and transfer it to the museum's site. He was keen to take up this cause and went to see the Round family to see what was possible. Unfortunately the discussions seemed to reach some kind of deadlock and for several years it looked as if The Limelight could not be saved. Nevertheless, during that period it was not demolished!

In 1993 Rounds Transport approached the Black Country Museum to see if they were still interested. By the end of that year museum staff were dismantling the cinema brick by brick and preparing to transfer it to the museum site, where a suitable location had been found. Once again the cinema would be "tucked away" – almost out of sight, and surrounded by its own yard.

The rebuilt Harts Hill Limelight Cinema was opened in the Black Country Museum in April 1955, and Maud and the Round Family came along to endorse it by confirming that it had been rebuilt correctly. Films were originally screened from 16mm prints, but now the Limelight has gone "digital" – what would John Revill have made of that?

Sedgley

Having looked at the little cinemas in Netherton and Harts Hill, we now move on to another area where the Black Country communites were very village-like. Before the local government boundaries of the late nineteenth century were drawn, Dudley's Staffordshire neighbours were the huge parishes of Sedgley and Kingswinford. We will explore them in that order. Within the ancient boundaries of Sedgley two "urban districts" were formed: Sedgley and Coseley. Our journey begins in the village of Lower Gornal, we climb western face of the Black Country's central ridge to bring us to Upper Gornal, take the Dudley-Wolverhampton road into the centre of modern Sedgley, and then descend the eastern flank of the ridge down into Coseley.

The cinemas of this area were often small and certainly intensely local. As will be seen, they were often known by their nicknames. They are the most difficult to research from the historian's point of view and here you will find the greatest number of gaps in this book's narrative. None of them exists as a cinema today. Yet despite both these factors, they possess colourful histories that have become legends. As someone says to a newspaper proprietor in a John Ford Western, "If you don't have the facts, print the legend!"

Lower Gornal

The Alexandra

Redhall Street, Lower Gornal, Sedgley

It is appropriate that our tour of the cinemas of the "central villages" of the Black Country should begin in Lower Gornal. The village, the legendary home of Aynuk and Ayli, maintained its Black Country character long enough to become a symbol of that culture. Two reasons, among others, may account for this. First its relative isolation, and secondly, the fact that the coal mining industry survived here at Baggeridge Colliery long after it had disappeared from the rest of the region.

Over a hundred years ago Doctor Hickin's Pit had worked the coal in the Redhall Road area – one of the many small pits that worked this part of the Black Country before the Earl of Dudley's new deep pit went into production at Baggeridge in 1912. The latter lasted until 1968, and in the time that has elapsed since then much evidence of having been a mining area has disappeared.

The man who brought the cinematograph to Lower Gornal and who chose to build a cinema in Redhall Street was Ernest Arthur Grenville Jones, an electrical engineer, who, at that time, lived in Pensnett. In March 1912 he registered a company called Alexandra Halls (Midlands) Ltd., with a capital of £500 and with three

Above: The "tin tabernacle" in Church Street, Netherton with was dismantled and taken to Lower Gornal to providse the auditorium of the Alexandra Cinema.

directors, himself, D. Jones and C.F. Webb. It seems that they hoped to own several cinemas but almost nothing is known about them. Did they hope to use existing buildings? Were they going to build something new? Surely, even then it was difficult to imagine that folks could open a few cinemas for £500!

Help came from an unexpected source. The Wesleyan Methodists in Church Street, Netherton, were about to dispose of their corrugated iron chapel. It was aleady a second-hand building as they had bought it in 1893 from a congregation in Birmingham. Such buildings were originally supplied as a prefabricated kit and they were built by erecting a basic wooden "skeleton" which could then be clad on the outside with sheets of corrugated iron. The inside was lined with wooden panels and the result was often quite snug. It was a relatively simple matter in 1912 to dismantle the chapel in Netherton and put it back up in Lower Gornal. A new front extension, probably built in brick, was probably put on the front of the building to provide an entrance foyer and a projection room.

In this way the construction of the Alexandra must have proceeded quickly. There seems to be no record of its construction or an exact opening date, but the Dudley Herald of 4th May 1912 records that the cinematograph licence had just been issued to the Alexandra and it can be assumed that it opened its doors as soon as possible after the granting of the licence.

The small hall held about five hundred people and was immediately successful. Many Gornal folk came twice weekly to see each programme and it became an established local social institution. It quickly earned the nickname, "The Bump", because of the noise from its slow-revving Crossley single cylinder gas engine which drove the generator in a shed at the side of the building. The stars of the silent screen became popular figures in Lower Gornal, and the cinema itself produced its own

legends: Uncle George, the drunken pianist, Ada at the cash desk, and Arlo, the chucker-out. One patron acquired local fame for laughing so much. His laughter apparently attracted further custom, so Jack Pugh was admitted free!

In 1931 the "talkies" were about to bring Lower Gornal's cinema up-to-date. It was planned that sound films would commence on Monday 31st August, but unfortunately a tragedy intervened. On the previous Thursday, 27th August 1931, Ernest Jones arrived at the cinema at about five o'clock to inspect the installation of the new "Imperial" sound equipment. Half an hour later, the operator, Francis Danks, from Shutt End, arrived and climbed into the operating room. By the time the first patrons were arriving, at about six o'clock, it was clear that something was going wrong as black smoke was pouring from the operating room. The fire itself seems to have started in the rewind room and although Ernest Jones and an assistant named Mr. Davenall, tried to extinguish the fire they were not having much success. Fires did occur in projection rooms and usually they could be brought under control. At some stage they must have realised the fire could not be brought under control and the important thing was to rescue Frank Danks. They also failed in this.

George Ball, who lived nearby, also tried to rescue the unfortunate projectionist. Eventually he succeeded, after reaching the room via a ladder to a window. By then the fire was so intense that the Bilston Fire Brigade could not prevent the entire destruction of the cinema. Frank Danks died the same night at Dudley Guest Hospital. Corrugated iron buildings contained a lot of wood and once this was burning the iron would usually buckle in the heat and the building would collapse.

Ernest Jones was badly burnt but he survived. Both men were non-smokers and the cause of the fire was never established. Mr. Jones was sent a bill from the Fire Brigade but claimed he had no assetts left with which to pay it!

It seems that Ernest Jones was determined to rebuild "The Bump", but once again the story of its reconstruction is "lost", and even the re-opening does not seem to have been recorded in any local paper. It probably reopened as a sound cinema about 1933, but was now built much more substantially. Meanwhile, Ernest Jones also became associated with the Castle Cinema, in Dudley High Street, for a few years.

In 1939 the cinema was acquired by Ken Jones and a Mr. W. H. Smith to be administered by Cinema Accessories Ltd., in other words; it had become a remote outpost of the Clifton circuit. Readers may wonder why the Clifton Circuit wanted to buy such a small cinema. Brand new Cliftons were built in Sedgley and Coseley, but what was the attraction of Lower Gornal. One theory is that Mr. Ernest Jones put it up for sale and it was built by a manager working on the Clifton circuit – possibly our Mr. Smith. Ken Jones was probabaly helping him out by bringing it into the Clifton

Left: The former Alexandra, Lower Gornal – awaiting demolition in 1981 after closing as The Throstles Club – a club for West Bromwich Albion supporters! It is not clear how much the Throstles Club altered the frontage of this building. There is still a large reward awaiting anyone who finds a picture of "The Bump" as a cinema!

network – the circuit already included many cinemas that were "managed" but not owned by the circuit.

At some stage the new BTP sound equipment was installed and every now and again it was refurbished in some minor way but essentially the Alexandra remained very unchanged and remarkably well supported, while other halls declined. By outliving places like the Regal, Wednesfield, it managed to inherit seats from the larger cinema!

Terry Ball, the grandson of George Ball who had valiantly rescued Frank Danks in the fire of 1931, joined the Alexandra at the age of fourteen in about 1949 and also experienced a fire - but one that was successfully contained and dealt with in the projection room. The manager at that time was Maxwell Gordon and if there was a fire the projectionist was supposed to report to the manager using a code: "Mr. Sands is in the cinema." Max Gordon started his career as projectionist at the Clifton, Sedgley, was promoted to manager at the Alexandra, and then went on to manage the Clifton at Fallings Park before returning to Sedgley to manage the cinema where his work began.

A Mike Friend recalls starting work for the Alexandra about 1958 as a fourteen year old posting the advertising bills over quite a wide area. He also assisted in stoking the boiler and general duties. He left for year but returned when he was about sixteen as a projectionist - assisting Mike Clarke. At the time the Alexandra was managed by Arthur Hodgetts. While he was there he remembers the first Sunday opening, and he remembers cinemascope being installed. Mike said that the area at the back of the auditorium provided with double seats for courting couples was known locally as "The Horse Box".

Another stalwart of The Bump was George Cooper. He started his career at the Clifton Sedgley as a trainee pro-

jectionist. He was often sent to the Alexandra to make sure there were always two operators in the box. He worked on the old Simplex machines that were notorious for over-heating. As fifteen year old he had his first experience of a projection room fire while at The Alexandra. He moved to the cinema full time in 1949 and stayed for about four years before going to the Clifton, Coseley. He returned to the Alexandra in 1955 to act as manager for about a year.

I remember visiting the Bump in 1965. My companion and I had walked through the countryside from Pensnett to see *"Help"* and after the show a member of the staff presented my companion with the poster from the display case at the front of the cinema — perhaps in recognition of the fact that we were foreigners. It had been a noisy audience and everyone seemed to know one another, but the Beatles then seemed as popular in Gornal as Pearl White or William S. Hart had once been. As we walked back to Dudley via the dark windswept wastes behind Gibbons Brickworks one had a strong feeling of having just visited a remote oasis.

Alas, it all came to an end on 24th September 1966 with a screening of *"Those Magnificent Men in Their Flying Machines"*. Generally a Clifton cinema would have had a prospective buyer before its closure was arranged and this was probably the case in Lower Gornal because the building had a further burst of life as the Gay Throstles Club. However, it seems noisy football club supporters upset the sedate atmosphere of Redhall Road because the Club closed in the early 1980s, and the building was then boarded-up. It was demolished about 1983 and some appartments were built on the site. The new appartments are called Alexandra Court.

YOUR LOCAL
CLIFTON CINEMA
LOWER GORNAL (Alexandra) —
Those Magnificent Men in Their
Flying Machines (U) 5.20 & 8.00.

The Picture House

Dudley Road, Upper Gornal, Sedgley

From Lower Gornal it is possible to climb the central ridge of the Black Country to Upper Gornal to join the main road from Dudley to Wolverhampton. At the point where Upper Gornal slides into Sedgley stood the Picture House, known to its patrons as "Jack Darby's".

Jack Darby was the licensee of the Leopard. He was a saddler by trade but came to this typical nineteenth century public house, with its own brewery at the rear of the premises, in 1905. At the time a large public hall stood next door, separated by a lane that took the trams to their depot behind that hall. The latter, known as "The Drill Hall", was built in the 1880s and its early life is described in volume two as it had pretensions of being Sedgley's first theatre!

The hall was turned into a cinema by a Mr. Lewis but, like "The Bump", its opening date is elusive. It seems likely that it opened late in 1911 or early in 1912. The earliest record I have found of its existence is a tiny note in the Dudley Herald stating that during May 1912 Mr. J. Lewis loaned the Picture Palace to local children for their spring pageant. About Mr. J. Lewis himself I have found nothing apart from the cryptic possibility that he may have later appeared as the proprietor/manager of a similarly obscure cinema enterprise in Wednesfield!

Clifford Brown's superb study of Wolverhampton Trolley-bus no. 637 passing a horse-drawn cart, taken on 31st March 1961, provides us with a glimpse of The Picture House after closure. The words "Picture House" seem to be falling from the front of the building, and some conversion work seems to have begun. Note the feedess to the overhead wires! (John Hughes Collection)

By the end of 1912 the cinema had been acquired by a Birmingham solicitor, Mr. Ernest Gilbert, who, with a friend, Fred Elvins, had registered the Midland Cinema Company on 27th November. They ran the Picture House for just over a year.

On 8th December 1913 Jack Darby took over. Along with his friends, Clifford Fellows and Joseph Eustace Fellows, he re-decorated the hall and "reopened" it. Jack Darby later acquired the Fellows Brothers' interests when they died. It was about the same size as the Alexandra and enjoyed a similar success. Possibly performances were quieter as the gas engine was at the rear of the cinema, and Sam Hartland's piano-accompaniments could be clearly heard.

Jack Darby retired from The Leopard in the mid-twenties, and handed The Picture House over to his son, Howard Darby, in the early thirties. Howard Darby took a partner, a Mr. Holmes, in 1936 and set about bringing The Picture House "up-to-date". A balcony was put in, which increased the hall's capacity to six hundred and thirty-one. A Western Electric sound system brought the talkies to Sedgley.

About the same time a brand new Clifton was being built in the centre of Sedgley, opening in May 1937, but this did not destroy the trade at the Picture House. In fact trade increased as the little cinemas had a reputation for warmth, and "order" was strictly maintained so that people could hear the soundtrack. The Clifton, like a few other super-cinemas, seemed cold and cavernous by comparison. During the Second World War the two cinemas shared the newsreels so relations between them cannot have been bad.

The Picture House carried on with its two programmes a week, two evening performances on a Saturday night and a children's matinee, often packed to capacity. Sometime early during the War a bomb dropped nearby and blew the neon-lighting off the front of the cinema. Howard Darby was in the A.R.P. (which had its HQ in the Tram Depot behind the cinema) and found the words "Picture House" torn off the front of the building. What did it matter? It was always known, and is still remembered, as "Jack Darby's". Just to cause a little confusion it was sometimes called the "Picture House and Hippodrome" in trade directories!

Mr. Holmes left the partnership sometime during the War and Howard Darby, and his wife, were left to run the place for the rest of its life. Although it was a small cinema they never regarded it as a "flea-pit". It was kept spotlessly clean by two sisters, Mrs. Britain and Mrs. Marsh, and the warmth and the atmosphere of an "orderly house" have already been mentioned.

During the troubled fifties Howard Darby still felt it was worth spending £4000 on re-decorating the cinema, replacing the Kalee projectors with new equipment capable of presenting cinemascope, and installing a wide screen. The remaining problem was one that always beset the independent exhibitor; one of obtaining films not already seen in Dudley or Wolverhampton which were modest trolley-bus journeys away, or at the Clifton. It was not possible to stay in business by endlessly reviving old favourites.

On 2nd January 1960 the chief operator, Jim Harrison, who had been there since the early thirties, projected the last show. The film was, *"The Mouse that Roared".* Then came the problem of finding a future use for the building as various manufacturers could not obtain planning permission to use the place. In the end it had to be leased for retail use only, and since then it has been an interior decorating/D.I.Y. store, although its exterior has remained basically unchanged right up to the present time. However, all trace of emergency exit doors on either side of the main entrance has disappeared and no sign of its past as a cinema exists inside the building.

Like "The Bump" and "Pages", "Jack Darby's" is still a local legend and details of its past are still the subject of argument in The Leopard or at the Sedgley and Upper Gornal Labour Club. Maybe someone still possesses a monthly programme the Picture House used to issue, headed "What's On". Howard Darby claimed they were the first to coin this title as a guide to forthcoming entertainment.

Below: The Clifton, Sedgley on Bingo in 1981.

The Clifton

The Bull Ring, Sedgley

About a quarter of a mile from the Picture House the Wolverhampton Road reaches the centre of the village of Sedgley at The Bull Ring. I do not know when bull-baiting last featured as entertainment in the village, but in the nineteen thirties this seemed an ideal site to build a super-cinema. Like other cinemas being planned at the time, this cinema was to have a large car park available and, as well as serving the host-community, there was a feeling that the middle-class patron would drive to a cinema, and to be situated half-way between two large towns was as good as being in the centre of one of them!

Sedgley's Clifton was designed by Roland Satchwell, and was built by the Wolverhampton contractor, H. J. Amies and Sons Ltd. The directors of Clifton Cinema (Sedgley) Ltd., were Sidney Clift, Leon Salberg, Ernest Roberts and Roland Satchwell. These names play a significant part in the Clifton story – as told in the introductory section of this book. By this time it was thought that Roland Satchwell had designed at least seventy cinemas!

The basic steel and concrete structure was concealed behind a particularly handsome frontage carried out in cream faience tiles with a low black dado. The use of a

corner site was exploited by continuing the cream faience across the front of the cafe and shops that extended round the corner into Ettymore Road. The four entrances beneath the canopy formed logical continuations of the lines of the four large vertical windows of the balcony lounge. The windows featured attractive leaded glass. The Clifton therefore has a much lighter, and less fortress-like presence than Roland Satchwell's work at Penn, or Fallings Park.

Much of the Clifton's equipment and fittings was common to other cinemas on the circuit. In this instance 1091 patrons could be entertained in Turner's latest tip-up seats, 779 in the stalls, and 312 in the circle. (This figure was fourteen less than appeared in trade directories!). As usual, BTH projectors and sound equipment were provided in the lofty operating room and BTH Deaf Aids could be obtained at the pay box.

The Clifton was opened on Monday 17th May 1937 by Captain Clift himself, and the proceedings commenced at 2.30 p.m. After the Pathe News and a cartoon the audience enjoyed *"San Francisco"* starring Clark Gable, Jeanette MacDonald and Spencer Tracy. A good quality opening brochure was produced outlining the programme and the details of the building. Programmes were changed twice weekly, and during the first few weeks favourites like Will Hay, George Formby, Jessie Matthews and Tarzan all appeared on the new screen.

The first manager was Mr. H.W.H. Crane. He had been in the cinema business since 1915 and came from a theatrical family – his father Harry Crane had managed the Grand Theatre, Birmingham, for a number of years. He had already worked for six years at the Scala and Castle cinemas, Dudley, so had established many friends in the area. He left Sedgley two years later to manage the Clifton at Coseley, where he stayed until its closure. The manager most strongly associated with the Sedgley Clifton was Mr. Maxwell Gordon who arrived after the closure of his Clifton at Fallings Park and supervised the cinema through its sad decline. At the time of the Sedgley Clifton's opening he had been its young chief operator. One Saturday morning matinee about 1970 he allowed me to view *"Oh! Mr. Porter"* as the sole occupant of the circle while the children in the stalls below maintained the traditional disorder.

Along with other Cliftons, the one at Sedgley provided variety shows and pop concerts in the fifties thus keeping alive the tradition of "live" theatrical use of cinema buildings, and, unlike some of its companions, it seemed to have a will to survive. When I first visited the Clifton, Sedgley, in the mid sixties, I found myself in a packed cinema enjoying a revival of *"Gone With The Wind"*. (Perhaps Clark Gable was popular in Sedgley!). However, by the mid seventies it seemed in a far less healthy state. It had outlived the Gaumont, Wolverhampton, and the Odeon, Dudley, but Bingo was being introduced for two nights a week.

Left: Clifton, Sedgley, balcony windows in 1997. *(Ned Williams)*

By 1978 quite a few seats had disappeared, which added an extra bizarre quality to sitting in a very empty cinema. By the final show only 845 seats remained in use. In the April of that year the building was acquired by the Jarglen Company, and Maxwell Gordon and his eleven staff were given their notice. Dudley Licensing Committee transferred the Bingo licence to Jarglen commenting, "There were no objections" but when they announced their intention of going over to bingo full-time some opposition was mobilised.

Although support for the films had dwindled to almost nothing, several local people opposed their total withdrawal, and I wrote a letter to Dudley's planning

chief on behalf of the local Film Society but our protests had no effect. Jarglen were merely doing what had become inevitable, and at least restored some social purpose to the building by running it successfully as a bingo hall.

The last films shown at the Clifton, Sedgley, were *"The Stud"* and *"The Anna Contract"* on Saturday 17th June 1978. After that Bingo was played seven nights a week without any significant changes being made to the building. When bingo ceased in January 1996 the building acquired another lease of life by becoming a Weatherspoons pub. The pub opened on 17th December 1998 and for a time featured a large 35mm cinema projector set up by the entrance!

On 3rd September 1997 I was able to make a survey of the Clifton, Sedgley, while it was awaiting sale. Purpose-built Bingo furniture still occupied the stalls, but the projection room had become a junk-filled pigeon loft.
The projection room has now been sealed-off altogether!

Coseley

The Coseley Picture House
(later known as The Cosy Cinema)

Ivy House Lane, Coseley

Sedgley's cinemas are not far from the crest of the central ridge that bisects the Black Country. What could have been more romantic after an evening at the Clifton, than a stroll over Sedgley Beacon to admire the twinkling lights of the conurbation? Where the base of the ridge meets the eastern plateau beneath the Beacon, where the sea of lights begins, lies the village of Coseley. At one time, Coseley could have been divided into smaller communities, such as Roseville, Deepfields and Daisy Bank; small hamlets with a history of mining. When the New Birmingham-Wolverhampton Road was built in the twenties it bisected Coseley in general, and a local road known as Ivy House Lane in particular. In this lane was "Page's", Coseley's equivalent to "Darby's" or "The Bump", and contemporary with them.

William Page, a cabinet-maker from Walsall, decided to build a cinema in Coseley in 1912. He formed a partnership with a Mr. Cook and they gained planning permission for their project in December 1912. The cinema is often said to have opened in that year but construction did not proceed quite as quickly as that!

Even so, Messrs. Page and Cook felt they were ready for business by the following March and applied for their licence. Four Coseley Urban District Councillors decided to make a prompt inspection of the place and one week later, at a meeting on 18th March, reported in favour of granting the licence subject to one or two suggested alterations being carried out. They made a second inspection four days later and the licence was issued. We can assume, therefore, that the Coseley Picture House, as it was then called, commenced business on 22nd March 1913. The name "Cosy Cinema" was not displayed on the cinema until after the Second World War, but everybody simply called it "Page's" anyway.

William Page lived opposite the cinema, and his son later lived in a bungalow built adjacent to it, so this close association with the cinema made its nickname inevitable. Mr. Cook's son-in-law later formed the other half of the partnership but he was bought out by Mr. Page, who ran it by himself until his death in the mid thirties, when the cinema passed to his son, William John Page.

William John Page had, in the meantime, taken over his father's cabinet-making and furnishing business in Walsall, although it seems that it was he who originally persuaded his father to build the cinema. W. J. Page's son, Victor Page, worked in his father's business by day and at his grandfather's cinema by night. Vic Page used to recall making the train journey from Walsall to

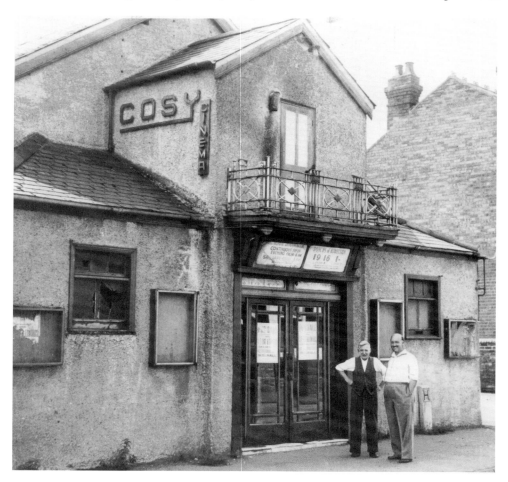

Left: The Cosy Cinema, Coseley, about 1958, after closure and awaiting sale. The gentleman on the left may be Mr. W. J. Page. (Express & Star)

Coseley, via Wolverhampton every night to assist his grandfather in the period following the First World War. He vividly remembered the sliding concertina gates at the front of the cinema, the little pay box in the porch, and the heat of the projection room. In the cramped rewinding room he used to assist Mr. Griffiths, the first operator at the cinema. In the best traditions of the business, the operator married the girl in the pay box, Ginny Oakley.

In those early days the front rows were bare benches, then upholstered benches, and tip up seats at the rear, and usherettes Lil Smith and Anna Beech, showed the patrons to their seats. Like many other cinemas, the Coseley Picture House used a gas engine to provide power for illumination, in the projectors, and the house lights, but the earliest projection equipment was hand-cranked, and some of the house lights were gas. Vic Page also had to fetch the films from Birmingham twice a week and carry the heavy cans of film from Deepfields station to the cinema. The shows usually consisted of a newsreel, a short comedy and then the feature, but serials like **"The Clutching Hand"** were also popular. The piano accompaniment was provided by a Mr. Cox, who was a painter and decorator during the day.

Children's matinees were presented on Tuesdays and Saturdays but the young patrons were not allowed to use the front entrance of the cinema. They stormed in from the side entrance and were by no means a quiet and docile audience. Even then the proprietors always had to be on the watch for "vandalism" and had to regularly check the screws in the seats!

Sound was installed in the early thirties, using Gyrotone equipment, and when popular musical films were being shown an ageing Mr. Page had to cry, "Standing Room Only". As some of the benches were replaced by more tip up seats the capacity of the little cinema fell from five hundred to four hundred. When William John Page took over he continued to modernise and improve the place and maintained the traditional personal approach to management, often standing near the pay box in evening suit and bow tie.

When Coseley's new Clifton opened in July 1939 trade was affected for about a month and then the old regulars started drifting back and business carried on briskly through the War years. In the 1940's a strong social scene existed in Coseley exploiting the two cinemas, dances at the British Restaurant, and refreshments at the old Hop And Barley. For a long time Arthur Grainger projected the films at the Picture House, and, in 1947, he was joined by a young assistant: fourteen year old Garton Hawkins who became a local legend as, "the little blackie in the operating room"! About 1950 W. J. Page sold the cinema to Messrs. L. Wilde and L. Poole and it officially became the Cosy Cinema.

Unfortunately, during the fifties the new proprietors were unable to keep up the payments on their private mortgage when the patrons drifted away, and the last

film was shown sometime during 1957. The building was re-possessed by W. J. Page, now in his eighties and, like many other gentlemen in the same situation, he now found it was difficult to dispose of the place. As usual the local council refused planning permission for the building to be used for light industry or warehousing. The Ministry allowed Mr. Page to appeal against this decision at an inquiry held on 21st May 1959. The local residents supported the Council's view but it seems that the Minister upheld the appeal, on the grounds that the building had several years of useful life ahead and should be put to some use until the site could be redeveloped. In the event it has become the Coseley Ex-Servicemen's Club, opened in 1961, and every now and again the residents of Ivy House Lane complain about parking problems and noise.

As a club the building has been transformed and anyone passing today would never guess it had once been a little cinema, but entertainment, of some kind, continues in the friendly atmosphere of the building which was once "Page's".

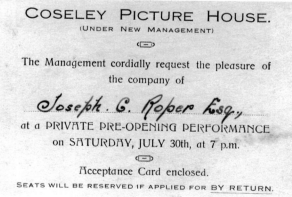

Two cards found in a collection left by Joseph Roper to his son John Roper, a well-known local solicitor and historian. The top one confirms that the Coseley Picture House did indeed open on 22nd March 1913, with an extra opportunity provided on the 24th if you missed it! The second refers to a "re-opening" and is assumed to refer to the transfer to W.J. Page's ownership.

The Clifton

Castle Street, Coseley

Coseley's cinema history follows the same pattern as Sedgley's. The small family-run picture house that had served the community since the early days of cinemas, found a new competitor with the arrival of a Clifton super-cinema in the late thirties. As in Sedgley, I feel the choice of this site had more to do with the emergence of private motor transport and the costs of building town-centre cinemas than with any inadequacy of the original cinema to serve its local community. True, Coseley's population was rising during the thirties, but I feel the directors of the Clifton Cinema (Coseley) Ltd. were more struck by the potential of a site overlooking the main artery of the conurbation, the Birmingham- Wolverhampton New Road. Some lack of confidence in the identity of Coseley is betrayed by their description of the cinema as, "Erected on the outskirts of the Staffordshire town of Bilston."!

The site was only a hundred yards from the centre of Roseville; in effect, the centre of Coseley. It was built at the Dudley end of Castle Street and seemed to face the traveller making his way towards Wolverhampton along the New Road. The frontage was an impressive blend of brickwork with stone facing around the three windows, and three sets of double doors, reached by a small flight of steps. The pleasing harmony of this elevation was not equalled by the view of the side and back of the cinema that greeted the traveller coming in the opposite direction. Here the massive brick walls loomed over the

blank spaces of the car park. The cinema's name in neon lights and a large hoarding advertising the programme did little to conceal how functional a cinema can be behind its facade when seen from this broadside view.

The building was designed by Roland Satchwell and erected by the Wolverhampton firm, Messrs. McKeand Smith and Company. It was built to hold 724 patrons in the stalls and 280 in the circle, but the capacity is usually quoted as 1050. Like other Cliftons it employed BTH equipment. Like the Regal in Wednesfield, it succeeded in giving its patrons an experience of luxury that few would have enjoyed in their own homes. Turner's tip up seats were upholstered in green, and the Super Wilton carpet was almost too good to walk on. When the finely designed proscenium curtains drew back they revealed a magnificent silver festoon curtain in front of the screen. Carpets and curtains were also supplied by W. W. Turner.

Since the opening of the Clifton, Sedgely, Leon Salberg had died, and Captain Clift was joined on the board of directors of this cinema by Messrs. Satchwell and Roberts, William Herbert Bull, normally associated with football, J. B. Share and C. W. Gray. The circuit now had over twenty cinemas operating in the Midlands and its opening somehow seemed less dramatic than the opening of the Regal, Wednesfield, in the circuit's infancy.

The opening took place on Saturday evening, 8th July 1939. The proceedings began with the National Anthem and then Ian Hannah, M.P., and Mr. Isaac Flavell, the

The Clifton, Coseley as illustrated in the opening Brochure.

Chairman of Coseley U.D.C. both said a few words. The latter was full of praise for the magnificent new building and stressed the educational value of the cinema to children. Ian Hannah felt there was something American about such a building. He added that he meant "American" in the best sense. A very British-made programme then followed consisting of **"South Riding"** starring Ralph Richardson and **"Oh! Mr. Porter"**, starring Will Hay, supported by Universal News. A special feature of the opening night was the free distribution of ice-cream!

The Clifton's new manager was Mr. Harry Crane, who had opened Sedgley's Clifton two years earlier. Apart from a period of service with the R.A.F. during the War, he stayed at the cinema for the entire twenty-four short years of its life, witnessing the sad decline in trade after the War. He added his own personal touch to the cinema by introducing two large tanks of tropical fish to the foyer. He also regularly changed into evening dress to greet the patrons. When trade faltered in the fifties a few one-night shows were tried. The first of these was on Tuesday 24th February 1959, and starred Jimmy Young, but already the Clifton's days were numbered.

The Cliftons found themselves standing on sites that were valuable for "redevelopment". The one at Fallings Park closed after a mere twenty-three years of life in 1961, followed a year later by the Regal, Wednesfield.

In 1962 a redevelopment company submitted plans to Coseley U.D.C. for a new shopping centre and bowling alley on the site. The plans were rejected but it seems that the cinema had already been sold, and its closure was by then inevitable.

The sad day came on 10th August 1963 when it closed with a screening of *"Nurse on Wheels"* starring Juliet Mills. Mr. Crane told the local paper, "Every one will be able to laugh for the last time, it really is a very funny film". I doubt that the staff laughed very much, for, as well as Mr. Crane, three other members of the staff of fifteen had been there since the opening and the rest had all been there for over ten years. As they stayed behind for a week or two to clear the building it must have been difficult to forget the happy years they had had together, and, ironically, the fate of their cinema as a building still remained unknown.

Coseley's Town Planning Committee seemed to be having second thoughts about redevelopment after some discussions with Staffordshire County Council. Upon a new application the developers gained approval to build six shops, a supermarket with a bowling alley above them, and flats and car parks on the surrounding land. The cinema was demolished by the end of 1963 and the wholesale redevelopment of Coseley's central area began the following year. The bowling alley did not materialise.

Below: A wartimne Sunday Concert at the Clifton ,Coseley, featuring a local orchestra and choir. These events were good fund-raisers and helped establish the prinicple of Sunday opening! (From the collection of Iris Turley).
Left: A Clifton Children's Club birthday postcard. (David Johnson)

Brierley Hill and District

Brierley Hill was home to Round Oak Steel Works, usually remembered as "The Earl's" as it had begun life as the Earl of Dudley's Ironworks. For the first three quarters of the twentieth century three Black Country towns: Bilston, Wednesbury and Brieley Hill were major steel-making communities and each of these towns was rather dominated by the local works, both in terms of the landscape and the numbers of people employed by them. Brierley Hill had a number of other firms connected with the iron and steel trade but was also well known as the home of Marsh & Baxters – manufacturers of hams and sausages. What emerges from all this is that Brierley Hill was a busy place – a thriving bustling industrial town – just the place to support a few cinemas. Today, at the beginning of the twentyfirst century, all this has changed, and the town is trying to regenerate and re-identify itself in the shadow of the new Merry Hill Shopping Complex – home to the Black Country's first multi-plex cinema.

When the old Brierley Hill Urban District Council was expanded way back in 1934 it took in surrounding townships where other cinemas were to be found. Brierley Hill UDC from 1934 onwards included Quarry Bank, where we have to tell the story of The Coronet, and Pensnett, Kingswinford and Wordsley – all once boasting cinemas! The cinemas in the central part of Brierley Hill are described in chronological order of arrival, and then we tour the surrounding area.

Brierley Hill

Early film presentations

Pat Collins regularly presented the fair at Brierley Hill Wakes from the 1890s to the 1950s. The first recorded visit of one of his bioscope shows was in 1909, but thanks to Southdown's writings in the World's Fair of the 1930s we have another account. (The identity of Southdown is discussed in the chaper on "Bioscope Days".

In the World's Fair of 30th October 1933 Southdown discusses his memories of Brierley Hill Wake and then adds:

"I wonder how many of the inhabitants of this old township can remember Mr. J.H. Bliss's American Bioscope visiting the Market Ground in 1907? This double wagon fronted show proved a big attraction during its stay. The exhibition was illuminated with a row of brass flare lamps on the outside and had a very nice four-figured organ of the trumpet variety. Mrs. Bliss's sister, Janey, was parading on the show with a clever knockabout comedian, Harold Reynolds. The pictures were always well varied, and on these Mr. Bliss

would lecture. He always struck me as being at his best when showing the once-famous picture, "The Bell Ringer's Daughter". He has had many members of his audience in tears on many occasions, and is equally good at making his audience roar with laughter at the excellent little comedies - which in those days were without subtitles. Although the illuminating power of the projector was supplied by two gas cylinders, the pictures were remarkably clear. It may be of interest to mention that the interior of the exhibition was illuminated with flare lamps before and after the exhibition. These were raised and lowered by means of a pulley and rope."

This is one of the few accounts found of a show by one of Pat's contemporaries. Unfortunately Southdown gives us no information about Mr. Bliss's show, nor any indication of whether it appeared at other Black Country venues.

The Queens Hall

High Street, Brierley Hill

Like many Black Country towns, Brierley Hill acquired a Town Hall before acquiring any modern local government status. It was opened in 1874, twenty years before the establishment of the Urban District Council, and the premises included a large "public hall" or "asembly room" that could be used for meetings and for entertainment. (Some kind of Public Hall had existed since 1867 on a site that later became the police station.)

Several interesting people leased the Town Hall on various occasions and it is difficult to know which of them might have first shown films. It is recorded that Professor Wood came in April 1900 – his first visit to the town – and he apparently gave phrenological readings downstairs during the day, and presented "animated pictures" upstairs in the evenings.

In 1910, when the Cinematograph Act came into force, the Town Hall's assembly room was leased to Mr. R. Colin for his presentations of film and variety. He had been using the hall since 1908 and he advertised these shows, and parallel ones at Nertherton's Public Hall as "The Tivoli". At various times, had also presented similar shows at the Empire, Dudley, and the Hippodrome, West Bromwich. Relations between Robert Colin and the Town Hall committee were often strained and in 1912 the committee decided to advertise for new lessees. They had five responses, including submissions from Irving Bosco and Howard Bishop who were competing with each other in Dudley, and Thomas Wood.

On 27th May 1912 the same hall reopened as "The Queens Hall", having been refurbished. The new successful lessees were Pooles Perfect Pictures, from Gloucester. They had also established themselves at the

Kings Hall, in Stourbridge. (Perhaps that is why they called their Brierley Hill operation "The Queens Hall".) Their first programme in Brierley Hill included **"The Charge of the Light Brigade"**. Admission was 3d and 6d, and twice nightly programmes were changed every Monday and Thursday. The manager was Cecil Couper.

Cecil Couper has been introduced in the first section of this book. He adopted Brierley Hill as his home and devoted the rest of his life, apart from army service, to local cinemas. About a year after arriving as manager, he took on the lease himself and made a great success of running the Queens Hall.

Although not a purpose-built cinema it enjoyed a long life. It survived into the sound era, by installing Morrison sound equipment and had the honour of introducing the talkies to Brierley Hill on 3rd February 1930, a month ahead of the Picture House. **"The Singing Fool"** was projected for the first three days of the week, and **"Sonny Boy"** for the following three days. They were projected by Harold Roberts.

Cecil Couper's son-in-law, Harold Roberts, learnt the business as an operator at the Queens Hall before taking on the Coronet, Quarry Bank in 1933, and it is not clear how much longer into the thirties the Queens Hall survived. All the indications are that it survived almost until the Second World War, apparently being run by a Mrs. Lamb who had graduated from the Palace. It seems as if the family and his staff struggled to maintain his little empire after Cecil Couper's death in 1937. Hence the fate of The Queens Hall, and The Palace, is a little obscure! Mr. Couper's daughter was of the opinion that when her mother finally abandoned the lease the local council were at a loss to know what to do with the hall!

Above: Film posters outside The Queens Hall and, below: The Palace, Brierley Hill. The cinema was behind the shop carrying film posters. *(Ken Rock Collection)*

The Palace

High Street/Church Street, Brierley Hill

Brierley Hill High Street came to an end at "The Five Ways", where Cottage Street, Mill Street and the top of Moor Street all meet. Continuing a journey from Dudley to Stourbrigde, along the old turnpike road, the traveller really finds himself in the top of Church Street. Today the Moor Centre occupies the quadrant between Moor Street and Church Street, but once the corner was occupied by The Horsehoes Hotel, and behind this, in the nineteenth century was a market place known as "The Old Boiler Yard". Portable theatres came to this yard or market place, and some of them might have stayed for quite a time. Their rather obscure history is told in volume two as they were concerned with theatrical entertainment. The story culminates in their replacement, in 1914, with a building from then on called The Palace.

The Palace was a timber framed corrugated iron building behind the Horseshoe Hotel. Variety and melodrama were popular at the Palace, usually referred

COUPERS' ENTERPRISES.

PALACE,
BRIERLEY HILL.

Proprietors: C. F. and M. Couper.

WEEK COMMENCING MARCH 9th.

Monday, Tuesday, Wednesday:

GLORIA SWANSON as

BLUEBEARD'S EIGHTH WIFE

Here's a picture bound to make your heart quicken to its startling climaxes —your eyes dance to its exquisite gowns and settings—your voice ring loud and long with enthusiastic praise. IT'S GLORIA SWANSON'S BEST. That makes it the best screen entertainment.

Thursday, Friday, Saturday:

BEBE DANIELS, DOROTHY MAC-KAIL, JAMES RENNIE and GEORGE FAWCETT, supported by an enormous star cast, present:

HIS CHILDREN'S CHILDREN

There's a big thought at the back of this startling picture, and a big situation in every part of it.

Usual Serials, Comedies & TOPICALS.

Prices as usual. 758

OLYMPIA,
WORDSLEY.

WEEK COMMENCING MARCH 9th.

Monday, Tuesday, Wed., at 7.15.

MATHESON LANG, supported by MDLLE. VALIA & HENRY VICTOR in

SLAVES OF DESTINY

Adapted from the Novel "Miranda of the Balcony," by A. E. W. Mason.

Thursday and Friday at 7.15.

Saturday at 6.20 and 8.40.

REX INGRAM'S

SCARAMOUCHE

The film that played to 240,000 people in eight weeks at the Tivoli, London.

The cast is over 10,000, headed by ALICE TERRY, RAMON NOVARRO, and LEWIS STONE.

For full details see special Bills.

NO ADVNCE IN PRICES.

Usual Comedies, Serials and Topicals.

Prices: 3d., 4d., 8d. and 1s. (reserved), the last two including Tax.

28

QUEEN'S,
BRIERLEY HILL.

Lessee ... ... CECIL F. COUPER

WEEK COMMENCING MARCH 9th.

Monday, Tuesday and Wednesday:

REX INGRAM'S

SCARAMOUCHE

The film that played to 240,000 in eight weeks at the Tivoli, London.

The Cast is over 10,000, headed ALICE TERRY, RAMON NOVARRO and LEWIS STONE.

NO ADVANCE IN PRICES.

Thurs. and Sat. 6.20 and 2.50

The one and only MATHESON supported by MDLLE. VALIA HENRY VICTOR in

SLAVES OF DESTINY

Adapted from the novel, "Miranda the Balcony," by A. E. W. Mason.

Usual Comedies, Serials and Topicals.

Prices: 3d., 4d., 8d. and 1s. reserved, the last two including Tax.

Above: A 1925 newspaper advert from the time when Cecil Couper was running The Palace, The Queens, and the Olympia in Wordsley.

Note that Cecil Couper describes himself as the lessee of The Queens, is ambiguous about his status at The Olympia, but makes it clear that he and his wife are joint proprietors at The Palace.

to as "The Blood Tub", but its manager, Mr. Goodhall did acquire cinematograph licences so some film must have been shown at The Palace during the First World War. It is thought that Cecil Couper acquired it just before the First World War and from then on it was more solidly used to present films.

It was never one hundred per cent wholeheartedly a cinema but after the War it was showing films much more regularly and advertised its programmes as far afield as Stourbridge and Tipton. In the mid-twenties, when Cecil Couper also took on the Olympia at Wordsley, the Limp and the Palace sometimes shared films.

The original building was damaged by fire sometime in the mid-twenties and was rebuilt more substantially of brick. It was reached via a passage-way from the High Street, the entrance being an arch with the pay box in the centre. Mr. Lamb projected the films, while Mrs. Lamb acted as cashier, assisted by Bernard Gash. Later the variety artistes, Kitty and Alfred Stewart came to help the Coupers run their various enterprises and Kitty Stewart played the piano at the Palace.

Sound was never installed at the Palace and therefore it is thought that it had returned to variety entertainment by the time of Cecil Couper's death in 1937. It seems to have "faded away" towards the end of that decade, and no trace of it exists today.

The Kinematograph Hall / Electric Picture Palace

Dudley Road, Brierley Hill

The Kinematograph Hall, Dudley Road, was almost next-door to the Round Oak Steel Works, and opposite the future site of the Danilo. Local residents remember it as "The Tin Shed", but information on the place has been very hard to find.

The Kinematograph Hall opened on Monday 10th November 1913 with *"Drummers of the Eighth"* - an American Civil War drama. A very brief mention in the local paper, the Brierley Hill Advertiser said: *"So far as the comfort of the public is concerned everything has been done to render this theatre ideal. It is artistically decorated in red and green, with seats upholstered in red plush."* Shows were twice nightly (7 and 9) and there were two three-day programmes per week. Prices were 2d, 4d and 6d, and a children's matinee was provided on Saturday afternoon. That is all we are told.

It appears to have been owned and built by Mr. D.W. Priest of Netherton and was large enough to accommodate six hundred patrons. Most puzzling of all is its subsequent demise. The cinema did not seem to advertise regularly, and it seems likely to have closed by the end of the First World War.

The Picture House
(later The Odeon)

High Street, Brierley Hill.

Brierley Hill's great claim to fame is that it was the home of the first cinema built by Oscar Deutsch; not his first Odeon, which came later, nor his first cinema, which had come earlier, but the first actually built for him. Oscar Deutsch joined forces with a local solicitor, Alfred Hawkins, to form the company to build the Picture House, and the architect was another local man: Stanley Griffiths from Stourbridge.

It was described as being in the "Assyrian Style", but was a fairly modest frontage by Odeon standards. The auditorium was set back from the High Street, and parallel to it. The frontage that greeted the patrons was merely the entrance to the pay box and crush hall.

It was opened by Thomas Williams, the Chairman of Brierley Hill U.D.C. on Monday 1st October 1928 with *"The Ghost Train"* plus *"Woman on Trial"*. Not to be outdone, Mr. Cooper presented the Ramon Navarro *"Ben Hur"* at the Palace on the same evening! However, the Picture House was the grandest cinema yet seen in Brierley Hill. Perhaps over-awed by its size, local people had worried about the safety of the balcony, but the new manager, Mr. A. C. Swift from the Grosvenor, Bloxwich, assured everybody that it was safe.

The Picture House began life with an orchestra led by a local composer, and pianist, Harold Hunt, but obviously the silent era was drawing to a close. The Picture House installed BTH equipment and opened for sound on Wednesday 12th March 1930 with **'The Rainbow Man'** proudly proclaiming: *"The only complete All British "talkie set" in this district — Made and assembled in the Midlands by Midland Engineers".*

The name "Picture House" was replaced by "Odeon" in January 1936. The original name was covered rather than removed, and was thus exposed again when the cinema was demolished. As it was smaller and slightly older than most Odeons, although younger than some of the halls absorbed by the circuit, it had the feeling of being a fairly remote outpost. In August 1951 when it was featured in "The Circle", the house magazine of the circuit, the Manager had taken a day off and the young chief operator, Tom Roberts, had acted as the cinema's ambassador! They concluded that it was "small but cosy".

One small claim to fame on the mighty Odeon circuit for Brierley Hill's cinema was that it had once been the responsibility of the circuits youngest-ever manager. Donald Pass was eighteen years old when he became manager at Brierley Hill. He started work there when it was the Picture House, way back in 1930, as a rewind boy, and returned as manager when it became the Odeon. He later managed the Odeons at Stourbridge and Dudley.

In the fifties Rank began to close cinemas like Brierley Hill's, and early in 1959 rumours abounded that it was to be included in a forthcoming auction. In the event the auction did not take place but the Brierley Hill Odeon was certainly up for sale. It was acquired by Stan Bastock, a trader at Brierley Hill's Market Hall. It closed without ceremony or comment on 25th July 1959 with *"Idle on Parade"* only having outlived the Forum, Pensnett, by a couple of months, and leaving the Danilo as Brierley Hill's sole surviving cinema. A Fine Fare supermarket was then built on the site.

Below: The Picture House, Brierley Hill, after the name "Odeon" had been placed over the original name. Note the auditorium is at right angles to the foyer and frontage.

(John Maltby)

Left: The interior of the Picture House/Odeon, Brierley Hill from the balcony. (John Maltby – CTA Archive.)

John Maltby, of Watford, took between three and six pictures of each Odeon as it opened or as it joined the circuit. Most of his 10"x8" glass negatives survive.

The Danilo

Dudley Road, Brierley Hill

Brierley Hill's only genuine super-cinema was the Danilo. Danilo (Brierley Hill) Ltd., was registered on 4th October 1935 with two directors; Mortimer Dent, and John Benton, of the Turks Head, Brierley Hill. It is thought to be designed by Ernest Roberts, and was built by William Jackson of Oldbury. It was a twelve hundred seater and, when new, must have seemed the most impressive building ever erected in Brierley Hill. It was equipped with sound by RCA.

It was opened on Monday 21st December 1936 by the Earl of Dudley, in the presence of George Formby, who was currently appearing on stage in Birmingham. The Earl of Dudley actually arrived just too late to make his opening speech and found that his son Viscount Ednam had deputized for him! George Formby had sung a song, and music had also been provided by the band of the Sixth Battalion of the South Staffordshire Regiment. Mr. R.H. Morgan, the Stourbridge M.P. who was interested in cinema matters, was present but Mortimer Dent seems to have been very self-efacing at these ceremonies. The first feature film shown was *"The Lady Consents"* and proceeds from the event were divided between the Dudley Guest Hospital and Corbett Hospital.

Not only was the Danilo's opening a major event in Brierley Hill's history, the cinema also managed to be at the centre of another interesting historic moment only two years later. On 25th September 1938 the Danilo played host to Paul Robeson. He had been invited to Brierley Hill by the town's prestigious Choral Society. The concert at The Danilo was a complete sell-out and once again crowds gathered outside the cinema long before the event, hoping to catch a glimpse of the black American star. Just to make sure everyone in Brierley Hill knew exacxtly who Paul Robeson was the cinema

screened his latest film, *"Sanders of the River"* during the previous week!

The concert opened with the orchestra playing The William Tell Overture, and other pieces, as a preface to the appearance of the choir – conducted by Stanley Adams, founder of the Choral Societgy. Paul Robeson then filled the remaining part of the first half of the concert. By the end of his appearance at the end of the second half of the show he had song ten songs – all accompanied by Lawrence Brown on solo piano. The 1200 strong audience managed to persuade him to sing another seven songs as an encore! It was an unforgetable show – and Paul Robeson only ever made one other appearance in the Black Country – at Wolverhampton's Civic Hall, in 1949. Local legend has it that Paul Robeson appeared at Brierley Hill for a fairly modest fee, and his appearance at The Danilo was probably the result of Dr. Campbell's influence and connections. Dr.Cambell was a well known local GP and Chairman of the Choral Society.

Whatever the pretensions of the Odeon, the Danilo, through size and modernity, was the town's most prestigious cinema. Muriel Morgan who went to work there as an usherette, from the Coronet, Quarry Bank, found herself working in a team of eight. The girls wore made-to-measure uniforms and it was the kind of place where brass buttons had to be polished. She remembers *"Love is a Many Splendoured Thing"* running for three weeks at the cinema and people queueing to see it several times. The usherettes never grew tired of the film either, nor weary of the audience crying.

Mortimer Dent occasionally visited the Danilo, usually accompanied by two large dogs, but ten years after it opened, the Danilo, along with the others on the circuit, was sold by Mr. Dent to Mr. Southan Morris' S.M. Super Cinemas Ltd. In turn it passed to the Essoldo Group but the name Danilo was retained until the end. As part of a large circuit, management seemed to change fairly frequently and no one particular named

The Danilo. Brierley Hill. (William Jackson Archive)

individual seems to have become well known locally through his work at the Danilo.

From 1959 onwards it was the only cinema left open in Brierley Hill, but I found it a rather impersonal and slightly run-down cinema when I visited it in the mid sixties. We went to see *"How The West Was Won"* and after the film had started we were annoyed not only by the three-lens process in which the film had been shot, which created a very distorted picture, but also a large mark across the picture suggesting the operator had left part of his bacon sandwich in the gate of the machine. When I complained I was told that it was a stain on the screen and the effect would be there throughout the film!

By then Essoldo Ltd. were already trying to obtain permission to operate Bingo. Dudley Council at first refused to grant permission but after an appeal and a public enquiry in 1967, permission was eventually obtained. The cinema which had once hosted Paul Robeson enjoyed one last moment of celebrity in Janaury 1968 when the film adaptation of James Joyce's "Ulysses" was shown for a fortnight. As the film had no certifcate each local Watch Committee had to decide whether it could be shown within its area.

Some towns banned it – others were indifferent – some agreed that it could be shown but only to patrons over the age of eigthteen. People flocked to see the film at Brierley Hill's Danilo but most came away somewhat disappointed.

The Danilo showed its last film, *"The Graduate"*, on 22nd February 1969. The facade, at entrance level, was then modernised with black and white tiles totally lacking in sympathy with the great expanse of brickwork that created the "Danilo-style", but generally the exterior of the building survived into the eighties without a great deal of alteration. Bingo was presented in the former Danilo from 1969 until June 1998, firstly by Mecca Bingo, then by Walker Bingo.

After Bingo had come and gone the Danilo began another life as a nightclub. The "Eclipse" nightclub opened in 2000 and closed June 2002. Six months later it re-opened as "The Club" on Fri 20th December 2002. More recently it has been renamed "The Deep" and then "Oxygen"! The building was sold – yet again – on 8th December 2010 at an auction for £150,000. As this book goes to press the former Danilo is reopening as the "Pulse Night Club" on 9th. July 2011. No one is betting that it will ever reopen as a cinema!

DANILO

Left: The interior of the Danilo, Brierley Hill, looking towards the screen, and looking back from the screen into the auditorium, giving some idea of the size of this cinema.
(William Jackson Archive)

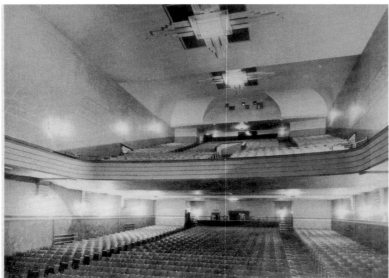

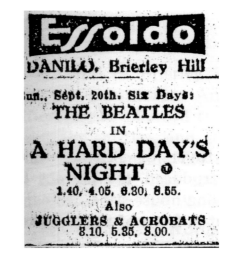

Essoldo
DANILO, Brierley Hill
un., Sept. 20th. Six Days:
THE BEATLES
IN
A HARD DAY'S
NIGHT
1.40, 4.05, 6.30, 8.55.
Also
JUGGLERS & ACROBATS
3.10, 5.35, 8.00.

THE FILM SENSATION OF ALL TIME!!
The uncut version of James Joyce's controversial
ULYSSES
(Special Local Watch Committee X cert licence)
ADULTS ONLY

Left: crowds form a queue outside the Danilo, Brierley Hill to see "Ulysses" in January 1968.
(Norman Robins)

Quarry Bank,

Quarry Bank was an independent "Urban District" from 1894 until 1934, whereas Pensnett, Kingswinford, and Wordsley were simply villages within the area administered until 1934 by Kingswinford Rural District Council. Therefore Quarry Bank is more of a place to reckoned with: something more than just a village!

The Coronet

High Street, Quarry Bank, Brierley Hill

Quarry Bank's first and only cinema was one of Cecil Couper's purpose-built mini-cinemas of the thirties, the other two being The Forum, Pensnett, and The Savoy, Netherton. It was designed by A. L. Horsburgh of Birmingham. The plans were approved in July 1932. It was built by Messrs. Batham and Beddall, well-known Brierley Hill building contractors. The four directors of The Quarry Bank Cinema Company, formed to run the Coronet, were Mr. and Mrs. Couper, their daughter, Irene, and her husband, Harold Roberts. His introduction to the Couper family seems to have been when he arrived at the Queens Hall to be a projectionist.

It was opened on 22nd February 1933 and every one of its five hundred seats was occupied by six o'clock. Many more people arrived and were unable to obtain seats! The ceremony was performed by Mr. J E. Dunn, who was President of the Quarry Bank Hospital Carnival Committee, and all the proceeds were given to that committee. The film presented was *"The Cuban Love Song"* but that was only presented for the one night. A normal three day run followed of *"New Moon"*, a Drury Lane Musical starring Lawrence Tibbett and Grace Moore.

It was a small cinema, with no balcony, despite originally offering seats at four prices, between four pence and a shilling. The frontage featured three vertical windows that gave an impression of there being a balcony but this was misleading. The two sets of double swing-doors in the centre of the facade were flanked by small shops. As in other Cecil Couper cinemas, Morrison sound equipment was installed but after the War this was replaced with the RCA system when some new Kalee II projectors were installed.

It was very much Harold Roberts' cinema. He had worked for his father-in-law at the Queens Hall, and presented the first talkie in Brierley Hill a few years before coming to the Coronet. He was well-liked by staff and patrons and a happy family atmosphere flourished at the Coronet throughout its life. For a time three sisters worked at the Coronet: Nelly Horton in the cash box in the main entrance, which led to the cheap seats, and Muriel Horton was an usherette. Muriel married Tommy Morgan who had started work as a page-boy, later worked at the Queens Hall, and then became an assistant operator at the Coronet. Various chief operators came and went, including Don Weston, George Horton and Jack Fletcher (who was Muriel Horton's brother-in-law!). Harold Roberts, of course, could project the films himself if necessary, but such was Harold's popularity that Tommy Morgan would go back in later years to help him out if required.

Right: The Coronet, Quarry Bank, decorated for the Queen's Coronation in June 1953. (Celia Couper)

An important night in the history of Quarry Bank was 19th December 1940 when land mines were dropped on the village, but did not explode. One dropped on the Liberal Club and the subsequent de-fusing and removal of the bomb has become the stuff of local legend. Most local people alive today who can recall that event begin their recollection with the words, "One night I was sitting in the Coronet when…" Other people talk about the children's matinees and the fact that the cheapest seats weren't seats at all – one just sat on mats on the floor beneath the screen!

In places like Cradley Heath Sunday-opening has never prevailed, even to the present day. However, the Coronet took advantage of Sunday-opening in Brierley Hill, after a campaign fought by the Odeon and Danilo, and opened seven days a week after the War.

One feels sorry for Harold Roberts as the nineteen-fifties brought the problems of declining audiences and even vandalism. In 1959 the Olympia, the Forum, and even the Odeon, all closed within the Brierley Hill area. His wife died about the same time. It seemed unlikely that Quarry Bank's little cinema could survive much longer.

Mr. Roberts put on the Coronet's final show on 20th February 1960: *"The Mouse That Roared"* starring Peter Sellers, supported by *"A Good Day For A Hanging"*. The advert for the last show at the Coronet gave the reader no clue that this cinema was about to close. Cinemas usually seem to have been rather coy about announcing their demise.

The Coronet had lasted twenty-seven years. Mr. Roberts' problems were not yet over. He applied for planning permission to convert the building into a factory and the application was refused. He then planned to convert it into a car showroom but again the application was turned down. The building changed hands several times before being demolished in January 1967 to make way for a petrol service station, which survived on the site for the next twenty years. In the end the petrol station disppeared as well and there is now housing on the site.

Wordsley

The Olympia

Brierley Hill Road, Wordsley

To the West of Brierley Hill lie the villages associated with the glass trade, Amblecote and Wordsley. The Clifton circuit planned to build a cinema in Amblecote during the thirties, and actually acquired some land to do so, but a cinema did not materialize. On the other hand, Wordlsey had supported a cinema of its own since before the First World War, and possibly felt no need of a Clifton.

The Olympia, Wordsley, was the property of Anthony Bailey (1872-1952). He owned a brewery in Brewery Street, now called Brierley Hill Road. The brewery had been built by Edward Oakes in the mid to late nineteenth century. Later mineral water was also produced at the brewery. In 1886 Anthony Bailey's father came to work at the brewery, and Anthony eventually learnt he art of producing mineral water. Later still Anthony was able to buy the brewery and surrounding buildings.

In 1912 he converted part of the premises into a cinema/theatre. According to an interview that Anthony Bailey gave to the late Jack Haden, he took advice from Ben Kennedy about doing this. It seems that Ben Kennedy may have supervised some of the conversion work in return for a three year lease on the building. It held about six hundred patrons and had stage facilities and dressing-rooms.

The Olympia opened on 23rd December 1912, presenting programmes of cine-variety, in the style favoured by Ben Kennedy. It closed again from June to August Bank Holiday 1913 for re-seating and was then leased to Benjamin Kennedy for a further six months. The County Express did report this reopening and said: *"The cinema has just reopened after a summer recess - during which time it was thoroughly cleaned and redecorated.*

Left: Crowds gather around Mr. Yapp, the blacksmith with premises on the right, to celebrate the end of the First World War. Meanwhile: on the left we catch a glimpse of the Olympia, Wordsley. Note the narrowness of Brierley Hill Road at this time. (Hazel Yapp)

The programme consists entirely of pictures. Special note is merited by the decorations on the stage, an array of graceful ferns and artificial flowers studded with electric lamps forming a most pleasing spectacle."

When Anthony Bailey spoke to Jack Haden about this he supplied a slightly different version of events. In his version Ben Kennedy's shows opened The Olympia from the start but many local people found the comedy was offensive and the audience rapidly declined. Kennedy reached the point where the small audiences did not warrant putting on the show and was about to quit. Anthony Bailey claims that he went to see Mr. Kennedy and sub-leased his own theatre back off his tenant for £2.50 per week! He also bought the cinematograph equipment from Mr. Kennedy and this led to the re-opening mentioned in the press when only films were shown. Apparently Mr. Kennedy and Mr. Bailey eventually came to a mutually acceptable arrangement, and Ben's brother Harry gave helpful advice on booking films and live acts. Anthony Bailey became so good in this capacity that Douglas Phelps at the Alhambra, Stourbridge became anxious about the competition!

In effect The Olympia was looked after by Mr. Bailey for the next decade, in which he felt he learned a great deal about the business. During this time the early pianist, Charley Matthews, had been followed by the violinist, Lena Wood. She became well known and attracted a large following.

About 1922 Anthony Bailey suffered a heart attack and had to think about devoting less energy to running The Olympia, particularly as the mineral water side of his business empire was also busy. A Mr. Roberts ran the cinema for few months but without great success so Anthony Bailey resumed control until finding someone who would buy it from him. In March 1923 he sold the Olympia to Cecil Couper for £4,500. On the day the cinema changed hands a special presentation was made to Mr. Bailey by Lena Wood. He was given a travelling bag bought by the orhestra and some of the regular patrons.(Lena Wood, the Olympia's violinist later played in broadcasting orchestras and lived in Stourbridge until 1982!)

Anthony Bailey later said that his greatest pleasure had been running the children's matinee shows. He tolerated the row generated by the youthful audience and gave every child a small Christmas present. He even collected old cowboy films specially for showing at the matinees. He aslo revealed that The Olympia had been at its busiest during 1919 and 1920. Sometimes he could not pack everyone in the cinema and had to employ a policeman at 8/- a night to control the queue.

Cecil Couper's background enabled him to continue the traditions of live variety at the "Limp", as it was known locally. The Coupers even ran a short "stock season" of plays at the Olympia, presented by the Charles Edwards Players in the late summer of 1929! Cecil Couper had installed Morrison sound equipment in the Olympia by

the autumn of 1931, but it is not clear what film was the first talkie shown in Wordsley.

The cinema had a habit of changing hands about every ten years. In 1934 it was taken over by Fred Leatham, this time in association with Eldon Firmstone. Mr. Firmstone, who lived nearby in Wordsley Manor, was an accordianist and claimed to be a cinema organist. He built his own private cinema at the Manor, at about the same time, and probably did not remain involved with the Olympia for very long. (See below.)

The restless Mr. Leatham stayed at the Olympia until about 1940 and then it was sold to a Mr. Bullock. Again there seems to have been some change of equipment, and for the rest of its life the cinema used the Worthytone sound system. Mr. Bullock tried hard to run an orderly house and had a like-minded chucker-out named Mick Masters. The latter ran the children's matinee and even during the Second World War found himself wading through monkey-nut shells after every performance to replace screws missing from the seats! One gentleman who was a child in Wordsley at the time can remember saving sixty-five pounds of waste paper to earn free admission to *"Gasbags"* starring the Crazy Gang.

Mr. Bullock ran the Limp through the fifties until it became impossible to go on. The last film, *"Maracaibo"* starring Cornel Wilde, was screened on 16th May 1959. (A fortnight before the closure of the Forum, Pensnett). Mr. Bullock sold the premises to a neighbouring die-casting firm.

The building was not demolished until 1969. (During demolition an 1858 foundation stone was uncovered). The site is now obscured by housing, and looking back now it is difficult to imagine films at the "Limp" One last word: For collectors of cinema nick-names, the Olympia is an interesting example. Many cinemas called "the Olympia" became known as "The Limp" but in Wordlsey many people called their picture house "The Snake". It was called this because the manager used to come in before the film started and shout, "Any of yo' who have snaked in here, can snake out again!"

Wordsley Manor: home to a private cinema!

WORDSLEY MANOR

Eldon Firmstone installed a Christie organ on the ground floor of Wordsley Manor in 1933, and opened his 50 seater cinema on the top floor in 1934 with the intention of running public shows every Sunday evening. He had grown up in a family owning local ironworks but showed little interest in industrial activity. He wanted to be a musician and an entertainer. Just before his death I went to Wordsley Manor to meet him and to talk about his cinema. Although he was keen to convince me that he had been a famous cinema organist, he could not supply the name of any cinema in which he had played – other than a one-night appearance at The Majestic, Cradley Heath.

He ran a few public film shows at Wordsley Manor but was then taken to task by the local magistrates who were upset that he did not have a cinematograph licence. He objected on the grounds that they were private shows. There were one or two more shows but they ceased without the dispute ever being resolved!

Kingswinford

The Grand

Market Street, Kingswinford.

Above: The Grand, Kingswinford.

Kingswinford seemed a smaller village than Wordsley in the days when cinemas were young. The electric tramway had linked Kingswinford with the outside world towards the end of 1900 but the journey to Brierley Hill meant a change of car at Brettle Lane or Scotts Green and it is difficult today to imagine how "separate" such communities once felt. Brickworks, fire-clay mines, desolate pit banks etc., all once separated the little village of Kingswinford from its neighbours.

In Market Street, on the road southwards to Wordsley and Stourbridge, stood a Market Hall. Just after the First World War a group of local businessmen led by the builder and timber merchant, Mr. Charles Coulson, decided this building would be ideally suitable for conversion to a picture palace. They were inspired by the success of other local cinemas, and invited Thomas Cooper of Blackheath to join them to provide some expertise. Together they formed Elysian Pictures.

It was planned that the Grand should open on Boxing Day 1919 but unfortunately it was not ready in time. It opened on Monday 5th January 1920, and the first programme included a five reel feature film, **"The Claw"**. Seats were 3d, 4d, 9d, and a one shilling, and the Grand featured an "orchestra", which was unusual for a place of its size where a trio would have been as much as could be expected. The pianist was James Hough, who later became manager for a time.

The opening did attract some attention in the Stourbridge newspapers:

The County Express of 3rd January 1920 wrote: *"A representative of the County Express has had the opportunity of inspecting the premises in company with Mr. D.H. Cox (one of the directors) and Mr. A.G. Wigley (manager) and was much impressed with the visit. The theatre possesses the greatest convenience and comfort for patrons, and the excellent arrangement of the seating and the slope of the floor will enable every member of the audience to have a clear and uninterrupted view of the screen. Tip-up seats have been introduced and there is a large number of plush chairs - the hall will accommodate 750 to 800 persons. There will be a change of picture in the second half of each week and a matinee on Saturday. The entrance to the cheap seats will be from Summer Street, and that to the other seats from the front of the building."*

The Stourbridge Observer of 10th January 1920 reported: - *"There were crowded audiences at the opening of the Grand, Kingswinford, on Monday evening, and the venture should be assured of success... The hall is very commodiously adapted and well heated. It has six exits and is electrically lit, and can accommodate 800 people. The floor is gradually elevated, giving everyone a fine view of the screen. There is some work on the exterior of the building still to be completed. The manager is Mr. A Wigley, and the operator is V. Reynolds from Dudley. The films will be changed twice weekly."*

Like many small cinemas in the more "remote" parts of the Black Country, its history is relatively obscure. It did not advertise regularly in the press, although occasionally special shows were mentioned in the Dudley Herald or sometimes the Stourbridge County Express. For example, on 11th May 1920 a free show was presented on "*The War Work of the Church Army*". In February 1924 the Canadian National Railway was recruiting for emigrants with a free showing of **"A *Land of Opportunity*",** but of the early fortunes of the Grand itself, one can learn very little.

It seems that by 1924 things were not going too well. All but Saturday shows may have been suspended for a few months. Elysian Pictures then seem to have decided to open again on a six day basis and appointed George Corbett as a manager for a time. Mr. Corbett tried to exercise some showmanship. When he screened *"The White Rose"*, his daughter, in her new silk dress, presented a paper white rose to every patron as they arrived. He was very artistic and was able to make his own posters to advertise the shows.

Sound was first introduced to the Grand, about 1930, on Edison Bell equipment but once again, the cinema seems to have run into difficulties. This time a Mr. Russell came to the rescue. Mr. Russell had previously been involved in travelling cinema shows in North Wales. He had come to the Midlands to install sound equipment in a cinema in Redditch. He came to the Grand to re-equip the cinema to a better standard and manage the place.

He removed the old bench seats, installed RCA equipment and much refurbished the place. The Grand re opened once again about 1935. Almost immediately he seems to have been given a lease on the 650 seater hall which was to run until about 1948. Mr. George Corbett was still around, and joined forces with Mr. Russell to print publicity material.

Mr. Russell died in 1937 and his wife assumed responsibility for his company, Selected Cinemas Amalgamation Ltd., and for running the Grand. It was difficult keeping the Grand going through the Second World War, but with the help of the chief, George Gregg, Mrs. Russell ran the Grand until the lease expired. It then closed once more.

The situation was resolved on this occasion by Thomas Cooper taking over Elysian Pictures and his son, Bernard, set about refurbishing the cinema yet again for another reopening. Two Kalee 12 projectors were installed, with B.A. sound and its last lease of life began about 1950. Once again the chief, now Ken Waterhouse, took a large part in running the Grand. It somehow survived the testing years at the very end of the fifties. Folks around today who can recall going to The Grand as chidren and teenagers present it as a fairly wild place at the end of the 1950s. The audience would often throw things at each other and at the screen and it was risky to go to the outside toilets by the boiler room in case your mates locked the doors while you were out there. After any potentially violent incident members of the audience would be frisked in case they were hiding peashooters or missiles on their person – such were those wild times in the life of a sedate village!

Thomas Cooper died in 1961 and the Grand continued to operate while the estate was settled. Remarkably, this took three years and the final show at the Grand did not take place until 26th September 1964. The cinema closed with **"*From Russia With Love*".** Even then the building remained empty for a time while rumours circulated about its redevelopment. Two months later the owners still denied that the site was for sale, "for the time being". Having just "faded-away" the building was eventually demolished and a new set of shops built on the site. The position of the cinema is now occupied by a branch of Boots.

Right: The Forum, Pensnett in Bingo days, in 1981. This little cinema where you might once have rubbed shoulders with Des O'Connor was demolished just as this book went to print in July 2011. (Ned Williams)

The Forum

Commonside, Pensnett

Pensnett was much closer to Brierley Hill than Wordsley or Kingswinford, but like the latter two villages, it existed in a strange hinterland of brick-fields, old iron-works, pit banks, canals and derelict land. The area has gradually been tamed in the twentieth century, covering all traces of the past with the relentless extension of successive waves of suburban sprawl. The centre of modern Pensnett developed on the main Dudley-Kingswinford Road, along which the electric trams first ran in December 1900, but the village also traditionally straggled along Commonside towards the back of Brierley Hill. It was here that Cecil Couper built the last of his "mini-super-cinemas" of the 1930's.

The Forum was built on land near the Queens Head on Commonside, on ground that had been the Victoria Football Ground. It was designed by Stanley Griffiths of Stourbridge and was built by J.M. Tate of Cradley Heath, like its predecessor on Mr. Couper's "circuit", the Savoy, Netherton. It held five hundred and fifty patrons on a single floor and was a simple straightforward building with just the barest hint of grandeur to make it feel "cinema-like".

The Forum opened on Wednesday 20th January 1937: the last cinema to open in the Brierley Hill area. It was opened by J.T. Higgs, Esq., President of the Midland Counties Mutual Benefit Society, and a well known local citizen, both in Brierley Hill and Pensnett itself. He made the usual remarks indicating that entertainment should try to be healthy, up-lifting and educational! Some more fitting remarks were made by Andrew Cooper who proclaimed, ..."The people of Brierley Hill...are indebted to Mr. and Mrs. Couper, and the directors of the firm, for several reasons. They had not built any huge cinemas, but what they had done was to erect buildings suitable for the district, the working man and his family, and the working man's pocket!" This was greeted with loud shouts of "Hear! Hear!" and there were further cheers when Andrew Cooper pointed out that 1937 was the Silver Jubilee of Mr. and Mrs. Couper's arrival in Brierley Hill.

The audience then watched *"Evergreen"* starring Jessie Matthews and Sonnie Hale. This was only presented as an opening show. The following night *"Queen of Hearts"* starring Gracie Fields, began a three day run. The proceeds from the first show were sent to the local hospital committee and everybody felt satisfied that Pensnett had arrived on the cinema map in fine style.

Cecil Couper was not present. He was very ill and was to die in a London Nursing Home later during 1937. The other directors of the Pensnett Forum were Mrs. Couper, Harold Roberts, the Couper's son-in-law who ran the Coronet, and a Mr. J. H. Hobson. The Forum was equipped with Morrison sound, which seemed generally favoured by Cecil Couper.

After Mr. Couper's death the Forum was usually looked after by Kitty Stewart, an old friend of the Coupers who had played the piano at the Palace and helped run the Olympia. Local legend has it that she could never bring herself to like the local dialect and local children used to infuriate her by asking, "Any sates?". "How do you spell that?" she used to reply. There is even a very distinctly local way of pronouncing the name "Forum", in which the emphasis is transferred to the second syllable.

About 1946 the Forum was sold to Fred Leatham. After acquiring the Rex in Wolverhampton, in August 1947, Fred Leatham asked Fred Ward to help him run the Forum. Fred Ward had worked for him as a manager at the Victoria, Horseley Heath. It appears that Fred Leatham favoured the RCA sound system, and this was installed at the Forum, as well as the Victoria and the Rex.

On 24th August 1952 Fred Leatham took over the Plaza in Dover and sold the Forum to Fred Ward and Ray Eggington. Mr. Eggington had worked as "Chief" at the Rex, having previously worked at places like the Coliseum, Wolverhampton, and the Alexandra, Lower Gornal. Messrs Ward & Eggington purchased the freehold of the cinema as opposed to simply taking it on a lease, and later were able to retire to Brighton while still landlords of a property in Pensnett!

Late in life the Forum did acquire one interesting claim to fame when a local girl named Phyllis Gill, a local beauty queen of the early 1950s, acquired a boy friend called Des O'Connor. They had met while working at Butlins, and during their courtship Des would hitch-hike to Pensnett to see her. They would spend time together in The Forum and later they married. Des went on to great fame and fortune as an entertainer! His autobiography mentions nothing of evenings in The Forum.

Like most small cinemas, it suffered a drastic decline in its fortunes at the end of the fifties. A coffee bar was installed upstairs, and there were often more people in the highly successful coffee bar than there were in the cinema.

The last film was shown on 30th May 1959, *"The Sun Also Rises"* starring Tyrone Power. Messrs. Ward and Eggington then put in a maple dance floor, and the Forum enjoyed a successful life as a ballroom for a couple of years. After that Bingo arrived and eventually the mighty Essoldo group, who presented Bingo a mile away at the Danilo, Brierley Hill, took on the lease.

Its survival as a Bingo Club, an oasis of bright light and social activity in Commonside, preserved the building as a monument to Cecil Couper and his brave belief in building little village cinemas at a time when everybody else believed in the super-cinemas. No converted chapels for Quarry Bank and Pensnett — they had purpose-built cinemas of which they could be proud. The Forum was finally demolished in June 2011.

Some Brierley Hill Mysteries and the Pensnett Hippodrome

The Kinematograph Year Books are obviously fallible however anxiously a researcher might wish them to be otherwise. Every now and again they seem to produce a cinema that has no other existence except between those attractive red covers, but such entries leave a question mark in the historian's mind. Two questions arise in relation to Brierley Hill.

In 1928 and 1929 the Kinematograph Year Books recorded the existence of the Market Place Picture House in Brierley Hill. It was said to be owned by Nottingham Pictures Ltd., a company associated with Mr. Shapeero. This gentleman ventured into the Black Country when acquiring cinemas like the Empire, Dudley, and Electric, Cape Hill, from Irving Bosco, at the beginning of the twenties. Is it possible that he planned to build a cinema in Brierley Hill or is the entry in the Year Book a mistake ?

The Indoor Market in Brierley Hill was opened on 20th December 1930 and investigation has revealed that it still owned by the Nottingham-based Shapeero family today – in 2011. It would seem likely therefore that Mr. Shapeero bought properties or sites that could be developed as cinemas during the 1920s, but towards the end of that decade when he sold his cinemsa to Denman Pictures Ltd. he lost interest in cinemas and specialised in markets. The 1928/29 entries on the Kine Year Book simply reflected an intention on Mr. Shapeero's part that did not materialise.

Almost throughout the twenties the Kine Year Books credited Kingswinford with two cinemas: The Grand and "The Picture House". Sometimes the latter was said to be owned by a Mr. M. Cooper. One possibility is that both entries were referring to the Grand and that the Mr. Cooper referred to was the Mr. Cooper from Blackheath as described above, or maybe it was just an incorrect entry.

One of the most intriguing mysteries of all concerns the possibility that Pensnett may have had a cinema long before Cecil Couper built the Forum! One tiny shred of evidence of this appears in a letter in a Tipton Herald of

January 1912. The letter is from Albert Edwards, sometime manager of Picture Halls at Dudley Port and *"one at Pensnett"*. We must assume that a manager of a Picture Hall would know where his building was located, but few other hints have been found of the existence Albert Edwards' "one at Pensnett"! The "hints" of its existence that I have encountered link Pensnett's ghost-like cinema with a chapel at Tansey Green, and with Jasper Tyrer of Oldbury as a possible proprietor.

This cinema carried the unlikely name: The Pensnett Hippodrome, and it appears to only advertise in the Brierley Hill Advertiser on one solitary occasion! – 10th January 1914. The advert tells us there was one house - from 7 to 9pm. Tickets were 2d, 4d 6d and 9d, and pictures were changed twice weekly. Jack Heffron - eccentric character comedian and dancer plus films: Mon - Weds: *"7 Years Bad Luck"*, *"The Switch Tower and Winter Sports in Finland"*. Thurs - Sat: *"Her Secret*," *"An Amateur Fireman"* etc....

Because it had advertised the paper gave a short report of the previous weeks films when they had been supported by Frank Leon, Brierley Hill's famous comedian! They also told readers: *"Since the new heating apparatus has been added the place is nice and cosy"*. This seems to imply that the cinema had been running for some time by the time this solitary advert appeared.

The Kingswinford and Pensnett Trade directory reproduced on back of the Alan Godfrey map of Pensnett calls it the PICTUREDROME and lists Alfred Edwards as the manager. Alan Godfrey's map is a reproduction of the 1903 map that is too early for our purposes, but a later map does show a chapel building opposite the Brickmaker's Arms in Tansey Green. The Picturedrome was probably established in the Sunday School building which had been at the back of this chapel – the chapel itself abandoned when its 'Independent Methodist' congregation moved to a new chapel in High Oak in 1893.

It looks as if we can say that between 1912 and 1914 The Picturedrome, Pensnett was operating as a cinema with a cine-variety programme. Maybe it survived for longer than that.

Right: The little auditorium of the private cinema created inside Wordlsey Manor by Eldon Firmstone in the 1930s. A miniature paybox was constructed outside this room.

(Ned Williams)

The Stour Vale

The Stour rises in the Clent Hills and becomes something worth calling a river by the time it reaches Halesowen. It head north towards Old Hill but then turns westwards and creates a valley between Cradley and Quarry Bank. It then separates Quarry Bank from The Lye and heads towards Stourbridge. Towns on the northern bank of The Stour were in Staffordshire; towns on the southern bank were in Worcestershire.

We will explore the cinemas of this area by going "upstream" – starting in Stourbridge, passing into The Lye and on to Halesowen. As a result of the strange 1974 frontiers of Dudley, our journey, in this section ends at a cinema normally associated with Quinton.

Stourbridge

Because Stourbridge is south of the Stour, and is therefore a Worcestershire town, it sometimes claims not to be in the Black Country. However, during the nineteenth century its industrialisation was rapid. Because the glass industry survived until recent times, it is often regarded as one of the principal industries of the area. The truth is, that by the middle of the nineteenth century, Stourbridge was dominated by the iron trades. The glass industry was really to be found north of the Stour in Amblecote and Wordsley.

The iron trade not only industrialised Stourbridge but also transformed the neighbouring villages of Lye and Wollescote, along the Stour Vale. The opening of the railway from Stourbridge Junction to Birmingham in 1867 not only served this area but also eventually turned Stourbridge and some of the towns of the Stour Vale into a dormitory of Birmingham in a way that was unknown in other parts of the BlacK Country.

By the beginning of this century industrialisation, transport, and housing development linked Stourbridge completely with the Black Country. Like its neighbours, the town first encountered moving pictures at Pat Collins' fairground or at the travelling shows presented at the Town Hall by Pooles of Gloucester and Professor Wood. In fact, Professor Wood continued to visit Stourbridge Town Hall until 1913, by which time he was permanently established in Bilston. Waller Jeff's New Century Pictures had been at the Town Hall in April 1905 and The Era reported that "several local scenes had been introduced." One wonders whether these might have included the legendary lost film made on the Kinver Light Railway?

At the Alhambra films could be seen from 1904 onwards, well before the passing of the Cinematograph Act. After passing of that act, Kings Hall rapidly established itself as the principle home of film entertainment before the First World War. Stourbridge then added a new cinema representing each epoch of cinema history until four cinemas served the twenty thousand inhabitants of Stourbridge at the beginning of the Second World War. The Scala arrived in the first flush of post First World War cinema building, the Central arrived at that glorious moment at the end of the silent era when every major cinema had an organ and an orchestra and quivered with anticipation of the coming of sound. The Danilo represented the following decade and the modern super-cinema. Meanwhile the Kings Hall had built a new "super" around itself.

Meanwhile, the story of the cinemas of The Lye is the typical story of Black Country village cinema. The small cinemas, that had successfully served the community since the earliest days, were challenged by a Clifton during the thirties. By the mid-sixties The Lye was without a single screen, leaving behind a nightmare for the cinema historian to try and unravel.

The cinemas of Stourbridge and The Lye are the only Black Country cinemas to have received the attention of a historian committing himself to print! In 1952 Chris Gittings, better known as Walter Gabriel of The Archers, researched the history of local cinemas and theatres and nearly thirty years later his work was published as a booklet by Dudley Teachers Centre. Chris Gittings, therefore, deserves to be recognised as a pioneer of local cinema history.

The Alhambra

Off the High Street, Stourbridge

Behind an inn called The Coach and Horses was an area known as Barlow's Yard. During the early nineteenth century this area was used by travelling showmen, and eventually the "Theatre Royal" was established there. The Theatre Royal, later known as The Alhambra, was built there, probably in the 1880's, by the travelling theatre company of Bennett and Patch.

By the end of the last century the widow, Mrs. Patch, was running the small wooden theatre until, upon her death, it was acquired by Douglas Phelps. Mr. Phelps was an actor who had tired of his nomadic life and decided to settle in Stourbridge with his wife, the actress Maude Linton, and run a permanent theatre. From 1900 to the First World War he brought opera, melodrama, musical comedy, and variety shows to the stage of Stourbridge's tiny theatre. The story is told in more detail in Volume Two.

Douglas Phelps was one of those entrepreneurs who experimented with film presentation in the years running up to the passing of the Cinematograph Act. In 1904 he invited Ediscope & Barnum's Electric Animated Pictures to present films for a week in October. British companies seemed to delight in evoking American names like Edison and Barnum when choosing an identity. Inviting such companies probably encouraged Phelps to invest in his own equipment.

On 21st April 1909 Douglas Phelps presented films at his theatre; *"Phelps Picture Plums": "The Grand National Steeplechase of 1909"*. During the following weeks films of football matches and the Boat Race were presented, as supporting attractions to programmes of variety acts. He used one hand-cranked, lime-lit, projector and by the Autumn of 1909 was advertising it as "Phelps Alhambrascope". The following year, when a kine licence was required before such entertainment could be offered, mains electricity was brought down Stourbridge High Street and the Alhambra became "Phelps Electric Theatre".

Douglas Phelps joined forces with Alfred Wall who had introduced cinematography to The Lye during 1910, and together they opened The Empire for the sole purpose of showing films, although their partnership was dissolved by the end of November 1910. The Alhambra continued to offer theatrical presentations, but the Empire seems to have been fairly short-lived, and by 1912 the Alhambra was very much involved in showing films again. "Phelp's Famous Electric Pictures" presented *"The Tale of Two Cities"* from 12th August 1912 onwards and this seemed to mark the Alhambra's return to the cinema business, and to serious competition with The Kings Hall.

As the Kings Hall emerged as the victor, the Alhambra presented fewer and fewer films. However, some of the films shown at the Alhambra would be of considerable interest today as they were shot in Stourbridge, often featuring visiting variety artistes. After the First World War very few films were shown at the Alhambra. An exception was the Canadian Pacific Railway's film that also appeared at the Grand, Kingswinford, in the early twenties.

Douglas Phelps seemed to keep The Alhambra very much his own personal supervision, although occasionally engaged in other ventures like The Empire, or his one-time interest in showing films at the Alhambra, Dudley Port. The Alhambra did, therefore sometimes have its own manager – such as Percy Victor who was there at the end of the First World War. Percy Victor was given a "farewell benefit" night at The Alhambra on 25th April 1919 and presumably continued his career elsewhere, or returned to the services of Ben Kennedy, for whom he had once been a booking agent. Douglas Phelps came on stage to express his gratitude to Percy Victor, but interestingly the new manager was John Phelps, probably Douglas Phelps' son. (The 1901 and 1911 censuses provide us with some information on the Phelps family. Douglas and Maude had two children and John was born in 1899 so would only be twenty years old when taking over the management of his father's theatre. The Phelps seemed to have lived "on the premises" as they give their address as "Theatre House".)

Douglas Phelps briefly flirted with films again in 1922 when he introduced back projection for a series of film shows that commenced on Bank Holiday Monday 7th August 1922. Shortly afterwards the Alhambra was

acquired by George Ray and he continued film shows for a time in 1923 while waiting to obtain a licence for further theatrical use. For the next five years George Ray ran the place as a theatre. When the building was condemned in 1929 he had enthusiastic plans to build a new playhouse but the recent opening of the Central Cinema nearby showed that theatres could no longer expect to lead the field in popular entertainment. The Alhambra closed its doors on 6th April 1929.

The Empire

Duke Street, Stourbridge

As stated in the previous chapter, Douglas Phelps, of the Alhambra, joined forces with Alfred Wall, of The Temp in The Lye, to provide Stourbridge with a hall entirely devoted to showing films. They acquired an old brewery warehouse in Duke Street, and converted it into The Empire.

At three o'clock on 3rd October 1910 the Empire had a grand opening, and thereafter presented twice nightly film shows. Mr. Weaver, who had played the piano at the Alhambra, accompanied the films at the Empire, and Chris Gittings recalls the auditorium as being very long and narrow, but provided with a raked floor. In his notes on local cinemas he recalls the smell of oranges, and the girls who dispensed, not only the oranges, but a range of refreshments including chocolates and ginger-beer.

Possibly the Empire was not quite the success Messrs. Wall and Phelps had hoped for. After a few weeks it closed, and the partnership was dissolved. It "reopened" on 17th December 1910 with shows presented by the Motiograph Picture Plays Syndicate and in the following year changed name to the Empire Picture Palace and then the New Picture Hall. It may well have closed by the end of 1912, but the Motiograph Syndicate later reappeared at The Temp in The Lye. Quite why The Empire did not become a more permanent part of the early cinema scene is a bit of a mystery. Maybe it simply could not compete with The Kings Hall.

The Kings Hall

New Road, Stourbridge

Messrs. Pooles of Gloucester regularly visited Stourbridge Town Hall with their travelling Myrioramas. After the passing of the Cinematograph Act they looked for premises in which to provide permanent regular film shows. Sometime during 1911 they decided to acquire the skating rink in New Road. This had opened as recently as 23rd October 1909 and was managed by Harry Wharton. The large corrugated iron building, completely transformed, was opened on 6th November 1911 for "Pooles Perfect Pictures" and "Vaudeville". A cockney named Teddy Day was taken on as the operator and he took charge of the Imperator projector, and the gas engine that was installed to provide power.

A Mr.Talbot was given the job of commissionaire and was sent out, in a smart uniform, to woo customers from the Alhambra. Within a few months of opening an arrangement was made with the owners of Longcroft Buildings in the High Street to use a passage from the High Street to New Road as an entrance to the cinema. Mr. Talbot could then face Frank Gittings, the Alhambra's "barker" in a nightly battle in Stourbridge High Street. The Kings Hall somehow managed to secure better films than the Alhambra and Frank Gittings had to sing the praises of his employer's programmes by describing them as "Slightly bent, but not broken!".

Ironically Frank Gittings' brother, Percy Gittings, sometimes worked for the Kings Hall. Brotherly loyalty should have inspired him to support the Alhambra, but in his time Percy had been a champion roller-skater in the rollerdrome that was now a cinema, and therefore maybe he felt his heart was in New Road. Percy Gittings sometimes provided sound effects for the silent films. For example during a film called *"Curse of War"* one scene featured an aeroplane being started up. Percy Gittings started up his motor cycle behind the screen with perfect synchronisation! During those early days only a piano, usually played by a Mr. Hull, provided the accompaniment but after the War an orchestra was engaged.

The Kings Hall was fairly large, and claimed to be able to seat one thousand five hundred patrons. In the theatrical tradition the most expensive seats, costing sixpence, were at the front, and for twopence one could sit in the balcony! The seating was later reorganised when the ground floor wss provided with a proper rake, with a reversed rake just in front of the screen.

When the Scala opened in 1920 the Kings Hall faced competition of an entirely new order. To compete with the Scala's orchestra led by Paul Rimmer, the Kings Hall engaged a proper orchestra of its own, led by Norris Stanley. Before the War Stourbridge had seen the "Battle of the Barkers", now the town enjoyed the competition between the rival cinema orchestras! There was also some rivalry between Harry Wharton and Harry Morris, the two cinema-managers, although they later changed places!

Although the Kings Hall was unimpressive from the outside it had quite a beautiful interior. Large hessian murals draped the walls, and together with the silk lanterns hanging from the ceiling, gave the hall an oriental atmosphere. Pooles' staff had smart uniforms and there was considerable pride in working at the Kings Hall. It had vanquished the Alhambra, had stood up to the Scala and, at the end of the twenties, was ready to compete with the new Central. As soon as part-sound films, using the Vitaphone system, with sound-on-disc,

Right:
The Kings,
Stourbridge,
September,
1956.
(Dudley
Archives)

were available the equipment was installed at the Kings Hall. However, by 8th July 1929 RCA equipment was installed and the Kings Hall brought proper "talkies" to Stourbridge with *"In Old Arizona"*.

The Kings Hall enjoyed good acoustics. Every Monday morning the Chief sat in the auditorium while the second operator ran the newly made-up programme through to check the timings and the sound settings. During the thirties the Chief was James Powell and towards the end of the decade the position passed from father to son when Bernard Powell took over. The latter worked at the Kings Hall while its new replacement was built around it.

The rebuilding of the Kings Hall was quite an amazing venture. The new super-cinema, to be called simply the "Kings" was designed by Stanley Griffiths, the only cinema the Stourbridge architect and writer designed for his home town. It was ingeniously planned so that the red brick shell of the building could be built over and around the original corrugated iron building. The Kings Hall then closed for a very brief period while the old structure was demolished inside the new, and the interior decoration completed. The main contractor was Joseph Hickman & Son of Brierley Hill and Mr. K. Friese-Green took responsibility for the interior, including the curtains and lighting. The new seating could accommodate eighteen hundred patrons, making it the town's largest cinema, and was arranged in stadium-style. The operating room was unfortunately low in relation to the highly-raked rear seats of the auditorium and it was possible for patrons to stand in the projector's beam!

Everything which had made the old Kings Hall a great success was retained in the new Kings: Simplex projectors, RCA sound equipment etc. Even so, the Chief, Bernard Powell, had to admit that some of the great intimacy and atmosphere of the original cinema was lost. The cinema also suffered from having a frontage facing the rather anonymous backwater of New Road, rather than the High Street. The frontage, therefore, relied for its effectiveness on a separate entrance hall and some prominent neon lighting. Once in the main building a spacious foyer led to a massive staircase rising to the stadium "balcony" and a large leaded-light window gave this foyer an atmosphere of some grandeur.

The grand opening was planned for Monday 4th September 1939 at 3 p.m. The Mayor, Councillor J. A. Mobberley, was invited to open the cinema and enjoy *"The Little Princess"* starring Shirley Temple, in glorious Technicolour. Unfortunately War was declared on 3rd September and all cinemas closed for a short period. The opening ceremony had to be indefinitely postponed, but normal shows were allowed to start on the following Saturday in Stourbridge and perhaps it is, therefore, more realistic to think of the Kings opening then, on 9th September 1939. Black-out regulations meant the neon lighting which was to be such a feature of the new Kings remained switched off.   It was not

switched on until April 1949, nearly ten years later! Harry Morris was followed at the Kings by Mr. Rothery-Ellis, who had managed the Opera House and Hippodrome, Dudley, for Benjamin Kennedy. He ran the Kings as if he was running a live theatre and with a confidence that suggested the Kings still thought itself better than the Odeon or Danilo.

Eventually the realities of the post-war world must have made it apparent that a town the size of Stourbridge could not support four fairly large cinemas. The Kings tried to preserve its superiority and, in the fifties, was the first cinema in town to present Cinemascope, on 6th September 1954. On 1st October 1956 the Kings was purchased by the Rank Organisation and it seems that the sole purpose of the purchase was closure and elimination of competition. Ex- Pooles staff naturally felt it would make more sense to close the Odeon and retain the Kings but I doubt if that was ever considered.

The Kings closed on Saturday 22nd June 1957 with *"Time Without Pity"* starring Michael Redgrave, supported by *"Fort Petticoat"* starring Audie Murphy. The Circuits Management Association, (The Rank Organisation), put a notice in the local paper stating: *"We regret to announce that due to the high Cinema Tax this theatre will be permanently closed after business today. The Management would like to thank Patrons for their past support!"*. The property was sold to Samuel Johnson, the coach hire firm who may have only used the car park. Since then it changed hands several times and lost all signs of ever having been a cinema. The huge red-brick building was a furniture store, and later a DIY store, before closing altogether. It was demolished in April 1984.

The Kings Hall, Harry Wharton and the Cinema Balls

Harry Wharton and the Poole Family seem to have been instrumental in organising the first Stourbridge Cinema and Theatrical Ball, held at the Town Hall on 11th March 1919. Cecil Couper sold tickets from the Queens Hall in Brierley Hill, and Percy Victor, who was managing the Alhambra for Douglas Phelps, joined the act to represent the "theatrical" side of the evening. Percy Victor also worked with Ben Kennedy as a booking agent but little else is known about him.

It seems to have been a great success. Miss Violet Hopson was invited to be the guest of honour and large crowds greeted her when she arrived at Stourbridge Town Station early in the afternoon. Her first port of call was The Kings Hall, which was screening a film in which she appeared. She was given a rapturous welcome, after which she retired to The Talbot Hotel to prepare herself for the evening event.

The Ball was so successful that the Pooles and Harry Wharton decided they could not wait for 1920 before organising another. Victor Percy had retired from the

Alhambra by this time, and Harry Wharton went ahead and booked the Town Hall for 21st October 1919. Once again Violet Hopson was going to be the guest of honour but other film actors were also invited. All seemed to be going well. The Kings Hall itself was refurbished in the September of 1919. The stage was pushed backwards providing space for 325 new tip up seats in the auditorium. All the old bench seats were treated to upholstery. Possibly the fact that a new cinema was being constructed in Stourbridge at the time - in the Lower High Street - prompted the Kings Hall to be keen about reasserting its supremacy. Unfortunately, at the last moment, the second Cinema & Theatrical Ball had to be cancelled, allegedly as a result of someone's illness.

Although the Kings Hall was not to enjoy a second visit from film-stars during 1919, Harry Wharton was probably not down-hearted. He was always able to think of alternatives: in July 1919 he had brought many customers to the Kings Hall by screening a film called "The Doings of ClanMcWharton" - a five hundred foot long film made locally featuring an entire cast of "artistes" from Stourbridge and The Lye! (Such a film would be a great archaeological find today.) The "Stourbridge Cinema Ball" concept was revived in 1920 and was successfully held on 3rd March at the Town Hall. The guest of honour was Violet Hopson once again. She made another spectacular arrival at Stourbridge Town Station but in much better weather conditions than in 1919. A short car journey through the crowds took her to the Kings Hall where her film, *"The Gentleman Runner"*, was about to be screened. When she later arrived at the Town Hall she found that Pooles had transported their scenic artists team up to Stourbridge from the HQ in Gloucester and they had transformed the Town Hall's interior into an oriental palace!

Among the guests at the Cinema Ball of 1920 was Douglas Phelps from the Alhambra. He spoke to Violet Hopson to remind her that she had once appeared as Natalie in a production of "The Merry Widow" presented by George Edwards' company at the Alhambra in February 1910. Violet Hopson (1891 - 1973) had been acting in silent movies from about 1910 onwards and had a prolific output. She appeared in at least four films in 1919!

The Scala (later known as The Savoy and The ABC)

Lower High Street, Stourbridge

The original Kings Hall may have established its dominant position as a cinema by the First World War but as soon as the War was over a local company was formed to provide a new purpose-built cinema in Lower High Street. The chairman of the Stourbridge Picture Playhouse Ltd., was George Parker of Birmingham and the Birmingham architect, Joseph Lawden, produced the plans. George Parker has already been encountered in this book in the chapter dealing with The Grove, Smethwick.

Work commenced in September 1919 following the demolition of some old malt houses, and the construction was carried out by a local builder, A. H. Guest Ltd. The auditorium, designed to hold eleven hundred patrons, was treated in a classical style with fluted pillars decorating the side walls. The exterior, which remained little changed over the years, was very attractive. Again the treatment was classical, with pillars flanking the entrance, and the brickwork above the entrance enhanced by the surrounding terra-cotta Hathernware tiling.

The Scala was opened on 11th October 1920 by Isobel Elsom, who was starring in the first feature film to be screened; *"The Edge of Beyond"*. Miss Elsom (1893 – 1981) appeared to be rather nervous although she was rapturously received by the audience. Everyone of the eleven hundred tip up seats were taken! In the event the main speech was made by Stourbridge's Deputy Mayor, Councillor Arthur Moody.

The Manager of the Scala was Harry Morris, and the orchestra was then led by Charles Bye. The competition between these gentlemen and their counterparts at the Kings Hall has already been mentioned. The Scala settled down to a routine of two programmes a week at prices that ranged from 1/3d in the balcony to 5d in the front stalls. The latter were reached from an entrance in Queen Street.

Left: The Scala at the top of Lower High Street, Stourbidge.
(From the Ken Rock postcard collection)

A settled existence seemed to come to an end with the closing of the silent era. During the thirties the Scala appears to have changed hands a number of times. When Western Electric equipment was installed and the first talkie screened on 12th May 1930, *"The Sky Hawk"*, the cinema was owned by a Mr. G. Hunter. By April 1936 it was calling itself the "New Scala" and appears to have been acquired by a group of Birmingham businessmen headed by B. T. Davis and H. Yoward. The same gentlemen were about to open a new super-cinema in Wolverhampton; the Penn. They installed a manager named Philip Cleife who later left to go to the new Clifton at Stone Cross.

At the beginning of the War it was acquired, or leased, by Fred Leatham after he had sold the Olympia, Wordsley, to Mr. Bullock. All this changing hands came to an end in September 1942 when it was acquired by ABC. By this time it must be remembered that the Central had become an Odeon, and the Kings and Danilo had provided Stourbridge with two very modern super-cinemas. The Scala now seated less than a thousand patrons and had become the smallest of the town's cinemas.

It was re-named the Savoy on 20th September 1943 and like the other "Savoys" has it later became the ABC. When Eric Johnson arrived in 1961 to manage the cinema the staff felt he had been sent to see if it was worth keeping open. The fifties had ended with Stourbridge's cinemas reduced to three. As it turned out, Eric Johnson's stay at the Savoy had a positive effect on the future of the cinema. Ironically he died in June 1978 just before work was finished on completely refurbishing his cinema, by which time it was the only cinema surviving in Stourbridge. Eric Johnson's death, at the age of 57, brought to an end a career that had begun with him joining ABC as a page-boy forty-five years earlier.

During his career at Stourbridge the Savoy /ABC had come close to closure at least once. In 1974 EMI had agreed to sell the cinema to Ladbrokes subject to an application to run the place as Bingo Club being approved. A great deal of local protest was generated and strong objections were raised when the application for a gaming licence was heard. Most of these protests were not considered relevant by the Court but, nevertheless, the application was turned down.

Ken Waterhouse, who had managed the Lyttleton, Halesowen, from 1964 to 1974 told the press on 21st.May 1974 that he was prepared to make a realistic offer for the cinema. The following year it was rumoured that the Classic Group was interested in purchasing the ABC. After this it was probably a relief to Eric Johnson that EMI seemed reconciled to keeping the cinema and, in 1978, started refurbishing the interior.

After Mr. Johnson's death Tim Williamson arrived to take up the post of manager. Coming from the large ABC in Walsall he was most impressed to find long

Above: Tommy Watkins, projectionist, and Tim Williamson, manager, outside the projection room at the ABC, Stourbridge in November, 1982.   *(Ned Williams)*

queues outside the little Stourbridge cinema, now reduced to holding 750 patrons. Over twenty thousand patrons came to the refurbished ABC to see *"Grease"* in 1978.

The ABC became one of the few remaining Black Country cinemas. Despite Tim Williamson's positive style of management its services were further curtailed. By the 1980s only the seats in the stalls were in use, reducing its capacity to 453. Saturday morning matinees ceased on 5th July 1980. Up in the operating box the assistant operators, Tom Watkins and Janet Bruton worked with ancient Ross GC3 machines that still used carbon arcs for illumination, and by 1982 the ABC was presenting single evening performances only, except during school holidays. The "Chief", Vic Court, retired from the ABC in 1982, having worked at this particular cinema for twenty-eight years. Soon after this Tim Williamson, the manager, tried to see if ABC wouldlease the cinema to him in the hope that he could keep it running.

The ABC showed its last film on 6th November 1982: Alan Parker's film called ***"Pink Floyd – The Wall."*** The film attracted a fairly youthful audience, but it was watched with enrapt attention – right to the very last frame, and I managed to persuade many members of the audience to sign a "thank you and farewell" card to Tim Williamson and his twelve staff that were facing redundancy. Tommy Watkins and Jan Bruton projected "The Wall", Miriam Moon sold the last tickets and Alice Jacobs and Edna Hill showed the last patrons to their seats.

The cinema was then boarded up and awaited a purchaser. A purchaser materialised in the form of W.T. Newman & Sons – local fruit and vegetable retailers who quickly started converting the cinema to retail use. While stripping the interior a rather strange mural was uncovered that appeared to date from the 1930s. Since that time various people have used the building – including the Co-op, and memories of its cinematic past are fading.

The Central (later the Odeon)

63 High Street, Stourbridge

As the national circuit, P.C.T./A.P.P.H. closed in on Dudley during the latter half of the 1920's, Sydney and Clifford Bray of the Criterion decided to sell out and concentrate their energies on the smaller towns of Halesowen and Stourbridge respectively. Clifford Bray set about forming a company to build a new cinema in Stourbridge, along the same lines that his brother had used to build the Criterion, Dudley.

F.J. Ballard became the chairman of the new company and local, Dudley based, companies and businessmen participated in the venture. Land was acquired in Stourbridge High Street consisting of part of the Old Fair Ground and part of the site of the old Conservative Club. This gave the cinema a narrow frontage to the High Street itself. The building was designed by the Dudley architects, Messrs. Webb and Gray, and was

constructed by the Dudley firm of A. J. Crump. The latter had his headquarters opposite the home of Sydney Bray, in Aston Road, and had been associated with the building of the Criterion. It was originally designed to hold fifteen hundred patrons, 900 in the stalls and 600 in the balcony.

During 1929 work proceeded quickly on the Central, and made local news when one of the balcony girders being swung into position from the High Street, slipped and struck several erectors, sending them flying to the ground. A. J. Crump's foreman, George Underwood, was largely responsible for seeing that the cinema was completed in time for the opening.

The Central was built at one of those moments in history when stylistic developments in cinema design were at a crossroads. In many respects the traditional theatrical conventions were incorporated into its design. For example the balcony had a horseshoe shaped front that extended almost to the proscenium arch. The ornamental plasterwork reproduced classical columns on the side walls and at either side of the screen, as favoured by the Scala, planned ten years earlier. In the centre of the orchestra pit a £4,000 Compton Organ was installed. It was a three manual, ten unit, organ and John Howlett was invited to open it.

The grand opening took place on 16th May 1929 with a film called *"Love's Crucifixion"*. In the absence of the Mayor of Stourbridge the ceremony was performed by the well known Stourbridge citizen, Ernest Stevens. As it happened, Alderman F. J. Ballard who opened the proceedings in his capacity as Chairman of the Company provided a "mayoral" presence as he was Mayor of Dudley at the time! Alderman Ballard stressed that, although the Central opened as a silent cinema, the company would keep abreast of any developments in the provision of sound. Meanwhile an excellent orchestra was provided under the leadership of Mr. Barrs Partridge, the Cradley Heath musician who had come to the Central from Birmingham's West End. And, of course, there was the Compton Organ. John Howlett had worked at two other cinemas since opening Dudley's Regent in the previous September. Alderman Ballard was full of praise for the young men at Webb and Gray, and for A. J. Crump's construction work, and Ernest Stevens was presented with a silver replica of the key to the cinema as a momento of the occasion.

Within just under a year of opening the original Simplex projectors found themselves being fitted with sound heads and Western Electric equipment was installed. Talkies arrived at the Central on 7th April 1930. For a short time the orchestra was retained to provide live musical interludes. Clifford Bray appears to have played some part in promoting the Central, at Kidderminster and both cinemas had much in common. (The history for the Kidderminster Central is detailed in Mercia Bioscope No.7).

Left: The Central, Stourbridge in December 1937 on becoming an "Odeon" (John Maltby)

The interior of The Central/Odeon Stourbridge
(John Maltby)

Clifford Bray, as General Manager of the company, and day-to-day manager of the cinema became a popular genial figure in Stourbridge. The proceeds from the first performance had gone to the Corbett Hospital and Mr. Bray continued to act as a fund-raiser for local charities by organising special shows at the Central. By the mid-thirties he began to suffer the effects of ill health. He died, aged 52, on 23rd April 1937 and a short time afterwards the Central was acquired by Oscar Deutsch. In January 1938 it adopted the name "Odeon". A few art-deco style light fittings were introduced to try and impose the Odeon style on the rather old-fashioned auditorium.

By comparison with the new Kings and the Danilo, opened in 1939 and 1940, the Odeon had an intimate atmosphere that made it a very pleasant cinema to visit. When more modern seating was installed, reducing its capacity to about eleven hundred, it seemed even more comfortable and cosy.

Like other Odeons, it ran Saturday morning matinees and the organ continued to be played by "Uncle Ken" at these events well into the post-war era. The organ was broken down and removed in 1958 and some parts of it are to be found locally in Netherton Parish Church.

Because the Odeon survived the sixties it seemed to have a kind of permanence that made the announcement of its closure, in 1973, come as something of a surprise. Perhaps the fact that only the five hundred seats in the balcony were being used should have warned us that the writing was on the wall.

The last show was presented on 16th June 1973. The programme consisted of a revival of **"Bonnie and Clyde"** supported by **"Blind Terror"**. The Chief, Joe Jones, had been at the Odeon for eighteen years, but that was a short time compared with the record of the commissionaire, George Crowther, who had been there thirty-four years, almost as long as it had been an Odeon. One interesting detail concerning the last show serves to illustrate how short the lifetime of a cinema could be. Among the people who had paid 44 new pence to see the last film was Sydney Ryder, who had paid 6 old pence to see the first film in 1929.

The shell of the Odeon survived closure and anyone seeing it from the back as they drove round Stourbridge Ring Road could easily think it was still a cinema. (Incidentally back views of the Kings and the ABC were also obtained from the circumnavigation of Stourbridge's amazing oneway inner ring road for a time!). In the High Street the entrance and canopy of the cinema were retained, but inside the building was been transformed into retail use for J.H. Stinger Ltd., a neighbouring furniture company. Later in the 1970s it was taken over by Owen Owen Ltd.

Of course when Owen Owen relinquished the building, in June 1990, Stourbridge citizens discovered they still had a fairly complete cinema on their doorstep and there was some opposition to its demolition when this became inevitable in April 1995 – five years later! Tiles from the floor of the foyer, displaying the Stourbridge coat of arms were removed and re-instated in the Crown Centre and a glass screen was taken to Himley Hall.

Above: The Danilo in 1940. (Keith Skone)

The Danilo

Hagley Road, Stourbridge

The site chosen on which to build the Danilo sloped down from Church Road to the Hagley Road where a large town house had stood. The Church Road end of the site had been occupied by two rows of back to back houses known as Copenhagen Place which had been condemned and then abandoned in about 1935. The spoil removed to provide a flat spce on which the cinema could be built was piled up at the Church Road end of the site to form a carpark.

The last cinema to be built in Stourbridge opened during the early part of the Second World War. Arriving on the scene so late, it represents the ultimate achievement of Ernest Roberts in producing cinemas in the modern style. It was also the last Danilo cinema to be opened by Mortimer Dent. Ernest Roberts designed the building to accommodate just under fourteen hundred patrons; 970 in the stalls and 410 in the balcony. The front elevation was carried out in rustic brickwork with stone dressings and heavy stone cornices. The five tall windows rising above the deep canopy had stained and leaded glass panes, admitting light to the balcony lounge. The four foot high letters of the cinema's name mounted above the stone cornice were made of stainless steel and could not be outlined in neon lighting due to black-ou restrictions! The cinema was built by William Jackson of Oldbury.

The steps up to the five pairs of entrance doors made the building seem very large and dignified from Hagley Road and once through those doors the patron found the interior treated in fine modern style. Concealed lighting and abstract designs in the fibrous plaster-work flattered a huge rectangular ante-proscenium. The forty-three foot wide stage was guarded by bright stage curtains and festooned screen curtains, all of which could be lit with varying effects.

The latest Ross GC projectors were installed and sound was supplied by RCA Photophone apparatus, much favoured by the Danilo circuit. If completed before the outbreak of War such a fine cinema would have enjoyed a very grand opening. In the circumstances the Danilo opened without ceremony on Whit Monday 13th May 1940 with *"At the Villa Rose"*. A sign of the times was that the programme included "All the latest War pictures and news".

At first the senior staff were propmoted and transferred from the Danilo at Brierley Hill. This included the manager, Harry Rudd, and the Chief Projectionist, eighteen year old George Salt. The staff, in their smart emerald green Danilo uniforms, greeted the patrons on opening day but the audience was smaller than had been expected because the Bank Holiday had been cancelled at the last minute.

As a result of the War there was a rapid turnover of staff which made the Danilo somehow more anonymous than the other Stourbridge cinemas, and less a part of the local community. It was the least-talked-about hall whenever I talked to Stourbridge people about their cinemas, although it was apparently popular during the War.

At the end of the War it passed from Mortimer Dent's control to the circuit of Mr. W. Southan Morris, and a

Above:The interior of the Danilo, Stourbridge.
(CTA Archives)

decade later it became part of the Essoldo group. Essoldo installed Cinemascope as from 22nd November 1954, and was first used to present *"The Coins in the Fountain"*. From February 1957 onwards it was advertised as, "The Danilo — An Essoldo Theatre". In the sixties the Essoldo Company seems to have been fairly interested in Bingo, and they closed the Danilo on 21st December 1963 to perform a very rapid conversion to Bingo. In fact they reopened for that purpose on 27th December!

The Danilo had closed with *"The Yellow Teddy Bears"*, a film about teenage pregnancies, and *"The Terror of Doctor Hitchcock "*. Its twenty-three year life as a cinema, was then almost been matched by its life as a Bingo hall. Bingo was not all "plain sailing" and the bingo provider changed several times. It eventually became a Coral Bingo and Social Club, and during that time much of the character of the building was well preserved. In fact, Coral refurbished the ex-cinema to a high standard. If you were lucky when you went there to play Bingo you may have met Harry, who once worked there as an operator. He was interviewed and appointed by Mortimer Dent himself and worked in most of the Danilo cinemas.

While in use as a Bingo club the former Danilo had the good fortune to host another "last picture show"! The Stourbridge Film Society decided to celebrate the 50th anniversary of the opening of the Danilo, so on a Sunday afternoon 13th May 1990, the circle came back to life for one last time as a cinema and a 16mm print of a Laurel & Hardy film was presented on a make-shift

screen. Several former members of staff attended this film show including George Salt who had been Chief Projectionist at the opening and from 1949 to 1955. His wife Betty had been an usherette, and was joined by Joan Groves who had also been an usherette, and Georgina Chatterton who had been a cashier in the 1940s. Also present was Derek Simmonds who had been a projectionist from 1952 to 1962. He had gone to greater fame as the proprietor of Derann Film Services. He and his wife Anne had opened a shop in Holly Hall, Dudley, to hire out 8mm copies of feature films, and later moved to premises near Top Church in Dudley.

Bingo kept the Danilo "alive" until June 1995, and after Bingo ceased there was hope that a local theatre company might take on the building and operate it as community theatre and arts centre – but that was not to be.

In August 1996 the former Danilo building opened as the Picturehouse Nightclub, and a year later it was planned to add a bowling alley to the facilities it provided.

The former Danilo was back in the news in 2007 when the premises were given permission to present lap dancing in a new club trading as "Barbarellas". As manager Chris Stanley explained to the press: *"The club would attract an older and more discerning audience."*

The Lye

Working our way eastwards from Stourbridge, the towns on either side of the Stour Vale form the southern boundary of the Black Country. Just outside Stourbridge we come to The Lye, a community of about thirteen thousand people, who usually included the definite article in the name of their town.

As in other small industrial communities of the Black Country that enjoyed an existence independent of the larger towns, it has been very difficult to assemble a reasonably complete history of the local cinemas. The Vic and the Temp both seemed to "come and go" more than most! Indeed, they are the Rosencrantz and Guildenstern of the local cinema scene; infuriating minor characters that are each often confused with the other! My story of The Lye's cinemas, therefore, differs from other published versions of the story. My research leads me to insist that the "Palace of Varieties" was the name given to Alfred Wall's operation in the Temperance Hall and not a separate place that later became the Victoria.

Records exist to show that Pat Collins brought his Wonderland bioscope show to The Lye in November 1908. There are aslo records of travelling theatres including The Lye on their tours so there is no doubt that the town was "on the map" as far as enertainment was concerned. The Lye's other claimto fame is that it was the birthplace of Cedric Hardwick – the local doctor's son who left the town and became a filmstar in Hollywood! A monument to Cedric Hardwick has now been erected close to Lye Cross.

The Temp

Church Street, The Lye

A Temperance Hall was built in The Lye in 1874, having been designed by the Stourbridge architect, Joseph Morris Gethin. During the first decade of this century concerts and variety shows were presented in the hall. A man named Alfred Wall seems to have tried showing films there.

On 16th April 1910 Alfred Wall opened the hall as the Lye Palace of Pictures and Variety, having obtained a permanent lease on the premises, and having had the place converted for such a purpose by Safety Bioscope Ltd. He told the press, *"This London company has fitted out a number of London theatres and halls, and the pictures seen at Lye will be of the same standard as seen in the Metropolis".* It is difficult to imagine what form the conversion took as The Temp did not seem particularly cinema-like even many years later! The ground floor was not raked and the balcony seemed chapel-like. Possibly it was a question of fitting a projection room that satisfied the requirements of the Cinematograph Act. For years the "box" at The Temp was little more than that, it was a tiny wooden structure hanging on the wall of the building!

Originally it held about 550 patrons, later this figure seemed to increase by a hundred, later still it decreased by a hundred. Alfred Wall later joined forces with Douglas Phelps and briefly opened The Empire in Stourbridge, but after that his name disappears from the scene. The Motiograph Picture Playhouse Syndicate

Left: The Temp, The Lye, 1971, after closure. Note how the projection box has been crudely cantilevered from the side of the building. (H.Cartwright Dudley Archives)

who took over the shows at The Empire also seem to have presented shows at the Palace by the beginning of the First World War.

By the middle of the War, when it was still known simply as The Palace, a Mr. T. Brookes was presenting cine-variety at the hall. After the War he was followed by Will Pritchard, a local carpenter. In the mid twenties the lease was obtained by Mr. J. Entwistle.

Mr. Entwistle was a local grocer who had opened his first shop about 1906 and built up a small chain of stores in the area. He ran The Temp, as it was called from then onwards, for thirty years and is still fondly remembered in The Lye. The trustees of the Temperance Society kept a watchful eye on the lessee of their hall but Mr. Entwistle earned the affection and respect of everybody. One patron claimed that he went to The Temp to enjoy a chat with Mr. Entwistle, rather than to see the films. He was devoted to his cinema, having acquired an interest in films from a brother-in-law who was in the business.

Music was supplied by "a first-class orchestra", and sometimes title songs were sung by Jesse Hackett. The stage was still used, and Cedric Hardwick made one of his earliest public appearances there. When Sir Cedric Hardwick returned to The Lye to open the community's first carnival he begged Mr. Entwistle to be allowed to take his wife to see The Temp!

Mr. Entwistle installed Gyrotone equipment, and brought the talkies to The Lye on 28th July 1930 with *"Voice of the City"*. The supporting film, *"Parade of the West"* was silent. After the War, in 1949, he installed the latest Mirrophonic Sound and his advertisement claimed, "Always A Good Show". It had to be : not only did the Trustees have to be satisfied, but The Temp was next-door to the Police Station, and many a policeman sought relaxation in the cinema.

It seems that Mr. Entwistle managed to continue running The Temp until 2nd June 1956, when he presented *"The Prodigal"*, starring Lana Turner. The following day the place was used for a talent contest and then the place appears to have remained dormant for a time.

The Temp reopened on 6th May 1957 with *"Calamity Jane"*. The person who had decided to run The Temp at this late stage was a Mr. Pointon, from the Garden Cinema, Bewdley. He rented it from Mr. Entwistle who still held the lease but its new life was short. It seems to have closed for the final time on 25th November 1957 with *"At War With The Army"*, starring Jerry Lewis and Dean Martin.

The building stood for another decade. I remember coming across it in the mid sixties, when the seating was still in place and vandalised projection equipment was rusting away in that odd little projection box. The Church Street area of the Lye has now been re-developed. Although everybody was stunned when the Temp closed, it has now passed into the world of fading local legends.

The Victoria

High Street, The Lye

As stated earlier, my research indicates the Palace was the name given, at various times, to the Temp. The Victoria was quite a different matter. It was a brand new purpose-built hall, and was never known by any other name, apart from the abbreviated form: the Vic. It was originally the brain-child of Joseph Heathcock, and was erected very quickly in the last two months of 1913.

Right: "The Vic" As new in 1913. (Dudley Archives)

Several cinemas of this period consisted of a simple and quickly-built auditorium obscured by a stylish frontage: The Cinema, Tipton, the Electric Palace, Bloxwich etc.

The auditorium was clad in corrugated iron, but it had an imposing frontage built of brick, treated in plaster, that survived almost unchanged for half a century. The stalls were properly raked, although it maintained the theatrical tradition of putting the best seats, the individual tip-ups, at the front. It had a proper balcony decorated with simple ornamental plaster-work. Eight hundred patrons could be accommodated. The architect, Hugh E. Folkes, of Stourbridge, had surely demonstrated that the "tin shed" type of cinema / theatre was capable of some elegance.

The New Victoria Theatre was opened on Monday 5th January 1914 by County Councillor J. T. Worton, a local draper. He recalled the past amusements of Lye residents, in particular cock-fighting and bull-baiting. He did not believe man existed only to work and sleep, so he was very pleased that Joseph Heathcock had provided The Lye with a proper theatre.

Joseph Heathcock, who had been connected with seaside pier entertainment for over twenty years, and who came from a well-known Stourbridge musical family, presented an opening programme of films that included *"Tapped Wires"*, *"A Surprise Encounter"* and *"Twixt Love and Fires"*. Music was provided by an orchestra led by Mr. H. Duffell. Seats were 2d, 4d, 6d, and 9d, with the best seats at the front. The County Advertisere told its readers that the projectionist was Mr. E. Preece who had come from The Theatre Royal in Shrewsbury.

By the autumn of 1915 Edward Lucas and Walter Williams from Cradley Heath were running the Victoria, and two years later Jack Arnold was presenting plays there plus films as part of variety shows. Of course these gentlemen may simply have been leasing The Vic. Jack Arnold seems to have stayed at The Vic longer than most, and seems to have lasted into the twenties, a decade in which I have been unable to trace the cinema's fortunes. During the 1919-1920 period The Vic was presenting week after week of variety entertainment, without any film input. In fact when the Vic did present a film called *"The End of The Road"* in September 1920 the manager, Jack Arnold, had to install projection equipment just for that week. The film was a drama featuring the consequences of sexually transmitted disease and as such was not being shown in many cinemas! Nobody under the age of fourteen was admitted while it being shown at The Vic, but its controversial nature ensured large audiences!

From November 1931 to April 1934 Sidney Bray was showing films at the Vic, then the story becomes confusing once again. Mr. Russell, previously mentioned in connection with The Grand, Kingswinford, may have shown films there briefly. Whether all this proceeded with any continuity, or whether The Vic was "dark" for various intervals is just not clear. Just before the Second World War it had a another spate of being used as a theatre, and this will be described in Volume Two.

According to Chris Gittings' history of local cinemas and theatres it was closed for a few years during the Second World War until opened for a short season of variety by a Wordsley - born playwright named Charles Hatton. From then on the story becomes confused and patchy once more. Several local people have suggested that the last film was shown there in the very early fifties, implying that there are gaps inthis story that still need filling. The building survived and continued to enjoy a varied and unpredictable career. By the beginning of the sixties it was being used as a rollerdrome and dance hall and probably even flirted with Bingo before demolition caught up with it in 1964.

When the Alan Godfery's series of maps came to publish one of The Lye, he had to base his map on a 1914 original – slightly later than the rest of his series. This has an advantage for the cinema enthusiast as it quite clearly marks the outline of The Vic as "picture theatre". Today the site is occupied by a Spar supermarket, but when looking at the map and comparing it with the location today it is interesting to note that the house next door to the Vic still exists! The map also shows the location of The Temp in Church Street, simply marked as "hall", and the future site of The Clifton is shown as vacant land on the corner of Valley Road.

The Clifton

High Street, The Lye

After the turbulent history of The Temp and The Vic it is relaxing to consider the straightforward story of the Clifton. Perhaps the only puzzle is the question of why the Clifton circuit built a luxury super-cinema in The Lye? However, when one considers the location of the other Black Country Cliftons at Sedgley, Coseley, Wednesfield and Fallings Park, it can be seen that the company favoured village sites and presumably felt that providing car parks would lure patrons from the larger towns.

The Clifton at The Lye was planned by Roland Satchwell. In my opinion his plan lacked the elegance of his work at Sedgley and Coseley, possibly because the front elevation did not exploit the effect of tall vertical windows above the canopy. However, it was treated in faience and was perhaps more "modern" than Roland Satchwell's other Black Country cinemas. The three double entrance doors were flanked by shops and the auditorium took advantage of the falling ground on the site. It did not, therefore, tower above its surroundings.

It was built by B. Whitehouse and Sons Ltd., whose only other cinema work in the Black Country was at the Warley Odeon. Internally it was a standard Clifton cinema, in other words BTH projection and sound equipment was installed. It was built to accommodate just over a thousand patrons, 726 in the stalls and 280 in

Above: Clifton, Lye, from opening brchure.

the balcony. It was, therefore, the smallest Clifton in the Black Country.

The directors of Clifton Cinema Lye Ltd., were Messrs Clift and Salberg as we would expect but the only other named director was Roland Satchwell, the architect. The absence of any other directors, and particularly the absence of a local director, was possibly ominous. Did it mean that few others thought it was worth inversting in this particular Clifton?

The Clifton opened on 8th February 1937 with *"Under Two Flags"* starring Ronald Colman, Claudette Colbert, Rosalind Russell, and "a cast of ten thousand". The opening ceremony was performed by R.H. Morgan, M.P., a man who had been present at so many other local cinema openings.

At the opening, the Manager was Mr. A.U. Morris, and the operator was Jim Davis, who was being groomed for management of The Regal, Wednesfield. Mr. Davis had a career that stretched back to being a "chocolate boy" for Pooles' early cinematograph shows. Later operators included Bernard Powell, who had previously worked for Gaumont British and Pooles, and Vic Court, who retired from the ABC, Stourbridge, in March 1982. The operators at the Clifton often had to provide technical assistance to Mr. Entwistle across the road at The Temp.

From War-time onwards The Clifton opened seven days a week unlike the cinemas of Cradley Heath, and also presented children's matinees on Saturday afternoon. As well as the Sunday show, The Clifton changed programmes twice weekly even in the early sixties.

As stated above, its life was uneventful. Cinemascope was installed in the fifties, and by the end of the decade it had outlived the Temp and The Vic. However, it still suffered a decline in its fortunes. In 1964 wrestling was presented on some nights as an alternative to film. The end came on 7th August 1965 with *"The Patsy"* starring Jerry Lewis, supported by *"Robinson Crusoe on Mars"*. The manageress at the time of closure was Mrs. King, and the chief operator was Vic Court who went on to work at the ABC Stourbridge.

It was one of the first Cliftons to close, and was apparently never regarded as a very profitable enterprise by people working within The Clifton circuit. Nevertheless there were several people interested in buying The Clifton once it had closed. Woodworth's, the Stourbridge-based toy retailers bought it and ran it as a warehouse until it was sold to the Price sisters who converted it to an indoor market.

Fortunately the building still exists, and today is in use as a market hall. A level floor had to be installed and the auditorium's interior destroyed but the basic exterior of the building has not been substantially changed.

Halesowen

On the Worcestershire banks of the Stour Vale, on the southern-most border of the Black Country lies the town of Halesowen. The town has a long history, particularly an ecclesiastical history associated with Halesowen Abbey. The survival of court rolls for the manor and for the borough have enabled a detailed history of medieval Halesowen to be constructed. Unfortunately the much more recent twentieth century history of the town's cinemas has not been so well documented!

Francis Brett Young, the well known local writer, described the area as, *"A bewildering mixture of beauty and squalor"*, a description that could be applied to almost any part of the Black Country from 1800 to the present day. Industry encroached on Halesowen via the Stour Vale, through which the Dudley Canal, and eventually the railway, passed. The sweated iron trades, such as the manufacture of nails grew up in the villages south of Dudley, Netherton, Old Hill and on to Halesowen, and as this cottage industry declined, factories grew up manufacturing tools such as scythes and spades, and the holloware trade. Until recent times the Stour Vale was dominated by the large factories of Walter Somers and the Halesowen Steel Company. Today new industrial estates carry on that tradition.

One man dominates the history of Halesowen's cinemas; Sidney Bray, who came not from the town itself, but from Dudley. He left no legend behind him to compare with Professor Wood in Bilston or Cecil Couper in Brierley Hill, yet he created one of the nicest Black Country cinemas; the Lyttleton, a super-cinema in the modern style reduced to the human proportions that were a realistic response to the entertainment needs of Black Country communities.

The Drill Hall

Newfield Lane (Furnaced Hill), Halesowen

In the County Advertiser for 28th January 1911 appeared the claim, *"Electric Pictures will be shown for the first time in Halesowen"*. They were to arrive on Monday 30th January, and the man who had leased the Drill Hall to show them was Sidney Bray, from Dudley. His brother-in-law, Wally Davies was in charge of the box office and was almost knocked over in the patrons' stampede to obtain seats! Mr. Bray himself stood outside shouting, "Two, Four and Sixpence, this way!".

Programmes were twice nightly, six days a week, except for one Tuesday each month when the Masons used the hall. At a Masonic Meeting Sidney Bray encountered a Mr. Harvey who became the chief operator. Mr. Harvey worked at the Drill Hall until moving to the Cosy Corner, where his son, Lawrence Harvey, started work as the rewind boy. The latter worked for Bernard Bray when the Picture House closed, thus illustrating the "family" nature of working for the Brays.

Ironically Sidney Bray was not really the first to show films at the Drill Hall. It had been used earlier by travelling film-shows. For example, on 20th December 1909 it had been used by Messrs. Gale and Polden, of London, to present a one day show of "animated pictures" on military subjects. However, Sidney Bray's shows at the Drill Hall were on a permanent regular basis.

What is not very clear is how long the Drill Hall was used as a cinema. It was certainly going strong after the First World War, when Bert Holden went there as the

Below: The Drill Hall, Halesowen, 1981.

pianist, and he and Lena Wood on the violin used to accompany the films. (Lena was better known for her work at The Olympia, Wordlsey.) There was also a time when the Drill Hall used to share serials with the Grand, Old Hill. The Manager had to take each episode over to Old Hill after it had been shown at the first house in Halesowen, and later bring it back for the second house. One night the film caught fire at Old Hill and the second house at the Drill Hall never saw that episode!

It seems likely that the Drill Hall was closed when the new Picture House was opened in 1927, or when Sidney Bray took over the Cosy Corner. Like several other Black Country halls, the Drill Hall claimed that the Black Country comedian, Billy Russell, made his debut there! The building still stands – long after all other buildings associated with the cinema busuness in Halesowen have disappeared.

The Kings Hall
(later the Cosy Corner)

Peckingham Street, Halesowen.

The Dudley Herald for 20th May 1911 records that Mr. Barnes of Smethwick had applied for permission to convert the Golden Cross Inn, Peckingham Street, into a Picture Palace. (This may have been the Mr. Barnes associated with the little cinema in Spinners End, Cradley Heath.) Whether this materialised as the Kings Hall is not clear, but Julian Hunt's recent history of Halesowen does clarify matters a little. No. 4 Peckingham Street had been The Golden Cross Inn - where the landlord, Joseph Nock had once provided music hall entertainment in a large outbuilding at the rear of the premises. The Golden Cross had closed in 1906 and the premises were subsequently rebuilt. However, it seems that the hall provided the basis for an auditorium for the Kings Hall/Cosy Corner Cinema. A new frontage absorbing the fronts of No.s 4 and 5 Peckingham Street seems to have been created in 1911 when the cinema came into being. This frontage had no particular cinema-like features but did include two shopfronts, and seems to have been designed by Dudley architect, A.T. Butler who designed one or two other cinema "conversions". The shopfront at "no.6" seems to have acquired a canopy at some stage (maybe 1919/20) and presumably formed the entrance to the cinema.

Whatever its origins, the Kings Hall seems to have been Halesowen's second cinema, and shows continued there until towards the end of the First World War. After the War it was purchased by Percy Dyche, a name associated with various cinemas in Birmingham, and whose only other venture in the Black Country was at the Beacon, Smethwick.

William Jackson, the building contractor from Langley, lavishly reconstructed the Kings Hall for Mr. Dyche and it re-opened at the end of 1920, or the very beginning of 1921, as the Cosy Corner. To live up to its new name it had plush tip up seats to hold four hundred and thirty

patrons, plus Axminster Carpets. It was managed by Frank Robbins.

Almost immediately, William Jackson assumed control and ownership of the Cosy Corner. It was not his only venture into the cinema business as he also ran the Regent, Langley, for a time. In July 1922 he appointed Will Tyrer as manager, and from then on the Cosy Corner prospered. Mrs. A. Lee of Halesowen, vividly recalls those times. Her mother and her sister worked there as usherettes and always looked very smart in their black dresses and white aprons. Mrs. Lee writes; *"Mr. Will Tyrer did a lot to liven things up, as he used to say. He introduced variety acts on stage such as conjuring or songs. Sometimes Will's own wife, who was a singer, would entertain the audience before the film started. I remember the queue stretching up to the top of Peckingham Street on Saturday nights, long before the doors were due to open. If there was a good performance on, there would be buskers outside the cinema, or the organ-grinder with his monkey".*

A report in the County Express of 9th June 1923 gives us a little picture of the life and times of a Black Country cinema of the early 1920s. Two musicians, Frank Nelson Raybould, a pianist, and James Robins, a cornetist, were suing the Cosy Corner Cinema Company for one weeks wages that they felt they should have been paid in lieu of notice. The manager, Wil Tyrer, insisted they had only been employed on a temporary trial basis for one week, after which they had been replaced by two other musicians. The registrar found in the musician's favour. What is interesting is that it suggests there was no shortage of cinema musicians at the time, and it gives some information about current wages and conditions. We learn that the pianist earned £2.50 per week and the cornetist earned £2 per week. One twelfth of a salary was paid for any additional matinee, rehearsals were expected and Mr. Raybould was given 3/6d to purchase sheet music.

Will Tyrer's success at the Cosy Corner caused trade to decline at the Drill Hall, and the latter introduced variety acts in order to compete. The Cosy Corner also had a good three-piece orchestra of drums, violin and piano. Wilf Hollyhead, who worked there for twelve months in 1923 as an operator, also recalls Will Tyrer's management. While he suffered the cramped conditions of the operating box, he had to admit everything there was of the best for the patrons. He recalls that during wet weather they used to put sheets over the stair-carpets in order to keep them clean!

At the end of the silent era the Cosy Corner was acquired by Sidney Bray. Although he had introduced talkies to Halesowen at the Picture House, he continued to run the Cosy Corner as a silent cinema. The pianist Bert Holden who had moved from the Drill Hall to the new Picture House in 1927 was now moved to the Cosy Corner, where he had to provide solo accompaniment to the film. Lawrence Harvey, who was trained at the Cosy Corner by his father, the "chief' at the time, has already been mentioned in the chapter on the Drill Hall. His wife, Lilly, worked at the Cosy Corner during the evening and in the local button factory by day. When the Cosy Corner closed she went to the Picture House!

The survival of the Cosy Corner into the sound era is curious. It seems likely that Sidney Bray, after his departure from the Criterion, Dudley, was keen to consolidate his position in Halesowen. Rather than modernise the Cosy Corner it seems that he wished to replace it with a brand new sound cinema, or, failing that, to build a brand new cinema elsewhere in Halesowen. The latter is what eventually happened.

By 1934 the Cosy Corner was no longer considered "structurally suitable for public exhibition" by Supt. Mobbs in his report to the licensing magistrates. The tiny operating and rewind room was particularly inadequate. At the beginning of March 1935 the kine licence had to be renewed and these objections were raised again. Sidney Bray protested that he was willing to extend the operating room and build a fire-proof rewind room but what he really wanted to do was build a new cinema.

The licence was renewed for nine months only, on Mr. Bray's undertaking that he would build a new cinema. Later in the year Mr. Bray found difficulty in securing land for a new super-cinema and in August he asked for an extension to the licence for the Cosy Corner and promised that he would spend £800 improving the place. His application was turned down so we must assume that the Cosy Corner closed at the end of 1935.

The premises were later converted to a Ladies' Clothes Shop but totally disappeared as Peckingham Street shared in the radical redevelopment of Halesowen's town centre. A pedestrianised Peckingham Street still exists and until recently Woolworths had a store on the approximate site of the cinema.

The Electric Theatre (Later The Picture House)

Stourbridge Road, Halesowen

Halesowen Cinemas Ltd., was registered on 25th July 1913 and it is thought that this was the company that built the Electric Theatre in Stourbridge Road. It was a corrugated iron, timber framed building, and had a seating capacity of nine hundred. This was not a venture launched by Sidney Bray, but by the Rose brothers of the Halesowen Steel Company. The four Rose brothers were named General, Major, Captain and Baron. Presumably the last named had most to do with running the cinema because it was known locally as "Baron's". It appears to have opened in 1913.

Sidney Bray seems to have acquired it in the early twenties, but then disaster struck. In the early hours of Thursday morning, 14th February 1924, fire mysteriously broke out in the cinema. A Mr. Garnet Clift, whose bedroom overlooked the cinema, raised the alarm and the local fire brigade, led by Captain Binfield, was on the scene within minutes. Fanned by strong winds the fire blazed furiously and it was five hours before it was completely extinguished. The building was completely destroyed, except for a brick-built shed that housed the gas engine and generator. Apparently the fire had not started in the operating box, and the operator arrived on the scene and managed to retrieve the films before the fire reached them! Another local legend tells that the film being shown that week was called *"Mighty Like A Rose"* and local wags claimed it was now "Mighty Like A Ruin".

Below: A picture taken from the church tower provides a glimpse of the original Picture House. (Ken Rock Collection)

Sidney Bray had to find a way of replacing the Electric Theatre and more than three years passed before the Picture House was completed in its place. The new building was designed by Halesowen architect, Stanley Beech, and was built to accommodate nine hundred patrons in a brick auditorium. It was built by J.M. Tate and Son of Cradley – builder of several local cinemas.

The Picture House opened on Monday 12th December 1927 with the film **"Second to None"**. Seats were 1/- and 9d in the balcony; 6d and 4d in the stalls. A full orchestra was provided, featuring Bert Holden from the Drill Hall. It has already been recorded how Lilly Harvey came to the Picture House from the Cosy Corner and later Sidney Bray asked her to persuade her husband to leave the Rex, Blackheath, and join the staff as the chief operator. He did so and stayed there until its closure.

The Picture House was the smartest cinema Halesowen had yet seen, and two years later had the privilege of introducing the talkies to the town. BTP equipment was installed and **"The Singing Fool"** arrived at the Picture House on 25th November 1929. After the Second World War Gaumont British Kalee projectors were put in, and a G. B. Sound system.

When Sidney Bray died in 1940, the Picture House and Lyttleton passed to his son, Bernard Bray, who also inherited the partnership with "Uncle Wally"; Wally Davies, at the Brownhills cinema. It was a straightforward matter for the two men to concentrate on running the three cinemas as before; Wally Davies in Brownhills, Bernard Bray in Halesowen.

Above: The Picture House, Stourbridge Road Halesowen. The chapel on the right – also seen on the previous page will give you your bearings as it still exists today. (P. Barnsley)

Bernard Bray ran the Halesowen cinemas successfully, but like most other independent cinema proprietors times proved difficult during the latter half of the fifties. He was interviewed by the Express and Star in April 1958 and in view of the difficulties at the Picture House, seemed anxious to sell it. A Mr. Brown, who had bought the Cosy Corner for his clothing business had been interested in buying it for use as a factory, but apparently planning permission had been refused.

There was a brief experiment in presenting wrestling in September 1961, but six day film presentation prevailed for the last few months of operation. (The Picture House had never opened on a Sunday.) After Bernard Bray's death it was possibly a relief to find that the Council wished to acquire the building in order to widen the Stourbridge Road.

The Picture House closed on 9th December 1961 with **"Pirate of the Black Hawk"** and one of my favourite "Z" films, **"Invasion of the Hell Creatures"**. The building was not immediately demolished, and during the mid sixties the Council leased the building to the Scala Bingo Club. Eventually it was sold to the Conservative Club who demolished it to provide space for a car park. The road was never widened.

193

The Lyttleton

Hagley Road, Hasbury, Halesowen

Halesowen's cinema history reached its zenith in the construction of the Lyttleton. In my opinion this was the ideal Black Country cinema. It had all the glamorous trappings of a super-cinema, but was built on a scale that seemed appropriate to the size of a Black Country community. Undoubtedly it was built by Sidney Bray to keep Gaumont British out of Halesowen, but it was really his son's cinema. Bernard Bray kept the Lyttleton under his personal supervision from the opening until his death.

At the conclusion of the story of the Cosy Corner we last encountered Sidney Bray searching for a site for a new super-cinema! A site was found at Hasbury, in "surburban" surroundings, on the Hagley Road, now eclipsed as a main road by Manor Way. For some reason unknown it was not designed by a local architect, but by Edward Wilford. He produced a cinema that held just over a thousand patrons, with an attractive frontage in rustic brick and contrasting faience. The balcony lounge windows extended the vertical lines of the four sets of double doors beneath a very rectangular canopy. On the left hand of the facade a large fin carried the name of the cinema in neon light. Neon lighting, and flood-lighting, made the Lyttleton very attractive at night, even at the end of its cinema career.

It is said that William Jackson expected to build the Lyttleton, but the lowest tender was supplied by Mr. J. Felton, who had rebuilt the Regent, Brownhills, when it

had been acquired by Sidney Bray and Wally Davies. It was certainly going to be a struggle to build the Lyttleton and costs had to be kept as low as possible while providing as fine a cinema as possible. The bricks used to build the auditorium came, second-hand, from the demolition of Her Majesty's Theatre in Walsall. It was built using the established practice of putting up structural steelwork and filling in with brick and concrete. The main girder arrived by rail at Rowley Regis and had a difficult journey by road to Hasbury!

John Felton calculated that he built the Lyttleton for £6,480. When it came to equipping the place everything was hired from Gaumont British rather than purchased outright. This included everything from the seats to the Gaumont Eclipse projectors and the British Acoustic Duosonic sound system. A pleasing sense of luxury was provided in the auditorium, the plaster-work painted in autumnal tones and concealed lighting used effectively.

The Lyttleton opened on Monday evening, 11th April 1938 with the film, *"Farewell Again"* starring Flora Robson. The ceremony was performed by Alderman Downing, the Mayor of Halesowen. Sidney Bray said that he felt quite a veteran, having presented films in the town for twenty-seven years, and he was glad his son would be looking after the new cinema. The official party posed for a photograph, reproduced on the next page, and when it was reproduced in the County Express the paper told its readers "The cinema has been built regardless of cost". As it happened this statement was true in a way other than in which it was intended. The Brays could not afford to pay Mr. Felton and he took possession of the building and presumably leased it

Right: The official party at the opening of the Lyttleton on 11th April 1938. Standing, left to right: Wally Davies, K. Choate (job architect), Bernard and Bessie Bray, John Felton, (the builder), and W. Harrison (electrical engineer). Seated: Mrs. Bray, The Mayor & Mayoress of Halesowen, Alderman and Mrs. Downing, and Sydney Bray. (From John Felton's collection.)

Right: The paybox and mural in the foyer at the Lyttleton were regarded as pretty "posh", although modest by Odeon standards. (John Felton's collection.)

Opposite page: The Lyttleton, Halesowen., 1938. (John Felton's collection)

back to the Brays to keep things going. As things improved it looks as if the Brays were able to obtain a mortgage in order to buy it back from Mr. Felton – but whatever the details of all this Mr. Felton, the Brays, and Wally Davies remained on good terms.

Bernard Bray ran the Lyttleton successfully. During the War it prospered as a result of the patronage of soldiers stationed nearby, and after the War it prided itself on keeping up-to-date. For example it was quick to install cinemascope in 1954. Its champions claim that it was the first to do so in the Black Country but it would appear that it was beaten by two weeks by The Plaza, Dudley.

After Bernard Bray's death in 1961, his wife, Edith Bray, ran the Lyttleton but it was not an easy task. When the Grand, Kingswinford, closed in 1964 Ken Waterhouse came to the Lyttleton. At the Grand he had been a chief operator with managerial responsibilities and his versatility and enterprise helped the Lyttleton survive. He fought hard to preserve the dwindling family audience, and the balcony at the Lyttleton continued to attract this audience providing one could maintain order in the stalls.

By the early seventies, Bernard Bray's daughters were running the Lyttleton. It was busier than it had been in the early sixties but companies interested in promoting Bingo Halls were prepared to offer high prices. The Lyttleton was sold to Ladbrokes in the autumn of 1973, but it continued to operate as a cinema until the company obtained a gaming licence the following summer. Ken Waterhouse found himself working for Ladbrokes with the prospect of Bingo approaching.

The Lyttleton closed on 1st June 1974 with *"The Intelligence Men"* plus *"Bless This House"*. The conversion proceeded with great haste, but the new proprietors did not touch the operating room, they simply truncated all the wiring! It was more important to provide new heating and new lighting as Bingo Clubs are invariably brightly lit.

After all this, Bingo was not a great success at the Lyttleton. So much so that the story of this cinema takes a surprising twist. Ladbrokes decided to show films again on four nights of the week, from Friday to Monday. This brought Sunday-opening to Halesowen for the first time. Bingo would take place from Tuesday to Thursday!

Restoring cinema facilities to the Lyttleton was not easy. The screen had been removed in October 1975 and now formed the screen in the Shenstone Theatre, in Halesowen's new library. It was used by the Halesowen Film Society. Three operators, Harry and George Siddall, and Steve Sidaway, had to collect equipment from all over the Midlands. Lights came from the Gaumont, Wednesbury, owned by Ladbrokes, chandeliers and a clock came from the Odeon, Stourbridge, and a new second-hand curtain came from Villa Cross.

Although the projection equipment existed, reconnecting it was a nightmare, and circuits were traced by making one's way along the plaster-work with a magnet to detect the metal conduit. It re-opened at the beginning of January 1976.

At first it was difficult to obtain a supply of suitable films, but Ladbrokes took showing films seriously, and even introduced Saturday morning matinees for children. Alas, during the summer, just as good programmes were being booked, Ladbrokes decided to make financial cutbacks and it was decided to abandon the film operation at the Lyttleton.

The second and final closure was on Monday 27th September 1976 with *"The Poseidon Adventure"* plus *"How to Steal A Diamond"*. The three operators who had put so much work into their task were heart-broken. The projection equipment was removed and "given away", and Bingo returned, but apparently still without great success.

Eventually the Lyttleton was sold to Harry Whitehouse, a Birmingham businessman who successfully ran Bingo at the Avion, Aldridge, and former Clifton, Perry Barr. [1] He brought success to Bingo at the Lyttleton and by the 1980s everyone believed the building was preserved. The exterior was still attractive, although shorn of some of its details. Even bingo eventually declined at the Lyttleton, and soon after ceased demolition was announced. The bull-dozers moved in on 6th February 1989.

Messrs Macarthy & Stone built fifty warden-controlled flats on the site of the Lyttleton and originally expressed an interest in seeing if there was any feature of the cinema that could be incorporated into their new building. Nothing came of that intention.

Unfortunately I only visited the Lyttleton once but it introduced me to courting-seats, which I had never encountered in London. The last such seat in the Black Country existed in the Royal, Cradley Heath, but none remained in cinema use by the mid 80s. (At the Lyttleton double seats were provided at the end of each row in the balcony and these were still there when the cinema was demolished.)

---

[1] There is further comment on Mr. Whitehouse in the chapter of The Avion, Aldridge.

Quinton

If one leaves Halesowen on the old road to Birmingham, one crosses The Stour and then climbs Mucklow Hill towards the city's outer suburbs – eventually coming to Quinton. Obviously we are no longer in the Stour Vale, and barely in the Black Country but because the 1966 boundary of Dudley was drawn to include this area we find we have one more cinema to explore – and a surviving one at that!

The Danilo
(later known as The Essoldo and the Classic, etc.
Now known as The Reel)

Hagley Road West, Quinton

Fortunately, at the time of writing, one cinema still flourishes as a "Gateway to the Black Country". This is The Reel, which stands above a high brick precipice on the side of the M5 Motorway. As northbound drivers pass below it they can see the Black Country open out ahead of them.

This cinema was originally part of the Danilo circuit, in fact it served as Mortimer Dent's Head Office as it was within easy reach of his Edgbaston home. Mortimer Dent's partner in building this particular Danilo was Colonel J. Baldwin Webb. The site chosen was in an area that was fast becoming a residential suburb of Birmingham, but at that time it was in Oldbury. The site was previously occupied by a mansion called "Apsley House", the home of industrialist Edwin Danks.

Plans were drawn by Andrew Mather, in the prevailing modern style, and were approved by the Council in February 1938. The contractor was T. Elvins, who had gained considerable expertise in building super-cinemas and had a specialised team working on such tasks. However, their only other excursion into the Black Country had been a decade earlier at the Beacon.

The 1600 seater cinema, with its apparently lengthy brick facade, opened on August Bank Holiday, 7th August 1939, apparently without official ceremony. The Majestic, Smethwick, re-opened on the same day. *"Charlie Chan In Honolulu"* could be heard in RCA High Fidelity Magic Sound for 6d, 1/- or 1/6d. Saturday afternoon matinees were introduced immediately, including the serial, *"Blake at Scotland Yard"*. The car park held five hundred cars: a sign of the times!

After the War the Danilo, along with the other cinemas on the circuit, passed to Mr. Southan Morris's S. M. Super Cinemas Ltd., but still retained its original name. It became part of the Essoldo group in 1951 and therefore took the name of the new proprietors from about 1954 onwards. The Essoldo Group installed

Cinemascope in 1955 and first used it to present "The Robe" commencing 17th January in that year, followed by "Three Coins in the Fountain".

The original Danilo name, in high stainless steel letters, was very much an integral part of the design of the front elevation and successive changes of name, and changing the canopy etc., have all spoilt its original harmony. It was given a £65,000 facelift by the Essoldo group in 1967.

After the local government reorganisation of Spring 1966 the Essoldo found itself not in Warley, as one might expect, but in Halesowen, Dudley, where there was no provision for granting Sunday licences! Special steps had to be taken in mid 1967 to enable the Essoldo to open seven days a week. Two years later rumours circulated about its possible closure, probably started by the fact that the motorway looked as if it was about to be built throught it. The manager, Michael Jackson, denied the rumour and promised further improvements to the cinema after the completion of the motorway.

In April 1972 it was sold to the Classic circuit and began calling itself the Halesowen Classic. A year later work began on tripling the cinema. At first the circle was kept open with the screen hanging from the ceiling to the front wall of the circle. This could accommodate 400 patrons while two 320 seater auditoria were constructed, at night, beneath it.

The Classic opened as a triple-screen cinema on 26th July 1973 with *"Cabaret" "The Ten Commandments"*

Below: Quinton's cinema when known as The Classic.

and *"The Sound of Music"*. It also started calling itself the Quinton Classic as references to Halesowen had confused potential patrons! The vacant space in the former front stalls was turned into a fourth auditorium, and opened Autumn 1978. Michael Jackson now found himself managing the Black Country's only quadruple cinema — and in 1979 won the Manager of the Year award within the Classic group. Michael Hands, the chief operator, won a similar award in his field. He had successfully installed "Sound Surround" equipment for *"Earthquake"*, and four-track stereo for *"Tommy"*. Further improvements heralded the eighties when a £10,000 Dolby stereo system was installed in Classic I during April 1980, first used for the Midlands premier of *"Hair"*. In 1984 armchair seating was introduced in some parts of the cinema.

Having been The Classic since 1972, the cinema went through another change of identity in 1986 when it became The Cannon. Three years later, on the cinema's fiftieth birthday the Deputy Mayor of Dudley, Councillor Woodall, came along to perform a post-dated opening ceremony – i.e. the ceremony that had not taken place in 1939! The ceremony included unveiling a plaque in the circle foyer. The film *"The Three Fugitives"* was shown to the guests invited to join the 50th Birthday. Earlier in the day Manager, Michael Jackson, and two of his staff: Florence Boffey and Margaret Friday, had cut a strip of film, in front of the cinema's canopy which carried the cinema's various names! Chief Projectionist Paul Daniels had been forced to postpone his holiday to make sure all went well on the cinema's birthday, so probably everybody felt they had adequately compensated for the lack of a proper ceremony in 1939.

After all these name-changes the cinema acquired some names that were even more confusing because of their historical associations. For example, The Cannon became "The ABC" in 1996, and in 2002 it became "The Odeon". (Trick question: How many cinemas in Dudley, using its present boundaries, have been called Odeon?)

In 2005 the Odeon Group bought UCI Cinemas and as a result of a Monopolies Commission ruling, eleven cinemas had to be sold. This led to Quinton's Odeon being sold to Curzon Cinemas of Loughborough who renamed it "The Reel". It survives as "The Reel", at the time of going to press.

Dudley's Multi-plexes

Merry Hill 10/Odeon

Multi-screened cinemas were pioneered in Britain by AMC who opened their first such cinema in Milton Keynes in 1985. The company could trace its history back to one family-run cinema in Kansas. It was in Kansas that their multi-screen concept began to develop – a single foyer and box office leading to an array of auditoria simply known as "screens". Their ambition was to reverse the decline in cinema-going, and provide a sense that they had changed the style in which films were presented.

The Black Country's first modern multi-screen cinema, or "multi-plex", was opened to the public as part of the Merry Hill Shopping Complex on Friday 14th October 1988. (There had been a private opening for The Mayor of Dudley, Councillor Celia Hough, on Wednesday 12th

November.) Nobody quite knew what to call it! Was it "The Merry Hill 10", or was it "The AMC"? most shows were sell-outs over the following weekend and AMC were already talking about opening a second cinema nearby if the success was maintained! In the ten separate "screens", about 2400 patrons could be accommodated.

Innovations included a general no-smoking policy, a return to separate shows as opposed to "continuous performances", and high standards of projection and sound, via large screens and modern audio systems. Equally important were large car-parks and great emphasis of selling refreshments!

AMC (American Multi Cinemas) had been working in Britain since 1984 and the ten screen Merry Hill cinema was their sixth, and the first in the West Midlands. Obviously the intention was to reverse declining cinema audience figures by introducing a new American approach to film-presentation. The fact that there was American thinking behind all this was reinforced by the fact that the cinema had staged an "Drive-In" presentation of "E.T." on the cinema's car park before opening the cinema! Plenty of people turned up to experiment with the idea of watching films from their cars, but the British climate provided them with a steady drizzle in which to experience it.

Below: The UCI ten-screen cinema at Merry Hill, Dudley in July 2001, having opened as the AMC cinema. (Ned Williams)

The first attempt at holding a Black Country Film Festival opened at the multiplex in Merry Hill with a premier of a film called *"The Feast of July"* based on an H.E. Bates novel. The film included scenes shot in the Black Country Museum and the Severn Valley Railway, plus some interior scenes that had been shot on the Pensnett Trading Estate.

In 2006 Merry Hill's multi-plex became "The Odeon", and was refurbished at the same time. Soon after this the cinema introduced "Senior Screenings" on Thursday mornings.

Showcase Cinemas

Castle Gate, Dudley

National Amusements, of Boston, Massachussetts, first appeared in the Black Country with their 12 screen multi-plex in Walsall, opened in 1989. In Walsall they built their cinema in land developed by the Black Country Development Corporation, chosen for its proximity to Junction 10 on the M6 motorway. In coming to Dudley they again chose a site that had been seriously "redeveloped". The old cricket ground which had occupied this area had been resting on fairly unstable ground undermined by limestone workings. The completion of work on the stabalising of this site coincided with the building and opening of the Dudley Southern Bypass. The traffic island at Castle Gate must have looked like another Junction 10 – here was freshly developed land, served by road infrastructure that made it accessible to a wide area and big population.

Showcase, Dudley, was built to seat 3000 patrons in fourteen "screens". Architecturally it showed some advance on the exterior developed at Junction 10. The centre of the cinema's frontage was designed in a style reminiscent of the arch surrounding a cinema screen. It was built by ZVI - a Birmingham construction company, and was designed by Ord Abbey and Hanson Rowe of Shrewsbury.

It opened at lunchtime on Friday 12th October 2001, opening with several new releases plus films that had already been playing in the Black Country. There was no opening ceremony or special screening to mark the occasion. Managing the new cinema was Mike Bowker, a local man, in charge of a staff which can range from sixteen to ninety at any one time, many of which work part time. Only three operators are employed - only one being on duty at a time!

Above: The entrance to the UCI Multi-plex at Merry Hill included a paybox that was rather open to the elements. This was later enclosed.

Right: The opening of the Black Country's first mult-screen cinema was supported by Beacon Radio, the Chitty Chitty Bang Bang car and the AMC bus!

(Ned Williams)

All auditoria were built in the "stadium" style including four "premier" screens which provided settee style double-seating at the back of the auditorium. These luxury seats are reached from doors from the "premier lounge" on the floor above the general foyer. (The only other Showcase cinemas having these features are to be found at Nottingham and Bluewater.) The foyer itself is fairly vast but is broken up by the staircase from the lounge. The building gives quite a different "general impression" to the Showcase at Junction 10. Near the front car park is a statue made to resemble a curled piece of film – a monument in memory of James Whale – the lad from Dudley who went off to become a Hollywood film director.

Below: Showcase, Dudley, photographed on the day it opened: Friday 12th October 2001. The four "premier Screens" include "double seats" – just like in the "Old Days"!

Bottom of page: Dudley's latest Odeon – the multi-plex at Merry Hill! All very confusing! Odeons existed in Dudley itself, Brierley Hill, and Stourbridge. The Plaza, Dudley, also used the name "Odeon" for a short time before closure.

Section 4
Cinemas of Wolverhampton

Queen's Square, Wolverhampton: Hippodrome to the left, Queens Cinema top right.

"Out of Darkness, cometh Light" might have been a slogan adopted by early cinematographers, but, in fac it is Wolverhampton's motto. Today the enlared Metropolitan Borough covers the entire north western corner of the Black Country, including, Tettenhall, Bilston and Wednesfield and even parts of Coseley. Like all the towns occupying the "corners" of the Black Country, Wolverhampton has traditionally regarded itself as slightly separate from its neighbours. Its coat-of-arms displays symbols of its pre-industrial past: its ancient educational and ecclesiastical institutions, the wool trade and early locksmithing. However, when Queen Victoria emerged from mourning to visit the town in 1866 she drove from the station to the town centre through an arch of coal. This was surely a realistic nineteenth century recognition of the fact that the town's wealth was built on coal and the resulting growth in manufacturing industry, and that the town was therefore, to all intents and purposes, a part of the Black Country. Wolverhampton's recent acquisition of "city" status has reinforced the Wulfrunian view that the place is in some way superior to its neighbours – the reality is that the whole of the Black Country is in "the same boat" – all struggling to deal with the decline of local industry.

Past growth and prosperity produced many fine buildings in Wolverhampton, and the continuing recklessness with which they have successively been replaced. However, some Georgian, Victorian, and Edwardian elements of the townscape have survived to mingle with post-war modern architecture; Cinemas have come and gone in the same way. Currently, in 2011, it is possible to come across the remains of The Pavilion, used as a cinema in the days before the First World War, and the great Odeon of 1937 vintage now listed and surviving as a banquetting suite.

Reflecting the size and importance of Wolverhampton, the town had a large number of cinemas. In this survey the cinemas of the town centre will be dealt with first, in chronological order of arrival. Then the cinemas of Wolverhampton's "inner suburbs" will be described, followed by those of the "outer suburbs". This destroys the over-all chronology but makes the identity of each cinema a little clearer. We will then proceed to Bilston and Wednesfield – both Black Country towns that were dragged screaming into Wolverhampton in the 1966 reorgansation of local government. By coming to Wednesfield last, this section can be concluded by taking a look at the Black Country's third multi-plex.

Films in Wolverhampton before 1910

Like most towns, Wolverhampton certainly saw films before the passing of the Cinematograph Act of 1910. In the section on Bioscope Days I have mentioned some of the visits of the early bioscope shows to Wolverhampton. Besides the fairground there were one or two other places where films appeared during the first decade of the twentieth century.

The very first occasion when Wulfrunians saw a film presentation was in December 1896 – the end of the year in which cinematography arrived in Britain. Harry Poole's travelling "Myriorama Show" presented a show at The Exchange Hall, Wolverhampton on Christmas Eve 1896 which included: "The Cinematograph; The World's latest Scientific Triumph". In reviewing this historic show the Express & Star simply told its readers, *"An important addition to the evening's enjoyment is the introduction of the cinematograph - by which invention animated photographs are recorded with marvellous accuracy."* So much for what might have been the very first presentation of cinematography in the Black Country!

Films were occasionally shown at the old Drill Hall in Stafford Street. I have no details of these shows but one Wulfrunian remembers being a small boy at one of these shows about 1905, and remembers being more fascinated by the beam of light and the temporary fireproof projection box erected in the middle of the hall than with the films themselves. It also seems fairly likely that travelling cinematograph shows came to the Agricultural Hall as described in the chapter on that establishment, and possibly to other public halls.

The Pavilion

Tower Street, Wolverhampton

The earliest "theatrical" shows seem to have taken place at the Pavilion. This was a variety theatre which was basically a fairly long low building stretching from Tower Street to Castle Street, and it seems to have opened about 1908. A small raked gallery was provided at the Tower Street end, where the building can still be seen to this day. Films were being shown by 1909 between the variety acts and people were being admitted for "a penny and a pass".

Whatever the relative importance of live variety and films, the Pavilion seems to have obtained a Cinematograph Licence after the passing of the Act and used to appear in the Kine Year Book when that first appeared. It is recorded as belonging to Messrs. Bennett & Stone and is said to have held 1500 patrons but that is very difficult to imagine even if they were all crammed onto bench seats.

The Pavilion seems to have closed during the middle of the First World War, and the building has seen a variety of uses since. The closure may have coincided with the departure of Mr. Percy Peter Lloyd - the manager. He went from The Pavilion to Kidderminster in 1916 where he managed The Picture House for Thomas Jackson of Whitmore Reans. In the 1920s Mr. Lloyd tried running a cinema of his own in Norfolk, but then returned to Kidderminster to the same cinema – but called The Futurist, and then owned by Benjamin Priest. Mr. Lloyd died in 1943 at the age of 68 – while still managing The Futurist. His son Ron Lloyd then ran the cinema until its closure in 1962. Ron Lloyd's son wrote to me from South Australia – like everyone else – he would love to more about The Pavilion.

In 1959 a gas-lit chandelier which used to hang from the ceiling forty years earlier was unearthed while the building was undergoing alterations. The frontage still has a theatrical look about it, but like the Electric/Imperial in Queen's Square, which also closed in the First World War, there are few people around today who can remember the place.

Left: The Pavilion, Tower Street, Wolverhampton, in 1981. At this time it had not been used as theatre or cinema for over sixty years   *(Ned Williams)*

The Electric Theatre
- later The Imperial

38 Queen's Square, Wolverhampton

In order to prepare premises that would fulfil the requirements of the 1910 Cinematograph Act, would-be cinema proprietors had to start work in 1909. Enterprise Developments Ltd. asked a London architect, Herbert H. Gissing, to draw up plans of a cinema they proposed opening in Queen's Square. The plans were approved on 8th December 1909 and involved making several alterations to the existing building. The frontage by Messrs Lewis & Barr was treated in pure white and looked wonderful when lit up at night. A raked floor had to be installed, a pay box at the entrance, and a small operating room immediately behind it, reached by climbing four steps. One description focussed on the heavy pile carpets and draperies supplied by Phillips & Jones of Wolverhampton, and the snug chairs. *"Handsomely uniformed attendants"* proved that no expense had been spared.

It was designed to accommodate three hundred people on benches and tip up seats reached from one side gangway. Nowadays it seems strange to imagine so many people squeezed into premises the size of a shop but at the time it was fairly typical of the places used for showing films in many high streets throughout the country. Such was the novelty of the picture house that the local magistrate issuing the licence for music and dancing in respect of the Electric Theatre could not understand what was happening. The licence was required as the silent films were to be accompanied "by a small piano, played by a lady artiste". The applicant, Mr. R. A. Willcock, assured the magistrate, Alderman Jones, that there would be no other music and certainly no dancing. Alderman Jones gave up, and turned his attention to the inflammability of films and their possible offensiveness. The owners offered to allow the Chief Constable to review the films privately every Monday morning if necessary!

Such was the rush to enter the cinema business that the Electric Theatre first opened to the public on 24th January 1910, and the opening programmme included **"Nero, or the Fall of Rome"**. The narrow cramped auditorium seems hardly to have provided enough space for a pianist to accompany the films, but apparently there was room behind the screen for a sink. The sink was used for washing cups, as patrons at some matinees could have cups of tea brought to their seats. Along with this image of a tea-drinking audience some Wulfrunians have recalled that the Electric showed many British films. When it opened the most expensive seats, which could be reserved, were a shilling: a high price in those days. By March the cinema was able to show films of Wolves matches almost as soon as they were over.

Business carried on at the Electric until about 1915 without any change. While being managed by a Mr. J.

B. Stephenson, it seems that a new company was formed to improve the place. Messrs. Imperial Playhouse Ltd. submitted new plans, by Frank Clark, for approval in November 1915. A new half-timbered facade was planned that would have given the cinema a more imposing frontage and would have made it seem less like a converted shop. It was also planned to move the screen so that it occupied the centre of the rear wall of the hall. This meant that the screen would have to stick out slightly across the existing rear exit to Cheapside. The plans were not given approval.

However, the Imperial Playhouse, as it wished to be called, carried on under its new name from 1916 until it closed sometime in 1918. Mr. Stephenson found a new job for a short while at the Coliseum in Blakenhall, and the little cinema became a shop. Many people remember the premises as Green & Hollins, the outfitters, a remember seeing ornamental plasterwork that been a feature of its cinema days. In recent years the premises have been used as bank.

Above: A much enlarged image from a postcard view of Queens Square, Wolverhampton taken just before the First World War shows a tram passing the front of The Electric Theatre. The carved frontage and central paybox seem to owe something to the bioscope tradition. It seems amazing that a shop-sized building could accommodate three hundred patrons!

(Bennett Clarke/Wolverhampton Archives)

Above: A "flier" from the Electric, and a "penny pass" to the Olympia – both from the John Roper Collection.

The Olympia

Thornley Street, Wolverhampton

The early shows at the Drill Hall in Stafford Street were probably presented by a Mr. & Mrs. Quigley, and to them goes the honour of the opening of Wolverhampton's second cinema. While the 1909 Cinematograph Bill was becoming law they seem to have been looking for suitable premises. The Thornley Street Odd-Works, not far from the Drill Hall, seemed ripe for conversion. The falling ground meant that an auditorium, constructed parallel to Broad Street, would have a natural rake. Plans, drawn by the architect Joseph Lavender, were submitted for approval in January 1910, and work began on altering the premises into a cinema.

Mr. James Joseph Quigley was a Derbyshire man who played for the County Cricket Team, but he now devoted himself to his future in Wolverhampton. He had recently married Frances Appleby, whose sister claimed to have shown films privately to Edward VII and Alexandra in Scotland. Frances had the interest in films and a flair for presenting them, he kept the books and ran the business side of the venture. Together they became the town's first cinema magnates.

The Olympia opened for business on 14th March 1910. It held eight hundred people, and in the theatrical tradition, the best seats were at the front, near the screen. The cheaper seats, benches with a back-rail, were at the rear of the hall. At first there was only one projector and programmes featured a gap between reels. Mr. Frank Whild was the musical director and sometimes sound effects were provided for the silent films. Early in its life the Olympia did present an early "talkie"; a man singing a song with sound provided by mechanically synchronised disc.

Ten years after opening their cinema, the Quigleys acquired the freehold of the property, and years later it was still owned by their daughter. Kine Weekly reported this fact in April 1920 and told its readers, *"The hall itself is of neat appearance and arrangement; they get a wonderfully clear picture, and it would be difficult to improve on the showing".* Kine Weekly was also impressed by the warm welcome the regular patrons extended to Frank Whild, who had been away on War Service, and had worked briefly at the Scala.

The Olympia managed to keep its regular customers and survive the growing competition from other cinemas in town by specialising in serials, strong melodramas and action films. It also received the very personal attention of its proprietors, who prided themselves on such matters as the brightness of their picture.

A new operating box, and loudspeaker room behind the screen, had to be added in 1930 when Western Electric Sound was installed. For many years the chief operator was Harry Poncherry. He was an electrical and mechanical genius. He came from a high-wire circus family but his inventive skill was just what was needed to help run a small cinema.

The Quigleys maintained their operating interest in The Olympia until early 1939. Mr. Quigley was then fifty-seven years old and decided to lease the cinema to C.S. Joseph. The latter's company, Pine Pictures, took over the Coliseum and the Olympia together and he announced plans to refurbish and revitalise them. Although Pine Pictures had inherited two of Wolverhampton's oldest cinemas, the popularity of film-going during the War meant that they were not such a

bad proposition. (The career of Cyril Joseph is sum-marised in the first section of this book.)

After the War the Olympia survived partly as a result of the enterprise of its manager, Charlie Kettle. It began to specialise in continental films and sometimes advertised as the "Olympia Continentale". In this he might have had little choice. As a small independent cinema within Cyril Joseph's group it was pretty low down the "pecking order" when it came to access to films. Mr. Kettle took the unusual step, for a cinema manager, of joining the committee of the town's Film Society soon after it was re-formed in 1948, I wonder if the expertise and help he offered the Society was repaid by members visiting his theatre to see some of the classics of the foreign cinema?

Towards the end of the 50's, C.S. Joseph began to pull out of the cinema business and Pine Pictures Ltd. was acquired by a Mr. Vincent Wareing. The arrival of Mr. Wareing led to the departure of Charlie Kettle, precipitated into retirement after a varied career in the management of Black Country cinemas. Ageing premises and declining audiences provided Mr. Wareing with problems, to which could be added the problems of fulfilling quota regulations. The Olympia gave up the struggle in July 1960. In this respect it was outlived by its original proprietor as Mr. Quigley lived until his eightieth year. In February 1962 he was buried in his adopted town. The last show, on 9th July 1960 had featured *A Lift to the Scaffold* supported by Fellini's *"Cabiria"*.

Above: The Olympia, Thornley Street, Wolverhampton seen just after closure. Vincent Wareing's posters claiming "You can't see films like these on the telly" still decorate the building. (WTC)

To this day the premises in Thornley Street bear flaking paintwork just about testifying to the existence of the Olympia Cinema, although subsequent lessees have put the premises to a variety of uses including a club – "The Planet". It even seems that one potential lessee had wanted to reopen the Olympia as a cinema, but could not obtain the lease. If he had done so it is tempting to wonder if the town's first cinema would have returned to life and survived to a greater age?

The Picture House

69 Victoria Street, Wolverhampton

While cinemas established themselves in Wolverhampton in 1910, other town-centre sites had to be found for conversion for the new mode of entertainment. A Wolverhampton architect, A. Eaton Painter was asked to produce plans for conversion of some premises at the back of the Villiers Club in Victoria Street. The plans, approved by the Council on 14th. November 1911, were commissioned by Messrs.

Evans, Brown and Myatt of the Villiers Club. This club was to be found next door to Hudsons, a leather goods shop. Work must have proceeded very quickly as little over a month later the Midland Evening News carried an advertisement for the opening of the Picture House at 6.00 p.m. on 21st December 1911, under the management of Clifford Wormersley.

It was usually known as the *"Little"* Picture House and many people remember the narrow entrance in Victoria Street and the corridor that led down to the cash desk and entrance to the hall. As in the Electric, Queens Square, there was a feeling of narrowness to the hall itself, and of a long slope down to the screen. It held about three hundred and fifty people and it could become quite hot when packed!

Within a couple of years of opening it had come within the growing empire of Thomas Jackson. Several local people have told me that he used to stand by the cash desk to welcome patrons and that one of his daughters played the piano accompaniment to the films, but I imagine that this figure was really one of the succession of managers.

After the War, Thomas Jackson seems to have planned to enlarge and improve the Picture House. He had plans prepared by Messrs. Hickton and Farmer, of Walsall and Birmingham, for a new overhead ventilation system, and extension to the auditorium, and for a new system of back projection to be installed behind the screen. The old projection room at the Victoria Street end of the hall was to become a fan chamber. As he was also planning to replace the Strand in Whitmore Reans with a new cinema, Mr. Jackson entered a partnership with a Mr. Allen to form Cinemas Consolidated Ltd.

Above: the staff of the "Little Picture House" pose in Victoria Street, Wolverhampton outside the narrow entrance that took patrons down to their cinema, just before the First World War.   (Ken Rock postcard)

Under the control of this new partnership work began on the Picture House, but in October 1922 the Licensing Justices refused to renew the music licence because proper sanitary accommodation was not available. For a time films were shown in silence while work on the alterations went on! It was officially reopened on 17th May 1923 and audiences were invited to enjoy the new "ray-less" pictures, and back projection was promoted as less likely to cause eye strain.

While audiences enjoyed the rather yellowish pictures that appeared on the cinema's translucent screen, the proprietors began to experience further financial problems. Jackson-Allen (Cinemas Consolidated) Ltd. was compulsorily wound up during 1923. The property had been conveyed to the Bank and to two trustees for the purpose of raising capital. The Bank now sold the property to recover its debt and ultimately the Picture House passed to the Midland Counties Circuit Ltd., along with the Coliseum, Dudley Road. This company seems to have been created exclusively to take over the cinemas of Thomas Jackson following his bankruptcy.

The Midland Counties Circuit sold the freehold to Beatties, the adjoining department store, in June 1926, but the Picutre House continued to operate as a cinema until plans for the expansion of Beatties' premises and rationalisation of the building line in Victoria Street led to its demise. While Beatties owned the freehold films were presented by the company then showing films at the West End in Whitmore Reans. It closed, just as sound films were reaching town, on 28th September 1929, and the last film was *"His House in Order"* starring Tallulah Bankhead. Demolition began a few days later on 2nd October.

However, a few reminders of the Little Picture House were incorporated into Beatties extensions. If you climb the stairs by the electrical department and look out the window it is possible to imagine where the Picture House stood, and for many years an elaborate piece of plaster work and ornate ceiling support on one of the walls of the electrical department also reminded customers of the cinema. This is no longer visible to the public.

The Picturedrome, later The Scala

Worcester Street, Wolverhampton

Sticking to the chronological sequence in which cinemas arrived in central Wolverhampton, we would now have to introduce the Coliseum on the Dudley Road, but that cinema is going to be desrcibed in a chapter dealing with cinemas that developed in Wolverhampton's inner suburbs.

While Thomas Jackson's "Picture House" and "Coliseum" were settling down to reasonable business in the two or three years that preceeded the First World War, other local businessmen planned bigger cinemas. Wolverhampton Picturedromes Ltd., led by F. Evans and G. Lewis, proposed to build a twelve hundred seater in Worcester Street. The plans, drawn by A. Eaton Painter, were submitted for approval in July 1913. Its rather grand frontage, featuring domes, arches and pillars, was the first such facade to bring the "cinema style" to Wolverhampton, and it had much in common with several cinemas being built in Birmingham at the same time. Behind the facade the auditorium had to be squeezed into a slightly triangular site but it was still thought possible to house 942 people downstairs plus 248 in the balcony.

Below: The Scala, Worcester Street, Wolverhampton.The photo was taken by Johan Van Leerzum who was cycling by and realised that the cinema was closing – so he leaned his bike against the fron of the building, crossed the road and took a photograph.

Left: The interior of The Scala in "Bingo Days" – about 1984. The floor has been put in at balcony level and patrons find themselves close to the ceiling and facing the top of the proscenium arch that once framed the screen.
(Ned Williams)

Opposite Page: A postcard picture of The Queens Picture House in the early 1920s. (Ken Rock)

Work must have proceeded apace during the second half of 1913, perhaps prompted by a desire to have the cinema open by Christmas. I have failed to find any advertised opening date but it was certainly opened in December of that year, having received its licence on the 8th of the month. It was certainly open for the Christmas week which began on Monday 22nd December. The programme included *"Dancing Lessons on Film"* which would seem an ideal film to show if the seats had not yet been installed! The mystery surrounding its exact opening is carried on into the years of the War. Whatever happened, it does not seem to have had a smooth start to life.

After the War it was bought very cheaply by Edgar Hounsell of Midland Amusements Company whose interests were mainly in West Bromwich. Oscar Deutsch is also believed to have been associated later with this Company, but not at the time of this Wolverhampton connection. It was re-named The Scala and Vic Hornblow was installed as manager. Some rebuilding, good management by Mr. Hornblow, and better programmes led to better box office success. A new orchestra, led by a Mr. Beard, was engaged.

Despite its success Edgar Hounsell soon seemed keen to dispose of the Scala. In 1920, in the middle of its most successful month of trading it had ever known, the cinema was sold to a firm calling themselves Midlands Entertainments Ltd. Vic Hornblow's services were retained but he only stayed till early 1921.

By the mid twenties it was acquired by a national circuit; Associated Provincial Picture Houses, who also owned the Queens and the Agricultural Hall, in the town. On 11th July 1925 A.P.P.H. closed the Scala for complete refurbishing, an operation they had just completed on the Agricultural Hall. It was reopened on 28th September 1925 with *"Winning Through"* and *"The Mirage"*. The advertisement declared, "Forty souvenirs to be given away nightly!"

Mr. C. Lloyd Davies, a name long associated with local cinemas, was the manager and Louis Ronnie was in charge of the orchestra. Apart from losing a few seats the Scala remained fairly unchanged over the years. When sound arrived British Acoustic equipment was installed. Its place in a national circuit provided stability and an uneventful life in terms of changes of ownership. It effectively served a population living in the Graisley area as well as serving the fringe of the town centre. The former area provided the "regulars" and when post-war movement led to a fall in that population the cinema's audience declined. Thus it was outlived for a few years by its flea-pit rivals!

The Scala closed on 1st December 1956 with Cornel Wilde's *"Beyond Mombasa"*. More significantly, it had revived James Whale's *"Bride of Frankenstein"* for the first two days of its final week of operation. The building was then put up for sale and began another chequered career similar to its early career as a cinema! It settled down, and survived, as a Bingo Hall, probably serving the population of the new rebuilt Graisley just across the Ring Road. Some of its original frontage survived. The Bingo hall's floor was at balcony level but the decorative plaster work of the ceiling and the top of the proscenium arch still reminded visitors of its cinema origins. Most of the frontage still survives in 2011.

The Queen's

Queen's Square, Wolverhampton

Every town seems to have had a favourite cinema that the populus took to its heart. Places like the West End and the Coliseum may have had their local following but usually a centrally sited cinema stood the best chance of being the premier picture house. Such a cinema had to aspire to respectability to win the middle classes to its cause. The Queens, in the centre of Wolverhampton, was just such a place. People who would not have dreamed of entering any other picture palace felt it was acceptable to visit The Queens. A "posh" atmosphere was obtained by incorporating such features as a tea room into the complex, but the elegance and "social safety" had to be spiced with a little of the vulgar excitement that film-going was really all about! In the twenties, which was the golden age of such cinemas, Hollywood's films themselves provided this same formula; a subtle blend of vulgarity, sophistication, and moral propriety!

The Queens, significantly, was part of a growing national circuit. It was built for Associated Provincial Picture Houses who specialised in providing this kind of cinema. Local xenophobia, just before the War, seemed to create a distrust of A.P.P.H. and they were constantly denying that they had any German connection. Up until 1914 many local cinemas had been pioneered by local men. Even A.P.P.H. were not as "foreign" as they seemed as will be made clear in the chapter on Walsall. The plans were produced by Messrs. Robert Atkinson and George Alexander, London architects, during 1913,

with a few modifications being made to the foyer and tea room in early 1914. Work on the building proceeded in 1914 and the contractor was Messrs. H. Willcock and Co.

On 30th September 1914 Wolverhampton's eighth cinema opened. (Including the Strand out in Whitmore Reans, and the Coloseum in Blakenhall, in the other seven.) The opening speech was made by Mr. A. E. Newbould of A.P.P.H. and he stressed his local connection and again denied any German sympathies. Indeed he had been born in Wolverhampton and had attended the local Art School. The Mayor, Alderman Bantock actually declared the cinema open, and the films that followed included *"Jelfs"* and *"Her Uncle"*. Norman Williams, from Covent Garden Opera House, sang *"Shipmates of Mine"* and *"Land of Hope and Glory"* to underline A.P.P.H.'s patriotism.

Accommodation was provided for just over one thousand people, slightly less than the Scala, but probably in greater luxury. Its frontage, dominated by three arched windows at balcony level, and its elegant foyer provided suitable grandeur for its imposing position at the top of Queen's Square. The cinema obviously took its name from this square. Other A.P.P.H. theatres were usually simply called "The Picture House", but this name was already used locally by the rival enterprise in Victoria Street. A commissionaire, page boys and ushers, in splended blue uniforms, greeted the patrons plus one solitary usherette, Edith Causer, who also helped out occasionally as a waitress in the cafe. She obtained the job through her sister Kate, who was an assistant in the operating room under the "chief", Mr. Collett.

QUEEN'S PICTURE HOUSE, WOLVERHAMPTON. No. 92

Managers came and went fairly quickly in the first few years but later individuals stayed for longer periods and became closely indentified with the cinema. In the early twenties it was the leader of the orchestra who was the personality most strongly associated with the cinema in most people's minds. This gentleman was Alfred Van Dam. Many people went to hear him play in his own right, as well as admire his accompaniment to the films.

Miss Causer had graduated from usherette to 3rd operator by the early twenties and used to open the projection room portholes when Van Dam was playing and used to sing along with the marvellous music. One day the manager sent a note up to the box saying, "Tell Miss Causer the orchestra is supplying all the music that is needed!"

It must have been a sad day when the talkies came to the Queens despite the excitement of the new medium. Unexpectedly, the Queens was not the first Wolverhampton cinema to be wired for sound, A.P.P.H. granted that honour to the Agricultural Hall. However, on 23rd September 1932 "*Weary River*" introduced the phenomenon to the Queens. Three members of the orchestra were retained on the staff.

Below: The interior of The Queens Picture House, Wolverhampton. (CTA Archives)

The cinema had been managed for a year by Cliff Lloyd-Davies from the Scala, but he was destined for the new Gaumont that September, so was replaced by Tom Lloyd. The latter stayed twenty-seven years until the cinema closed. His long stay, and Cliff Lloyd-Davies' long stay at The Gaumont later joined by Mr. Felton at the Odeon, earned them the local nick-name, "The Three Musketeers". Successfully they managed the local cinemas and promoted the films shown, for quarter of a century.

The Queens was provided with Western Electric sound and through the thirties and forties continued to hold its own against newcomers like the Odeon and Savoy. The Earl of Dudley, and occasionally his guest, The Prince of Wales, came to the Queens without any special fuss being made, and several generations of courting couples regularly went to the cinema or the cafe. Future husbands and wives actually met at the Queens, proposals were made there, and even honeymoons often started there! Although its "golden age" may have been the twenties, each subsequent decade provided people with memories of the place right up to its closure at the end of the fifties.

By the mid fifties the owners, the Circuits Management Association of the Rank Organisation, were undergoing the first of their endless series of rationalisations. Thus Dudley's Criterion disappeared as early as 1956, and Wolverhampton's Scala had closed by the end of that year. In July 1957 Rank revealed plans for converting The Queens into a ballroom, but these were apparently shelved in September when snags arose over licensing.

210

Right: The tea room at balcony level in The Queens Picture House, Wolverhampton, added a touch of class – all part of the company's plan to take the cinema business "up market "with much improved standards of customer service. (WTC)

In May 1958, it was announced that the cinema would be auctioned. A month later, in the London auction room of Goddard and Smith, it was withdrawn when bidding reached £74,000, probably about £6,000 short of the reserve. For a while it seemed a private sale might still take place, but by the end of the year it was clear no sale would take place and that Rank themselves would re-develop the site.

The end came on 7th February 1959. The final programme was *"The Square Peg"* starring Norman Wisdom, plus *"The Lavender Mob"* starring Alec Guinness. The restaurant remained open while "alterations" commenced. It was to become a dance hall after all. The £30,000 conversion was planned by Dennis Patterson and K. W. Brookes of the Harry Weedon Partnership, and was carried out by A. W. Gibbons and Son of Coventry.

Ironically the conversion made the place seem more "theatrical" inside than it had looked for years in the view of the Express and Star reporter. He viewed the place as the scaffolding was being removed in May 1959. Deep reds and blues, and gilt panelling created this atmosphere. The strongly horseshoe-shaped balcony where courting couples had once sat in the double-seats, was retained and linked to the dance-floor at the former screen end of the hall. The Canadian maple dance floor was installed at the level of former rear stalls. As the stalls were steeply raked this left considerable space under the floor at the screen end, but brought the dancers nearer to the original ceiling which was retained. The lavish plaster work was "lost" by being painted all over in midnight blue. Someone remarked that it would make an ideal intimate cinema!

The Queens Ballroom opened on 15th May 1959 but lasted just under a decade. For some it had strong nostalgia as a dance hall, but generally there was a flood of nostalgic letters in the local press about the place as a cinema when, almost another decade later, the building was demolished. Demolition began in 1977 but staggered on into 1978. Even on a valuable town centre site it seemed that a cinema could just "fade away" rather than promptly disappear. The site was redeveloped in 1980 by Lloyds Bank. Behind the bank is a car park suggesting the "footprint" of the cinema's auditorium.

The New Theatre Royal
- later The Clifton

Bilston Street, Wolverhampton

The centre of Wolverhampton did not witness the building of a 1920s cinema. The Globe out at Horseley Fields opened in 1927 but was rather remote from the town's centre. Events at the end of the 1920s bring us back to the town centre, but confuse the issue by also being part of the town's theatre history. (The story of the New Theatre Royal in all its incarnations, and the story of The Empire will be told in volume Two.)

When a cinema earns the nickname, "The Blood Tub" we do not expect to find it standing on a prime site in the town centre but the Clifton was just such a contrary place. The building enjoyed an extraordinary history. It was built on the site of a slaughter-house and opened in 1865 as The Prince of Wales Theatre, providing music hall entertainment. It was also known at various times as The Star, the Hippodrome and The New Theatre Royal, to distinguish it from the former Theatre Royal that stood at the end of Garrick Street. It was equally well

The New Theatre Royal/The Clifton presenting Bingo in Bilston Street, Wolverhampton. (Lionel J Lee)

known as The Blood Tub, in honour of the stirring melodramas presented, and "Kimberley's" after one of the proprietor's; Mrs. Kimberley.

In 1913 the building caught fire, not for the first time, and the rebuilding that followed created the frontage that survived until the 1980s. The plans were drawn up by Marcus Brown in 1914 and the work was completed the same year. It reopened with Mrs. Kimberley's *"Australian Nell"* and the proceeds went to a war-fund. The ornate plaster work across the front of the building seemed more appropriate to a theatre than a cinema and the interior certainly always retained its theatrical atmosphere.

On 23rd August 1928 Leon Salberg, proprietor of Birmingham's Alexandra Theatre, purchased it for £25,000 and decided to concentrate on higher class drama, revues and pantomime. Repertory Theatre was presented just as the "talkies" were beginning to take the world by storm. Leon Salberg decided to join the craze and converted his theatre into a cinema. The last play was presented on 25th May 1931 and the conversions took less than a month. The plans had been drawn up by Satchwell and Roberts and had to contend with problems such as improving sight lines in the circle. This was solved by modifying the upper circle, or balcony, reducing its previous figure of 274. A screen was dropped at the front of the stage and an operating box was constructed right up in the roof of the building. The resulting angle of projection was ridiculously steep.

Even with the screen angled it was impossible to prevent some distortion or loss of focus. With such

impossible projection conditions it seems fitting that the only chief operator who could be found who would not suffer vertigo was a man with one eye: Tom Edkins. Special appertures were cut in the machines but it was never very satisfactory. A Western Electric sound system was put in. As the stage took up a fairly large proportion of its size, the building only held just over a thousand patrons.

The cinema opened on 15th June 1931 with *"The Widow From Chicago"*, not long before the Empire began a short period of showing films. Thus the decade of the "super-cinema" began with two of the town's theatres courting the new improved medium. Whether it was intended to show films at the New Theatre Royal for long I am not quite sure.

In mid 1930 Cinema Proprietors Ltd., the partnership of Leon Salberg and Sidney Clift, proposed re-developing the site on the opposite side of Bilston Street as a huge 3,000 seater to be called "The Garrick". Again this was to be designed by Messrs. Satchwell and Roberts. If it had materialised in their ownership it is not clear what might have become of the New Theatre Royal.

However, before this plan had progressed very far ABC seem to have entered the picture. A new set of plans for a cinema was finally submitted to the local authority the following year, by Leon Salberg, but these were drawn by William Glen — ABC's resident architect. Next we hear that ABC themselves were to build their own "Savoy" on the site, but some "special relationship" presumably existed between ABC and Messrs. Salberg and Clift because the New Theatre Royal was then leased to ABC while the Savoy was being built.

When this lease expired, and the Savoy was open, the cinema returned to Cinema Proprietors. Presumably it retained the name "New Theatre Royal", rather than "The Clifton", to avoid confusion with the Clifton at Fallings Park. For the first decade of its life it had been managed by Harry Warburton, but about 1940/1941 Howard Smith became the manager, and licensee of the Clifton Bar at the Tower Street end of the theatre. He remained there until its closure as a cinema.

In the summer of 1948 the "New Theatre Royal" name plates were removed from the front of the building while it was repainted. As from 19th September it was to be known as The Clifton, but as the building was known by so many of its names this made little difference to anybody. A more important problem was to find suitable films to show there now that the two major circuits had tighter control over the availability of film, and a more monopolistic control of town centre cinemas.

The Clifton began its long association with revivals, foreign films and films rejected by ABC and Rank. Thus films such as *"All Quiet on the Western Front"* reappeared in Wolverhampton and the work of Bunuel, Bergman and Fellini popped up among cheap horror films and dubbed Italian epics. In September 1949 Howard Smith actually approached the town's film society and begged its members to support the Midlands premiere of *"Paisa"* at the Clifton. Sadly the middle classes who supported such films in the rarified atmosphere of the Film Society rarely seemed to venture into the Olympia or the Clifton to see the same material. When I arrived in the area in 1962 I was amazed to be able to see films that I had previously gone to the Academy in London to see, but often had to sit through a Harrison Marks supporting film to enjoy a Bergman classic!

The Clifton seemed such a tatty contrast to the ABC opposite, but its theatrical atmosphere was far more exciting than the plainess of the ABC. It was obvious its days were numbered. The Clifton circuit disposed of both the Clifton and the Rosum, Walsall, to Star Associated Holdings in February 1966.

The final show for the old proprietors was on 12th February with a magnificent double bill, *"Curse of the Fly"* and one of my favourites, *"Duel of the Space Monsters"* but it seems probable that Star Holdings ran the place as a cinema for a further week. The last show was therefore probably on 19th February, but as it was not advertised I have been unable to find out what was shown.

It was transformed into a Bingo Hall even more quickly than it had been transformed from a theatre to a cinema. The screen and orchestra pit disappeared and an attempt was made to streamline the interior of the auditorium and give it a feeling of brightness and luxury. It opened for Bingo on 3rd March 1966, and survived for a decade in which it was taken over by E.M.I. Bingo; ABC's second association with the site.

By 1978 the building was being declared unsafe and was acquired by the County Council as part of the process of acquiring land associated with extensions to the final phase of the town's ring road. For the last two or three years of its existence it presented a very sad and dejected face to cinema-goers emerging from the ABC. One even wished it had survived longer as a Bingo Hall.

Demolition began early in 1981 but even that proceeded slowly until W. Jones and Son replaced the original contractor in April. Work then speeded up in a dramatic way. The eastern wall of the building was ripped away exposing a magnificent side-elevation transect of the building from projection box, through both circles, down to the stage. A huge gas-engined generator was unearthed beneath the stalls, and on 5th April 1981 the frontage came down; leaded windows, art-nouveau tiles on the staircases, bronze doors, and decorative plaster work all disappeared without any ceremony.

The Agricultural Hall and the Gaumont

Snow Hill, Wolverhampton

Following a chronological pattern it is logical to proceed to a description of the Gaumont, Wolverhampton's first "modern" cinema, but the story and chronology are complicated by the fact that-the Gaumont was built on the site of the Agricultural Hall and that story takes us back to the early days of cinema, just before the First World War.

The Agricultural Hall was built in 1863 at Snow Hill, the junction of the roads from Bilston and Dudley — the corner itself determining the distinctive curved frontage of the Hall, and later of the Gaumont. A weekly corn market was held there and above the building's entrance was a decorative device featuring a stook of corn, a plough and agricultural produce. Various additions were made to the building as time went on and it could be used for public meetings, conferences, exhibitions etc.

Early travelling cinematograph shows were put on at the hall. For example, Poole's travelling shows came there. The hall was used by the Birmingham showman Waller Jeffs in 1908 as the finishing line in a marathon race from The Curzon Hall in Birmingham. Irving Bosco

Right: Demolition of the Clifton gets underway in 1981.
During the demolition it was possible to see the various stages through which the building had been changed over the years.
The history of the building as a theatre is told in Volume 2.
(Express & Star)

Above: The Agricultural Hall, Snow Hill. The statue has since moved to West Park.

organized the race in connection with the Wolverhampton Cycling and Athletic Club. It was filmed from a car supplied by Charles Clark and Sons. The film of the event was certainly shown at the Curzon Hall but it is not clear if it was also screened at the Agricultural Hall.

From 1910 onwards, while the town's early cinemas were emerging, the Hall seems to have concentrated on concerts and public meetings. The touring film-exhibitors usually occupied the hall during the winter. For example in September 1912 a new season of "Perfect Pictures and Vaudeville" is advertised to start on the thirtieth of that month. The presenters call themselves "Pictureland" but it may have been Poole's. At Christmas 1912 this gave way to a film presentation of *"From the Manger to the Cross"*. A very pious attitude was adopted towards this, and it must have been more like attending a religious meeting than going to the pictures. It seems to mark the hall's determination to become a picture palace. During 1913 it closed for proper modification to a cinema. Plans were drawn up by Norfolk and Prior of Catford and a new raked floor capable of holding 1248 patrons was provided. The magnificent foyer and crush hall with fountain provided many patrons with lasting memory of the cinema. It opened, in its new form, sometime during the latter half of 1913, coming half way between the openings of the Picture House and the Picturedrome in terms of a chronological account of the town centre's cinemas.

The proprietor was the Wolverhampton Playhouse Company but this local name disguised a firm that had its headquarters at the Rink Cinema, Finsbury Park, in North London. The company later became North Metropolitan Theatres, but by 1919, the Agricultural Hall had been acquired by Associated Provincial Picture Houses, who owned the Queen's, and later the Scala.

Several managers came and went, but from 1924 to 1927 Fred Studd ran the Hall. While he was there in September 1924, a film caught fire in the projector. The operator, Mr. Fielding, managed to contain the situation but the last two reels of the film were destroyed. A common enough cinema story of that period, but two factors were interesting. First, this "red-hot" piece of film was suitably, *"Sodom and Gomorrah"* and secondly, the resourceful Mr. Studd managed to acquire two replacement reels within ninety minutes and the doors were opened to allow the audience to see the end of the film!

During his stay at the Agricultural Hall Cinema, as it was called, Fred Studd saw the place refurbished. It closed for a few months for this to be carried out, and reopened on 13th July 1925 with *"The Snob"* starring John Gilbert. Although not originally a purpose-built cinema it had become a cinema in quite a grand way. Its huge auditorium could hold eighteen hundred people and its entrance hall had an elegance to rival the Queens. There was also a three manual straight organ to accompany the films in silent days. It is not surprising therefore that the Agricultural Hall was the first cinema in the town to present sound films. These arrived in 1929.

Despite all this nothing could really disguise the fact that the place was a rather old Victorian building, and, perhaps naturally to its owners, it seemed to be sitting on an ideal site for a new 1930's style super-cinema. Thus its days were numbered. The last film was shown there on 19th September 1931 and the building was demolished to make way for the new Gaumont.

The Gaumont

The demolition men began their work on the Agricultural Hall on 21st April 1931, the Monday after the last show. A.P.P.H.'s successor's, Gaumont British, owned three sites in Wolverhampton; the Queens, the Scala and the old Agricultural Hall and, as stated in the last section, the site at Snow Hill provided an ideal location for a new super-cinema. The architect, W. E. Trent, who designed a number of Gaumonts, drew up the plans which were given local approval in July 1931, and work was carried out as quickly as possible. Meanwhile G.B. maintained their presence on three sites by using the Hippodrome, formerly The Empire theatre.

The builders were McLaughlin and Harvey Limited, and their foreman was named James Risk! However, construction went smoothly and soon the towering structural steelwork dominated the corner of Snow Hill. The balcony girder alone weighed thirty-five tons, yet it only took ten weeks to erect the steelwork. The hall was horseshoe shaped and was built to accommodate nearly two thousand people, six hundred and fifty of which were in the balcony. The age of the "super- cinema" had truly arrived in Wolverhampton.

The large sweeping exterior wall was of brick, relieved by narrow horizontal bands and a canopy ran the entire length of the wall facing the town centre. A canopy, nearly the width of the pavement, covered the entrance where two columns headed skywards to the illuminated sign, "Gaumont Palace", at roof level. Three pairs of swing doors led into the walnut-panelled entrance hall and further doors led to a crush corridor that circled the rear of the stalls.

Above: The interior of the Agricultural Hall Cinema.   (Wolverhampton Archives)

In the auditorium the walls were lined with fabric in pastel shades of green, fawn and gold, which was thought to enhance the acoustics of the theatre. The dado was deep blue and the tip up seats were upholstered in a rose moquette. The ceiling had a small central dome and throughout the theatre elaborate and novel lighting was deployed. Most of the ornamentation was concentrated around the proscenium and the stage was fully equipped for theatrical use.

Up in the projection room two of the latest Gaumont machines were installed and Western Electric sound apparatus was brought along from temporary use at the Hippodrome. The final touch was the provision of a Compton organ, a 3c/7 model, housed in a special chamber under the stage. The console rose on an electric lift.

The huge half page advertisement in the Express and Star announced that the opening would take place on Monday 5th September 1932, fifty weeks after the Agricultural Hall had closed. It was opened by the Mayor, Alderman J. Haddock and the film shown was ***"A Night Like This"*** supported by ***"Northern Lights"*** and ***"Mickey's Troubles"***. On the opening day Frederick Bayco played the Compton organ.

The first patron to buy a ticket at The Gaumont was Ted Bailey of Jefcock Road. He had stood for hours at the front of the queue and bought his ticket for one shilling, He kept his half of the ticket in the back of his pocket watch and was invited back at the 25th Anniversary Show to sit in the same seat without further payment!

Wolverhampton thus acquired a super-cinema of which it could be proud fairly early in the decade associated with such buildings. Like the Queens, it had a certain respectability and style about it. It also provided a cafe which, in this case, closed before the cinema did. However, it never seemed to command the same devotion as the Queens. Mr. Shawcross came to manage it having served earlier at the Queens and was already well-known in the town. He left to manage the Dunstall and Cliff Lloyd-Davies began his long reign.

By the end of the thirties the Gaumont had stood by and watched two more large super-cinemas join it in the town centre but the popularity of film-going during the Second World War kept them all busy and produced special events in the cinema's life. For example, on 18th September 1944, the film **"This Happy Breed"** was screened after which the local auctioneers, Bussey and Swallow, ran a sale of donated goods, including a captured Nazi flag, to raise money for the local "Comforts Fund".

In 1945 the Gaumont was selected for the world premier of George Formby's **"I Didn't Do It"** and from then onwards various premiers were put on as special late night shows to raise money for various charities. In the 1950's the cinema decided to make greater use of its stage facilities and tried to obtain the necessary licence. Each year this was opposed by the Grand Theatre and some years the licence was granted, some years it was not.

The 25th Anniversary of the opening of the Gaumont was celebrated quite lavishly in September 1957. Patrons were given a "special edition" of "Gaumont News". This four page newspaper stated:

"What has happened since the Gaumont opened in 1932? Well, the Gaumont has done practically everything in the past quarter of a century. Hundreds of good films have come and gone, stars of stage, screen and radio have visited at all times of the day and night. More recently the premises have resounded to the strains of rock and roll, and there has even been full scale variety shows.... And the Compton organ has been played by such famous people as Reg Dixon and Ralph Rapley. The organ in fact was in prominent use the night that Carroll Levis "discovered" singer John McHugh.

In its 25 years the Gaumont has had only five managers. By far the best known was Cliff Lloyd Davies. He came to Wolverhampton is 1924, having managed several London cinemas, and became manager of The Scala. Five years later he went to The Queens, and in 1933 came to the Gaumont. He was a popular Father Christmas in local hospitals and started the cinema's Saturday Morning Club.

When the cinema first opened the manager was Harry

Shawcross who first came to the town to manage The Queens in 1926, did relief work, and then managed The Regent, Dudley, before coming to The Gaumont for a year. In 1938 he went to The Dunstall Cinema and then The Penn, where he worked for 14 years up to his retirement. The third manager was Mr. P.J. Thornton, who only stayed eighteen months, before handing on to Mr. Ted Hainge, who stayed for the same length of time. The fifth manager was Joe Alexander who started at the Gaumont in May 1957.

Joe Alexander was a Dudley man who entered the business in 1938 and who had managed the Odeon, Dudley, for eleven years from 1944 to 1955."

The paper went on to introduce many of the staff at The Gaumont, starting with Bill Taylor, the Chief Projectionist. He started as a page boy in a Birmingham cinema, and had worked for thirty two years for Gaumont, sixteen of which were at The Gaumont, Wolverhampton. Youngest member of staff was George Newnes who had joined the projection room staff just after leaving school at Easter 1957. Other staff mentioned included Isabella Govan, chied cashier, and Gladys Hill who had also worked at The Scala and The Coliseum. Albert Morris was the boilerman and general handyman, and sixty nine year old Nellie Munger was one of the cleaners who deserved a mention. She had started her career as a waitress in the café at The Queens, and had then transferred to The Agricultural Hall – where she stayed on the site for 39 years apart from the year spent at The Hippodrome while the Gaumont was being built – a good cross section of local cinema history!

Joe Alexander, who had organised The Gaumont's twenty fifth birthday, was the man who really built up the rock and roll aspect of life at The Gaumont. This started on Saturday morning matinees, which later became "teen matinees", and then band contests, and finally a long series of one night concerts featuring all the pop and rock and roll stars of the day from Cliff Richard to The Beatles.

In the auditorium itself a little drama was provided in 1965 when a policeman's killer was arrested in the rear stalls. On stage occasional concerts were presented. One evening in the mid sixties I tried in vain to fight my way through Snow Hill to reach the Film Society but the traffic was at a standstill and policemen and screaming girls blocked my way. The Beatles were appearing at the Gaumont, in the wake of Bill Haley and Henry Hall! The Gaumont also tried late night film shows, firstly in the early sixties, with films such as a revival of the Boris Karloff **"Frankenstein"** and the Bela Lugosi **"Dracula"** and then in the late sixties, with foreign films such as Bunuel's **"Viridiana** '. Saturday morning matinees for teenagers were tried featuring material like **"Rock Around The Clock"** which by then was considered rather tame!

In the seventies it seemed unlikely that the Rank Organisation would wish to keep both the Gaumont and the Odeon running in the town centre while audiences were allegedly dwindling. Many local people felt the Gaumont was the more attractive of the two cinemas and that its stage facilities were a valuable part of the town's entertainment provision. The Gaumont went through a bad period when its programmes were dominated by sex films and oddities. One wet afternoon I sat in the huge cinema with three old pensioners, two wearing dirty raincoats, snoozing through Fellini's *"Satyricon"*.

When the Odeon was chosen for tripling it was clear that the Gaumont would eventually be abandoned. It carried on bravely under the careful management of Colin Hunter, who would later go to the Odeon. The last live show featured Cliff Richard on 11th October 1973.

Colin Hunter made sure the Gaumont went out in fine style. A Rodgers theatre organ was installed for the final

week, provided by the Wolverhampton Organ Centre, and on the very last night, six hundred patrons heard it played by Graeme Hawkins. The show consisted of Mario Lanza's *"The Great Caruso"* plus **"Gene Kelly's** *Singing In The Rain"*. On the 10th November 1973 at 10.40 p.m. precisely the local paper's film critic, Ray Seaton, switched off the power after everyone had joined in singing Auld Lang Syne, and the Gaumont was dead.

The demolition men were supposed to be ready to pounce on the building to clear the potential real estate as quickly as possible but the Gaumont did not completely vanish until the following spring. To everybody's amazement the redevelopment of the site took a long time to materialise. Eventually Allied Carpet's new store graced the corner of Snow Hill. In time Allied Carpets left the site and today a branch of Wilkinson's occipies this location.

Above: The Gaumont, Snow Hill, Wolverhampton, on its impressive corner site in about 1962 – photographed by its manager!.
(Joe Alexander)

Right: The interior of the Gaumont as seen from the balcony. The picture does not do justice to the grandeur of the screen surround.
(Author's Collection)

217

The Empire/Hippodrome

Queen's Square, Wolverhampton

This building was primarily a theatre but it was used for a year as a full-time cinema and therefore has to be included in this survey. Its theatrical history goes back to the middle of the nineteenth century when entertainment in the Music Hall style was provided on the site in the Cheapside Tavern. On 22nd May 1897 the "Gaiety Syndicate" of Birmingham made an application for the rebuilding of the tavern as a proper theatre. It closed in its original form, on 17th July 1897.

The new "Empire Palace of Varieties" cost £30,000 to build and turned out to be a magnificent place. The architects were Messrs. Owen and Ward of Birmingham and they provided the theatre with a bizarre frontage, even by Victorian standards. It should be compared with the same architects' work on Her Majesty's Theatre, Walsall. The Empire was crowned with a golden dome, rising above a row of small cupolas across the top of the facade, and the facade itself featured Moorish windows! Somehow it had a capacity for nearly two thousand people, at least half of the patrons being crammed into a huge gallery.

The Empire opened on 5th December 1898 and many music hall stars appeared there. It was also used for meetings and people like Ben Tillett — the dock workers' leader with a voice like silver, and General Booth of the Salvation Army also stood on its stage. Like many variety theatres, films were occasionally shown and during the summer of 1910 the Empire had presented film matinees every afternoon using the name "Cinematinees". It closed briefly very early in 1921, reopening on 21st February of that year as the Hippodrome.

Ten years later it started its short career as a cinema. Variety entertainment ceased on 19th September 1931 and the theatre closed for a week while the equipment from the Agricultural Hall was installed. Keeping the Western Electric Sound System in use was apparently one of the main reasons for transferring the cinema shows to the Hippodrome while Gaumont British built the new Gaumont. Film shows commenced beneath the golden dome on 28th September with **"Derelict"** and **"No Lady"** starring Lupino Lane.

Harry Shawcross managed the Hippodrome while the Gaumont was being built and then, with the equipment, went back to Snow Hill. The last film show was on 27th August 1932, **"The Impatient Maiden"** and the theatre then closed for another week for conversion back to its original use. It reopened as a variety theatre on the same night as the Gaumont opened its doors; 5th September 1932.

Once again great names appeared live on the Hippodrome's stage. Somehow its pantomimes were always second to the ones at the Grand, but in later years it gained prestige with some of the bands who gave concerts there, including a visit by Louis Armstrong. On Sunday morning, 19th February 1956, the building was destroyed by fire, although the bar survived! For a while, the site was an eyesore but eventually it was redeveloped and a furniture store was built. More recently the site has been occupied by Yates Wine Lodge.

Above: Monthly film guide produced by GB for the Hippodrome while it was a cinema. Left: The Hippodrome, on the corner of Queen's Square and North Street in the 1930s. This building was only used as a full-time cinema for a year while the Savoy was being built. (Ken Rock)

The Odeon

Skinner Street, Wolverhampton

Cinema building reached its zenith in Wolverhampton with the construction of two super-cinemas in the mid-thirties, the ABC's "Savoy" and Oscar Deutsch's "Odeon". For those who love the super-cinema, the Odeon is undoubtedly a very fine example and a classic example of what could be expected from Harry Weedon's architectural practice. The individual architect in charge of the project was P. J. Price, but, as with the Odeon, Dudley, it is Harry Weedon's name that will always be associated with the building and its style.

The front elevation of the building is dominated by a tower and the biscuit coloured faience alternated with thin green tiles. At a pedestrian level black faience and the canopy provide a horizontal base from which the verticals soar skywards. Every part of the building was functional. For example, the tower contained the air intake for the air conditioning system, as well as "flying the flag" in the form of the neon light, in the characteristic lettering we associate with the name "Odeon". The huge auditorium could hold just under two thousand patrons (1272 in the stalls and 668 in the circle) and featured a fairly simple decorative style. A series of rectangular "frames" across the walls and ceiling guide ones eyes towards the screen. Standard BTH equipment was fitted. The general contractors were Housing Ltd.

The cinema was opened on 11th September 1937 and despite the fact that so many of his cinemas were opening at that time, Oscar Deutsch himself attended the ceremony. This was performed by the Mayor of Wolverhampton, Councillor Sir Charles Mander, and was followed by a musical interlude provided by the band and pipers of the First Battalion, King's Own Scottish Borderers. The film was *"Dark Journey"* starring Conrad Veidt and Vivien Leigh.

The first manager at the Odeon was Edward Pike from the Odeon, Perry Barr. A couple of years later he was replaced by Percy Stanwick but its best known manager was Reg Felton.

The first chief operator was Frank Harvey and he remained there until 1950. He was followed by John Warrilow who gave twenty-five years service as an operator and had in fact been in the industry locally since 1929 when he had started as a page boy at the Queens. Often people gave long periods of service at the super-cinemas whose existence was more stable than that of older, smaller theatres. Back in 1967 Colin Hunter came to Wolverhampton to look after the Gaumont and Odeon, and continued to manage the Odeon until its closure. His quiet dedication to the cinema was much appreciated.

Childrens matinees began at the Odeon on 19th August 1944, after the Odeon, Dunstall, and the Gaumont, and survived until 12th July 1980, the last such show in the Black Country. Like the Gaumont, the Odeon occasionally ran late-night premieres and special promotions. In the sixties a few late-night shows were put on for the Wolverhampton Film Society, using the balcony seats only, presenting films like Godard's *"Weekend"*. Like other cinemas it celebrated significant birthdays, and on its fortieth birthday in 1977 ran a week of one night double bills of film-classics. We went to the Odeon four times in one week!

The major event in the cinema's history was its tripling in the early seventies. Modernisation and refurbishing was planned way back in 1968 but the early seventies brought in the fashion of dividing cinemas into smaller units. On 4th August 1973 the stalls were closed and the £40,000 conversion work began. The three screens came to life on 7th October 1973, with *"Live and Let Die"* on Screen 1, now seen from 622 seats in the former circle, *"Fist of Fury"* in Screen 2, which only held ninety-six seats, and *"Sleuth"* in the 111 seater,

Right: A local photographer, Bennett Clarke took several pictures of the Odeon in Skinner Street while it was under construction. This one was dated 3rd. June 1937. An earlier view is shown on page 49.

(Cyril Parker)

Top Left: The Odeon, Skinner Street, Wolverhampton: The exterior of the building photographed on 8th September 1937. Top Right: The foyer photographed at the same time. Left: The auditorium seen from the balcony photographed on the same occasion. All three photographs by John Maltby, who was paid by Odeon Cinemas to record each building as they were completed or brought into the circuit.

Bottom left: The interior of The Odeon in Bingo days when the décor was very bright and cheerful. Every surface of the plasterwork was picked out in a different bright colour! Note the staircase introduced to provide access to the balcony from the stalls. A single auditorium had to be re-created after film presentation ceased as the cinema had been "tripled"

(Ned Williams)

Screen 3. Screens 2 and 3 were tucked beneath the former balcony and shared a new projection box. Rather unusually the seats in the front stalls were left in place but I do not know if they were ever used to seat patrons watching Screen 1. When the cinema reopened with three screens three sets of local triplets were invited to help publicise the event: the Tunneys of Tettenhall, the Allibands of Netherton and the Lowes of Shifnal. The Express & Star photographed them outside the cinema.

The Odeon repeatedly sought a licence to serve drinks. Their first application was turned down in 1974 but in February 1981 they were successful and a bar was built in the ground floor crush hall.

Inside, the Odeon's conversion was more pleasant than many others, outside the Odeon was still a pleasure to behold. At the time producing "Cinemas of the Black Country" in 1982 the future of Wolverhampton's Odeon as a cinema was threatened by the plan to convert the premises to a Bingo and Social Club. Outline planning permission for the scheme had been obtained some time before and therefore, to some extent, approval was fairly automatic. The cinema wa still open when I used it to host the launch of "Cinemas of the Black Country" on 24th October 1982.

The Odeon closed on 4th June 1983. The last films shown were: *"The Boys in Blue"* in Screen 1, *"Table For Five"* in Screen 2, and *"Nutcracker"* in Screen 3.The staff, including Colin Hunter, the Manager, were made redundant. Colin had worked in the Gaumont and Odeon since 1967. Mrs. Peggy Wood, the Assistant Manager, had served in local cinemas since starting at the Gaumont, Wednesbury. Alan Merrick, the chief operator had started at the Odeon, Bilston, in 1948.

Work then began on converting the cinema to become a Bingo and Social Club, which, of course, meant putting back a single auditorium. The conversion, which may have cost as much as £500,000, restored many of the cinema's original features, and, by coincidence, was taking place at the same times as the town's theatre was being refurbished. The Grand reopened at the end of August 1983, and The Odeon reopened for Bingo with a "public preview" on 3rd September. The official reopening took place on Friday 9th September and bingo-players sat down in splendid brightly lit surroundings. The rectangular "arches" of ornamental plasterwork had been repainted in a dazzling style – every surface picked out in a different colour. Bright colours abounded, and the balcony, now reached by a new staircase from the stalls, had been re-seated. The company's sound engineer, Bernard Weaver, who had supervised some of the conversion work, had started as a pageboy at the Odeon in the 1930s and had later progressed to Chief Operator at The Odeon, Perry Bar. The closure of Wolverhampton's Odeon in the autumn of 1983 left only one cinema in town centre – The ABC.

Top Rank, and then Mecca Bingo, continued in the former Odeon until 31st October 2007, by which time the building was "listed". This protected the building but made it more difficult to find a new use. After a year or two in which it looked unlikely that a new use could be found, the former Odeon was refurbished and reopened as a banqueting and conference suite.

Below: Colin Hunter sells tickets to the last chidren's matinee to take place at the Odeon in July 1980. *(Ned Williams)*

The Savoy, later The ABC and The Cannon

Corner of Garrick Street and Bilston Street, Wolverhampton.

As mentioned in the chapter on The New Theatre Royal, ABC had some interest in providing a cinema in this area from the early thirties onwards, probably purchasing the site from Leon Salberg, who provided ABC with a screen in Wolverhampton at the New Theatre Royal, while the new cinema was being built.

The site had been vacant for some time when ABC submitted William Glen's plans to the local council for approval in January 1936, and it took nearly two years for the cinema to be completed, beaten by several months by its rival new super-cinema, the Odeon!

The contrast between the early "modernism" of the Gaumont, only a few yards away, and the later "modernism" of the ABC built only five years after, was quite interesting. Glen's design was very austere and simple, possibly even forbidding in its lack of decoration and its massive expanses of brickwork. The pleasing geometry of this simplicity can only really be appreciated now that surrounding buildings have been demolished and roads widened. As the traveller walked along Garrick Street, the massive brick built structure was intended to have all the majesty of an ocean liner seen alongside its berth!

Apparently, while it was being built, by W.H. Jones & Son of Coventry, it was intended that it would be known as The Regal, but by the end of 1937 the name "Savoy" was adopted. The Savoy, therefore, opened on 20th December 1937 with a programme consisting of **"Let's Make A Night Of It"** starring Charles Rogers and June Clyde, plus **"Last Train from Madrid"** starring Lew

Ayres and Dorothy Lamour. The opening was performed by the mayor, Councillor R.E. Probert. Although he did not say so at the time, the Mayor was no stranger to cinemas, as he had once been Managing Director of the Dunstall Cinema Company. Mr. A.S. Moss of ABC presided at the opening, and at the reception held afterwards at the Victoria Hotel. Everyone seemed very impressed with the latest cinema, admiring the autumnal shades of the internal decor and the size of the cantilevered circle, capable of holding 622 patrons. (Another 1155 could be seated in the stalls). The acoustics did fine justice to the sound provided by the Western Electric system.

The Savoy was the last town centre cinema to open in Wolverhampton, although two other large cinemas were to open in the suburbs. With its completion one could say that the town was now well served by cinemas and that the major circuits, Odeon, Gaumont British, and A.B.C. were all now represented and ready to "do battle". The other striking thing about the Savoy was its contrast to the Clifton directly opposite on the other side of Bilston Street. Rarely can two such contrasting establishments have faced one another.

As a modern super-cinema The Savoy had a less hectic life than many a smaller or older theatre, and the managers of the Savoy never seem to have become as well known locally as their counterparts in the Rank cinemas. Children's matinees on Saturday mornings did not begin until 1948, over a decade after the cinema's opening. In later years it merely confused eveybody with its name changes!

In the 1950's as cinemas began to experience the challenge from television, The Savoy went in for the usual promotional activities. For example Manager L. Spurgh challenged a member of the public to come forward and sit alone in the theatre through a midnight showing of **"The Phantom of the Rue Morgue"**. Mrs.

Left: The MGM Cannon, still known to most folks as the ABC Wolverhampton, in October 1991, just before closure.

(Ned Williams)

Pat Evans volunteered and photographs of her reaction to the film appeared in the local weekly paper. A more interesting event occurred in January 1951 when Manager Ken Hall screened a 16 mm copy of **"Annie Get Your Gun"** to a bedridden 81 year old Wolverhampton woman who, in 1888, had met Annie Oakley and Buffalo Bill in person.

In December 1960 the name "Savoy" was dropped and "ABC" adopted in line with company policy throughout the country. In the same month seven years later the cinema was celebrating its thirtieth birthday, and the special cake was cut by the mayor, Councillor E. Fullwood. Manager Ron Trevor ran a competition in which one had to guess how many miles of film had been projected at the cinema in thirty years. The answer was 104,500 miles.

In July 1968 ABC celebrated the success of its local protege, Euan Lloyd, by asking him to personally introduce **"Shalako"**, a film he had produced, before it was screened. Perhaps a more significant sign of the times came in December when "The Clock", A.BC's fifth pub, opened on the corner of the theatre, on the site once occupied by the cafe. Its name referred to the clock in Golden Square where ABC had its headquarters, a reference that was rather lost on the local public.

The major event in the cinema's history unfolded in the mid-seventies. EMI, now owners of the ABC circuit, had tripled and twinned a number of theatres before turning their attention to Wolverhampton. The ABC was surveyed early in 1973, but by the summer of the same year it seemed that the proposals would be shelved. Meanwhile Rank unfolded similar plans for the Odeon. EMI then changed their minds and decided to triple the ABC after all.

The cinema closed on 27th April 1974 and work began on providing two small cinemas under the existing circle and a centralised projection box to serve them. The stalls had been closed since the February but the cinema naturally wished to close completely for only the shortest possible length of time. ABC 1, the former circle now holding 590 patrons, used the existing projection box and screen. ABC 2 was provided with seats for 127 patrons, and ABC 3 seats 97. The entrance foyer was also slightly modified. The new complex opened on Monday 13th May 1974.

ABCs 2 and 3 never seemed effective – there was something mean and rather lop-sided about them, but Screen 1 was less affected by the tripling porocess. Perhaps by the end of the eigties one was supposed to simply be grateful that Wolverhampton still had a cinema.

In its guise as The Cannon, the cinema closed on a dismal wet Thursday evening on 17th October 1991. It had been the subject of much attention and debate in the letters column of the local paper, but the staff of the cinema showed little interest in marking the occasion in any public way. The Manageress did hold a party for her staff after the last film had been shown, but remained in her office while the public were in the building for the last time. The last films shown were **"Robin Hood"**, **"Jacob's Ladder"** and **"Out for Justice"** – each dispensing just the kind of "nastiness" that had deterred many people from film-going! The only member of staff I met on that night who expressed any sadness was Doreen Raynor, in the sales kiosk – who had previously worked at Wolverhampton's Olympia and Clifton.

Below: The rear entrance to Wolverhampton's ABC was as smart as the front entrance in Bilston Street, as seen in this 17th May 1961 study of trolleybus no.622 passing the cinema. (Clifford Brown via John Hughes)

Above:Doreen Raynor and Barbara Williams stand at the paybox at the MGM Cannon better known as The ABC, Wolverhampton, on 13th October 1991 – four days before closure.
(Ned Williams)

The Light House

Fryer Street, Wolverhampton.

On the 18th October 1991, the day after the Cannon (formerly the ABC) closed its doors to the cinema-going public of Wolverhampton, a new cinema opened. At 5.30.pm the first patrons trooped into the Light House Cinema to see **"Edward Scissorhands"**. (Incidently, this was not the advertised programme!) The Light House was a new 200-seater auditorium built inside the Chubb Building – a restored nineteenth century industrial building close to the town centre.

The Light House had been showing films since 1986 as a joint venture between the local council and the Polytechnic, and its first shows were presented in a tiny room in the Wolverhampton Art Gallery. Later shows were moved, in 1989, to the Arena Theatre. Its aim had been to nurture a "film-consciousness" in Wolverhampton – an aim long cherished in the town's pre-war and post-war film societies. In the 1960s the British Film Institute had proposed the idea of "Regional Film Theatres" to take the work of the National Film Theatre to the provinces. Wolverhampton had been considered for such a film theatre but nothing came of the idea. The Light House Media Centre therefore was a bold venture, and its survival despite a sometimes chequered history has been remarkable. Much of this has been the result the work of its director – Frank Challenger, who showed great determination and ingenuity in keeping the light flickering on a cinema screen in Wolverhampton.

In February 1992 The Studio Cinema was opened, providing The Light House with two screens. Two years later the Light House Media Centre was re-established as an independent company, financially supported by Council and University.

On Thursday 11th Oct 2001 The Light House celebrated its tenth anniversary with a few words from Norman Davies, Leader of Wolverhampton City Council, and a packed house for a free presentation of **"Moulin Rouge"** - Some refurbishment and repainting had just been completed and cinema was then back on seven day opening after a period of three-day opening. Since then it has continued to provide excellent film-going opportunities for Wulfrunians. At the time of going to press The Light House was preparing to celebrate its twenty-fifth anniversary.

Left: Kevin Robinson takes down the last programme details from the canopy of the MGM Cannon (ABC) as the last show begins on 17th October 1991. (Ned Williams)

Wolverhampton's Suburbs

Wolverhampton's Inner Suburbs

Today Wolverhampton's city centre is very clearly defined by the Ring Road. Just outside the ring road were Wolverhampton's first suburbs, all developed as industrial suburbs of the mid to late nineteenth century. The large working-class populations of these suburbs were assumed to provide a potential cinema audience, and each of the cinemas described in this section were pretty individualistic with fairly complex histories. We start in Whitmore Reans, north west of the city centre, move on the Blakenhall in the south west and then reach Horseley Fields on the east of the city centre.

The Strand /West End/Park/Rex

Coleman Street, Whitmore Reans, Wolverhampton

The entire history of Whitmore Reans as an industrial suburb of Wolverhampton is a fascinating subject although an outsider to the area would be privileged to have even heard of the place. Today, new signs have been erected to welcome people to "Whitmore Reans", but the place must have changed beyond all recognition in the last two decades and the last generation that properly recognised it as a place in its own right has passed on or moved away! The latter are the people who still carry with them the legends of Whitmore Reans' own cinema. Redevelopment has totally obscured even the site of the cinema, but the legend lives on.

Long ago, at the end of the Edwardian era, there lived a baker and confectioner in Whitmore Reans named Thomas Jackson. On the site of his bakehouse he decided to build a picture house. Some plans were drawn by William Oliver in the early summer of 1912 and conversion of the bakehouse proceeded very quickly because the Strand was opened on Monday 22nd July of that year. The first show was at three o'clock but normally shows were to be presented twice nightly, at seven and nine o'clock. For the payment of 2d, 3d or 6d the Strand promised *"Finest, Steadiest and Most Up-To- Date Pictures Will Be Shown!"*. By the autumn of 1912 Marcus Brown had provided plans for further extensions and better use of the site was made, making the place more like a cinema. (Following a similar pattern of development as Jackson's venture in Blakenhall; the Coliseum).

The little 350 seater was now well established in Whitmore Reans. The entrance, or front of the theatre was in Coleman Street, opposite the junction of Gatis Street and Evans Street, but only a stone's throw from the hub of the local community at "Leicester Square"

Both the cinema and Thomas Jackson prospered, as detailed elsewhere. By the early nineteentwenties it was

Above: Staff at The Strand, Whitmore Reans, pose for a photograph. The only people identified are the manager, Mr. Van Lachterop in the top hat, and Emma Cartwright bottom right. (WTC)

obviously worth rebuilding the place on a larger, grander scale. During the latter half of 1922, plans were being drawn up to build the new cinema. Unfortunately, however, this coincided with the period of Thomas Jackson's financial problems, already detailed in relation to the Little Picture House in Victoria Street. The new cinema was to be built by Edward Garfield to the plans of Leonard Voisey, whose design was formally approved on 10th October 1922. A company was formed called the West End Cinema Company, by these two gentlemen, plus four others and they acquired the Strand. The "others" included the elusive George Parker, a man who dabbled in many cinema ventures including some within the Clifton Circuit.The licence was transferred from a Mrs. Baker to Edward Garfield and for a little while longer the Strand continued to show films. The renewal of this licence was refused on 24th September 1923 because no work had yet started on either improving the Strand or building its successor. It seems that work on building the "West End" began soon afterwards. Edward Garfield had an interest in other cinemas at that time, for example, Ye Arden cinema in Solihull.

Leonard Voisey's plans provided Whitmore Reans with a building grand enough to be recognised as a proper purpose-built cinema. A flight of steps up to a double set of swing doors, a canopy and a tall facade greeted patrons, and the furnisher, Mr. W. Turner provided seven hundred and fifty seats in the new auditorium, which included a balcony. One ex-operator complained to me that the only way out of the re-wind room was back through the projection room and, that in the event of fire, you would have had to escape through the fire itself. Meanwhile, patrons inside the building were beguiled by broad staircases, a cosy lounge with orange walls and blue and gold Chesterfields.

The West End formally opened on Saturday afternoon 29th August 1925. Mr. Berresford, the manager, greeted the Mayor, Councillor J. Clark, on behalf of the directors, Messrs. Garfield and Voisey and the others under the chairmanship of a Mr. Parker. The event was an ominous warning that the cinema could expect a chequered career because the audience was very small. Everyone had gone to watch the Wolves in their first match of the new season! The cinema made a better start on the following Monday, 31st August, when it opened properly for business with *"The Flaming Forties"*.

Edward Garfield's company ran the West End for the next decade. During that time, sound was installed and "talkies" commenced on 13th April 1930, probably at first using a BTH system. Later, Western Electric sound heads were fitted. The popularity of live music at the West End is illustrated by the fact that three years later the orchestra was "re-instated" on Friday evening for a time.

From the early 1930's onwards, the West End Cinema Company leased the cinema to various people. One well remembered lessee was Captain Bert Riego who commanded the Saturday afternoon matinees with his striking presence. As usual, children came away with sweets and comics. About 1936 the enterprise was acquired by F. S. Sandover whom we meet elsewhere in this book in connection with the Regent, Langley Green.

From 1934 onwards the cinema enjoyed the privilege of being the monthly meeting place of the Wolverhampton Film Society, and on one Wednesday night each month, classics like *"The Cabinet of Dr. Caligari"* and *"Battleship Potemkin"* flickered across its screen.

Towards the end of the thirties it becomes increasingly hard to unravel the history of the West End through a number of apparent changes of ownership or lease. For a time it was leased by E. K. Hawtin, the Cannock-based businessman who ventured into the Black Country to run such places as the Globe, Horseley Fields and the Alhambra in Bilston. Early during the War a Mr. Funnell appears and Walter Palmer jointly managed both the West End and the Globe. Then Mr. Funnell seems to have become associated with Messrs. E. A. Oakey and H. Godsall. The latter pair as 0. G. Pictures Ltd. assumed control of the West End during the middle of the War.

O.G. Pictures Ltd. brought an organ to the West End, a Hammond Model A, with a home-made surround of glass panels that could be illuminated by lamps of various colours. It was set up just below the centre of the screen as there was no stage and the screen itself was virtually on the rear wall of the hall. Stan Bannister crossed the town from the Coliseum to become the new manager and with him he brought Arthur Collett to play the organ. If the picture was a good one, the combination of Mr. Bannister's talent at promoting custom and Arthur Collett's performance on the organ, could bring people from all over the town to Whitmore Rean's little cinema.

The organist also helped out in the projection room and was shocked by the age of the equipment. The old Ross projectors with hand-fed arcs could hardly be neglected for a moment and although Western Electric sound heads had been installed the old sound-on-disc equipment was still in position. Possibly the problem of reinvesting in the cinema's improvement caused the various changes of ownership. On Sunday 16th January 1944 the West End became the Park cinema, taking its name from its proximity to West Park. On the Saturday it had been the West End, the next day it had a new name, but for most local people the old name stuck. The new proprietors were the Marks Circuit, the Manchester firm that six months earlier had relinquished the Globe.

Left: The Rex/West End in the late 1950s when used as a warehouse.   *(CTA Archives)*

There were now one hundred less seats (650) than provided way back in 1925 but the general feeling was that the cinema continued to remain remarkably unchanged. It was sometimes more difficult to book a good film than to fill the cinema and with this kind of problem a small suburban flea-pit struggled into the post-war era. As the Park, the cinema closed in July 1947.

The phoenix rose from the ashes very quickly. Fred Leatham reopened the cinema on 10th August 1947 as the Rex with the announcement in the local paper, *"The management welcomes back old and new patrons to Whitmore Reans' "Little Super-Cinema"."* Some refurbishing of the cinema had taken place and an RCA sound system was now installed. It opened in fine style with *"Kismet"* starring Marlene Deitrich and Ronald Coleman. At the time, the government was trying to introduce a tax on American films and the Americans were threatening to refuse to send films to Britain, but such matters seemed a long way from life in Whitmore Reans.

Life did not run smoothly at the Rex for very long. By January 1953 the cinema was up for sale once more. It was to be auctioned at the Grand Hotel, Birmingham on 20th January by Messrs. Harris and Gillow. The reserve was £10,000 and the top bid fell just four hundred pounds short of this figure. This seemed to give the agents confidence that the cinema would soon be sold. However, nothing seemed to come of it and Mr. Leatham struggled on until early in 1956. The cinema then closed for six months while Mr. Leatham had trouble disposing of the Victoria in Tipton.

Below: The Coliseum, Dudley Road, Wolverhampton, in its final days as an Asian cinema. (Terry Cresswell, CTA)

Remarkably, the Rex reopened once more. Cinemascope was added and on 30th June 1956, the cinema returned to life with *"The Student Prince"*. The final respite was short and the Rex closed for ever in December 1956. The building remained unused for a time and then became a warehouse used by Woolworth's. Since then the whole of Whitmore Reans has undergone considerable changes and Coleman Street no longer reaches Leicester Square. The one-time position of the Rex is obscured by the new Avion Shopping Precinct. Its history across four changes of name, two buildings, countless proprietors, lessees and managers, its first association with Thomas Jackson, its final association with Fred Leatham and everything from organ to Cinemascope, make it one of the most fascinating cinemas of the Black Country. What Odeon has a story to compare with it?

The Coliseum

Dudley Road, Blakenhall, Wolverhampton

The little cinema on the Dudley Road that was being demolished in April 1980 was the inspiration for starting *"Cinemas of the Black Country"*. The demolition contractor's bonfire made me realise that the story of our local cinemas had to be sorted out before it was all too late. There was something significant in the fact that the building was in a sorry state and nobody seemed sad to see it go. Surely, if only the story could be unravelled, it would reveal that even a little flea-pit would have once had its day, and been as proud a picture house as any mighty Odeon. Its glory could have reflected the vitality of the area in which it had been built, now a twilight zone on the outer fringe of town, shorn of any suburban purpose, swallowed by ring roads and the changing pattern of the town's life.

227

In the decade before the First World War, Blakenhall was an important suburb of Wolverhampton. Many of the town's famous firms had their factories there and the network of late Victorian and Edwardian streets housed a large working class population.

Nowadays only the Ring Road seems to separate Blakenhall from the town centre but in those days it was a tram-journey away and it seemed perfectly reasonable to build a cinema on the Dudley Road, the main artery of the area, to serve a local need. The man who brought the cinema to Blakenhall was Wolverhampton's cinema entrepreneur, Thomas Jackson, possibly inspired by his success in Whitmore Reans, a similar "suburb" on the west side of town. He planned a cinema on the site of a stone-mason's yard, and the local architect, Williarm Oliver, drew up plans which were submitted for approval in May 1912. The single storey auditorium was set back from the Dudley Road and only a narrow entrance reached the street alongside some shops. It was a simple building with a Belfast roof.

The grand opening took place on 14th November 1912, in time for Christmas. There were to be new programmes three times a week and admission to the twice nightly shows ranged from 2d to 6d. A Children's matinee was held on Saturday afternoons.

In July 1913 William Oliver produced more plans for Thomas Jackson in which he sought to extend the cinema up to the Dudley Road with a much more imposing frontage, pitched roof and a small balcony. This extension turned the shell of the cinema into the building that lasted until 1980. Later in 1913 it was improved still further by adding a canopy-style shelter across the front of the cinema and down the side of the cinema in Bell Place. This time the architect was Marcus Brown.

One Blakenhall resident recalls that the first manager was a Mr. Walker but that he was replaced by a Mr. Williams. As a child about to leave school just before the First World War he remembers assisting the operator, Mr. Jesse Lewis, occasionally running errands to the Strand in Whitmore Reans. The doorman, Bill Hall, was a well known local character as he weighed twenty stone or more! The cinema's place in the life of Blakenhall is emphasized by the screening of film taken of a comic football match played on the Sunbeam Football Pitch, and the fact that the cinema's staff used to participate in the annual Blakenhall Carnival. One manager, in those early days, was Charles Norton, and his fifteen year old son Percy began work at the "Col", later working at a number of local cinemas until retiring from the Penn fifty-six years later.

Thomas Jackson regularly visited the Coliseum, in his chauffeur-driven car. One night he raced to the cinema thinking that it was on fire but the blaze was at the Star Motor Works nearby in Frederick Street. After the War, Thomas Jackson formed a partnership called Cinemas Consolidated Ltd., and the Coliseum, like his other cinemas, floundered as the partnership encountered

difficulties in 1923. The Coliseum, along with the Little Picture House in Victoria Street, were taken over by the Midland Counties Circuit. The latter company ran the place for the rest of its silent-cinema life, and was controlled by Mr. Thompson, who had been appointed official receiver after Mr. Jackson's bankruptcy.

In the twenties music was provided by an orchestra under the direction of Claude Fenn-Leyland, who came from the Palace, Walsall, and a two-manual orchestral organ was in use. However, with the coming of sound the cinema went through another change of ownership. The Quigleys, of the Olympia, Thornley Street, acquired the cinema from the Midland Counties Circuit as a twenty-first birthday present for their daughter Madge, in mid 1930.

Madge Quigley spent as much money as the cinema had cost on renovating the place. It was re-seated and the canopy outside was renewed. New bronze doors were installed that lasted until April 1980. The local architect Marcus Brown, planned a "new horn recess" behind the screen for the new loudspeakers, and a bright new Coliseum reopened with *Gold-Diggers of Broadway* on the 24th November 1930. Sound was by Western Electric.

The Coliseum held just over eight hundred patrons and for a time was personally supervised by Miss Quigley assisted by usherettes in the balcony and male chuckers-out downstairs. Miss Quigley married in 1934 and therefore had less time to devote to her cinema as the thirties went on. Her marriage, and her father's retirement, led to the disposal of both the Olympia and the Coliseum to a new lessee.

C. S. Joseph's Pine Pictures took over both cinemas in 1939. He felt that they were both doing poor business and that the areas they served had declined in prosperity during the thirties. Mr. Joseph set about building up business again. He improved the programmes, set up "promotions" and publicity. For example, the first fifty ladies coming to see *The White Rose* were given hankies to cry into! Unconsciously the cinema had "moved" and was now one of four on the fringe of the centre of Wolverhampton, along with the Olympia, the Globe and the Scala. Blakenhall was no longer significantly separated from the centre of town.

The Coliseum continued one other interesting tradition that had begun with Madge Quigley's management. It continued to be run by women. The Manageress from 1940 to 1955 was Mrs. Eleanor Webster. She was assisted by Mrs. Gladys Hill, the cashier, and five usherettes. In the projection box the operators were Irene Batty and Maisie Carter. The chief, George Darby, was the only man on the premises!

By the mid-fifties time seemed to have caught up with the Coliseum again, and its audiences were declining. It closed on 17th January 1959 with *Naked Alibi* and a *Zorro* serial. However, Pine Pictures Ltd. was sold to Mr. Vincent Wareing, and reopened on 6th. June of the same year with *"Carry On Nurse"*. The Canopy of the building boldly exclaimed, "Back from the Telly"! It closed, for the second time that year, on the 19th December with *"Horrors of the Black Museum "*.

Having suffered two closures in 1959 it seems surprising that the building stood for another twenty years! History repeated itself as Blakenhall revived in the sixties and new tower blocks rose into the sky by the Dudley Road. Several people developed schemes for using the Coliseum. In the early sixties it seemed that it might become an indoor golf school, but the state of the building always deterred would-be developers.

In the end the new Indian community in Blakenhall came to the rescue and the cinema once again served its local community as it had done in its early days. Ajit Singh and his two brothers acquired the lease in 1963 and reopened with Indian films, after virtually rebuilding the cinema within the existing shell.

A decade later they found themselves threatened by the advance of the new Ring Road. The cinema clung on to a precarious existence through several years of uncertainty. The blight caused by the impending Ring Road meant that little money could realistically be spent on the place. Towards the end of the seventies it looked very sorry for itself and it entered the eighties waiting for the demolition men. As I said at the beginning of this chapter; when they arrived in April, I began the research for this book. The fortunes of the Coliseum rose and fell many times. For many more years many Wulfrunians will not even be aware that it has gone! Despite that bonfire, every day that I worked on the book over the next three years people assured me that the "Col" was still there. No wonder such cinemas become legends.

The Globe, later the Carlton

Horseley Fields, Wolverhampton

There is a distinct feeling as one walks down Horseley Fields today that it was in an area quite remote from the life of the centre, somewhat reinforced by the presence of the modern ring road. Like the Coliseum in Blakenhall, there is feeling that this cinema never shared the bustle of town-centre life, and that the cinema belonged to its own inner suburb that has also now disappeared.

The eastern approach to the town is visually the most depressing way to encounter Wolverhampton. Perhaps it was different when this cinema's neon lights were the "brightest in town", as one fan of the Carlton informed me.

The Globe was promoted by Captain W. J. A. Cresswell and his father-in-law, Mr. Hawthorn. The building on the site in Horseley Fields was formerly Hollingsworth's

Pork Sausage and Pie Factory. (They still had a factory nearby until recently.) The local architect, Marcus Brown, drew up plans for converting the building to a cinema and these were approved on 9th June 1926. A new roof was provided, a small foyer put in, with a projection room above it, plus an entrance in Mary Ann Street to provide access to the bench seats at the screen end of the auditorium, but basically the outline of the building did not change very much. There was only a tiny orchestra pit and narrow stage with the screen mounted on the rear wall.

To make the entrance a little more imposing an overhanging canopy was planned while the local contractor, H. J. Amies, was working on the conversion. It had a hanging iron framework, was glazed and bore the name of the cinema. Again, it was the design work of Marcus Brown. When all was ready and the cinema prepared to open one local paper apparently ran a story headlined, "From Pigs to Pictures", which did not please Captain Cresswell very much.

On 24th January 1927 the Globe was opened by Mayor of Wolverhampton, Alderman F. A. Willcock, at the matinee performance. The first film was *"The Midnight Sun"*, a film of pre-war Russia. Captain Cresswell welcomed the Mayor and the latter praised good wholesome entertainment. He dismissed crime thrillers with the words, "We don't want the rising generation shown how to become burglars". Chief Constable Webster was also present and, addressing himself to the

Below: The Carlton, Horseley Fields.(WTC)

229

natives of Horsely Fields with a broad smile declared, "You now have a church, a pub, and a cinema, what more do you want?" (The Globe was sited opposite Mount Zion Church and that has also disappeared).

The Globe advertised *"Amusing, instructive and wholesome pictures, with orchestral music, in comfort — at popular prices"*, and from 1927 onwards that is just what it did, although the orchestra disappeared about four years later and B.T.H. sound equipment was installed. It was a small cinema, holding about six hundred people, and for the first decade of its existence it had an uneventful life.

About the middle of 1937 it seems that Captain Cresswell decided to dispose of his cinema. This plunged the place into a series of changes of ownership over the next six years. By the end of 1937 it was owned by Mr. Hawtin of Cannock, and he had an extension put on the Mary Ann Street side of the building, principally as a garage, and built a car park at the rear of the building stretching from Mary Ann Street to Gough Street. At the beginning of the Second World War a Mr. Funnell was involved, and the cinema was associated with the West End in Whitmore Reans for a time. Mr. Walter Palmer, managed both cinemas for a short time and engaged Ron Farr as a re-wind boy following a rapid turnover of lads in this position. Forty years later Mr. Farr can still remember crawling under the stage in the darkness to manually wind the curtains at the right moment.

The cinema was thriving during the War, with long queues outside, just like the super-cinemas, but that did not seem to stop the confusing changes that seem to have taken place in the Globe's ownership, plus short periods of closure. On 10th November 1941 it reopened after closing briefly for refurbishing, this time under the banner of the Marks Circuit, a Manchester firm also represented locally at the Regent, Tipton.

Two years later it closed again. On 13th June 1943 it presented its last show as The Globe. On Sunday 14th November of that year it reopened as The Carlton. The first film was *"International Squadron"*, starring Ronald Reagan. The cinema was now in the hands of H. F. N. Burton, of Walsall, and, at last, had found an owner who was going to stay to the bitter end.

When the War was over Norman Burton improved the cinema and put up its new name in neon light. The little six hundred seater marched on into the post-war era. Although it advertised regularly I have spoken to many Wulfrunian cinema-goers of that period who seem unaware of the Carlton's existence, perhaps indicating how remote Horseley Fields seemed, or the unfair way it was dismissed as a flea-pit. By early 1960 Norman Burton was in ill health and the cinema was put up for sale.

The Carlton closed on 2nd April 1960, the last film being *"Tommy the Toreador"*. The building was sold to Bergs of Wolverhampton, owners of The Household

Stores, and Mr. J. Berg found himself trying to give away six hundred tip-up seats.

I am not sure how long it survived as a warehouse. However, it was eventually demolished, and a new building, occupied by a credit company, was built on the site in a Horsely Fields that has become increasingly derelict and uninhabited. That building survives and one passes it on the approach to the new Novotel, but there is no longer any reminder that a cinema once stood on the site.

Wolverhampton's Outer Suburbs.

Three cinemas were built sufficiently far from the centre of Wolverhampton to earn the right to be dealt with separately. Three were the products of 1930's cinema building when suburban sites were often a popular choice. The first of the three cinemas described here was to be found in Dunstall – next door to Whitmore Reans, so ably served by The Rex. Dunstall was really a nineteenth century suburb created to provide homes for Wolverhampton's railway workers, but in choosing their site on the Stafford Road, the proprietors probably also had their eyes on the growth of Wolverhampton's new suburbs as Bushbury, Oxley and Low Hill. The cinemas in Fallings Park and Penn were definitely built to serve an outer-suburban population reflectin the great expansion of Wolvarhampton in the 1930s.

The Dunstall Picture House/Odeon

Stafford Road, Dunstall, Wolverhampton

The Rex, Whitmore Reans, and the cinema built on the Stafford Road both served industrial suburbs on the north western side of the town, in the "good ol' days" when the girls who worked at Courtaulds were courted by the young men who worked on the railway at Stafford Road Works.

Leaving Wolverhampton by the Stafford Road the traveller at one time passed the G.W.R.'s factory, much extended across Dunstall Hill in the early thirties, then crossed the valley of the Smestow where the canal and railway viaduct now dominate the scene, and then climbed out of the valley after passing the Electric Construction Company's works on the right. On a site opposite the junction with the road to Bushbury four local businessmen decided to build a cinema.

The project began as the brainchild of Jack Roper and John Tyler. Jack Roper was a local fishmonger who

Above: The Dunstall Cinema, better known as The Odeon, Stafford Road, Wolverhampton, on 10th December 1937.

(John Maltby, CTA Archives)

developed an interest in the cinema, particularly its technical aspects. At one time he ran a mobile cinema putting on shows at hospitals. He often visited the projection room at Wood's Palace in Bilston, saying to Harry Bayliss, who was working there, "One day I will have a cinema of my own". John Tyler was a businessman from Willenhall. He was proprietor of the Dale, which had opened in 1932 and in many respects the Dunstall was modelled on the Dale, which, in turn, was inspired by Wood's Palace! Dr. Hamp and R.E. Probert, a local butcher, completed the team. The latter becoming chairman of the board. At the time the cinema opened he was a local councillor. When he became mayor of the town he performed the opening of two other cinemas!

The cinema, which was going to cost about £20,000, was designed by Mr. Hurley Robinson whose work at the Dale and Wood's Palace was already appreciated by the directors. The plans were approved early in 1934 and construction began in the spring in the hope that the contractors, J. & F. Wootton, could have the work completed by the autumn.

Construction proceeded quickly. Harry Bayliss, the young operator then at Wood's Palace, remembers watching the huge circle girder being swung into place while the Stafford Road was closed to traffic. Jack Roper's dream of having his own cinema was becoming a reality. A few months later Harry Bayliss was offered the job of chief operator at the new cinema, thus becoming Wolverhampton's youngest "chief". It was a large building, holding 1400 patrons, and at the time, its facade was described as "bold and dignified" but unfortunately over the years its snowcreted frontage suffered the ravages of the weather. Four main entrance doors were approached by a few steps under a steel canopy. The spacious auditorium featured a slightly rising floor for the front stalls and a huge screen was placed 30 feet in front of the nearest seat. The stage, 19 feet deep provided some facilities for live presentations.

When Harry Bayliss arrived a month before the cinema was due to open he recalled that no one knew which

curtain was to be hung to the left and which to the right. No-one ever knew whether they were hung correctly! There was a rush to complete the building. Bryan's Adamanta worked hard to finish the fibrous plaster work and internal paint work. Even so, it is believed that paintwork was wet on some of the exit doors as the first show began! Harry Bayliss found himself in a huge operating suite of no less than seven rooms extending the whole width of the building above the balcony foyer. The contrast with the conditions he had worked in at the Palace was staggering. The Western Electric Wide Range system was quite awsome, and together with the Kalee Eleven projectors, gave Mr. Bayliss the feeling that he had stepped into a mighty Rolls Royce. Another show piece was the rectifier supplying current for the High Intensity arcs. This was supplied by the E.C.C. — the firm situated directly opposite the cinema on the other side of the road.

The opening was arranged for Monday afternoon, 19th November 1934. The cinema was to be declared open by the mayor, Councillor Morris Christopher, but the event was to be made more exciting by a personal appearance of Winifred Shotter. She was the British star of the opening film *"Lilies Of The Field"*.

Unfortunately the 19th November turned out to be a foggy day in London and Winifred Shotter's train was late in arriving at Wolverhampton. She was met by the Mayor and whisked away to the Victoria Hotel for a meal. Tension mounted at the cinema where every seat was taken and the operator nervously waited to start the show. Three-quarters of an hour late, manager Roland Matthews was able to welcome the star to the Dunstall Picture House and she said a few words to the audience before the show, concluding with "I haven't seen it myself so I cannot tell you anything about it". Whether she stayed to see it on this occasion is not recorded. The first screening of *"Lilies Of The Field"* raised £45 for local charities.

As they were running late, the second house had to follow the first as soon as the audience could leave, and the second audience reach their seats. Dr. Hamp's wife thoughtfully took some sandwiches to the men in the operating box. After such a hectic start the Dunstall settled down quickly, but its independent life was short.

In the opening brochure the company declared, *"The Dunstall is a non-combine, privately owned super-cinema not bound by mass control, routine and the general regulations which are inseparable from the officialdom of the large organisation ...."*. Bold declarations of independence were not enough! Two years later the cinema was absorbed by the Odeon circuit, becoming the Dunstall Odeon, and in 1942 the name simply became Odeon. Harry Bayliss remembers John Maltby coming to the cinema to take the official photographs for the Odeon records. John Maltby set up his plate camera, opened the shutter, and then walked round the operating room with a lamp in his hand to illuminate the shadowy areas. He explained that his movements would not register on the negative unless he stood still for several seconds!

One aspect of life in a large circuit was the sharing of newsreels. The newsreel was shared with the Odeon in the town centre and the lad who was the youngest operator at that cinema had to collect the newsreel from the railway station on Sunday afternoon and then shuttle it back and forth between Skinner Street and Dunstall on an Odeon bicycle. Meanwhile, Harry Bayliss kept his operating room spotless and one assistant told me, "The floor had to be polished so brightly that you could see the usherettes knickers reflected in it!".

Several managers came and went, including Harry Shawcross, associated with several local cinemas, who went from Dunstall to the Penn. Its last manager was none other than Cliff Lloyd who had come to Wolverhampton to manage the Scala in 1925 and had managed the Queens and Gaumont before coming to Dunstall. The head cleaner, Doris Price joined the cinema in 1936 and stayed there throughout its life. The "chief", Harry Bayliss left in 1950, but that was not the last he saw of his beloved cinema.

The Black Country Bugle of 1st February 2001 included a feature on memories of the Dunstall Odeon. Gladys Carter (nee Guy) was interviewed by the paper about the time she had worked at the cinema along with her sisters, June and Elaine Guy. They worked as usherettes and ice-cream girls, along with Mrs. Farqhar, Mrs. Venables, Mrs. Astbury and Mrs. Trubshaw. The projectionists at the time were Dennis Dillon and Leslie Scott. The latter would take part in "promotions" by dressing up and appearing in the foyer to advertise forhtcoming films. Gladys herself recalled the weight of the overall that she had to wear, the crush at the Saturday morning children's matinees and the checks that had to be made to make sure customers were not trying to get into the cinema via the emergency exits.

As the Rank Organisation continued to find reasons for abandoning its cinemas throughout the fifties, the future did not look too bright for Dunstall's Odeon. After closing the Queens and the Scala in the town centre Rank announced that they were really only interested in town centre cinemas and therefore the Odeon Dunstall would be the next to go! The closure was announced for 5th November 1960.

Below: The Penn Cinema, Warstones Road, Wolverhampton – the town's most-loved suburban cinema! 3rd March 1973- just before closure. (Terry Cresswell)

With a great sense of history, Harry Bayliss was invited back to show the last programme, even though he now worked outside the industry. He has the rare distinction of having projected the first and last film in a cinema, events separated by a mere twenty-six years. The last programme consisted of ***"The Savage Innocents"*** and ***"Dead Lucky"***.

After this sad day the cinema was more "dead" than "lucky" as it remained empty and unused for over a year. It was not wide enough to become a twelve lane bowling alley and Rank already had one cinema in town converted to a dance hall. Eventually bingo saved the day and the hall reopened for Top Rank Bingo on 16th February 1962.

As a bingo hall it passed to the Hutchinson Group (Surewin Bingo) in 1971 and survived for another decade. The exterior became shabby but the bright lights and atmosphere inside provided a valued social amenity to the residents of Dunstall and Bushbury. Meanwhile the Stafford Road was being widened, and on both sides of the cinema great changes were being made to the landscape. Bingo was last played in the old cinema on 23rd September 1981 and on the following night a brand new Surewin Bingo Club opened in a purpose-built hall a few hundred yards away in Bushbury Lane.

On 19th November 1981, forty-seven years after the cinema's opening, the demolition contractor, J. J. Gallagher of Birmingham moved in. By the end of the year only some rubble remained. Sheltered housing has been built on the site.

The Penn Cinema

Warstones Road, Penn, Wolverhampton

When Harry Shawcross left the Dunstall in 1938 to go to the Penn cinema, he found himself in a much less industrialised part of the town. Here was the truly "suburban" cinema, surrounded by pleasant inter-war housing estates of tree-lined avenues and semis. In the thirties the Clifton and Danilo circuits had contemplated such sites, the Clifton at Fallings Park being the only one to materialise, so it was left to an independent to promote this suburban super-cinema and to see it become a success.

The Penn Cinema Company was formed by a Birmingham accountant, B.T. Davis, in association with the architect, Roland Satchwell and a number of local men, G. T. (Tommy) Whitehouse, who supplied the locally made Baggeridge Bricks to build the place, and Mr. French, the electrical engineer. Mr. H. Yoward occupied the chair. B. T. Davis did not have much to do with the cinemas of the Black Country but in Birmingham his interest in cinemas was well known. He figured largely in the local branch of the Cinema Exhibitors Association and became the CEA President in 1947/8. In many respects the Penn was "his" cinema, but Mr. Whitehouse apparently liked to bring his friends on tours of the projection room to admire what he regarded as "his" cinema!

As the building took shape in 1937 it began to look like a typical Roland Satchwell cinema of the period. It was fairly plain and its solid rectangular form was undisguised. Five large vertical windows to the balcony foyer provided relief to its huge brick frontage. It was built to provide accommodation for 1122 patrons. The Penn cinema was opened on 27th December 1937 by Geoffrey Mander M.P. The first film was *"A Day At The Races"* featuring the Marx Brothers. After the show the directors entertained one hundred and twenty guests at the Bradmore Hotel.

Up in the projection room behind the Ross projectors was the new chief operator, Mr. Cyril Moore. He had started his cinema career at the Coliseum and had worked in at least three other Wolverhampton cinemas before coming to the Penn. Like Harry Bayliss at the Dunstall, he had the distinction of showing the first and last films screened at his cinema. He gave over thirty-five years of devoted service to the Penn, inspiring affection and the respect of his colleagues. At the age of sixty-three, the closure of the cinema forced his retirement. He was presented with a replica "Oscar" to mark the event. A replica "Oscar" was appropriate because the Penn used a picture of an Oscar on its monthly programmes. Some of his friends felt that the closure of the cinema had broken Cyril's heart and when he died just under a year later a screen-shaped wreath appeared at the funeral to pay tribute to his dedication to the cinema.

Returning to the chronological history of the Penn, we must go back to its early life. The first manager, Mr. Rogers, was replaced, as we have already noted, in 1938, by Harry Shawcross. The patrons of the Penn now enjoyed the attention of a man who was the epitome of a cinema manager. He ran the cinema with attention to discipline regarding his staff and with a personal welcome for his customers. He ran the Penn until the early fifties.

When war broke out, Mr. Shawcross had to remove the sign from the front of the cinema and the building was "fortified" with piles of sand bags placed across its frontage. The home guard, the police, and the ARP all used the premises and the shows carried on. Childrens matinees were popular at the Penn and were only suspended during the war for a short period of three weeks. Sunday concerts were also put on and proved quite popular.

During 1939 and 1940 The Penn was used on Sunday by the local Methodists who eventually built Springdale Methodist Church in Warstones Drive.

Below: The interior of The Penn, seen from the balcony. *(CTA Archives)*

Opposite page: The staff at The Penn in the 1950s. Front row: Eric Turvey (2nd Projectionist), Cyril Moore (Chief Porjectionist), Gordon Mintern (Manager), Mrs. Mintern (Cashier), Mrs. Pope (Sales) and Mrs. Goodway (in charge of cleaners).
(Eric Turvey Collection)

B.T. Davis seemed keen to maintain his cinema and after the war there seemed to be more reinvestment in the Penn than in many independent cinemas. As well as refurbishing the auditorium, the Penn also saw several major changes in the projection room. The theatre's acoustics were good and the Western Electric Sound System worked well but in July 1948 the projectors themselves were replaced with Simplex machines with Peerless Magnon arcs. Three years later the Penn became the first cinema in the country to install Philips F.P.7 projectors with a Philips sound system. The Penn's huge screen also had to be modified, with some difficulty, to accommodate Cinemascope.

A certain pride could therefore be felt in working at the Penn. The only problem that remained unsolved since its opening was the question of heating the place! This problem was finally solved by Gordon Mintern, the cinema's manager from the early 50's onwards. He managed to make the Penn a warm place. It says something for the loyalty of the Penn's patrons that they endured the coldness of their cinema through the War years and its aftermath! Gordon Mintern would also have liked to install an organ at the Penn but he was not allowed to do so.

While other cinemas began to flounder as the 1950's unfolded, the Penn continued to do good business. It was certainly easier to park at the Penn than in the town centre and often people caught up with a film there having missed it at its earlier town centre screening. Local patrons patiently waited for the big epics like *"The Ten Commandments"* and *"Ben Hur"* or popular musicals, to reach their nearest screen. Coffee and drinks could be obtained during the interval and the personal atmosphere continued to give the cinema a pleasant ambience.

Gordon Mintern left during the mid sixties and Frank Crane became the manager. He maintained the traditions of the Penn for the remainder of its life, a period when its possible closure was often the subject of rumour and most of Wolverhampton's other remaining cinemas succumbed. As early as 1966 B.T. Davis was busy publicly denying that the Penn would close so that the site could be redeveloped.

Another figure to join the Penn for the last seven years of its life, was Percy Norton. We have first encountered him at the Coliseum where he started work before the First World War. At one time he had managed the Little Picture House in Victoria Street and the Palace, West Bromwich, but he had left the cinema business in 1931. He returned in the mid sixties to become second operator at the Penn. He was slightly older than the chief, Cyril Moore, and retired a short while before the cinema's closure. One ex-assistant operator from the Penn later called his budgies Cyril and Percy in memory of the grand old men from the operating room!

One sign of the times came at the end of the sixties. Childrens matinees had been running since the cinema opened but they ceased with the final show on 26th April 1969. Average audiences were still two to three hundred children, but Frank Crane explained to the local press that it was no longer possible to obtain suitable films.

As the cinema bravely lived on into the seventies rumours about its closure became more frequent and more intense. Film supply problems meant the Penn could not sometimes show material that suited it needs. I remember being one of an audience of four watching a sub-titled print of *"Onibaba"* one sad evening.

In March 1972, local residents held a "Save the Penn" public meeting and tried to push forward the idea that the cinema could provide community facilities and need not be the victim of redevelopment. Interest in the cinema led to increased attendances in 1972 but meanwhile a London property company, Old Burlington Street Estates, relentlessly pursued its plans for purchase and redevelopment. The original plan for a 10,000 square foot supermarket, shops and car park was modified and resubmitted for the council's approval later in 1972. The new plan proposed included a few amenities such as squash courts. Councillor Frank Clapham of the planning committee declared "I think any hope of it continuing as a cinema is out".

B.T. Davis was growing old, the future of the cinema industry seemed uncertain, the continual yearly reinvestment in the cinema had slowed down and economies had been made. To be offered a quarter of a million pounds for a cinema in such a situation was to make an offer that no independent proprietor could refuse. The council saw no possibility of intervening and thus planning applications were granted, the cinema was bought and its closure announced.

Cyril Moore laced up the projectors for the last time on 24th March 1973, with Dick Emery's film *"Ooh, You Are Awful"*, Frank Crane and his staff of fifteen were to be made redundant, after throwing a farewell party at the cinema after the last show. There were sad farewells, marking not only Cyril Moore's retirement, but also a goodbye to people such as Violet Goodway who had been head-cleaner at the Penn for thirty-four years.

Many of the cinema's fittings were sold. The projectors are alleged to have gone to India. Gordon Mintern returned and preserved the curtains and clock. They could later be seen at the Regal, Henley-on-Thames. The demolition men quickly knocked down the building and a new MacMarket went up on the site. (This became an International Stores, then Somefield, and now The Co-op.

There must be many ghosts that haunt the site and many memories of the cinema surviving in the area! For a suburban cinema it had some great times. For example in 1960 a midnight matinee had been presented to raise money for Boys Clubs. Richard Attenborough came along to introduce, in person, his film *"I'm Alright Jack "*. It was an unfortunate choice of film as its political content led to a mighty row between B.T. Davis, the Birmingham accountant and businessman, and Wolverhampton's Mayor, an engine driver who disliked the film's attitude towards the working class! But of such bizarre moments is the story of a local cinema made. The Penn proves that cinemas were not just bricks, mortar and electrical equipment; they were also the result of the personalities of the people who ran them and visited them.

Eric Turvey in the projection room at The Penn.   (Eric Turvey Collection)

The Clifton, Fallings Park

Cannock Road, Fallings Park, Wolverhampton.

This cinema had the distinction of being the last to open in Wolverhampton and enjoyed a short life of only twenty-three years. It occupied a good site on the Cannock Road, which was one of several sites considered by the Clifton circuit for cinema building in the mid thirties. Plans drawn by Messrs. Satchwell and Roberts had been approved as early as March 1934, but the cinema actually built was the result of new plans drawn in 1936! The builder was H.J. Amies & Sons, of Wolverhampton.

Approaching the cinema from the town centre it presented itself with a rather castle-like frontage as two octagonal towers seemed to grace each side of the flight of steps up to the three sets of swing doors. The large expanses of brickwork were plain but the three high vertical windows above the canopied entrance gave it a certain grace. Their leaded panes let light into the balcony foyer but there were no windows at the projection room floor level, nor in the sides of the cinema. Like several other cinemas by Satchwell and Roberts it expressed a great feeling of solidity. It seated 826 in the stalls, and 340 in the balcony.

The Directors of Clifton Cinema (Fallings Park) Ltd., were Sidney Clift, the late Leon Salberg, replaced with Harold Brown who was executor of the late Leon Salberg's estate, J.B.Share, and Archibald Bishop (proprietor of the Cinema de Luxe in Walsall).

As the building neared completion, Alex Tuck moved over from the Regal, Wednesfield to prepare for the opening. Alex Tuck was one of the Clifton Circuit's senior managers, having begun his cinema career at 14 in one of his father's five cinemas.

The Clifton, Fallings Park, was declared open on 24th October 1938. The visitors were welcomed by Captain Clift, and the Mayor, Councillor Probert, performed the opening ceremony. This one time director of the Dunstall Cinema had previously opened the ABC during his year of office. The first films shown were *"The Trail of Portia Merriman"* and Sonja Henie's *"Happy Landing"* – a programme that ran for the first three days.

Below: The imposing frontage of The Clifton, Fallings Park, photographed on the cinema's 21st birthday in 1959. (Express & Star)

Like the other Clifton cinemas it was provided with BTH equipment and one operator recalled that a mushroom shaped light fitting at one time obscured the operator's sight lines. The building accommodated 1186 patrons and looked to the large estates on each side of the Cannock Road to provide the custom. It provided some competition for the Dunstall cinema and even for the Regal, Captain Clift's own cinema in Wednesfield, but such was the industry's optimism at that time. Mr. Kenyon took over from Mr. Tuck just before the War and enjoyed a fairly long association with this cinema.

It is possible that The Clifton, Fallings Park, did not live up to Sidney Clift's financial expectations. The cinema was sold to Midland Leaseholdings who leased it back to the original company. In turn the company paid Cinema Accessories to manage and run the cinema.

Graham Simmonds, who eventually became the Clifton's chief, began work there as a trainee in 1953. At the time it was still a busy place and queues could still be seen around the building. He recalls how spick and span the projection room had to be. For £1.50 a week he spent the first eighteen months polishing the floor. The pride and sense of purpose enjoyed by the cinema was soon to be eroded.

The Clifton did last long enough to enjoy a twenty-first birthday party in 1959. A special programme brochure was produced and **"Carry On Teacher"** was presented for the week commencing 25th October, follwowed by other "Carry On" films. For one "Carry On" film Charles Hawtry made a personal appearance at Fallings Park and was entertained by the cinema's directors. The manager, Maxwell Gordon, later of the Clifton, Sedgley, expressed the hope that ".... you will continue to find many happy hours at this cinema during the years to come". However, its fortunes were rapidly declining.

Above: Charles Hawtry visits the Clifton Fallings Park during its week of "Carry On" films screened to celebrate the cinema's 21st birthday in October 1959. On the left is Max Gordon and his wife. Max had managed several Cliftons. In the centre of the picture we see Frank and Denise Holmes, Sidney Clift's son-in-law and daughter.
(Doug Withers' collection)

As the decade closed, staff were reduced, bingo was briefly tried at afternoon sessions and the prospect of putting on wrestling was considered but rejected. At one time rumours circulated that an American firm was considering buying the premises from Midland Leaseholdings Ltd., who owned the Clifton. The family clientele that had once come to the cinema had disappeared and the takings were often ridiculous.

The end came fairly abruptly. Some demolition contractors appeared — also spreading rumours about the closure of the Regal, Wednesfield, and not long afterwards the final show was announced. The last film was shown on 4th November 1961; **"Can Can"** starring Frank Sinatra and Shirley MacLaine, and after the National Anthem, Auld Lang Syne was played from the projection room. Demolition followed immediately and the site was then redeveloped as a Fine Fare supermarket. Since that time the supermarket has been operated by Somerfield and now The Co-op.

The smell of fish and chips can no longer rise from the back row one night a week as the girls from the Ever Ready eat their tea and take in a film. The natives of Fallings Park have had to look further afield for entertainment in the swinging sixties and ever after.

Wolverhampton's Unbuilt Cinemas

In every Black Country town there must have been various proposals made regarding cinemas that never came to be built. It might be interesting to consider what might have happened in Wolverhampton and leave readers to imagine the similar examples that occurred throughout the conurbation. Perhaps thirty or forty cinemas were planned in the region that never materialised.

During the pre-First World War period the local architect Marcus Brown drew plans for at least two unbuilt cinemas. For George Lovatt he designed a cinema in 1912 that was to be built in Church Street, not far from the Picturedrome. When nothing came of it, Mr. Lovatt possibly fulfilled his dreams of cinema-proprietorship by running the Gem in Dudley for a short time. Marcus Brown also designed a small cinema that someone proposed building in Heath Town. The minute books of Heath Town UDC do contain an item dated 18th March 1914 in which we learn that the Heath Town Picture Palace Company had enertained the idea of building a cinema on the Wolverhampton Road.

A very attractive little cinema was planned by Frank Clark for a Mr. W. H. Maynard. This would have been built in Owen Road, Penn Fields, but unfortunately, nothing came of it.

Twenty years later at the height of the "craze" for building super-cinemas at least two were planned in Wolverhampton, but not built. A large fifteen hundred seater should have occupied Graisley Hill on the Penn Road and the Plaza, Tettenhall, should have been built at Newbridge. Both cinemas were planned by Roland Satchwell in 1935 for the Clifton Circuit. Both ran into delays in gaining planning approval although the Tettenhall cinema was approved on appeal. By early 1938 the land at Newbridge seems to have been sold to the Danilo Circuit and Mr. Hurley Robinson had drawn up some more plans. Again, nothing came of it. This gives some indication of the possible number of proposals that local circuits may have had for super-cinemas.

Even in recent times, proposals to build cinemas have caused interesting speculation. In 1966 the Classic Cinema Group talked about opening a brand new purpose-built five hundred seater cinema as part of the Hammerson Group's new Wulfrun Centre. About the same time there was talk of a West Midlands Regional Film Theatre coming to Wolverhampton. When this did not materialise the Wolverhampton Film Society ventured into several schemes to build a local arts centre that would have included cinema facilities, none of which materialised.

Below: Staff at The Clifton, Fallings Park, icluding Graham Simmonds, T. Glover, and T. Harley, and Mrs. E. Douglas projectionists,

Plus usherettes , cashiers and cleaners In front of them all is Mr. A. Doodwin – the "theatre formen". (Graham Simmonds Collection)

Wednesfield

Heading eastwards from Wolverhampton along the old road to Lichfield one comes to the one-time village of Wednesfield, almost encircled by the Wyrley and Essington Canal. Wednesfield was a small independent "urban district" until local government reorganisation of 1966. The village was often associated with a particular specialism within the iron trades – the making of traps. (A trap factory from Wednesfield is now to be found in the Black Country Living Museum.) This community, with its fine Saxon name, at one time saw itself as quite remote and distinct from Wolverhampton and its Urban District Council tried to fight the overspill advance of Big Brother Wolverhampton towards the fields of Ashmore Park.

It can come as no surprise to find that such a place supported two cinemas of great individuality and that these cinemas are much loved and remembered by those who lived in Wednesfield in the "good old days". Cinema historians won't be surprised to find there was even a third cinema in Wednesfield whose history is almost totally obscure!

The Regal

High Street, Wednesfield

Rather than deal with Wednesfield's cinemas chronologically let us consider the Regal first because it seems to be passionately remembered with great affection, and its story can be told in more detail. For many people it was the finest building in Wednesfield and in the mid-thirties was a symbol of the community's march into the modern world. The site, on the corner of the High Street was possibly the site of one of Wednesfield's early manor houses and was selected by Captain Clift and Leon Salberg for one of their early "Clifton" cinemas. Why the name Regal was adopted rather than "Clifton", is not quite clear, but Messrs Salberg and Clifton had just formed a partnership called "Regalia Cinemas", and the Clifton Circuit had not yet quite materialised. As it happens the cinemas were built by individual companies and were linked into a "circuit" by the services of a management company. Despite having formed Regalia Cinemas, the Wednesfield cinema was actually built by The Regal Cinema (Wednesfield) Ltd., but Captain Clift and Leon Salberg had the major financial interest in it. The company secretary was Harold Brown, an accountant, who became a major figure in the Clifton Circuit.

The Wolverhampton building contractor, H. J. Amies & Sons erected the cinema, the first of several for Captain Clift and the plans were prepared by Roland Satchwell. Stage facilities were provided as well as luxurious accommodation for 1028 patrons. Like the later Cliftons it was equipped with BTH apparatus. As children came out of the Sunday School at the Parish Church, almost opposite the Regal, each week they counted the new

Courses of brickwork to record the progress made by this huge new edifice.

In the Autumn of 1935 Alex Tuck came over to the new Regal to become the new manager. He had been at the Dunstall Cinema since April 1935, but had previously enjoyed a career in the industry that went back a quarter of a century. He had started work as a chocolate boy in a cinema in Selby owned by his father and had experience of most aspects of cinema work on the way up to management. He prepared the Regal for its official opening on 14th October 1935.

Unlike other cinemas that opted to open during the afternoon, the Regal chose to commence work at 7.30 p.m. that Monday night. It was an interesting evening. The feature film, Jack Hulbert and Fay Wray in *"Bulldog Jack"* plus supporting film, cartoon and Universal News were preceeded by events reflecting Captain Clift's sense of history. First of all, R.H. Morgan, the Stourbridge M.P. formally opened the cinema. He had recently been campaigning in Parliament for a reduction in Entertainment Tax, a cause dear to the heart of Captain Clift and the Cinema Exhibitors Association, of which he was an active member. Then none other than Waller Jeffs was asked to introduce a screening of two of his early films, one made in 1908 of *"Veterans of the Indian Mutiny "* and the other made in 1909 of the *"Stratford-On-Avon Shakespeare Festival"*. Mr. Jeffs was in his seventies and it was then thirty-five years since he brought his film shows to the Midlands, but he had recently become associated with Captain Clift and Leon Salberg by being manager of their newly acquired cinema in Stratford. It is appropriate that six years before his death he was invited back to the West Midlands to show this Wednesfield audience his early pioneering work. (See the note on Waller Jeffs in Section One.)

The Regal was an immediate success in Wednesfield, faring much better than the other Clifton cinemas that opened in village-like communities already served by smaller, older independent cinemas, e.g. Sedgley and Coseley. Perhaps it was well served by its managers. Alex Tuck left after three years to open the Clifton at Fallings Park and then to become a circuit supervisor. His replacement, Mr. H.J.E. Davis, was the man who became indelibly associated with the Regal for the rest of its life. Like Alex Tuck he had entered the industry as a chocolate boy, working for Poole's Theatres Ltd. at Stourbridge and in Edinburgh. He worked on the last "Myriorama" there and on the first "talkie". He joined the Clifton Circuit in February 1937 as the Chief Operator at the new cinema in Lye and began to prepare for a managerial post.

His style of management was characterised by diligence, organisation and efficiency rather than charisma, but he was a practical man who could both appear in smart evening dress to see the patrons arrive, and who could understand the "electrics" and operating side of his cinema's life. During the war he organised many concerts for the benefit of several charities and during one Christmas season the Regal's stage facilities

Above: The Regal, Wednesfield, as illustrated in the cinema's opening brochure.

were enjoyed by a full blooded pantomime, **"Babes In The Wood"** featuring Delia Neil as Robin Hood!

Mr. Davis was also at the Regal when the "*Great Nixon*" came to town. He was billed as *"the world's master mind reader, astrologist and original blindfold wonder"* and appeared at various Clifton cinemas. A local publican, James Howe of The Angel, was asked to hide an article somewhere in Wednesfield. The Great Nixon, blindfolded, then walked through the town, followed by a growing procession, until he "found" it. In the evenings he performed his mind reading act on stage, between the films.

After the war, the Regal continued to be busy. Many local people have emphasised to me that its luxury, in particular its carpeted floors and warmth, were far more inviting than many a local home. Its doormen gave you the feeling you were entering an expensive hotel and yet it was truly "your" local cinema. Mr. Davis in immaculate evening dress and greased jet black hair always stood at the foot of the stairs to the balcony. Often, Harry Taylor, the chief operator, leaned on the radiator. Outside, the commissionaire, Albert Brookes, looked after the patrons. Albert Brookes became another well-remembered personality associated with the Regal. If he evicted some nuisance from the cinema, that nuisance would never succeed in entering the Regal again. Mrs. Benton and her fellow cleaners kept the place spotless, Albert maintained good behaviour!

Local community feeling ran high in the 1950's with the publication of a small broadsheet, "The Wednesfield News". As from April 1954 Mr. Davis made sure the Regal's programmes and special events such as children's painting competitions, were given publicity in this paper. In 1956 he organised a special 21st Anniversary Programme, presenting **"The Student Prince"** on Monday 15th October. (The 14th October, being a Sunday, only featured a one-day screening of **"The Red Badge of Courage "**).

The Regal seemed to be surviving. Its neighbouring Clifton cinema at Fallings Park had closed suddenly and the demolition men had been heard muttering "It's the Regal next!". However, Mr. Davis felt his cinema was "safe". Since Captain Clift's death, it had been in the hands of "Clifton Cinemas Management Ltd.". Unknown to Mr. Davis, Newbold Securities, the Solihull firm that had purchased and demolished the Clifton, Fallings Park, were also intending to do the same in Wednesfield.

The end came very quickly and at short notice. The "Wednesfield News" interviewed a shaken Mr. Davis in the office he had occupied for twenty-seven years, and on 17th March 1962, *"The Naked Edge"*, starring Gary Cooper had the honour of being the last film to be shown. It was followed by a party for the staff and then the Regal was dead. Albert Brookes looked after the place for several weeks while various items were

Left: Jim Davis, manager of The Regal, Wednesfield, stands at the kiosk during a quiet moment. (Mrs. Charlesworth;s Collection)

Centre: Albert Brookes puts his cap on the step, outside The Regal and poses for a picture with two usherettes. Albert was a fine example of what is known locally as a "chucker-outer". (Author's Collection)

Bottom left: An advert for The Great Nixon's apperance at The Regal, Wednesfield He appeared at a number of local Clifton cinemas..

salvaged for use in other Clifton cinemas. For example, it seems that some of the seats went to the Alexandra, Lower Gornal.

The demolition men moved in, despite protests from the Wednesfield community. Ironically the new Fine Fare supermarket building that was erected on the site, was of roughly the same proportions as the once elegant and beautiful cinema. The store is currently a Co-op.

The Ideal

Rookery Street, Wednesfield

Wednesfield's two cinemas were as alike as chalk and cheese! The Regal is the historian's dream: everyone remembers it, plenty of documentation concerning it survives and its birth and death can be clearly and precisely located. The Ideal is just the opposite; it is a historian's nightmare, putting a few facts together seems like constructing a dinosaur from a few random bones.

Ironically a rebuilt version of the building still stands, defiantly greeting travellers from Wolverhampton as they come into Wednesfield after crossing the Wyrley and Essington Canal. It is on the main road that abruptly swings into the High Street where the Regal once stood. Today it is a Carpet Store and a few remnants of the decor reminded visitors of its past until a fire destroyed them.

In the nineteenth century the building was a chapel, built in 1852, and used by the Methodists until 1886. The building may have had a variety of uses in the following years but by the early twentieth century seems to have become some kind of public hall.

It has been impossible to pinpoint the exact date when the hall became a cinema. The earliest mention of it as the "Electric Theatre" appears in the Midland Evening News of 15th. November 1912 when it is described as being *"in business"* and pursuing a policy of *"Civility and the latest pictures"*. Advertisements in the same paper appear in January 1913 and the entertainment column states, *"The new Picture House in Wednesfield has certainly "caught on" with the local people."* This implies it had opened as a cinema at the beginning of November 1912.

The surviving Wednesfield UDC records do not seem to record the issue of cinematograph licences, but the Minutes of the UDC do mention the submission of plans for *"the erection of a gallery at the Electric Theatre in Rookery Street"* on 17th August 1914. The plans were drawn by H. Marcus Brown, a Wolverhampton architect who seemed to have a record of producing such work at other cinemas. The plans were approved, and in the Register of Plans submitted to the UDC we have the additonal information that the cinema was owned at the time by Mr. Marchant – as later recalled by Joe Purshouse. (See below.)

For most of its life this little cinema enjoyed the services of a local man named Joe Purshouse, known as "Joper". He started work at the cinema at the age of eight in 1917 and his father had worked there before that. At the time the cinema was owned by a Mr. Marchant and later a Mr. Aldridge but Joe's father effectively ran the place. Joe worked at Sidbotham's trap works by day and at the cinema by night. He started by re-winding the films and doing jobs like fetching the comics and oranges for distribution at the children's matinees. The operator, George Ainsworth, taught Joe that side of the business.

As a silent cinema the audience entered the auditorium from the canal-end of the building and the screen was at the end nearest Rookery Street. Its proximity to the canal meant that it must have been one of the few cinemas where the patrons' entertainment was sometimes marred by the noise of canal boats chugging past! It is not clear when it was first called "The Ideal", but some 1922 plans drawn by Messrs. Boswell & Tomkins were submitted to Wednesfield UDC in 1922 on behalf of the Ideal Cinema Company. The plans, which are described in the register simply as "Alterations to Cinema", were approved. But this indicates the time from which it may have been known as The Ideal.

About 1931 the cinema was acquired by John France, a building contractor, from Trench in Shropshire. It seems that this could also be when it became the "Ideal", and possibly John France had ambitious plans for rebuilding a larger and more luxurious cinema on the site. In the event The Ideal carried on showing silent films while Wednesfield's new "super-cinema", the Regal, was built a few hundred yards away. This was not a death blow to the little cinema as many people went to The Ideal at the beginning of the week for a cheap night out and then to the Regal at the end of the week. Even at the end of the week The Ideal took the "overspill" turned away by the Regal!

Below, Wednesfield's little cinema appears in all its glory on this pre-First World War postcard. *(Stan Webb Collection)*

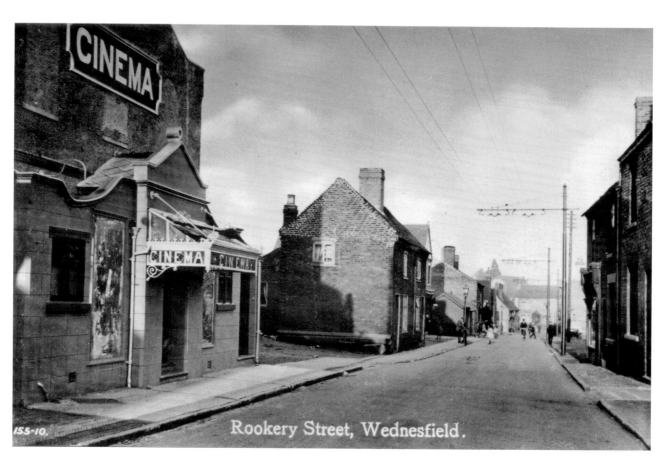

Rookery Street, Wednesfield.

243

The Ideal was rebuilt towards the end of the thirties and turned into a sound cinema. The screen was now installed at the "canal end" and a porch and projection room built at the new "front" of the cinema. Two Kershaw Kalee 8 projectors provided the picture and Gyrotone equipment provided the sound. A raked floor and tip up seats added to the transformation, but it still only held about three hundred and fifty patrons.

It seems likely that John France died before the alterations were completed and the cinema was left in the hands of the trustees of his estate. His daughter, Maisie Withington was in charge but in reality Joe Purshouse and Frank Britten still ran the place. During the War Joe often ran it virtually single-handed, sometimes staying up all night waiting for sound engineers to come over from Coleshill to look at the Gyrotone equipment when it went wrong. Frank Britten was the son of Enoch Frank Britten who had also managed the cinema. The younger Frank Britten appears to have worked alongside Ernie Beckett in the projection room. Ernie's wife Betty Beckett, was known to work in the box office.

At some stage the executors of the estate of John France sold the cinema to a Mr. Sankey, and in turn he sold it to William Severn, a waste paper merchant from Solihull. It remains a mystery why such a small local cinema continually found itself owned by proprietors from far afield. In William Severn's case it seemed that it was the nearest cinema he could find that he could afford. He was fanatically interested in the cinema as a hobby and seemed obsessed with the idea of running a real cinema. He had bought some projection equipment at a house sale at Blythe Hall, Solihull after the death of a Mr. Bird, a one-time High Sheriff of Warwickshire. With this equipment and an organ, he built his own private cinema at his home. Somehow, this was not enough to satisfy him and his desire for a real cinema lead him to purchase The Ideal.

Joe Purshouse, and Mr. Britten, from the nearby fish shop, still helped manage the place, and Mr. Severn, or his son, popped over whenever they could to keep a proprietorial eye on it. If technical troubles arose help was often forthcoming from the operating room at the Regal. In this way The Ideal survived into that difficult decade; the fifties. For a while it competed with the Regal by having details of its programmes printed in printed in the little "Wednesfield News" but the announcements ceased in the summer of 1954. Hard times had come to The Ideal and as far as I can work out the last film was probably shown in the autumn of 1957. Mr. Severn, then in his sixties, suffered a long period of ill health but still believed his cinema could return to life.

In 1959 he bravely refurbished and partially re-equipped the place but during the summer of that year vandals broke in and wrought £500 worth of damage, slashed the new screen, stole the curtains and smashed heating and lighting fittings. The reopening that Mr. Severn had planned for that September never took place.

Just before the Regal closed in March 1962, The Ideal entered a brief new lease of life as a dance hall! Tommy Burton's Rock and Roll Group came over from Bilston to open the place and dancers jived on the raked floor. Tommy Burton went on to acquire fame at the keyboard but the poor old Ideal could not survive as a place of entertainment. At least it has enjoyed a sedate retirement as a carpet store.

As sketchy as this outline of the cinema's life has turned out to be, one fact about The Ideal is known to every proud inhabitant of Wednesfield. This fact, now legend, concerns the nickname by which the Ideal was always known: "The Smack".

The Tivoli/Palace Electric Theatre

Hall Street, Wednesfield

The third site of cinematic entertainment in Wednesfield is even more obscure. Apparently a building in Hall Street was used for showing films before the First World War and several people have referred to it as "The Tivoli" but one of the few pieces of evidence I have discovered of its existence is a small entry in "The Bioscope" for 2nd June 1910. It is described as having opened during the previous week and, under Bert Dawes' management, was bringing films and variety to the people of Wednesfield. In "The Bioscope" magazine it is called the Palace Electric Theatre, but I have never heard it called by that name in the village. One cryptic reference to a Mr. Lewis in a reference to the cinema in Upper Gornal (later known as "Jack Darby's") suggested that this Mr. Lewis might also have been connected with the cinema in Hall Street, Wednesfield.

Mr. Lewis is mentioned in an entry in Wednesfield UDC Minutes on 7th May 1910. It records, "The plan of Mr. J. Lewis for the erection of an electric theatre in Hall Street was approved and passed.

Whether it continued to show films when the "new" electric theatre opened in Rookery Street, I do not know. Its existence can be likened to the Pensnett Hippodrome or the obscure picture theatre at the Round Oak end of Brierley Hill. It has come and gone but left little record of its existence. However, the building survived and by the 1980s was in use as garage mainly servicing commercial vehicles. In the garage it was still possible to see the portholes of the projection room to prove its ancestry!

*Opposite page:
Although the little
cinema in Hall
Street, Wednesfield,
seems "lost and
forgotten" this ticket
to the children's
matinee survives!
Note that children
will enter and leave
the cinema in single
file!
(John Roper
Collection)*

*Top right: The Ideal as a carpet
warehouse in 1982 – before the
fire. (Ned Williams)*

*Centre: Frank Britten and Ernie
Beckett in the projection room at
The Ideal. (Christine Stanistreet)*

*Bottom right: The interior of The
Ideal on 28th August 1962, taken
while the building was being
converted into a dance hall
(Express & Star).*

Cineworld

Bentley Way, Wednesfield

The Black Country's third multi-plex was opened in Wednesfield – not because the developers had heard of The Regal, The Smack, or The Tivoli, but because a retail park was being created at Bentley Bridge on land "rescued" by the Black Country Development Corporation. The cinema proprietors were probably more influenced by its proximity to Wolverhampton – a target recognised by several players in the world of multi-screen cinemas, including Hoyt's, the Australian company who had hoped to open on the Low Level Station site.

Cine-UK felt Bentley Bridge was close enough to Wolverhampton to justify building their cinema in black and gold bricks – the colours of The Wolves! The £8m venture was to include fourteen screens, of varying sizes with the box office and refreshments housed in a central atrium. Altogether the 14 screens could accommodate over two thousand patrons.

Cineworld opened to the public on 10th October 1997. Meanwhile a private opening ceremony had been held on Wednesday 8th October, when "stars" from the Wolves football team were guests of honour. The guests

inluded manager Mark McGhee, director John Richards, and some well known Wolves veterans such as Bert Williams and Peter Broadbent. They were all greeted by Cine UK's chief executive, Steve Weiner. Everyone was keen to congratulate Cine UK on their fourth British multi-plex.

Films shown as the cinema opened included, *"The Game"*, *"Hercules"*, *"Air Force One"*, *"My Best Friend's Wedding"* and *"Men in Black"*. Several screens were used for Bollywood films and "junior screenings" were introduced on Saturday mornings, to which the accompanying adult was admitted free! At first the programming at Cineworld was a bit more adventurous than at the other local multi-plexes, but this has become less so as time passed. For anyone who believes that cinema queues are a thing of the past they should trying visiting Cineworld on an "Orange Wednesday"! ("Two for one" for tickets ordered by mobile phone.)

As in the other local multi-plexes the audience is often young and sometimes noisy and restless – and sometimes addicted to misuse of mobile phones.

Left: Dave Shipley, the "launch manager" at Cineworld, Bentley Bridge, Wednesfield, poses for the camera in one of the larger screens in the compex, in October 1997just before the cinema was opened.
(Express & Star.)

Above:
Cineworld,
Wednesfield.
(N. Williams)

Above: Norman Newnes seen at his last day of work at Cineworld in Janaury 2007. He retired after working almost half a century as a projectionist in local cinemas. He started work at the Gaumont, Wolverhampton, at Easter 1957 straight from school. Three years later he transferred to The Odeon, Skinner Street, where he stayed until the cinema closed. He then worked at The ABC, Walsall until that closed in 1991. after a four year break he began his final stint at Cineworld.

As a reirement gift he was presented with a wide-screen television!

(Express and Star)

Bilston

Today, Bilston is part of the City of Wolverhampton, having lost its "independence" in 1966. In October 1980 Bilston's blast furnace, Lizzie, was ceremoniously demolished, and a symbol of the town's past as an important iron and steel-making community vanished from the Black Country landscape. Two centuries earlier, Iron-mad Wilkinson had brought iron-making to the area and built furnaces by the canal near Bradley. Bilston had developed and prospered in a way that reflected the identity of the Black Country - man's exploitation of coal, iron and labour. Its products became world famous: cast iron baths, domestic cookers, etc.

The market towns that had been important before the Industrial Revolution often acquired "Borough" status long before the new industrial communities like Bilston, but travelling showmen recognised the size of their population and identified a potential audience waiting for entertainment. Captain Payne erected his bioscope show on Bilston Market Place in July 1898, and the reason that we know this is that it caught fire and managed to earn a mention in the local press who otherwise would have ignored its presence.

Later Professor Wood and his son came to the old "Urban District" of Bilston and their story unfolds in the following account of Bilston's cinemas, along with other Bilstonians who brought light and shadows to the town's screens for about half a century. Bilston no longer has its giant steelworks and Bilston no longer has an operating cinema.

The Town Hall and The Drill Hall,

The principle room in Bilston Town Hall was used by Professor Wood for his winter tours of industrial Britain from the turn of the century onwards. He presented demonstrations of mesmerism and phrenology and advised the audience on their health, while his son, Thomas Reay Wood, projected elaborate magic lantern slides and short films. Entertainment gradually supplanted the lectures and by 1909 Professor Wood

Right: Bilston Town Hall, with Lichfield Street on the right and Church Street on the left – both home to cinemas. The sign on the Town Hal welcomes patrons to Wood's Picture Palace – a large upstairs room rented by the Wood Family for cinema use – and now fully restored to its former glory.

(Author's Collection)

advertised his show as a *"Musical and Pictorial Combination"* and promised that the films *"will delight and please you - a thousand laughs in ninety minutes."* Elaborate heavy generating equipment had to be set up to project the films and it is implied that sound was sometimes provided with early phonographic synchronisation. To put on such a show on a travelling basis must have been quite hectic and perhaps the "coming to rest" in Bilston, with the passing of the Cinematograph Act, was quite a blessing. From 1910 onwards Joseph Wood and Son leased the room for film shows on a regular basis.

For the next decade, the room at the Town Hall was advertised as "Wood's Palace" and a sign to that effect appeared on the exterior of the building. The shows continued until 1921 and ceased with the opening of the new "Wood's Palace" just across the road in Lichfield Street. In recent years the Town Hall has been restored and the upstairs room once used by the Wood family is beautifully refurbished. Tea dances are enjoyed where the Annual Cinema Ball was once held.

After the passing of the Cinematograph Act a licence was issued to the Drill Hall in Mount Pleasant, almost next door to the Theatre Royal. I assume occasional film shows were presented there up until the First World War but I have been unable to locate any detailed information concerning them.

According to a brief item in The Era of 9th. October 1909 the Picture Palace, Bilston, was being used by Edison & Barnum's Pictures - this was a travelling cinematograph company - at some stage taken over by Ben Kennedy, so it looks as if this might have another example of Ben Kennedy "popping up" and was nothing to do with the Wood family. The Era implies that the films at The Picture Palace, i.e. The Drill Hall, may have commenced on 27th September 1909.

The Drill Hall is now the Robin Hood Club and still brings live entertainment to the centre of Bilston.

The Electric Palace/The Grand

Church Street, Bilston

The little cinema in Church Street, later the furniture shop of J. Forrester & Sons Ltd., was Bilston's most short lived cinema. It was opened about 1913, by a Mr. Hallet, to provide an income for his three single daughters after his death. The Bilston Electric Theatre Ltd. was registered in May 1913 with a capital of £2000. Although it only held about three hundred and fifty people, it had a small balcony with an operating box underneath and was typical of the small "electric theatres" opened in such premises just before the First World War.

In the autumn of 1919 it was taken over by Joseph Wood & Son who ran it until the spring of 1921, although it was only across the road from their own shows in the Town Hall. At the same time their new Palace was being completed just round the corner of Lichfield Street, but they relinquished their shows in the Electric Palace about six months before their new cinema opened while taking a lease on the Alhambra a few hundred yards down the High Street! The little cinema was acquired by J. Forrester and adapted for use as a furniture sale room. At first the appearance of the building altered very little but now there are very few traces of the furniture shop once having been a cinema. Some cinemas closed just after the War when their licences were no longer renewed as they failed to meet safety regulations and this may have been another factor in its demise.

Above:Church Street, Bilston, with the Town Hall on the left and The Grand cinema on the right. Note the name "Grand Cinema" appears immediately beneath a sign using the name "Electric Palace".

(Wolverhampton Archives)

The Alhambra

Church Street, Bilston

It is interesting that parts of Bilston's other pre-World War One cinema, the Alhambra, are still standing today although its "temporary closure" seems ever more likely to remain permanent. It probably opened before the Electric Palace but the precise date of its opening is lost in the general obscurity surrounding the rapid expansion of the cinema interests of Wolverhampton's Thomas Jackson. It may well have opened on Thursday 7th November 1912 with the show, **"On the Brink of the Abyss"**. This is the earliest show for which I have found an advertisement.

The auditorium, on a single raked floor, held about six hundred patrons but looking at its brickwork in the 1980s it appeared to have undergone several alterations. The entrance onto Bilston's High Street was separate from the auditorium and formed the central part of a parade of shops, lacking the grandeur of a facade appropriate to a cinema.

Left: Thomas Jackson advertises the Alhambra and its latest programme from the back of a cart. The cart is standing in Bilston market place in front of Pat Collins' "Joy Wheel" during Wakes Week – a rival form of pleasure! (Author's Collection)

Thomas Jackson's financial difficulties followed the First World War, but when Joseph Wood and Sons acquired the lease of the Alhambra and began showing their programmes from September 1921 onwards, the freehold was already in somebody else's hands. Although not really very far from the Town Hall, the Electric, or the new Wood's Palace, that end of Church Street must have served a different community because the Woods continued to operate the Alhambra until their lease expired in the Spring of 1927, by which time they were building their new replacement for it on the opposite side of the street.

After 1927 the Alhambra began a long series of changes of tenants designed to send the cinema historian crazy! Among those who showed films there were H. J. Whittaker, T.A. Webb, and E.K. Hawtin of Cannock. Mr. Hawtin acquired, or leased, various Black Country cinemas during the thirties. At a time when the super-cinema was making its presence felt he seemed to be building up a small empire of relatively unimposing halls. However he took his role of cinema magnate seriously and for example, in July 1937 he, his wife and his daughters took the staff of the Alhambra and the Forum, Cannock, on a Sunday outing to Aberystwyth at his own expense! Ironically, there had been talk of replacing the Alhambra with a modern super-cinema in the mid thirties but it had come to nothing.

The changes in ownership, or lessee, continued during the forties, by the end of which it seems that the freehold was in the hands of H.J. Barlow of Wednesbury, trading as Magnet Cinemas. Early in 1950 Sidney Saunders took on a lease to run the Alhambra. He had resigned as manager of the Essoldo in Penge to come to Bilston. Perhaps the Alhambra failed to realise his dreams! About two years later it seems that he relinquished the lease and Mr. Barlow sold the cinema to Mr. and Mrs. Woodroffe.

The Alhambra now took on a new lease of life. It was refurbished by Modernisation Ltd. With its smart interior and the excellent Western Electric sound the Woodroffes felt that they could put on the best shows in Bilston. Even modernised inside, the Alhambra was still an old building and featured problems like damp. A stream ran under the floor near the screen and when its beautiful clear waters rose they needed pumping out now and again. However, Mrs. Woodroffe was ably helped in running the Alhambra by several dedicated staff who had survived the various changes of proprietor.

During the fifties, the Alhambra had still been a busy little cinema but by the beginning of the sixties life had become much more difficult and new business was sought. First of all bingo was tried on three evenings a week, but by 1964 the Odeon could provide much grander facilities for bingo. Asian films were screened on Sunday afternoons for the Indian community. The Woodroffes probably gave up showing English language films towards the end of 1963, out-living the Savoy by a short time but succumbing before the Odeon.

It was sold to a group of Indian businessmen and when the licence became due for renewal in 1964 it was in the name of Leslie Taff of the Regal, Darlaston. He had been associated with screening Indian films at the Regal, but apparently did not in fact renew the Alhambra's licence. Instead, the cinema was used for private shows and to gain admission, one had to be a member of the Eastern Film Society. In August 1968 the Express and Star reported that complaints had been made about the discomfort, dirt and dampness at the Alhambra. However, J.S. Sidhu, for the lessees, protested that it was clean and had just been redecorated despite the fact that it was only open three nights a week.

Open on a part-time basis for private shows of Indian films, the Alhambra limped into the seventies to become Bilston's last surviving cinema. Then it became "temporarily closed" awaiting refurbishment. Although I sometimes heard rumours that it could reopen I found it difficult to believe it would ever happen. Most of the building still existed while this enigmatic question mark hung over its fate. In April 1982 a planning application was submitted to the council to turn the front portion of the building into a clothes shop. In the process this was separated from the auditorium, most of which was demolished.

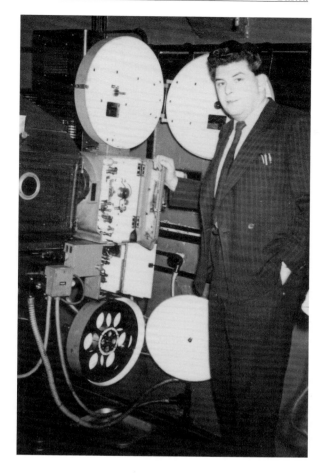

The entrance to The Alhambra was rather lost in the middle of this parade of shops in Church Street – beneath the double window.
The two pictures on the left show the interior of The Alhambra after work carried out by Modernisation Ltd.
(Pictures supplied by Doris Woodroffe)

Top right: Les Spratt in the projection room at The Alhambra. Sid Saunders brought Les up from London to join the Hassall family in running the Alhambra. He hoped that Les would be his chief engineer on the circuit he dreamed of building! Les helped several local flea pits to keep their ancient machinery running.
(Author's collection)

251

Wood's Palace/The Palace, later The Odeon

Lichfield Street, Bilston

As stated previously, while the Woods were taking on the Alhambra, in 1921, they were also busily putting the finishing touches to their brand new "Palace" in Lichfield Street. They had always called their shows in the Town Hall, "Wood's Palace", but the new building was going to be truly worthy of the name. It was the top show place in Bilston.

I imagine that it would have been built earlier but for the intervention of the First World War. The War created shortages of labour and material and restrictions on the kind of building work that could be undertaken. There were also doubts being expressed about the continuation of the new medium's popularity, and therefore the new hall was equipped as a fine theatre as well as a cinema, although its magnificent stage facilities were relatively little used.

Mr. Hurley Robinson was engaged as the architect and it was built by J. Hickin and Sons at a cost of £30,000. The interior design was by Val Prince. To Lichfield Street it presented a beautiful Renaissance-style facade, and the front elevation was treated in white faience. A cafe and billiard hall shared the facade but these have since ceased operation. Even so the entire frontage still has a unity that makes it an impressive part of the street scene, thanks to recent restoration work.

The interior designer was carried away, filling the great arch-roofed auditorium with luxurious colour and atmosphere. Val Prince himself wrote, *"The colour schemes are strong, but I feel harmonious — orange, black, violet and blue, toned with a pearly irridescence.*

The wall panels are erratic, but, I hope, not aggressive on either side of the proscenium are painted panels emblematic of song and dance, strong in colour, but designed to stand amongst the brilliance surround of orange. The seating, in rich purple, and painted draw-curtains in the same tone, pulls the whole together."

Fourteen hundred tip up seats were provided in the stalls and balcony, both fully raked and the screen was set back behind the proscenium. An orchestra pit was provided to accommodate up to twenty musicians and dressing rooms were provided off stage for theatrical use. With everything provided on such a splendid scale it is interesting to note that the original operating room was small and almost inadequate. The hall's own generators were supplied by the E.C.C. of Wolverhampton, and a Kalee Indomitable projector and a Powers No. 6 provided the shows for many years.

Messrs. Wood were described as "plucky promoters", and Kine Weekly stated that it opened, "at a time when others are holding back". The opening took place on 17th November 1921 and the ceremony was performed by Councillor Haddock, who was presented with a souvenir key by the contractor. On stage were the oldest shareholder in the venture, Professor Wood in his mid-seventies, and the youngest, his grand-daughter Angela, who was one year old exactly! The Professor said that many people had said that they were making it too fine for Bilston, but he thought that Bilston people deserved as fine a palace as anybody in the world. The first public show followed later that evening with *"The Old Nest"*.

The orchestra, under the director of Mr. Salisbury, soon acquired a reputation for good music at Woods Palace and it must have been an impressive cinema to visit during the silent era. On 14th October 1929 Woods Palace announced its "first 100% talking film" in the form of *"On Trial"*. Possibly this indicates that some

Right: Wood's Palace in Lichfield Street, Bilston. Note the lamps, beacons etc. This picture was taken about 1927, when trams still traversed Lichfield Street.

(Angela Bird)

Everything about Woods Palace seemed to establish a new level of luxury and stylishness. Above, a picture of the scene that greeted the patron. Doors to the stalls straight ahead – past the portrait of Professor Wood, up the stairs for the balcony. (Angela Bird's collection)

films had already been shown with short sound sequences or maybe it represents the gradual introduction of sound technology, and that this film still used a "sound on disc" system. Much more fuss was made on 11th November 1929 when *"The Singing Fool"* opened for six days. BTH sound equipment was installed at Woods Palace, and to improve the acoustics of the hall celotex panels were hung on the walls over Val Prince's murals. A larger screen was installed in July 1930, larger than anything in neighbouring Wolverhampton.

By the time the cinema celebrated its twelfth birthday in 1933 it had been refurbished throughout. The Mayors of Wolverhampton and Bilston came along to a birthday party and screening of *"The Good Companions"*.

Professor Wood had long since retired to North Wales and had died in 1927 before the advent of sound. His son Thomas Wood always maintained a presence at the Palace despite his busy civic life and the fact that day to day running of his cinema interests had to be delegated to managers. In 1936 "T.R." decided to retire, and on 29th August 1936 the cinema, along with his other halls, were leased to Cyril Joseph. As from September it simply became "The Palace" and very quickly the lease was transferred to Oscar Deutsch and the cinema became part of the Odeon circuit.

Traditions die hard, and even as the Bilston Odeon, it continued to be known as "Wood's". The building itself underwent little change and continued to thrive as a result of capable management by Billy Tyrer who had long association with Black Country cinemas including service in Oldbury and Halesowen.

Billy Tyrer organised successful war-time Sunday concerts in his Odeon that made good use of its stage facilities and throughout the forties it was still Bilston's number one cinema as its place on the circuit guaranteed good films relatively early in their release.

When the twenty-one year lease expired the Rank Organisation exercised their option to renew it and in the October that year, 1957, they installed £2000 worth of automatic projection equipment. The small operating room in which Reg Lloyd, the chief operator in the thirties, had struggled to do his best was at last enlarged to a reasonable size.

Only seven years later the closure of the Odeon as a cinema was announced. The last film was shown on 22nd February 1964 and it was *"Heavens Above"*, starring Peter Sellers. Conversion for use as a Bingo Hall was put in hand immediately and the Top Rank Bingo Club opened on 5th March. The opening was performed by Pat Astley, and hundreds had to be turned away!

The freehold still belonged to Woods Picture Halls, but in 1971, the Rank Organisation made a deal involving five properties (which included the Dunstall Odeon) and not only was their lease terminated, but the freehold

itself was sold to the Hutchinson group, operating as Surewin Bingo. For a decade it survived, the exterior was repainted, but the auditorium still had an atmosphere laden with the cinema's history. The "W" monogram in the ornamental plaster work, gold on a blue background, still dominated the proscenium arch and the staff talked about dusty old volumes on phrenology and medicine which had recently been found in a haunted office. A few days after I had laughed about the idea of Professor Wood's ghost still patrolling the cinema, I came across an article in the Express and Star for 17th January 1964 announcing the closure. The article added that the cinema had "a long standing reputation for being haunted".

By the early 1980s Woods Palace was closed for extensive refurbishment by United Leisure in order to reopen as the Cascade Bingo and Social Club. After bingo had ceased the former cinema was taken over by the family running the furniture shop next door. It was presented as "The Imperial Banquetting Suite", and mainly catered for Asian wedding parties. They, in turn, sold it to the Ramill family in about 2007 and there was another major refurbishment, but no change in name.

Now smart in a cream colour scheme, dazzling chandelier etc…the interior is back in business but with no signs of the original cinema auditorium visible. Meanwhile the exterior has been restored to a more cinema-like appearance, especially with the restoration of the doors and canopy and other details.

Although it still stands as a monument to the Woods, father and son, I would like to think that others who gave loyal service to the cinema could also be remembered. Some kind of record could be claimed by Sally Price who started work at the Palace as an usherette when it opened in 1921 and gave almost fifty years unbroken service, including work as projectionist and later cashier, until her retirement in March 1971. Within her working life many other local cinemas had completely come and gone!

Above: Wood's Palace – the frontage fully restored in 2010 – including the lamps and beacons! (Ned Williams)

The Theatre Royal

Mount Pleasant, Bilston

The Theatre Royal opened in 1902 and only became a "proper" cinema in 1932, so the reader may wonder why an account of its history appears apparently out of chronological order. The reason is that the history of entertainment in Bilston revolves around the development of the Wood Family's empire. It so happens that the Theatre Royal was acquired by Wood's Picture Halls for the sum of £3000 in 1924. In other words, they bought the theatre half way between opening their two purpose-built cinemas; the Palace and the Savoy.

Let us go back to the theatre's beginning. It was built on the site of an earlier theatre, at the time when Music Hall was enjoying its heyday. The proprietor, Mr. H. Battersby, called his new hall the Theatre Royal as, in 1902, Edward VII's coronation had made such names rather popular. Nearly seven hundred people could be accommodated in the stalls and balcony, the latter shaped like a huge horse-shoe in the style more associated with theatres than cinemas. (A more detailed account of the building's complicated history as a theatre is provided in Volume Two.)

After the passing of the Cinematograph Act, E.C. Jazon acquired a kine licence and films were introduced between the variety acts. About 1912 it was called, for a short time, "The Royal Hippodrome and Picture House" but variety and drama still filled the bills. Strong melodrama was popular in Bilston, but touring Shakespearian productions were also presented. Mr. Jazon is something of a mystery character, but he did promote "cine-variety" in the same way at Wednesbury's Theatre Royal.

It was closed for a time in 1924 when Thomas Wood acquired it, but reopened on Boxing Day of that year with a review called **"Cheer Up"**. At the time, variety acts occasionally supported the films at the Palace but, as described in the chapter on Thomas Wood, he was no stranger to the live theatre and already had many contacts in that business. He was also a patron of the local Bilston Operatic Society and as from 1927, they also began to use the Royal for their annual shows. Thomas Wood installed Mr. Arthur Holland, the man who had produced "Cheer Up", as his first manager. Under his management the Royal continued its theatrical career with great success until the advent of the "talkies" stole the patrons who had previously supported live entertainment.

The Royal closed for a time in 1932 but was slightly rebuilt and refurbished with a view to reopening as a cinema. A BTH sound system was installed and Ross projectors were mounted behind the screen. Back projection was considered quite a novelty, although "ray-less" pictures had been seen earlier in Wolverhampton and Dudley. Its short life as a cinema

Above: Two usherettes from Woods Palace, Bilston, in its "Odeon" days meet Avril Noon, the Wolverhampton Chronicle Personality Queen, on 9th November 1963. Two "runners-up" from the same contest came along too: Marianne Preece and Marilyn Lewis. In her role as Miss Bloxwich, Marianne rode an elephant when Billy Smart's Circus came to Walsall. It's all show business!

began with a presentation of James Whale's **"Frankenstein"**, starring Boris Karloff, probably chosen to continue the tradition of melodrama rather than to celebrate the Dudley-born film-maker's success.

Four years later in August 1936, the Theatre Royal was leased to Cyril Joseph's "Astel Pictures" and it soon reverted to being a theatre. About 1941, Mr. Joseph transferred Jack Riskit from the Palace, Wednesbury, to the position of manager at the Royal. More information about Jack Riskit and the use of this site for theatrical entertainment is contained in Volume Two.

Astel Pictures, as Cyril Joseph's company was called, must have been quite relieved when the lease expired in 1957. He was certainly not interested in renewing it and Thomas Wood's son, Reay Wood, announced to the press that the theatre would not reopen after its usual summer closure.

255

The Royal was put up for sale by auction but failed to reach its reserve price. Eventually the local authority bought it and towards the end of 1961 the building was demolished. The site is now a car park. After the demolition, Councillor Beards told the Public Works Committee that nobody had regretted its passing. Surely someone must have felt nostalgia when recalling its theatrical history, and a few perhaps remembered those rear projected pictures.

Above: The Royal in Mount Pleasant, Bilston about 1910. On the left is The Drill Hall, also used briefly for showing films.
(Wolverhampton Archives)

The Savoy

Church Street, Bilston

As we have seen already, Messrs. Wood expanded their cinema empire to the other end of the Church Street with their acquisition of a lease on the Alhambra. This lease expired in the spring of 1927, but by then Thomas Wood had already made plans to continue his company's presence in that part of Bilston.

In the November of 1926 Mr. Hurley Robinson had drawn up plans for a new Alhambra to be built on a site on the opposite side of the road to the old one. He produced a far less imposing plan than he had drawn up for the Palace. In fact, he followed the Alhambra's tradition of hiding the auditorium well behind an entrance foyer that formed a central part of a parade of shops. Impressive columns guarded a small vestibule between numbers 45 and 49 High Street and this gave access to the two pairs of swing doors that led to a long

main entrance hall. The auditorium held only seven hundred and fifty patrons. There was no circle but the four rows of seats furthest from the screen were higher than the rest of the hall and were reached via a separate entrance. The front rows were raked upwards towards the screen to improve viewing. It had similarities therefore with the Regent, Dudley, planned at about the same time, suggesting a fashion for the "stadium" style.

Mr. Hurley Robinson improved on Woods Palace in one respect: a more generous operating room was planned situated above the pay box and that long entrance hall. The latest Kalee machines were installed in it. The orchestra pit held five performers and a deep stage was provided. All this was built by J. Hickin & Sons of Willenhall, the contractors who had built the Palace. The only problem that remained was what to call the new cinema as the old Alhambra was going to continue using that name. Thomas Wood organised a competition in which future patrons had to select their favourite name and by this process the cinema became the Savoy.

The Savoy opened on 10th October 1927 and the ceremony was performed by the seven year old Angela Wood, who had been carried on to the stage of Wood's Palace by her grandfather on her first birthday. Thomas Wood spoke of his regret that the Professor had not lived to see the completion of the Savoy. Councillor W. M. Hughes, chairman of the Urban District Council lent a civic presence to the proceedings. The first film shown was *"Remember"*, a story based on a song by Irving Berlin.

The silent film era was coming to a close and the Savoy, along with the other Wood's Picture Halls, was converted to sound, using the BTH system. It also shared their fate in 1936 when they were all leased to Cyril Joseph for the next twenty-one years. Mr. Joseph's company, Astel Pictures, ran the Savoy, the Theatre Royal and Bradley's cinema, until that lease expired. In the case of the Savoy, this was for the greater part of its life.

Thus, in August 1957, the Savoy returned to the fold and Reay Wood, Thomas Wood's son, found himself running it in the hope that a buyer would materialise. The proprietors of the Alhambra had taken the opportunity to acquire the Forum, Bradley, but no-one seemed keen to acquire the Savoy. Presumably as an economy, the Savoy ceased advertising in the local press in 1959 and in the July of that year, the Express and Star reported that the building was for sale. Reay Wood was helped by his manager, Reg Lloyd, who had worked there since leaving the operating box at Woods Palace where he had been a well-liked "chief". The cinema outlived him and towards the end of its life it was run by Mr. Fullwood, the chief operator. It seems that the Savoy limped on until June 1962.

Once sold, the building was demolished to make way for a Tesco supermarket, but even today, a remnant of Mr. Hurley Robinson's building can be seen clinging to the edge of the frontage. After a short life as a supermarket, the premises became a Weatherspoon's pub. The rear portion of the pub, still occupies the "footprint" of the Savoy's auditorium, and therefore some sections of wall may also date back to The Savoy. As a cinema it lacked the dignity and prestige of Wood's Palace, and the longevity and idiosyncrasy of the Alhambra. However, it did have a nickname, "the Savvy" and this suggests that it meant something personal to its patrons and deserves to be remembered.

Below: The Savoy, Church Street, Bilston. Wolverhampton trolleybus no. 480 passes The Greyhound inn on 15th April 1961, as the Savoy struggles on for another year under Reay Wood's control. The Alhambra was almost opposite..
(Clifford Brown via John Hughes)

The Queen's Picture House, later known as The Forum

Salop Street, Bradley, Bilston

One last cinema must be included in our survey of Bilston, but as it was really in the village of Bradley it had more in common with the cinemas in similar small Black Country villages. In other words, it served a distinct community quite separate from its counterparts nearer the centre of Bilston. However, while its patrons may have been local people, for most of its existence its ownership linked its history with that of Bilston's cinemas.

The original proprietor was a man called Ernest Hall and the building was erected by Messrs. Crewe of Dudley, at the same time as Wood's Palace was being built. The Queen's opened before the Palace but was probably far enough away to avoid any feeling of competition. The South Staffordshire Times exclaimed, *"The Town which has no cinema is out of date. Bradley is now abreast of the times and on Monday night a commodious cinema is to be opened within its borders".*

The first show began at 6.30 p.m. on 17th October 1921, featuring Madge Titheradge and C.M. Hallard in *"His Story"*. The supporting programme included Charlie Chaplin's *"Shoulder Arms"*, Pathe News and the first episode of a serial, *"The Invisible Hand"*. Prices were 5d, 9d and 1/-, which I suggest were rather high, even if all six hundred seats were upholstered, and the lofty auditorium enjoyed the wonder of electric lighting and good ventilation! For 1/-, patrons could sit in the small "balconette" and the cheapest seats, although upholstered were only benches. Later, when the seating was improved, the cinema's capacity was reduced to about three hundred and fifty. A small orchestra accompanied films at the Queen's, not quite on the scale of Wood's Palace, but grand enough for Bradley!

Towards the end of the twenties the cinema was acquired by Wood's Picture Halls and thus, when sound arrived, BTH equipment was installed, as in their other cinemas. From 1936 onwards it was leased to Cyril Joseph's Astel Pictures and in his hands, a new foyer was added to the original building and it became the Forum.

When Cyril Joseph's lease expired in 1957 the Forum was acquired by Mr. and Mrs. Woodroffe of the Alhambra. They redecorated the inside of the cinema and put in a new screen and reopened with a Tommy Steele film. Ironically, the Forum seems to have ceased advertising in the local press at about this time, but perhaps this was a realistic reflection of how such cinemas were used. Nobody travelled from far afield to an obscure second-run cinema, but if the community in the immediate vicinity supported your venture you could be a success. The Woodroffe's enjoyed this kind of very local success both in Bradley and in Princes End at a time when other cinemas felt their audience had deserted them for commercial television. A second run film could fill the Forum provided it had plenty of action.

When the audience figures did begin to decline in the sixties, bingo was introduced for half the week. The Forum ceased showing films altogether some time during the summer of 1964, although Mrs. Woodroffe continued to renew the cinematograph licence and the equipment was not removed immediately. In August 1964 about fifty young people, led by Bilston Grammar School pupil, Linda Bayliss, converged on the cinema in a demonstration to demand its reopening. Mrs. Woodroffe responded by explaining that bingo was played five nights a week and a dance was held on one night. Monday night was free and could possibly be used for a youth club, showing films when available.

I do not think anything came of this and the Forum was whole-heartedly devoted to bingo after that. Mr. and Mrs. Woodroffe retired in the early seventies and the club was then operated by Jarglen Ltd. After bingo the premises became a snooker club and it still survives in that guise. The corner entrance is no longer used and there is no sense of being in a former cinema auditorium when in the building.

A Gaumont British usherette in uniform provided – plus torch! The "Odeon" style can be seen on page 255.

Section 5
Cinemas of Walsall

Walsall occupies a position in the north-eastern corner of the Black Country, corresponding to Wolverhampton in the north-west. Like Wolverhampton, it has a background and history that slightly separates it from the Black Country, but industrial development and the patterns of urban growth have united it with the area where the presence of the Ten Yard Seam of coal was more obvious. In this section of the survey the cinemas of Central Walsall itself will be considered first, followed by cinemas further afield, including Walsall's multiplex at Bentley. Bloxwich deserves separate attention before moving on to the former "urban districts" of Willenhall and Darlaston. The modern Metropolitan Borough of Walsall also takes in Aldridge and Brownhills – rich in cinema history – and not really part of the Black Country. Howver, it makes sense to include them as the people who appear in the histories of the cinemas in those areas are encountered elsewhere in this book. For example, Thomas Jackson, from his base at The Strand, Whitmore Reans, in Wolver-hampton, developed interests in Walsall, like the cinema shown above, and out at Bloxwich. People who ran cinemas in Brownhills, also ran cinemas in Dudley and Halesowen!

Above: Staff at Walsall's Picture Palace in The Square sometime after 1912. The picture makes an interesting comparison with the photograph taken outside The Strand, Whitmore Reans, another cinema pioneered by Thomas Jackson (See page 225).
The manager, in top hat, and projection staff stand at the back, cashiers and usherettes are seated, pages sit on the ground clutching their trays of Fry's chocolates, and doormen (chucker-outers) frame the group. The men with bow ties may be musicians.
(Elizabeth Hazel's collection)

Central Walsall

With Pat Collins' connections with Walsall and Bloxwich it would be very surprising if his fairground bioscope shows did not play a part in bringing the earliest film shows to this corner of the Black Country. Film shows were also to be found in public halls. For example, for six days in January 1903 a show was put on in Walsall Town Hall. The drama-feature was *"The Sand Man"*, but it was supported by colour film of the Delhi Durbar. Unfortunately the contemporary advertisements do not reveal who was presenting the show. Professor Wood certainly came to Willenhall and Bloxwich and so may have come to Walsall, but usually mentioned himself in the advertising! A press report indicates that the show was popular, but possibly not particularly unusual. We will probably never know who showed the first film in Walsall.

Thus when the Cinematograph Act became law at the beginning of 1910, films were already familiar to the people of Walsall. Messrs. Melville and Stuart put on shows, with piano accompaniment by Selwyn Hay, at the Town Hall, from Christmas 1909 through to the New Year. Films had already been presented at the Imperial and, although not a purpose-built cinema, the Imperial has the strongest claim to being Walsall's first cinema by probably being the first to operate with a kine licence.

From then on Walsall's cinemas developed on similar lines to other Black Country towns, with the Palace and De Luxe opening near the town centre before the First World War. They were joined by the Grand's defection from theatre to films, and by comrades in the "suburbs" at Caldmore Green and Bloxwich. The Picture House, which had sister cinemas in Wolverhampton, Willenhall and Wednesbury was delayed by the War and problems arising out of a site so close to the waters of Walsall's mighty river, the Tame. For a cinema built above a river it, and its successors, were strangely cursed by fire!

Although ABC acquired four halls in the town and set about replacing Her Majesty's Theatre with the Savoy, an excellent example of the large 1930's super- cinema, the "modern" style never quite arrived in Walsall as in other towns of comparable size. Oscar Deutsch did not build an Odeon there and the Clifton circuit built nothing closer than the Rosum at Leamore, although at one time had proposed building a large cinema at the point where the Walsall-West Bromwich road crossed The Broadway.

Nevertheless, by the end of the thirties, six cinemas flourished within the fairly compact centre of the town, plus others within easy reach.

Writing about her cinema going in Walsall, Eileen Stables recalls:
"I can still vividly remember the happy hours I spent with a friend during the Second World War at the cinemas of Walsall. Practically every night saw us at the "flicks" and neither our school work nor morals ever seemed to suffer.

As the Palace has long since closed, it can now be said that I had a relative there who was an usherette who let us in, via the fire doors, free of charge, in the absence of the manageress. Being a cinema that changed its programmes three times a week, i.e. Monday, Thursday and Sunday, and showing rather ancient films, that was our entrance to three trips of Hollywood fantasy, and how we thrived on it. Her two complimentary tickets to the Classic or the Savoy provided us with two more shows.

In those days it was a continuous performance and many was the time we went in at 2.00 p.m. and watched the wartime classics through three times (the relation bringing us a sandwich at 5.00 p.m.). Our signal for the "free admission" was to stand outside Taylors Record Shop in the Old Square and watch the little window, high above the foyer (if one could call it that at the Palace, for let's face it — it was pretty low on the list — just one above the Classic). When my cousin's head appeared at the window, we would shoot round to the fire doors and into another world.

The Classic "De Luxe" let us use the free pass, but we were never very happy there. The fact that we had been told it was infested with mice may have had something to do with it. As the pass took us upstairs, we had a brave feeling that maybe the rodents wouldn't have the audacity to invade that hierarchy. I distinctly remember seeing the great Bing Crosby in "Bells of St Mary's" at the Classic.

How strange it seems now that one could walk into a cinema in those days half way through a film, immediately get engrossed, watch round to the exact word you caught as you sat down and then get up and say "Come on, this is where we came in".

Nowadays I never cease to wonder how two young girls used to walk through a blacked-out town, full of GI's, Dutch soldiers and other allied troops, up the Birchills Hill, and never have a care in the world, no muggings in those days. If Antonio and his hot potato machine happened to be outside the Grand (before the fire) we would, if funds permitted, buy a hot potato each to eat on the way home. They were like nectar. Only one night we were scared, that was after seeing "Maria Marten and the Murder in the Red Barn". We ran past the iron foundry in Birchills Street that night!

As we got older and the war finished, we graduated to boy friends. Then it was the New Picture House on the Bridge or the very elite Savoy. Of course the boyfriend worth cultivating was the one that took you "upstairs in the one and nines". That carpet on the staircase was sheer luxury. And how strange it now seems that every cinema in town could leave the "stills" in glass cases all day and night and they remained intact. To be given a spare still was like receiving a medal, to be filed away with the weekly Picturegoer."

The Imperial

Darwall Street, Walsall

To the Imperial goes the honour of first showing films in Walsall on a regular basis, following the passing of the Cinematograph Act. On 1st January 1910 films were being presented there nightly by the American Bioscope Company.

The building had started life as an Agricultural Hall, built in the 1860's. It was later rebuilt, and was reopened in 1887 as St. Georges Hall. In turn, in 1889, it became the Imperial Theatre. The successive changes had reduced the building in size but, at the turn of the century it still held about one thousand five hundred people. I am not quite sure at what stage it acquired its present frontage but there is something about its appearance that seems to owe more to the theatrical traditions and the public-hall tradition, than to any cinema-style.

It became the property of the Walsall Theatre Company, but from 1910 onwards seemed wholeheartedly devoted to an existence as a cinema, unaffected by the opening of the Palace and the De Luxe. During the twenties it headed its advertisements, "The Royal Academy of "Reel" Life"! Such was its dedication to silent movies it seemed reluctant to have to abandon them. Although W.T.C. quickly installed sound at the Palace they left the Imperial to make a virtue out of silence: "Silence Pictures Supreme", claimed the Imperial's advertisements. Sound, by Western Electric, eventually arrived on 20th October 1930 with *"All Quiet On The Western Front"*.

In April 1936 ABC took over the four halls in Walsall owned by W.T.C. Their little triangular motif appeared on either side of the entrance, but the exterior of the building seems to have undergone very little change over the years. Even by the 1980s, as an EMI Bingo Club, the name "Imperial" still existed, on part of the facade.

During the Second World War a small office on the left of the foyer was used as a signing-on point for the local fire-watchers. Before going on duty the fire-watchers were allowed to see the evening's programme free of charge and were also allowed to spend part of the night sleeping upstairs at the back of the cinema in the room used by the usherettes. On many occasions the fire-watchers on stand-by heard a buzzing noise in the auditorium and would come down to find the manager, Sammy Hipkiss, cleaning his cinema with the vacuum cleaner! Apparently he just loved doing it.

The Imperial may have been Walsall's first cinema but its prestige seems to have diminished over the years. It went sound fourteen months after the arrival of the first "talkie" in town. By the mid-fifties the installation of cinemascope took place a year after ABC had bought the wide screen to the Savoy. Eventually *"Bedevilled"* filled the Imperial's new wide screen on 29th August 1955. At this time the Imperial held just over eleven hundred patrons — about half the number accommodated at the Savoy. ABC then closed The Palace, which held a similar number of patrons but for some reason the Imperial survived.

Below: The Imperial, Walsall, in 1946
(Kevin Wheelan Collection)

Although small and old-fashioned the Imperial seemed a popular cinema right into the sixties. My one and only visit to the cinema was early in 1967 when I joined a packed house to see Vincent Price pretending to be Richard III in *"Tower of London"*. One felt glad that a cinema still existed to bring such obscure gems to the Black Country after Wolverhampton's Clifton had closed.

During 1965 the Indo-Pakistani Muslim Welfare Association hired the Imperial for Sunday morning shows. This created a little crisis because Sunday opening was permitted in Walsall on the understanding that children were not admitted to a cinema before five o'clock. (Presumably after attending Sunday School). Great concern was expressed when it was realised that Muslim children were possibly seeing films in the Imperial on Sunday mornings. The Council seemed reluctant to alter their rule without consulting local clergy. A change was opposed by Councillor O'Hare on the grounds that it would be, "Another intrusion into the sanctity of the Sabbath." The Imperial had closed by the time the rule was relaxed.

When the cinema's demise was announced someone obviously decided that its farewell to Walsall should be presented in a style appropriate to the cinema's seniority. For the four weeks preceeding closure the Imperial ran a "Big Film Month", reviving many of the favourites that had been popular there, such as *"The Ten Commandments"*. This culminated with its final film show on 4th May 1968 featuring *"Assignment K"* and the superb, *"Cat Balou"*

The Electric Theatre, better known as The Palace, as built.
(Ken Rock postcard collection)

The manager, Mr. R. Maher, stayed on to see the eighty year old building enjoy a "face lift", but once again it was the interior of the building that must have received the attention. He then prepared the Imperial for its opening as a Bingo Hall on 23rd May 1968. The interior was painted in strong lurid colours and the balcony was retained although not used.

Bingo ceased in the former Imperial about 1996, and the building was reopened as a Weatherspoon pub in March 1997.

(NB the story of the Griffiths brothers in relation to the history of The Imperial is told in the section on cinema staff.

The Palace

The Square, Walsall

As soon as the Cinematograph Bill became law an attempt was made to create a chain of Black Country cinemas. Electric Picture Palaces (Midlands) Ltd., with a proposed share capital of £50,000 set out to build six theatres, in Walsall, West Bromwich, Smethwick, Darlaston, Wolverhampton and Handsworth. Only two of these materialized, and Walsall's was the first. The directors were from London but the company's office was in Birmingham. The company's architects were Hickton and Farmer, of Walsall.

No time was wasted on building The Palace, Walsall. The builder was S. Wootton of Bloxwich and most of the sub-contractors were local firms. It was erected in three months but, nevertheless, lived up to its name. It was built to accommodate just over a thousand patrons and was solidly constructed from brick. (No wooden frame and corrugated iron for the Palace!). The Walsall Observer described it in some detail:

"The outer elevations present an attractive scheme executed in modelled fibrous plasterwork, the open Loggia front having Corinthian columns carrying an open ballustrade surrounding the dome, from the centre of which arises a figure of Electra...."

On entering the main doors, on the left is the manager's office, and next comes a lounge, luxuriously furnished with upholstered bays in green, and the floor is covered with a rich Rose du Barry carpet From the lounge, in which refreshments are provided, the theatre proper is approached. This is a magnificent building with tip up seats, and is carpeted. The seats are upholstered in two shades of green and the walls and ceiling are panelled and finished in red paper, while the beautiful electric torches are shaded with pink silk hankerchiefs...."

The paper made only one complaint: "The building is a most imposing one, and it is to be regretted that it could not be found a place in a more prominent thoroughfare of the town."

The Square was not far from The Bridge and therefore the Palace was in a reasonably central position, but was often regarded as being "tucked away". Today the site is obscured by the development of a new shopping precinct.

The Palace opened on 12th April 1910; Walsall's first "purpose-built" cinema. The ceremony was performed by Lady Holden in the presence of an influential gathering which included the Mayor. Mr. Harry Farmer, of Hickton and Farmer, was presented with a silver rose bowl and everyone congratulated everybody else. In the words of The Bioscope: "An exhibition of pictures followed, some remarkably fine films being shown."

One of the early features of the programmes at The Palace was "sequence pictures". These were not "serials", but involved the same characters in a series of self-contained stories. They were projected by a Mr. Robinson on two Pathe projectors from his fireproof operating room. The resident manager was Alex Grant but the company also employed Mr. H. Stanley Marks, from Pathe Freres, as General Manager. This gentleman probably found his job more demanding when the company's second "Palace", in West Bromwich, was opened a month later.

Right: The Palace, Walsall, in 1946, under ABC ownership. Note how the original entrance was retained even when the cinema was much enlarged. (Kevin Wheelan)

Sometime in 1912 these two "Palaces" were taken over by United Electric Theatres, the grand circuit of six cinemas never becoming a reality for the original company. The new proprietors redecorated the cinema and offered free afternoon tea to patrons in the stalls.

They described themselves as "The only fashionable Picture Theatre in Walsall", and, "The Rendezvous of the elite". Continuous performances ran from 3 p.m. to 10.30 p.m. but the full orchestra only accompanied the evening screenings. This usually implied that most of the musicians were part-timers who rushed to the evening performance after their "day job".

It seems that not everything went well for the Palace. It was probably acquired by Thomas Jackson, the Wolverhampton baker and confectioner whose empire had spread to the Walsall area, to include the De Luxe and the Palace, Bloxwich. It may have closed for a time while Thomas Jackson tried to renovate the place. Such a task may have been specially difficult during the War and it seems that it was not reopened until 17th December 1917. The occasion was marked by a showing of D. W. Griffiths' *"Intolerance"*. After the war, the Palace adopted the slogan, "The House With A Big Following".

In March 1920 this slogan was replaced in the advertisements with "The House that is Becoming Different", and after Easter this became "The House That Is Now Different". The changing slogan does not do justice to the work Thomas Jackson undertook. The theatre was turned round! The screen had originally been at the entrance end of the auditorium. It was now transferred to the other end to which a twenty-five foot extension had been added. A new balcony was built over the main entrance, reached by broad staircases, and the projection box was moved. Much of the work was

accomplished while shows continued, much to the pride of the manager, Mr. Reynolds Benjamin.

The new Palace reopened on 3rd April 1920 and *"Spiral of Death"* filled the new washable silk screen with light from the Powers No. 2 projectors. The orchestra was now directed by Claude Fenn-Leyland, late of the London Opera House. The financial strain may have been the beginning of Thomas Jackson's downfall but the cinema was packed that Easter Monday.

Along with the De Luxe in Stafford Street, the Palace was acquired by L. A. Thomson's "Midland Counties Circuit" when Thomas Jackson's empire was dissolved in 1922/3. There it remained until it was taken over by Walsall Theatres Company in the summer of 1930. W.T.C. briefly closed the Palace in order to install the BTH sound system, and reopened on 4th August 1930, with *"The Gold Diggers of Broadway"*. The Palace must have become accustomed to changing hands every six or seven years because on 1st April 1936 it was taken over by ABC. The cinema then held one thousand, one hundred and sixty-four patrons.

Like the ABC's Imperial, the Palace eventually found itself overshadowed by the company's brand new Savoy. It only screened the best releases when they were on their second time round. However, its proximity to the Picture House and the Empire meant that during the Second World War when all three cinemas enjoyed long queues, The Palace gratefully accepted the patrons who were unsuccessful in getting in at the other two places!

When audiences faltered it was natural that ABC should prune at least one of its three cinemas surviving in Walsall. The Imperial was an older building but the Palace was the first to be abandoned. The last show was on 24th September 1955 and featured Norman Wisdom's second film, *"One Good Turn"*. The last advertisement carried a "thank you" to the patrons for their loyal support. Possibly the question of redeveloping the site was more relevant to its closure than a real loss of patrons. Five days later the site was sold to the Walsall Observer, becoming the Commercial Printing Department. The new owner's canteen occupied the site of the balcony. As mentioned earlier, the site has since been redeveloped and all traces of the Palace have gone.

Cinema de Luxe, later The Classic

Stafford Street, Walsall

For a couple of years after the passing of the Cinematograph Act the citizens of Walsall only had the Imperial and The Palace to provide them with a choice of cinematic entertainment. However, on Monday 23rd December 1912, Walsall's third cinema opened in Stafford Street, not quite so close to the town centre. The cinema only had a very narrow frontage to Stafford Sreet, and a flight of steps led into its foyer – the auditorium being well behind this.

The Cinema de Luxe appears to have been built by Thomas Jackson in his first flush of success after opening the Strand, in Wolverhampton, five months earlier. It was opened by Walsall's mayor, Councillor John Venables, and held about one thousand patrons. Little seems to be recorded of its early history although it seems that Thomas Jackson was keen to enlarge the place, but his plans were held up by the First World War. The work was done in 1920, increasing its capacity to about one thousand five hundred. As suggested elsewhere, the strain of enlarging both his Walsall cinemas just after the First World War may have been the cause of Thomas Jackson's financial problems.

After Thomas Jackson's financial collapse in 1923, the cinema was administered by the Midland Counties Circuit, as was the Palace. When they were put up for sale, it can be assumed that the Walsall Theatres Company did not want the De Luxe. It was bought by a neighbouring garage proprietor and motor-car dealer, Mr. T. Birch.

Sound was installed in November 1931 using the Western Electric Mirrophonic system. The De Luxe, the last cinema in Walsall to introduce the "talkies", showed its first sound film, *"The Easiest Way"* on 30th November 1931. The new proprietor probably gradually improved the seating and its capacity fell to about eight hundred and fifty, and later to about a hundred less than that. Miss Minnie Wallace, who had been a secretary in the garage, was later given the job of managing the place, knowing that she would be one of the few women given the opportunity to occupy such a position.

When the De Luxe was sold to the Clifton Circuit Miss Wallace retained her position of manageress and worked for that company until the mid-sixties. The cinema ceased to be the De Luxe on Sunday 25th February 1940, Sunday opening being allowed during the Second World War, despite strong denunciations of such practices in Walsall. The cinema was then redecorated and refurbished by the Clifton Circuit and some technical changes were made although the cinema's equipment continued to be rather antiquated. The cinema reopened as The Classic on 4th March 1940 with *"OHMS"* starring John Mills. The new name implied that the cinema intended making a virtue out of showing old films! It was going to be policy to show the "classics"; films that had already proved popular in Walsall. The advertising also described the three hour double feature programmes at other cinemas as "wearisome" and announced that The Classic would specialise in two hour shows consisting of a feature supported by only a short and Universal News. Patrons were to be charged sixpence downstairs or a shilling in the balcony.

Miss Wallis became secretary of Walsall's War Aid Committee, organising variety shows, concerts and dances for war-time charities. After 1945 she carried on such work for local charities. Tommy Trinder, George Formby, Norman Wisdom and bandleaders, Billy Cotton and Joe Loss, all found themselves answering Miss Wallis's charity call. In 1951 Miss Wallis was presented to Princess Margaret as a "cinema manager and charity worker".

The Classic was literally overshadowed by The Savoy and naturally seemed something of a "flea-pit" by comparison, but it had its own pride and a determination not to give up too easily in the fifties. It celebrated the Coronation by being lavishly decorated externally and by reducing seat prices to one shilling downstairs, two shillings upstairs. Mr. Moseley who went to the cinema as third operator and had risen to second operator, assured me that the sound and picture were always the best that could be obtained on the rather old equipment provided. He and his chief, Bill Prescott, had to be on their toes to get the best from their Kalee 8 projectors with BTH arcs, although helped by good maintenance by the Clifton Circuit engineers.

The age of the building and its slightly awkward site added to its problems and the Classic finally gave up the struggle to survive on Sunday 22nd June 1958. The last show was a one day only presentation of *"Johnny You're Wanted"* and *"Phantom from 10,000 Leagues"*.

By the 1980s the building was occupied by the Mazda Price Supermarket and was not obviously an ex-cinema until one stood well away from the frontage to be able to see the roofline. Until November 1981 the operating box could be seen clearly projecting through the forward slope of this roof, but was removed after fire had destroyed part of the building. Sometime after the fire the rest of the building was demolished.

Right: The narrow front of The Cinema De Luxe is rather lost beneath all this advertising, but the steep flight of steps into the entrance can be clearly seen.   (National Film Archive)

The Rink, The Arcade and The Grand

Three other establishments presented films in Walsall before the First World War. For convenience they will be dealt with together in this section.

The Rink, as its name suggests, was a converted skating rink in Darwall Street, not far from the Imperial. It opened on Saturday 10th May 1913 with **"Broken Wings"** and **"Undine"**. The following week brought a forty minute silent version of **"Romeo & Juliet"**. It claimed to hold two thousand patrons at two and three pence a time. (In 1913 seats at The Palace were one shilling, sixpence and threepence!).

The Walsall Observer reported: *"The Skating Rink has been admirably adapted to the requirements of a Picture House"*. However it does not seem to have been

A great success, or its licence fell foul of safety regulations, because films at "The Rink" seem to have ceased fairly quickly, probably within a year of opening. It was managed by one Alfred Jacobs, but beyond that I have discovered very little!

A kine licence was also issued for a time before the First World War to W.T. Comer of the Arcade. Mr. Comer was an optician, and one of the original tenants of Walsall's Arcade. During 1913 or 1914 he may have organised film shows in the Assembly Rooms at the Arcade but I have not found them advertised, nor recorded elsewhere.

Walsall Theatre Company has already been mentioned in relation to the Imperial and the Palace. At the time when these two places were pioneering film entertainment in Walsall, the two theatres owned by W.T.C.; the Grand and Her Majesty's, were still presenting drama and variety. By 1912 W.T.C. thought it worth acquring a kine licence for Her Majesty's Theatre and successfully showed a twice-nightly film programme there during the summer.

Mr. Westwood of W.T.C. declared that he had decided the cinema was here to stay, and that Walsall could support another cinema. The Grand, in Park Street, which had been built as a theatre in 1890 was therefore closed in 1912 to be converted to a cinema.

Four hundred and fifty new tip up seats were installed in the stalls. The seats in the circle were regarded as too good to change and the gallery was left as it was, to provide cheap seats, apart from a section used to house

the operating box. New heating was installed to overcome its reputation as a cold theatre and a new screen was mounted behind the proscenium arch.

The Grand opened as a cinema on 4th November 1912 with **"The Mysteries of Paris"** but did not formerly change its name to "Grand Picture House" until the following May. Ironically by this time some variety acts had crept back into the three hour programmes! It had an orchestra led by a Mr. Blakemore, and could accommodate about one thousand five hundred patrons. It occasionally returned to theatrical use in subsequent years and was presenting plays when sound films arrived at Walsall's cinemas. It was briefly closed in mid 1931 and reopened on 15th June, with *"Just Imagine"* as the Grand Talkie Theatre.

When it was acquired by ABC in April 1936 it served a useful purpose in maintaining their presence at that end of the town while they demolished Her Majesty's Theatre and replaced it with the Savoy. The Grand closed on Saturday 1st October 1938 and the Savoy opened two days later. The final show featured **"Sea Devils"**, starring Victor McLagen.

The Grand languished for a short time and was then reopened as a live theatre, by Pat Collins Junior, Pat Collins' grandson. Unfortunately it was destroyed by a fire in 1939.

Below: The Grand in Park Street, Walsall, next to the entrance to the railway station. Not Her Majesty's Theatre in the background. (J.S. Webb collection)

The Picture House — Gaumont — Odeon

Bridge Street, Walsall

Just before the First World War, Associated Provincial Picture Houses began work on a prestige cinema for Walsall. This was to be The Picture House in Bridge Street, virtually built over the River Tame itself. The site had formerly been part of the George Hotel, an old coaching inn, right in the centre of town. The foundations were laid and then the problems began.

First of all construction had to be suspended during the War, due to shortage of labour and materials, then building restrictions. By the time work could resume the foundations were flooded and expensive piles had to be sunk to try and put things right. A.P.P.H. had managed to open their cinemas in Wolverhampton, Willenhall and Wednesbury and were doubtless keen to open in Walsall as quickly as possible. Eventually the contractors were working at nights and on Sundays to try and finish the cinema. Even then the frontage was not quite finished in time.

The front elevation of the cinema was particularly handsome. It was faced in cream glazed faience and was dominated by marble pillars above the main entrance doors. The lofty windows of the cafe at balcony level, and the ballastrades, added to the effect of grandeur. The foyer was panelled in oak, there were lifts to the balcony level and the best seats were of a cosy armchair type. Everything suggested luxury and good taste to reassure the middle classes that A.P.P.H. had made cinema-going respectable. The architect were Percy, Browne, and Glover.

The Picture House opened on 29th July 1920 in the presence of Walsall's Mayor. Mr. Darbyshire, of A.P.P.H., made a speech explaining why Walsall deserved such a fine cinema. He said,

"Many of her sons have devoted their brains to the development of the picture industry. Dr. Jupp, who was the first to conceive of the idea of the super-cinema was a native of the town, while many senior men in A.P.P.H. were born locally. Walsall men had shown America how to build Picture Houses and when the history of cinematography came to be written Walsall would occupy a high and honourable place"

It is interesting to see the term "super-cinema" in use so early. The Picture House held one thousand five hundred patrons and was therefore a "super" in the numerical sense, but I think A.P.P.H. were referring to the luxury, refinement, good quality music, fine cafe and general "atmosphere" of their cinema when using the term.

The first film shown was called **"*Woman*"** and the orchestra provided musical accompaniment that included themes by Strauss, Wagner and Gounod. The orchestra's director was a Signor Cinganelli. The proceedings culminated in the presentation of a gift of £100 to the mayor by A.P.P.H. for the War Memorial Fund. (The Walsall Theatre Company immediately gave a similar amount!)

The Picture House confidently settled into its role in Walsall's life. It overlooked the principal town centre tram terminus and no doubt filled everyone with awe. The only distraction was a huge advertisement for the Imperial, and its programmes, standing alongside the Picture House's facade. When the cinema had been built the old City and Midland Bank buildings next door had been truncated and its new gable end was entirely devoted to the Imperial's advertisement!

Flooded foundations and war-time delays had no doubt been forgotten by 1923. On the evening of 1st September of that year the audience in the Picture House saw William S. Hart's film ***"Travellin' On"***. After the performance the manager, Mr. Pain, inspected the premises, locked up and went home. He was summoned early Sunday morning to find his sumptuous theatre was reduced to a wreck by fire. During the night a P.C. Lewis had smelt burning but could not locate the fire. He had aroused the landlord of the George, and the two men suddenly saw a tongue of flames shoot out of a ventilator cover on the cinema's roof. The Fire Brigade worked for an hour and a half bringing the fire under control, rescuing two kittens and damping down the wreckage.

Above : An architect's sketch of The Picture House, Walsall.   *(Kevin Wheelan)*

A.P.P.H. had now been absorbed by its associate P.C.T. and the company resolutely took up the task of rebuilding the Picture House. Once again it was built on a grand and luxurious scale. The new interior seemed brighter, and a rich Renaissance-style ceiling was added. Oak panelling was retained and the foyer still featured its old-time fireplace. The proscenium was flanked by two new electric pedestal lights, capable of flooding the entire stage in light and the screen could now be drawn up into a fly tower if the stage was required. At the same time, the seating capacity was increased to one thousand seven hundred. P.C.T. claimed it was second in size only to their Regent in Brighton. The Picture House opened, for the second time, on 26th December 1924, with **"Down to the Sea in Ships"** and once again it had been a great rush to have everything finished. Everyone worked all hours right up to the last minute.

After such an exciting career, Walsall's Picture House deserved the honour of being the first Black Country cinema to have a Wurlitzer installed, indeed, it was the first Wurlitzer in any British cinema. The two manual, six unit instrument was opened by Jack Courtney in 1925. The Picture House was also the first Walsall cinema to present the "talkies". *"The Singing Fool"* was shown on 26th August 1929 and the film drew massive queues to the cinema all week. The Picture House used the Western Electric system. P.C.T. eventually became part of Gaumont British and the cinema was fitted with the latest G.B. Kalee 21 projectors.

The name, "The Picture House", was retained until July 1948 and then it quietly became the Gaumont. Perhaps the name seemed more "modern". Despite the relative newness of the Savoy, the Gaumont still had its own special quality. Projectionist John McLeod, who joined the cinema just after its change of name, and who worked there for a decade, recalled:

"Of course, the Gaumont had one major advantage over other cinemas in Walsall: it possessed a restaurant, as well as a private room that could be hired for special occasions (The Oak Room). What a thrill it was to take that special girlfriend for a meal in the lush surroundings, before plying her with the most expensive box of chocolates, in the best seats. The seats at the front of the circle were like theatre-boxes with seats just for two."

Meanwhile the projectionists apparently flirted with the chambermaids from the George Hotel. The latter's quarters were clearly visible from the operating room and each party no doubt felt sympathy for others, each assigned to remote parts of buildings! During John McLeod's time in the operating room he saw the Wurlitzer taken out of the theatre. Its departure, in 1955, seemed to mark the beginning of the period of decline. He had often been able to sit at the organ's console on Sunday mornings and imagine the well known organists who had occupied the same seat; Arnold Loxam, Hubert Selby and Wilf Gregory. Like the organ at The Regal,

Darlaston, Walsall's Wurlitzer had starred in radio broadcasts. Today the organ is in the Congregational Church at Beer, Devon.

The Gaumont changed its name once again; on 22nd October 1965 it became the Odeon. Whether its fortunes would have declined, or whether it would have survived to this day, we shall never know because once again fire destroyed the building. Unfortunately the Odeon had not long been completely modernised. It had closed in May 1967 for the interior to be re-modelled at a cost of £70,000. New seats, carpets, new silver curtain, and a new larger screen were installed. The old timber fireplace in the foyer that survived the fire of 1923 was abandoned, the restaurant was rebuilt and even the marble pillars were replaced with Hoganas tiling. Two hundred and forty seats had been lost in the modernisation but it was still a reasonably sizeable theatre.

It "reopened" on 26th June 1967 with a special gala performance of **"Casino Royale"** and the manager, Philip Cross, probably felt confident that the much-renewed cinema would last for decades. The following week **"Privilege"** was screened and many young folk in Walsall went to see themselves or their friends appearing as "extras" in the parts of the film shot in Birmingham.

Less than four years later all the modernised interior was destroyed when fire broke out on the night of Tuesday 2nd March 1971. **"Hello Dolly"** was being presented that week, but the fire broke out while the cinema was empty. Eighty firemen from several Brigades tackled the dramatic fire, at the height of which, the roof caved in and collapsed. When Philip Cross was summoned to the scene he felt he was watching a nightmare. He went into the cinema's office to retrieve money and records while the auditorium still blazed. As before, the front of the cinema was relatively little affected.

It was one of the worst fires ever known in the centre of Walsall and it was a miracle that it did not spread to the Walsall Observer offices or the George Hotel. At first there seemed to be no evidence that it was anything but an accident but later a man was convicted for arson. From Bridge Street it seemed as if the Odeon was still in existence, although the frontage was partly boarded-up. Behind the facade the remains of the auditorium were demolished and thus it remained for a year or two until the site was sold and redeveloped. The Savoy/ABC, was thus left as Walsall's sole surviving cinema, and the Bridge Picture House, as it was often known, has passed into history.

The Empire

Freer Street, Walsall

After the opening of The Picture House in 1920 there was no further cinema building in the centre of Walsall for over a decade. The same could not be said of the other major Black Country towns, and it is interesting to wonder why this was so. The only genuine "super-cinema", of the style expected of the 1930's, to be built in the centre of Walsall was the Savoy, opened in 1938. The only town-centre cinema to open between 1920 and 1938 was the Empire.

The Empire was built on the site of Walsall's Temperance Hall in Freer Street. This building had been erected in 1866. In December 1931 a poorly attended farewell gathering was held in the hall, presided over by Alderman Joseph Leckie to mark the sale of the hall. He recalled the more active days of the Temperance Movement and the decline of the hall. The decline had followed the collapse of the roof about 1921. The Movement had never financially recovered after facing the cost of repairs. It was bought by a Mr. T. Jackson who set about turning the ruin into a new cinema at a cost of £13,500. Mr. T. Jackson was a resident of Bournemouth, not to be confused with Thomas Jackson, the Wolverhampton cinema proprietor who had ventured into Walsall at the De Luxe and the Palace.

The new cinema was designed by J. H. Hickton and the work was carried out by J. & F. Wootton, of Bloxwich. The frontage of the original building was used, but was totally transformed by a white cement facing over the brickwork, effectively contrasting with marble terrazzo steps and plinths. The pairs of handsome recessed swing doors replaced the old entrances. A raked floor had to be installed in the stalls, plus nine hundred upholstered seats. Three hundred such seats were positioned in the balcony. The walls and ceilings were decorated in eau de nil, ivory and gold, while each side wall contained six panels, each of which was filled with a landscape mural.

Mr. Jackson hoped to open the Empire on 24th August 1933, but in fact it opened the following Monday: 28th August 1933. Naturally it was built as a sound cinema, using the Western Electric system, and the opening programme featured the musical comedy, **"Letting In The Sunshine"**, directed by Lupino Lane. It was supported by **"Slightly Married"** described as a "ticklish comedy of married life" and Universal News. Although no organ was installed in the Empire the proprietors did the next best thing: they showed a short sound film of Jesse Crawford playing a Wurlitzer!

Mr. Jackson did not remain the proprietor of the Empire for very long. In February 1936 a film renter named Henry Smith introduced Mr. Jackson to Captain Clift as a would-be purchaser of the Empire. The negotiations ceased but were resumed in 1937, when Captain Clift finally agreed to purchase the Empire for £20,000. The

Empire then became part of the Clifton circuit. When the Rosum at Leamore was opened in 1936, and the De Luxe was acquired in 1939, the Clifton circuit had quite a presence in Walsall although the name "Clifton" never appeared there. The Empire and The Classic (one time De Luxe) shared newsreels during the War as a result of being part of the same circuit, but in many ways they seemed to pursue their independent ways.

Although The Empire was less prominent in Walsall's screen world than the Savoy/ABC or The Gaumont one manager, Gerald Palmer, later defended its position:

"Though an unpretentious cinema, it was popular with Walsall film-goers, and films like "The Seventh Veil", "The Blue Lamp" and "The Wicked Lady" were amomg those that made box-office records in the days when capacity houses were the rule rather than the exception. Diana Dors, as a Rank starlet, opened my Clifton Saturday Morning Childrens Club in 1948."

During the fifties patrons may have guessed that the Empire and the Rosum were part of the same circuit because both cinemas installed cinemascope simultaneously. The Empire brought *"The Robe"* to central Walsall on 4th October 1954, one day after the Rosum. Such was its success that it had to be brought back for a further run a few weeks later. The Empire was the first *town-centre* cinema in Walsall to present cinemascope.

Below: The Empire, Freer Street, Walsall, in 1964 on the eve of closure.

(Walsall Observer)

When Clifton cinemas started closing in the early sixties rumours began to circulate about the future of the Empire. Even managers were kept completely "in the dark" until the last moment. When *"Cleopatra"* was screened at the Empire on 24th October 1964 Clifton Cinemas would still not confirm or deny that the cinema was closing! In the event, that show was the last, and the cinema only remained empty and unused for a very short time. The Clifton Circuit often kept a cinema open right up to the moment when its future alternative ownership was confirmed. This often led to closures seeming very "abrupt". In February 1965 the buildng was demolished.

The area around Freer Street and Leicester Square has been fairly dramatically redeveloped and all trace of the Empire has disappeared.

The Savoy - ABC - Cannon

Town End Bank, Walsall

The history of Walsall's super-cinema begins with the history of its predecessor; Her Majesty's Theatre. The latter was opened by Sir William Pearman Smith in March 1900 for Walsall Theatre Company. Its bizarre architectural eclecticism dominated Town End Bank, at the top of Park Street. Two thousand people could be accommodated in this colossal structure, which had taken Messrs. Whittaker & Co., of Dudley, nearly four years to build. It was designed by Messrs. Owen and

Ward of Birmingham and had a suitably ornate interior and proscenium arch. The first show was *"The Belle Of New York"* and there followed many quality plays and pantomimes.

Leading actors of the day, such as John Forbes-Robinson and Laurence Irving came to Walsall to appear at Her Majesty's Theatre and when drama gave way to the popularity of Variety, Charlie Chaplin is said to have appeared there in *"Casey's Court"*. Like other theatres, Her Majesty's obtained a kine licence and occasionally showed films between variety acts. Their popularity led the proprietors to devote The Grand to showing films. Her Majesty's survived as a theatre until about 1933 but then spent most of its time showing films. Along with the other W.T.C. properties, it was acquired by ABC in April 1936. I assume their intention from the start was to demolish the building and replace it with a modern purpose-built super-cinema.

William Glen, ABC's principal architect, produced an elegant cinema that would dominate Town End Bank with its simple sweeping straightforwardness just as dramatically as the exotic theatre had done. Once again it was to be a large building, holding 1358 patrons in the stalls, and 811 in the circle. It was built by Messrs. Fox & Co. of Norton-on-Tees. There was some participation by the local architects Messrs. Hickton and Madeley.

Below: The Savoy, Walsall, in 1946.
(Kevin Wheelan)

The five pairs of swing doors across the semi-circular entrance to the cinema led the patron to a large foyer with a terrazzo floor. The walls and ceilings were pink with blue and gold relief. These colours were continued in the auditorium. Around the screen and proscenium arch there was a decorative scheme in dark blue and gold and the screen itself was draped in gold silk that rose in billowing festoons.

The new cinema, the Savoy, opened on 3rd October 1938 and the ceremony was performed by Walsall's Mayor, Dr. E.P. Drabble. He had opened the Avion at Aldridge a week or two earlier but gave this task a distinctive quality by welcoming Sir William Pearman Smith to the stage and recalling Sir William's similar function when the theatre had opened thirty-eight years before. The opening programme featured **"A Yank at Oxford"** starring Robert Taylor and Vivien Leigh. The Newsreel showed Mr. Chamberlain at Munich and the audience heard the Prime Minister's voice, via the wonders of the Western Electric Mirrophonic Sound, announce, on his return, that there would be peace in their time. The opening party then went off to a reception at the George Hotel.

The Savoy was the last cinema to open in Walsall, forgetting the Rex and the Showcase for a moment, and thus, the ABC circuit owned the first cinema in Walsall, the first purpose-built cinema in Walsall and the last purpose-built cinema in Walsall. Like many super-cinemas built by the major circuits towards the end of the thirties the Savoy has had a fairly uneventful history and suffered no major changes until the seventies.

The ABC's Minors Club started at the Savoy on 20th April 1948. On one of the annual celebrations of the club's anniversary, its eleventh, the cinema presented a premier of the N.C.F.F.'s production, **"The Cat Gang"**. Shows continued until 1980. The name "Savoy" was dropped in favour of ABC at the end of 1960, but such details do not add up to an exciting history!

The major event in the cinema's life came in 1973. During the summer it closed for three months for tripling. Screen 1 was the first to reopen as this made use of the balcony, now reduced in capacity to five hundred, and the existing projection box and screen. It opened on 30th September 1973 with **"Love Thy Neighbour"**. Screen 2, a 278 seater, and Screen 3, a 143 seater opened on Friday 16th November with **"Man At The Top"** and **"Scorpio"** respectively. On 17th November, the ABC re-started their Minors Club in Screen 1 and presented the first show free of charge.

A new manager, Mr. Alex Wright, took charge of the three screens and the tripling marked the departure of Mr. Frank Attoe. The latter had enjoyed quite a long association with the Black Country in several cinemas, while working for ABC. One assistant manager from this cinema moved on to greater things. Euan Lloyd became a successful film producer, making films like **"Shalako"** and **"The Wild Geese"**.

Like its fellow survivor, the ABC, Wolverhampton, it now was eventually equiped with modern Philips projectors and sound, and although the tripling changed the interior, the exterior was only slightly modified by the presence of a modern canopy.

By surviving the closures of the sixties and seventies, the cinema was able to make something of celebrating its forty fifth anniversary on 3rd October 1983. To mark the occasion Euan Lloyd returned to Walsall and two of his films, "Who Dares Wins", and "The Wild Geese" were given special screenings in Screen 3. Euan was keen to talk about forthcoming productions rather than his past in Walsall, but manager Bernard Riley kept everyone's attention on the historic nature of the event by producing a traditional cinema birthday cake.

In 1986 The ABC became The Cannon, like its counterpart in Wolverhampton. Everything seemed set to continue, but everything changed with the opening of the Showcase cinema at the nearby motorway junction in 1989. Seat prices at The Cannon were slashed to £1 to try and retain customers. Closure eventually seemed inevitable. When it was announced there was a 5000 signature petition produced demanding that the cinema be saved but the operations director of MGM, Cannon's parent company, insisted the cinema was no longer viable.

The Cannon closed on Thursday 18th November 1993, with three films to choose from: **"Rising Sun", "Tina", and "The Fugitive".** The advert in Thursday's Express & Star warned readers that this would be the final shows and their "last chance to see a feature film for £1".

Cannon had exercised quite a monopoly on local screens up until that point, but continued to show films at Wolverhampton, Quinton, and Cannock for a little while longer.

The Cannon was not demolished until the beginning of 1995. The area was cleared to make way for the Town Wharf Development, and to everyone's delight the building erected on the site of the former theatre and cinema was designed to recall architectural features of the earlier buildings. It was first occupied by Woolworths.

PICTURE-PLAY-HOUSE

THE GRASS ORPHAN | THURS to SAT | THE CRIMSON CHALLENGE

MATINEE at 2 O'CLOCK

Left: Two doormen stand outside the Picture Playhouse, Caldmore Green, Walsall, soon after the cinema opened. This was another Black Country cinema where the directors of the company were chaired by George Parker – the mysterious Birmingham entrepreneur. Mr. Parker was also associated with The Scala, Stourbridge where the owners also flirted with the name "Picture Playhouse". (V.J. Bulman collection)

Out in Walsall's Suburbs.

The Caldmore Green Picture Playhouse later known as The Forum

Caldmore Green, Walsall

Caldmore Green is one of those fringe areas of a town that neither belongs to the centre nor to the outer suburbs. Yet it has a confident identity of its own, perhaps to be compared with places like Blakenhall and Whitmore Reans in Wolverhampton, both of which supported their own cinemas.

The Caldmore Green Picture Playhouse unceremoniously opened some time in November or December 1915. The first show advertised in the Walsall Observer was *"Life's Highway"* which commenced on 27th December, but in the same issue of the paper as the advertisement was the report, *"Opened*

a few weeks ago, the Caldmore Green Picture Playhouse is achieving great success, and large audiences have been delighted with the atmosphere of cosiness and warmth which pervades the hall".

Manager Harry Parr was in charge of the cinema, which could seat up to eight hundred patrons. Its name was not quite such a mouthful when one remembers the name of the district is always pronounced "Karma Green". However it later abbreviated its name to Caldmore Green Picture House. Like many others, it boasted, throughout the twenties, that it had the finest screen in the Midlands and showed the "Best Selected Masterpieces". It also claimed that it was easily reached by tram from Darlaston and West Bromwich and may well have drawn patrons from a wide area.

It is not clear whether the cinema was purpose-built or converted from an existing building. Probably it was a case of building a purpose-built auditorium, and creating an entrance by converting existing retail premises. The auditorium was at right angles to the foyer and main entrance which faced the Green. The auditorium had no balcony but the rear seats were separately raked in the "stadium" style. The projection room was approximately level with the screen.

On 14th April 1930 BTH sound equipment came into use, making Caldmore Green's little cinema the second in Walsall to introduce the "talkies". The following year it was acquired by Sheridan Film Services and changed its name to the Forum on 24th December 1931. The same company also acquired the Alhambra, Dudley Port, at about the same time. Later, both cinemas were transferred from Sheridan Film Services to S.T. Cinemas when Mr. Suffolk went into partnership with Mr. Thornton.

All went well for a time, but eventually events overtook the Forum. After the Second World War the Forum found itself very much "the last in line" and films had been seen at practically every other local cinema by the time they reached Caldmore Green. Mr. Suffolk opted for older films, that had the added virtue of being cheaper, but the resulting poor programmes drove patrons away.

In 1950 Mr. Suffolk appointed Frank Harvey as manager and gave him a month to study the cinema and report on its state. Frank Harvey had enjoyed a distinguished career in the projection rooms of the Odeon circuit. He had been at Wolverhampton Odeon from its opening in 1937 until coming to the Forum. Little wonder he found the place very "run down" by comparison. Apart from recognising the results of poor programming, Frank Harvey also recognised the folly of charging five different prices for seats ranging from 1/6 to 3/-. The prices were also too high.

As it happened, Mr. Suffolk sold both the Alhambra, Dudley Port, and the Forum at the end of 1951, and the new proprietor allowed the manager to institute some reforms. The new proprietor was Horace Miller from Leicester. He booked better programmes and later passed that responsibility to Frank Harvey. Meanwhile, the latter had introduced a two price system, seats for 1/- and 1/6. Matters greatly improved straight away. Even the family audience returned and queues were seen in Caldmore Green for popular films like *"Seven Brides for Seven Brothers"*.

Horace Miller then set about improving the Forum. He installed a new wide screen and new proscenium arch. A colour lighting system complemented the new silver satin curtains. The BTH equipment was removed and the latest G.B. Kalee 20 projectors with President arcs were installed plus G.B. Duosonic Sound. All the work was entirely carried out over one weekend between Saturday night and the Monday performance! With its fine modern equipment it could now legitimately claim "The Brightest Screen In The Midlands", and with its energetic manager, often present in the foyer, in the grand tradition, the Forum continued to prosper through that difficult era. Frank Harvey left in 1958 and Horace Miller sold the cinema to Vincent Wareing. It closed for

a fortnight in June 1958, presumably coinciding with the change of ownership.

Vincent Wareing's excursion into the Black Country did not go well. As well as the Forum, he acquired the Palace, Great Bridge, and the Coliseum and Olympia Wolverhampton. In all these cases he found himself running cinemas which were rapidly declining in patronage. Sadly, the Forum showed its last film on 28th May 1960. It closed with *"Northwest Frontier"*. Today, the auditorium is a warehouse for the Walsall Lithographic Company. The foyer became a restaurant but suffered a fire in 1979, but was rebuilt to provide offices for the local housing association. The canopy and arched brickwork over the windows of the manager's office still suggest the presence of an ex-cinema.

The Rosum

Leamore

Half way between Walsall and Bloxwich the trams, and later the trolleybuses passed through Leamore. In the mid thirties, Edgar Summers, a local accountant, felt that this was an ideal spot for a super-cinema. It was to be called the Rosum, named after his wife, Rose Summers. To find the necessary funds, Edgar Summers joined forces with Sidney Clift and the architect, Ernest Roberts, to form Rosumclift Cinemas Ltd.

Planning and construction followed very quickly. Legend has it that the plans produced by Ernest Roberts were identical to the plans of the Clifton, Wellington. The legend goes on to make this "fact" responsible for periodic flooding of the cinema's boiler rooms, as the Rosum was built on sloping ground, apparently quite different from the Clifton's site! Work began in December 1935 and the Rosum was completed in about eight months by J. & F. Wootton of Bloxwich. In fact, it was ready about ten days before the opening.

The building stands flush with its neighbours, with a portico over the street. The frontage was white stone, later painted grey. Its simplicity reflected a "modern" style that was also to be found in the interior, but looked imposing when beautified by neon lighting. Above the three double swing doors the cinema's name appeared, occupying the position where the balcony foyer's windows were normally to be found on a Satchwell and Roberts cinema.

The auditorium, with its fine sweeping lines of plain plaster work by Bryan's Adamanta, held 808 patrons in the stalls and 392 patrons in the balcony. Turner's tip up seats were provided in three different shades of upholstery and the effect, looking back across the hall from the stage was a series of diagonal rows of each particular colour. Up in the projection room, the new "chief operator", Bill Lockett, who had come from the

Left: The Rosum at Leamore decorated for the Coronation of Elizabeth II in June 1953. (Doug Withers)

Grosvenor, found BTH projection and sound equipment. In nearly all respects it was a typical "Clifton" cinema.

Invitations were dispatched for the Rosum's opening on 24th August 1936. The ceremony was to be performed by Walsall's Mayor, Councillor Fletcher, and the Houston Sisters, the stars of the first film. At 5.30 p.m. on the great day the Houston Sisters had not arrived. The GPO provided a land line to loudspeakers in the auditorium and the audience could hear the Scottish accent of Renee Houston speaking from Leicester Square in London. "Hello Walsall", she said, "We are very proud that our picture has been chosen to open the Rosum".

The audience had to be satisfied with the presence on stage of Councillor Fletcher, Edgar Summers, Captain Clift and Ernest Roberts! In the audience was Pat Collins, fairground showman and sometime cinema proprietor. The ceremony was followed by Mark Stone and Ida Barr, live on stage, and eventually the Houston Sisters' film *"Happy Days Are Here Again"* on the screen. A film was made of the opening and this was shown in the cinema on the next three anniversaries of the event. The film still exists today in Walsall History Centre's local collection.

Leamore's cinema was a success and fully justified Edgar Summers' hopes. Sometimes the programmes

enjoyed a local success for local reasons. For example, a film called *"Black Diamonds"* did well because the manager, Percy Rogers, exploited the local interest in coal-mining, and used tubs and track from a local pit to put on a promotional display. The Rosum also used its limited stage facilities to occasionally mount variety acts or bands to complement some films. The Great Nixon, who also visited the Regal, Wednesfield, came to the Rosum and stayed with Bill Lockett and his wife. They learned no secrets of his mind reading act.

The Rosum continued to prosper through the War, with female staff in the operating room. When Mr. Lockett returned from the services in 1947 he was offered the icecream business! On Sunday 3rd October 1954 the Rosum introduced Cinemascope to Walsall with *"The Robe "*. The adaptation to cinemascope was undertaken at the same time as The Empire in Freer Street.

Things began to decline in the sixties and Bingo was introduced on Tuesday and Friday nights for a time. The Star Group expressed an interest in buying the Rosum, but it took some time to agree to the terms of sale. Eventually the Star Group acquired both the Rosum and the Clifton, Wolverhampton. The last film was shown on 16th April 1966 and was *"Mary Poppins".* As soon as the last film was re-wound, the contractors moved in to convert the interior for use as a full-time Bingo and Social Club.

Bingo started on 21st April 1966 and continued for nearly forty years. It became an EMI Bingo and Social Club in March 1975 and the auditorium remained preserved although the canopy was eventually removed, which further emphasised the plainess of the Rosum's frontage. The building still dominates Leamore, but excited patrons no longer cross the road and queue in the elegant trolleybus waiting shelter on the opposite side of the road. Nevermind, the last trolleybus ran in 1970. Today even Bingo is a thing of the past and in recent years the cinema building has been a "Farm Produce" freezer centre.

The Rex and The Raj

Stafford Street, Walsall

Indian films were first shown in Walsall at the Imperial in 1965 on Sunday mornings and at the ABC. Their success led Surinder Kumar to investigate the possibility of creating a cinema specifically for that purpose.

In 1974 St. Patrick's Church Hall, Stafford Street, was acquired and planning permission was obtained to convert the building into a cinema. This revived the ancient tradition of converting such buildings into cinemas! A raked floor was installed, which pushed the rear seats well towards the ceiling and a small operating room was built over the entrance. Two ancient BTH machines came to life every Sunday until video enticed the audience away and shows were abandoned in 1981. It was called The Rex but the name did not appear on the building. I enjoyed one conducted tour of the building during the summer of 1980, which gave me the impression of time-travelling back to the fifties and venturing into a village "flea-pit".

In 1977 Tarsem Singh Dhami planned to build a four hundred seater cinema at Pleck on the site of the Bescott Petrol Station. It was an ambitious project which would have created a brand new purpose-built cinema as part of a community centre. It would have shown English language and Indian films but was continually opposed by Walsall Council. It would have enjoyed that most princely of names: The Raj.

The Rex, Walsall, 1981 (N.Williams)

Above: The Rosum, on Bingo, in 1981.

The Showcase Cinema

The Black Country's second multi-plex is just inside the Walsall boundary and therefore quailfies to be described here while we tour "outer Walsall". When the cinema was first advertised the proprietors did not quite seem to know where their new cinema was? Was it in Bentley? Darlaston? Walsall? All these places were mentioned. The truth was, that as far as the American proprietors were concerned it was at Junction 10 on the M6 Motorway. It was if they had spread out a map of the West Midlands on a desk in their offices in Boston, focussed on the motorway network, and decided that Junction 10 was within easy reach of about two million people. They may have been encouraged to select this location by the Black Country Development Corporation, who needed new businesses come and occupy their territory. Like all land assembled by BCDC there was a large element of contamination to deal with, and the presence of mine shafts. However, the Corporations job was to face these challenges and bring such areas back into use.

National Amusements already had three multi-plexes running in Britain by the time thay had embarked on the project at Junction 10. (Nottingham, Derby and Peterborough). The cinema at Junction 10 was to have twelve screens – two screens more than the multi-plex at Merry Hill. National Screen Amusements also claimed that their patent "rocking seat" made their cinemas more comfortable than those of their competitors. Dolby stereo sound, and large screens were also going to demonstrate the high standards that a multi-plex cinema could now expect to reach. The cinema was built by Messrs. Bowmer & Kirkland, who had built the first thee, Showcase cinemas, and was designed by the Abbey Hanson Rowe Partnership, based in Shrewsbury.

The new multi-plex at Junction 10 was opened by the Mayor of Walsall, Councillor Reg Farrell, and Ira A. Korff, the company's Chief Executive, at a special evening gala presentation on 24th August 1989. The film shown was **"Mystic Pizza"**, starring Julia Roberts. The cinema opened to the public on the next day.

Above: "Showcase Cinemas", at Junction 10 on the M6 motorway, near Walsall, waiting for the first patrons on 25th. August 1989.

Left: One of the twelve screens at The Showcase featuring the famous "rocking" chairs.

Bottom left: The first paying customers arrive at the modern style paybox at The Showcase (Ned Williams) on Friday morning 25th August 1989. Films include "The Return of the Musketeers", "The Karate Kid", "Police Academy 6", "Bull Durham", "Kick Boxer", "Land Before Time, "Three Fugitives" "Batman" and "The Three Fugitives". The author, who had bought the first ticket, was thrown out of the cinema after taking this picture. Permission for photography could only be granted from Head Office in Boston.
(Ned Williams)

Bloxwich

Bloxwich was, for many years, in the Foreign of Walsall, and in terms of the history of modern local government, never enjoyed the kind of independence that Wednesfield experienced in relation to Wolverhampton. Nevertheless, it was a community that was proud of its own history and identity and tended to feel "separate" from Walsall.

Professor Wood brought his "animated pictures" to Bloxwich and presented them in the hall that had once been the Sunday School behind the Wesley an chapel in Park Road, in the early years of this century. He reappears in the history of Bloxwich's cinemas later and joins the familiar names of the other men who showed films in Bloxwich: Thomas Jackson, Pat Collins and Oscar Deutsch!

The Electric Palace

165 High Street, Bloxwich

The Electric Palace was opened by Alhambra Picture Palaces Ltd., a company established by Thomas Jackson to open The Alhambra, Bilston, and this one in Bloxwich, following his first steps into the cinema business at the Strand in Whitmore Reans, Wolverhampton. It was a small hall, holding four hundred patrons, and it is not clear whether it was a conversion of an existing building or was purpose-built. The earliest show I have found advertised for the Electric Palace was for Monday 30th December 1912, when *"Romance of the Coast"* was being screened.

Therefore it would appear to have opened early in December 1912 – more or less at the same time as its counterpart in Bilston. It seems likely that the cinema consisted of an auditorium clad corrugated iron, with a brick-built frontage housing the entrance and foyer.

The cinema may not have been a great success, or the facilities simply inadequate, because it closed the following Spring for some improvements to be made! It reopened on 12th May 1913, with *"Quo Vadis".* The Walsall Observer reported, *"Extensive alterations have been carried out in the building, and a balcony has been provided, no expense being spared to ensure the comfort of patrons."* Perhaps the addition of a balcony indicates that the venture was actually successful.

From that date onwards shows were presented twice nightly, with matinees on Mondays, Tuesdays and Wednesdays. Seats cost 2d, 3d and 4d downstairs, or 6d and 9d in the balcony: a bewildering range of prices for a small cinema. Thomas Jackson formed a new company in 1913 called Wolverhampton, Walsall and District Cinemas and the Bloxwich Electric Palace became part of the empire of the new company.

Towards the end or just after the First World War the cinema was sold to Pat Collins, who was making Bloxwich the headquarters of his fairground organisation at about the same time. It was also a time when Pat Collins was acquiring various cinemas, including two others in the Black Country. Pat Collins "diversified" during and after the First World War and "started again" by making Bloxwich his home and headquarters. As this little cinema was "right on his doorstep" it seems that he quickly resolved to turn it into a flagship cinema in a brand new building.

The last film shown in the Electric Palace was *"The Tatters",* screened on Saturday 3rd December 1921. It was then demolished to make way for Pat Collins's brand new cinema; the Grosvenor.

Below: The Electric Palace, Bloxwich.

The Grosvenor, later known as The Odeon

High Street, Bloxwich

Pat Collins obviously wished to build a cinema of which he could feel proud in his adopted home of Bloxwich. His new cinema was to be called The Grosvenor, and was designed by Hickton and Farmer of Walsall, and built by J. & F. Wootton, at a cost of £12,000. While it was being built, Pat Collins showed films at The Central, as described later. Messrs. Hickton & Farmer had designed about thirty cinemas since 1910 and the Grosvenor was a very pleasing example of their work. The early twenties produced some very attractive Black Country cinemas even if the trade was going through uncertain times.

The frontage of the Grosvenor was treated in a classical style, finished in Hathernware terracotta. It was built to hold a thousand patrons. Four swing doors gave access to a reasonably spacious entrance hall with staircases on each side to the balcony floor. It was opened on 11th December 1922 and Lady Arthur Grosvenor, of Chester, came along to perform the ceremony. Ironically, Pat Collins, who had just become Walsall's M.P., could not be present. Lady Grosvenor praised her absent friend and admired the hall. The Mayor of Walsall, and Rev. Father H. McDonnell also spoke, and the latter expressed the hope that Pat would make his way to the House of Lords, to become Lord Bloxwich! The film that followed was *“The Three Musketeers”*, and the proceeds enabled £26.00 to be sent to Walsall Y.M.C.A.

Below: The Grosvenor, Bloxwich

(John Maltby)

The operators found themselves working in fairly cramped circumstances in a room at the back of the stalls, crammed between the staircases. Legend has it that tall patrons could cast a shadow across the screen! In 1929 Pat Collins appointed young Bill Lockett as third operator and in the 1980s Mr. Lockett could remember the sound-on-disc system coming to the Grosvenor in July 1930. Western Electric equipment was used and *"Innocents of Paris"* brought the talkies to Bloxwich on 14th July.

Maintaining the arcs while setting up discs and dealing with reel changes every ten minutes made life difficult in the small operating box. Life became much easier in December 1931 when sound-on-film arrived and twenty minutes worth of film was put on one spool. The new equipment was inaugurated on Boxing Day with the film *"To Oblige A Lady"*.

Pat Collins continued to run the Grosvenor several years after selling his other two Black Country cinemas, but in 1935 he sold it to Oscar Deutsch and it became an Odeon on 17th July of that year. A number of independent cinemas became Odeons at this time – including Woods Palace in Bilston, and the Dunstall Cinema, Wolverhampton. As an Odeon it survived the round of closures that put several old cinemas to death in 1956, but three years later it was sold to a Sunderland firm engaged in light industry. The company acquired the Picture House, Willenhall, at the same time. The last film *"Operation Amsterdam"*, was shown on 2nd May 1959, just before celebrations were being organised locally to celebrate the centenary of Pat Collins' birth.

The building has survived. For many years it became increasingly dilapidated, but at the end of the 1970s it was transformed. The original frontage was been given a face lift, but in essence was "preserved", and the premises then operated as a discotheque-styled nightclub using the name "Flix". After the nightclub venture ceased the building went through several other uses before becoming a youth centre.

Below: Pat Collins and his manager on the steps of The Grosvenor just before the opening in 1922. *(Author's collection)*

Right: The interior of The Grosvenor, Bloxwich, photo-graphed by John Maltby as the time that the cinema was brought into the Odeon circuit.

Below: The ex-chapel building used as "The Central", Bloxwich, photographed in 1981. (Ned Williams)

The Central

Park Road, Bloxwich

Not long after the opening of the Electric Palace a local company was formed called the Bloxwich Picture Company. It was registered on 2nd June 1913, with a capital of £2,000. The directors were Samuel Wilkes, Jonah Wilkes, A. J. Wilkes, J. F. W. Binns and Jesse and Frederick Wootton, the builders. Many of the remaining shares were bought by the employees in Samuel Wilkes' lock works.

The company intended to build a cinema more or less on the site of Professor Wood's early shows, referred to earlier. In Park Road a large Wesleyan chapel, built in 1838, had been made redundant by the erection of a more modern chapel elsewhere. By extending this chapel backwards to include the Sunday school building visited by Professor Wood, it was possible to produce a cinema capable of holding five hundred patrons. A raked floor was put in and a small stage provided facilities for cine-variety. Naturally, the work was carried out by J. & F. Wootton.

As the Central Picture Palace it must have opened late in 1913 and one Harry Morris found himself managing the new rival to the Electric Palace. During 1915 and 1916 it was leased to Tom Wood and to some local people it is remembered as the Central, to others it is remembered as "Woods Palace". Harry Gilmore managed the cinema about this time. Harry later worked at the Alexandra Theatre in Birmingham for Leon Salberg where he did fourteen seasons as the pantomime cat! He was a talented set painter. He died in Bloxwich in March 1959 at the age of 77. By the end of the War the original company seemed to have resumed showing the films.

It may have then closed for a short time because on 5th December 1921 we find that it was "reopened" by Pat Collins who wished to continue showing films in Bloxwich while the Grosvenor was being built. Pat Collins' shows continued for exactly one year and the Central closed just before the Grosvenor opened.

Pat Collins then used the Central as a store and a place where his fairground rides could be repaired. In 1937 it was sold to Bert Britain who converted it to a garage. It was then used by Mid Air equipment, and has been in industrial use ever since. The frontage of the cinema, which was basically the frontage of the original chapel, has remained almost unchanged. One interesting story concerning the Central tells of the tomb of two children buried beneath the central aisle when the raked floor was installed. They were the children of a Wesleyan minister, and they had died of diphtheria. When Bert Britain removed the raked floor in 1937 he discovered their grave. He had them removed and reburied in a more suitable place to everyone's satisfaction.

279

Willenhall

Travelling anticlockwise around Walsall from Bloxwich one encounters the towns of Willenhall, Darlaston and Wednesbury, the latter now being in Sandwell. The development of the tramway system tied them to Walsall but they are not in any way "suburbs" of Walsall. Each has a distinct history of its own. Willenhall is particularly associated with the manufacture of locks and relishes the nickname "Humpshire" in memory of the locksmiths bent over their tasks. By the beginning of this century both Willenhall and Darlaston were "Urban Districts" each with a population of about 20,000. Cinemas were quickly provided to serve this population.

Willenhall's cinema history is one in which each successive cinema strives to be better than the one it hopes to replace, although little record survives of the first two enterprises.

The White City

Hall Street, Willenhall

Soon after the passing of the Cinematograph Act Fred Redfern opened Willenhall's first cinema in a disused Catholic Church in Hall Street. It had been abandoned when the Catholics moved to a new church, but returned to life as "The White City". It had a balcony and claimed to be capable of holding 700 patrons.

Short films were punctuated with variety acts, some of which were organised as local talent competitions, with prizes for the performer who gained the loudest applause. Teddy Hall assisted Mr. Redfern as the White City generally did good business. It was unpretentious but was not particularly daunted by the opening of the Coliseum. The top of the picture at the Coliseum struck the low ceiling and the White City made much of this by claiming that their films were projected entirely on the screen! It seems to have closed sometime during the First World War, after the new Picture House had raised local expectations of what a cinema should be. The name is still a legend in Willenhall, although the building was demolished sometime ago, after further life as a steel stock-holding warehouse.

The Gomer Street Hall

The White City was not Willenhall's only experience of early cinematography. Another hall was used for magic lantern shows and early films in Gomer Street. It was to be found next to the Falcon Inn and was possibly a former chapel. When A.P.P.H. opened their cinema in Stafford Street some local residents were careful to call it the *New* Picture House, to distinguish it from this older one. It seems likely, however, by that time films were no longer being shown in Gomer Street.

The Coliseum and The Dale

Bilston Street, Willenhall

The Coliseum was the first cinema in Willenhall worthy of being described as such! It was opened about 1913 or 1914 by Mr. H. Johnson, and used a barn-like building close to Dale House, the home of the Hinks Family. A smart foyer was built in which flowers and mirrors created a favourable impression on the patrons, but the single floored auditorium was still very barn-like and its low ceiling has already been mentioned. Not only was the top of the picture hitting the ceiling but the audience also seemed to suffer the noise from the projector. At first a pianist competed with the buzz from the machines but he was later replaced by a gramaphone.

The "Collie", as it was known, held about 400 patrons. It ran popular childrens matinees and Mr. Johnson distributed little conicle bags of sweets to his young customers paying a penny on the benches or tuppence for a seat. Each week one sweet bag contained a sixpence! Mr. Johnson's son acted as projectionist and a great time was had by all.

When the Picture House opened, the Coliseum was partially eclipsed, just as the White City had been. After the War Thomas Wood presented the programmes, advertising it as Wood's Coliseum until July 1921. It was acquired by Herbert Anthony but Thomas Wood continued to advise and assist with the bookings. About 1925 a Mr. Samson tried his hand at running it for a year or two and then it passed to a Mr. and Mrs. Campbell.

Mrs. Campbell was very business-like and ran the box office. It seems that they ran the Collie until its demise. The talkies arrive at the Picture House and the future looked bleak. Then the last member of the Hinks Family, a Mrs. Price, died and the entire estate, including Dale House and the cinema, were put up for sale. The Coliseum closed its trellis gate for the last time in 1931 or early in 1932.

The premises were purchased by John Tyler, a successful plumber and builder and decorator supplier in Willenhall. John Tyler, and his daughter Norah, were keen to build a brand new super-cinema on the site of the Coliseum and the malt-house at the back of Dale House. In continuing the endless competition between each of Willenhall's successive cinemas this was to be finer than the Picture House and was inspired by Mr. Tyler's admiration for Wood's Palace. It would seem that the Tylers took on the Coliseum as a "going concern" as documents in the Country Record Office include notes by the County Architect to the effect that Norah Tyler was "proprietor" of The Coliseum as late as January 1932.

Plans for the new cinema, the Dale, were therefore prepared by Mr. Hurley Robinson and it is believed to have been built by Messrs. J. & F. Wootton. To make good use of the site the Dale had to abandon the usual concept of a grand frontage, and the entrance and foyer extended from the main auditorium towards the corner of Dimingsdale and Bilston Street, like a snake emerging from a basket. The auditorium held one thousand, one hundred and fifty patrons in attractive surroundings. The balcony held 275 patrons.

The Dale was opened on Monday 31st October 1932 with **"Viennese Nights"** in Technicolour and the wonders of Western Electric sound. The ceremony was performed by Councillor J.H. Harper, Chairman of Willenhall U.D.C. The entire proceeds of this matinee, nearly £51, were donated to the local Nursing Association. A packed cinema heard Councillor Evans of the Licensing Committe claim that the Tylers had created a cinema worthy of the richest corporations. John Tyler became a director of the Dunstall Cinema Company, and both cinemas were proud of their independence, though John Tyler did not live long to enjoy them.

The Dale passed to his daughter, Norah Tyler, but she died in 1945. The Dale was then acquired by Messrs. J.L. and A.H. Brain who had just acquired the Avion cinema at Aldridge (26th September 1938 to 30th December 1967). From then on the fortunes of the Dale and the Avion were linked. The new owners left the Dale in the capable hands of the manager, Arthur Holland, who had come from Bilston's Theatre Royal.

The Dale and the Avion closed on the same day, 30th December 1967, with *"Lt. Robinson Crusoe"*. The closure also brought an end to Sunday shows of Indian films, organised by Tarsem Singh Dhami. It had outlived the Picture House and was a fine cinema so many Willenhall people were sad to see it close. A few protests were made by local councillors about its conversion to a Bingo Club, but, nevertheless, it opened for Bingo on 16th February 1968.

Bingo was still being played in the Dale in the 1980s. Despite some alterations, the auditorium and many details of the building still had a strong cinema-like atmosphere, and all the seats in the balcony were retained.

After Bingo had come and gone, The Dale was redeveloped as a Weatherspoon's pub in the mid 1990s. Many details of the building as a cinema have been retained.

Below: The Dale, Willenhall, photographed by Bennett Clarke about 1945. The use of the corner site to produce an elegantly curved entrance is clearly seen.
(Wolverhampton Archives)

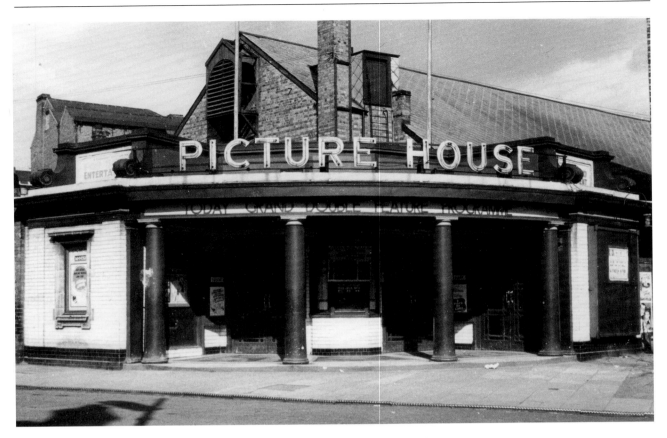

Above: The Picture House, Willenhall, photographed just after the Second World War. (Bob Hosier)

The Picture House

Stafford Street, Willnehall

The cinemas built by A.P.P.H. were usually intended to introduce a grandeur and respectability to cinema-going in the towns they selected. In Walsall and Wolverhampton perhaps there was a middle class and affluent class of artisans ready to respond. Perhaps the situation in Willenhall was different. Whatever the reason, Willenhall's Picture House was relatively modest. It was small, only holding 736 patrons and was never quite finished!

The First World War had begun as construction was getting underway and the cafe and shops that should have complimented its frontage were never built. The entrance and foyer never effectively concealed the outline of the auditorium but patrons have told me that the interior was elegant and dignified. It opened on 19th April 1915.

After the War, in 1919, the Picture House was used to present local war heroes with clocks and watches as a token of the town's esteem. The male contribution to the War was reflected in the fact that the manager, Mr. Astbury, had to appoint a lady, Edith Johnson, as the chief operator. She remembers the cinema being called "the New'un" at the time to distinguish itself from "the owd'un" in Gomer Street.

From 1920 to 1926 The Picture House used the services of a young violinist named Ebenezer James Lloyd. He was always in great demand and also played at Woods Palace in Bilston, the Picturedrome, Darlaston and the Queens, Wolverhampton. It is easy to forget how a good quality musician could really act as a draw to the audience in silent film days.

As a result of A.P.P.H. being absorbed by its associate P.C.T. the cinema became part of a large national circuit, even if it was only a minor outpost of one. R.C.A. sound equipment was installed in 1929 and the first talkie in Willenhall was *"Black Waters"*. The film was presented for three days commencing 11th November 1929. One young lady who jumped the queue to get in to see it felt the picture was appropriately murky and could not understand where the sound was coming from!

The film that everyone was waiting to see was *"The Singing Fool"* and that was presented for the second three days of that week which meant that some keen Willenhall film fans had already dashed over to Bilston to see it at Woods Palace where it had been playing since the Monday. Woods Palace and the Picture House, Willenhall, often seemed to be competing with one another. At the former, films usually played for six days, but the Picture House favoured two three-day programmes per week. Woods Palace responded by changing its supporting film half way through the week! Through the thirties and forties, Willenhall was well served by the Picture House and the Dale, and queues were common irrespective of how many patrons were tempted by films in Bilston, Wolverhampton, or Walsall!

When Sunday opening started in Willenhall the Picture House was allowed to present films on a Sunday providing, *"....a film on Road Safety, Public Health, National or Local Government Services, or a religious subject, shall be included in at least every fourth programme."* (This is recorded in the archives of Rank Organisation licensing records in Cinema Theatre Association Archive.)

By the mid- fifties, the Rank Organisation, who had inherited ex P.C.T. halls via Gaumont British, were beginning to close their smaller and older cinemas. The Picture House was a victim of the same "rationalisation plan" as the Odeon, Bloxwich. It closed on 2nd May 1959, with ***"Storm Over the Nile"*** The same firm bought both cinemas.

Sometime later it was demolished, and a supermarket was then built on the site.

Darlaston

Darlaston is a typical industrial community of the Black Country. Until recently 85% of its working population was engaged in the manufacturing industry. Large firms like Rubery Owen and GKN dominated its well-being until recent unemployment has turned such a world "topsy-turvy". Ironically the centre of Darlaston has gone through its first major redevelopment just as jobs have disappeared. It is therefore difficult to visit Darlaston and imagine the busy factory-dominated town that existed as its first cinemas came into existence.

Darlaston Wake welcomed many of the great travelling shows of the late nineteenth century – some of which will be described in Volume Two. Pat Collins soon brought the Darlaston fairs under his control in the 1890s and his bioscope shows would have come to Darlaston in the first decade of the twentieth century.

The Queen's Hall

Willenhall Street, Darlaston

As in other similar towns, films were first shown in Darlaston in permanent buildings in the local "variety hall"; the Queen's Hall. The building was on the site of a Wesleyan Sunday School, or was a conversion of that building, and had been in business since the 1890's. "Animated Pictures" were presented between variety acts before the passing of the Cinematograph Act, and subsequently the Queen's Hall obtained a kine licence.

One elderly resident of Darlaston recalls that the films were projected from a make-shift platform erected above the paybox at the rear of the hall. He also recalls that the evening's show included variety acts, melodrama and films. Perhaps its greatest claim to fame is that Billy Russell, the Black Country comedian, worked there about 1910.

It is not clear who owned the Queen's Hall; one record says it was a Manchester firm, another says it was Ben Kennedy. Nor is it clear when the hall closed. Shows probably ceased at the end of, or just after, the First World War. If the Queen's Hall had any rival in claiming to show the first films in Darlaston, it would be Professor Wood. He probably visited the Town Hall once a year as his winter tour brought him through the Black Country.

Left: Parkes & Mainwaring produced three colour bills for local independent cinemas such as this crowded advertsiement for the Picturedrome's triple progreamme week in August 1953.

The Picturedrome

Crescent Road, Darlaston

Darlaston's two pre-First World War cinemas opened within a few months of each other in 1911, and both have histories that have been relatively obscure and difficult to trace. The Picturedrome appears to have been purpose-built and was an imposing building. Its dome was a feature of the Darlaston skyline for many years and its white plastered frontage was most impressive. Its arch-roofed auditorium could hold up to nine hundred patrons.

The local magistrates issued a licence for the Picturedrome on 24th May 1911 and the cinema must have opened straight away, or in June. Although no record of the opening has been found, the Walsall Observer later mentions the cinema in connection with local Coronation festivities.

"On Monday (26th June 1911) about 550 children attending the Central School visited the new Picturedrome in Darlaston where a special programme of pictures, including some fine films of the Coronation procession, were shown. The scholars thoroughly enjoyed themselves and further batches of children from other schools visited the Picturedrome during the week."

Below: A postcard view of The Crescent, Darlaston, before the First World War, provides us with a good view of The Picturedrome as bulit. (Ken Rock)

The new cinema became known as "the Drome", and was probably owned and run by a George Williams. In 1922 he sold it to Mr. Brettell of the Hockley Picture House Company, thus beginning the Brettell family's long association with cinema entertainment in Darlaston. Mr. Brettell and Mr. Olliver later formed Colmore Entertainments, running the Picturedrome for the rest of its life and building the Regal in Pinfold Street.

The Olympia just managed to introduce talkies to Darlaston ahead of the Drome, but Western Electric equipment was installed in the autumn of 1930 and the two cinemas competed on equal terms once more. In the end, the Olympia was the first to close! In the summer of 1956 the Picturedrome was refurbished by Modernisation Ltd., and the proscenium was widened to accommodate cinemascope and wide screen presentation. It certainly looked smart for its final battle for survival. Leslie Taff managed both the Picturedrome and the Regal in their final years.

Unfortunately, the Picturedrome closed on 2nd February 1959 with **"Escort West"** and **"Guns, Girls and Gangsters".** The building was not demolished until the late summer of 1963 and the site is now a car park. A short service road crosses the car park to the rear of the shops in King Street. In 1981 one of the three names being considered by Walsall Council for this road was Picturedrome Way. There is a Danilo Road in Cannock but I do not think any other Black Country road has been named after a cinema.

Right: This picture, taken in August 1963, shows The Picture-drome, Darlaston in its final form, shorn of its dome, and its decorated frontage It was demolished soon after this picture was taken. (Howard Madeley).

The Olympia

Blockall, Darlaston

The Olympia, known as "the Limp", also has origins clouded in mystery. The locally held opinion that it opened very shortly after the Picturedrome is borne out by a short report in the Express and Star, at the time of its closure, stating that the first film, ***"Death Before Disaster"*** was shown on 15th October 1911. Unfortunately I have found no other documented verification of this.

Part of the site was once occupied by the Bell Street Chapel and the Trustees of this Chapel were given permission to sell the site in March 1910. A large "L" shaped building was erected, the short "base" of the "L" forming the entrance to the larger part of the building. It seems to have been erected by a Mr. Laycock who intended opening it as a skating rink. It never opened for that purpose, and in July 1912 a new company was formed by Mr. Laycock, and a partner, to take over the premises in the name of Olympia (Darlaston) Ltd., and convert the building to a picture palace. It is, of course, quite possible that films had been shown at the Skating Rink since the October of 1911. Before the new company was formed, an application for a kine licence had been turned down in March 1912, and structural alterations demanded. A composite version of the story would then suggest that films may have been shown at the Skating Rink from October 1911 to March 1912. It would then have closed for proper reconstruction as a cinema.

Whatever the truth about the early course of events, it is certain that in 1912 the local builder, William Taylor Lees, transformed the skating rink into a luxurious picture palace. The conversion was designed by Messrs. Joynson Brothers, a Darlaston architectural practice that had offices adjoining the Picturedrome.

In this form the Olympia opened on 19th October 1912. The Wednesbury Herald, published on the same day, described the building as follows:

"The outside is pleasing but unobtrusive, and gives little idea of the extent of the interior. There is a large entrance hall containing a booking office and swing doors give access to a commodious lounge and refreshment buffet. This lounge is known as the Crush Hall and is one of the most striking features of the Olympia, being of considerable size, with a large lantern roof.... It is comfortably furnished and has a staircase leading there from to a cosy dancing room, built above the entrance hall.

The hall itself is a revelation, with its beautiful arched roof, gently sloping floor and general air of roomy comfort".

Bernard Williams, later a carpenter and joiner for W. T. Lees, was a choirboy at the time at All Saints Church. It was thought appropriate at the time that a new building should be given a parson's blessing, with full choral support. Mr. Williams went along as part of the choir, and with Sam Hampton conducting, they fulfilled this duty. Even an official blessing could not save the Olympia from the problem of subterranean fires. The cinema was built over some coal that was addicted to spontaneous combustion, possibly stimulated by the weight of the building above it.

In 1913 or 1914 the seats and flooring had to be removed and the whole floor was concreted over. The danger of "wild fire" became one of the legends associated with the cinema, but did not deter Pat Collins from acquiring the cinema at the end of the First World War. He may have been present at the opening of the cinema in 1912 but probably did not acquire it until venturing into the Black Country cinema business about 1919 with the Olympia and the Alhambra, Dudley Port.

The Olympia, Darlaston, in 1952 – in ABC days. Manager: Norman Langley, behind him Joe Butler, chief projectionist, who provided the photographs.

For several years it was managed for Pat Collins by Walter Mould. It is known that Walter Mould took the staff of the Olympia for a grand outing to Llangollen by motor-charabanc on 8th August 1920. Pat Collins could not join the party but he helped pay for the trip!

By the end of 1926 it seems that Pat Collins wished to dispose of his two "old" Black Country cinemas. The Olympia was bought by C.D. Cinemas, the partnership run by Mortimer Dent and Joseph Cohen. Two years later the partnership was dissolved and most of the halls belonging to C.D. Cinemas were sold to ABC. As well as acquiring smart new cinemas like the one at Edgbaston, ABC found themselves running a strange assortment of converted music halls and skating rinks — including the Olympia. ABC installed sound, the R.C.A. system, in the summer of 1930, just ahead of "the Drome". For many years its capacity was quoted as 969 which made it slightly bigger than its rival, but, of course, both cinemas were outclassed by the arrival of the Regal in 1938.

Blockall is away from the centre of Darlaston and possibly the Limp successfully fulfilled a local need. ABC certainly showed no predisposition to close it until the fifties. The cinema starred on the front cover of the ABC staff magazine in June 1950 when a picture showed a group of ABC staff and National Coal Board staff about to make their annual inspection of the state of the subterranean fire!

The end came very suddenly on 10th December 1955 with *"Thousands Cheer"* starring Gene Kelly. *"Calamity Jane"* starring Doris Day had been booked for the following week but an advertisement appeared stating that the theatre had "closed for redecoration and alterations". Whether there was any intention of reopening it, or whether the subterranean fire was becoming too much to put up with, we will probably never know.

For a time the building was used as a car showroom but was derelict by the time it was demolished in the mid sixties. Walsall Council have redeveloped the area with new housing, after reassuring themselves that the problem of the subterranean fire has been resolved.

The Regal

Pinfold Street, Darlaston

A brand new super-cinema came to Darlaston at the end of the thirties, not promoted by Oscar Deutsch, who would have regarded Darlaston as too small, or by the Clifton circuit, but by Colmore Entertainments, who already owned the Picturedrome.

The chairman of Colmore Entertainments was Mr. C.O. Brettell, who had purchased The Picturedrome for his

Hockley Picture Palace Co., in 1922. His fellow directors were his wife, who booked films for the company's cinemas, and Mr. V. Olliver, at one time associated with the Palace, West Bromwich.

The Brettell and Olliver families had inter-married, and Mr. Olliver's son, John, managed the Picturedrome while the new cinema was being planned. Messrs. Brettell and Olliver had been instrumental in building the Tower, West Bromwich, but their other cinema activities had been in Birmingham. By 1938 they controlled a dozen halls.

Darlaston's new cinema was to be called The Regal. It was designed by Ernest Roberts, by now a bold exponent of the simple functionalism of the modern style. 193,000 bricks produced by the Bentley Hall Brick Company formed its massive rectangular walls. The frontage, in reconstructed stone, continued the emphasis on plain rectangular forms. The four pairs of double swing doors were well-recessed behind the building line, increasing the amount of shelter beneath the canopy.

The auditorium held 1043 patrons downstairs, and 372 in the balcony. Ernest Roberts had excelled himself with the design of the interior, and Bryans Adamanta had reproduced his bold flowing lines in plaster painted green, gold and rose pink. Horizontal shading lined the wall below the balcony level and near the ceiling an abstract "border" led from the curtained balcony exit right to the finely moulded ante-proscenium. The Wilton carpeting was green, black and old gold, matching the green appliqued curtains. When there were parted they revealed a festooned screen curtain in flaming gold. The seats were also upholstered in gold.

The Regal was constructed by J. & F. Wootton Ltd., and was possibly the last cinema they built. Equipment was supplied by Kalee Ltd., and Western Electric Mirrophonic sound system was installed. The "cherry on the top of the cake" was a Compton Theatrone electronic organ, a two-manual instrument that survived in the Regal until just after films ceased to be shown.

The opening took place on Monday 19th September 1938. Miss Thelma White, "the golden-voiced accordionist", appeared on stage, followed by a Micky Mouse cartoon on the screen. Then came a grand organ recital by Leslie Taff and the feature film; *"Make A Wish"*, starring the child-actor Bobbie Breen. It does not seem that any opening ceremony was performed.

The manager, John Olliver, had moved "across town" from the Picturedrome, but Leslie Taff, the organist, was given managerial responsibility fairly soon after the opening. The cinema became very much associated with Leslie Taff. During the War he broadcast many organ concerts for the BBC, some of which were made on the Regal's organ. He also organised Sunday concerts and variety shows, making good use of the stage and dressing room facilities. Patrons must have come from far afield to the Regal.

Leslie Taff devoted the rest of his career to the Regal, presenting films, playing the organ, organising shows and even a pantomime. Later he presented wrestling, Indian films and, finally, Bingo. When the Compton organ became unreliable and spares were difficult to obtain he could no longer play at the Regal, but after its removal in 1965 a Bird organ was installed to entertain the bingo players.

The Eastern Film Society, led by J. S. Sidhu, started by showing a few films at Wolverhampton's Wulfrun Hall in 1955, moved briefly to the Picturedrome and then to the Regal. The first Indian film shown at the Regal was *"Ladki"*, which played to an audience of 316 on 11th September 1955. The last Indian film was shown on 23rd June 1963 and the E.F.S. moved to the Alhambra, Bilston. By this time Bingo was being introduced on Tuesday and Friday nights and on Sunday afternoons.

The last film was a single performance on Saturday 1st February 1964. The main feature was ***"Duel of the Titans"*** starring Steve Reeves and Gordon Scott, supported by *"The Ringer"*. The next day Bingo began "full-time". For some unknown reason, it was called The Regent Cinema Bingo Club, unless the advertisement was misprinted.

Twenty years later, the Regal was still playing Bingo. Only minor alterations had been made to both the exterior and the interior of the building. It was managed by Leslie Taff's son, David, and still owned by Colmore Entertainments. The Regal seemed a very permanent feature of the Darlaston landscape throughout the years when industry melted away, but nothing lasts forever! In April 1994 arsonists set fire to the Regal and the resulting damage meant that the building had to be demolished.

Above Left: The Regal, Darlaston in 1962 – in Bingo days.
(Alan Price)

Left: The interior of The Regal, Darlaston, when new, including a glimpse of the Compton organ console.
(Keith Skone)

Aldridge and Brownhills

To the east of Walsall we find the communities of Aldridge and Brownhills. The latter included the small township of Walsall Wood. The presence of collieries and brickworks made these places seem to have much in common with their counterparts in the Black Country, yet they seem quite "remote" and I felt no compulsion to include them in "Cinemas of the Black Country" in 1982. Since then I have realised that the four cinemas once to be found in this area were very "connected" to those in the Black Country, and now I have to include them on the grounds that since 1974 this area has been part of the Metropolitan Borough of Walsall.

Brownhills had run its own affairs as an Urban District sine 1894. Aldridge was not even given that status until 1934. In 1966 the two Urban Districts were amalgamated but in 1974 they simply found themselves absorbed into the new realm of Walsall MBC, and therefore part of the new County of West Midlands. Historically they had been part of south Staffordshire. Brownhills was home to two cinemas and Aldridge had one. Remarkably Walsall Wood also had just one tiny cinema. I will deal with them in that order.

The Avion

Anchor Road, Aldridge.

Half way between Walsall and Aldridge was Walsall Airport, later used as the research and development headquarters of Tube Investments. This aeronautical connection inspired the cinema builders of Aldridge to adopt the name "Avion" for their new enterprise.

The man behind the Avion was Albert Brain. He had been involved in the cinema business elsewhere and was one of the directors of the cinema built at Scotts Corner, near Great Barr. It was called the Beacon and was embraced by the Clifton Circuit. It seems that Albert Brain still wanted to establish his own empire – of which the Avion in Aldridge was just going to be the first step. He also set up Midland Constructions (1938) Ltd., and this company was going to build the cinemas.

Albert Brain's fellow director was Roland Satchwell, the architect mentioned many times in these pages. Builder and architect therefore combined to provide us with The Avion, but they needed some directors who could contribute some expertise and experience in actually running the cinema. It seems quite clear that they did not want to use Cinema Accessories Ltd., which would have brought them into the Clifton orbit. The other three directors, therefore, were Charles W. Cooke, John Copeland, and A.L.Glyde – Mr. Copeland's son-in-law. Messrs Cooke and Copeland had worked together since 1913 when they had opened The Elite at Bordesley Green.

Construction of The Avion began early in 1938 and was expected to take four months. Roland Satchwell's design has often compared to the Odeon style because of the use of cream faience tiling and his exploitation of classical geometry. The effect of the lettering, narrow strips of green tiling, and the well proportioned canopy also added to the Odeon-like quality. It was designed to accommodate 1050 patrons and included two hundred double seats! A pleasant art-deco interior was provided, and the technical equipment came from B.T.H.

The Avion opened at 2.30.pm on Monday 26th September 1938 and huge crowds turned out to see George Formby take part in the event. Councillor Drabble – the Mayor of Walsall, and the Mayor-elect, conducted the actual opening. The latter was none other than Alderman Pat Collins. Councillor Rowley of Aldridge UDC also had to have a say, and Roland Satchwell had the last word. The audience then watched a short film and British Movietone News before being allowed to greet George Formby. George sang at least two songs before making his own speech and was then mobbed by the audience as he tried to leave the stage via the auditorium. Watching the feature film *"I See Ice"* must have seemed an anti-climax even if it did star George Formby.

After the dramatic opening, The Avion settled down to presenting two three-day programmes per week, under the management of Victor MacDonald. He stayed at The Avion for about four years before going to the Empress, Sutton Coldfield, for Albert Brain. George Davidson was promoted from the projection room to replace him. George had quite a large part-time staff, including the usherettes in their smart green and gold uniforms. One became well known locally as "The AA Girl" – because if she caught any patrons talking she would shout, "Hey, hey", and they would immediately stop! Another was known as "The Corset Girl" because she was always saying, "Yo' cor sit 'ere."

As soon as the War was over, a few changes began to take place. In 1945 the cinema was "sold" from the original company to a new Aldridge Cinema Company headed by Albert Brain and his brother Leslie. In fact it was Leslie Brain who now seemed to be "in the driving seat" and as a result of his endeavours the new company then bought The Dale cinema in Willenhall from the trustees of the estate of the late Norah Tyler. This purchase was completed in 1946, and the Dale became the "head office" of both cinemas. In charge of this office, on a day-to-day basis was Harry Russell.

Harry Russell's first encounter with the cinema business had been at The Palace, Brownhills, where he had turned sheet music for the resident pianist. Harry eventually had a day job at the Mid Cannock Colliery, but in his own time he worked at all the cinemas in Aldridge and Brownhills – sometimes in the projection rooms, sometimes collecting and returning films. There were even occasions where he worked at more than one cinema at the same time. For example, during the war

Top left: The Avion, Aldridge, about 1990, in Bingo days, in its smart cream tiles and pale green stripes and lettering. (Ned Williams)

Left: The interior of The Avion, looking towards the screen, from a picture used in the opening brochure. (Author's collection)

he helped Enoch Simpson run the Walsall Wood Cinema while occasionally relieving George Davidson at The Avion!

Although based at The Dale, Willenhall, Harry Russell spent more and more time at the Avion, where he also began presenting variety shows and concerts. He even took these shows out to local factories to provide lunchtime entertainment. If life was not already too full, he also found himself concerned with the well-being of The Palace, Walsall Wood, when that little cinema became the third member of the group.

In the 1950s The Avion was upgraded with BTH SupaSound and Cinemascope was installed. Harry never tired of trying new things – adding variety acts between the films on Sunday nights and experimenting with Skiffle Sessions on Sunday afternoons. Every now and again films were replaced completely by live "Variety" for a week. During one such week Harry booked a young Des O'Conner for eighteen shillings. Harry Russell also forged links between the cinema and the

community. For example he went to see the Headmaster of the Druids Heath Boys School and arranged for them to attend the cinema at a special price.

By the mid 1960s the audiences seemed to be seriously declining, and the second half of 1967 was particularly bad. There was no option but to close, and the last films were shown on Saturday 30th December 1967. The final programme consisted of "Follow Me Boys", supported by "Wind in the Willows". The Dale, Willenhall, closed on the same day, and all three properties were put up for sale. A Mr. Robert Gillette purchased the Avion, Dale and remains of the Palace, Walsall Wood. Mr. Gillette owned a company trading as Legalite and was interested in casinos and bingo clubs.

Bingo was brought to the former Avion cinema by Mr. Gillette, but in 1973 he sold out to Harry Whitehouse – owner of a number of Bingo clubs, and last encountered in this book in the account of the fate of The Lyttleton, Halesowen. Harry Whitehouse had been a successful businessman engaged in the world of electro-plating. In his retirement he "discovered" Bingo, and decided to go into it as a second career! His first venture was at The Dorchester Club, in Temple Street, Wolverhampton.

Harry's son, Bob, took over the management of the club in the former Avion, and even when it was leased to Jarglen, and then Gala, he remained as its manager – putting in more than thirty years to this task.

On Friday 26th September 2008, four local history enthusiasts (John Sale, Albert Gill, Len Boulton, and Harry Denmant) hired the Aldridge Social Club to mount a celebration of the seventieth anniversary of the opening of The Avion. Bob Whitehouse was the Guest of Honour. He died the following February at the age of 61, but the social evening of 26th September had left him in no doubt that his service to Aldridge and the Avion in particular had not gone unnoticed. That event brought a number of people associated with The Avion together for the last time. For example Marion Boot, nee Bickley, was present. She was there on the day the cinema opened and had met her future husband while queuing to obtain George Formby's autograph. She later worked at The Avion.

Bingo ceased at the former Avion in August 2009, bringing seventy-one years of history to a close. As this book goes to press the building faces an uncertain future. Rumours have ranged from its possible reopening as a Weatherspoon's pub, to its complete demolition to enable Morrison's supermarket to extend its carpark.

Below: The Palace, Brownhills, photographed in October 1924. Wood was use to clad the frontage, but the roof and walls were clad with corrugated iron. The projection room, mounted over the entrance left a lot to be desired. (John Felton's collection)

The Palace

Brownhills

Brownhills may have been "on the map" in bioscope days, and therefore the first films seen by the local inhabitants were probably presented by travelling showmen. There is some evidence that the Twigdon Family's bioscope travelled in the area in the 1900s, which is interesting in the light of their association with film-presentation in Cheslyn Hay. The Jervis family also travelled in the mining villages of Cannock Chase and may have travelled a little further to come to Brownhills and Walsall Wood. Any attempts to travel further west would mean invasion of the Pat Collins's territory!

Meanwhile, in the heart of the Black Country Sidney Bray, of Dudley, was becoming interested in the business of showing films. His first public shows were at the Drill Hall in Halesowen, and The Temperance Hall in Langley, and the gradual introduction of films at The Criterion in Dudley itself. Why Sidney Bray then decided to build a cinema in Brownhills is a mystery. It is even possible that someone else started the project in Brownhills and Sidney Bray took it over.

The Palace was a purpose-built cinema in the "tin shed" tradition. The auditorium, clad in corrugated iron on the outside, and wooden panelling on the inside, was built with a wooden frontage set back from the road. There was no balcony but the rear seats were on a raked floor, separated from the cheaper seats by a step. Like other cinemas of this kind, The Palace generated its own power from a gas engine. When it rained the noise of the rain hitting the roof was accompanied by the thump of the gas engine and the music of the three-piece orchestra.

Thanks to one local citizen who kept a diary at the time, we have been able to learn that The Palace opened on 23rd December 1912. Brownhills was so far from any town publishing a weekly paper that its opening seems to have gone un-noticed by the outside world. The life and times of The Palace can only be glimpsed via the memories of local people, now largely deceased, who remembered their cinema in terms of the people who worked there, and who also worked alongside them in local pits and brickworks.

For example, the silent films were apparently accompanied by the Jones Brothers – Len on the cello, Sam on the violin, and Fred on the piano. Fred Jones married Nancy Dorricott who worked in the paybox and was still alive in the beginning of the 1980s when "Cinemas of the Black Country" was being researched. Fred recalled that the teenager who turned the pages of his sheet music was the young Harry Russell, who later managed The Avion, Aldridge, and Dale, Willenhall! Len and Sam Jones could also sing and they introduced variety acts to The Palace. Something about The Palace attracted such folks because for a time it was managed by Mr. & Mrs. Beckett who had first come to Brownhills at The Wake – as "Lightening Charlie and Starlight Nell". Two operators remembered from silent days were Jessie Shrigley and Joseph Clegg.

By the mid 1920s Sidney Bray was much pre-occupied with his cinema interests in Dudley and Halesowen. Sidney had married Flossie Davies and her brother Wally was brought into the business. In 1924 he was formally made Sidney Bray's business partner, and its seems that he had to take particular responsibility for their interests in Brownhills. As the 1920s progressed this became even more important with the arrival of competition in the form of The Regent. The introduction of "sound" became the centrepiece of this rivalry, and the Palace opted for the Melotone system after a brief flirtation with sound-on-disc.

The competition between The Palace and The Regent ceased in 1932 when Wally Davies and Sidney Bray bought the latter. This marked a decline in the fortunes of The Palace and soon it was closed altogether in the summer months. Later still the winter opening was restricted to just a Thursday/Friday/Saturday operation. The Palace enjoyed one more moment of glory, and that was when it returned to six-day opening while The Regent was improved and rebuilt in 1938.

It is thought that the Palace closed in the Summer of 1939, but did resume its three-day film shows in the Autumn of that year. The story goes that one night a heavy snowfall, in late 1939 or early 1940, caused the roof to collapse and that marked the end of its existence. Official documents in the County Record Office include a report written by the County Architect, Mr. K. Murray, in March 1939 when he commented: *"It is an entirely wooden structure covered on the outside in corrugated iron. It is seated for about 513 persons, and the whole structure is showing signs of decay...   ...the whole of the building and its fittings and furniture require drastic repair."* Later in August 1939 he said:

"I inspected the Palace cinema today in the company of the Chairman of the Justices, and have stated my opinion that this building, which is of very unsatisfactory construction, and in very decrepit condition, is not up to the standard which would justify the issue or renewal of a Cinematograph licence."

As the licence ran from 13th December it is possible that that The Palace kept running up till that date. Even so, it has not been possible to date its demise precisely.

The Regent

High Street, Brownhills.

The history of the Jervis Family is quite complicated and I have explored it as fully as possible in "Midland Fairground Families", published in 1996. A Thomas Jervis had nine children, and graduated in his own lifetime from market trader to fairground showman. Three of his sons; Tom, Miles, and Edward, travelled in the Cannock Chase area and became involved in the history of local cinemas.

Ted Jervis converted a market hall at Chasetown to cinema use, but then sold it to his brother Miles. Tom built up a portable cinema/bioscope in Heath Hayes but decided to stay and later rebuilt the enterprise in brick. Tom and Miles together took over The Palace in Walsall Wood in about 1919, but in about 1924 sold it to Ted. From Walsall Wood it seems as if Ted decided to take on Sidney Bray and Wally Davies in Brownhills.

Ted Jervis acquired a site in Brownhills High Street and set about building the cinema himself. He was assisted by his staff in Walsall Wood, and by out-of-work miners grateful for any work they could get. It seems to have been a case of building the auditorium behind existing shops and providing an entrance via a narrow passage to the High Street. It seems typical of this area that the opening has gone unrecorded. One source has suggested the cinema was completed by the September of 1927, another has claimed that The Regent opened in 1928. Its existence is first recorded in a Kine Year Book in 1929 – confirming that 1928 is the latest that it could have opened. Not long after opening the "sound war" broke out between The Regent and The Palace, with The Regent adopting the Marshall system.

After all this Ted Jervis had another bout of the wanderlust, and The Regent was sold to his competitors in 1931! (Ted set off to run a small circuit of cinemas near the North Wales border.) Sidney Bray and Wally Davies put Jack Turner in charge of their two Brownhills cinemas, and Jack installed his brother, Charlie, in The Regent's projection room. Sometimes Charlie was assisted by Tommy Bridgen, and sometimes by Harry Russell.

Right: The Regent, Brownhills, thought to have been photographed at the end of the Second World War. (John Felton collection)

Sidney Bray and Wally Davies then decided to radically improve The Regent, and to run down The Palace. Plans were drawn by Messrs. Cleland & Hayward of Wolverhampton and it was proposed that the existing small balconette be turned into a proper circle, and the auditorium roof would have to be raised. By demolishing some old shops the cinema could be give a new modern frontage – even incorporating a fin! The work had to be carried out in two stages and while this was going on The Palace was brought back into six-day use. In its new form The Regent would hold over six hundred patrons – 468 in the stalls and 148 in the circle.

The contractor used to rebuild The Regent was John Felton, who went on to build The Lyttleton, Halesowen, for Sidney Bray, and who became a close friend of both Sidney Bray and Wally Davies. The precise date of the new Regent's opening in 1936 is as obscure as its original opening, but it is thought to have been on 25th May. In the April of 1938 the County Architect came to see what had been done. Where there were supposed to be 468 seats in the stalls he found 560 seats, and in the balcony he found 160 where there should have been 148! He was not even sure if the plans had ever been given official approval.

This possibly led him to keep a watchful eye on The Regent. He was driving past the cinema in September 1940 when he noticed more alterations were taking place. The County Architect wrote to the Licensing justices to say that… *"considerable alterations are being made to the building despite no plans having been submitted or approved. This is not the first time that the proprietors of this cinema have adopted this attitude."*

Sidney Bray died in 1940 and his share in The Regent passed to his son, Bernard Bray. The thirty-year old Bernard was busy managing The Lyttleton, Halesowen, and therefore matters in Brownhills were very much left to Wally Davies, and the manager, Jack Turner, joined by Dennis Toddington in the box.

In 1954 Messrs Turner and Toddington adapted The Regent for Cinemascope and stereophonic sound – ahead of most of the colleagues in Staffordshire. *"The Robe"* opened at The Regent on 12th July 1954. For a short time The Regent felt confident enough to advertise in The Walsall Observber! Later Bernard Bray and Wally Davies used the fact that Cinemascope films were in short supply to justify their breaking of the Quota Regulations obliging them to show 30% British films. Bernard Bray complained to the press, *"We have been penalised because we were too progressive and wanted to bring The Regent right up to date."*

Bernard Bray died in 1959, leaving Wally Davies to run The Regent. Wally was sixty-eight and was uncertain of The Regent's future. Rumours were circulating that Brownhills' High Street might be redeveloped. Wally Davies, by this time, was assisted in booking films etc by Miles Jervis – the grandson of the Miles Jervis mentioned in connection with cinemas and fairground matters in this area. In the end Wally Davies parted with The Regent to Miles Jervis III in 1961. The latter was assisted for a few months by Dennis Toddington, the projectionist, and then Miles installed his own manager: Mr. W.J. Jelly.

Whatever Miles Jervis' hopes for The Regent, Mr. Jelly was determined to make it a success, with hopes that the cinema would be further improved. He created a very well supported children's matinee club and secured more popular films. No doubt he was disappointed to learn that The Regent was going to be compulsorily purchased by the local council and redevelopment of the site was going to go ahead.

The Regent closed on 29th September 1962 with John Ford's masterpiece, **"The Man Who Shot Liberty Valance"**. The cinema was then boarded up to await demolition, which began a year later. The site was redeveloped as The Ravens Court Shopping Precinct. Miles Jervis III redirected his attention to his father's

293

cinemas in West Bromwich and the enthusiastic Mr. Jelly eventually found himself looking after The Haven cinema in Stourport for the Jervises. Meanwhile Wally Davies had died in 1972 in Dudley, leaving a scrapbook containing the only photographs I have ever seen of Brownhill's cinemas.

Below: A Saturday morning matinee at The Regent, Brownhills, probably presented by Mr. Jelly just before the cinema's closure in 1962. (Mile Jervis)

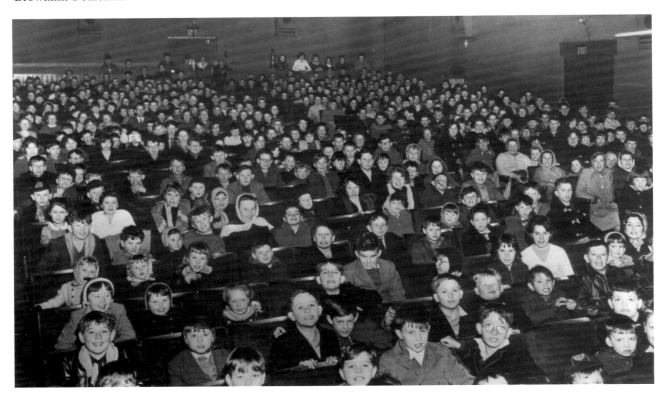

The Palace

Brookland Road, Walsall Wood.

Research into cinema history is difficult in Brownhills – but it becomes even more difficult in the little township of Walsall Wood. In this case both the opening and closure of the local cinema are both buried in obscurity!

The late Bob Wareing, a local film and cinema enthusiast, once showed me some ledgers of Britannic Films – a Birmingham-based film-renting company once owned by his father. The ledgers related to the years September 1916 to September 1918 and listed the films rented out by this company to many cinemas in the West Midlands. During that period Britannic Films regularly supplied Messrs. Nicklin & Barker with films for showing at their Walsall Wood Picture House. If they were in business at Walsall Wood in 1916, I think it can be safely assumed their cinema had opened before the First World War began – and therefore probably dates from the 1912-1914 period.

I also interviewed Dolly Hood who had worked at the cinema as a cleaner for Mr. Nicklin, and whoremembered it being sold to Miles Jervis. She had been born in 1902 and lived in Brookland Road. She claimed the that she remembered seeing cinema being built on land she had once played upon as a child.

Although nothing has yet been found out about Messrs. Nicklin & Barker, we do a little about Miles and Tom Jervis who bought the cinema from them in about 1919. (An early rate book relating to Walsall Wood records that in 1919 the "picture palace" was owned by the Jervis Brothers.) As stated in the previous chapter, Ted Jervis ran a cinema in the former Market Hall at Chasetown, later sold to his brother Miles. Miles and Tom purchased the Walsall Wood cinema together, but then Tom moves on and Miles buys his share in it. Miles goes on to build his brand new cinema at Chase Terrace in 1925, by which time the Walsall Wood cinema is in the hands of Ted Jervis. The latter is more interested in building The Regent, Brownhills, and passes the Walsall Wood cinema on to Enoch Simpson!

Enoch Simpson acquired The Palace, Walsall Wood, about 1927 or 1928. The cinema's existence is first acknowledged by the Kine Year Books in 1930, when in Mr. Simpson's ownership, it is listed as accommodating 1100 patrons. The benches must have been tightly packed in Mr. Simpson's time! Apparently some shows were so well supported that extra chairs had to be borrowed from neighbouring houses. The cinema's popularity spread beyond Walsall Wood and legend has it that patrons from Clayhanger reached the cinema via the railway track!

294

Enoch Simpson ran The Palace with the assistance of his three sons, Young Enoch, Edgar and Ernest. The cinema also played a large part in the life of the Hatton family, and naturally we shouldn't be surprised to see that Harry Russell also comes into the story at this stage. He came along to play non-synchronised music on gramophone records at the end of the silent era and stayed while a Gyrotone sound system was installed. At a later date he assisted Enoch Simpson with film-booking.

After the Second World War the Leslie Brain took over The Palace – adding it to the Avion and The Dale, Willenhall to form his trio of cinemas. A separate company was formed to take on the ownership of the Palace, Walsall Wood, and the directors were named as Leslie Brain, Harry Russell, and a Mr. Nightingale. "Old Enoch" had died by this time and The Palace had been run by his sons, Young Enoch and Ernest. The new owners provided a new link between Harry Russell and The Palace, but he decided to appoint Jeff Collins to carry out the day-to-day management of the cinema. Jeff had started work at The Palace in 1940 at the age of fourteen. Like everyone else he was a part-timer and his "day job" was at the Walsall Wood Colliery. He was Chief Projectionist during the latter part of the war, although still in his teens. Jeff eventually brought his wife, Dorothy, into the paybox, and recruited other men from the colliery to work in the projection box. These included Alan Clift, Malcolm Corfield, Roy Dukes, Ray Hudson, and Terry Gill. The latter was one of the last lads to be trained at The Palace. Years later Roy Dukes' most vivid memory of working there was the fact that the screen curtains had to be manually opened before each performance – they could not opened mechanically by the flick of a switch in the box!

The Walsall Wood Cinema Company was anxious to rebuild The Palace as soon as conditions made it possible. Unfortunately the cinema had to be closed for about six months while this was carried out. The Palace

acquired a new brick frontage and a new larger projection box. I assume the original building consisted of a corrugated iron auditorium with a timber frontage but the absence of plans, and conflicting memories of those who knew The Palace, make it impossible to be certain. The rebuild, that took place in about 1950 was undertaken by the Hardy Brothers of Aldridge – and one of the brothers went on to become a well known local house-builder. Old Kalee 6 projectors were replaced with Kalee 8 machines and a new BTH sound system was installed.

All this investment in Walsall Wood's little cinema indicated that everyone involved believed it had a future, but somehow the cinema never recovered from its sixth months of closure. Business never returned to what it had been. The fortunes of the cinema declined as the 1950s progressed.

Readers who have followed the difficulties of researching the history of cinemas in this area will not be surprised to learn that it has been impossible to be sure the date of the cinema's closure. Having discussed this with many people who have all provided conflicting accounts, I would tend to believe it closed in about 1954. One source was convinced the cinema survived until 1959, another believed it lasted until 1964. In their recent booklet "Memories of Old Walsall Wood", the respected local authors, John Sale and Bill Mayo, who published the book in 2000, have concluded that The Palace closed in June 1957.

Another problem is that the cinema stood empty for a long time after it had closed while planning permission was unsuccessfully sought for alternative uses. It was included in the sale of the company's three cinemas to Mr. Gillette in 1967, and was probably demolished the following year. A small block of flats called Lee Court was built on the site.

Right: The Palace, Walsall Wood, about 1950, after its post-war rebuild. Obviously pictures of the Palace are very rare! (Eric Poxon)

Left: The interior of The Palace, Walsall Wood, about 1950. These are the curtains that had to be opened manually before each performance. (Eric Poxon)

Left: The man who had worked in all four cinemas of Aldridge and Brownhills was Harry Rusell whose cinema career began by turning pages for the musicians at The Palace, Brownhills. He was best known as the manager of The Avion. Here we see him in the box office at The Avion with George (named after Geroge Formby)- a donkey that used to graze behind the cinema and became a "regular". (From the Harry Russell collection)

Below: Every flea pit worthy of the name took disinfecting the premises seriously! Specific products were made for the purpose.

Section 6
Cinemas of South Staffordshire

Above: The Picture House, Heath Hayes.

The Black Country has traditionally been regarded as part of South Staffordshire, even although it included a detached part of Worcestershire. The southernmost towns of the Black Country; Stourbridge and Halesowen, were also in Worcestershire. The local government area designated as "South Staffordshire" today was formed in 1974 by amalgamating Cannock Rural District, in the north, with Seisdon Rural District in the south. A more general sense of what constitutes South Staffordshire would include a small part of what is now within the boundaries of Lichfield District Council.

Cinema builders took little account of civic boundaries; they simply looked for settlements that might prove viable in providing an audience. Therefore in this book it has seemed reasonable to go beyond the boundaries of the Black Country, and take in the cinemas built in the surrounding area of South Staffordshire.

This means looking at the cinemas built in and around Cannock Chase, and to be comprehensive I must include the village of Kinver. It will soon be seen that all this is justified by the fact that many names of people associated with Black Country cinemas will also appear in this section.

I will start the survey in Cannock, and the roam the Chase to look at cinemas in the smaller towns of the coalfield: Hednesford, Blackfords, Chase Terrace, Chasetown, and Heath Hayes. Heading back towards the Black Country I will take quick look at the curious cinema history of Cheslyn Hay. As we circle the Black Country, we find that settlements like Codsall and Wombourne are devoid of any cinema history, but right in the southernmost part of South Staffordshire we find the little village of Kinver once was home to a cinema.

Cannock

We can be fairly certain that the citizens of Cannock first saw films in the bioscope shows that travelled through the area. For example, Pat Collins brought his Wonderland bioscope show to Cannock and opened on ground in Market Hall Street opposite where the hippodrome was eventually built. Waller Jeffs' "New Century Pictures" also came to Cannock for two days in November 1910 and were shown in the "New Hall".

What is surprising is that there does not seem to have been a rush in 1910, as the Cinematograph Act came into force, to open a cinema in Cannock. In 1912 Cannock became home to a theatrical venture but as we will see below, thanks to Ben Kennedy the project soon also becomes part of local cinema history.

Pat Collins on Cannock Chase.

Pat Collins, the Walsall-based showman, seems to have had some success in taking control of fairs in the Cannock Chase area at the time when he was also presenting his own bioscope shows as part of the fair. It seems likely, therefore that one or other of his "Wonderland" shows, of 1907 and 1908 vintage were seen on The Chase before 1910.

At the Cannock Wakes of October 1911 Pat's advertisement in the local press specifically states that "Wonderland" will part of the fair. As a result of the 1910 Cinematograph Act it is tempting to assume that the show did not include films on this occasion. The main attraction on the show seems to have been a revival of "Pepper's Famous Ghost Illusion". However, in the small print the advertisement adds that the show will also include "the best and latest living pictures".

The Hippodrome
- later The Forum

Market Hall Street, Cannock.

Cannock's principal theatre experienced a shaky start. A London-based firm commenced construction, but once the basic outer walls had been completed construction came to a halt. The man who came to the rescue in this situation was none other than Benjamin Kennedy, at the height of his expansion into the Black Country and beyond. He joined forces with a Mr. T. C. Langstaff of Hednesford, and construction continued. A Mr. Davenport, who joined the team completing the interior of the theatre, went on to become its first stage manager.

Ben Kennedy announced that The Hippodrome would open on Easter Monday - 8th April 1912, and, as in his other theatres, would present programmes of films plus variety acts, twice nightly. The Hippodrome itself was described by the local newspaper as *"handsome and imposing"..... "No expense having been spared in the erection of the building, which would not only be a credit and an ornament to the town, but would permit the engagement of the best companies."*

The first show included John P. Franklyn's Western Girls, plus a vocalist and comedian, and the film ***"The Little Railroad Queen".***

After initial success audiences declined and some put this down to the theatre's poor heating. Whatever the reason, Ben Kennedy seemed keen to lease the theatre by the Autumn of 1914. A Richard Jones took over the lease and reopened in February 1915 with the intention of focussing on film entertainment, but quickly reverted to "cine-variety". Richard Jones also reduced admission prices and experimented with "night-workers matinees" on Wednesday and Friday mornings. Richard Jones did not renew his lease in February 1916.

At one stage the proprietor of the Cannock Picture Palace, Walsall Road, leased the Hippodrome so that he could continue showing films while his cinema was redecorated! Miles and Ted Jervis took over in 1916 but gave up at the end of January 1917, and seemed to have used the stage rather than the screen. Later in 1917 Percy Millar ran the Hippodrome and it seemed to settle into a routine of presenting drama and variety from then until the early 1920s. During the second half of the 1920s there were many more openings and closures. (See Volume Two)

When the theatre reopened for the countless time on 1st February 1932 it was wired for sound and had become The Forum - now under the control of Cannock businessman - Mr. E. K. Hawtin. Mr. Hawtin's arrival marks a period of steady use of the building as a cinema. As we have seen earlier in this book, Mr. Hawtin later acquired cinemas in Wolverhampton and Bilston, but had been connected with the cinema business since 1911, when he assisted his father in running a cinema in Selly Oak, Birmingham. Although The Forum then enjoyed a more stable existence as a cinema, the stage facilities were still used once a year by the Cannock Amateur Operatic Society.

Sunday opening came to The Forum on 28th August 1942 and proved very popular. In 1948 Eric Poxon joined the staff at The Forum as Second Operator, and has been able to confirm that The Forum was busy as a cinema in the early post-war period despite competition from The Danilo, to which he defected a year later. At the time Mr. Hawtin's daughter, Betty, was really running The Forum as her father was more interested in his racehorses! The Hawtin family ran The Forum as a cinema until 1955, when he then converted it into a dance hall. The last films were shown on 11th September 1955. The final programme had included the film ***"Marty"*** starring Ernest Borgnine.

Perhaps surprisingly The Forum did have another period of being used as theatre while in Council ownership, but the building was finally demolished in 1985.

The Cannock Picture Palace
Also known as The Essoldo, the Cannon and Electric Picture House

Walsall Road, Cannock.

The Cannock Picture Palace opened on 6th April 1914 – two years after The Hippodrome. It was designed by Mr. Joynson, encountered elsewhere in this book in describing the history of the cinemas of Wednesbury and Darlaston, and had been built by T. Elvins & Son. It accommodated 650 patrons on a single raked floor. The proprietors described themselves as The Cannock Picturedrome Company, who had appointed Frank Williams as their manager.

The opening programme included a Max Linder film, *"Max Wishes He Hadn't",* and the first part of two sequence pictures; "Fight for Millions" and "A Modern Girl". The press commented on the quality of the projection, and the orchestra, and the cinema was immediately well supported.

At the end of the First World War there was a slight change of name and the cinema became The Cannock Picture House, a name then used for the next fifty years! This may have been the result of the cinema changing hands and being slightly rebuilt. The new owners appear to have been Paramount Picture Theatres Ltd.

Early in 1920 there was a more radical rebuilding of the cinema based on plans produced by Marcus Brown of Wolverhampton. The cinema closed in October 1919 for this to happen, and it was reopened on 8th March 1920. The roof and ceiling of the cinema were raised by twelve feet and a balcony was installed. This enabled the cinema to hold 800 patrons downstairs, with 400 in the balcony. The contractors were T. Elvins & Son once again.

The talkies were introduced to Cannock at the Picture House on 16th December 1929 with a film called *"Broadway".* This may have used the "sound on disc" system as the projectionist, Mr. Cope couldn't cope! Despite several months training Mr. Cope suffered several technical hitches on the first night. Sound on film probably arrived in January 1930 with *"The Singing Fool",* but all is not clear because a Western Electric sound system was added in November 1931.

In November 1931 Paramount Picture Theatres sold The Cannock Picture House to Mr. Charles Deeming of Coalville, Leicestershire. This marked the departure of Frank Williams and the arrival of a new manager – Tom Gribble – who claimed to have gained experience of cinema management in Bilston and Wednesbury. Frank Williams re-enters our story when we take a look at the Tivoli, Hednesford.

Charles Deeming ran The Picture House until the Spring of 1938 when he sold it to Mr. McDonald who was already associated with The Carlton, Sparkbrook, and The Coliseum, Saltley, and had managed his father's cinema; The Regal, Handsworth. Mr. McDonald senior had built of The Empress cinema in the Cannock Chase Military Camp, and the family was familiar with the Cannock area. Tom Gribble left to look after a new cinema Charles Deeming had opened in Coalville, and Mr. McDonald took over personal supervision of his newly acquired cinema. He improved the standard of films booked for The Picture House and made a success of competing with both the Danilo and The Forum. For example, when *"Gone With The Wind"* came to The Picture House in November 1942 he ran it for three weeks. It returned to the cinema on at least six occasions!

Below: Cannock;s "Picture House" as The Essoldo, September 1969.   (CTA Archive)

Mr. McDonald's original intention of managing The Picture House himself was eventually modified with the appointment of Mr. Sam Cooke in 1940 as manager, but for a time either gentleman might personally greet you as you entered the cinema! Mr. McDonald also steadily maintained and improved his cinema, regularly redecorating it, fitting a larger screen etc…In November 1954 he installed Cinemascope. In 1955 the frontage of the cinema was modernised.

Mr. McDonald died in March 1962 at the age of fifty-nine. The ownership of The Picture House passed to his wife, Ada Elizabeth, although Mr. Cooke continued to provide management for about four years, when he was followed by Mr. Graham Gittings. Mrs. McDonald continued her late husband's policy of continuing to invest in the cinema despite the fact that audiences were generally declining. She also remained committed to showing films, as opposed to introducing Bingo. Even so, in September 1968 she was persuaded to sell The Picture House to the Essoldo group – the company that had already bought Cannock's Danilo in which they were presenting Bingo.

On 7th September 1969, after a further refurbishment, the cinema re-opened as The Essoldo. From that time onwards, only the stalls were used, although seating reached new heights of luxury and the screen was enlarged once more. Seating capacity was reduced to just over four hundred. As the Essoldo entered the seventies there was confidence that the cinema was suitably "modern", and that audience figures were healthy. Even so, in 1972 the cinema changed hands again and became part of the Tigon Group, and was "re-badged" as "The Classic". The new owners even introduced children's matinees.

Below: The Electric Palace, Cannock. December 2009. (CTA Archives)

Twelve months later the 140 Classic cinemas operating nationwide changed hands, but in Cannock the name was retained. Having survived a period in which many Black Country cinemas had closed, Cannock's sole surviving cinema eventually reached the era of tripling and twinning. At the end of 1977 it was announced that The Classic would acquire a second screen by building a new auditorium at the back of the existing one. "Screen Two" opened to the public on Sunday 5th March 1978 with Paul Newman in *"Slap Shot"*. (On the previous day Screen Two had been used for a private preview of *"Abba, the Movie"*.) Screen two accommodated 180 patrons.

The Classic group changed hands again in 1979, but the cinema still retained its name. Yet another take-over resulted in the cinema becoming part of the Cannon Group. The cinema's name was not changed to "The Cannon" until 1985, by which time the cinema industry seemed in a much deeper crisis although attendances were sustained in Cannock. By the 1990s Cannock could consider itself lucky – and "unusual" – to still have a cinema! The longer it has survived the more remarkable Cannock's cinema has become.

When all looked lost in 2004, the cinema was acquired by Kailash Suri of the Curzon, Loughborough, who had also taken over The Majestic at Bridgnorth. This led to the reintroduction of the name, "The Picture House". However Mr. Suri was not able to reverse the fortunes of the cinema in Cannock, even if he had done so elsewhere. The Picture House closed on 24th Feb 2005, and seven staff were made redundant. The site was scheduled for multi-purpose redevelopment. In August 2005 permission was to build a £50m leisure complex on the site - to include a six-screen cinema, so perhaps the demise of The Picture House was going to lead to an even brighter cinema future for Cannock.

The proposed leisure centre did not materialise for various reasons, but the remarkable thing is that the closed cinema has come back to life! On Friday 13th November 2009 The Electric Palace Picture House, Walsall Road, Cannock, was re-opened in grand style. After five years "in the dark", local property developer Fred Pritchard, re-opened the cinema in a much refurbished form - in strong blue and silver colour schemes. The opening film was *"2012"* - a marathon end-of-the world blockbuster scheduled to start at 8.00.pm. Queues built up outside the cinema from about 6.30.pm onwards while a privileged group of invited guests were allowed in to make their way to the balcony and its entertainment suite! About sixty seats in "sofa style" are provided in this balcony while the stalls holds just over 220 patrons in reasonably spacious seating, but in rather long unbroken rows.

The opening was being held to raise funds for the charity Help for Heroes which explained the number of Army Cadets present. The queue - standing out in the drizzle - took a long time to process as the ticket seller was also selling refreshments which seemed strange as smartly dressed new staff in blue uniforms seemed abundant. Once inside the environment seemed very bright and shiny and long corridors laid with blue carpet led to the back of the main auditorium - part of the original 1914 structure of the cinema, but now looking very smart with its restrained plasterwork painted dark blue. The smaller auditorium, which holds about 170 patrons, was not being used on opening night.

Manageress Tracy Massey was present to greet some of the guests and patrons and Graeme Cotton, in evening dress was "everywhere". Graeme stepped in as the cinema's "operator", although that seemed to involve a lot more than simply projecting the films. Tracy was Manageress in the twilight years of the cinema in the early part of the decade when it was being run as part of the Loughborough based Curzon group, and was obviously pleased to be back in business. Graham was exuding enthusiasm for the new project.

Quite an elaborate opening ceremony was presented at the front of the stalls. Graeme Cotton welcomed everyone and whipped up the audience's enthusiasm for the return of the films to Cannock. Fred Pritchard also spoke and told everyone that re-opening a cinema was much more exciting than being a property developer. A local councillor cut a ribbon - and all that was only the beginning! We were also introduced to young Ben Wilby, a local actor who appeared in the film *"Nativity"*, shown at the cinema just before Christmas 2009. It is not every day that an eloquent ten-year old takes part in opening a cinema! This was followed by a raffle in which the winning ticket was selected by local singer Fay Bray who had acquired some television-based fame. Fay also 'belted out' three songs before the film eventually hit the screen. The audience seemed very positive about the cinema's return to life. The event was probably quite a contrast to the more formal openings of the past - and certainly had an atmosphere that it is difficult to achieve in a vast multi-plex.

The Danilo

High Green, Cannock

Mortimer Dent's fifth Danilo was built in Cannock. Like all the others it was registered as a separate company, and was registered in August 1937. The cinema was built on the site of the Manor House, which was demolished in 1936. Mr.Hawtin of The Forum, and Mr. Deeming of The Picture House were opposed to the building of the Danilo, as might be expected, and they were joined by Mr. Williams who even felt his enterprises in Hednesford might be affected. Whether influenced by the protests, or not, the Council refused planning permission.

Charles Howard Stanley, the company secretary for Danilo cinemas, made a second application to use this site. This time he was given permission to proceed with a guarded recommendation that he only be granted a cine licence if the completed building proved satisfactory, and that it had to be completed by the end of June 1938.

Progress was slightly hampered by arguments with Cannock UDC who remained owners of the land on which the cinema was being built. Ernest Roberts planned a cinema to hold 1378 patrons. There were disputes about the width of emergency exit doors and the width of gangways. At the same time there was a shortage of structural steel with which to build the cinema's basic framework! The builders were Thomas Jackson of Langley Green, who had built other Danilos. There was no possibility that they could complete the cinema by June 1938.

The cinema was designed to incorporate a stage, eighty feet in width, and a few dressing rooms, and was to have its own car park.

It was opened on Saturday 25th February 1939 by Major General Sir John Brown, supported by the Chairman of Cannock UDC, Mr. H. J. Foster. Julie Suedo provided a "star appearance" and military band music was provided by the Band of the 6th Battalion, South Staffordshire Regiment. Films included *"Everybody Sing"* and *"Two Hearts in Wartime"*.

Proper public programmes began on Monday 27th February with *"Too Hot to Handle"* starring Clark Gable and Myrna Loy, and the cinema was managed by P.J. Mills who had come from Guildford. Two three-day programmes were to be presented each week, and the cinema was to close on Sundays. (Sunday opening was eventually permitted on 30th August 1942, on a temporary basis.)

Like the other Danilos, the one in Cannock was sold to S.M.Associated Cinemas in 1946, although it's original name was retained. After the War, the management of the cinema passed to Mr. Highlands, and it was he who introduced Children's' Saturday morning matinees,

Above: The Danilo, Cannock about 1960.
(Express & Star)

known as "The Chums' Club". Mr. Highlands stayed until 1953 when Mr. Haddock, from Blackpool, followed him.

Cinemascope, with stereophonic sound, was introduced on 7th February 1955 with *"The Robe"*, by which time the cinema had become part of the Essoldo Circuit, but again with no change of name. The second half of the 1950s showed a continuous decline in attendances, but the 1960s witnessed the introduction of one-night stage shows – and this brought many stars to Cannock's Danilo. The first show was on Thursday 24th March 1960 and was simply called "Top Twenty Hit Parade". Next came a very successful sell-out Cliff Richard show, followed by Roller-Drome in Wolverhampton, and his task was to make the cinema even more attractive to teenage audiences. Attendances generally seemed to be improving and the auditorium was actually redecorated for the first time in many years!

But by 1966 the decline seemed to have set in again. Wrestling was occasionally presented as an experiment.

Meanwhile the planners were considering new retail developments for Cannock. The last film show was scheduled for Wednesday 31st 1969 when the Danilo would show *"Monte Carlo of Bust"* starring Tony Curtis, Peter Cook and Susan Hampshire. The adverts stated, *"All film programmes are now discontinued until further notice – but BIG BINGO will continue."*

Bingo ceased in February 1970 and by the end of that year the cinema had been demolished, although then immortalised in a street name!

The Central Cinema

Blackfords, near Cannock

Half way between Cannock on Hednesford, along the back road, is the area known as Blackfords. It was here that a Mr.Richard Jones decided to build a cinema next door to his existing hotel.

The Central Cinema House, as it was first called, opened on 14th April 1913 with a Vitagraph production of *"Romeo and Juliet"*. Councillor J. Hunter of Cannock UDC performed the opening ceremony and expressed his view that films were generally very educational and therefore should be commended. The sixty official guests were then entertained in The Central Hotel.

The Central was a small cinema, holding about 350 patrons on a single floor. Unfortunately no architect or builder has been identified.

Richard Jones also took on the Empire, Hednesford, briefly, but by 1917 seemed keen to relinquish his cinema interests. After a brief period of closure in order to refurbish the building The Central opened for a second time on 26th March 1917 under the management of the Cannock Picture House (Paramount Pictures). They did not hold on to it for long as it was sold again in 1919 to a Mr Taylor, who was also showing films at the Palace, Cheslyn Hay.

At least Mr.Taylor continued to run The Central until February 1924. The next owner was Mr. H Smith, a resident of Blackpool. Mr. Smith was responsible for bringing the talkies to Blackfords. They were introduced on 15th December 1930 with *"The Rogue Song"*, featuring Laurel and Hardy. However six years at The Central seemed a long time and later in 1930 we find that Mr.Smith was leasing his cinema to others. Various people took a lease, and some carried out improvements to the cinema.

Below: Isaiah Bate says farewell to the Central.

Sometime in the mid thirties The Central was leased to Isaiah Bates and his partner, Mr. Roobottom. Their partnership was dissolved in April 1944 and Isaiah Bate took on the sole ownership and management of the cinema. In many peoples' memories he is the man most associated with The Central.

Isaiah Bates and his wife ran The Central for the rest of its life. At first business was good, but by the 1950s it was seriously declining. With regret the Bates presented the last film show on Saturday 4th June, one week after the last show at Heath Hayes' little cinema. The last show was attended by Florrie Mears who had also been at the first show back in 1913. She had gone to the cinema twice a week throughout its life and had always sat in the same seat.

The cinema stood empty for a few years, and was then used by a taxi and car-hire firm. After that it was used as a kitchen and bathroom centre, but since then it has been demolished.

Hednesford.

Hednesford was right in the heart of the Cannock Chase Coalfield and was surrounded by big pits. The town had two cinemas.

The Tivoli

Anglesey Street, Hednesford.

The Tivoli began life as a skating rink, built about 1910 by Roland Barton. He eventually started showing films on the premises on two nights per week. This was made more obvious in 1912 when it became known as The Electric Picture Palace, but skating was still enjoyed on two nights a week. Roland Barton's commitment to roller-skating is reflected in the fact that for a few years it reverted to being called "The Rink".

Roland Barton relinquished his rink/cinema at the end of 1931 and sold the building to Frank Williams whom we last met at Cannock's Picture House. Frank Williams undertook considerable alterations to the building that included the provision of a raked floor and the installation of sound projectors and Western Electric equipment. On Monday 11th January 1932 his cinema opened as The Tivoli – a proper sound cinema. The programme featured *"Alibi"* – a British detective film, and *"The Dawn Trail"*, a Buck Jones western.

Frank Williams had inherited a large wooden structure and was anxious to rebuild the cinema in a more substantial manner when finances permitted. This took place in April 1938 and the building was thoroughly modernised by Messrs. Linford of Cannock. The alterations included the installation of a balcony, increasing its capacity to over seven hundred.

Frank Williams ran The Tivoli until August 1944 when he sold it to C.J. Griffiths and George Cockburn, trading as C&G Cinemas. Mr. Griffiths was a native of Walsall, and had entered the business as a pageboy at The Grand. He had progressed to projection room work and had worked in Wednesbury, Darlaston and then Coalville before coming to Hednesford.

Early in 1950 Mr. Griffiths died but George Cockburn carried on running the cinema for the rest of the year. In December 1950 The Tivoli was sold to Kennedy Theatres Ltd. of Dudley Hippodrome fame. Bryan Kennedy was put in charge of The Tivoli, having gained some experience at The Plaza, West Bromwich.

The Kennedy's had financial worries of their own and in 1954 they sold The Tivoli to Miles Jervis II. A guide to who's who in the Jervis family is provided elsewhere.

In this case we are talking about Miles – the son of Miles Jervis, of fairground origins, who opened the cinema in Chase Terrace. Miles Jervis II was an enterprising showman and he tried various methods of building and preserving an audience at The Tivoli. Perhaps it was remarkable that he managed to keep it going until 1963.

On 9th March 1963 The Tivoli closed with *"Watch It Sailor"*, supported by *"Gunmen from Laredo"*. In the following week seats and equipment was removed and the building was sold to Cannock UDC. It was then demolished and a supermarket, market stalls and a carpark were developed on the site. In recent years the site has been occupied by a Co-op.

Below: The Anglesey Hotel still exists but is no longer a hotel. Its presence helps to establish our bearings as this area of Hednesford has changed over the years. In the background – in Anglesey Street we can see The Tivoli as it was at the beginning of the 1960s.

(Eric Poxon collection)

The Empire
also known as The Picture House

Rugeley Road, Hednesford.

In 1911 Frederick Montague Barber, an amusement caterer and auctioneer, purchased the former "Public Rooms" in Hednesford. His aim was to convert them for use as a cinema or theatre, and he managed to have his "New Empire" open by the October of 1911. At first the emphasis was on drama and variety but sometime in 1912 films began to be shown.

Mr. Barber's health failed in 1913 and he passed the operation of the New Empire to a Mr. Maddox, a Worcester-based showman with four other theatres under his control. By the end of 1914 control had passed to Richard Jones, last encountered at The Central at Blackfords. He was more interested in running the place as a cinema, and it "re-opened" as The Empire Picture Palace" on 14th December 1914.

After three years Richard Jones passed The Empire on to Paramount Pictures who were running the Cannock Picture House. They revamped the cinema and held their re-opening on 22nd December 1917. Tip-up upholstered seats now filled the cinema, and provided comfort for up to 600 patrons, 200 of which were in a balcony in double seats. To conform to the naming policy established in Cannock, the Empire was re-christened "The Picture House Hednesford". Talkies came to the Hednesford Picture Palace on 3rd. November 1930 with *"The Desert Song"* starring John Boles.

By 1932 the Picture house had been acquired by Miles Jervis I, from Chasetown, and a year later he changed the name of the cinema back to "The Empire". Almost immediately the cinema was taken over by Frank Williams, who had also acquired The Tivoli. Frank Williams undertook a thorough refurbishment of The Empire and staged another "re-opening".

As we have seen in describing the fate of The Tivoli, Frank Williams retired in 1944 when both his cinemas were passed to Messrs. Griffiths & Cockburn. The Tivoli and Empire had become "twins" – the fate of one was the fate of the other. Perhaps the Empire had been allowed to become a little shabbier. During 1950 The Empire, while being run by George Cockburn almost lost its licence, but improvements were put in hand and it survived to be sold, like The Tivoli, to Kennedy Theatres.

Under Bryan Kennedy's management there was another attempt to refurbish The Empire, and seating capacity was reduced to 450. Generally, the Kennedys seem to have been pleased to pass the Hednesford cinemas on to Miles Jervis II. Even Miles could do little to restore the fortunes of The Empire, and it closed on 16th June 1957 with *"Satellite in the Sky"*. He did not find it easy to dispose of the building, although in 1960 the local Spiritualists were persuaded to come and use if for their services.

The Spiritualists stayed about three years and then the former Empire was demolished. A garage was opened on the site.

Below: The Chase Cinema, Chase Terrace.

The Chase Cinema

Sankey's Corner, Chase Terrace.

There was little to be found at Chase Terrace when Miles Jervis I decided to build a purpose-built cinema at the crossroads at Sankey's Corner. An elegant brick built edifice was erected as an expression of confidence in the future development of the area. It could hold 700 patrons in the stalls and balcony.

It opened on 19th October 1925, with evening performances only during the week, and two shows on Saturday as it was anticipated that most patrons worked in the local pits. Certainly most of the staff had "day jobs" in the pits. Miles's confidence was rewarded and the cinema quickly became a success. In fact, on the opening day all seven hundred seats were taken and Doctor Horton of Chasetown provided an opening speech for the occasion. There were musical items as well as films in the programme that followed.

The Chase Cinema was able to introduce the talkies in October 1930, and the original Kalee 12 projectors were adapted to work with British Acoustic sound. Apart from the later introduction of Xenon lamps in the projectors, the conversion to sound was probably the only modernisation experienced by The Chase Cinema! The cinema became particularly associated with Miles' wife, Ann Jervis who became a fixture in the box office, while her husband returned to fairground activities such as running some amusements on The Lickey Hills.

Miles Jervis I died in 1948 but Ann carried on with The Chase Cinema even although audiences began to decline. In September 1960 Bingo was introduced on Sunday evenings – no doubt under the influence of her son, Young Miles, who was always resourceful when it came to keeping cinemas going. Ann retired in 1969 at the age of eighty, and the cinema was leased to Regent Entertainments. They decided to offer Bingo on three nights a week, and to show films on the other three. In this way The Chase Cinema lasted longer than most in similar locations.

The Chase Cinema closed on 26th July 1975 with *"Flesh Gordon"* – a few months short of its fiftieth birthday. The building was eventually sold and demolished and sheltered accommodation was built on the site. The building has been named "Jervis Court".

The Palace
also known as The Plaza

High Street, Chasetown.

Chasetown grew into a typical late nineteenth century mining village with the development of the Cannock Chase Coalfield, and the Marquis of Anglesey's pits later operated by the Cannock Chase Colliery Company in particular. A population of miners attracted travelling showmen and the Chasetown Wakes became an important date in the calendar, having started in about 1865. It is reasonable to assume that bioscope shows came to this wake, but we would be lucky to find any written record of this.

The Jervis family was among those who were tempted to travel among the small abut growing Chase communities, and for some reason Edward Jervis decided it would be a good idea to present film shows on Saturday nights in the market hall in Chasetown High Street. Years later when I interviewed Miles Jervis II he recalled being taken to his uncle's shows in this hall, perhaps igniting his own interest in the cinema business, but he was not quite sure what had brought Uncle Ted to Chasetown. Ted's mother, Mary Jervis, died on 26th September 1914 and is buried in Chasetown Cemetery. Her death certificate states her address as simply, "High Street, Chasetown". Is this proof that by 1914 some of the Jervises lived in their vans parked close to the market hall used on Saturdays for the film-shows?

Ted Jervis's film shows in Chasetown were eventually increased to six-nights a week and the market hall was presented as The Palace de Luxe Cinematographic Theatre – or simply, "The Palace". After the First World War Ted persuaded his brother, Miles, to take over The Palace, and Ted disappeared from the area for five years.

Miles, as we have seen above, built The Chase Cinema at Chase Terrace in 1925 and this may have led to some loss of interest in the little cinema in Chasetown, and in 1927 he bought the Alhambra, Dudley Port from Pat Collins. By the end of the silent era it may well have closed or been mothballed. A report written in 1936 concerning the cinema's ability to meet its licensing requirements implies that cinema may have been closed for us much as ten years at that time.

At some stage in 1936 it did reopen as a sound cinema, and adopted the name, "The Plaza". It was managed by Billy Burke whose sister Eileen married Miles Jervis II! In the great tradition of such cinemas, it does not seem to have ever advertised or attempted to lift its profile beyond the immediate locality. The life and times of The Plaza are still a mystery! It has to be assumed that it remained in the ownership of Miles Jervis I, and after his death in 1948, it passed to Ann Jervis.

The Plaza seems to have survived until the early of mid 1950s, and may have been run for a while by Mary Jervis – daughter of Miles I and Ann – and her husband, Bill Stevens. The few people I managed to talk to who had worked in The Plaza could shed no more light on the subject.

Today the building that was once Chasetown's cinema is used a gymnasium and bears no sign that it was ever once used as a cinema.

The Palace
also known as the Picture House

Hednesford Road, Heath Hayes.

Edward Jervis was established in Chasetown by 1914. In 1915 he applied for a cinematograph licence for a "moveable structure" to be erected at Heath Hayes, on the Hednesford Road, but very close to the crossroads where it met the main road from Cannock to Lichfield. It is very tempting to conclude that this "moveable structure" was a portable cinema/bioscope show that had been travelled by Ted Jervis before the passing of the Cinematograph Act. The one poor quality image we have of this cinema does indicate that it was in the "portable theatre style". (See next page)

On 1st. August 1915 The Palace, Heath Hayes, opened its doors and commenced business. Ted was assisted by his manager, Fred Benton, who also played the violin in the orchestra, which was just as well as Ted was still occupied in Chasetown, and possibly had other interests. At the end of the First World War Ted wanted to travel again so he persuaded his brother Tom to take over The Palace.

Tom Jervis married Florence Dobson and had three children. When Florence died in 1902 he married her younger sister, Nell. Nell and Tom went onto have ten more children. (Florence and Nell Dobson were daughters of old Tom Dobson of Birmingham who founded a fairground family dynasty.) The first six children born to Tom and Nell were born at many different locations indicating that the family was still travelling. The seventh child, Ernest, was born in 1918 and his birth certificate records that he was born in the van behind the cinema at Heath Hayes. This is proof that Tom had settled in Heath Hayes at that time and was ready to take over his brother's cinema. In fact Tom had come to the area in 1916 and joined his brother in a short-lived theatrical venture at Cannock's Hippodrome.

Tom and Nell eventually left their van and moved into a house in Norton Road, and by the mid 1920s Tom was feeling fairly dissatisfied with his fairly primitive cinema. In the second half of the 1920s the Jervises were all showing their determination to build themselves new cinemas. Miles opened The Chase Cinema, and Ted was back in the area and building The Regent, Brownhills. Tom decided to adopt Ted's "self-build" approach. With the help of local miners, on strike, or on the dole, Tom replaced his old portable cinema with a brand new brick-built building. The plans were first drawn up in 1925, and were officially approved in the March of that year, but the new cinema may not have opened until 1928. It is not clear for how long the old cinema remained in use while its replacement was being built.

The new cinema was to be called "The Picture House", and was built to accommodate 387 patrons downstairs plus 80 in the balcony. Tom's daughter Flora later recalled than the introduction of the talkies had seemed more significant that the opening of The Picture House, but perhaps that was because the arrival of the talkies threw her, and her fellow musicians, out of work! Many of Tom's family worked in his cinema. Nell worked in the paybox and Ernest did the accounts. Flora's sister Josephine learnt to be a projectionist, following in the

Below: This postcard view of Five Ways at Heath Hayes provides a glimpse of the Picture House.

footsteps of her husband, Vic Jackson. After the war the cinema was managed by Jack Jervis. Nell was widowed in 1937 but continued to run the family's cinema right until its closure.

The Second World War was a busy time for the Heath Hayes Picture House, and extra seating had to be found. After the war the cinema tried to maintain attendance by adopting a three two-day programmes a week schedule, but remained shut on Sundays. The Bates family at Blackfords, and the Jervises at Heath Hayes found themselves in the same predicament and both cinemas reached the point in the 1950s where they were running at a loss. They both closed within a week of each other.

The last film was shown at Heath Hayes on Saturday 2nd May 1959 – it was *"Seven Brides for Seven Brothers"*, and villagers packed the cinema to enjoy the film and say goodbye to their cinema. The cinema remained empty for a year or so while permission was sought to change its use. It then had a period of industrial use before becoming a carpet sales room.

Above: A poor quality picture of the original "portable" cinema erected in Hednesford Road, Heath Hayes – but perhaps a glimpse of the kind of structure we will meet again in Volume Two as we look as portable theatres.

Cheslyn Hay

The village of Cheslyn Hay lies to the south of Cannock, and like the towns mentioned above, it had its share of collieries and brickworks. It is as difficult now to imagine such things as it to imagine that the village once had a cinema!

The Britannia Hall - The Palace - The Palladium

Rosemary Road, Cheslyn Hay.

The earliest record of films being presented in Cheslyn Hay seems to be an advertisement in the Cannock Chase Courier for 27th January 1912. This is headed, "Twigdon's Electric Pictures" and it announces that they will be presenting films in the Britannia Hall for a few weeks with thrice weekly changes on programmes.

Enthusiasts of bioscope history will immediately recognise the name Twigdon and be delighted to learn that they settled for a while in Cheslyn Hay in that period after the 1910 Cinematograph Act had come into force - a time when such enterprises had to abandon their travelling habits and try showing films on a slightly more permanent basis. That they intended changing their programme every third night seems to suggest they hoped the locals would indulge in a lot of film-going! They also announced they would be providing a children's matinee at 3 o'clock on Saturday afternoons and on Sunday evening there would be "grand sacred music concert". The latter is an indication that they still retained the bioscope's organ from its travelling days and that they had adopted the Sunday concert idea that many other showmen exploited to good effect.

Left: Once again a poor quality picture but at least a rare glimpse of the Britannia Hall at Cheslyn Hay.

The origins of the building used by the Twigdons are obscure. It seems to have once been known as "St. Georges Hall", and had been bought by a Mr. Thomas Thacker in the late 1890s. He made various additions to the building including provision of a market hall, and entered a partnership with a Mr. Glover. At this stage the original building seems to have become home to visiting theatrical companies and became known as "The Britannia Hall". For example in August 1898 the Cannock Chase Courier reported that "The Vicar's Daughter" was being staged at The Britannia Hall.

The hall seems to have been a long narrow building with a sloping floor that simply followed the fall of the ground. However, the Courier's report, mentioned above, added that, *"The theatre is well fitted, well lighted and the scenery is good."*

Returning to the Twigdon's arrival in 1912, it is annoying that we do not know what was meant by the phrase "for a few weeks". This gives us no idea how long Cheslyn Hay's first cinema survived. The adverts continue on a weekly basis until the middle of April. Interestingly it does tie up with the only known picture of the cinema where the name "New Britannia Picture Company" appears over the door. However the word "new", and the use of the name "Palace" that can also be seen in this picture, suggests that someone else may have taken over by the time the picture was taken.

During the first four months of 1912 while the Twigdons were showing films in Cheslyn Hay a couple of things happened that may have affected their success. They already faced competition from the Electric Palace at Hednesford and the Electric Theatre on the Walsall Road at Cannock - both renewed their cinematograph licenses at the beginning of 1912. On Easter Monday, 8th April 1912 the Hippodrome Cannock finally opened and it may simply be coincidence that this seems to the point at which Twigdons stop their shows. Whether entertainment opportunities in Cannock could affect those in Cheslyn Hay must have been tested when the Holland family presented their "Picture Palace" on Cannock Wakes Ground for a couple of weeks at the end of February. Once again this seems to be an instance of a bioscope show continuing to travel in this post-Cinematograph Act period. Another irony is that the Hollands and Twigdons were both from the East Midlands - strange that they should be on each other's doorstep here in the West Midlands.

The Britannia Hall seems to disappear for a time from the pages of the Cannock Chase Courier after April 1912 - but for one more mention. An advertisement appears on 20th April informing readers that the operetta *"Cinderella"* will be presented for two nights at the hall on 24th and 25th of that month. The show was presented by members of the South Staffordshire Women's Association, led by Mrs. Minifie Hawkins and Miss Hampton. Another little twist to this tale is that among the helpers listed as assisting the ladies put on this show is none other than Mr. A. Twigdon!

Leon Bucknall's extensive research into the history of cinemas in the Cannock area picks up the story in 1915 when again an advertisement appears in the local paper in November telling us that films are being shown at The Palace, Cheslyn Hay. He also came across an interesting advertisement of January 1916 that announced that a benefit evening was being held at The Palace for the projectionist who had just enlisted.

After the First World War The Palace became The Palladium, which suggests a change of ownership, and probably some improvement to the interior of the hall. Prices of admission rose and advertisements claimed the place was now more cosy and refined. The new proprietor was F. Taylor who was also running the cinema at Blackford's, and he appears to have run both halls from 1920 to 1924. Someone else must have taken over in the August of 1924, but it changed hands again in 1926 when a Mrs. Griffin took over. Whether the freehold changed hands or it was simply a matter passing on the lease is never clear in the history of little village cinemas and their chequered lives, but the Cheslyn Hay cinema seems to have more than its fair share of changing hands, refurbishments and reopenings.

There was another reopening on 22nd August 1930 following another "transformation". Accompaniment now seemed to be provided by an "orchestra" - but not for long, because in the October of that year it was announced that the talkies would be coming to Cheslyn Hay. The first sound film was presented during week commencing 6th October 1930, for three days and was *"The Rainbow Man"*. For the second three days the film was *"Red Hot Rhythm"*.

An announcement in November 1930 indicated that Messrs Wright-Pitchford and Cooke-Rogers were now the proprietors of The Palladium, but is not clear whether they had been so since the August of 1930, or whether this represented yet another change. The introduction of talkies seems to have been a success, although Leon Bucknall is of the opinion that the folks in Cheslyn Hay were definitely prepared by this time to take advantage of other cinemas further afield, thanks to improvements in local bus services. One sign that maybe all was not well is that the management introduced dances on Wednesday evenings and proclaimed that they were the "Palladium Cinema and Ballroom". Perhaps this indicates that the floor of the building no longer followed the slope of the ground!

In January 1932 it was announced that the cinema equipment at The Palladium was being sold by auction as "the owner was leaving the district" - and this is generally understood to be the demise of film presentation in Cheslyn Hay. Certainly many local people recall that the building was empty for a long time and may not have come to life again until after the War when a Mr. Jones converted the premises to a garage, later known as Bart's Motors. No traces of the building survive today.

Kinver

Kinver has no connection with the Cannock Chase area, but it is in South Staffordshire and is therefore included here. It is southwest of the Black Country – with which it has strong connections. This soon becomes clear as we look at the history of Kinver's little cinema.

The Kinema

The High Street, Kinver.

Ben Priest (1881-1954) was the proprietor of a nut and bolt factory in Old Hill, but he eventually came to live in Kinver. In 1919 he was persuaded to invest in the production of a film called "Bladys of the Stewponey". Much of the film was shot in Kinver so everybody in the village must have been aware of this strange phenomenon called "cinema", even if they had not been to Kidderminster or Stourbridge to see such things for themselves.

About the same time that "Bladys" was being made, a company was formed called Kinver Entertainments Ltd., with the intention of building a cinema in Kinver. The Managing Director of the company was Stanley Smith, who became known in the village at the time as "Cinema Smith". A good site was found on which to build the cinema – next to the White Hart, right in the centre of the village. Messrs. Webb & Gray, the Dudley based architects drew up the plans and construction began. The same architects designed the Centrals in Kidderminster and Stourbridge, and the Majestic, Cradley Heath, which were all quite grand, but here in Kinver the cinema was to be a very basic shed-like auditorium with a Belfast roof, and a fairly modest frontage. All seats were to be on a single raked floor, and the projection room was to be inside the main structure – at the back of the hall. It was built by W. Basterfield, the local builder, and wasn't quite finished by opening day!

The Kinver Kinema opened on Monday 9th May 1921 at 4.p.m. The ceremony began outside the cinema, and was presided over by Councillor Ballard of Dudley. This gentleman was later a director of the companies that built the cinemas mentioned above, and therefore it is tempting to believe that he might have invested in The Kinema. However, this does not seem to be so because in his speech that afternoon he told the crowds that he had advised the Kinema directors that they were undertaking a very risky venture!

The task of unlocking the cinema's door with a silver key and declaring it open was given to Mrs. Goodyear of Wombourne. She was the daughter of another prominent Dudley businessman, once again emphasising Dudley connections. Councillor Ballard had even mentioned his delight at seeing so many Dudley people present. Mr. A .E. Timmins then replied

on behalf of the Kinema directors and claimed that he had been particularly instrumental in propelling the

Kinema into existence and that it was he who had appointed Stanley Smith to manage the project.

The first film was "Queen of the Sea", but a more significant part of the programme was a locally made film about the Enville Races. This film provided an opportunity for many local people to see themselves on the screen – in their very own local cinema! After all this there was a "second house" at 7.p.m. and the Kinema settled into its two shows a night, two three nightly programmes, per week. The County Express reported:
"The new Kinema…. is a thoroughly up to date picture theatre in every respect. It is centrally heated and will provide accommodation for 500, all of whom will be in full view of the screen, and every seat is of the comfortable tip-up variety."

Despite the hopes of Mr. Kimmins and Stanley Smith, the Kinema does not seem to have come up to their expectations. In other words, Councillor Ballard's comments had been well-founded. It was even known for shows to be cancelled if less than twelve people turned up. With the cinema on the verge of closing, it seems that Ben Priest stepped in and bought it.

It is not clear when Ben Priest acquired the Kinema, nor why he did so. He did not incorporate it into his "group" of cinemas that consisted of the one in Old Hill, plus two in Kidderminster, nor did put under the supervision of his manager, George Smith. Equally it is not clear how long he kept it going! It seems to have closed before the end of the 1920s. Perhaps he abandoned it to concentrate on introducing sound into his other cinemas as the 1930s progressed.

The Kinema only came to life again when the Second World War commenced and Ben Priest loaned it to the Fire Service. The cinema's screen was at the High Street end of the building, and this had to be destroyed so that doors could be installed to make the building serve its new function. The raked floor must also have been removed. After the war the former Kinema stood empty and unused once again. Ben Priest died in 1954 and the following year his nephew, Cecil Jackson, sold the building to a Mr. Sidney Hillman.

Sidney Hillman was from Wordsley, where, in his teens he had worked in the re-wind room at the Olympia for Mr. Bullock. From 1940 to 1946 he was in the RAF, but when he returned to Wordsley Mr. Bullock offered him a partnership in the Olympia, providing he also worked in the projection room. He then progressed to acquiring the Ritz cinema in Market Drayton from Fred Leatham in 1950. When the Kinema became available in 1955 he was keen to buy it and establish a cinema nearer home.

Sidney Hillam carried out most of the work on the old Kinema building himself, while travelling to and from Market Drayton on his motorbike. A new roof was built, and the auditorium was "turned round" so that a new projection room had to be built on the outside of the building at the front. Ross projectors from a Cannock cinema were installed, seats from a Wimbledon cinema, and a RCA sound system. RCA also supplied a multi-format screen. The cinema could now accommodate 396 patrons.

The new Kinema opened on Monday 2nd April 1956 with **"The Student Prince"** – in colour and Cinemascope. Sidney Hillman was as optimistic about the cinema as his predecessors had been in 1921. This optimism was based on the fact that the village was now much larger, and if he advertised in the County Express, based in Stourbridge, he was certain he could win patrons from a wide area. His adverts carried the message: "Drive out to the Kinema, Kinver – the City Cinema in the Country"!

Sidney Hillman appointed two operators – George Morgan from Brierley Hill, and Pierre Baskerville, plus loyal part-time staff from the village. Towards the end of the 1950s they noticed that audience figures were declining, and Mr. Hillman was beginning to make economies. History was repeating itself.

The Kinema closed on a Saturday in August 1961, but no-one seems sure of the precise date! Being part of its rapid decline was demoralising and the staff felt it had simply faded away and therefore did not heed the date. After closure film stills and the times of performances were still on display in the foyer, indicating that it may have closed at short notice. Sidney Hillman himself could never put a more precise date on the closure.

The building was demolished in 1964, after purchase by the local council. A health clinic was built on the site – leaving me with a desire to put a plaque on its wall to commemorate the Kinema and the dreams of Stanley Smith, Ben Priest, and Sidney Hillman.

Right: The Kinema at Kinver, probably photographed in the 1930s while the cinema was shut. To the left is The White Harte – used as a location in "Bladys of the Stewponey" – see text. (Author's collection)

Right: Sid Hillman greets a group of pensioners who have come to see his rebuilt version of the Kinema at Kinver in the late 1950s. The forthcoming attractions advertising in the background features "Teenage Rebel" which may not have been their kind of film. (Sid Hillman's collection)

Acknowledgements and Resources

Research into local cinema history begins in the pages of *the Kinematograph Year Book* — an annual trade directory that provides a mine of information. I have extensively used a local private collection of KYB's and the collection in Birmingham Reference Library. *Kine Weekly*, the trade's magazine is also useful, and I have consulted copies at the British Film Institute and the National Newspaper Collection at Colindale. Other more obscure sources include *"The Era"*, and *"The Bioscope"*, not forgetting *"The World's Fair"*.

Local newspapers are invaluable and the Black Country Archives have good collections. *(The Express and Star,* and the *County Express* allowed me to use their own archives in the days before they trransferred such material to local archives.)* In recent years the Black Country Bugle has published much material to encourage intereat in local cinemas etc. Local government records, like plans, licences, council minutes etc. are again invaluable but not always available. Some authorities have committed official vandalism with their own archives, particularly on the two recent occasions of local government reorganisation. Perhaps, on the other hand, we should be grateful for everythins that has survived.

I have had much assistance from the following libraries: Wolverhampton, Walsall, Bilston, Wednesbury, West Bromwich, Tipton, Smethwick, Dudley, Halesowen, Brierley Hill, Stourbridge, and, across the border, in Birmingham and at Staffordshire County Record Office. Staff have often helped me find information that they themselves did not know they had! Sandwell Planning Department concealed a good archive at Wigmore House at one time and I must thank the two ladies who unlocked some of its treasures for me. Since the 1980s nearly all these resources have been brought together in the specialist archive and local history centres. I thank the local archives for making photographs available and allowing me to use them.

I hope individuals will accept a huge "thank you" directed at everybody. I particularly have to thank a host of individuals who have talked to me, written to me, and phoned me, to help assemble the story that follows. (It could not have been compiled from archives alone.) Chris and Rosemary Clegg of the *Mercia Cinema Society* gave much assistance and encouragement. This society has recently been merged with the Cinema Theatre Association. The CTA was helpful first time round and has been so again in preparing this new book. In 1982 I thanked Hugh Sykes, Tony Moss, Terry Cresswell, Kevin Wheelan, Keith Skone, Alan Moore, Allen Eyles, Norman Robins, Eurwyn Jones and Richard Gray. This time round I am grateful for help from Clive Polden, the association's current archivist.

The following members of the Black Country Society helped me in 1982: John Brimble, Dave Whyley, Andy

Rutter, Peter Glews, and Keith Hodgkins. Since then other BCS members have provided assistance including Stan Hill, who chaired the Society for many years and edited *"The Blackcountyrman"*.

Obviously over the years that have passed since 1982 many more people have added to what is now included in this book, including those I met while working on *"Cinemas of Aldridge & Brownhills"*, and *"The Kinema at Kinver"*. In recent times I am grateful for help from John Vincent Smith, Hazel Yapp, Derek Reckard, F. Geobey, Eric Poxon, Leon Bucknall and John Sale. Doug Withers, Brian Hornsey, and Norman Robins have made big contributions. There seems no way in which I could name everybody who has assisted in some way or other, and as a result of a shortage of space I have not been able to reproduce the names thanked at the front of *"Cinemas of the Black Country"*.

Quite an army of people have assisted and advised during the production of this book and offered all kinds of help, as they did during the production of *"Cinemas of the Black Country"*. Family support has been invaluable over the years, and this project - consisting of two books - has been greatly supported by my partner, Terri Baker-Mills.

Readers may feel that they would like to find out more about the following specialist organisations:

The Cinema Theatre Association.

For those interested in the history of cinema buildings a worthy organisation is the Cinema Theatre Association, founded in 1967 to promote serious study of all aspects of their design and operation. Regular visits and meetings, plus a bi-monthly newsletter are provided. The CTA has a good archive currently based in East London,and has a website. Membership enquiries should be addressed to Neville Taylor, Flat 1, 128 Glouscester Terrace, London, W2 6HP.

The Black Country Society.

This society unites everyone who has an interest in the past, present and future of the Black Country. The society holds regular talks during the Autumn and Winter, and activities like trips and guided walks during the Summer. The Society publishes an excellent quarterly magazine called "The Blackcountryman". Enquiries should be addressed to the BCS, P.O.Box 71, Kingswinford, Dudley, DY6 9YN.

I am always pleased to hear from readers and hope that some will keep up with me via my website: **www.nedwilliams.co.uk**

312